SPIRIT POSSESSION IN JUDAISM

Raphael Patai Series in Jewish Folklore and Anthropology

A complete listing of the books in this series can be found at the back of this volume.

General Editor:
Dan Ben-Amos
University of Pennsylvania

Advisory Editors:
Jane S. Gerber
City University of New York

Barbara Kirshenblatt-Gimblett
New York University

Aliza Shenhar
University of Haifa

Amnon Shiloah
Hebrew University

Harvey E. Goldberg
Hebrew University

Samuel G. Armistead
University of California, Davis

Guy H. Haskell
Emory University

SPIRIT POSSESSION IN JUDAISM

Cases and Contexts from the Middle Ages to the Present

Edited by
MATT GOLDISH

With a foreword by
Erika Bourguignon

and an introduction by
Joseph Dan

Wayne State University Press
Detroit

Copyright © 2003 by Wayne State University Press,
Detroit, Michigan 48201. All rights are reserved.
No part of this book may be reproduced without formal permission.
Manufactured in the United States of America.

Library of Congress Cataloging-in-Publication Data

Spirit possession in Judaism : cases and contexts from the Middle Ages to the present / edited by Matt Goldish.
    p. cm. — (Raphael Patai series in Jewish folklore and anthropology)
Includes bibliographical references and index.
  ISBN 0-8143-3003-7
  1. Spirit possession—Judaism. 2. Judaism—Doctrines. I. Goldish, Matt.
II. Series.
  BM645.S65 S75 2003
  296.3'16—dc21
                                             2002010171

CONTENTS

Foreword   9
ERIKA BOURGUIGNON

Preface   11
MATT GOLDISH

Section I: Historical and Phenomenological Background

Prologue   25

Introduction   27
JOSEPH DAN

The Taming of the Deviants and Beyond: An Analysis of *Dybbuk* Possession and Exorcism in Judaism   41
YORAM BILU

Possession and Exorcism in the Magical Texts of the Cairo Geniza   73
JONATHAN SEIDEL

Section II: The Sixteenth Century

Prologue   99

Benevolent Spirit Possession in Sixteenth-Century Safed   101
LAWRENCE FINE

City of the Dead: Spirit Possession in Sixteenth-Century Safed   124
J. H. CHAJES

Pneumatic Mystical Possession and the Eschatology of the Soul
in Lurianic Kabbalah   159
MENACHEM KALLUS

Maggidim, Spirits, and Women in Rabbi Hayyim Vital's *Book of Visions*   186
MORRIS M. FAIERSTEIN

A Spirit Possession Tale as an Account of the Equivocal Insertion
of Rabbi Hayyim Vital into the Role of Messiah   197
HARRIS LENOWITZ

Section III: The Seventeenth and Eighteenth Centuries

Prologue   215

Vision and Possession: Nathan of Gaza's Earliest Prophecies in
Historical Context   217
MATT GOLDISH

Kabbalah and Jewish Exorcism in Seventeenth-Century Italian
Jewish Communities: The Case of Rabbi Moses Zacuto   237
RONI WEINSTEIN

Dybbuk and *Devekut* in the *Shivhe ha-Besht*: Toward a Phenomenology of Madness in Early Hasidism   257
ZVI MARK

Section IV: The Nineteenth and Twentieth Centuries

Prologue   305

Love and Death in a Contemporary *Dybbuk* Story: Personal Narrative and the Female Voice   307
TAMAR ALEXANDER

Dybbuk, Aslai, Zar: The Cultural Distinctiveness and Historical
Situatedness of Possession Illnesses in Three Jewish Milieus   346
YORAM BILU

Appendices

Appendix A: Texts concerning Spirit Possession in Sixteenth-Century Safed 367
J. H. Chajes

Appendix B: Lurianic Texts concerning "His Portion and His Neighbor's Portion"—A Moral Problem 385
Menachem Kallus

Appendix C: Lurianic Texts concerning the Hazards of the Self-Rectification of the Incomplete *Tzaddik* 403
Menachem Kallus

Appendix D: Lurianic Texts concerning Rabbi Hayyim Vital and His Psychical Experience 407
Menachem Kallus

Appendix E: On the Possession of Rabbi Hayyim Vital from His *Book of Visions*, book 5, chapter 12 415
Morris M. Faierstein

Appendix F: Texts from Vital's Autobiography concerning the Vision of Pillars 417
Harris Lenowitz

Appendix G: Selections from *Sefer ha-Hezyonot*, by Rabbi Hayyim Vital 421
Harris Lenowitz

Appendix H: From *Sha'ar Ru'ah ha-Kodesh* (The Gate of Holy Spirit), by Rabbi Hayyim Vital 437
Matt Goldish

Appendix I: On How the Spirits of the Dead Enter the Bodies of the Living, from *Sefer Nishmat Hayyim*, by Rabbi Manasseh ben Israel, book 3, chapter 10 441
Matt Goldish

Bibliographical Essay 445

Glossary 449

Contributors 455

Index 457

FOREWORD

ERIKA BOURGUIGNON

The phenomenon of spirit possession we know from many parts of the world, yet this fine volume, by focusing on the topic in Judaism in different times and places, fills a void. It brings together for the first time the great variety of beliefs and practices surrounding spirit possession in Judaism. As a result, this volume raises important new questions and topics for research. The scholarship assembled here not only contributes to the study of Judaism but is of potential significance for cross-cultural research.

It is particularly striking that we have here chapters (such as the five dealing with the mystics of Safed) based on ancient texts together with complex metaphysical elaborations, on the one hand, and on the other, accounts of beliefs and practices observed in contemporary Israeli life.

Although the volume begins with and emphasizes the Middle Ages, we know that beliefs and practices surrounding spirit possession are much older. Flavius Josephus and Philo Judeus, like the New Testament authors, speak of possession and exorcism in the time of the Roman occupation of Galilee. Where the latter refer to demons, the former, representing a more sophisticated view of the day, speak of the souls of dead sinners that come to possess people, a view implying some version of a concern with punishment after death similar, it appears, to interpretations of dybbuk possessions. Yet the Moroccan tradition, as shown by Yoram Bilu, is one in which evil spirits rather than dead sinners possess their victims. Elsewhere Bilu has spoken of the Moroccan practice of using children as trance mediums. The classicist Sarah Johnston has recently written about such practices in ancient Greece.[1]

The continuities through time and the connections with surrounding peoples are fascinating, as are the truly unique aspects of Jewish cosmology and metaphysics. For example, the idea of spirit possession is generally paired with the idea of a soul that is replaced, temporarily, by an invading entity. The kabbalistic idea of sparks of a soul that can coexist with the host's soul is quite special. Here the possession does not involve a change of consciousness, nor necessarily an awareness of it, nor any public demonstration of the gifts thus acquired. Referring to such an "invasion" as *ibbur* (impregnation) is quite distinct from the idea of a domination or takeover, which the English word *possession* implies. But *ibbur* is used for negative possession as well. The recent story of the widow of Dimona who claimed to be "possessed" by her dead husband thus gives us a woman impregnated by her husband, or is it pregnant with her husband? In another contemporary case, as told here by Tamar Alexander, of a young woman possessed by her boyfriend's dead girlfriend, the exorcist—the rabbi's wife—claims to see the possessing spirit curled up inside her like a fetus. She is not only impregnated but pregnant.

This case also shows us two other important features, one ethnographic, the other methodological. Ethnographically, we see the astonishing mixtures of cultures and traditions taking place among several immigrant communities in Israel. Methodologically, we can contrast this study, in which Alexander obtains several reports from participants to create a complex picture, and the many studies based on texts, which are necessarily incomplete and represent the point of view of the author.

Given the significance of these materials, this volume will surely stimulate much further research into a fascinating topic, or rather a series of related topics.

Notes

1. Yoram Bilu, "Pondering the Princes of Oil: New Light on an Old Problem," *Journal of Anthropological Research* 37:3 (1982): 269–78. Reprinted in *Megamot* 27:3 (1982): 102–23. Sarah I. Johnston, "Charming Children: The Use of the Child in Ancient Divination," *Arethusa* 34 (2001): 97–117.

PREFACE

MATT GOLDISH, OHIO STATE UNIVERSITY

> It was then that I saw Amparo.... I saw her fling herself into the midst of the dancing, stop, her abnormally tense face looking upward, her neck rigid. Then, oblivious, she launched into a lewd saraband, her hands miming the offer of her own body. "A Pomba Gira, a Pomba Gira!" some shouted, delighted by the miracle, since until then the she-devil had not made her presence known.... The gira was coming to an end. I left the platform and ran to Amparo. Agliè was already there, delicately massaging her temples. "How embarrassing!" Amparo said. "I don't believe in it, I didn't want to. How could I have done this?"
> —Umberto Eco, *Foucault's Pendulum*

Spirit possession presents an irresistible subject for the scholar—but also an almost unmitigated series of paradoxes and conundrums. What other topic offers the theatrical quality, the geographical, temporal, and phenomenological breadth, the psychological complexity, the religious import, and indeed the genuine mystery that one finds in possession? There is now an extensive literature on the subject by specialists in psychology, anthropology, sociology, folklore, history, religion, and mysticism. The continued fascination possession holds for a broad audience is expressed not only through the popularity of these studies and their lowbrow "New Age" counterparts but also by cultural events such as films like *The Exorcist* and *Being John Malkovich*, the revival of An-ski's play *The Dybbuk* in Israel and America, television's *X-Files* and *Psi Factor*, and the recent uproar surrounding the possession and exorcism of a Dimona woman. On the other hand, there continue to be many societies in which possession is so common and integral to traditional life that it does not attract much attention at all.

Terms and Types

A spirit possession is a phenomenon in which a person (or those close to a person) believes that an alien spirit, either a ghost of a dead human or a disembodied spirit of another type, has entered the person and controls or influences some or all of the person's actions and thoughts, while the person's own spirit or soul is partially or fully dormant. This definition differs from some versions offered by earlier scholars because it does not attempt to affirm or deny any actual change in states of consciousness or physical control in the subject. Recent studies speak of possession in terms of perception, or belief, which clears the way for the most open-minded approach to descriptions and explanations. This definition also avoids the question of a spirit's ability to coerce the subject in any number of ways, by asserting only that the subject's own spirit or soul is conceived not to be functioning in whole or part.

Use of the possession idiom obviously requires that the society in question hold some conception of disembodied spirits. The society must also have a conception of such spirits entering living bodies and influencing them. Most of the time this means societies that have some communal picture of a supernatural or spiritual realm beyond the visible world. When examining possession reports, one often finds rather complex understandings of the relationship between physical and spiritual worlds underlying the description of events.

Possession beliefs exist among a great many of the world's societies, both in the past and the present. In Christianity the conception is usually of possession by evil spirits, probably because this phenomenon is described in many passages of the New Testament. There is also, however, a succession of prophetic Christian possession movements in the early modern period. In the present volume, conceptions of unwanted possessions are referred to as negative or malevolent. Judaism, Islam, and some other cultures conceive of negative, neutral, or even positive (benevolent) possessions. All these types receive ample attention in the following essays. We will similarly learn about exorcisms—those ceremonies designed to drive malevolent spirits away—and about the techniques used by mystics to attract possession by benevolent spirits.

Several main types of spirits in the Jewish context are discussed throughout this volume. *Ru'ah* is a generic word for spirits; it is the oldest and most basic term for a possessing entity, usually a malevolent one. One of the major contributions of the Safed context was the publicity and development of benevolent possession concepts, including the *maggid*, a heavenly mentor granted to great kabbalists; the *ibbur*, a usually undetected additional righteous soul that came to help rectify one's sins (though one occasionally finds a malevolent *ibbur*); and the closely related *gilgul*, the soul that repeatedly "rolls over" into new bodies after the death of old ones through metempsychosis and is sometimes placed in possession contexts.

Finally, and best known, is the relatively late term *dybbuk*, a malevolent spirit, generally that of a dead person, that adheres to and controls an unwilling subject.

History

It is impossible to attempt any statement about the history of possession ideas in the hundreds of societies that hold them, but I will say something brief about their background in Christianity and Islam as well as Judaism.

The Hebrew Bible (the Old Testament) does not speak of anything truly similar to spirit possessions in the sense described above. However, it does supply some of the terminology later used for possessing entities—for example, *ru'ah* (wind, breath, or spirit)—and a complex set of conceptions about the spiritual world. One passage that might potentially be understood to refer to a possession concerns King Saul who, upon the anointing of David in his place, was divested of the spirit of God, which was replaced with an "evil spirit" (*ru'ah ra'ah*; 1 Sam. 16:13–16). This, however, could well refer simply to bitterness. Other passages concerning *ru'ah* in humans are similarly unclear.

Jewish society in the Land of Israel during Jesus' time, on the other hand, appears to have had an already well-developed conception of malevolent possessions, for the Gospels refer repeatedly to the casting out of demons. The contexts imply that this was an act of healing that could be carried out only by men who were both holy and informed of the technique. The subjects were considered mad when they were under the influence of these "devils," and it is likely that we are dealing in some cases with victims of psychological and well as physical illnesses (see, for example, Luke 13:10–13; Matt. 12:22).

The Roman Church adopted official positions expressing belief in possession and exorcism, the latter being possible only by an ordained priest, indicating its complete sacralization in Catholic theology. These dogmas have not been withdrawn, and indeed, official exorcists of the Church have been very much in the American news of late. Most other Christian denominations have possession beliefs as well. Nevertheless, possession accounts and exorcisms appear to have been relatively rare in the Middle Ages. They explode onto the European scene at the same time Jewish possessions appear in significant numbers, in the sixteenth century.

For both Judaism and Christianity, the sixteenth and seventeenth centuries were the heyday of possession accounts. Since the early eighteenth century there have been occasional individual possessions and small clusters in both Christian and Jewish society, but the general trend has been away from the possession idiom. It may be that the symptoms and accounts influenced each other until they became dissonant; or perhaps the symptoms, although they might have appeared in some people throughout history, were generally interpreted as possession only in specific settings and times, for reasons scholars have been theorizing about for years.

The situation in Islam was somewhat different. While there are traditions of popular neutral and negative possessions in some Muslim lands, particularly North Africa, the main known possessions were benevolent ones, deliberately fomented by Sufi mystics. The techniques and meaning of such possession conceptions were described by Sufis in the Middle Ages as a long-standing tradition, and this apparently did not change much through at least the nineteenth century.

Explicating the history of possession and exorcism ideas is hampered by the problems of relating possession *events* to possession *accounts*. One never knows how many events perceived by subjects or observers as possessions occurred in any given society. One only has the accounts to rely on, which tend to be tendentious and polemical in nature. It is thus necessary to apply great skill and thoughtfulness to the interpretation of these accounts. The present volume offers a rare opportunity to understand the problem of events versus accounts in the chapter by Tamar Alexander. She reports on a case in which she had the opportunity to interview all those involved, and we can only imagine what the rest of our cases would look like if we were able to see them in the same light.

Disciplinary Approaches

Possession events and accounts can be approached, like any other phenomenon, from a variety of perspectives. Those most widely applied by scholars are the following.

Religion. The religious dimensions of possession and exorcism are among the most highly visible. Since the spiritual world is the realm of religion, and the major outbreaks of possession occurred in early modern times, when the natural and supernatural worlds began to be distinguished, the role of religious ideas looms large in possession accounts and scholarship. Often the possessing souls describe their travails as the result of religious transgressions, and their expulsion has a sacral character not only in Christianity and Judaism but in other cultures as well.

Anthropology. Anthropologists have tended to take a particular interest in the possession ideas of less industrialized societies, such as those of

Haiti, Brazil, Morocco, and Ethiopia. Anthropologists have been particularly interested in the *function* of possession and exorcism beliefs in each culture. Usually, both possession and exorcism are understood in terms of social control by the elite and rebellion or a quest for status by the dispossessed.

Medicine. It appears clear that many of the symptoms associated with possessions are in fact related to physical malfunctions and disease. Convulsions and fainting are the most obvious—they were probably often the result of either epilepsy or high fever. Thus the exorcist functioned as a physician, attempting to cure with supernatural remedies illnesses believed to have been caused by supernatural agents. Unfortunately, subjects often died of their diseases; and what is more, the formulae for exorcism often included the burning of poisonous materials under the subject's nostrils, which itself caused a subject's death more than once.

Psychology. Psychological explanations of possession are almost as common in scholarship as religious ones. The stresses of life, especially in the rapidly changing world of the sixteenth and seventeenth centuries, may well have created the conditions for apparent possession states. In the parlance of the time, those possessed were often considered madmen; some were said to suffer from melancholy or unfortunate astrological effects. Later the terminology for the possessed mindset was that of hysteria. In recent years there has been some discussion among psychologists about whether possession is or is not a psychological illness requiring a cure. Clearly, much of the key to possession ideas rests in the unlocking of human psychological traits, both voluntary and involuntary.

History. Historians are often interested in knowing why possession accounts suddenly appear in certain settings and what conditions at that place and time made this the preferred explanation of symptoms. Sometimes possession accounts prove extremely useful for understanding relationships between popular and elite culture, men and women, Christians and Jews, or mystics and ordinary people, among other things. Occasionally there are larger historical lessons to be learned from possession accounts, such as those of the nuns at Loudun, those occurring in Safed, or those connected with Salem witch accusations.

Folklore and Literature. The folklorist and literary scholar are most interested in the accounts of possession, whether they are oral or written. How do the tales relate to other beliefs and stories in that society and in other societies? Of what does the storyteller want to convince the audience, and what strategies does that person employ for the purpose? If there are multiple accounts, how does each relate to the others? Often there is a kind of conversation among accounts across time and space. One even finds the literary account presented in a play by the Yiddish writer An-ski influencing actual possession accounts—a bonanza of potential for folkloristic and literary interpretation.

Gender. Whether or not one accepts the caveats of Dr. Faierstein in this volume, who claims Jewish possession subjects were not mainly women, there is no doubt that in both Jewish and Christian tales women make up a sizeable proportion of possession subjects. The most common explanation for this fact, and undoubtedly a largely correct one, is that possession both empowered women and freed them from social mores, if only for a time. In this context, the possessed Jewish women who acted as advisors and mediums, of whom several appear in this volume, are particularly interesting. A further gender issue concerns the psychological significance of male spirits possessing women and vice versa.

This Volume

The essays presented here are by no means exhaustive, but they cover a wide range of possession accounts and beliefs in the Jewish world from the Middle Ages to the present. With its multiplicity of approaches, texts, and contexts, this book contributes to scholarship in a variety of fields. It certainly expands the horizons of those interested specifically in Jewish spirit possession cases. The larger community of scholars studying spirit possession in other cultures should also benefit from seeing the many approaches brought together here. Possessions are often discussed from only one point of view in a given work—psychology, anthropology, history—creating a tendency to explain a broad and complex phenomenon from a limited perspective. Here we have an opportunity to see how scholars from very different disciplines approach possession material. The Jewish cases and their background can also be fruitfully compared with cases from other cultures. The volume will be particularly useful to students of the Safed mystical community of the sixteenth century, to which no fewer than five essays are dedicated here. Those concerned with contemporary possessions, including the Dimona case, will find original and highly significant material herein. I am particularly proud to offer English readers the opportunity to profit from the scholarship of several brilliant Israeli scholars: Tamar Alexander, Yoram Bilu, Joseph Dan, Menachem Kallus, Roni Weinstein, and Zvi Mark. The essays by Bilu, Dan, Weinstein, and Kallus were composed in English and edited by me. Tamar Alexander's essay was translated by Harris Lenowitz and me, and Zvi Mark's essay was translated by me.

Since one of the features of the present work is its wide range of disciplinary approaches, I have chosen to leave in a fair amount of overlap, not only in the analyses themselves but also in the introductions to spirit possession and its causes presented by each author. One will find, for example, that Tamar Alexander covers much of the same background as Joseph Dan or Yoram Bilu, but she presents the material from the point of view of a folklorist, while Dan's perspective is that of a mystical and literary scholar and Bilu's is that of an anthropologist and psychologist. Even authors discussing precisely the same text, such as Morris Faierstein and Harris Lenowitz on R. Hayyim Vital's *Sefer ha-Hezyonot* (Book of Visions), are so different in their approaches that the juxtaposition of perspectives is very useful.

We may turn now to the contents of this volume in search of directions to explore. In the first section, Joseph Dan offers an introductory essay on the relationship between particular metaphysical beliefs and the appearance of widespread spirit possession accounts in Judaism, especially in the sixteenth century. A reprint of the well-known study by Yoram Bilu explains the forms and functions of Jewish spirit possessions, focusing on their use for social control. Jonathan Seidel contributes a complementary discussion of spirit possession and exorcisms in medieval Judaism, particularly as they are portrayed in texts from the Cairo Genizah. This background allows us to think carefully about what is new and what is less so during the first large wave of possession accounts from the sixteenth century while leaving us with some still unresolved issues.

The five essays that follow in section II, dealing with possessions in the Safedian and Lurianic contexts, constitute a major contribution to our knowledge of sixteenth-century Jewish thought as well as to the issue of spirit possession. Lawrence Fine opens this section with a general description of benevolent possession phenomena in Safed and lays a framework for the following chapters. J. H. Chajes carries on the discussion of what possessions meant in Safed, linking them to the larger kabbalistic milieu with its special view of relationships between dead and living souls. This line of investigations is carried into the tangled literary remains of the Luria school by Menachem Kallus, who shows how possession was part of the complex Lurianic theory of soul roots and "impregnations." Morris Faierstein presents a revisionist view of the whole Safedian context with his contention that possessions were not, in fact, a matter of any great significance or frequency in Safed. Finally, Harris Lenowitz, stepping back from the mystical viewpoint into that of human relationships, speaks about the role of a possession in Damascus in the formation of Rabbi Hayyim Vital's messianic self-image and his dealings with the Jewish community.

Possessions continued to be a significant part of Jewish life in the seventeenth and eighteenth centuries. In my contribution, which begins section III, I describe how Nathan of Gaza, the prophet of Shabbatai Zvi, was publicly possessed at the beginning of the movement, and how this affected the growth of Sabbateanism. Roni Weinstein discusses the possession cases connected with Rabbi Moses Zacuto, a leading kabbalist of the seventeenth century, explaining the centrality of social and gender elements. Zvi Mark examines possession in the formation of early Hasidism, positing a close relationship between possession, prophecy, and madness as they are portrayed in the *Shivhe ha-Besht*. This essay exemplifies the way possession tales fit into broad cultural contexts by bringing together important elements in modernization and eighteenth-century thought in general.

Possessions have played specific social and religious functions in Jewish communities up through the present, and the last two essays, in section IV, deal with these more recent phenomena. Tamar Alexander offers a unique and highly enlightening insight into the cultural politics of possession in the present. She has actually interviewed several principal characters in a contemporary possession episode, and her results permit an astonishing cross-section of three-dimensional human actors not available in literary accounts. Finally, Yoram Bilu contributes an essay on types of possession as they are presently found among certain national and cultural groups in Israel, featuring a discussion of the recent case involving a Dimona woman that made headlines in Israel for weeks.

A bibliographical essay at the end of the volume offers a selection of important works about spirit possession texts for further reading. The Text Appendixes, also found at the end of the book, present English translations of primary sources relating to specific essays. These, added to the many texts quoted in the chapters, give readers a good range of primary sources to consider. Finally, a glossary contains definitions of specialized terms and abbreviations commonly used in the text.

While we are still far from conclusive views on the interpretation of possession, the studies here can help us formulate at least a historical overview. Jewish spirit possessions of the malevolent type were known in the ancient and medieval periods, but our sources do not generally offer narrative tales about them. Rather, what has been preserved is a series of technical statements about exorcism. In the sixteenth century we encounter an explosion of possessions, both malevolent and benevolent, learned and popular, in the Mediterranean region. Reasons for the outburst may be connected with the development of metempsychosis doctrines, changing social and religious patterns, and the influence of Christianity, in which widespread accounts of malevolent possessions occur at this time. Malevolent possession accounts remain part of Jewish culture in both Ashkenaz and the East from this time until the present, appearing generally in spatial and temporal clusters. Benevolent possessions cluster in the Safed/Damascus area in the later sixteenth and early seventeenth centuries, then again under the impact of Sabbateanism from the mid-seventeenth century to the early eighteenth century. After that they are found in the Hasidic context, but seldom elsewhere. Malevolent possessions known in the twentieth century seem to be heavily culturally determined, but the ability of academic scholars to examine them firsthand opens new vistas for the study of possession in Judaism.

Together, the studies presented here can help us approach many of the interpretive questions with which possession research struggles. We see how issues of psychology and theology interact with concerns of literature, history, and cultural politics in specific spirit possession cases. We remain far from any unified "explanation" of possession, but this in itself is a sort of explanation. The meaning of possession, like that of all human activity, exists on a multitude of planes, the examination of which can teach us a great deal about ourselves, our fellow humans, and the societies we create. May we all be possessed by the spirit of inquiry and excitement for deeper knowledge that permeates this volume.

I would like to thank all those who contributed their essays. I must also thank Wayne State University Press and its director, Arthur Evans, for their willingness to take the project on. Jennifer Baise of WSUP and Robin DuBlanc did an astounding job with our extremely unruly typescript, and I am deeply grateful to them. I have learned a great deal in the process of preparing this book, and I hope people will learn a great deal from reading it.

A NOTE ON SPELLING

Some of the words in this text that were originally written using Hebrew characters have been rendered in the Latin alphabet a number of different ways, depending on the system of transliteration used by the authors of these essays. Similarly, Hebrew names have been rendered in both Anglicized and transliterated forms in this book, according to the desires of the author or the tenor of the text. The following are some of the equivalencies:

Aaron = Aharon
Abraham = Avraham
Benjamin = Binyamin
Elijah = Eliahu
Isaac = Yitzhak
Israel = Yisrael
Jacob = Ya'akov or Yakov
Joseph = Yosef
Joshua = Yehoshua
Moses = Moshe
Samuel = Shmuel
Solomon = Shlomo

Section I
Historical and Phenomenological Background

Prologue

The literary traces of ancient and medieval Jewish popular religious culture are relatively sparse, making it difficult to know much about spirit possession beliefs or exorcisms in those periods. There is, however, sufficient evidence that possessions and exorcisms were to be found among the Hebrews and their medieval descendants. As we have seen in the preface, varied evidence attests to these phenomena in the New Testament and contemporary sources. After the fall of Jerusalem in 70 c.e., the Jews were increasingly dispersed in the Mediterranean and Europe, many in societies that had their own possession beliefs.

It is not surprising to learn, then, that the rabbinic literature of late antiquity and the early Middle Ages, as well as the great storehouse of documents from the Cairo Genizah, contain scattered evidence of continuity in these phenomena. Possessions and exorcisms appear to have been of interest in popular rather than scholarly circles for the most part, connected mainly with magical healing practices. The high Middle Ages offer little new material, and it is only in the sixteenth century, with the onset of the Christian "Age of the Demoniac," that Jewish accounts become more common or begin to offer any larger narrative structure.

When this did occur, however, starting particularly in Palestine and Italy, possessions and exorcisms became fairly widespread and culturally significant. There were many reasons for this development. One was the evolving conceptions of the human soul and the afterlife in kabbalistic ontology; kabbalistic schools were concentrated in Palestine and Italy after the Spanish Expulsion. Another factor was the increased degree of intellectual relations between Jews and their Christian and Muslim neighbors at a time when the Christians, in particular, were experiencing an enormous outbreak of possession events. A third direction for inquiry is the rapidly changing world of that period, when accepted beliefs about the world and God were being challenged by the voyages of discovery, the inquiries of the humanists, the Protestant Reformation, the scientific revolution, and the military successes of the Muslim Ottomans. Possessions at such a time of dwindling certainties might be taken as a symptom of identity displacement.

Because possession and exorcism became regular features of Jewish literature in the sixteenth century and afterward, they can be studied phenomenologically as well as historically. One can investigate the psychological profiles of possession subjects, exorcists, observers, and reporters. The purposes or social functions of possession narratives can be surmised. Similarly, assessing the relationships and similarities between Jewish cases and those in other societies becomes possible.

This section contains three chapters. The first is the introduction by Joseph Dan, who explores the changing mystical and literary conceptualizations underlying possession beliefs between the Middle Ages and the early modern period. The second essay is Yoram Bilu's well-known study about the functions of possession and exorcism in Jewish society. The third chapter is by Jonathan Seidel. He steps back to explore the late ancient and early medieval accounts of exorcisms, laying more detailed groundwork for understanding the major change that would come afterward.

Introduction

JOSEPH DAN

I

If there were any doubt about the importance of the subject to which this volume is dedicated, events in Israel in March 1999 (after most of the studies included here were written) must put them to rest. Those events proved that whatever the *dybbuk* may be, it is present and active around us today and has accompanied all of us into the new millennium.

Judith, a widowed mother of eight in the southern Israeli town of Dimona,[1] claimed that the spirit of her husband, who had died two and a half years previously, had entered her and continued to reside in her body. Several rabbis to whom she applied for help turned her down. Finally, Rabbi David Basri, the head of the Shalom Yeshivah in Jerusalem, agreed to perform the exorcism ceremony and free her from the spirit. The procedure was carried out in the presence of about a hundred people. It was also broadcast live and uncensored by a private radio station and filmed on video. Later it was rebroadcast several times on other radio stations and even on national television.[2]

The most notable effect of this event—though hardly a surprising one—was that in the weeks after this broadcast thousands of people called the media or the courts of various rabbis claiming to be victims of the same affliction. Others testified that a wife, a daughter, a mother, or a sister demonstrated all the symptoms of a *dybbuk* possession. Interest in the phenomenon declined after a few weeks, yet the episode serves as one more example of "mystical-kabbalistic superstition" which, according to the secular majority of Israelis, characterizes the worldview of the ultraorthodox. They particularly associate such beliefs with those who originate from Arab countries and who are represented by the vigorous new political party in Israel, Shas.[3]

The subject of the *dybbuk*, or, to use its more traditional name, the *ru'ah*[4] (*dybbuk* became dominant only after the appearance of a play by that title from the Yiddish author An-ski) is a continuous and continuing tradition in Jewish culture. Its history since the sixteenth century can in fact be regarded as a unified whole. It should be studied, therefore, by utilizing the texts of these centuries, without for a moment forgetting the many previous centuries from which it is absent.

Is the *dybbuk* a historical phenomenon or a psychological one? Does one studying the narratives describing the *dybbuk* employ biography and expulsion as elements in a consistent psychological and cultural phenomenon? Or is it an expression of one particular phase in the development of people's understanding of themselves and their souls, characteristic of a specific period, milieu, and religious-literary atmosphere? Some of the studies in this collection tend to present the first view and some the second. It is not my purpose in this introduction to survey the extant literature. Rather, it is hoped that the accumulated material in the present studies and the extensive bibliography each of them presents will combine to show the current stage of research in the field. Here I would like instead to explain my attitude concerning the fundamental nature of the problem.

An analysis of this issue must include more than the known materials concerning *dybbuk* narratives and the conceptions of human psychology that are expressed or implied therein. It must also take into account the material that is absent—where, when, and in what circumstances we do *not* find references to such narratives. One cannot deal with the prominence of *dybbuk* stories in the rich and variegated hagiographic literature of the sixteenth century without reflecting on the scarcity of such narratives in the even more rich and variegated hagiographic narratives of Hasidism in the nineteenth century. We have literally thousands of narratives in the Talmuds and midrashim, which cover the period of a millennium. Why is it that not one of them tells about a *dybbuk* and its exorcism? If we assume—as some studies have done—that the phenomenon represents basic needs of human psychological expression, why was it absent for such long periods?

One constructive approach to the subject is to start from the very beginning. It is true that any concept of beginning in the history of ideas and cultures is arbitrary, because everything is always based on previous materials, language, and conceptions. Yet it is possible to pinpoint rather accurately the earliest expression in Judaism of the concept that souls can move from one body to another—reincarnation or transmutation of souls—of which the *dybbuk* is a particular example. In order to arrive at the concept of the *dybbuk*, which stipulates that two souls can reside in one body, it must first be accepted that souls are constant while bodies are transient. In this sense, the *dybbuk* is one element within a wider picture of the belief in reincarnation. Reincarnation generally conceives of the return of the soul in a new body, while the *dybbuk* is conceived as a soul entering an already-occupied body.

It is well known that the first example from Jewish culture of a positive presentation of the reincarnation idea is found in the *Sefer ha-Bahir*, the earliest book of the Kabbalah, which was written around 1185.[5] The anonymous author attributed to Rabbi Aqiba an interpretation of the verse in Ecclesiastes "A generation goes and a generation comes" according to which the generation that goes is the same as that which comes—that is, the same souls return again and again. This is followed by an elaborate parable in which physical bodies are referred to as garments that change while the body—that is, the soul—remains.[6]

How can we explain the fact that Judaism existed for at least two millennia, producing a vast literature of every possible genre, without ever, even marginally, expressing the concept of reincarnation?[7] The idea of reincarnation was very well known, if not universally accepted, for many centuries. Its usage by Indian writers made its way west, and its Platonic adaptations had great influence. Reincarnation was a significant feature in the classical treasury of spiritual concepts, open and accessible to anyone who wished to use it. The fact that Jewish scholars did not do so cannot be viewed as a result of their ignorance of it. They could have adopted it had they any interest in it. Yet they did not do so until the late twelfth century, and even then in a most marginal and esoteric manner. Most of the kabbalists who followed the *Bahir* did not refer to it in any way. The Zohar utilized it but never made it a central concept.[8] Only in the sixteenth century, in works like the *Galya Raza*[9] and, most notably, in the Lurianic Kabbalah, did it achieve a central position; yet even many Lurianic kabbalists did not give it a meaningful place in their systems.

Why did the *Bahir* accept what many centuries of Jewish writers ignored or rejected? A case has been made that it was influenced by the Catharist heresy in southern France in the twelfth century.[10] This thesis, however, has yet to be confirmed; it is in fact highly doubtful, especially since in previous generations the idea was easily available. Reincarnation did not first appear in proximity to a Jewish cultural center in the twelfth century. The problem is not whence Jewish thinkers appropriated the reincarnation idea but why. The opportunity was always there—it was the need for it that was absent. Yet an analysis of the innovative, even revolutionary kabbalistic worldview of the *Bahir* does not seem to indicate any necessity for this concept. The many kabbalistic notions that were the main features of Bahiric innovations—the world of the ten *sefirot*, the feminine divine power, the image of the devil, the divine tree—none of these is dependent on or even closely tied to the concept of the transmigration of souls. If the few sections dealing with it were deleted from the book, the history of kabbalistic thought would hardly change.

The only answer I can offer to this question is that it is tied up with the personality of the author of the *Bahir*: he was innovative in many ways, including his conception of the Shekhinah as feminine; so perhaps he expressed his rebellious, unconventional attitude in this realm as well. This is not a very profound historical answer, but sometimes the less dramatic answers may be the correct ones.

The analogy with the *dybbuk* is rather clear. In this case as well we are dealing with a conception that was available to Jewish writers long before the first narrative appeared in the sixteenth century. Particularly in the Christian world the concept of exorcism was quite common. References to it may even be found in the New Testament itself.[11] Jews in Christian countries could, if they wished, have adopted it long before this. Yet unlike the *Bahir* and the idea of reincarnation, in this case we cannot point at one definite source as the first to introduce the narrative genre into Judaism. It seems to appear contemporaneously in several places, so that the assumption that there was one primary source for the rest is a very difficult case to make.

II

Most of the preserved *dybbuk* narratives are embedded in a hagiographic context. This fact was obscured from the public conception of the subject because the playwright An-ski's dramatic presentation neglected this context; nor did it connect the plot with the personality of an outstanding scholar or leader. But most of the early versions of the *dybbuk* narrative from the sixteenth and seventeenth centuries feature a well-known leader at their center and are in many cases hagiographic. This is clear, for instance, in the cases of Rabbi Isaac Luria and Rabbi Hayyim Vital, the great sixteenth-century Safed kabbalists, and also in the narrative of *Shalshelet ha-Kabbalah* by Gedalia ibn Yahia. The latter book includes some of the most important early hagiographic stories concerning medieval figures, including Rashi and Nahmanides. It is evident that the *dybbuk* narratives are connected to the history of Jewish hagiography in content, plot, and characters, and are part of the history of this literary genre.

Little note has been taken of the fact that medieval Jewish literature is surprisingly short on hagiographic material concerning notable Jews of its own period. Medieval sources abound with stories about biblical heroes:

some old, some adapted or expanded, and some new. The same is true for the figures of the great talmudic sages, particularly the *tanaim*, around whom vast and complex narratives were woven, especially in kabbalistic literature. Yet we find hardly any tales about medieval scholars, writers, and leaders. Most of the stories about them originate in the sixteenth century or later—often much later. Thus, for instance, we are now in possession of a large and variegated body of stories about Abraham Ibn Ezra, the poor, enigmatic wandering scholar. All these stories are found in late works, many of them quite modern. The large cycle of stories about the mysterious thirty-six hidden righteous people for whom the world exists are found only in fairly late sources. Kabbalists became a subject of hagiography only in the sixteenth century, when they also began to be associated with miraculous and magical events, the raw material for their hagiographic biographies.[12]

There is one important exception to this general tendency: the great cycle of hagiographic tales centered around Rabbi Samuel the Pious, his son Rabbi Judah the Pious, and other leaders of Ashkenazi Jewry in the twelfth and thirteenth centuries. These stories are found in a fifteenth-century Hebrew collection, though later they became known best in the Yiddish version included in the famous *Ma'aseh Buch*. It can be proven that many of these stories developed gradually and have their roots in the authentic writings of the Kalonymids (the clan from which R. Samuel and R. Judah derived).[13] This is one case in which it can be shown that a hagiographic cycle developed gradually during the thirteenth and fourteenth centuries, receiving its present shape in Hebrew and Yiddish in the fifteenth and sixteenth centuries. These stories—like the whole literary corpus of the Kalonymids tradition, at the center of which stands the *Sefer Hasidim*—specialized in tales of demons and witches, spirits and ghosts, and a vast array of supernatural occurrences.

The souls of the dead appear in these narratives very often, sometimes in the dreams of the living and sometimes as separate entities: revealing secrets, instructing, and occasionally threatening.[14] This is a context that invites stories about exorcisms and *dybbuks*, both by its content and by its literary presentation. Its heroes are masters at controlling the realms of demons and spirits. Nevertheless, no *dybbuk* story can be found in this cycle or its offshoots. These German Pietists (Haside Ashkenaz) were intensely interested in the subject of sins and their punishment in the next world, and spirits who visit the world of the living often recount their experiences. All the constituent materials of a *dybbuk* narrative can be found here in abundance. They were also open to miraculous stories of their non-Jewish neighbors, and many narratives are undoubtedly borrowed from the folktales of the surrounding culture. Despite all these factors, however, the concept of the *dybbuk* is absent both from their theoretical discussions of the soul and its fate (such as Eleazar of Worms's *The Wisdom of the Soul*)[15] and from the narratives included in their works or told about them by later generations. Thus even in this remarkable and almost unique example of medieval Jewish hagiography about medieval leaders, the subject of the *dybbuk* is completely absent. It should be emphasized, however, that in the early versions of these narratives the figures are anonymous; only in the late medieval and early modern redactions do the leaders of Ashkenazi Jewry assume the role of hagiographic heroes.

A historian of Jewish narrative literature must therefore view the sudden appearance of *dybbuk* narratives in the sixteenth century as part of the larger phenomenon of the flourishing of Jewish hagiography in that period, in contrast to the situation in the Middle Ages.[16] We no longer use causal terminology in history, and in this case certainly there is no basis for proposing that the two phenomena are dependent on each other in a causal fashion. But it can be stated that they both take shape in Hebrew literature in close proximity and constitute segments of the historical, literary, and ideological transformations that Judaism underwent in the sixteenth century.

The fact that there is no causal relationship between these two bodies of literature, hagiographies and *dybbuk* tales, is proven clearly by two examples already mentioned: (1) the fact that the cycle of hagiographic narratives that developed in the Middle Ages around the leaders of the Haside Ashkenaz does not include the *dybbuk* genre; and (2) the fact that, centuries later, the vast body of hagiographic narratives that took shape in the nineteenth and early twentieth centuries around the modern Hasidic movement does not include it in a manner proportionate to the vast number of supernatural stories presented in Hasidic literature. The *dybbuk* constitutes an important element in several Hebrew hagiographic cycles but not in all of them or even in most of them. It is wrong therefore to say that wherever there is hagiographic creativity the *dybbuk* may be found. Many other factors are undoubtedly relevant no less than the hagiographic environment; yet this relationship should not be overlooked.

III

The next subject that must be examined is conceptions of the human soul that lead to the development of a *dybbuk* narrative. Several preconditions can be outlined for the belief in the intrusion of one person's soul into another's living body possessing its own soul.

First, there must be a belief in the possibility of a soul existing without a body. This concept is basic to all systems of thought that include belief in an afterlife. Originally, the Aristotelian conception of the integral ties between the soul (or souls) and the functions of the body could be viewed as prohibiting such a conception, but later interpretations of that system by medieval theologians postulated that the uniquely human aspect of the soul could exist on its own. This element can therefore be regarded as universal as far as this discussion is concerned.

Second, there must be a belief in the possibility that the soul of a departed person can wander in the created world and act or appear within it. There are several schools of late antiquity and the Middle Ages that do not support such a view, but they are usually the realm of intellectuals or scientists and do not dominate folk beliefs.

The basic concept, which ultimately opened the gate for the development of various *dybbuk* conceptions, appeared, as Scholem has shown, in late-thirteenth-century Kabbalah.[17] Here the idea that the soul is not just one entity but may be broken into various components, called in this period *nitzotzot*, found a place in kabbalistic literature. In a thirteenth-century text published by Scholem we find the idea that parts of the souls of sinners, who are obligated to undergo transmigration, may join a "new" soul in one body and together constitute that person's soul.[18] These parts of the souls of the sinners are those involved in the process of sinning; the parts involved in the performance of commandments remain meanwhile in their proper place in the divine world. The sinful sparks try to influence the "new" soul to behave in a way that will assist them to atone for their transgressions in previous incarnations and thus achieve the purpose of their return to earth. In this brief text we have an almost complete set of foundations for a *dybbuk* narrative: an unharmonious meeting of "pure" and "impure" elements of the psyche in one body, struggling to achieve their often conflicting goals through the behavior of the body in which they are lodged together. Various formulations of such ideas are found in the *Tikkune Zohar, Ta'ame ha-Mitzvot,* and other sources relating to the great surge of kabbalistic creativity in the Age of the Zohar and immediately after it.

Despite the wealth of material in this vein, the subject still remained marginal and esoteric within the Kabbalah and even more so in Jewish culture as a whole, which at that time offered only remote, hidden corners to the ideas of the kabbalists. Only in sixteenth-century Safed did these ideas surface, develop, and became central in the Kabbalah. What is more, because the Kabbalah was swiftly becoming the dominant component of Jewish culture at this time, these conceptions had an impact on intellectual as well as popular strata of Jewish society.

The most central historical point is that in these sources from the height of Spanish Kabbalah, the psychological doctrines that enabled the development of *dybbuk* narratives were completely integrated in the history of kabbalistic literature. They had no chance to influence the wider public, where the dominant ideology was that of the Jewish rationalists, who opposed all notions of transmigration of souls. This adds another element that may help us understand why the sixteenth century saw the appearance of *dybbuk* narratives: this was the period in which the Kabbalah broke out of its esoteric corners in Jewish culture to achieve a central place on the stage of Jewish creativity.

This conclusion is supported by the fact that the kabbalistic origins of the *dybbuk* concept are highly prominent in the later *dybbuk* narratives, from the centrality of the Luria school in the development of the genre to the kabbalistic aura with which An-Ski endowed it in his modern play. This does not mean that some narratives couldn't have been influenced by Christian exorcism concepts or practices or other external and internal sources. But the main context of the *dybbuk* throughout its history has been and remains the world of kabbalistic ideas and terminology. While we should not ignore other possible factors that might have contributed elements in this body of literature, there seems to be no doubt that it developed essentially and predominantly *within* Judaism, basing itself on the conceptions of the soul and its fate that prevailed among the various schools of the kabbalists.

IV

The history of the structure of the soul in kabbalistic literature is actually a history of the language used to describe the soul. The soul itself—whatever it may "really" be—did not change during this period or any other period. The terminology used to describe it, however, underwent complex processes of development and transformation. *Gilgul, ibbur,* and *nitzotzot* are words selected by particular groups, within the framework of their theories, to describe real or imagined phenomena. Therefore, the *ru'ah,* or *dybbuk,* should also be conceived as a linguistic phenomenon, representing the terminology prevalent at a certain time and place. A dictionary should define this term as one of diagnosis, or self-diagnosis, of physical seizures. Scores of causes can bring on a seizure, many of them known, some perhaps unknown. There are many types of seizures, and these may be described by separate or common terms. The *dybbuk* is not a *cause* for seizure. It is the linguistic element used by the afflicted, or the people surrounding them, to designate the phenomenon. Once examples of such occurrences become widely known, people may use the terminology to designate an increasing number of cases of this common affliction. Historical study should be directed, therefore, toward discovering the circumstances in which such terminology became prevalent after being completely unknown for many centuries.

The major spiritual phenomena that have to be taken into account in trying to establish the background for the emergence of the *dybbuk* narratives are thus:

1. The popularization of the Kabbalah and its emergence as the dominant spiritual power in Jewish religious culture, which began in the sixteenth century and culminated in the seventeenth and eighteenth. Jewish rationalistic philosophy ceased to have a meaningful place in Jewish religious thought following the destruction of its great center in Spain. It almost disappeared under the impact of the accusation that Averroism contributed to the mass conversion of Spanish Jews to Christianity by weakening the practical aspect of Jewish tradition.[19] The kabbalistic concept of the soul became increasingly popular and influential. It should be emphasized, however, that this process had only begun in the sixteenth century and did not penetrate into popular social strata at that time; it happened for the most part in the concentrations of kabbalist communities found in Italy and the Land of Israel. On the other hand, it may be suggested that the withdrawal from Jewish rationalistic concepts, especially those of Maimonides, opened the gates for such ideas generally and enabled them to flourish with little opposition.
2. The great surge of dualistic worldviews and demonology in Christian Europe in the late fifteenth century, which intensified in the sixteenth, seventeenth, and early eighteenth centuries. This surge, which is marked mainly by the witch-hunts,[20] understood possession by demons to be one of the most common tactics used by Satan for taking over human souls. It is very difficult to disassociate the Jewish phenomenon from the widespread events in Christian Europe, yet it should be taken into account that belief in the *dybbuk* is found in the sixteenth and seventeenth centuries mainly in countries governed by Islam and not directly affected by the European

witch craze. One can never prove a negative; it is impossible to demonstrate that there was no influence of Christian dualism on the emergence of the Jewish phenomenon. But it is important to emphasize that we do not find the *dybbuk* in the great centers of Christian struggle against Satan in Europe, and we do find them in places rather remote from this. In the details of possession and the rituals associated with it, it is difficult to find anything that indicates a relationship with the main ideas of European demonology.

3. The emergence of Hebrew hagiographic literature. *Dybbuk* narratives celebrate a hero, a great spiritual leader who saves a suffering soul and overcomes an element of evil—an obvious constituent of hagiographic stories.

V

An interesting and instructive analogy to the *dybbuk* narratives can be found in the history of the *golem* narratives in Jewish thought and literature. The concept of the possibility of creating a human being out of the earth, using scientific and magical means, emerged in Hebrew esoteric and kabbalistic literature in a period slightly earlier than that of the *gilgul* and *ibbur*. It appears in the second half of the twelfth century, first in the writings of the German Pietists and later in a few early kabbalistic works in the thirteenth century.[21] The concept became part of the kabbalistic understanding of the *Sefer Yetzirah*, though most of the kabbalistic commentaries on this work completely ignored it. These sources, which comprise but a handful of pages in the vast literature of the Kabbalah between the thirteenth and the eighteenth centuries, did not include the concept that a homonuculus could be created as a servant who will fulfil particular functions.

The image of the *golem* as a servant emerges for the first time in a sixteenth-century hagiographic narrative about Rabbi Samuel the Pious, the father of Rabbi Judah Hasid. This was the earliest known cycle of hagiographic narratives describing a group of medieval sages (discussed above in the context of *dybbuk*), which served as a basis for the stories about these sages in the Yiddish *Ma'aseh Buch*. Hardly a trace of the story of Rabbi Samuel creating a *golem* to use as a servant remained in the published Yiddish version, but in the older Hebrew source it is clearer, though it is obvious that this Hebrew version was also heavily censored. In the next few generations a thin thread of narratives on the subject can be traced in hagiographic-kabbalistic literature until it erupted with great power in the early twentieth century in Yehuda Yudl Rosenberg's fictional hagiography about the Maharal of Prague (1909).[22] From there the tale made its way into European literatures, constituting probably the most prominent Hebrew contribution to the literature of the twentieth century. Rosenberg believed his own soul to be the reincarnation of the Maharal's, a belief that enabled him to invent a small library of pseudo-Maharal writings, which he published under his spiritual ancestor's name. The *golem* of Maharal is thus a modern example of hagiography and self-hagiography fused together, based on a dormant, marginal, esoteric, and kabbalistic concept from the thirteenth century, which found its expression in modern hagiographic literature.

A different kind of analogy can be found in the development of the concept of the *tzaddik* in modern Hasidism.[23] In this case as well, a modern movement developed ideas inherent in the early Kabbalah. In Hasidism, traditions concerning the theoretical role of the ninth *sefirah*, *Yesod* or *tzaddik*, were forged into a new doctrine discussed in several Hasidic theological works. Its full expression, however, can be found in the vast hagiographic literature produced by the Hasidim in the nineteenth and twentieth centuries.

The spread and development of hagiographic literature in Judaism in modern times had an impact on various cultural developments, some of them seemingly unrelated to the literary genre. The appearance of the *dybbuk* narratives can be connected with this phenomenon. Hagiography may have been the result of the popularization of kabbalistic literature and worldviews in Judaism after the expulsion of the Jews from Spain and the great transformations that separate early modern Jewish history from the medieval period. Yet it should be remembered that when dealing with the *dybbuk* phenomenon we are not following and describing actual events— we are only attempting to understand the development of the language used to describe phenomena.

Language, on the other hand, also influences events. After the *dybbuk* in Dimona, thousands of people felt that they were afflicted by the same type of intrusive spirit. Were they really afflicted? And if they were, was a *dybbuk* the cause? We do not know, and we shall never know. All we can do is follow the history of people using a certain linguistic element and try to understand the circumstances that led them to do so.[24] The essays in this volume may suggest as many new questions as solutions, but they constitute an important exploration into the issues.

Notes

1. It is tempting, but completely wrong, to view the name of this town as conducive to demoniac possession. It is a town founded in the 1950s in the Negev, and its name is derived from the list of Levites' towns in Josh. 21:35. The Hebrew terms for demons and spirits do not include the letters used for this realm in European languages. Near the city there is an ultramodern scientific institute and an atomic research complex.

2. The event was intensively covered by the Israeli news media. I am relying in this description on the article published in the ultraorthodox Haredi weekly, *LaMishpahah* (For the Family), 29 April 1999, 9–11. This source is the only one that did not ridicule the event and did not insert it into the intense political debate in Israel before the elections of 17 May, in which a great victory was achieved by the ultraorthodox parties, especially the Sefardi one, Shas. The editors of this weekly chose a very careful course in describing the event. They quote half a dozen well-known contemporary rabbis who criticized the whole affair and published a detailed interview with a rabbi who has good knowledge of the history of the subject—especially the Lurianic sources—but does not himself believe in it.

3. In the previous elections campaign, in 1996, Shas was accused of using amulets, blessings, and curses by rabbis who were famous for their supernatural powers to induce people to vote for its leaders. This party has now an image—in the eyes of its opponents—of using superstition to enhance its political power.

4. "Spirit." Most of the sources from the sixteenth and seventeenth centuries use just this term, and the titles of the narratives dedicated to it are *Ma'aseh ha-Ru'ah* and the like. The term *dybbuk* is derived from the Yiddish usage of the Hebrew term, and it is an abbreviation of the the phrase *dybbuk ra*, an evil possession.

5. The date can be fixed rather accurately. We find in the *Bahir* reliance on the mid-twelfth-century works of Abraham bar Hiyya, and very probably on those of Abraham ibn Ezra and the early translations of Judah ibn Tibbon (about that, see below). It could not, therefore, be written before 1180–85, while soon after it is used by later kabbalists. See Gershom Scholem, *Origins of the Kabbalah* (Princeton: Princeton University Press, 1986), 63–65 and passim; and J. Dan, *Jewish Mysticism*, vol. 2, *The Middle Ages* (Northvale, N.J.: Aronson, 1998), 1–18.

6. See *Bahir*, ed. R. Margaliot (Jerusalem: Mosad ha-Rav Kook, 1978), 121–22. Gershom Scholem dedicated a detailed study to the concept of *gilgul* in the *Bahir*, the Zohar and other kabbalistic works. See *On the Mystical Shape of the Godhead* (New York: Schocken, 1991), 197–250.

7. We probably have a few references before the *Bahir* to this concept in a critical manner, objecting to this belief; Saadia Gaon, in his *Emunot ve-De'ot*, chap. 6, criticized Jews who believe in it. There may have been groups of Jews who accepted metempsychosis, but Jewish theology consistently ignored or rejected it.

8. See Scholem, *Mystical Shape of the Godhead*, 207–28. According to his analysis, the author of the Zohar was one of the kabbalists who tried to minimize the scope and meaning of metempsychosis, while the author of the later parts of

the Zohar, the *Raya Mehemna,* and *Tikkune Zohar* elaborated and developed the doctrine.

9. Rachel Elior, "The Doctrine of Metempsychosis in *Galya Raza*" (in Hebrew), in *Studies in Jewish Mysticism, Philosophy, and Ethical Literature Presented to Isaiah Tishby,* ed. J. Dan and J. Hacker (Jerusalem: Magnes, 1986), 207–40.

10. Shulamit Shahar, "Catharism and the Beginning of the Kabbalah" (in Hebrew), *Tarbiz* 40 (1971): 483–507.

11. See Matt. 10:1; Luke 11:14.

12. There is an essential difference between Judaism and Christianity concerning this literary genre. Early in its history the Church established the norms for endowing its exceptional figures with the position of sainthood, and the process entailed a judicious procedure in which the person's biography had to be presented in great detail and thoroughly documented. It insisted that examples of supernatural events be included in the life of a candidate of such a position. The result was that followers of great teachers and leaders took pains to record (or in some cases invent) the exceptional deeds of their heroes. Christian hagiography is therefore much more elaborate and purposeful than the parallel Jewish examples.

13. See on this cycle I. Meitlis, "The Cycle of *Shevahim* on Rabbi Samuel and Rabbi Judah the Pious" (in Yiddish), *Di Goldene Kite* 23 (1955): 218–34; idem, *Das Ma'assebuch* (Berlin: R. Mass, 1933); J. Dan, "The Jerusalem Manuscript 3182 and the Story of the Jerusalemite" (in Hebrew), *Kiryat Sefer* 51 (1976): 492–98; and M. Gaster, *The Ma'aseh Book* (Phildelphia: Jewish Publication Society, 1946). Sara Zfatman wrote an M.A. thesis on the Hebrew sources of the *Ma'aseh Buch,* and dealt with it in many of her studies.

14. The important monograph on Jewish demonology and witchcraft, Joshua Trachtenberg's *Jewish Magic and Superstition* (Philadelphia: Jewish Publication Society, 1939), is based mainly on this material.

15. Jerusalem: Pe'er ha-Sefer, 1968.

16. I have studied the history of the *sifrut ha-shevahim* (the Hebrew term for hagiography) in several works in Hebrew. See *The Hebrew Story in the Middle Ages* (Jerusalem: Keter, 1974), 158–62, 238–52, and passim; *The Hasidic Story* (Jerusalem: Keter, 1975); "The History of *Sifrut ha-Shevahim,*" *Jerusalem Studies in Jewish Folklore* 1 (1981; in Hebrew): 82–100; and "*Sifrut ha-Shevahim*: East and West," *Peamim* 26 (1987; in Hebrew): 77–86.

17. See Gershom Scholem, "*Gilgul*: The Transmigration of Souls," in idem, *On the Mystical Shape of the Godhead,* revised ed., ed. J. Chipman, trans. J. Neugroschel (New York: Schocken, 1991), 215–220.

18. G. Scholem, "Sidrei de-Shimushei Raba," *Tarbiz* 16 (1945): 135–50.

19. On Jewish philosophy and the expulsion, see J. Dan, *Ethical and Homiletical Literature* (in Hebrew) (Jerusalem: Keter, 1975), 167–81.

20. A comprehensive recent study of this phenomenon is Robin Briggs, *Witches and Neighbors: The Social and Cultural Context of European Witchcraft* (New York: Viking, 1996).

21. The notion that the *golem* concept is to be found in ancient Judaism is erroneous. Scholem believed that a hint of such a possibility can be found in the ancient *Sefer Yetzirah* is unacceptable. The phrase near the end of the book, "and he [Abraham] was successful" cannot be an indication for this. The narratives in BT Sanhedrin (65b) about Rava, Rabbi Hoshaia, and Rabbi Hanina refer to a different concept: the scientific quest for creating living things, which preoccupied several scientists in the Greco-Roman world. See Gershom Scholem, "The Idea of the Golem," in idem, *On the Kabbalah and Its Symbolism* (New York: Schocken, 1965), 165–67; and, following him, M. Idel, *Golem* (Albany: State University of New York Press, 1990); See also P. Schaefer's convincing analysis, "The Magic of the *Golem*: The Early Development of the *Golem* Legend," *Journal of Jewish Studies* 36 (1995): 261ff.; J. Dan, *The Unique Cherub Circle* (Tübingen: J.C.B. Mohr (Paul Siebeck), 1999), 31–38.

22. Rosenberg published his *Nifle'ot Maharal* in Lemberg in 1909. Scholem assembled the various legends that preceded Rosenberg and then described the book as "not popular legends but tendentious modern fiction." See Scholem, "The Idea of the Golem," 198–204, esp. 203, n. 1.

23. On the doctrine of the *tzaddik*, see Rivkah Shatz-Uffenheimer, *Hasidism as Mysticism: Quietistic Elements in Eighteenth Century Hasidic Thought* (Princeton: Princeton University Press, 1993), 272–77 and passim; and see the next note.

24. Rivkah Shatz, "The Doctrine of the *Tzaddik* in Rabbi Elimelekh of Lyzhansk" (in Hebrew), *Molad* 18 (1960): 365–78; Rachel Elior, "Between *Yesh* and *Ayin*: The Doctrine of the *Tzaddik* in the Works of Jacob Isaac, the Seer of Lublin," in *Jewish History: Essays in Honour of Chimen Abramsky*, ed. Ada Rapoport-Albert and Steven J. Zipperstein (London: Peter Halban, 1988), 393–455; David Assaf, *The Way of Kingship: Rabbi Israel of Rizhin* (Jerusalem: Merkaz Shazar, 1997; in Hebrew); and J. Dan, *Messianism in Modern Judaism* (Tel Aviv: MOD, 1999; in Hebrew), 150–203.

The Taming of the Deviants and Beyond: An Analysis of *Dybbuk* Possession and Exorcism in Judaism

YORAM BILU

Documented cases of *dybbuk*[1] possession appear in Jewish sources from the sixteenth century A.D. to the first decades of the twentieth century. Since these sources have usually been inaccessible to the general scholar, this uniquely Jewish variant of spirit possession has been largely the subject of literary rather than scientific investigation. Ansky[2] and Singer[3] popularized the *dybbuk* phenomenon by emphasizing its colorful and dramatic nature; Ansky's play *The Dybbuk* (subtitled *Between Two Worlds*) was the first to be preformed by the Hebrew National Theater and had widespread success. Recently, a scholar of Judaic studies collected and annotated what appears to be the vast majority of the reported cases of *dybbuk* possession.[4] Most of these reports are to be found in mystically oriented exegeses of the Holy Scriptures and in books of Hasidic tales, usually written to praise and commemorate a renowned rabbi or sage. Some cases are more detailed and were published in special brochures or booklets, the titles of which attest to their dramatic quality, for example, "Awful Tales," "Terrible Deeds of the Spirit." These provocative titles had their effect—the brochures were published in numerous editions.

In this essay I shall attempt to clarify the *dybbuk* phenomenon in terms of some of its psychocultural components. My study is based on an analysis of sixty-three documented cases over the nearly four-hundred-year span in which *dybbuk* possession thrived in various parts of the Jewish world. Most of the cases seem to be authentic, located as they are in known coordinates of time and space. The reports were usually written by eyewitnesses, some of whom actively participated in the expulsion of the *dybbuk*; many of the victims and exorcists were identified by name, and in some instances the documents were signed by distinguished witnesses testifying to their accuracy. As ethnographic accounts, however, these reports leave much to be desired. Laconic and obscure on some points, overly elaborated and embellished on others, they were written from a definite ideological stance, which imbues them with strong moral overtones. Still, an appreciation of the literary instruction of the documents can contribute to an understanding of the *dybbuk* phenomenon *within its sociocultural context* if the motivation underlying it is correctly deciphered and interpreted.

A *methodological* problem involves the high variability of the sample, composed of cases so far removed in time and place. My analysis will therefore remain on a relatively molar level, concentrating on the commonalities among the various Jewish communities in which the *dybbuk* appeared. One factor that seems to mitigate potentially misleading effects of the variability of the cases is the very stability of the *dybbuk* phenomenon over time and space. The behavioral patterns of the possessed, whether in sixteenth-century Palestine or nineteenth-century Poland, bear a remarkable resemblance (although again the literary construction of the cases might have contributed to this resemblance). Throughout its history, *dybbuk* possession was conceived as a disease, and the possessing spirits were negatively evaluated in contrast to possession phenomena in many other ethnic groups[5]; possession by *dybbuk* did not undergo a transformation into the ceremonial context of a possession cult, wherein possession is not stigmatized but socially approved and the adept seeks to establish a symbiotic relationship with a possessing agent.[6]

Dybbuk possession, by definition, involved spirits of the dead as possessing agents. Although Jews were possessed by demons as long as two millennia ago (as the exorcisms by Jesus demonstrate) and as recently as this century,[7] cases of demonic possession were never considered to fall within the framework of the *dybbuk* phenomenon. The latter is based on a kabbalistic doctrine of transmigration of souls (*gilgul*), which explains why it appeared in mystically oriented Sephardic as well as Ashkenazic circles. The doctrine of transmigration emerged in Jewish mysticism in the twelfth century and rapidly became a core concept.[8] The mystics of that era contended that the spirit of a deceased person might transmigrate into a newborn human (and also, although rarely, into animal and inanimate forms) as retribution for certain transgressions the person committed during his lifetime. Although considered a severe punishment, transmigration signified a divine mercy as well, since it was meant to rehabilitate and purify the sinner's spirit by virtue of his reformed behavior in his new lifetime. In sixteenth-century Kabbalah, the idea of the transmigration of souls became a universal law. The doctrine relevant for possession was developed in the second half of the thirteenth century, when the concept was expanded to include the entry of a spirit into a living person after he was born. According to this doctrine, not only wicked spirits but also righteous ones took possession of people (themselves innocent and just) in order to complete their quota of good deeds required for entry into Paradise. But the designation *dybbuk* was reserved for the spirits of the wicked who penetrated humans in order to find refuge from persecution. Since these were spirits of sinners, they were doomed to remain in limbo, wandering between the two worlds without being allowed to enter Hell. (In Jewish tradition, Hell was not considered a place of eternal torment, but of temporary retribution from which some could enter Paradise.) In this limbo, the spirits were exposed to ruthless persecution by angelic and demonic beings. Thus, the inhabitation of humans gave the spirits temporary shelter as well as a unique opportunity to be purified, thereby to gain access to the world of the dead, as the description of the exorcistic ritual will later show. It should be noted that the term *dybbuk* was introduced during the seventeenth century to designate this type of possession and was employed by the Askenazic Jews only. Sephardic Jews adhere to the terminology of the early kabbalistic literature, in which the possessing agent was named "evil spirit."

The fact that the cases of *dybbuk* possession appeared in the second half of the sixteenth century, almost three hundred years after the theosophical foundation underlying it had been established, has not yet been explained. It may be that such an interval is required for novel, "disembodied ideas" to be transformed into a set of tangible behaviors; the onset may have been precipitated by specific circumstances within the Jewish milieu (such as the dispersion of the Jews following their traumatic exile from Spain in 1492) or outside it (the witch craze in Europe); or finally, the cases of the sixteenth century may simply have been the first to have been written down, as part of the general proliferation of Jewish literature in that era.[9] Coordinated interdisciplinary research by Judaica scholars and social scientists should suggest answers to this question.

In any event, the first reports of *dybbuk* possession came from sixteenth-century Sephardic communities in Safed, Palestine (the cradle of that century's Lurianic Kabbalah), and in Italy. In the seventeenth century, cases were reported in Safed, Damascus, and Cairo, and later in Turkey and Italy. Only toward the end of the seventeenth century did the first eastern European cases appear, but in the eighteenth and nineteenth centuries mystically oriented Hasidic communities, mainly in Poland and Russia but also in Germany, Hungary, and Lithuania, supplied most of the case reports. Throughout this period, cases from the Mideast continued to appear in print. In the eighteenth century, for example, Jerusalem, Tiberias, Damascus, Beirut, and Baghdad were represented on the *dybbuk* map. The last cases to be documented appeared in the first decades of the twentieth century in Lithuania, Palestine (Jaffa and Jerusalem), and Baghdad. Whereas the timing of the onset of *dybbuk* possession has not been fully explained, its disappearance was apparently related to the gradual disintegration of Jewish traditional centers in Europe as a consequence of modernization and emigration, and finally their physical extermination during the Holocaust. The mass emigration of Jews from the Moslem orbit to modern Israel brought an end to possession in those areas as well.

Despite the vast cultural differences between East and West in Judaism, all the communities in which *dybbuk* possession appeared shared a common tradition with a "complex of commandments which governed the day to day discipline of the Jew, his piety, his morals, his rules for personal life at home, in the synagogue and in the market place."[10] Indeed, it might be argued in somewhat tautological fashion that the very appearance of *dybbuk* possession in these communities points to a certain degree of common mystically oriented understanding. Only a few reported cases emereged from a nonmystical matrix.[11]

In analyzing *dybbuk* possession, I have found it profitable, following Obeyesekere[12] and Crapanzano,[13] to conceive of it as an idiom for articulating and structuring certain inchoate experiences and events. An idiom, according to Crapanzano, "provides the basis for those schemata by which reality is interpreted."[14] An act of articulation separates events from the flow of experience and renders them meaningful. When these events are construed on a phenomenological level within a culturally shared idiom, the entire experience undergoes "symbolization":[15] "Chaos [is] fashioned into cosmos."[16] Borrowing Crapanzano's terms, I view the articulatory function of the *dybbuk* spirits as essentially "vectorial." That is, the spirits are a vehicle for articulating unacceptable, conflict-precipitating desires and demands. Since the idiom of possession is culturally constituted, this articulation may result in relief for the actor. He does not suffer "the consequences of his idiom" as a Western paranoid does (even while both are considered sick in their respective cultures).

Although I am concerned in this essay with both individual motivation and societal cultural constraints, my emphasis is on the latter—the collective (or control) level. This is partially due to the fact that I am dealing with written documents rather than with actual cases observed in vivo. Starting with the assumption that the desires and demands underlying *dybbuk* possession constituted a threatening challenge to the Jewish traditional way of life, I shall depict the impressive dialectical process by means of which deviance was transformed into a conformity-strengthening vehicle, a process involving three levels of control: (1) the articulation of unacceptable desires within the possession idiom, the tenor of which was set by an externalized, ego-alien agent; (2) the rectification of individual deviance through the exorcism of the *dybbuk*; (3) the strengthening of conformity of the community by way of the moral implication of the *dybbuk* episodes.

In what follows, I shall analyze these three levels of control in detail, drawing on examples from the case reports. I shall then attempt to locate the possessed within a psychiatric diagnostic category in the light of their social roles in the cultural matrix from which the phenomenon emerged. Finally, some implications for the analysis of culture-specific syndromes will be discussed.

First Level of Control: Outwardly Directed Cultural Molding of Aberrant Impulses

Through the *dybbuk* idiom forbidden wishes were articulated and symbolized in a way that considerably decreased their potential threat both to the individual and the community. From a psychodynamic point of view, this process can be formulated in terms of projection,[17] whereby repressed impulses found expression in an externalized (although internally located) entity—the possessing spirit. What were the cardinal impulses underlying the articulated scheme of the *dybbuk*? One need not be a devoted Freudian to single out sexual wishes as a major motivating force behind this type of possession. Open expressions of sexuality were strictly regulated and curtailed in Jewish traditional communities of former centuries,[18] leaving few nondeviant forms of expression (without resulting, however, in an overall devaluation of sexuality). Since a discussion of these regulations and prohibitions, relevant as it may be to an understanding of the cultural matrix from which the *dybbuk* phenomenon emereged, is beyond the scope of this essay, I shall focus here instead on the textual evidence of sexual themes in the documented cases.

Dybbuk Possession as an Articulation of Sexual Urges

According to Crapanzano[19] and Spiro,[20] the elements in the idiom of spirit possession must constitute appropriate metaphorical representations of the impulses putatively underlying them—there must be some degree of congruence between symbol and referent. Such congruence is pronounced in the phenomenon under discussion, in that an act of penetration is essential both to *dybbuk* possession (and spirit possession in general) and sexual intercourse. So compelling is this congruence that the scholars who elaborated the theosophical doctrine underlying the *dybbuk* could not disregard it. The first kabbalists linked transmigration specifically with sexual transgressions,[21] and in Jewish mystical texts the residence of a spirit in a human being was designated "impregnation" (*ibbur*).

The sexual meaning of penetration in spirit possession is even more accurately (and therefore more convincingly) conveyed when the genders of the dramatis personae, penetrator and penetrated, correspond with those in a standard heterosexual act. Hypothetically, since spirits and victims alike are unequivocally sex-typed, four gender combinations are possible. What is their distribution in the cases under discussion? The sample consists of forty-one female victims and twenty-two male victims. The ratio of almost two to one is consistent with massive evidence for the preponderance of women among the possessed in a greater variety of culturally unrelated social groups.[22] Explanations of this recurrent finding usually emphasize the culturally defined inequality of the female role in male-oriented societies,[23] which is also consistent with Jewish mystical traditions concerning spirit possession. The author of *'Emek Hamelech* (The Valley of the King), a kabbalistic text, argues that women were excessively vulnerable to possession because "the impurity stemming from the serpent still abounds in them." Here an allusion is made to Eve's primordial sin of succumbing to the temptation of the snake, the nature of which temptation was blatantly sexual, according to mystically oriented sources.[24] In another text, *Minhat Eliahu* (The Gift of Elijah), the relative immunity of men to possession is attributed to the fact that "a man cannot refrain from the sin of nocturnal pollution, out of which demons are engendered; these creatures always encircle him, so how can [the possessing spirit] enter him?" Male sexuality procreates demons that haunt wandering human spirits and dispel them. This cosmological proposition, which is verified by many *dybbukim* in the recitations of their ordeals, is based on a conception of male sexuality as outer-oriented, rendering men relatively immune to penetration, in contrast to women, who are relatively accessible to penetration because their sexuality is inner-oriented, a point to which I shall return below.

The gender distribution of the spirits is even more one-sided. Fifty-eight of the spirits (92 percent) were male; only five of the spirits (6 percent) were female. As a result, the most prevalent gender combination in the sample is that of a male spirit with a female human (thirty-six cases). This too is a recurrent finding cross-culturally.[25] Second in frequency is the male-male combination (twenty-two cases). Significantly, all five female spirits penetrated women. Hence, most of the *dybbukim* comply with the heterosexual or, less frequently, the male homosexual metaphors; female spirits rarely assume the role of a possessing agent, but when they do the idiom is exclusively female homosexuality. The penetration of a male human by a female spirit, which is the least plausible alternative as long as sexuality is the guiding metaphor, is left an empty category, even though it is hypothetically feasible. It should be noted that female-in-male possession is not *universally* an empty category. In various forms of socially approved ceremonial (institutionalized) possession, as in Afro-American religions[26] and North African Muslim cults,[27] the pattern is quite common. The difference apparently lies in the moral dimension, as to whether the possessing entity is positively or negatively evaluated. When the possession is positively or ambivalently valued, female-in-male possession can occur because the possessed-to-be is alleged to "open" himself up to it. The prevailing images in these cases are of sexual seduction and willing consent, tending sometimes to lasting romantic alliances and marriage. When the possessing agent is negatively evaluated, so that possession is considered an illness rather than a sought-for religious accomplishment, the implicit sexual image is of rape rather than of consensual indulgence. And whereas males can rape females or other males, females cannot rape males. Indeed, the self-reports of some female victims in the samplings include descriptions of experiences that closely resemble rape. An eleven-year-old girl from nineteenth-century Jerusalem described a violent struggle in which "I stumbled, I was pushed, then I had to lie down and was turned over." A seventeen-year-old adolescent girl in Baghdad at the turn of the century experienced "something like a big cat [that] fell on my hips, in between the shoulders, stretching me in order to force its way into me." Both victims were virgins, for whom the metaphor of possession-as-rape seems particularly applicable, since penetration is difficult both physically and, given the premarriage moral purity accorded to females, mentally.[28]

Unlike the organ of departure, which toward the climax of the exorcistic ritual is stereotypically located by the exorcist in one of the toes, the penetrated organ is seldom described. When it is mentioned, it is most frequently the vagina (four cases, each of the victims married women). The evasive, reluctant language used in these cases (for example, "it is disgraceful to say") suggests that other such penetrations were left unreported. The only case that involved penetration through the anus was of a male spirit taking possession of a male adolescent. The selection of these erogenous zones further implicates the sexual meaning of *dybbuk* possession.

Generally speaking, *dybbuk* possession is a drama of the young. When the victim's age is explicitly indicated (in about 20 percent of the cases), it does not exceed thirty-five. When age is not specified, age-linked status categories of the victims, which appear in most of the case reports, included "babies,"[29] "children," "girls," "virgins," "young men," and "women." No mention is made of older adults. Female victims in the sample were predominantly newly married young women. In sum, the sample reveals the victims' ages to be those at which sexuality emerges as a potent drive. The spirits, although older than their victims in most cases, were originally those of people who died quite young. The few cases of possession by an elderly man's spirit clearly represent a different, more positively valued type of possession. These spirits belonged to righteous people who required only minor rehabilitation. They utilized the possession episode to deliver reproachful messages to the community and were willing to depart peacefully once their mission was completed.

The sample also reveals that male victims were generally younger than female victims. About 75 percent of the former were less than twenty years old, as opposed to 49 percent of the latter. Among the female victims the largest subcategory was of "women," a term usually used for married women, whereas only two male victims were explicitly described as married. Of these, one was a young religious scholar from Mogalnitsa, Poland, who was possessed eight weeks after marriage, the other—a borderline case of *dybbuk* possession—also a religious scholar, from nineteenth-century Jerusalem, obsessively haunted by the spirit of a Christian minister without being unequivocally possessed by it. Thus, women were liable to possession over a relatively wide age range, particularly after being married. Indeed, in those cases where the penetrated organ of the female victim was mentioned, the site of entry was further specified as the "opening" of the vagina, normally formed during the wedding night and symbolic of the consummation of sexuality. In a case report from nineteenth-century Stolovitsch, Poland, entitled "A Terrible Happening" (*Ma'aseh Nora'ah*),[30] the spirit explicitly states that "as long as she [the victim] is a virgin, we are forbidden to approach her, but when she is married, then we shall have our share too." In contrast, the marriage of a man afforded him a kind of prophylaxis, a relative immunity to *dybbukim*. Thus, the emergence of sexuality and the consummation of the sexual act have different meanings for the sexes vis-à-vis the *dybbuk* phenomenon: whereas consummation for the male turns him into a penetrator, thereby rendering him almost impenetrable, the female, by having been sexually "opened" and penetrated, becomes all the more accessible to penetration. These meanings correspond, of course, with transcultural images of male and female sexuality[31] and are implicit in the kabbalistic texts I cited above.

The sexual implications of the *dybbuk* phenomenon, as "emically" reflected in the motivations of the possessing spirits, are represented throughout the case reports. A gentle spirit from seventeenth-century

Cairo "entered a woman for his passion." Other spirits described the possession by using the verbs "to come to" and "to know," which in biblical Hebrew were euphemisms for sexual relations. One of the aforementioned Stolovitsch spirits testified that "he never touched [the girl] as a husband does." The most lucid and elaborated example is a turn-of-the-century Baghdad mystical text. The author gives instructions for identifying male-in-female possession with reference to the following conditions: "If she sees in her dream a man standing against her, or lying with her; or inflaming her heart with the passion of intercourse; or rubbing her genitalia or anus . . . or preventing her from having sex with her husband in order not to be sexually penetrated by him." It is hard to imagine a more straightforward exposition of the sexual wishes attributed to the spirit. Assuming that those sexual proclivities represented the repressed sexual fantasies of the possessed, the thin, almost nonexistent cover of the disguise is surprising. In all likelihood, the motivations expressed did not have to undergo desexualization because the externally located idiom of the *dybbuk* rendered their manifestation safe. In other words, the centrifugal (inner to outer) transformational disguise, rooted as it was in a sociocultural construction of reality, was so effective as to make any *content* transformation superfluous.

The sexual motivations underlying *dybbuk* possession can be examined more specifically as reflected in the *sins* of both participants in the possession episode. That the victims' wrongdoings, considered the precipitating factor for possession, were nevertheless laconically portrayed is not surprising, in that these were the only behavioral aspects of the case from which the possessed was deemed responsible—the only ones that did not fall under the idiomatic cover of the *dybbuk*. The sexual transgressions of the victims, if mentioned at all, seem mild, even negligible, when compared to those of the possessing spirits. Against a background of expressions of libidinal desires by the victims rarely going beyond a caress, a kiss, or obscene utterances, the accounts of the scandalous misconduct of the spirits during their human lifetimes represent, from a psychodynamic point of view, acting out in fantasy of the most forbidden repressed (or suppressed) sexual urges. To illustrate the spirits' uninhibited sexual profligacy, I should like to return to the Baghdad corpus of cases, which provide the most detailed and colorful descriptions of Jewish possession. The misconduct of a spirit possessing his own sister is described as follows: "He was tender of age but a veteran in vices and wickedness as a hundred-year-old. Very handsome was he, and the generals loved him, because he was ready to satisfy their desires, as well as those of their wives, and he took his hire from both sides. Some prostitutes would solicit him to do with them whatever he craved, from whichever side he preferred, any time he wanted, even during their menstruation period." It was no wonder, then, that "since he is long experienced in adultery and prostitution, he cannot calm down even now [after death, being a spirit] and he lies with his sister whenever he desires." In another Baghdad case, a person was possessed by Shabbatai Zvi, the notorious false Messiah of the seventeenth century. It is significant that the major sins for which he became a wandering spirit involved promiscuous sexual misconduct. He admitted that he had sinned with Gentile and menstruous women as well as with prostitutes, that he had committed adultery, that he encouraged a young disciple of his to have sex with his wife, and that he had practiced sodomy wrapped with his prayer shawl and phylacteries. These cases were, indeed, the most extreme examples of sexual misconduct, but many other spirits, particularly in the first documented cases of the sixteenth century, were characterized as lecherous profligates. Some of them were specifically identified as pimps and rapists. It seems that the most dark, unutterable desires were projected onto the spirits, thereby gaining cathartic outlet.

Another socially accepted channel supplied by the *dybbuk* idiom for the verbal expression of sexual wishes derived from the special ontological status of the spirits, which afforded them extraordinary skills of divination. These skills were employed to unravel cosmological aspects of the afterlife, foretell future events, and expose and denounce hidden sinners in the community. The spirits' revelations, particularly in the last regard, were saturated with sexual content. From the sixteenth century on, possessing spirits identified adulterers and homosexuals among the observers and generally criticized the growing sexual permissiveness of the community: "in our time, half of the women are disloyal to their husbands," complained a Baghdad spirit. This preoccupation with sexual matters, presented as virtuous reproach, constituted another socially acceptable outlet for forbidden wishes.

The acting out of sexual urges within the *dybbuk* idiom was not limited to the fantasy level. As in other cultural variants of possession, uncontrollable ecstatic behaviors, sometimes mimicking the violent convulsions of epileptic seizures, were prevalent in *dybbuk* cases. The rhythmical fits resembled the grand paroxysms of *hysteria major* of the nineteenth century, so minutely described by Charcot and others.[32] Whereas in ceremonial possession "ecstatic possession seizures were sometimes explicitly interpreted as acts of mystical sexual intercourse between the subject and his . . . possessing spirits,"[33] this interpretation was never made in *dybbuk* reports. In some early, prototypical cases, however, the sexual connotations of paroxysmic behavior are implied in the texts. For example, a spirit in a woman from Safed in the sixteenth century indicated his readiness to depart through the big toe "by bringing her [the victim's] feet up and down in successive movement, time after time, and with these violent movements her gown fell from her feet and thighs so that she was contemptibly exposed." By itself, this description might seem an insufficient basis for interpreting the seizures as a simulation of intercourse, but in this case the spirit had penetrated through the victim's vagina, and when asked by the rabbis if he did not fear her husband's wrath, insolently replied: "Not at all! Since her husband is not here but in Saloniki." Psychodynamically, then, this might have been a well-organized sexual fantasy, of which fits were an integral part. Another early case involved the spirit of an Italian shepherd, a Gentile, who took possession of a twenty-five-year-old woman "when her husband . . . had to go." Here also the woman was penetrated through the vagina, at night. She was depicted as lying breathless, open-mouthed in her bed, "all her organs . . . in agony and . . . shaking forcefully and jerking as if fever-stricken."

The heterosexual aspects of *dybbuk* possession were thus revealed through the constructed idiom of a male spirit penetrating a female human, providing various paths for the expression of sexually loaded content on the verbal and psychomotor levels. The victim's overt prepossession behavior—his moral transgressions, left uncovered by the idiomatic shield—gave only a scant indication of the contained sexuality.

Showing the same correspondence of sexual patterns and gender combination, descriptions of male-in-male possession—which constitute about a third of the sample—disclose homosexual themes with varying degrees of explicitness. (The penetration of the spirit itself can of course be viewed as homosexually motivated.) The town of Nikolsburg, in Moravia, provided two classic *dybbuk* cases in the seventeenth and eighteenth centuries. In one case, after the spirit had been exorcised, he presented himself to his victim and "held his small finger, through which [he] had been expelled, and embraced him like a man fondling his friend's hand with affection and desire." In the other, according to a story in *Ma'aseh Buch* (in Yiddish, The Book of Tales), considered by some the first documented *dybbuk* case, the spirit that took possession of a young adult accused two of his friends of practicing homosexuality. To the astonishment of the crowd gathered around, both immediately admitted their sin. The aforementioned spirit of Shabbatai Zvi, whose most shocking transgression was self-portrayed as pederasty, took possession of a young Baghdad male in the beginning of the twentieth century. In another Baghdad male-in-male possession, the spirit confessed that "on the Holy Sabbath, he committed pederasty in the orchard of village B." The spirit was allowed to take possession of the victim because the latter, "when he was still a child, went with his father to village B and entered the same orchard in which I committed my sin. There, on Sabbath, he had picked [a fruit] from the same tree under which I committed pederasty." When viewed psychodynamically, the sins of the spirit and his victim—picking a fruit on Saturday is a transgression of the Sabbath rest laws—fit neatly together to produce a coherent fantasy. Given the identical coordinates of time and space, the metaphor of plucking a forbidden fruit can be considered a very cogent symbolic substitute for the homosexual event. This correspondence might hint at a childhood recollection of an actual homosexual experience (under the same tree in the orchard of village B), barred from consciousness by attributing it projectively to the spirit and by translating it metaphorically into a desexualized equivalent.

An explicit association between male-in-male possession and homosexuality is revealed in the case from nineteenth-century Mogalnitsa already cited. A few weeks after his marriage, a religious student fell into a severe depression following his harassment (but not yet possession) by a spirit. As later revealed by the young man, this was the spirit of a man who had attempted during his lifetime to molest him sexually. The sick student said he had not succumbed to the seduction, which he had promised to keep secret. Despite his promise, he revealed this intimate information to his rabbis during his illness, whereupon the spirit took possession of him. Assuming that the spirit possession represented the acting out in fantasy of a homosexual impulse, the timing of the episode is singularly significant. It might be speculated that the young groom was flooded with "homosexual panic" when he had to display heterosexual behavior incompatible with his homosexual proclivities. Wedding time was also a critical period—but now for a spirit's *departure*—in one of the rare cases of female-in-female possession from the Baghdad corpus. The victim was a seventeen-year-old fatherless girl brought up and surrounded by female figures. The possessing spirit, which had tenaciously endured the healer's persecution, eventually gave its promise to depart from the victim once she married, during the time of defloration. The idea, already cited above, that the spirit's entry and the husband's sexual penetration are mutually exclusive is presented here quite explicitly. (It is worth noting that in classical Greece marriage was a recommended cure for hysteria, which was allegedly caused by disordered sexuality—the product of a "wandering womb").[34]

A discussion of the sexual urges implicit in the *dybbuk* cases would be incomplete without a consideration of oedipal themes, which, according to Freud's classical analysis[35] of a case of demonic possession in the seventeenth century, may play a major role in the phenomenon. If one considers the possession agent to be a father image or representation, the male-in-female form of *dybbuk* possession might reflect a symbolic realization of female oedipal desires toward the father. Since most of the case descriptions contain only skimpy and fragmented background information as to the spirit's characteristics, it is impossible to examine the father-as-spirit hypothesis except in its direct, undisguised manifestation—that in which the possessing agent was the spirit of the victim's father. Two of the thirty-six victims of male-in-female possession were possessed by their fathers, whereas none of the twenty-two male victims was thus possessed.

The first case, which I have already discussed in another context, involved a multiple possession of incestuous nature. First the spirit of the brother, whose sexual licentiousness in his lifetime was boundless, penetrated his sister, who explicitly experienced possession as a sexual assault or rape. The second possessing spirit was the father's, whose posthumous persecution was related to the fact that he has been tempted by a married woman to commit adultery. This sin, which caused his spirit to wander and seek refuge in his daughter's body, might very well have represented the girl's fantasy of tempting her father. The unexpected epilogue of this case report converges in an intriguing way with the ending of the original Oedipus myth: of the transmigration of the brother's spirit into the body of a newborn baby, it is said, "and he who is wise as the Blessed One to understand the meaning of things. For He plagued the boy with smallpox that maimed his face and blinded his two beautiful eyes . . . so that he would never be involved in pederasty nor in adultery." Nor in incest, one is tempted to add.

The second case, which involved a famous Hasidic rabbi and his beloved daughter in nineteenth-century Russia, is too complex to be represented in detail here.[36] The core of this tragic drama involved the rabbi's boundless love for his daughter Eidel, whom he preferred over his other children (boys included!), and his pathetic attempts to disregard or repair "Satan's mischievous interference that prevented her from being born a male." That he considered Eidel a boy was reflected in such extraordinary gestures as adorning her with male religious artifacts—specifically, his phylacteries.[37] In the light of this intimate relationship, colored moreover by the rabbi's loving but tragically short-lived relationship with his own mother, it is no wonder that Eidel could not accept the accession by inheritance of one of her brothers to the throne of the Hasidic court when their father passed away. The climax of the bitter struggle between two siblings came in an exorcistic ritual in which Eidel, possessed by a spirit who claimed to be her father (but considered an impostor by her adversaries), confronted the rabbi-exorcist, her brother. Under the shield of the *dybbuk*, she desperately fought to discredit her brother's moral authority. Eventually, however, her father's strong voice faded away and she was defeated. Following the exorcism, she lived in complete apathy, dissociated from her surroundings. Eidel's son, a famous rabbi in his own sake, was born blind! The oedipal theme, interwoven with such related themes as sibling rivalry and sex-role conflict, appears as a leitmotif of the plot, which is no less dramatic or bizarre than any by Singer.

Nonsexual Aberrant Impulses Articulated within the Dybbuk Idiom

The *dybbuk* idiom also served as a culturally molded outlet for nonsexual urges and desires whose expression was forbidden in Jewish communities. In fact, the emergence of such desires can partially be understood as a reaction to the strict, instinct-suppressing regulations governing all spheres of communal life, based as these were on rigid religious codes and prohibitions. Overt expressions of such desires would have undermined the very foundations of the Jewish way of life. As with sexuality, these urges received only minimal expression on the nonidiomatic (therefore undisguised) level of the victims' prepossession misconduct. The majority of their misdeeds were associated with such religious transgressions as not fulfilling one of the Sabbath duties, disregarding a prayer, or misusing a ritual artifact. Other, more serious, transgressions, usually committed by women, included doubting the validity of episodes of Jewish history (Exodus, for example) or diverting a spouse from religious studies to mundane affairs. But these appear negligible in comparison with the spirits' (nonsexual) sinfulness during their lifetimes. *Dybbukim* of this type make an impressive gallery of infamous characters—apostates who converted to Christianity, informers who handed Jews and their property over to Gentile authorities, robbers and thieves. Four of the *dybbukim*-to-be committed suicide—an inexpiable sin according to Jewish law—and five were notorious criminals and murderers of fellow Jews. Thus, a *dybbuk* from eighteenth-century Detmold, Germany, admitted that he had killed two Jews with his own hands and caused the death of three others. A female spirit who took possession of a girl in Radin, Lithuania, at the beginning of the twentieth century confessed that she had strangled two Jewish children. The first *dybbuk* from Nikolsburg, who was the head of a Jewish community in his home town, cold-bloodedly murdered two rabbis who reproached him for his bad manners. There was even a biblical murderer: a *dybbuk* from the shtetl of Koznitz identified himself as the man who had initiated the stoning of the prophet Zechariah.

The merging of these exemplars of uninhibited licentiousness (some of whom boasted that none of the 613 commandments regulating Jewish life was observed by them) with their victims, modest sinners at worst, can be explicated within two frames of reference. From the perspective of *control*—essentially the perspective of the participants' conscious mind—the fact that a person drank without blessing was possessed by the spirit of an apostate constituted a warning signal indicating where ostensibly innocent negligence of commands might lead. The view that "one transgression brings on another" and "of one ill come many" was soberly acknowledged and gloomily repeated by Jewish rabbis. From a *psychodynamic* perspective on deviance, it might again be argued that the victim's humble sins were the visible part of a mental iceberg of darker, unutterable desires, which found idiomatic expression and metaphorical outlet in the profligate *dybbuk*. Apart from the reported sinfulness of the spirits, the behaviors of the victims while possessed—while presumably controlled by the spirits—cogently reflected the nature of these hidden subversive wishes. Not only did many of the victims actively avoid basic ritual duties, they made violent attempts to desecrate the most sacred symbols of the Jewish religion. When taken to the synagogue, for example, where many of these symbols were located, the possessed would jerk and contort violently, spit on holy books and artifacts, insult and physically attack the shocked worshippers. Obversely, they were irresistibly attracted to Christian sacred paraphernalia. Kissing the New Testament, "eating and praying as the Gentiles do," and compulsively making the sign of the cross were repeated symptoms. It should be pointed out that most of these extreme antireligious behaviors were enacted by males, on whom rested the lion's share of the burden of Jewish commandments.

Whether or not these behaviors and underlying subversive wishes were specifically expressions of a yearning to be released from the cumbersome yoke of religious law, they would certainly have constituted a threatening challenge to the essence of the Jewish way of life had they not been attributed to an external agent. The fact that they, like aberrant sexual impulses and their associated behaviors, were culturally molded into the *dybbuk* idiom, substantially mitigating the harm done to the community, is what I mean by the "first level of control" in the process by which deviance was combated.

Second Level of Control: Rectification of Deviance by Exorcism

By enabling individuals to articulate forbidden inner urges through an externalized, ego-alien agent, the *dybbuk* idiom significantly decreased their destructive potential. As to the behavioral *manifestation* of deviance, however, the contrary was true. The fact that the evil spirit of an outstanding sinner was considered the motivating agent underlying the victim's behavior served to accentuate and dramatize the deviant nature of the possession episode: the possessed publicly engaged in the behavior that was considered blasphemous even to think about. The danger therefore existed that these behaviors might be added to the observers' repertoire. Through the *dybbuk*, the inexpressible became possible and real. In order to assure that the potential for such behavior was not actualized, the *dybbuk* had to be exorcised. Deviance had to be rectified. That this was, indeed, the ordinary consequence of the exorcistic ritual suggests that exorcism was a traditional and effective equivalent of individual psychotherapy.

As in other cultural variants of spirit possession wherein the invading agent was considered evil and the alliance with it forced and undesirable,[38] the exorcism of the *dybbuk* was understood to require the strict observance of a set sequence of steps, which perforce culminated in its expulsion.[39] Its uniquely Jewish, culture-bound aspects were prominently expressed in the therapeutic phase. The exorcist was a mystically oriented rabbi, whether a kabbalist or a Hasidic *tzaddik* (a pious, holy man). Often the exorcism was performed in the synagogue with the active participation of a *minyan* (a kind of religious quorum—a group of ten male adults without which public prayer could not take place). Jewish sacred paraphernalia were generally employed during the critical stages of the exorcism in order to facilitate the expulsion of the spirit.

Even though successful exorcism was the rule in cases of *dybbuk* possession, the rabbi-*dybbuk* encounter was usually depicted as a long, bitter, emotionally charged, and exhausting struggle. The healer had to mobilize all the stamina, sagacity, and resourcefulness at his disposal to overpower his insidious adversary, for whom, it should be recalled, the victim's body constituted a longed-for refuge from the incessant and merciless persecution of the vindictive angels of destruction.

The exorcistic ritual was performed in a fixed, graded order, with milder measures of verbal coaxing of the spirit giving way to adjurations and decrees of excommunication against it. Coercive methods of fumigating or beating the *dybbuk* were resorted to only after the aforementioned verbal alternatives had been exhausted. When a synagogue was the arena for the exorcistic ritual, its dramatic nature was particularly enhanced. In this public setting, the rabbi's performance was accompanied by an orchestrated set of activities performed by the audience. These included the taking out of the Torah scrolls from the ark, the blowing of ritual ram's horns, and the successive lighting and extinguishing of black candles. The quorum participated in special prayers and incantations. Sometimes the victim was tied and laid down in front of the ark. The tension in the crowded synagogue (even non-Jews occasionally came to observe the extraordinary scene) mounted gradually with each step or "round" in the rabbi-*dybbuk* struggle until it exploded ecstatically with the spirit's forced exit.

The first step of the exorcistic ritual was aimed at ascertaining the authenticity of the case as one of *dybbuk* possession. This was particularly necessary when the spirit deliberately concealed his presence. In questionable cases, various indications were used as diagnostic criteria, such as speaking without moving the lips, the swelling of peripheral organs (for example, the neck or breasts), and bodily sensations of extra heaviness. Sometimes more sophisticated, quasi-medical examinations were made. For example, the exorcist might look for a particular pattern of pulse in the victim's forearm, indicative of the spirit. Once the differential diagnosis was completed, the healer turned to the second step, in which the spirit was identified and compelled to disclose background information concerning his transgressions, the circumstances of his death, and his vicissitudes between that event and the onset of possession. It was assumed that without communicating with the spirit and retrieving these identifying details, successful exorcism was not possible.[40] The *dybbuk*'s recitations concerning his experiences as a wandering spirit were overwhelmingly impressive in their disclosure and detailed description of various aspects of Jewish cosmology. For the participants in the exorcistic ritual, this was a unique opportunity to witness "directly" an entity with special ontological status, reporting from the "other world" and specifying its nature.

Following the inquiry, a lengthy negotiation took place between the parties. The exorcist tried to gain the spirit's consent to free the victim or, at least, discuss the conditions for its departure. This was the most crucial phase in the ritual, the one that determined its consequence. Against the rabbi's resourceful application of exorcistic devices, the *dybbuk* assumed an obstinate position from the outset, disobeying the exorcist's commands, deriding and depreciating his authority, and occasionally attacking him physically. (More often the spirit directed his violence at the victim.) The spirit's insidiousness was particularly revealed in those instances where its readiness to depart was followed by a stubborn refusal. To counteract his adversary's deceitfulness, the rabbi would compel the spirit to pledge its readiness to leave with a public oath, sworn over a handkerchief to guarantee the departure.

For the *dybbuk* to be expelled, certain conditions had to be fulfilled. These usually involved activities aimed at redeeming the spirit from his liminal position. Whether they were requested by the spirit or initiated by the rabbi, these postexorcistic obligations were to be performed mainly by the possessed. They included the observance of certain mourning rituals for the *dybbuk*, the donation of a meal for poor religious students, sacrificial slaughter, and the lighting of memorial candles. Sometimes the rabbi himself and other participants in the exorcistic ritual would promise to recite prayers for the *dybbuk*'s spiritual redemption. These activities were performed from one to twelve months after the exorcism. Their omission would render the formerly possessed victim liable to further assaults by the spirit.

A hot debate over the body site of the spirit's departure often terminated the negotiations phase. The *dybbuk* would try to transform his coming defeat into partial victory by causing major damage to the organ through which he departed. Stereotypically, his preferences, strongly opposed by the exorcist, were an eye, ear, mouth, or limbs. Departure through one of these might have rendered the victim blind, deaf, mute, lame, or paralyzed. Under the healer's pressure, the spirit agreed to leave through one of the fingers or, most often, one of the big toes, where its exit was not deemed hazardous.

The tension that accumulated during the various stages of the exorcistic ritual was climatically discharged with the *dybbuk*'s departure. Even though successful exorcisms were immediately reflected in the victim's regaining ordinary consciousness, additional signs were sought to validate the spirit's expulsion. Without them, no one could guarantee that the insidious *dybbuk* would not reenter its victim. A small scar on the big toe or a sharp pain in the toe, an exploding sound in the air or, most impressively, a broken window were frequent manifestations of the departure. In the case reports, this final stage of the exorcism was particularly overdramatized. For example, a *dybbuk* exorcised from a child in seventeeth-century Constantinople "shaked the house, and forced his way into a dish which he moved to and fro, downward and upward several times . . . [then the spirit] violently rolled the dish away from the house and it fell upon a pitcher which was broken into pieces."

Following the exorcism, the formerly possessed, weak and exhausted, was carefully guarded against further assaults by the spirit. He was arrayed with amulets and encircled by religious students who recited prayers around him until he was altogether recovered from the possession episode.

Judging from the sample of reported cases, exorcism was highly efficacious psychotherapy. More than 90 percent of the possessed were completely, irreversibly cured. (The success rate in the general population might have been lower, of course, if failures were underrepresented in the written reports.) When failure was admitted, it was usually associated with the exorcist's shortcomings rather than with the incurable nature of the disease. Thus, after two futile attempts to exorcise a *dybbuk*, a Hasidic rabbi from Lithuania candidly admitted that "I learnt that it is not my mission to exorcise spirits, therefore I stopped." It was probably his lack of assertiveness that underlay his failure, as implied in the *dybbuk*'s remark: "At first I feared him, but later on the situation was reversed, and he was afraid of me." Three cases of death following exorcism were attributed to the spirit's rancorous, ruthless revenge for having been expelled. The fact that all three were early-sixteenth-century cases might be taken as an indication of the novelty of the phenomenon, as evidenced by the difficulties in coping with it. The delicate relations between the dramatis personae in their complementary roles had yet to be settled and regulated.[41] Since it was mentioned more than once that a spirit would try to strangle its host, the possibility that asphyxiation by "overfumigation" was the cause of death seems reasonable.

The therapeutic effectiveness of *dybbuk* exorcism was revealed most strikingly in terms of the *contrasting effect* it produced. Typically, the symptom-free former victim displayed new, positively valued behaviors that had not been in his repertoire before the possession episode. This was particularly true in cases of extreme antireligious sentiments voiced by male victims, but it also held for profligate women tamed into penitence and strict observance of commands. Through the idiom of *dybbuk* exorcism, change could be formulated as an abrupt transformation whereby deviant identity was expunged and replaced by a positive conformist one. In the first case from Nikolsburg, for example, a male adolescent who could not pray for six years became, shortly after exorcism, "a new creature, a faithful observer of the commandments, blessed with good health, and erudite in the Torah." A child from nineteenth-century Pressburg who, during possession, used to tear Jewish sacred artifacts and kiss Christian holy books, became "a disciplined person who followed the right way all his life."

Thus, the exorcism of the *dybbuk* caused deviant behavior to be replaced by exemplary behavior. The rectification of individual deviance through exorcism, depicted here as a traditional (and more effective) equivalent of individual psychotherapy, represents the "second level of control" in the process I am describing.

Third Level of Control: Strengthening of Conformity in the Community through the Dybbuk Episode

The implications of *dybbuk* possession and exorcism were too far-reaching to be exhausted by the aspect of individual control. A major difference between curing rituals in traditional societies and modern psychotherapies lies in the fact that the rectification of deviance in the former did not take place in a social vacuum.[42] It often had profound reverberations in the social world and contributed to its reorganization. In this manner, deviance was harnessed to enhance social control and conformity in the community.

The elaborate cultural processing of the *dybbuk* made it a powerful vehicle for enhancing obedience and discouraging deviance, largely by virtue of the multifaceted manifestation of the idea of *reward and punishment* expressed within the idiom. As an ideological doctrine, the principle of the transmigration of souls provided a solution to the question of the "ill-fated righteous," a problem of great significance in Jewish history, both in the individual and society. A present-day Hasidic book (*Shomer Emunim*), for example, contends that the victims of the Inquisition in Spain and Portugal were inhabited by the transmigrated souls of the First Temple Israelites, who had engaged in idolatry. By the same token, the persecution of Jews in czarist Russia was meant to rectify the evildoing that had precipitated the destruction of the Second Temple. Finally, the Holocaust is alluded to as the ultimate rectification!

The *dybbuk* idiom contained within it two levels of retribution. By attributing the penetration of the spirit to the host's past transgressions, moderate though they might have been, a clear principle of retribution was established, which contributed to social control. The second, more severe form of retribution was of course reserved for the *dybbuk* itself, brutally and multifariously punished for its sins, its suffering minutely described before the audience of the exorcistic ritual. These included both the quality of their deaths in this world and their sufferings in the hereafter. Thus, the majority of possessing spirits were originally persons who had died young, very often of unnatural causes. A few had committed suicide (in a case from seventeenth-century Constantinople, the spirit was identified as "a vicious apostate, involved in ugly affairs, who killed himself because he could not find rest from his wrongdoings"); others were hung, drowned, or massacred by Gentiles (the aforementioned *dybbuk* of Koznitz was the first to be killed by invading Babylonians). Some of the spirits reported particularly agonizing deaths. A vicious sorcerer whose spirit took possession of the girl in Stolovitsch died after he had fallen into the wheel of a grinding mill. His arms were mutilated and his back broken. The young Baghdadi whose spirit possessed his sister lost his foot while serving in the Turkish army during World War I: "So intense was his suffering that he was rolling on the ground forward and backward.[43] No remedy could cure him until gangrene inflicted upon him a bizarre death."

But it was the reported vicissitudes of the spirits in the hereafter that provided the most comprehensive and impressive accounts of retribution. It bears repeating, in this context, that these episodes offered a unique encounter between the living and the dead until then almost nonexistent in Judaism. The spirit's recitation was one of the high points in the exorcistic ritual precisely because it constituted dramatic and emotionally charged *evidential confirmation*[44] of metaphysical beliefs concerning the nature of the "other world." Jewish traditional cosmology was confronted, as it were, with empirical reality and translated into everyday language.

The spirits described their persecutions by angels of destruction and demons in such realistic detail as to make the mere thought of committing a sin frightening. In the early cases from the Mediterranean area, for example, they were reported to be hit with sticks of fire, "each blow caus[ing] them unparalleled agony, just like that of a living person whose flesh is cut, little by little, with a knife until he passes away." A spirit from the shtetl of Korets was torn from its body by the angels of destruction, to be successively swallowed and spit out by demons; then it was ground in a mill and had to transmigrate into a pig and other animals. The Baghdad cases from the turn of the century again supply the most detailed descriptions. The spirit of Shabbatai Zvi, for example, was beaten in his tomb for twelve years. Afterwards he was transmigrated into a wild animal, "and every Friday, from two o'clock to half past four in the afternoon, he was condemned to a cell of boiling excrement." Another spirit was flogged by thirty-five angels of destruction fifteen hours a day, "and the remaining nine hours I had to spend in a desolate desert full of snakes and scorpions that bit and ate my flesh for four years." The spirit of an adulterous woman from Baghdad gave the most detailed account of her postmortem punishments. At first she was beaten incessantly with sticks of fire for three days. Then she had to stand trial before the grand jury in Heaven. Upon refusing to answer the charges, she was beaten until she dissolved into ashes. Her sentence was to be handed over to the vindictive angels for a hundred years in punishment for a hundred incidents of adultery. The latter flogged her twenty-seven times a day and seventeen times each night, the sum, forty-four, equaling the numerical value of the Hebrew word for blood, (*dam*), to remind her that she did not cease her sexual misconduct even during her menstrual period. In addition, she had to chop trees each night to fuel a furnace on which she was burnt for three hours in front of the celestial jury. Only on Saturdays could she rest, though chained and imprisoned; spirits who had desecrated the Sabbath were persecuted on Saturdays as well.

The credibility of the accounts was enhanced by the realistic quality of the spirits' descriptions of the "other world." The garments of its inhabitants, the structure of the Heavenly Court (including exact measurements of the rooms in which it was located), even the form of certain sections of Hell, into which some spirits were allowed temporary entrance, were portrayed in detail. All this information supplied a convincing context for conveying the idea that in the coming world, regulated by principles of reward and punishment, the righteous were prosperous and the wicked doomed. It is hardly surprising, indeed, that some exorcists could not let this rare opportunity pass without seeking to elicit information concerning matters unrelated to the exorcism itself. In some reports, intellectually curious rabbis sought from the *dybbuk* an elucidation of the laws of the universe. In one of the Baghdad cases, for example, the exorcist asked the spirit: "Tell me whether the sun rolls upon heaven like a ball, or does it break its way through it, or does it pass underneath, in the air of this world." Sometimes the spirits were employed to solve such unsettled cosmological issues as this: "Since it is known that in heaven night is no less bright than day, is there any difference between the two and how can the sunrise be recognized?"

The impact of the spirits' recitations was all the greater when the setting of the exorcism was public. Aware of the effect of the formidable spectacle, some of the exorcists spared no effort to increase the size of their audience. Thus, a nineteenth-century Hasidic rabbi, who originally thought to exorcise the *dybbuk* with only the participation of a quorum, changed his mind and decided to make the exorcism public "so that many people would observe and repent." The same reason underlay another exorcist's command that the *dybbuk* confess in front of an audience, even though his sins had already been recited privately. It seems evident that a major motivation for writing and publishing *dybbuk* episodes was the need to promulgate their moral lesson. Although the proliferation of brochures and pamphlets dealing with *dybbukim* was partially due to their dramatic plots, in which dreadful adventures, suffering and agony, sex and violence, relief and salvation, on both real and celestial levels, all played a part, the published accounts also served as an important means of indoctrination and strengthening community conformity. In most of the publications, the latter tendency was clearly indicated as, for example, in one of the first documented cases from Safed: "It is important for them [the audience] to subdue their hearts before heaven, and to fear doomsday, since everything is taken into account, and there is no refuge in *Sheol* [the underworld]."

Apart from testifying to their tantalizing sufferings, the *dybbukim* also served as direct agents of social control by exposing sinners in the audience and by demanding stricter observance of the commandments. All these activities, embedded within the dramatic, sometimes shocking spectacle of the exorcism, electrified the observers and produced immediate effects. An early report from Safed ends: "many people were present, all of them weeping, as the fear of doomsday fell upon them; and the whole country was strongly moved." In an Italian case of the seventeenth century, the spirit exposed the sins of people in the community, whereupon "all of them whole-heartedly repented, having learned that the spirit revealed their most profound secrets." A hundred years later, in Nikolsburg, an eyewitness reported that "the extent of penitence, experienced by the large crowd, was inconceivable." In fact, deep sentiments of compunction and repentance as aftereffects of exorcism were reported in most of the cases. In some of the accounts, even non-Jews were moved to repent.

In this way, the circle was closed. Symptoms representing aberrant wishes that, if directly expressed, would have damaged the foundations of Jewish life, were transformed into a conformity-enhancing device. This dialectical transformation could only have happened, moreover, in close-knit, traditional communities, which monitored and governed the entire living environment of each of their members. In my concluding remarks, I shall elaborate on this functionalist argument at some length.

In addition to expressing the principle of reward and punishment, the *dybbuk* idiom served as a means of validating the status and enhancing the sociopolitical prestige of certain individuals. The moral authority of the rabbi-exorcists, in particular, was indisputably confirmed by the fact that the spirits eventually acknowledged their authority and submitted to it. Sometimes it was hinted that this acknowledgment was based on information that the spirit had gathered in Heaven. The spiritual ascendency of well-known Hasidic rabbis was convincingly confirmed by the spirits even when those rabbis were not involved in their exorcism. Thus, a *dybbuk* from Peelts in Poland complained that ever since a certain Hasidic rabbi had passed away *dybbuk* cases had multiplied, implying that only the late rabbi could redeem the spirits. A temporary exit from the girl he had possessed was explained by this spirit as a desperate attempt to gain salvation on the rabbi's tomb. This attempt failed when thousands of souls assembled in the cemetery for the same purpose, and he could not get through. The manipulative use of *dybbuk* cases to enhance status was particularly evident in the context of power struggles between individuals, groups, or sects. Rabbi Hayyim Vital, a renowned student of Rabbi Isaac Luria Ashkenazi (the founder of a major tradition of Kabbalah in sixteenth-century Safed), was assisted by a *dybbuk* in Damascus in his bitter struggles with other mystically oriented rabbis, the spirit denouncing his foes while praising and exalting Rabbi Hayyim. Delicate status ratings were construed out of the differential skillfulness of rabbi-exorcists. In one Hasidic source, for example, it was contended that the Belzer rabbi could exorcise spirits only in the vicinity of his hometown, and that his exorcistic interventions took several weeks. The rabbi from Rozin, in contrast, had no geographical limits to his exorcistic skill, nor had he to spend more than a few hours to expel a spirit. The superiority of the latter was thus displayed. The bitter conflicts between Hasidism and their opponents (*Mitnagedim*) found expression in *dybbuk* cases when spirits of persons who had insulted Hasidic rabbis described their consequential sufferings and repented their sins.[45] In the struggles over control within Hasidic courts, *dybbuk* cases were again manipulatively exploited, as reflected in the aforementioned case of Eidel, who roundly criticized her brother, the leader of a Hasidic sect, under the cover of *dybbuk* possession.

Ultimately, the validation of the moral ascendancy of religious leaders through the *dybbuk* idiom contributed to social control: the rabbi, more than any other figure, served to maintain the Jewish identity of his community. Moreover, the exorcistic ritual reinforced traditional status rankings based on age and sex variables. The rabbi-exorcists, males by definition, were typically middle-aged or old. The possessed, mostly females, were usually quite young. The exorcistic ritual constituted a conservative mechanism that facilitated the perpetuation of the traditional status hierarchy in the community.

Conclusions: Dybbuk Possession as a Culture-Specific Syndrome

My analysis of *dybbuk* possession and exorcism, with its healing, functionalistic, control-oriented emphasis, obviously needs to be qualified. The conditions must be specified under which deviance may undergo a transformation such that it enhances conformity. By elucidating and circumscribing these conditions, moreover, in the dialectical process by means of which personally and socially disruptive experiences were harnessed to contribute to the maintenance of the social order, some insight may be gained into the nature and limits of "culture-specific syndromes." Since the process necessarily involves an elaborate, coordinated interplay between individuals and societal institutions, the analysis should encompass both levels. Specifically, the recruitment into the *social role* of the possessed, with its culturally prescribed role definitions and script, should be explicated.

With regard to the societal level, I have already emphasized that the *dybbuk* phenomenon appeared in close-knit, traditional communities that exerted extensive control over their members. This would appear to be a necessary condition for the success of a deviance-transforming idiom. The fact that deviants could be so smoothly tamed reflects a major dimension of this control. With regard to the individual level, I have argued, in line with general psychodynamic reasoning, that the enactment of the role of the possessed served to express and partially gratify urges otherwise unfulfilled. Even beyond the articulation of forbidden impulses within a culturally constituted and socially accepted idiom, however, the possessed—precisely because of their suffering—enjoyed considerable secondary gain. Some of the *dybbuk* victims shrewdly exploited their conditions to become the focus of general attention, to elicit sentiments of respect, pity, and awe, and to be pampered and cared for. So conspicuous was this secondary gain that in some cases people were reported consciously simulating *dybbuk* possession in order to gain material rewards and sympathy from onlookers.

So much for the *motivation* of individuals to enter the role of the possessed. But a crucial selection factor in the enactment of any social role concerns the *ability* or *skill* to generate the socially prescribed behaviors involved in that role.[46] Since the *dybbuk* role embodied a complicated set of behaviors, culturally defined and constrained (and compellingly conditioned by the complementary role of the exorcist), its enactment called for certain assets that only a select group of "deviants" possessed. Thus, it is highly unlikely that the severely disturbed (that is, psychotics) could comply with the elaborate behavioral specifications and constraints of the *dybbuk* role. (Recall the highly structured stages of the exorcism.) In the Hobbesian (or Freudian) sense of a constant battle between individual impulses and societal control, the *dybbuk* epoch clearly represented the triumph of society. But the triumphant endeavor itself was limited to those individuals who were willing and able to articulate their aberrant wishes and inner conflicts within the *dybbuk* idiom. Even in Jewish traditional communities, where conformity to sociocultural dicta was powerfully enforced, only *some* deviants could be tamed so effectively.

Who were those willing and able individuals? According to contemporary psychiatric diagnostic systems, most of them would probably be labeled "hysterics." But hysteria, as Krohn puts it,[47] is an "elusive category" given the multitude of contexts in which it has been applied and of meanings ascribed to it. In his insightful effort to elucidate and decipher the core dynamics underlying hysterical variants across time and cultures, Krohn analyzes hysteria using formulations that seem tailor-made for explication of *dybbuk* cases. He begins with the thesis that "hysteria can be variably defined as a disorder which plays out *dominant current culture identities, often to a marginal but never to a socially alienating extreme,* in an attempt to promote the myth of passivity" (153; my emphasis). He defines the "myth of passivity" as "an attempt to disown, both internally and interpersonally, responsibility in the broadest sense for thoughts, acts and impulses" (153). In Jewish traditional communities, *dybbuk* possession was just such a myth. The ability of the hysteric to resolve individual conflicts by astutely using the dominant forms of the culture attests, according to Krohn, to "his capacity for good reality testing, impulse control and interpersonal sensitivity . . . the capacity to regress and to be flamboyant within the bounds of convention . . . [and] the resiliency and advanced development and differentiation definitional of the hysterical ego" (162). It is not surprising, therefore, that hysterics were rarely considered substantially deviant. Moreover, "in living on the myths treasured by his reference group, the hysteric becomes a *living advocate of the moral and stylistic positions of the culture, a 'yes' man for the social axioms of his milieu*. . . . In remaining for psychological reasons within the limits of convention, they are a *natural conservative force*" (208; my emphasis). This seems a very appropriate summary of the analysis of *dybbuk* possession and exorcism I have presented.

The intimate liaison between "emically" deviant individuals and sociocultural dicta as formulated by Krohn and as exemplified by *dybbuk* possession may constitute a basis for delineating a distinct subgroup within the broad category of culture-specific syndromes.[48] That individuals in this subgroup may be considered hysterical from a Western psychiatric perspective does not invalidate, in my opinion, their inclusion in this category. Hysteria in the above formulation is defined in terms of *dynamics* and *psychological mechanisms* rather than in terms of symptomatic content. The fact that most culture-specific syndromes are reducible to psychiatric diagnoses insofar as processes are examined is widely acknowledged.[49] "Most such 'ethnic psychoses,'" contends Wallace, "which reflect in their behavior the specific cultural content of the victim's society are simply local varieties of a common disease process to which human beings are vulnerable."[50] Not only is it justified to consider *dybbuk* possession an example of culture-specific syndromes but, in some respects, it might serve as the prototype of "pure cases" in this category. To be considered culture-specific in the precise, restrictive sense exemplified by *dybbuk* possession, then, a syndrome should meet the following criteria, of which not a few of the disorders so designated fall short.

It should be considered a disease (or a social deviance) on the "emic," native level. This apparently trivial requirement eliminates some of Krohn's cultural variants of hysteria, such as shamanism and overlapping cases of ceremonial possession (see Langness's suggested distinction between "hysterical psychoses" and "possession").[51]

The cultural processing of the syndrome should be manifested in the form of specific, meticulously followed role behaviors, through which a dominant set of beliefs is personified and "empirically validated." To what extent culture participates in the formation of symptoms is crucial, since *some* cultural coloring is typical of many recognized psychiatric disturbances as manifested in ethnically distinct groups.[52] Even though classical culture-specific syndromes such as *amok, latah, koro*, and *negi negi* "are learned, patterned, recurrent and culturally transmitted,"[53] their enactment does not necessitate the same extent of structuring as is required in the case of the *dybbuk* possession. In particular, indigenous *etiologies*, esoteric and culturally unique as they may appear to the Westerner, cannot constitute a basis for designating a disease entity culture-specific in the restrictive sense suggested here, insofar as they are not *fully* expressed on the visible, "participational" level.[54] *Susto*, another culture-specific syndrome, derives its cultural distinctiveness primarily from its peculiar etiology—soul loss—rather than its symptoms, which include "listlessness, loss of appetite, and withdrawal from social interaction."[55] What appears to Uzzell to be "the most important characteristic of *susto* as an illness role . . . [,] its flexibility,"[56] removes it from the *dybbuk*-type subgroup of culture-specific syndromes. In contrast to the *dybbuk, susto*, "in terms of performance . . . is very loose script indeed."[57] I am well aware of the fact that the *dybbuk* would probably appear more flexible in vivo than it does in the written texts. Still, especially during the elaborate exorcistic ritual but also before it, the acting out and personification of an entity deeply rooted in a complicated cosmological belief system must necessarily have called for a high level of structuring. This also seems to hold true for other forms of possession-as-illness.[58]

The syndrome should be utterly curable. Culture-specific syndromes such as the *dybbuk* are syndromes with which a culture is able to cope. Since they emerge from a cultural idiom, accepted as part of the prevailing belief system, the elements in the idiom can be manipulated to regain conformity. The symptoms are not idiosyncratically construed but rather derive their form and significance from a set of public symbols shared by all members of the community. From onset to cure, the script of a *dybbuk*-type culture-specific syndrome takes a predetermined course, well known to the participants. As I have already stated, only a small subgroup of potential deviants (one may call them "the truly cultural deviants") are able to resolve their inner conflicts by personifying cosmological identities and themes. This personification requires, on the one hand, that there exists in the community a potent, widely accepted cosmology, and on the other hand, that these individuals possess personal attributes (for example, good reaction testing) that seriously disturbed people do not possess. Consequently, this would exclude any psychotic disorder from the subgroup suggested here even though benign forms of psychosis are represented among culture-specific syndromes.[59] (That malign psychosis is not liable to *heavy* cultural processing was demonstrated in various anthropological studies.[60] Whether basically hysteric or not, those individuals who are capable of molding their inner conflicts in the service of society are only moderately disturbed.

The syndrome should not persist following substantial sociocultural changes. By definition, any culture-specific syndrome is vulnerable to more than superficial modifications in the sociocultural constellation of factors from which it emerged. This is all the more true for "pure cases," modeled on *dybbuk* possession, as they epitomize core elements of a traditional cosmology. When the cosmology decays—when society uses other incompatible idioms—the syndrome is doomed to disappear.

In addition to these conditions, it appears that a state of *disassociation* or, more broadly, *altered consciousness*, plays a major role in the "pure-case" culture-specific syndromes, constituting a psychic matrix conducive to the display of cultural identities markedly at odds with the "regular" self. Indeed, disassociation is amenable to a multitude of cultural interpretations and elaborations, according to Bourguignon.[61] Her illuminating distinction between "trance" and "possession" is frequently represented in various classifications of culture-bound syndromes[62] in which possession syndromes explicitly appear.

In all of this, I do not mean to suggest that the traditional classification of culture-specific syndromes should be narrowed. Rather, I mean to call attention to "pure forms" of cultural disorders that comply with the above criteria and that may be designated "culture-dictated syndromes." This subdivision of culture-specific syndromes may be viewed as located at the extreme end of a continuum representing the extent to which culture intervenes with symptomatic content, the other pole of which involved minimal cultural coloring of the disorder.

In sum, I have argued that *dybbuk* possession is an example of a subgroup within culture-specific syndromes that involved a kind of working alliance between society and a selected group of deviants. In the process, through which deviance was transformed into enhanced conformity, the possessed played a conservative role, endorsing cultural dicta and contributing to social stability. I think it reasonable to assume that culture-specific syndromes such as the *dybbuk* were prevalent in times of crisis precipitated by rapid sociocultural changes; in line with this thesis, their enactment would have constituted a valuable resource of society in protecting and revalidating its endangered myths. (This assumption might be a promising lead in understanding the enigmatic onset of *dybbuk* possession.) Beyond a crucial amount of cultural change, however, this societal mechanism of defense would fail. Indeed, the disappearance of cases of *dybbuk* possession attests to the profound attenuation of the Jewish traditional way of life in our time. With the exception of secluded ultraorthodox communities (where, indeed, the possibility that rare, unreported cases of *dybbuk* possession still appear cannot be ruled out), no more does Jewish traditional culture pervasively control and monitor the lives of Jews, nor does it offer potent, acceptable idioms for articulating inner experiences and conflicts. As a result, it has lost its capacity to mold and rectify deviance with the vitality and vigor exhibited in *dybbuk* possession and exorcism.

Notes

Originally published in *Psychoanalytic Study of Society* 11 (1985): 1–32. The notes and text have been modified to conform to the format of the present volume. Reprinted by permission.

1. In Hebrew, the verb *davok* means "to cleave" or "to stick." The noun *dybbuk* (pl. *dybbukim*) designates an external agent "clinging" to a person.
2. S. Ansky, *The Dybbuk* (New York: Liveright, 1926).
3. I. B. Singer, *Satan in Goray* (New York: Noonday, 1959).
4. See G. Nigal, "The Dybbuk in Jewish Mysticism" (in Hebrew), *Da'at* 4 (1980): 75–100
5. See *Religion, Altered States of Consciousness and Social Change*, ed. E. Bourguignon (Columbus: Ohio State University Press, 1973); *Case Studies in Spirit Possession*, ed. V. Gattison and V. Crapanzano (New York: John Wiley & Sons, 1977).
6. See E. Bourguignon, *Possession* (Corta Madera, Calif.: Chandler & Sharp, 1976); Y. Bilu, "The Moroccan Demon in Israel: The Case of 'Evil Spirit Disease,'" *Ethos* 8 (1980): 24–39, esp. 36.
7. See Bilu, "Moroccan Demon" for demonic possession among Moroccan Jews.
8. See *Encyclopedia Judaica* 7:573–77, s.v. "*Gilgul*," by G. Scholem.
9. This proliferation was probably related to recently introduced printing devices. Former centuries were relatively mute in contrast
10. B. Z. Bokser, *The Jewish Mystical Tradition* (New York: Pilgrim, 1981), 22.
11. Hasidism, founded by Rabbi Israel Ba'al Shem Tov (The Besht) in the first half of the eighteenth century, is a movement clearly based on mystical ideas. Unlike mystical trends in former centuries, it quickly became a mass movement, the centrality of which has persisted in Judaism up to the present.
12. G. Obeyesekere, "The Idiom of Demonic Possession: A Case Study," *Social Science and Medicine* 4 (1970): 97–111.
13. Crapanzano, introduction to Gattison and Crapanzano, *Case Studies*.

14. Ibid., 11.

15. E. T. Gendlin, "A Theory of Personality Change," in *Personality Change*, ed. P. Worchel and D. Byrne (New York: John Wiley & Sons, 1964).

16. R. A. Shweder, "Rethinking Culture and Personality, Part III," *Ethos* 2 (1980): 64.

17. For an elaborate discussion of culturally constituted projection, see M. E. Spiro, *Burmese Supernaturalism* (Englewood Cliffs, N.J.: Prentice-Hall, 1967), 77. Crapanzano, introduction, in contrast, contends that the Western metaphor of projection involves dimensions different from those associated with the articulated idiom of spirit possession. In the latter, "the tenor [of the metaphor] is located outside the individual from the start" (12).

18. M. Zborowski and E. Herzog, *Life Is with People: The Culture of the Shtetl* (New York: Schocken, 1962), 134–38.

19. Gattison and Crapanzano, *Case Studies*, 18.

20. Spiro, *Burmese Supernaturalism*, 72.

21. "*Gilgul.*"

22. Bilu, "Moroccan Demon"; Bourguignon, *Altered States*; I. M. Lewis, *Ecstatic Religion: An Anthropological Study of Spirit Possession and Shamanism* (Baltimore: Penguin, 1971); T. K. Oesterreich, *Possession, Demoniacal and Other* (New York: Richard Smith, 1930); R. H. Smith, foreword to Crapanzano and Gattison, *Case Studies*; S. S. Walker, *Ceremonial Spirit Possession in Africa and Afro-America* (Leiden: E.J. Brill, 1972).

23. See Lewis, *Ecstatic Religion*; idem, "Spirit Possession and Deprivation Cults," *Man* 1(1966): 307–29.

24. R. L. Rubenstein, *The Religious Imagination: A Study in Psychoanalysis of Jewish Theology* (Boston: Beacon Press, 1968), 54.

25. Oesterreich, *Possession*, 21.

26. See E. Pressel, "Umbanda in São Paolo: Religious Innovation in a Developing Society," in Bourguignon, *Altered States*.

27. V. Crapanzano, *The Hamadsha: A Study in Moroccan Ethnopsychiatry* (Berkeley: University of California Press, 1973); idem, "Mohammed and Dawia: Possession in Morocco," in Crapanzano and Garrison, *Case Studies*, 141–76.

28. See B. Beit-Hallahmi, "*The Turn of the Screw* and *The Exorcist*: Demoniacal Possession and Childhood Purity," *American Imago* 33 (1976): 296–303; D. H. Dwyer, *Images and Self-Images: Males and Females in Morocco* (New York: Columbia University Press, 1978).

29. In traditional Jewish terms, children up to the age of ten might have been so designated.

30. This episode was apparently a major source for Ansky's play.

31. Dwyer, *Images and Self-Images*, 165–84.

32. See C. Smith Rosenberg, "The Hysterical Woman: Sex Roles and Role Conflict in 19th Century America," *Social Research* 39 (1972): 652–77.

33. Lewis, *Ecstatic Religion*, 58.

34. L. P. Ullman and L. Krasner, *A Psychological Approach to Abnormal Behavior* (Englewood Cliffs, N.J.: Prentice Hall, 1969), 110.

35. S. Freud, "A Seventeenth Century Demonological Neurosis," in *Freud: Studies in Parapsychology*, ed. P. Rieff (New York: Collier Books, 1963).

36. I shall present it in full length in another paper.

37. Phylacteries (*tefillin*) are sacred ornaments that all male Jews from their thirteenth birthday on are commanded to wear during morning prayers.

38. See Oesterreich, *Possession*, 103.

39. See Bilu, "Moroccan Demon"; R. Patai, "Exorcism and Xenoglossia among the Safed Kabbalists," *Journal of American Folklore* 91 (1978): 823–35.

40. Bilu, "Moroccan Demon," 36.

41. On the other hand, *all* the first cases were written in a matter-of-fact style with no evidence of wonder at the bizarre, unprecedented occurrence. As was stated earlier, the question of the onset of the *dybbuk* phenomenon is still unsettled.

42. See Crapanzano, *Hamadsha*, 215; idem, introduction, 33; J. G. Kennedy, "Nubian Zar Ceremonies as Psychotherapy," *Human Organization* 4 (1967):185–94; D. Landy, ed., *Culture, Disease and Healing: Studies in Medical Anthropology* (New York: Macmillan, 1977); F. E. Torrey, *The Mind Game: Witchdoctors and Psychiatrists* (New York: Emerson Hall, 1972).

43. Here an interesting correspondence is implied between his death and sexual behavior.

44. See Spiro, *Burmese Supernaturalism*.

45. On the same use of possession in the struggle between Catholics and Protestants, see Oesterreich, *Possession*, 30.

46. Ullman and Krasner, *Psychological Approach*, 71.

47. A. Krohn, *Hysteria: The Elusive Neurosis* (New York: International Universities Press, 1978). Page references are hereafter cited in the text.

48. Also called "culture-bound syndromes" (Lebra and Yap), "exotic psychotic syndromes" (Arieti), and "hysterical psychoses" (Langness), to mention but a few such designations.

49. See A. Kiev, *Transcultural Psychiatry* (New York: Free Press, 1973).

50. A. Wallace, *Culture and Personality*, 2d ed. (New York: Random House, 1970), 218–19.

51. L. L. Langness, "Hysterical Psychoses and Possession," in *Culture-Bound Syndromes in Ethnopsychiatry and Alternative Therapies*, ed. W. P. Lebra (Honolulu: University of Hawaii Press, 1976).

52. See A. Kiev, *Magic, Faith, and Healing*; idem, *Transcultural Psychiatry*; M. K. Opler, *Culture and Mental Health* (New York: Macmillan, 1959).

53. Langness, "Hysterical Psychoses," 60.

54. Bilu, "Moroccan Demon," 31.

55. See D. Uzzell, "Susto Revisited: Illness as a Strategic Role," *American Ethnologist* 1 (1974): 369; J. P. Gillin, "Magical Fright," in *Social Studies and Per-*

sonality: A Case Book, ed. Y. A. Cohen (New York: Holt, Rinehart & Winston, 1961); A. J. Rubel, "The Epidemiology of a Folk-Illness: Susto in Hispanic America,"*Ethnology* 3 (1964):268–83.

56. Uzzell, "Susto Revisited," 372.

57. Ibid.

58. Bilu, "Moroccan Demon"; G. Obeyesekere, "Psychocultural Exegesis of a Case of Spirit Possession in Sri Lanka," in Crapanzano and Gattison, *Case Studies*, 235–94.

59. See *The American Handbook of Psychiatry*, ed. S. Arieti (New York: Basic Books, 1959); Langness, "Hysterical Psychoses."

60. See, for example, R. B. Edgerton, "Conceptions of Psychosis in Four East-African Societies," *American Anthropologist* 68(1966): 408–25; J. Murphy, "Psychiatric Labeling in Cross-Cultural Perspectives," *Science* 191 (1976): 1019–28.

61. Bourguignon, *Altered States*; idem, "Possession and Trance in Cross-Cultural Study of Mental Health," in Lebra, *Culture-Bound Syndromes*.

62. See Kiev, *Magic, Faith, and Healing*; P. M. Yap, "The Culture-Bound Reactive Syndromes," in *Mental Health Research in Asia and the Pacific*, ed. W. Caudill and T. Y. Lin (Honolulu: East-West Center Press, 1969).

Possession and Exorcism in the Magical Texts of the Cairo Geniza

JONATHAN SEIDEL

This essay describes the rituals of power in the Cairo Geniza documents, which claim to rid afflicted people of ghosts, spirits, and demons. My intent is to look at the exorcisms in the Geniza with an eye to earlier and later traditions of spirit expulsion. We do not find extensive narratives or documentary case histories of spirit possession and performative exorcisms in these materials, but the Geniza texts do form an important prelude to the medieval and early modern materials. They constitute a significant backdrop to the majority of exorcism stories in this volume, that is, narrative accounts of spirit possession in early modern Judaism. This essay should thus provide some textual and historical background to the accounts from Safed and post-Lurianic kabbalistic circles.

I am also interested in the specific phenomenology of possession and the language of the ritual texts that were written for the purpose of ending possession. Along the way, I will address the constellation of issues associated with Jewish spirit possession and exorcism in general: the Greco-Roman background to the rhetorical style and poetics of the texts, the character and moral status of the afflicting spirits, "healing," the process of adjuration, and the historiolaic or mythic power of the formulae.

The Setting for Spirit Possession and Exorcism in Late Antiquity

A preliminary question in the history of possession in Judaism is the problem of spirit possession and its cultural and psychological setting. A study of the recent social scientific literature on possession and exorcism (Bourguignon, Crapanzano, Bilu, Kapferer, I. M. Lewis[1]) reveals five aspects of this field over which scholars differ: (1) criteria for identification of possession; (2) causes of demon possession; (3) the culture in which the possessed live and the ways in which the possessed interact with society; (4) how exorcisms "work," that is, their performance and its interpretation; and (5) the consequences of the healing, or how the exorcist was understood to reestablish social or individual equilibrium through exorcism. In the absence of detailed narratives of possession and exorcism that are found in Greco-Roman literature and are (relatively) abundant in sixteenth- and seventeenth-century Jewish texts, what are we to make of short prescriptions for spirit expulsion? What are the assumptions of the scribes who produce such amulets or prescriptions? Are they, in fact, identical with the ritualists who would have performed a public or private exorcism? And when the predominant type of spirits are malignant or evil, can we find volitional possession, that is, mediumship that is instrumental in divination or prophecy?

Let me begin my response to these questions with an ancient Roman text, a rather humorous account of an exorcist found in Lucian's *Lover of Lies* (14–18)

> It is ridiculous of you, Ion said, to doubt everything. You know, I should really like to ask you what you have to say about all those who deliver men possessed by daemons from their terrible predicament by—and there is no doubt about it—exorcising them! No need for me to dwell on this. Everybody knows about the Syrian from Palestine, the expert in these matters, and how many people he took care of—those who collapsed before the full moon, those who rolled their eyes, those whose mouths filled with foam—and yet he made them well and sent them home in a normal frame of mind, having healed them from whatever plagued them, *for a substantial fee.* They lie there and he stands beside them and asks, "Where do you come from? Whence did you enter this body?" The patient himself says nothing, but the daemon answers, either in Greek or in a foreign language, depending on the country he comes from, and tells him how and from where he entered this person. Then he swears an oath, and if the daemon does not obey, he threatens him and drives him out. As a matter of fact, I saw one coming out, all black and smoky.[2]

This narrative resembles many exorcism tales from late antiquity and corresponds roughly to the prescriptive texts that invoke a variety of significant deities and powers to expel spirits.[3] There is no "magic book" or text-based oath here, no need to resort to a manual. While the text demonstrates a rather skeptical outlook concerning the facility and nature of exorcism in late antiquity, it does not question ritual per se or magical powers in general. The allusion to exorcism professionals is no surprise in an era in which a variety of healers solved physical and psychological problems for a fee. As an indication of their popularity and success in late antiquity and the early medieval period, there is no shortage of ritual texts that promise relief and success.[4]

Unlike the later narrative accounts of possession and exorcism detailed in this volume and in recent scholarship, the Cairo Geniza materials contain no firsthand accounts of powerful practitioners, whether clerical or lay, expelling ghosts or performing exorcisms in public. We have no way of knowing whether these rituals were public discourse or the handbooks for a private practice, nor whether there was a regulation of healer/exorcists or of certified demon expellers, nor even whether there was some sort of certification program. The Babylonian Talmud (*Shabbat* 66a–b) indicates that an expert amulet maker must be proven in healing. The practitioners may have advertised successful cures, but there might have been simply an empiricism of word-of-mouth acceptance.[5] We have more tales of exorcism-by-heroes in the talmudic midrashic literature and many more in early modern texts.

The texts that I have examined do not fall into the *dybbuk* model as suggested by Yoram Bilu, nor into Erika Bourgignon's paradigm.[6] These possession texts are clearly distinct from the later tradition of *dybbuk* with which we are familiar—that tradition of a wandering spirit, usually a well-known sinner, who took temporary refuge in the body of a living person. They are much closer to earlier Greco-Roman accounts of demons or ghosts who inhabit or "cling" to a person against his or her will. They are similar to some of the "Solomonic" exorcisms that circulated in late antiquity.[7] Descriptions of possession of this type are found in handbooks designed to guide the expert in identifying the nature of spirits and liberating the possessed, especially in exorcistic handbooks.[8]

Because of the vast diversity of the Geniza fragments and the difficulty with dating them and situating them in the Mediterranean world of late antiquity and early medieval times, one cannot present exacting, historically situated analyses but simply comment on the language, style, and function of these ritual texts. While they are scribal and clearly examples of working magic,[9] I see them as instances of the history of early medieval Jewish psychological medicine as well, and as expressions of the folk that have little to do with scholasticism at all.

Exorcism and Mediumship in Early Judaism

The immediate Jewish background to the Geniza materials in talmudic and midrashic literature emerges from lively tales of exorcism, necromancy,[10] and spirits. The world of the late antique rabbis is one of fluidity between the realm of the living and the dead and of encounters with disembodied entities that can affect and infect humans, plants, and animals. Not only can certain skilled rabbis communicate with the dead but rabbinic experts must be able to expel or kill malevolent or troublesome spirits wherever they occur. One *ma'aseh* (episode), which is found in its earliest and fullest form in the midrash *VaYikra Rabbah* (24.3), attributes public healing powers to "Abba [father] Yosi son of Yohanan man of Tzaitor."[11] In fact, numerous tales of powerful actions against demons are associated with the title *Abba*.[12]

Rabbinic fascination with the spirits of the dead and the story of Saul, Samuel, and the female ritual specialist at Ein Dor centers on the types of necromancy and the classification of the one who seeks the dead—the *Doresh el ha-Metim* in Hebrew.[13] The rabbis are ostensibly interested in necromancy not only because sages can accomplish this communication between worlds but for legal purposes: to discover the nature of the biblical prohibition, so that a *psak din* (legal ruling) might help clarify what is appropriate Jewish activity and what is not.

A text found in BT Sanhedrin (65b) mentions, in the midst of a discussion of aspects of magical powers and necromancy, those who fast so that an impure spirit (*Ru'ah Tum'ah*) might rest upon them.[14] Rabbi Akiba laments this practice, and it is his lament that leads me to inquire here about the historicity of such practices and rituals that have an opposite purpose—namely, to expel impure spirits.[15] In a cosmos in which people might attract spirits through ritual, it seems logical to assume that they would ascribe power to rituals and ritualists who expel similar spirits. Volitional possession also might assist someone in the commission of evil.

Another account describing spirit visitation in slightly different language is found in the midrash *Pirke de-Rabbi Eliezer* and shows the ambivalence toward the role of Samael—a heavenly being representing the personification of the serpent in this case—in compelling human beings to do evil:

> To what might this matter be compared? To a man in whom there is an evil spirit [*ru'ah ra'ah*]. All the deeds which he does, or all the words which he utters, does he speak of his own mind? Does he not act only according to the mind of the evil spirit which possesses him? So it was with the serpent. All the deeds which it did and all the words which it spoke it did not speak without the mind of Samael. Concerning him, the Scripture says "The wicked is felled by his own evil." (*Pirke de-Rabbi Eliezer*, chap. 12)

The "man in whom there is an evil spirit" is apparently not held accountable for his actions. Jews and Christians alike blamed evil actions in certain instances on either an "evil spirit" or the "evil eye," the latter emerging only from a human being.[16]

How entrenched is this motif of "possession" in ancient Judaism? One of the latent subtexts underlying this theme is, to my mind, the biblical motif of the troubled king. The major biblical figure who is compelled by an evil spirit, whose "curse" is attributed to the operations of a foreign force is, of course, King Saul. Saul's choices are doomed because his charisma has departed: "But the spirit of the Lord departed from Saul and an evil spirit from the Lord troubled him" (1 Sam. 18:12). Saul, who is a *Nabi*, which in the context of 1 Sam. 10:5–6 clearly means an ecstatic, trancing, possessed prophet, is notably troubled by this evil spirit, if not completely possessed by it.

It is not clear, however, from 1 Sam. 16:23 ("So whenever the evil spirit from God came upon Saul, David would take the lyre and play with his hand, and Saul would be relieved and feel restored and the evil spirit would depart from him") whether David is performing exorcism or simply calming a terribly troubled man.[17] An "evil spirit" afflicts Saul, but it does not take over his personality in toto. It is a significant cultural datum that David attempts to cure Saul through music therapy, to rid him of the evil spirit as Orpheus charms humans, animals, and spirits in Greek tradition. Music plays an important role in creating a state of altered consciousness to make possession possible as well as a role in charming a spirit or forcing it to come out of the body.[18] David may thus have served as an implicit model for the magician-exorcist.

Mediumship is the opposite, voluntary side of possession and posed a different set of issues for the rabbis. The talmudic condemnation of contacting an "impure" spirit with the accompanying desire to invoke the Shekhinah anticipates the later discomfort with mediumship and the desire to be attached to or possessed by a *dybbuk*.[19] In this case the "attached" spirit is conjured and invoked. I would see this type of willful possession as confirming the value of supernatural visitation found so often in ethnographies of mediumship and divination in cultural anthropology. I. M. Lewis and others have recognized in certain societies two forms of possession: one that is "central" and valued, and one that is peripheral and undesirable. In the case of the former, the spirits are thought to be benign and sympathetic, whereas in the latter the spirits are perceived as malignant and dangerous.[20]

The hints of both valued and undesirable types of possession in the talmudic era may adumbrate similar developments in later Judaism. A recent article by Yoram Bilu tackles the categorization of spirit possession in Judaism.[21] Bilu writes against the categorical bifurcation of altered states of consciousness proposed by Erika Bourguignon.[22] As Bilu has so wisely observed in his essay, "positive" cases of spirit encounters or possession are willfully sought, since the spirit is believed to contribute to the well-being of the medium, the practitioner, and the community.

In light of these developments in the later Jewish tradition, the larger background of mediumship and positive relations with spirits in the talmudic period becomes especially significant. In Greco-Roman papyri it is the untarnished youth who is able to host the desired spirit of divination and mantic insight.[23] In Arabic literature there are treatises devoted to beneficial familiar spirits who are helpful and inspiring muses, assistants in the poetic enterprise.[24] There appears to be a close connection between the poet (*sha'ir*) and the magician/bard (*kahin*); in early Islam panegyric poetry was recited ritually against the enemy in battle. I bring this point here because there appear to be in the Geniza fragments (in Judeo-Arabic) partial texts concerning invocation of angels to assist in healing and appeals to the supernatural assistant to help the local exorcist. The military character of the Geniza spells designed to intimidate demons resembles this genre of Arabic poetry as well as the rhetorical style of the spells in the Greek papyri.

Many encounters with angels are clearly beneficial in those texts in the Geniza that fall within the *Hekhalot* genre, the mystical description of the heavenly chariot based on Ezekiel 1.[25] Indeed, divination by means of angels seems to be quite beneficial and indicative of what might be considered "portable prophecy" in late antiquity. The spiritual virtuoso can become a medium for a muse at any auspicious place at an auspicious time. Both angels and demons can be informative, but it is the *Sar ha-Torah* (Prince of the Torah) whom one invokes to help one learn Torah and improve memory.

"Willful" possession for the sake of ecstatic prophecy or healing is not attested in the Geniza texts, even though Karaites such as Kirkisani (10th c.) claim that Rabbanites are practicing such things. *Ibbur* in the sense of spiritual impregnation finds literary expression only much later. Rather, we find several important texts that ask that the Prince of Torah, in the form of Metatron (a high-level angel discussed in the Talmud and midrash), help the initiate gain "instant Torah." He might thus be construed as an entity that "possesses" a person. Here is one example: "I [X son of Y] so that I learn Torah and cling to wisdom so that I learn Torah and never forget your Name, I say: 'Metatron, *Sar ha-Panim* [Prince of the Face (of God)] who is Prince of the Torah Amiel is your name KNYNYA is your name M'Hom 'Itimon Piskon Stregron is your name, your name which is similar to that of your Lord' ".[26]

I take Torah here in the "maggidic" sense, that is, one not only acquires Torah skills or data but the vision and prophetic understanding that accompanies revelation, as a number of scholars have demonstrated in their studies of the *Sar ha-Torah*.[27] In the Geniza texts, we find continuity with the ancient *Merkabah* (Chariot) and *Hekhalot* (Chambers) traditions based on Ezekiel's vision.[28] I also see the persistence of Metatron as the *Sar Torah* as a later trajectory of the angelic intercessor (familiar spirit?) in the Judeo-Islamic world.[29] This entire motif represents a Judaic version of ancient Greco-Roman traditions about contacting a medium or using a familiar to gain oracular information in an altered state of consciousness, whether trance-possessed or simply entranced, but not possessed.[30] It might be seen as a safe, theologically acceptable means of allowing possession by the gods or lesser divine beings.

Rebuking and Threatening Demons

Ancient exorcists sometimes had to "interview" or torture a demon to properly identify its role in possession and affliction.[31] There is no fact finding or interviewing in the Geniza exorcisms, but there are coercive threats that cover a number of demonic species. The technology of the spells appears to group these types of malevolencies together, providing the practitioner with catchall rhetoric. The Geniza documents that I have surveyed in all of the Shaked and Naveh volumes as well as the Shaked and Schäfer volumes[32] do not indicate that practitioners sought possession by an evil demon or that they invoked an "impure spirit" to rest upon them or their clients for mantic purposes. In this sense the documents are clearly different from the Solomonic tales of identification and expulsion and from divinatory materials in the Hellenistic magical tradition.[33]

Most demonological texts in the Geniza—and there are dozens—concern the "conquest" (*kibush*) of demons in order to dispose of them.[34] The conquest consists of scripted ritual action combined with traditional, "proven" rhetorical formulae and magical language. Much of the Geniza material appears to be on a trajectory of what might be termed "Jewish liturgical exorcism" in line with the antidemonic psalms found at Qumran. There is little of the *Testament of Solomon* tradition, in which the practitioner plays the role of interviewer and learns how to banish the unwelcome visitor. There are several fragments of an early medieval book entitled *Sefer Kevitzat ha-Ruhot* (The Book of the Gathering of Spirits),[35] concerned with gathering and controlling demons—like hordes that can be dominated and directed. There are also fragments of demonological handbooks that are in fact "scribal" productions and highly conservative of earlier rhetorical formulae.

In these works the exorcist becomes a mythic hero set in opposition to cosmic threats that are manifest in local, often corporeal situations. The Geniza magician is a linguistic specialist who harnesses the forces of good through knowledge of the pronunciation of divine names and language. His role is a time-honored Jewish function, one that addresses the ongoing cosmic war of the Divine and the Demonic. But he never places the healing or exorcism in the *Olam ha-Ba* (World to Come) or Messianic era, in contradistinction to the exorcistic healings of Jesus, which are contextualized with eschatological meaning.[36]

The power dynamics in the Geniza texts include the whole range of relationships: elimination of demons that are identified with fevers, aches, and diseases (in keeping with Mesopotamian demonology and spirit medicine); "encounters" with demons who can then be asked about the future (similar to adjuration of communicating angels, such as the request to see an *Ov* oracle in the book *Sefer ha-Razim*); and use of demons who serve as mechanisms of divination, such as the "Princes of the Thumb" or "Princes of Oil."

The latter refers to demons who reveal information after being invoked with mixtures of oil and water. The mixture of oil and water in a pot serves as the ritual basis for an exorcism in an exorcistic text preserved in the Gaster collection that can serve to illustrate this type of encounter.[37]

> To drive a demon out of a person: One should recite the psalm "Why O Lord do you stand so far away?" [Psalm 10] over a new pot filled with drawn water, and put into it a little olive oil, and say [the psalm] nine times, and one should wash in [the oil and water] and direct his mind to the Name that emerges from [this psalm] and shall say: "May it be Your will ALMTZ that you should remove every illness and every demon from N. son of N. now and forever. And the name that comes out . . .

Much more common than these forms, however, especially in the Geniza amulets, is the term *rgd*, which in Akkadian indicates scaring away: to rebuke, scream at, noisily coerce (compare Dead Sea Scrolls, Genesis Apocrypon 1 QapGen 20:38ff). In the magical bowls from Mesopotamia one finds release terminology, especially *ryp*; this usage appears in some of the Geniza amulets as well. The ritualist expels or divorces demons; he rarely asks them to be on his side as one might request an angelic friend or a speaking *maggid* spirit. One might ask to "clothe oneself in the Name" in order to gain divinatory powers or to heal, but one does not seek to have impure spirits take over one's personality in these texts.[38]

The Language and Rhetoric of Exorcism

There are several terms in the Geniza amulets and prescriptions that might come close to our English "exorcism." I might note here that the term *exorcism* itself derived from *orizo*, which in its connotation of adjuring demons is attested no earlier than the first century B.C.E. *Exorkizo* is a specialized term attested in curse tablets and when used with the verb *exelthein*, "to come out," connotes an exorcism in the technical sense.[39] Kotansky has studied numerous primary exorcistic texts in Greek that correspond closely in style and content with the Geniza materials.[40] Exorcism as a ritual praxis has ancient Near Eastern roots, and there were professional exorcists in Mesopotamia. The closest Hebrew term, which has Akkadian antecedents, is the term *rgd*: "rebuke" or "scold." The New Testament commonly portrays Jesus as "rebuking" demons.[41] *Ga'ar* seems to be an activity of ritually embarrassing or scaring demons out of the afflicted. One Geniza amulet (Jewish Theological Seminary of America, New York [JTSA ENA], Ms. 1177.16, line 34) mentions a servant of the angel Gabriel named *ktrgd Ga'ariel*, an angel specifically symbolizing God's exorcistic power. Another Semitic term for exorcism recalls the language of divorce: *ard*, unilateral expulsion of an unwanted being.

What emerges in the rabbinic and late antique Hebrew, Aramaic, and Greek texts is the contractual relationship between the exorciser and the demon or negative spirit being exorcised. The "contract" is drawn up exclusively by the healer/ritualist, with supernatural witnesses. Hence, serial adjurations of the Jewish God in the Greek materials found in early Judeo-Greek texts appear in the context of curses and defixiones. Kotansky has clearly shown that the term *ard* mirrors the Semitic *gca*, meaning "to adjure" in the context of an oath. Such contracts are "binding," made effective by performative ritual that always includes recitation of the Divine Name. In late antiquity the exorcism texts, especially those of the Aramaic magical bowls, contain legal formulae that "divorce" the demon as if the possessed and the spirit had in fact been legally married.[42]

What of the exorcist's medical function? The Geniza exorcisms do not much resemble the type of expulsion found in the Book of Tobit, with its explicit herbal recommendations, but Raphael, the angelic hero of the story, does appear in those texts.[43] Nor do the Geniza exorcisms list the herbal or medicinal particulars found in the medical-magical treatise *Sword of Moses*, fragments of which were found in the Geniza.[44] Shaked and Naveh have noted in their more recent study of Geniza amulets that the source of the possession is not always clear in these texts; it might be a generic disease that lies behind a variety of illnesses, or it might be attributable to witchcraft.[45]

Here are three exorcisms that exemplify the classical Geniza formulae of address and adjuration and expulsion. The first is:

> Selah, Selah, Selah Hallelujah In the Name of the God of Israel.
>
> For the sake of your loving kindness and your truth. *Yah* God, the God of the armies of Israel, drive out all evil spirits and afflictions and all blows and all harmful spirits and every Satan and all grief and all pain and all kinds of spirits and demons. In the Name of *Ehyeh asher Ehyeh*, who spoke and the world came into being. In the name of He who, when the sea heard His voice it split, when the fire heard it, it was extinguished, when the rocks heard, they broke, [when] the stone heard it, it exploded. I adjure you spirit and demon, in the Name of the *Shem ha-Meforash* who sits on the wings of the wind [2 Sam. 22:11], who sits on clouds. *Yah* is His Name who sits in thick clouds of the skies who sits in the heaven of heavens. Further I adjure you all spirits and all demons and all harmful spirits and all Satans and all grief and all pain and all kinds of troubles. In the Name of Michael, Gabriel, Raphael, Suriel, Nuriel, Baraqiel; what is more, [I adjure you] all spirits and demons and harmful spirits. In the name of . . . (Cambridge University, Taylor-Schechter Geniza Collection, MS. K.1.68)[46]

This is a classic exorcistic amulet from the Geniza replicated in style and rhetoric many times in a conservative manner rather typical of magical texts. The Geniza exorcisms, whether singular amulets or fragments of larger magical "books," are excellent examples of practical ritual spells written for an individual. They utilize biblical quotations that emphasize breaking, cracking, and smashing the alien force and generally avoid elaborate "*historiolae*," mythological narrations of power performed by a victorious deity that in turn empower the spell or incantation. In the Greek papyri the spells contain much more extensive tales of the primordial exorcists and divine demon fighters.[47] In early medieval Christian exorcisms the practitioner identifies with the power of the Christ in expelling the enemy, essentially becoming Jesus for the moment.[48] Exorcisms in the

Geniza magical books contain some *historiolae*,[49] but more frequently the Geniza texts are short on narration. Rather, they offer short, comprehensive lists of inflicting spirits who, once named, identified, and classified, can be expelled.

Here is an example of a classical exorcistic text that might be considered exemplary of the healing exorcism.

> An Amulet for a Bride.
> Write: In the name of YHVH *Sabaot* and in the name of these angels. Three times Qadosh. In the name of Sadqiel Azriel, Paqmiel, Tzafiel. In the name of *yhs*, who increases the convulsion of the bone [?] May you disperse and loosen and uproot all evil spirits, male and female; the spirit of the fox [?] the spirit of the gang [?] the spirit of the noisy movement, the spirit of he who causes damage, the spirit that flies, the spirit that dwells, the spirit of the chill, the spirit of the gates of the heart, the spirit of the stomach, the spirit of the breastbone, the spirit of he who harms and the eye of any creature and all spirits of pain and suffering from the body of N. b. N from the 248 limbs that are in her. Amen Amen Hallelujah. Tested.[50]

Here spirits are practically identified with illness—consistent with legions of Mesopotamian demononic taxonomies. A note about the morality of possession and exorcism is appropriate here. Not all possessing entities have acquired moral characteristics. A possessing entity, whether a catalyst of disease or the "dis-ease" itself, need not be considered ipso facto "evil."[51] Nor is the gender of the visiting entity fixed. And while it is women (mostly young) who are the most common victims of possession, the demons are both female and male, at least in the earliest texts.

The third exorcism is as follows:

> In your name O Lord of Hosts, God of Israel, Enthroned on the Cherubim, the Explicit Name, by the Seventy names of God, Compassionate and Merciful, God who wounds and heals: Send healing and have mercy on Bunayna bint Yaman and send her complete recovery. Upon your compassion and faithfulness, in you I trust God of Israel, answer me in my time of trouble. I adjure you spirits and demonesses, evil eye, evil affliction, evil satan, and all kinds of visitations; in the name of *Ehyeh asher Ehyeh* who causes the entire world to quake; by the name that the sea heard and was split, that the fire heard and was quenched, that the boulders heard and were shattered, and that the stone heard and exploded— SO SHALL YOU LEAVE, depart and go away and shall not touch Bunayna

bat Yaman from this day and forever AMEN AMEN AMEN SELAH. By your name O Merciful One may there be healing from heaven for Bunayna bat Yaman and may she be healed by the mercy of heaven and may she be healthy and free of any evil eye, evil spirits, evil plague, evil diseases, afflictions, chastisements, fever and chills, and any blasts and harmful spirits. I swear by you and adjure you in the name of Gabriel, Michael, Raphael, to move and depart from Bunayna bat Yaman from her body, from her head, from her temples, and from the two hundred and forty-eight organs that are in her. AMEN, AMEN, SELAH HALLELUJAH . . .[52]

Physician or Rabbi? The Exorcist and Settings for Exorcism

Shaked and Naveh have noted that the word generally associated with demons in these Geniza documents, *Bish* (usually translated as "evil"), might also be read *bush*, "illness." It is also not clear that demons are to be identified with disease as they are in the Assyrian and Babylonian taxonomies of disease. Is there a demonic etiology of disease in these texts? Yes, but it seems more likely that demons trigger the mechanisms of disease, as the healer/shaman must trigger the mechanisms of healing by first dispensing with the demon, beginning with identification and expulsion. This dynamic of making room for the "healing" by expelling the illness is cross-cultural and global; it is a process that can be mastered by any man or woman from any socioeconomic background.[53] In the case of the Geniza materials, it appears that the scribes are not very literate, and while they revere important and powerful talmudic rabbis, they may not have been educated rabbis themselves. They may rather have combined healing with other low-paying professions.

What, then, might be the historical and social context of early Jewish exorcism and the healing of possessed individuals? What relationship might counterpossession rituals have to regular prayer in places of Jewish assembly? Did healing supplications come to replace public or private exorcism? We have practically no evidence of healing centers or clinics in late antiquity or in the Geonic period.[54] While we cannot argue from silence, it would seem that local healing was centered in homes, not community sponsored "clinics" or medical centers. From official Geonic responses in the halakhic literature we know that the Ge'onim were very wary of Karaite charges of practicing magic. There could be no public countenance of amulet writing or healing ceremonies.[55] Nevertheless, if we assume that the rabbis were not necessarily the all-powerful religious magistrates of small communities and certainly not omnipotent adjudicators in the hundreds of tiny hamlets, we may still not exclude the possibility that synagogues (smaller places of assembly in the towns or countryside) may have been "healing centers" before they were under the domination of rabbis.[56]

Roy Kotansky makes the intriguing suggestion that some forms of exorcism or necromancy might have been performed at synagogues in Antioch in Syria.[57] Kotansky's hypothesis comes from his reading of Shaye Cohen's work concerning the synagogues of Antioch and the accusations by Chrysostom that many Christians were seeking healing there, perhaps based on the synagogues' being built around the graves of Maccabean martyrs.[58] Here necromancy and exorcism might come together: invoking the spirits of the powerful military ancestors to accomplish powerful healings. If the dead served as intermediaries between heaven and earth, as Cohen suggests, they are not sources of impurity, and a healer might call them "up" or "down" in order to accomplish other near-impossible tasks. Rabbis need not sanction this type of healing.

Indeed, rabbinic discourse on exorcism acknowledges the performative, perhaps illusionist ritual power of the action but not necessarily its reality. In the frequently quoted episode found in the midrash, Yohanan ben Zakkai explicitly (though perhaps with tongue in cheek) compares the ritual of the *Parah Adumah* (Red Heifer) to exorcism.[59] In that famous account, the efficacy of exorcism is *assumed*. Exorcism develops a local priestly character in the medieval period: a miniature priestly setting of ritual implements, the use of appropriate "Names of Power," the invocation of powerful assistants, and collaboration with cosmic forces.

In summary, I would argue that the Geniza documents relevant to possession reveal that illness, whose cause is assumed to be demonic or spiritual, is the major concern. Among the published texts we find several good examples of prescriptive exorcistic amulets that resemble the formulaic Greco-Roman exorcisms, especially those in the "Solomonic" tradition, but some also sound like the rhetoric of the magical bowls from Iraq. These prescriptive exorcisms contain neither narrative of specific cases of possession nor long *historiolae* but, rather, short biblical quotations and allusions to the forces of breaking, smashing, and cracking—actions that the healer might indeed have acted out. These texts, while rhetorically similar, are written for certain families and (most often) young women. They advertise a "proven" ability to conquer or expel the malevolent forces. A further study of the linguistic setting and medical use of these texts and their meaning in both the Islamic and Christian worlds remains a desideratum.[60]

Notes

1. See bibliography at the end of this volume, and Bruce Kapferer, *A Celebration of Demons: Exorcism and the Aesthetics of Healing in Sri Lanka* (Washington, D.C.: Smithsonian Press, 1991). One of Kapferer's unique contributions to the theory of performed exorcisms is that he has shown how the healer and the patient enter into a simultaneous trance that culminates in the loss and reconstruction of the self, a formula that is instrumental in the healing process. See also Kapferer, "Mind, Self, and Other in Demonic Illness: The Negation and Construction of the Self," *American Ethnologist* 6 (1979): 110–33.

2. Translated by Georg Luck in *Arcana Mundi: Magic and the Occult in the Greek and Roman Worlds* (Baltimore: Johns Hopkins University Press, 1985), 109. For a general discussion of spirit possession in the Greco-Roman world, see Eric R. Dodds, *The Greeks and the Irrational* (Berkeley: University of California Press, 1951); and H. Jackson's commentary, "Some Notes on the Testament of Solomon," *Journal for the Study of Judaism* 19 (1988): 19–60. On the constellation of madness, disease, and possession in classical literature, see, most recently, Ruth Padel, *In and Out of the Mind: Greek Images of the Tragic Self* (Princeton: Princeton University Press, 1992). The New Testament demoniacs (for example, Mark 1:24) demonstrate that at least some Jews believed that the possessed was not wholly taken over by the demon, but that the demon was of the self of that person as well.

3. See the still suggestive and thorough treatment of the subject by C. Bonner, "The Technique of Exorcism," *Harvard Theological Review* 36 (1943): 39–49 as well as his study of Jesus' exorcisms, "Traces of Thaumaturgic Technique in the Miracles," *Harvard Theological Review* 20 (1927):171–81. More recently, see the excellent introduction to exorcism in R. Merkelbach, *Abrasax: ausgewahlte Papyri religiosen und magischen Inhalts*, vol. 4, *Exorzismen und judisch/christlich beeinflusste Texte*, Papyrologica Coloniensia 17.4 (Opladen: Westdeutscher Verlag, 1997).

4. Roy Kotansky has translated and studied numerous exorcistic amulets from the Greco-Roman world. See esp. "Greek Exorcistic Amulets," in *Ancient Magic and Ritual Power*, ed. M. Meyer and P. Mirecki (Leiden: E.J. Brill, 1995), 243–278; and "Remnants of a Liturgical Exorcism on a Gem," *Le Muse'on* 108 (1995): 143–56.

5. Exorcists in contemporary Israel have marketed their skills and made a decent living simply through community acclamation and acceptance—without the media. See Yoram Bilu's chapter in this volume on the recent (1999) exorcism in Dimona as well as various articles on healers in the Israeli press.

6. See Erika Bourguignon, *Possession* (San Francisco: Chandler and Sharp, 1976). See also the recent collection of essays on spirit possession, *Spirits in Culture, History, and, Mind* ed. J. M. Mageo and A. Howard (New York: Routledge, 1996).

7. See the excellent recent studies of this tradition by David Duling, "Solomon, Exorcism, and the Son of David," *Harvard Theological Review* 68 (1975): 235–52; and Duling, "The Eleazar Miracle and Solomon's Magical Wisdom in

Flavius Josephus' *Antiquitates Judaicae*," *Harvard Theological Review* 78 (1985): 42–49. On "Solomonic" exorcism and magic in the Christian world, see Richard Greenfield, "A Contribution to the Study of Paleaelogan Magic," in *Byzantine Magic*, ed. Henry Maguire (Washington, D.C.: Dumbarton Oaks, 1995), 117–54.

8. See, for example, the Great Magical Papyrus of Paris (*Papyri Graecae Magicae*, ed. Karl Preisendanz et al. [Stuttgart: B.G. Teubner, 1973], Text #4). The second exorcism of the Paris exorcism manual adjures demons to "come out of" the afflicted and recommends the construction of a tin lamella amulet. The various formulae of the spells usually end with the imperative *ekselthe*. One of the best studies of the language of the Greek exorcisms remains Samuel Eitrem, *Some Notes on the Demonology of the New Testament*, In *Symbolae Osloenses Suppl* vol. 20, 2d ed. (Oslo: Universitsforlaget, 1966). See also W. L. Knox, "Jewish Liturgical Exorcism," *Harvard Theological Review* 31 (1938): 191–203. Daniel Sperber treats the rabbinic background of some of the Greco-Roman exoricisms in "Some Rabbinic Themes in Magical Papyri," *Journal for the Study of Judaism* 16 (1985): 93–103.

9. Michael Swartz, *Scholastic Magic* (Princeton: Princeton University Press, 1996) has recently termed the *Hekhalot* and Geniza materials "scholastic magic," which does justice to the writing and scribal aspects of these texts but as a generic phrase does not fully describe the popular component of the activity of these writers. Swartz's discussion of ritual in the *Hekhalot* texts is very helpful and his work, along with that of Elliot Ginsburg, provides the model for further discussion.

10. I will not concern myself with necromancy per se in this chapter but simply take note of the rather serious interest in classification in the Palestinian Talmud. Concerning the types of necromancers and their actions, see PT Sanhedrin 25c/40–45.

11. Abba Yosi of Tzaitor was sitting and studying at the mouth of a public fountain. A particular spirit that lived there appeared to him and said:

> You know that for a long time I've been living here and all the while you were coming and going, you and your wives, evening and morning you were never injured. Now you should know that a certain evil spirit wants to live here and he will injure people." [Abba Yosi] said, "What should we do?" And the spirit responded: "Go and warn the residents and say to them, 'Whoever has a shovel or a spade shall all come out here tomorrow and observe the surface of the water,' and when they see that the water is disturbed let them strike irons together and call out 'Our side wins!' And don't let them leave the place until they see a clot of blood on the surface of the water." . . . When [the residents of the town] noticed a disturbance on the water they struck their iron implements together and cried "Our side wins! Our side wins!" And they didn't leave the spot until they saw a type of clot of blood on the surface of the water. (*Leviticus Rabbah* 24.3)

A parallel and much more succinct version of this story is found in *Midrash Tanhuma*, ed. Salomon Buber (Vilna: Romm, 1885): 77. See also the discussion of this story and other tales of rabbinic demon expelling by Meir Bar-Ilan, "Expulsion of Demons by Rabbis: On the Magical Activities of the Sages of the Talmud" (in Hebrew), *Da'at* 34 (winter 1995): 17–31. On water demons (a common explanation of polluted or unsafe public wells and drinking systems), see T. Canaan, "Haunted Springs and Water Demons in Palestine," *Journal of the Palestine Oriental Society* 1 (1920–21): 153–70. The *Shabriri* demon was particularly associated with unsafe water and is mentioned in both the Talmud and in Geniza texts. See PT Terumot 8.5–6; 45c–46a; and Raphael Patai's treatment of water in *On Jewish Folklore* (Detroit: Wayne State University Press, 1983); and in the Geniza materials see, inter alia, Shaul Shaked and Joseph Naveh, *Magic Spells and Formulae: Aramaic Incantations of Late Antiquity* (Jerusalem: Magnes Press, 1993), Geniza 10, p. 155.

12. That is, one need not be ordained a rabbi to have extraordinary powers like a master of Torah. The honorific *Abba*, clearly not given to any ordinary father, seems to designate a holy man with magisterial spiritual power. See further the comments of Bar-Ilan, "Expulsion of Demons," 26. The notion of a good demon informing the "connected" specialist is known in Greco-Roman texts as well.

13. One type of *Doresh* is the *Nish'al ba-golgoleth* (one who consults the dead by means of a skull). The other is the *Ma'aleh be-zekhuro* which is identified with the *Ov*. I treat the history of the interpretation of these figures in rabbinic literature in my "Studies in Ancient Jewish Magic" (Ph.D. diss., University of California–Berkeley, 1996).

14. The *Shoel Ov*. Is this not the same figure as "the one who Consults the Dead [*Doresh el ha-Metim*]?" [It should be taken as] *Doresh Le-metim*. This means one who starves himself and spends the night in a cemetery so that an unclean spirit [Soncino: "of a demon"] may rest upon him [Soncino, following Rash"i: "to enable him to tell the future."] If one who starves himself so that a *Ru'ah Tum'ah* may rest upon him has his wish granted, he who fasts that the Pure Spirit may rest upon him—how much more should his desire be fulfilled! But alas, our sins have driven it [the Shekhinah] away from us as it is written: "But your iniquities have separated between you and your God." An impure spirit apparently causes different behaviors than an "evil" one.

15. This practice resonates with tomb visitations, and we do have later attestations of pilgrimages to tombs in early Islamic times, ostensibly to pray to invoke spirits of the dead at holy sites. For a good study of the meanings of the tomb visitations, *hillulah*, and the efficacy of prayer and dreams at the tombs of the saints, see I. Ben-Ami, *Saint Veneration among the Jews in Morocco* (Detroit: Wayne State University Press, 1998), 93–124.

16. See R. Kilmer's monograph on the evil eye in ancient Judaism, *The Evil Eye in the Bible and Rabbinic Literature* (New York: Ktav, 1994). In the Greek Papyrii (PGM 9) there is a clear distinction made between psychological disturbance—that is, possession—spirits of the air, and the evil eye. See further M. Dickie's

discussion of possession and the evil eye in Byzantine magic in "The Fathers of the Church and the Evil Eye," in Maguire, *Byzantine Magic*, 9–34.

17. See Gilbert Rouget's suggestive treatment of David's music therapy in relation to Saul's troubles, *Music and Trance: A Theory of the Relations between Music and Possession* (Chicago: University of Chicago Press, 1985). Rouget argues that the lyre that David plays conjures the evil spirit to cease its affliction of the tragic king, but that this is not exorcism since there are no classical incantations. His performance is rather in the Near Eastern tradition of music therapy with stringed instruments, following the studies of the musicologist W. Farmer, "The Music of Ancient Mespotamia," in *The New Oxford History of Music*, vol. 1 (Oxford: Oxford University Press, 1957), 228–54.

18. On this particular dynamic of music and possession in antiquity and cross-culturally, see Rouget, *Music and Trance*. His discussion of exorcism and music (157–66) is particularly helpful in making distinctions between behavior that evidences a state of trance and possession by a foreign malevolent force.

19. See Gershom Scholem's classic discussion of the origins of this concept in his article in the *Encyclopedia Judaica* s.v. "Dibbuk." Scholem's claim that the usage of this term as an attached, afflicting spirit first occurs in Yiddish in 1680 needs investigation. Gedaliah Nigal, in his study of the literature of exorcism and *dybbuk* tales ("The *Dybbuk* in Jewish Mystical Literature" (in Hebrew), *Da'at* 4 [1981]: 75–100) mentions an early documentary case referred to in *Shalshelet ha-Kabbalah*. There are several references to "*dybbuk*" in the Geniza, including a phrase in one amulet of unknown provenance that mentions a charm "*Le-dibbuk u-le-hibbuk*." I see these Geniza terms as simply the expression of affliction, but without the extended narrative and expanded meanings of the later figure of the *dybbuk*. There are simple exorcisms for the angry or unfulfilled ghosts in the Greek papyri and Near Eastern exorcistic texts. On the issue of afflicting ghosts in the ancient Near East and rituals to remove and appease them, see, most recently, JoAnn Scurlock, "Ghosts in the Ancient Near East: Weak or Powerful?" *Hebrew Union College Annual* 68 (1997): 77–96. I would like to thank Dr. Scurlock for clarifying a number of issues related to ghost propitiation and ritual in a variety of texts relevant to this essay.

20. I. M. Lewis, *Ecstatic Religion* (Hammondsworth, Eng.: Penguin, 1971). Peripheral possession does not support the goals of the society.

21. Yoram Bilu, "*Dybbuk* and *Maggid*: Two Cultural Patterns of Altered Consciousness in Judaism," *Association for Jewish Studies Review* 21.2 (1996): 341–66. This article demonstrates the importance of using anthropological tools of analysis in understanding the construction of altered consciousness in Jewish history. Bilu has surveyed the important literature on dysfunction, psychopathology, trance, and possession. The exorcisms of the type found in the Cairo Geniza do not fall easily within Bilu's typology. See also the fundamental and seminal essay, s.v. "Maggid" by Joseph Dan in the *Encyclopedia Judaica*, as well as his essay on "Samael, Lillith and the Problem of Evil," *Association of Jewish Studies Review* 5 (1980): 17–40.

22. Erika Bourguignon, *Religion, Altered States of Consciousness, and Social Change* (Columbus: Ohio State University Press, 1973), as well as her classic essay, "Religion, the Self, the Behavioral Environment, and the Theory of Spirit Possession," in *Context and Meaning in Cultural Anthropology*, ed. Melford Spiro (Glencoe, N.Y.: Free Press,1965), chap. 2.

23. On the magical assistant, spiritual and human, in the Greek papyri, see Leda Ciraolo, "Supernatural Assistants in the Greek Magical Papyrii," in Meyer and Mirecki, *Ancient Magic*, 279–96. See also my discussion of the relationship of divination and magic in rabbinic literature and their status in halakhah: Seidel, "Charming Criminals," in ibid., 145–66.

24. For example, *The Treatise of Familiar Spirits and Demons by Abu Amir ibn shuhaid al-Ashjaii, al Andalusi*, ed. James Monroe (Los Angeles: University of California Press, 1971). The *kahin* figure of pre-Islamic Arabia no doubt continued to function in the Middle East as an ecstatic healer/shaman figure. His companion spirit is known as *tabi* or *sahib*. See the still useful overview of the *kahin* and his psychosocial context in the *Shorter Encyclopedia of Islam* (Leiden: E.J. Brill, 1974), 206–07. The Geniza amulet scribes do not appear to promote themselves as inspired ecstatics who work with familiar spirits, but this does not preclude the possibility that clients went to ecstatic healers and consulted scribes for healing.

25. Rebecca Lesses has shown (following Rachel Elior, Peter Schäfer, and others) that adjuring helpful angels is within the prerogative of the practitioner, and "speaking with angels" is a constructive cultural endeavor in this textual community. See her "Speaking with Angels: Jewish and Greco-Egyptian Revelatory Adjurations," *Harvard Theological Review* 89.1(1996): 41–60.

26. Cambridge University Library, Taylor-Schechter Genizah Collection (hereafter TS), K1.19. Steven Wasserstrom has found a similar text in the appendix to volume one of Solomon Gaster's edition of the *Sword of Moses* (New York: Shocken, 1919): 330–36. See also his comments on Metatron as a domesticated spirit who helps in apotropaic functions: Wasserstrom, *Between Muslim and Jew* (Princeton: Princeton University Press, 1995), 190. This integration of cosmic angels with domesticated healers is, in my view, a perfect medium for the healer who advertises his intimate relation with enormous angels. The amulets seem to reflect this "marketing" technique.

27. See esp. Michael Swartz's original work on the redaction of the *Sar Torah* texts in his *Mystical Prayer in Ancient Judaism* (Tübingen: Mohr-Siebeck, 1995) as well as his chapter on this subject in *Scholastic Magic*. Joseph Dan has argued convincingly that *Sar Torah* mysticism is one of the three major genres of ancient Jewish mysticism. See his *Three Types of Ancient Jewish Mysticism* (Tel Aviv: MOD Books, 1993). Dan was the first to highlight the intersection of mysticism, divination, and magic in this literature, a matrix that still needs further analysis and study.

28. See also Swartz, *Scholastic Magic*, 62–149 on *Sar Torah*. Steven Wasserstrom traces the figure of Metatron as an intercessor in Islamic magic in his *Be-*

tween Muslim and Jew, 167–202. Wasserstrom's work provides the new standard for interpreting Jewish mystical and magical figures and motifs in the Islamic world.

29. See Wasserstrom, *Between Muslim and Jew*, 189–90.

30. See the history of this theme in the Greek world in Rouget's *Music and Trance*, esp. chaps. 5, 7. The latter chapter, on the role of music in trance dancing among the Arabs, is critical for studies of demonic and nondemonic possession in the Islamic world, and hence in the world of the Geniza.

31. As in the *Testament of Solomon*. See the translation of D. C. Duling in J. H. Charlesworth, *Old Testament Pseudepigrapha* (New York: Doubleday, 1983), 1:935–87. Exorcists in this model would have been expert diagnosticians.

32. Shaul Shaked and Peter Schäfer, *Magische Texte aus der Kairoer Geniza*, 3 vols. (Tübingen: Mohr-Siebeck, 1994–97). I have not had the opportunity to examine the third volume in depth but have examined some of these texts on microfilm. Giuseppe Veltri treats some forthcoming materials in his book *Magie und Halakha* (Tübingen: Mohr-Siebeck, 1997), 261–75. Veltri sees Jewish exorcism as a trajectory of Hellenistic Jewish folk medicine (224–25).

33. On the relationship with angels in general in *Hekhalot* literature and the perception of angelic beings, see Rachel Elior, "Mysticism, Magic, and Angelology," *Jewish Studies Quarterly* 1.1 (1993–94): 3–53.

34. See, for example, Joseph Naveh, "A Good Subduing" (in Hebrew), *Tarbiz* 54 (1985): 367–87.

35. These were first published by Scholem in his study of Judeo-Arabic magic, "Some Sources of Jewish-Arabic Demonology," *Journal of Jewish Studies* 16 (1965): 1–13.

36. Jesus' expulsion of demons from "demoniacs" has been studied from the perspective of healers within oppressive imperial cultures. See Paul Hollenbach, "Jesus, Demoniacs, and Public Authorities: A Socio-Historical Study," *Journal of the American Academy of Religion* 49.4 (1981): 569–88.

37. The texts concerning this type of demonology have been studied by Samuel Daiches, *Babylonian Oil Magic in the Talmud and in the Later Jewish Literature* (London: Jews' College, 1913); and Joseph Dan, "The Princes of Thumb and Cup," (in Hebrew) *Tarbiz* 32.4 (1963): 359–69. There are additional hydromantic and oil divination texts emerging from the new publications.

38. The prehistory of maggidism and prophetic Kabbalah needs more scholarly attention. For the time being, see the publications of Moshe Idel and Lawrence Fine, among others. These phenomena of maggidism include angelic corporealized speaking books or *Shekhinah*-as-Sefer visitation or "automatic" writing as one finds in the strata of the Zohar. This is possession by a transmigrated soul or *gilgul* of a deceased sage, who in a sense never dies but "becomes his book" and inhabits the willing psyche of another incarnation of his soul root, to use the zoharic terminology. Cordovero writes an entire treatise on maggidic revelation and angels. "A man can become a prince, a king, or a prophet," he claims, if a man

is blessed with this type of spirit possession. (Patai [206] from Cordovero, *Derisha b'Inyanei ha Malakhim*.) I have not found any extended request for "clothing" oneself in the angel or vice versa but an interest in pronouncing divine names with the intention of clothing oneself in the *Shem ha-Meforash*. This garbing oneself in the name appears to be part of a larger Gnostic tradition of the *Malbush*, the Divine Garment (concomittant with the Divine Crowning or sealing) that is characteristic of a stream of late antique Jewish ritual practice.

39. Kotansky and Jordan, "A Solomonic Exorcism," 55, where they cite an example from Gregory the Thaumaturge, *Precatio et exorcismus* (PatrGr. 36.734) "I adjure you all unclean spirits by Elohim, Adonai, Sabaoth, to come out and depart from the servant of God, so and so."

40. Kotansky, "Greek Exorcistic Amulets," 29. There are Geniza texts that are formulaically identical to the Greek materials, suggesting significant "interconfessional" or interritualistic communication among the healers.

41. See Klaus Thraede's discussion of the New Testament exorcisms: "Exorzismus," *RAC* 7 (1969): 44–117.

42. The classic treatment of this legal language in the magical bowls is by Baruch Levine, "The Language of the Magical Bowls," in *A History of the Jews in Babylonia*, ed. Jacob Neusner (Leiden: E.J. Brill, 1970), 343–75. More recently, and more specifically concerning the language of the Geniza marriage, divorce, and magic documents, see Mordechai Friedman, *Ribbui Nashim be-Yisrael: Mekorot Hadashim mi-Genizat Qahir* (Jerusalem: Mosad Bialik, 1986) and his earlier English-language study: *Jewish Marriage in Palestine: A Cairo Geniza Study*, 2 vols. (Tel Aviv: Tel-Aviv University Press, Jewish Theological Seminary, 1980).

43. Raphael is frequently invoked or mentioned as the agent of exorcism and the agency of healing. Raphael's role in 1 Enoch is healing the wounds inflicted by fallen angels. He is "over" all diseases and wounds of the children of the people (1 Enoch 40:9) The Geniza texts do not have elaborate *historiolae* with Raphael as the star, as he functions in the Book of Tobit, where he is an angelic physician. In Akkadian texts he is a messenger of healing from Ea. See Paul E. Dion, "Raphael l'exorciste." *Biblica* 57, no. 3 (1967): 399–413. Was Raphael the patron angel of folk healers at one time or were all angels capable of bringing freedom from the demonic aspect of disease? All four guardian angels, amongst others, are invoked in Geniza exorcisms.

44. See *Magische Texte aus der Kairoer Geniza* as well as the translation in Schäfer's series on Hekhalot literature, *Übersetzung der Hekhalot-Literatur*, ed. P. Schäfer, K. Hermann, et al. (Tübingen: Mohr-Siebeck, 1995), Band 4, 7–17.

45. Shaked and Naveh, *Magic Spells and Formulae*, 31–39. See also Veltri's chapter on magic and medicine in his *Magie und Halakha* (262–66), where he demonstrates how Jewish medicine encompassed Galenic and folk medical traditions in the late antique and early Gaonic period. The theory of disease in the magical handbooks clearly encompasses a demonological framework, though it is not limited to such a background or grid of explanation.

46. Shaked and Naveh, *Amulets and Magical Bowls*, Geniza 4: 223–224. Compare the text of an exorcism found on a magical bowl:

> In the name of the Lord of salvations. Designated is this bowl for the sealing of the house of this Geyonai bar Mamai, that there flee from him the evil Lilith, in the name of YHWH El has scattered; the Lilith, the male Lilis and the female Liliths, the Hag and the Ghul. . . . Hear and obey and come forth from the house and the dwelling of this Geyonai bar Mamai from Rasnoi, his wife , the daughter of Marath. I place you under oath [*umit alikhin*] by the honor of your father and by the honor of your mother. . . . I make you swear [*mashb'ana likhin*] by the Strong One of Abraham, by the Rock of Isaac, by the Shaddai of Jacob . . . to turn away from this Rasnoi, daughter of Marath and from Geyonai, her husband.
>
> (J. A. Montgomery, *Aramaic Incantation Texts from Nippur* [Philadelphia: University Museum, 1913], 154–60)

This text is also discussed by Baruch Levine in his "Appendix: The Language of the Magic Bowls," in *A History of the Jews of Babylonia*, J. Neusner (Leiden: E.J. Brill, 1970), 5:347–51.

47. On the Jewish elements in these tales and spells, see, most recently, H. D. Betz, "Jewish Magic in the Greek Papyri PGM VII:260–271," in *Envisioning Magic*, ed. P. Schäfer and H. Kippenberg (Leiden: E.J. Brill, 1997), 45–64. Betz discusses the evidence for iatromagic, adjuring the wandering womb and uterus, in both Greek papyri and Hebrew Geniza materials (for example, from TS K.1.157), which is also discussed by Schäfer and Shaked, *Magische Texte*, 1:112–13.

48. See Richard Kieckheffer's recent study of medieval exorcisms and conjurations, *Forbidden Rites: A Necromancer's Manual of the Fifteenth Century* (University Park: Pennsylvania State University Press, 1998), esp. 126–53. Kieckheffer shows that early exorcistic formulae resemble Jewish and Arabic Geniza conjurations and, most significantly, the necromantic conjurations of early modern times are based on the language and formulae of the earlier medieval exorcisms. He does not study Jewish magic, language, and rhetoric in depth in this work.

49. See L. Schiffman and M. Swartz, trans. *Hebrew and Aramaic Incantation Texts from the Cairo Geniza* (Sheffield: Sheffield Academic Press, 1993); and David Frankfurter, "Narrating Power: The Theory and Practice of the Magical Historiola," in Meyer and Mirecki, *Ancient Magic and Ritual Power*, 457ff.

50. TS K1.143. Shaked and Naveh, *Magical Spells and Formulae*, Geniza 18: 189–209.

51. That is, the antisocial and dysfunctional behavior attributed to demonic etiology may not necessarily carry the weight of moral evil. Saul's afflicting spirit, *ru'ah ra'*, appears to be part of his a priori "problem" and the cause of his tragedy and his perverse tendencies toward self-destruction. The Bible presents Saul as

one of the trancing prophets who has charisma but whose ability to keep the Spirit of God close is weak. *Ruhin bishin*, "evil spirits," can be read "spirits of illness" in many cases in the texts. Illness may enter a sinner more easily, and explanations of misfortune and sickness are often attached to moral weakness or sin; but possession is not necessarily related to sin. There are a number of cultural factors that precipitate possession, including misery in a particular family situation (most commonly incest, rape, and abuse). See Janice Boddy's study of the Zar Cult, *Wombs and Alien Spirits* (Madison: University of Wisconsin Press, 1989), for an excellent study of the cultural codes of possession and the ending of possession in an African society.

52. TS K1.127 (parallel to Ts 143.427.1–17). Schiffman and Swartz, *Incantation Texts*, 113–15.

53. Ruth S. Freed and Stanley A. Freed, in their outstanding study of ghosts and rituals for expelling ghosts in rural India, have shown that healers/curers/exorcists can come from all classes of society. *Ghosts: Life and Death in North India* (Washington, D.C.: American Museum of Natural History, 1993), 201–06. Historians have not yet been able to locate the class of Geniza scribal exorcists, but from the paleography, we can see that the scribes were usually not highly skilled or literate, let alone educated. See Shaked and Naveh, *Magic Spells and Formulae* (introduction) on the possible education and social status of the Geniza magicians.

54. A solid study of early medieval Jewish magic and medicine, especially in Islamic Spain and the Mediterranean, remains a desideratum.

55. On the intellectual climate of the Ge'onim, see, most recently, the discussion in Robert Brody, *The Geonim of Babylonia and the Shaping of Medieval Culture* (New Haven: Yale University Press, 1998), esp. 144–45. Brody notes all the relevant passages in Hai Gaon concerning magic, especially *Hekhalot* mysticism and magic praxis.

56. Shaye Cohen has demonstrated the likelihood that synagogues existed independently of rabbinic leadership and hegemony at one time: "Were Pharisees and Rabbis the leaders of Communal Prayer and Torah Study in Antiquity?" in *Echoes of Many Texts: Essays in Honor of Lou Silberman*, ed. W. Dever and J. E. Wright (Atlanta: Scholars Press, 1997), 99–114.

57. Kotansky, "Greek Exorcistic Amulets."

58. "Pagan and Christian Evidence on the Ancient Synagogue," in *The Synagogue in Late Antiquity*, ed. Lee Levine (New York: American Schools of Oriental Research/Jewish Theological Seminary, 1987), where John Chrysostom is quoted extensively concerning Christians flocking to synagogues for healing.

59. *Pesikta deRav Kahana*, ed. B. Mandelbaum (New York: Jewish Theological Seminary, 1987), 1:4.7, p. 74; *Pesiqta Rabbati* 14.4, ed. Friedman and M. Guedemann (Vienna, 1880), 65a; *Midrash Tanhuma*, ed. S. Buber (Vilna, 1885); *Numbers Rabbah* 19.8. A brief overview of rabbinic exorcism can be found in P. Alexander, "Incantations and Books of Magic," in E. Schürer, *The History of the Jewish People in the Age of Christ*, rev. ed., ed. G. Vermes, F. Millar, and M. Goodman (Edinburgh: T&T Clark, 1986), 3.1:341–43. See now the more extensive treatment of Meir

Bar-Ilan, "Exorcism by Rabbis: Talmudic Sages and Magic," (in Hebrew) *Da'at* 34 (1995): 5–15.

60. Veltri's work, growing out of that of Schäfer and Shaked, is an excellent beginning. I am currently examining the formation of magical books in medieval Jewish life and how they contributed to both the "folk" medicine of the time and the more classical academic medicine in Spain and the Mediterranean. These Geniza fragments are for the most part sections of larger "books" that were used by the folk healers. They exist in Judeo-Arabic, Aramaic, Hebrew, Ladino, and Yiddish.

Section II
The Sixteenth Century

Prologue

It is hard to know how widespread possessions and exorcisms were in the ancient and medieval Jewish world, but what is certain is that we have very few narrative accounts from this earlier period. In the sixteenth century, especially in the circles of the great kabbalists in Palestine and Italy, this situation changes radically. Just as the "Age of the Demoniac" dawns on the Christian world at this time, it is an age rife with possessions and exorcisms in the Jewish world as well. The idioms for possession (*ibbur*, *dybbuk*, *maggid*, *ru'ah*) and the models of both events and accounts are formulated at this time.

The earliest and largest group of narrative possession accounts preserved is that pertaining to the important circle of mystics living in the Galilean town of Safed and its environs. One can trace the phenomenon into Safed with the arrival of Rabbi Joseph Karo, a towering rabbinic figure who was expelled from Spain as a child, lived for a long period in Greece, and immigrated to Safed in the 1530s. Before his arrival in Palestine he was already privileged by visits from a heavenly mentor, a *maggid*, which possessed him and spoke through his mouth. In Safed Karo performed the first known exorcism in the Safed context, on the victim of a less benign possession. Thus Karo is connected with both "positive," willful possession and "negative," malevolent possession.

Under the influence of Rabbi Isaac Luria, who arrived in Safed from Egypt around 1570, not only did accounts of possession and exorcism multiply but a whole kabbalistic theology of possession was elaborated on the basis of Luria's teachings about the soul. These became a permanent legacy of possession ideas in learned Jewish culture—and to a degree in popular culture—forever after.

There are five essays in this section. In the first, Lawrence Fine offers a general introduction to possession ideas and models in Safed. He focuses particularly on the benevolent possessions by *maggidim* among the Luria circle and the techniques involved in achieving these. J. H. Chajes investigates the context of Safed possessions in more detail, examining several cases in depth and exploring the idea that this city emphasized the proximity of the living and the dead in both mystical and physical terms. Menachem Kallus tightens the focus on the Luria circle even further, offering a detailed account of the theology and psychology underlying their understanding of the soul. Kallus ultimately traces not only the mystical position articulated by Luria and Vital but also the specific manner in which the entire possession phenomenon became fully integrated into their system of thought. An interesting counterpoint to all these discussions is presented by Morris Faierstein, who argues that possession and exorcism were in fact quite marginal in Safed, and that many scholars' conclusions about gender and possession in the Jewish context are false. He bases these points mainly on the amazing spiritual diary of Rabbi Hayyim Vital, the chief disciple of Luria. Finally, Harris Lenowitz further exploits the Vital diary to investigate Vital's use of possession in his quest for a messianic identity.

As a group, these essays not only offer the deepest investigation of Safed possession issues currently available, they also tell us a great deal about the spiritual life of the Safed mystics. They are critical for understanding the direction of spirit possession and exorcism narratives as they developed in the ensuing centuries.

Benevolent Spirit Possession in Sixteenth-Century Safed

LAWRENCE FINE

Among the most significant manifestations of the great kabbalistic renaissance that took place in the Galilean village of Safed during the sixteenth century was the practice of mystical techniques that involved various forms of spirit possession. Spirit possession, or spirit mediumship of one type or another is encountered both in literate and nonliterate traditions and may be defined in a fairly broad way as "any altered or unusual state of consciousness and allied behavior that is indigenously interpreted in terms of the influence of an alien spirit, demon, or deity."[1] Among the wide range of altered states of consciousness to which the history of mysticism attests, the one most frequently associated with spirit possession is trance. For our purposes trance can be described as "a condition of dissociation, characterized by the lack of voluntary movement and frequently by automatisms in act and thought, illustrated by hypnotic and mediumistic conditions."[2] In such an experience individuals feel detached from the frames of reference that form the basis for their normal understanding of the world. As the Balinese say, such an individual is "away," literally separated from his or her own usual behavior as well as from companionship and community.

The possessed behave as if another personality—some spirit or soul—has entered their body and assumed some degree of control. Typically, there are dramatic changes in voice, body movement, and general physiognomy. While possession can be somnambulistic, where the possessed remembers nothing of what occurred, it is just as likely for it to involve lucidity, where everything is remembered. Spirit possession can be undesirable, in cases where individuals are believed to be seized or attacked against their will by an evil spirit or afflicted with a physical or emotional illness. As other chapters in this volume make clear, Safed sources themselves attest to such experiences, that is, malevolent or demonic possession requiring professional, ritualized exorcism. Indeed, this is what comes to mind for most people when they think of spirit possession. In many cultures, however, possession may also be a *desirable* state, one to be cultivated and practiced out of a variety of motivations. Here the spirits are *sympathetic*, and communication with them is socially, morally, and religiously acceptable. In contrast, demonic possession is usually regarded as violating the social, moral, and religious order of things.

This study encompasses four Safed practices in which adepts sought to achieve a benevolent and desired state of possession.

1. The "journeys" of Moses Cordovero (1522–70) and Solomon Alkabets (c. 1505–84) to the gravesites of ancient prophets and sages buried in the environs of Safed. Such mystical "peregrinations" or *gerushin* (literally, "exiles") resulted in a form of involuntary speech in which Cordovero and Alkabets would suddenly find themselves uttering kabbalistic interpretations of Torah.
2. The practice of Joseph Karo (1488–1575) to recite *mishnayot* (paragraphs of Mishnah) by heart, as a result of which his *maggid* or mentor-angel would speak through Karo's own voice.
3. The technique of Isaac Luria (1534–72) to prostrate oneself upon the grave of a departed sage so as to commune with the latter's soul, a practice known as *yihudim*.
4. The practice of Hayyim Vital (1542–1620) to recite *mishnayot* so as to commune with the soul of the ancient sage who authored the particular Mishnah teaching.

As we will see, these various experiences were clearly regarded as positive insofar as they enabled an individual to reach beyond the limitations of the material world to a world construed as constituting a deeper reality. And they were unquestionably socially desirable, inasmuch as one's status appears to have depended, to some degree at least, on the success at achieving such experiences.

Each of these practices has been the subject of scholarly inquiry.[3] My purpose in the present study is thus not a discrete, detailed analysis of any one of these techniques but rather an examination of them as a cluster or constellation of closely related typological phenomena. What can we learn by considering these various rites in relationship to one another and against the backdrop of the broader themes motivating the kabbalists of sixteenth-century Safed? My method will be to subject these practices to a morphological analysis in which I identify and compare their most significant features.

Qualifying Rites

Unusual states of consciousness—in the context of mystical experience—do not typically descend upon an individual "out of the blue" but, as already suggested, they can be cultivated in an intentional and purposeful manner. In the practices with which we are concerned, such purposefulness is evidenced by the explicit conviction that successful practice cannot be achieved unless a person has first rendered himself fit by means of proper conduct. For example, Karo's angelic mentor, or *maggid*, frequently informs Karo that the *maggid* will speak to him (and *through* him, as we shall see) only if he behaves properly. Indeed, this conditionality is one of the central dynamics of the *maggid*'s relationship to Karo. The *maggid* never tires of reproaching Karo for failing to meet the long list of moral and ritual standards that the *maggid* prescribes, while at other times the *maggid* indulges in exaggerated praise of Karo for his proper behavior. Here is a brief sample of the *maggid*'s expectations:

> First of all you must take care never to allow your thoughts to dwell on anything other than the Mishnah, the Torah and the precepts. If any other thought enters your heart, cast it away. Take care to have no other thought in mind during your prayers except the actual words of the prayers, not even thoughts of the Torah and the precepts. Take care never to speak an unnecessary word, whether by day or by night. Take care never to speak anything that leads to laughter and if you hear such, never laugh. This includes the admonition never to scoff at all. Never lose your temper over merely material things. Take care to eat no meat at all for forty days. . . . Be gentle in your replies to all men. Never be proud. Be exceedingly low in spirit. . . . Take care not to enjoy your eating and drinking and your marital relations. It should be as if demons were compelling you to eat that food or perform that act. . . . Have your sins always in mind and be anxious because of them. . . . Happy are you in that you have been warned. Reveal it to your friends and they, too, will wake up. Was it a good thing that you failed to read the Mishnah yesterday? Was it good that you have been so careless lately about thinking about the Torah? . . . How can you wish for me to converse with you when you eat horseradish? Be careful, therefore, to eat only a little. . . . If you will improve your behavior I shall reveal to you the mysteries of reincarnation.[4]

In the case of Isaac Luria, the attainment of divine inspiration of any type—particularly the highly esoteric, specialized practice of *yihudim*—

was dependent on the cultivation of a wide range of moral and spiritual qualities. Luria himself played an indispensable role in the lives of his circle of disciples by serving as their physician of the soul. Before they could practice rituals that were intended to enable them to bind their souls to the divine realm, his disciples had first to mend their own souls and to cleanse them of all imperfection. No individual whose own soul had failed to achieve a certain level of perfection was worthy of engaging in the practice of *yihudim*. A person had to undergo a period during which he cultivated certain spiritual and moral traits and atoned for whatever transgressions he might have committed. Luria, for example, was particularly convinced that anger prevented a person from achieving divine inspiration: "The quality of anger, aside from serving as an obstacle to mystical inspiration altogether, [has other injurious consequences] . . . all other transgressions injure only a single limb of the body, whereas the quality of anger injures the soul in its entirety, altering its character completely."[5] Likewise, sadness and depression hinder an individual's ability to experience divine inspiration: "Melancholia, by itself, is an exceedingly unpleasant quality of personality, particularly in the case of an individual whose intention is to acquire esoteric knowledge and experience the Holy Spirit (*ru'ah ha-kodesh*). There is nothing which impedes mystical inspiration—even for someone who is otherwise worthy of it—as much as the quality of sadness."[6]

In addition, Luria provided his followers with highly detailed rituals of atonement. These penitential acts were known as *tikkune avonot* (amends of sins), whose purpose was "to mend his soul" and "cleanse him from the filth of the disease of his sins."[7] According to Luria, the polluted nature of the body, partaking as it does of the imperfections of the material world, frustrates the human ambition to gain access to the sacred.[8] But the weapons of ascetic piety—significant regimens of fasting, receiving lashes, sitting in the dust—are potent enough to cleanse the soul of the stain that clings to it. Luria himself was regarded by his disciples as the diagnostician and healer of diseased souls. He did what any good physician would do: he carefully diagnosed his "patient's" specific spiritual malady and prescribed the appropriate penitential cure.[9] For Luria, impurity of the soul was not only a situation entailing guilt and shame—essentially moral categories—but an *ontological* condition that radically affected the whole of one's being. The most important consequence of the defiled state was that it rendered an individual unfit, ineligible for divine inspiration. Only by first cleansing *himself*, by divesting himself of the evil that clings to him, could an adept ever hope to engage in the task of ridding the world of its impurity as well as to become a repository of the holy.

Rites of Preparation and Transition

In addition to moral and ritual qualification, from a structural point of view mystical techniques almost invariably require an initial stage in which a person deliberately negotiates a *transition* from a normal mode of activity to an extraordinary one. I am drawing a distinction here between qualifying activities that may take place over a long period of time and preparatory rites that are an intrinsic part of the practice of a technique itself. Thus, for example, Joseph Karo's accounts repeatedly stress the requirement for Karo to ready himself by depriving his body of all pleasure, especially food and drink, not only as a general matter but most especially in the period *immediately* leading up to practice. Moreover, the recitation of Mishnah texts should take place at night because he needs to deprive himself of sleep to induce the *maggid* to manifest itself:

> The eve of the Sabbath, 29th of *Iyyar*, portion *Be-Midbar Sinai*. I ate but little and drank the same and I studied the Mishnah at the beginning of the night. I then slept until daybreak so that when I awoke the sun was shining. I was very upset, saying to myself: "Why did I not arise during the night so that the word should come to me as beforetimes?" Nevertheless, I began to rehearse the Mishnah and I studied five chapters. As I was reading the Mishnah the voice of my beloved knocked in my mouth and the lyre sang of itself. It began by saying: "The Lord is with you wherever you go, and the Lord will prosper whatever you have done and will do, but you must cleave to Me and to My Torah and to My Mishnah at all times, not as you have done this night. For, although you did sanctify yourself in your food and drink, yet you slept like a sluggard, . . . and you did not follow your good habit of rising to study the Mishnah.[10]

Hayyim Vital's practice of reciting Mishnah required detachment from ordinary life through the achievement of solitude and by cutting oneself off from all material sensation. Vital's accounts provide us with a detailed description of how to go about this.

> You already know that all types of inspiration require a person to be alone in a house so that his mind will not be distracted. The individual must seclude himself mentally to the farthest limits, and divest his body from his soul as if he does not feel that he is clothed in matter at all—as though he is only soul. The more he separates himself from matter the more his inspiration will be increased. If he senses any voice or movement that disturbs his concentration, or if any material thought comes to him of his

own accord, this will stop his soul's concentration on the upper realms. And he will not gain any inspiration whatsoever insofar as the supernal holiness does not rest upon a person while he is [still] clinging to matter, be it even a hairsbreadth [of attachment to matter]. Therefore, prophecy or the Holy Spirit is called deep sleep or dream or vision. The end of the matter is that he who wants the Holy Spirit to rest upon him, if he does not become adept at completely divesting his soul from his body, the Holy Spirit will not do so.[11]

The process of preparation and transition is somewhat less obvious in the case of the practice of *gerushin*, but even here we learn that one is supposed to *train* oneself by journeying in the proper manner: "... how to train oneself in the practice ... One should wander, as if exiled, from place to place, purely for the sake of Heaven, and thereby make oneself a vessel for the Shekhinah in exile.... Thus one should humble one's heart and bind it to the Torah.... And if one trudges on foot from place to place, without horse or cart, so much the better."[12]

Such rituals of mental and physical preparation serve as means by which a person leaves off this world for the sake of entering another one. Victor Turner argued, as is well known, that rituals such as rites of passage, pilgrimages, festivals, and certain mystical experiences involve a transition between two fixed states. Following the earlier work of Arnold Van Gennep, Turner labeled this transitional state as liminal, meaning a condition of "in-betweenness" or limbo as one deliberately passes out of normal social life, dissolves existing ties to community and everyday reality, and enters into a new life—even if only a temporary one.[13] Techniques that intend such a transition have little in common with experiences that are purported to come about in a completely spontaneous, unsolicited way. While in the case of the practice of *gerushin*, or Luria's practice of *yihudim*, we do not have the same kind of elaborate preparatory instructions provided by Hayyim Vital, even in these instances the process of journeying to a gravesite and physically isolating oneself there, cut off from social community, preferably in the dead of night in the case of the *yihudim*, serve similar purposes.

Possession

In every one of the techniques under consideration, successful practice resulted in a mental and physiological condition in which individuals were not in complete control over their bodies but rather were possessed by some spirit or soul other than their own. The most significant and central manifestation of this was speech automatism, a universal element in each and every one of these four practices. Such speech automatism, or "automatic speech," is attested in numerous cultures across time and space and is frequently a characteristic of possession experiences, both benevolent and malevolent. Involuntary speech was at the heart of Cordovero and Alkabets's experiences of peregrination: "Again we wandered on the 15th day of *Shevat*, my master and myself alone, and the words of Torah were *shining in us and the words were spoken of themselves.* We went as far as the tomb of Rabbi Joseph of Yokrat and on our return we discussed the verse [Mic. 7:15] 'According to the days of thy coming out of the land of Egypt will I show him.' For my master asked . . . and replied. . . . Thereupon I commented . . . and my master added to this by saying . . . enlarging very much on the subject because the words were shining forth of themselves."[14] According to this, Cordovero and Alkabets carried on a virtual exegetical conversation with one another in this manner. Cordovero goes out of his way to confirm the involuntary nature of these experiences: "these things are all supernal, infused without reflection whatsoever; they are sweeter than honey, the gift of the Queen [that is, the Shekhinah] to those that wander with her in exile."[15]

The voice that spoke out of their mouths was none other than the Shekhinah, the female aspect of divinity believed by the kabbalists to be exiled or separated from her lover and male counterpart, *Tiferet. Malkhut*, or Shekhinah, as is well known, is associated in Kabbalah with the receptive divine female who possesses no light or vitality of her own. Instead, she is filled with the nourishment she receives from the ten *sefirot* above her. The harmony that ideally characterizes the relationship between Shekhinah and *Tiferet* (along with all the other *sefirot*) is interrupted as a result of human sin. The Shekhinah is cut off from her source of nourishment and remains separated or "exiled" from the rest of the *sefirot*. Even though earlier kabbalists had spoken of the exile of the Shekhinah (*galut ha-Shekhinah*), it was the Safed kabbalists, now especially consumed by a sense of guilt and responsibility, who took up these notions with even greater fervor. By their self-imposed wanderings, an act of "exile," Cordovero and Alkabets were able to express the suffering to which the Shekhinah is herself subjected and to fully identify with that suffering. Thus, Cordovero writes that his teacher Alkabets "decided upon the innovation that in the summer months especially we should on occasion walk barefooted in the mystery of the Shekhinah."[16]

This identification was taken a significant step further by their belief that it was the Shekhinah herself who spoke through their own voices in the course of these peregrinations. As the culminating point of the self-revelatory process within God, the Shekhinah was imagined as the fully articulate aspect of divinity, symbolized by the "speech" of God. Thus, she is considered to be the ultimate source of virtually all vocal and prophetic revelation. The *gerushin* served, then, as a ritualized technique by which an adept rendered himself fit to be possessed by the physical and vocalized manifestation of the Shekhinah.

It is the Shekhinah, as well, whom Joseph Karo identifies with the maggidic or angelic voice that speaks through him in the course of his experiences. We have already seen that in Karo's case the manifestation of the *maggid* depended on Karo's recitation of the Mishnah. Karo, a master of rabbinic law, would recite from memory large amounts of Mishnah, following which his mentor-angel would suddenly begin speaking to him. Even more, however, Karo regarded this voice as the Mishnah itself, that is, as the Mishnah *personified*. The identification of Mishnah and Shekhinah is explained by the fact that the former, like the latter, is representative of Oral Torah according to kabbalistic teaching. That is to say, each signifies the *speech* of God, the full unfolding of God's vocal revelation.[17] In a report by Solomon Alkabets, describing his witnessing of Karo's maggidic experiences in the company of a group of companions in Turkey, we learn explicitly that Karo is invested with the spirit of the Shekhinah/Mishnah:

> No sooner had we studied two tractates of the Mishnah than our Creator smote us so that we heard a voice speaking out of the mouth of the saint, may his light shine. It was a loud voice with letters clearly enunciated. All the companions heard the voice, but were unable to understand what was said. It was an exceedingly pleasant voice, becoming increasingly strong. We all fell upon our faces and none of us had any spirit left in him because of our great dread and awe. The voice began to address us, saying: "Friends, choicest of the choice, peace to you beloved companions. Happy are you and happy those that bore you. Happy are you in this world and happy in the next that you resolved to adorn Me on this night. For these many years had My head fallen with none to comfort Me. . . . I am the Mishnah, the mother who chastises her children and I have come to converse with you. . . . All these things did we hear with our own ears and much more of a like nature, all matters of wisdom and great promise. We all broke into tears at the great joy we had experienced and when we heard of the anguish of the Shekhinah because of our sins, her voice like that of an invalid in her entreaties."[18]

As the most complex form of benevolent spirit possession we know from sixteenth-century Safed, Isaac Luria's practice of *yihudim* deserves special attention. As with the other techniques discussed here, the practice of *yihudim* was intended to be an independent exercise, detached altogether from the context of traditional daily prayer. There were two places in which they were to be performed: at the grave of a *tzaddik* (a "saintly" or righteous person) or in one's own home. The purpose of performing these exercises at the grave was that one of the essential goals of the *yihudim* was to commune with the soul of a departed *tzaddik*. They could be carried out at home, but a yet greater degree of purity on the part of the adept was then necessary to bring about the desired communion of souls. From Hayyim Vital, Luria's chief disciple, we have the following description of this technique:

> Be aware that in the case of all possible *yihudim*, if you perform the *yihud* by stretching yourself out on the *tzaddik*'s actual grave, you should contemplatively intend that by virtue of your stretching out on top of him you also cause the *tzaddik* to stretch out his lower soul [*nefesh*], which will then spread out in his bones that are in the grave: [whereupon] he comes "alive" and his bones become like a body to the soul that is stretched and spread out within them. This [particular] soul is the one that remains over the grave, as is known, which is the secret meaning of: "And his soul mourneth over him" [Job 14:22]. And it is as if this *tzaddik* lives in body and soul at this moment. And if you perform the *yihudim* in your house, without prostration, there is no need to practice the contemplative intention indicated above. However, you must always concentrate upon raising up your soul [*nefesh*] and that of the *tzaddik* while they are bound to one another, your soul included with his, regardless of whether you perform the *yihudim* while prostrated at the grave or while at home. You must also concentrate your attention upon that [soul] root within Adam from which both your soul and that of the *tzaddik* derive. And concentrate upon arousing that root, for it is the "limb" within Adam from which the soul of this *tzaddik* originates. By doing so you can raise up his soul through the mystery of the "female waters."[19]

We discover here what is certainly a most unusual, even extraordinary ritual, not the sort of thing we are accustomed to coming across in Jewish practice. There are three parts to this technique when performed at the grave itself. First, the adept activates the lower soul of the *tzaddik* that hovers above the grave, enlivening or animating the latter's bones by stretching himself out on the grave. Following this, he concentrates on binding his own lower soul (and potentially higher levels of soul as well) to that of the *tzaddik*. Finally, while in this state of intimate cleaving of soul to soul, he concentrates on raising up both of their souls to the upper realms by concentrating on their common soul root within Adam's original soul. The difference between performing this at the grave as opposed to one's home is that in the latter instance it is unnecessary to carry out the first of these three steps. Even in this case, though, it is still possible to cleave to the soul of the *tzaddik*.

The quasi-magical nature of this practice is evident. What distinguishes it, in part, from actual magic is that the physical act by itself does not suffice to accomplish the intended goals. No simple formulaic incantation or mechanical gesture satisfies the adept's desire to arouse the dead. Rather, an elaborate and sustained contemplative effort is required. Not only are the methods spiritual in nature but the ultimate goals are as well. This rite, then, should not be mistaken for necromancy, the divinatory art of magically conjuring up the souls of the dead. Necromancy has as its main purpose communication with the dead for the purpose of obtaining information—typically concerning what the future holds in store. The broad mystical goals associated with the *yihudim* point to a far more subtle and complex phenomenon. Nevertheless, the theurgic tendency so fundamental to all forms of theosophical Kabbalah may be said to be taken in this case to something of an extreme.

In addition to communion with the soul of a deceased individual, the *yihudim* involve concentrating on an intricate array of divine names. These names correspond to the sefirotic configurations of divine vitality known in Lurianic Kabbalah as *partzufim*. The combining and unification of these divine qualities—in particular, masculine and feminine dimensions—is brought about through formally structured contemplation on the names themselves. The *partzufim* and the names of God to which they correspond constitute a vast and complex map of the divine structure; they are linguistic symbols denoting various discrete concentrations of divine power. As such, they are not really names in the conventional sense but possess a fullness of meaning that normal language cannot convey. In a way strikingly reminiscent of Abulafian mysticism, Luria's divine names are, to a significant extent, beyond rational understanding altogether.[20] For the contemplative adept, however, to exercise one's concentration successfully upon them is to realign theurgically the structure of divinity.[21]

What kind of experience did individuals have in the course of practicing the *yihudim*? What were the effects upon the psyche and body of the adept, and what were the ultimate consequences of this practice?[22] We learn from Hayyim Vital that in the course of concentrating on divine names the flow of divine power stimulated by the unification of two of the *partzufim*, *Ze'ir Anpin* (masculine gradation) and *Nukba de-Ze'ir* (female gradation), constitutes the source of mystical inspiration that the successful adept attains—either in the form of prophecy (*nevu'ah*) or the Holy Spirit (*ru'ah ha-kodesh*). Vital does not distinguish clearly between these two terms; they appear to be used virtually interchangeably, each being a form of inspiration or illumination (*hasagah*). Nevertheless, given their historical usages, there is no question that prophecy was held to be a more exalted experience, although it was more rarely attained than the experience of *ru'ah ha-kodesh*. "All of the prophecy that prophets experience derives only from [the *sefirot* of] *Netzah*, *Hod*, and *Yesod* within *Ze'ir Anpin*—because from there an illumination shines upon *Malkhut*, the feminine [aspect of *Ze'ir Anpin*]. From this illumination prophets draw their prophecy. . . . There is no comprehension for any prophet to see except by means of *Nukba de-Ze'ir*."[23]

That prophetic inspiration derives from *Nukba de-Ze'ir* is in complete accord with the traditional kabbalistic notion that most prophecy is mediated through the feminine, or *Malkhut*. Based on a tradition in the Babylonian Talmud (*Yevamot* 49b), according to which "all the prophets looked through a glass [mirror] that did not shine [*aspaklariah she-enah me'irah*], but Moses looked through a glass that shined [*aspaklariah she-me'irah*]," the kabbalists associated Moses' prophecy with the divine masculine and that of all others with the feminine.[24] Uniting the masculine and feminine *partzufim* contemplatively infuses an individual with divine inspiration and enables him to speak words of prophecy. The spirit of prophecy begins to rest upon him and manifests itself through spontaneous unreflected speech. Prophetic utterance such as this requires great power of concentration and is not achieved easily: "There is one who begins to achieve some degree of inspiration, and the Spirit (*ha-ru'ah*) rests upon him. But it does not possess perfection with which to cause the voice of prophecy and the Holy Spirit to dwell upon his lips and tongue. Without speaking, he only feels at the moment of *yihud* that his hair stands up, his body and limbs shake, his lips tremble—but the power of speaking is not in his mouth."[25]

This condition may afflict an individual only after he has already achieved a degree of inspiration. The Spirit speaks within him but does not manifest itself vocally in any external way. Luria thus prescribed several particular *yihudim* whose specific function was to invest the adept in need of special assistance with the power to bring forth prophetic speech: "If the person who performs *yihudim* has already obtained some arousal on the part of his soul, which speaks to him by means of some *yihud* that he has performed, but he does not yet have the strength to bring forth [actual] speech upon his lips from the potential to the actual—he should perform this *yihud* before he does the other one."[26]

Although Vital writes in one place that "God will reveal to him the wondrous things from His Torah," the speech itself, that the contemplative either hears from without or utters with his own mouth, derives from the *tzaddik* with whom he is communing: "On account of these *yihudim*, they [the *tzaddikim*] reveal to them secrets of the Torah and matters having to do with the future."[27] Elsewhere, this process if described in the following way: "And how is this mystery of cleaving [*devekut*] performed? Let a righteous person stretch out on the grave of one of the *tanna'im* [rabbis from the period of the Mishnah], or one of the prophets, and cleave with his lower soul (*nafsho*) to that of the *tzaddik*, and with his spirit to his spirit. Then the *tanna* begins to speak with him as a person talks to a friend—and answers all that he asks, revealing to him all the mysteries of the Torah."[28]

The successful practitioner is compared to an angel on high who is in a position to gain access to heavenly mysteries: "There is no doubt that if the individual always practices these meditations, he will be as one of the angels on high who minister in heaven. And he will attain knowledge of all that he wishes, especially if he does not cease, [but] concentrates continuously, not separating his thought [from this meditation]. And everything depends upon the power of his concentration and his cleaving (*hitdabkuto*) above."[29]

What do we know about Luria's own performance of this technique? According to one account given by Hayyim Vital, on a certain occasion Luria communed with the soul of the talmudic sage, Rabbi Yannai:

> On the first of the intermediate days of Passover I traveled with him [Luria] to a certain village known as Akbarah. We entered the cave of Rabbi Yannai [by walking] through an orchard. A spring flowed from the entrance of the cave itself, the entrance being exceedingly narrow . . . and there his soul cleaved to that of Rabbi Yannai. In the course of his words Rabbi Yannai said to him that "I, Rabbi Yannai, am the inhabitant of this gravesite. Know that God, may He be blessed, has said to you, 'Go and tell this person, Hayyim Vital, who has accompanied you, that he should guard against slander, evil gossip, and idle conversation, and that he ought to behave exceedingly humble, and that I will be with him wherever he is.'"[30]

Other evidence depicting Luria's practice is found in the collection of hagiographic traditions about Luria, *Shivhe ha-Ari*:

> Once the Rabbi went to prostrate himself upon the grave of Shemayah and Avtalyon in Gush Halav,[31] at a distance of one *parsa*, for the purpose

of inquiring of them the true secrets of the Torah, for such was his custom. Whenever he desired to speak with a prophet or a certain *tanna*, he would travel to his grave and lay himself down upon it with outstretched arms and feet, "putting his mouth upon his mouth . . ." [2 Kings 4:34], as did Elisha with Habakkuk.[32] He would concentrate upon a *yihud*, and elevate the lower soul, spirit, and super-soul of this *tzaddik* through the mystery of the "female waters." . . . He would bind his [own] lower soul, spirit, and super-soul to those of the *tzaddik*, and bring about supernal unification. By means of the *yihud* the soul of this *tzaddik* would be invested with a new light, greater than that which he had previously [during his life]. In this way the dry bones that lie in the grave revived. The soul, spirit, and super-soul of that *tzaddik* descended to his bones, bringing him to actual life , [and] speaking with him as a man speaks to his neighbor, revealing to him all the secrets of the Torah concerning which he asks of him. All of these *yihudim* are in my possession, written down, praised be God. For the Rabbi transmitted them to his disciples, all ten of whom successfully practiced them. As a consequence, the *tzaddikim* [with whom they commune] spoke to them, answering all their questions. However, they possessed the strength to do this only during the Rabbi's lifetime. After his death their efforts were without success, with the exception of our teacher, Rabbi Hayyim Calabrese, may God protect and preserve him, who successfully practices them to this day.[33]

Finally, in connection with Luria's practice of this technique, another passage from *Shivhe ha-Ari* attests to Luria's close identification with Rabbi Shimon bar Yohai, the second-century rabbinic sage believed by kabbalistic tradition to have composed the Zohar. Here we learn that Luria was possessed by the soul of this teacher in the course of performing these exercises at the latter's grave in Meron, a short distance from Safed:

> He [Luria] used to stretch himself out on the tomb of the *tanna* [Shimon bar Yohai], and he knew how to cleave spirit to spirit, and to concentrate on binding and raising up his soul [*nishmato*] with that of the *tanna* in the mystery of "female waters" until he brought about unity above. Afterwards, the soul of the *tanna* descended into his [Luria's] body, and he [Shimon bar Yohai] would speak with him, revealing to him all that he had learned in the academy on high, as a man speaks with his neighbor.[34]

The most extensive accounts of individual experiences in the practice of *yihudim* come from Hayyim Vital. The phenomena of involuntary speech and, more generally, loss of bodily control are vividly attested in Vital's descriptions, of which the following is a brief sample:

> Then a great dread and trembling seized hold of all my limbs and my hands trembled. My lips, too, were trembling in a highly exaggerated manner, moving quickly and concurrently, and with great speed as if a voice was perched on my tongue between my lips. It said with great speed more than a hundred times: "What can I say? What can I say?" I tried to steady myself and prevent my lips from moving but was unable to still them at all. . . . All this was said at a great speed, repeatedly, many times, utterly wondrous, while I was in a waking state and while prostrated in the sepulcher of Abbaye . . .[35]

After having achieved a level of inspiration in which he heard the external voices of others speaking *to* him, Vital entered a more intense stage of experience in which he was overcome with physical trembling and began to utter short phrases repeatedly and quickly in the manner of uncontrolled speech. The identity of the voice is left undetermined, though there is no doubt that he is invested with the voice of another, insofar as it was "as if a voice was perched on my tongue between my lips." In addition to the physical manifestations described in this account, we noted earlier the sensation that one's hair stands on end. Descriptions such as these are remarkably reminiscent of accounts of ecstatic experience in Abulafian literature. For example, in *Sitre Torah* Abulafia writes: "Know that so long as you combine letters rapidly, and the hairs of your head do not all stand up in trembling, you have not yet attained one of the levels of the spirit in which all of the limbs [of the body] are moved, and you have not known even His existence, let alone His essence."[36]

Similarly, in Abulafia's treatise *Otzar Eden Ganuz*: "The hairs of your head will begin to stand up . . . and all your body will begin to tremble, and your limbs will begin to shake, and you will fear a tremendous fear, and the fear of God shall cover you. . . . And the body will tremble, like the rider who races the horse, who is glad and joyful, while the horse trembles beneath him."[37]

Abulafian experiences attest as well to speech automatism. In *Sha'are Tzedek*, speech is described as emanating from an individual's inner heart: "Behold, like the speech that emerges from my heart and comes to my lips, forcing them to move; and I said that perchance, God forbid, it is a spirit of folly that has entered me, and I perceive it speaking wisdom. I said that this is certainly the spirit of wisdom."[38]

In the case of the *yihudim* a person ritually enacted a death for the purpose of life. By going to a cemetery and stretching out one's body upon a grave an individual resembles one who has died. Yet, by doing so, he *revitalizes* the body of the deceased person. What is more, an adept enjoys his own personal spiritual rejuvenation through the ascent of his soul above. Indeed, the living and the dead assist one another. By their contemplative pilgrimages to the grave the living are able to animate the dead such that the souls of the latter ascend on high, while by cleaving "soul to soul" the mystical adept is also able to journey to the world above and to enjoy communion with the celestial realms. These exercises made it possible for both the living and the dead to avoid the normal consequences of death by preserving a relationship with each other, a relationship based on spiritual kinship, cleaving, and communication. In some respects this mutually beneficial "exchange of gifts" between the living and the dead parallels the attitudes of medieval Christians toward their saints. As Patrick Geary wrote of European Christianity:

> Death marked a transition, a change in status, but not an end. The living continued to owe them [the dead] certain obligations, the most important that of *memoria*, remembrance. . . . For one category of the dead, those venerated saints, prayers *for* changed to prayers *to*. These "very special dead" in the phrase of Peter Brown, could act as intercessors on behalf of the living before God. But this difference was one of degree, not of kind. All the dead interacted with the living, continuing to aid them, to warn or admonish them. . . . The dead were present among the living through liturgical commemoration, in dreams and visions, and in their physical remains, especially the tombs and relics of the saints. Omnipresent, they were drawn into every aspect of life.[39]

Geary's notion that for medieval Christians the physical remains of the dead—including their tombs—constituted relics deserving of veneration is suggestive as well in the case of the *yihudim*.[40] As Peter Brown put it in connection with the veneration of graves in late antiquity: "The graves of the saints—whether these were the solemn rock tombs of the Jewish patriarchs in the Holy Land, or, in Christian circles, tombs, fragments of bodies, or even physical objects that had made contact with those bodies—were privileged places, where the contrasted poles of Heaven and Earth met."[41] The numerous gravesites and tombstones that dotted the landscape of Safed and its environs were not merely physical reminders of the saintly dead but sites vested with sacrality, *holy* in the sense that they made access to the realm of the divine especially possible. As such the landscape as a whole took on a sacral quality; to journey to a gravesite, or from one gravesite to another, was quite literally a matter of religious pilgrimage.

While Hayyim Vital practiced the *yihudim* as a disciple of Isaac Luria, he also devised his own distinctive technique for investing himself with the soul or spirit of deceased sages. Vital's technique of Mishnah recitation also attests to an experience characterized by spirit possession entailing automatic speech. Vital clearly adapted features from both Joseph Karo's practice of maggidic revelation and Luria's *yihudim*. From Karo he borrowed the use of the Mishnah as an object of contemplative focus and as the vehicle through which he achieved experiences of spirit possession. Whereas Karo's technique was to recite from memory significant amounts of *mishnayot*, Vital preferred to repeat over and over again a single teaching (or paragraph) of Mishnah. It was presumably his teacher Luria's influence that led him to strive to become possessed by some particular rabbinic sage from the past. And true to his highly eclectic temperament, Vital almost surely drew on his knowledge of Abulafian techniques for the instructions concerning the physical preparations[42] for such an experience, with which he begins the passage below:

> Seclude yourself in an isolated house . . . [and] wrap yourself in a prayer-shawl, and sit and close your eyes, divesting yourself of the material world as if your soul had left your body, and was ascending to heaven. Following this abstraction [from matter], recite whichever single Mishnah that you wish, many times in uninterrupted succession. Concentrate your mind upon attaching your soul to that of the *tanna* mentioned in the Mishnah. And this is what you should concentrate your mind upon: That your mouth is an instrument which articulates the letters of the text of this Mishnah. The soul becomes a throne so that in it there may be invested the soul of this *tanna*, the author of the Mishnah, and so that his soul will be invested in your own. When you become exhausted from reciting the text of the Mishnah—if you are worthy of it—it is possible that the soul of this *tanna* will become invested within your mouth while you are reciting the Mishnah. And then while you are still reading the Mishnah he will speak with your mouth and offer you a salutation of peace. Everything that you then think of asking him will he answer you. He will speak with your mouth and your ears will hear his words. It is not you yourself speaking, but he is the one who speaks. This is the meaning of: "The spirit of the Lord speaks by me and His word is upon my tongue" [2 Sam. 23:2].[43]

We are struck by the fact that all four of the experiences described here are decidedly *oral*—as well as *aural*—in nature. It is the speaking of words that engenders the experiences in each of the techniques. While there are certainly examples of pneumatic techniques from Safed involving *visionary* experiences—such as appearances of the Shekhinah and visions of light— the techniques in question here betray the degree to which the *linguistic* dominated this particular culture.[44] Virtually everywhere we turn we find spoken language as the most potent force for animating the psyche and the imagination. In various guises divinity is no further than one's throat, "knocking" in the mouth, gathered upon the lips.

Revelatory Gnosis

The final feature of spirit possession that I wish to consider—and that I believe helps us understand the proliferation and significance of such experiences in sixteenth-century Safed—is the revelatory nature of this phenomenon. One of the several ways in which kabbalists traditionally laid claim to authority for their teachings was direct, personal revelation of one type or another. This type of claim was already made on behalf of the earliest constellation of Provençal kabbalists, including Abraham ben Isaac (d. about 1179), president of the rabbinical court at Narbonne, his son-in-law Abraham ben David of Posquieres (d. 1198), the most prominent rabbi of his time in southern France, the latter's son Isaac the Blind, and Jacob ha-Nazir. These are the individuals whose teachings were transplanted into Spain by their disciples around the beginning of the thirteenth century. A number of slightly varying traditions reporting that these early kabbalists experienced the "appearance of the Holy Spirit" and revelations from the prophet Elijah first appear, however, a century later, about the year 1300. In the Zohar, as well, Shimon bar Yohai is depicted as a charismatic personality who possesses the spiritual power enabling him to engage in discourse with angelic spirits, the souls of the departed righteous, and Elijah. As Isaiah Tishby wrote, Shimon bar Yohai "is portrayed as the expert in mysteries, to whom all secret paths are made plain by means of revelations from heaven, and the circle of his fellow disciples, thirsting for knowledge of the hidden world, sits in the dust at his feet in order to receive instructions from his lips. Knowledge of the unknown is the magic wand whose power enables him to rule over the upper and lower worlds."[45]

Although there were earlier kabbalists whom tradition regarded as having derived their knowledge in this way, it was not until the fifteenth and sixteenth centuries that activity of this type proliferated. As Moshe

Idel demonstrated, the appearance of an influential anonymously authored book entitled *Sefer ha-Meshiv*, written in Spain sometime in the second half of the fifteenth century, occupies an important place in these developments.[46] According to *Sefer ha-Meshiv*, various authors employed magical means—including fasting and the recitation of divine names—to induce angelic revelations. Such techniques were believed to be the proper and reliable fashion by which to gain divine knowledge for the purpose of composing a book. People who used such techniques were like the prophets of old, writing under the power of divine inspiration. There is a very strong likelihood that this book influenced individuals such as Joseph Taitatzak, Solomon Molkho, and others living in the Byzantine areas of the Ottoman Empire to write in such a pneumatic style. It is also certain that *Sefer ha-Meshiv* was well known among a wide range of Safed kabbalists, including Ovadiah Hamon, Moses Cordovero, Hayyim Vital, and probably Isaac Luria. While the latter certainly did not employ the more magical techniques described in this book, repudiating as he did this kind of "practical Kabbalah," he clearly shared its views about the centrality of celestial revelations from Elijah, angels, and other heavenly agents, the possibility of experiencing automatic speech, and the utter unreliability of purely intellectual approaches to kabbalistic truth. *Galya Raza*, an anonymous treatise on the transmigration of souls written probably in either Greece or Turkey between 1543 and 1553, also attests in an interesting manner to the growing phenomenon of kabbalistic composition under the auspices of pneumatic inspiration.[47]

Notions of charismatic authority and divine inspiration also played a central role in the life of another Jewish community, one at a physical and cultural remove from the Byzantine/Turkish orbit. A vibrant circle of kabbalists emerged by the middle of the sixteenth century in the area of the High Atlas Mountains and the Draa Valley in southern Morocco.[48] Comprised of indigenous Jews whose families had lived in this area for centuries along with a smaller number of new immigrants from the Iberian Peninsula, these kabbalists both preserved older traditions from Spain and developed new ones. A wide range of evidence attests to the fact that these individuals cultivated some of the kinds of experiences we have been discussing: revelations of the prophet Elijah, attainment of the Holy Spirit, visionary dreams, and the composition of texts under the auspices of heavenly inspiration.

The profound interest in these kinds of phenomena on the part of the kabbalists of Draa, along with a pattern of venerating individuals adept at such practices, shares certain striking similarities with practices of the Muslim Berbers, or more precisely, Marabouts, among whom the Jewish community of southern Morocco lived. There is reason to suppose that the Jews of southern Morocco, surrounded by this religious culture, appropriated various elements of it. We know, further, that in the sixteenth century a good number of North African kabbalists, including those from the region of Draa, migrated to Jerusalem and Safed by way of Egypt. For example, Joseph ibn Tabul and Abraham ben Eliezer ha-Levi Berukhim, both Moroccan kabbalists, settled in Safed and became prominent disciples of Isaac Luria.

There is no question, then, that in the post-Expulsion period the phenomenon of divine inspiration and direct revelation assumed a place of enormous importance in at least several kabbalistic circles, none more significant than Safed itself. It is precisely against this backdrop that we can better understand the enthusiasm for benevolent spirit possession in sixteenth-century Safed. Safed cultivated a climate that was highly hospitable to individuals who sought kabbalistic knowledge by such extraordinary means. Isaac Luria, in particular, must be regarded as the most important figure in this development. In Luria we see a rich and full realization of this tendency. Luria stood out because he was perceived as a virtuoso at such activity, as one who was gifted beyond compare.

The ability of individuals to reveal knowledge disclosed to them in the course of possession experiences such as we have described is intimately connected at the same time to the well-known eschatological enthusiasm that permeated Safed. Many Safed kabbalists believed that the year 1575 would witness the beginning of the messianic age. According to the Lurianists, for example, sin and exile had caused the exile of the inner secrets of the Torah. In the messianic age, however, these mysteries would be fully revealed once again. Whereas now only fragments of the Torah's mysteries were available, in the messianic future Israel would gain knowledge of the Torah in all its dimensions and depth. Increasing knowledge of the secret mysteries of the Torah was regarded not merely as a sign of the coming messianic age but also as a means by which to facilitate the redemption. As such, extraordinary ways of acquiring such knowledge—particularly spirit possession—were highly prized.

Notes

1. Victor Crapanzano, "Spirit Possession," in *The Encyclopedia of Religion*, ed. M. Eliade (New York, Macmillan, 1987), 14:12. An excellent bibliography on this subject accompanies the article. For an extended discussion of the issues raised

here, see V. Crapanzano and V. Garrison, eds., *Case Studies in Spirit Possession* (New York, John Wiley & Sons, 1977), esp. the editors' introductory essay.

2. *Penguin Dictionary of Psychology* (Hammondsworth, Eng.: Penguin, 1971), 38.

3. Concerning Cordovero and Alkabets's experiences of *gerushin*, as well as for a full-length study of Karo's *maggid*, see R. J. Z. Werblowsky, *Joseph Karo: Lawyer and Mystic* (Oxford: Oxford University Press, 1962), 50–55 and passim. Luria's practice of *yihudim* is studied in L. Fine, "The Contemplative Practice of Yihudim in Lurianic Kabbalah," in *Jewish Spirituality*, ed. A. Green (New York: Crossroad, 1987), 2:64–98. For a study of Vital's practice of reciting Mishnah, see L. Fine, "Recitation of Mishnah as a Vehicle for Mystical Inspiration: A Contemplative Technique Taught by Hayyim Vital," *Revue des études juives* 141 (1982): 183–99. For yet another practice related to these, see L. Fine, "Maggidic Revelation in the Teachings of Isaac Luria," in *Mystics, Philosophers, and Politicians*, ed. J. Reinharz and D. Swetchinski (Durham: University Press of North Carolina, 1982), 141–57. A general account of kabbalistic life in sixteenth-century Safed is found in L. Fine, *Safed Spirituality* (New York: Paulist Press, 1984).

4. Joseph Karo, *Maggid Mesharim* (Amsterdam, 1704), 1a–b. This translation is from L. Jacobs, *Jewish Mystical Testimonies* (New York: Schocken, 1976), 130–33.

5. *Sha'ar Ru'ah ha-Kodesh* of the *Shemonah She'arim* (hereafter *SRH*), 33. All references to Hayyim Vital's *Shemonah She'arim* are to the Yehudah Ashlag edition (Tel Aviv, n.p., 1962).

6. *SRH*, 33.

7. *SRH*, 39. See Fine, "Contemplative Practice," 74–78.

8. See L. Fine, "Purifying the Body in the Name of the Soul: The Problem of the Body in Sixteenth-Century Kabbalah," in *People of the Body—Jews and Judaism from an Embodied Perspective*, ed. H. Eilberg-Schwartz (Albany: State University of New York Press, 1992), 117–42.

9. See L. Fine, "The Art of Metoposcopy: A Study in Isaac Luria's Charismatic Knowledge," *Association for Jewish Studies Review* 11 (1986): 79–101.

10. Jacobs, *Jewish Mystical Testimonies*, 118.

11. Fine, "Recitation of Mishnah," 189.

12. Werblowsky, *Karo*, 52.

13. On the concept of liminality in the work of Victor Turner, see, for example, "Pilgrimages as Social Processes," in idem, *Dramas, Fields and Metaphors: Symbolic Action in Human Society* (Ithaca: Cornell University Press, 1974): 166–230; idem, "Liminality and Communitas," in his *Ritual Process: Structure and Anti-Structure* (Chicago: University of Chicago Press, 1969): 94–130; and along with Edith Turner, *Image and Pilgrimage in Christian Culture* (Oxford: Oxford University Press, 1978).

14. Werblowsky, 53.

15. Ibid.

16. Ibid., 51.

17. It appears, however, that in Karo's case the term Shekhinah is not used to represent *Malkhut*, the tenth *sephirah*, per se. As Werblowsky has shown, for

Karo it always refers to a secondary or "lower Shekhinah." In this regard Karo is in agreement with Moses Cordovero's definition of Mishnah as being "second to *Malkhut,*" that is, as a *lower* manifestation than the tenth *sephirah*. See Werblowsky, *Karo,* 271; and Fine, "Recitation of Mishnah," 194–95.

18. Jacobs, *Jewish Mystical Testimonies,* 124–26.

19. *SRH,* 75.

20. Concerning the combining of letters and names in Abulafian tradition, see Moshe Idel, *The Mystical Experience in Abraham Abulafia* (New York: State University of New York Press, 1988), esp. 13–52.

21. For examples of this aspect of the *yihudim,* see Fine, "Contemplative Practice," 83–87.

22. The partial answers we are able to provide to these questions derive from two kinds of sources. First, we rely upon fragmentary and incidental statements in the theoretical accounts describing the *yihudim* in Vital's *Sha'ar Ru'ah ha-Kodesh* and *Sha'ar ha-Yihudim* (Jerusalem: Mekor Hayyim, 1970). Second, Vital has recorded some of his own experiences in *Sha'ar ha-Gilgulim* (*Shemonah She'arim*) and in his dream-diary, *Sefer ha-Hezyonot,* ed. A. Z. Aescoly (Jerusalem: Mosad ha-Rav Kook, 1954).

23. *Sha'ar ha-Yihudim,* 1.

24. See the elaborate discussion of these and related issues in Elliot Wolfson, *Through a Speculum That Shines* (Princeton: Princeton University Press, 1994), 270–317, 377–80, and passim.

25. *Sha'ar ha-Yihudim,* 5.

26. *SRH,* 115–16.

27. *Sha'ar ha-Yihudim,* 3.

28. *Sefer Toledot ha-Ari,* ed. M. Benayahu (Jerusalem: Ben-Zvi Institute, 1967), 157, n. 6.

29. *SRH,* 143.

30. This passage occurs in both *Sha'ar ha-Gilgulim* (of the *Shemonah She'arim*), 126, and *Sefer ha-Hezyonot,* 135–36.

31. Shemayah and Avtalyon were sages and colleagues of the late first century B.C.E. They constituted the fourth of the *zugot* (pairs) of sages, and they are said to have received rabbinic tradition from Judah ben Tabbai and Simeon ben Shetah. Shemayah was *nasi* (president) and Avtalyon was *av bet din* (head of the court) of the ancient Sanhedrin. The tradition according to which they were buried in the village of Gush Halav, not far from Safed, is an old one, despite the fact that their activities are not associated with this place. Various testimony from the early thirteenth century forward reports on their graves in Gush Halav. See Zev Vilnay, *Matzevot Kodesh be-Eretz Yisra'el* (Jerusalem: Ahi'ever, 1986), 1:50–54.

32. The text refers here to the incident in Second Kings, chapter four, in which the prophet Elisha revives the dead child of a Shunammite woman: "Then he went up and lay upon the child, putting his mouth upon his mouth, his eyes upon his eyes, and his hands upon his hands; and as he stretched himself upon him, the flesh of the child became warm." According to a legendary motif in the Zohar

(1:7b; 2:44a–45a)—upon which the text under discussion apparently draws—the revived child was the prophet Habakkuk.

33. *Shivhe ha-Ari* (Bardejov: n.p., 1929), 5. Concerning this book, see Joseph Dan, *Ha-Sippur ha-Ivri be-Yemei ha-Beenayim* (Jerusalem: Keter, 1975), 238–51.

34. *Shivhe ha-Ari*, 17. See as well the account given in Benayahu, *Sefer Toldot ha-Ari*, 157.

35. *Sefer ha-Hezyonot*, 170–72. This translation is adapted from Jacobs, *Jewish Mystical Testimonies*, 131–33. A slightly different version is found in *SRH*, 140–41. Abbaye was among the most important Babylonian sages. His gravesite, according to kabbalistic tradition, is in the village of Avnit, northeast of Safed. Vital describes this site in *Sha'ar ha-Gilgulim*, 85. See Vilnay, *Matzevot Kodesh*, 231–33.

36. Quoted in Idel, *Mystical Experience*, 75.

37. Ibid. The anonymous author of the Abulafian treatise *Sha'are Tzedek* also writes that "great trembling seized me, and I could not gather strength, and my hairs stood up." See Idel, *Kabbalah—New Perspectives* (New Haven: Yale University Press, 1988), 76.

38. Idel, *Mystical Experience*, 85. See also evidence of automatic speech in the writings of Isaac of Acre in Idel, *Mystical Experience*, 85.

39. Patrick Geary, *Living with the Dead in the Middle Ages* (Ithaca: Cornell University Press, 1994), 2. See also 77–92 where Geary frames the relationship between Christian saints and those who venerate them in terms of the model of gift exchange, such as I have suggested here in connection with the *yihudim*.

40. This connection has already been made by Pinchas Giller, "Recovering the Sanctity of the Galilee: The Veneration of Sacred Relics in Classical Kabbalah," *Journal of Jewish Thought and Philosophy* 4 (1996): 147–69.

41. Peter Brown, *The Cult of the Saints* (Chicago: University of Chicago Press, 1981), 3.

42. See Idel, *Mystical Experience*, 37–41.

43. MS. 749, folios 10v-20v, British Museum, London contains the text of the fourth chapter of Vital's book *Sha'are Kedushah*, deliberately omitted by the original printer of this book, a practice followed by subsequent printers as well. The section from which this passage is taken is found on folios 16r–16v. This text was published for the first time in my article "Recitation of Mishnah."

44. For an extensive study of the visionary in Jewish mystical sources, see Wolfson, *Through a Speculum*. As Wolfson aptly points out, the visionary and the oral are not mutually exclusive, and we find numerous examples in which they are combined.

45. Isaiah Tishby, *Wisdom of the Zohar* (Oxford: Littman Library, 1989), 1:10.

46. Idel, *Kabbalah*, 237–40; idem, "Inquiries into the Doctrine of *Sefer ha-Meshiv*" (in Hebrew), *Sefunot* 17 (1983): 185–266.

47. See Rachel Elior, "The Doctrine of Transmigration in *Galya Raza*," in *Essential Papers on Kabbalah*, ed. L. Fine (New York: New York University Press, 1995), 243–69.

48. Concerning the history of the kabbalists of Morocco, see R. Elior, "The Kabbalists of Draa" (in Hebrew), *Pe'amim* 24 (1985): 36–73; M. Hallamish, "On the Categories of Kabbalistic Composition in Morocco" (in Hebrew), *Pe'amim* 15 (1983): 29–46; and M. Idel, "The Beginnings of Kabbalah in North Africa" (in Hebrew), *Pe'amim* 43 (1990): 4–15.

City of the Dead:
Spirit Possession in Sixteenth-Century Safed

J. H. CHAJES

> Several times I was with my teacher, z"l, walking in the field, and he would say to me: "Here is a man by the name of so-and-so, and he is righteous and a scholar, and due to such-and-such a sin that he committed in his life, he has now transmigrated into this stone, or this plant. . . . My teacher, z"l, never knew this person, though when we inquired after the deceased, we found his words accurate and true. There is no point in going on at length about these matters, since no book could contain them. Sometimes he would gaze from a distance of 500 handsbreadths at a particular grave, one among twenty thousand others, and would see the soul [*nefesh*] of the dead there interred, standing upon the grave. He would then say to us, "in that grave is buried such-and-such a man by the name of so-and-so, and they are punishing him with such-and-such a punishment for such-and-such a crime. We would inquire after that man, and found his words to be true. [There are] so many and great examples of this that one cannot imagine.[1]

R. Hayyim Vital recalls in this passage—one of many of its kind—how his teacher, R. Isaac Luria, constantly beheld the dead in his midst.[2] Luria would *gaze* at the dead, and *see the soul . . . standing upon the grave*; in the paragraphs that follow this passage in *Sha'ar ha-Gilgulim* (Gate of Transmigrations), Vital reiterates that Luria saw these individuals "with his eyes" and did not merely feel their presence or conjure them up with the aid of his "sacred imagination."[3] For Luria, the dead mingled with the living and appeared with transparent immediacy in the rocks and trees of Safed and, of course, in and about its graves, marked and unmarked.

City of the Dead

Safed, then as now, is a city that lives with its dead, its stone domiciles and synagogues poised on sloping hills that are home to "twenty thousand" dead, whose graves begin only a few steps beyond the homes of the living. Safed embraces its graveyard, which, like the stage of an amphitheater, is always within view, commanding one's attention. Not far in the distance, every denizen of Safed can see hills filled with the graves of rabbinic-era sages, culminating with Mt. Meron, graced with the remains of R. Shimon bar Yohai, Moses of the mystics, and, in their eyes, author of their "Bible," the Zohar.[4]

Sixteenth-century Safed was a city shared by the living and the dead, a sacred space that might be compared to the sixteenth-century Spanish churches, "where the dead were relentlessly buried under the worshipers' feet."[5] Many who made their way to Safed did so in order to partake in this sacred space and the special benefits it afforded their souls. R. Moshe Alsheikh, Vital's teacher in rabbinics,[6] described Safed in his *Hazut Kashah* (Terrible Vision) of 1591 as a city

> which has forever been a city of interred dead, to which people from throughout the lands of exile came to die, and from a holy place, a city of our God from the day of its founding, to die there and there be buried, which has within it many more than 600,000 men, not including the bones of men continuously brought, beyond measure to the righteous in its midst, for "there is no end to its corpses" [Nah. 3:3]. Who from all the cities of the exile, near and far, does not have in her [Safed] a father or brother, son or daughter, mother or sister, or some other of their flesh, them or their bones.[7]

According to others, being in Safed was conducive to penetrating the secrets of the Torah as well as to achieving a good death. R. Abraham Azulai, born in Fez (1570) to a Castilian family, wrote the following about Safed around 1619, some twenty years after his arrival in the Land of Israel:

> Safed is also 21 and with the word itself 22,[8] corresponding to the 22 letters of the Torah, alluding to Safed's being ready and receptive to the attainment of the depth of the Torah and its secrets, for there is no purer air in the whole of the Land of Israel than the air in Safed. . . . And Safed is also gematria (570),[9] to allude that all who dwell in Safed have an advantage over all other cities in the Land of Israel. And one who dies and is buried there, since it is a high place with air purer and cleaner than any city in the Land of Israel, his soul therefore speedily sails and flies to the Cave of Makhpelah[10] in order to pass from there to the lower Garden of Eden.[11]

Mystical experience and death, according to Azulai, are Safed's specialities.[12] The literature produced in this hothouse of morbid ecstasy is replete with encounters with apparitions of the dead, encounters at once mystical and moribund.[13] Few, however, could aspire to the powers of Luria to behold with their own eyes such apparitions before them. Vital's accounts of Luria's abilities certainly underscore their exceptional nature.

Though few could see the dead as did Luria,[14] Safed and its environs remained a region with death underfoot, whose relics did much to attract the leading lights of the Jewish world in the course of the sixteenth century. By virtue of its unique appeal as well as its economic health,[15] Safed soon outstripped every other center in the Land of Israel both in the quantity and "quality"[16] of its population. According to the *Mufassal Defterler*, or detailed registers of the cadastral surveys undertaken by the Ottomans in Palestine, Safed's Jewish population tripled between 1525 and 1555, from 232 to 716 households.[17] During that time, the composition of the population changed markedly as well. By mid-century, *Mustarib* (native Arabic-speaking) Jews were no longer the large majority of the Jewish population. Their absolute number in fact declined, as Jews from Portugal, Cordoba, Aragon, Seville, Calabria, and other lands added hundreds of new households to the community. *Conversos* also chose to settle in Safed in substantial numbers.[18] Safed thus took on a cosmopolitan character, with a strong European—and particularly Iberian—component. These new Safedians seem to have arrived bearing a particularly intense preoccupation with death, a characteristic of Spanish culture that has often been noted by scholars.[19] We do know that the Iberian Jews who produced zoharic literature in the late thirteenth and early fourteenth centuries had a more positive, sacral orientation to the grave and its denizens than did their Ashkenazic counterparts, for whom the world of the dead "was an abode of dread and danger."[20] Indeed, it was the zoharic *image* of the Galilee and its holy relics that attracted many of these figures to Safed in the sixteenth century.

While they could not see the dead hovering over graves or suffering in their transmigrations into the minerals, plants, and animals around them, these new residents of Safed did have one way of encountering the dead face to face, "not in a dream, but while wide awake."[21] The dead appeared to the living of Safed chiefly through a process of displacement. The dead could become visible to all by commandeering the bodies of the living and making them their own. For the first time in Jewish history, possession by the dead—by ghosts—became the most common variety of spirit possession in sixteenth-century Safed. While the identification of a possessing spirit as a ghost seems to have been frequent among late medieval and early modern Christians, clerical authorities generally suppressed such notions when summoned to begin the process of exorcism.[22] In so doing, they were following theological traditions going back to Augustine that denied this possibility.[23] Such clerical objections did not, however, entirely succeed in eliminating the phenomenon of possession by the dead.[24] Thus, while Christian clerics attempted to suppress the notion that the dead could possess the bodies of the living, Jewish religious authorities came to regard spirit possession as typically resulting from just such an etiology. The dead appeared to the living Jews of Safed *in* the living Jews of Safed.

After more than a millennium for which we have no extant Jewish spirit possession narratives, a dozen or more such narratives treat cases that ostensibly occurred in the sixteenth century.[25] Of them, more than half treat cases in Safed, while the remainder chronicle cases that took place on the Italian peninsula. While my approach to these narratives is similar to that adopted by recent historians of hagiographic literature and therefore not committed to ascertaining the historicity of the "facts" involved so much as determining how the accounts of these facts reflect the mentality of their producers,[26] it is still important to carefully delineate the provenance of the sources for these early cases to insure that we do not confuse sources *about* sixteenth-century Safedian cases—but produced later and elsewhere—with sources written then and there. My examination of these early sources has, in fact, led me to conclude that they are best treated in two distinct discussions. The first, which follows here, will attempt to learn something about Safedian culture in the mid-sixteenth century through a reading of these sources; the second, which I have treated elsewhere,[27] examines the *uses* of these possession narratives in seventeenth-century works and their role in bolstering the aims of authors and editors engaged in various polemical, didactic, and hagiographic enterprises.

Let us begin with a brief bibliographic survey of these narratives. The earliest extant manuscripts that include accounts from the sixteenth century are of seventeenth-century provenance. These include copies of earlier, no longer extant manuscripts and new works composed in the seventeenth century that include possession accounts. Examples of the former include *Tzafnat Pa'aneah* (Decipherer of Mysteries) of Judah Hallewa, a work composed in 1545 that survives only in a single, later copy.[28] Vital's memoirs, known as *Sefer ha-Hezyonot* (Book of Visions) (and later as *Shivhe R. Hayyim Vital* [Praises of R. Hayyim Vital]), also contain references to Safedian cases of the 1570s as well as to a 1609 Damascus case.[29] Far more numerous are examples of the latter, including manuscripts of Jacob Zemah's *Ranu le-Ya'akov* (Joy for Jacob) and *Meshivat Nafesh* (Restoration of the Soul), Samuel Garmison's *Darkhe No'am* (Ways of Pleasantness), and Joseph Sambari's *Divre Yosef* (Words of Joseph). Zemah and Garmison included two Safedian cases in which Vital was the exorcist, while Sambari included four Safedian cases in his chronicle of its "golden age."

Turning to printed works, we find that a Safedian case figures in only one work printed in the sixteenth century: *Ma'ase ha-Shem* (Acts of the Lord) of R. Eliezer Ashkenazi, published in Venice in 1582. Gedalia ibn Yahia's *Shalshelet ha-Kabbalah* (Chain of Tradition), published in Venice in 1586, recounts ibn Yahia's own experience with a possessed woman in Ferrara and mentions a multiple possession case in Ancona but includes no Safedian cases.[30] At the cusp of the sixteenth and seventeenth century, the *Ma'aseh Buch* (Story Book) appeared in Basel, featuring a possession narrative that, in Sambari's version, was reported as having taken place in Safed.[31] It was only in the seventeenth century that the classic Safedian accounts began to be published widely: from Joseph Delmedigo's 1628 *Ta'alumot Hokhmah* (Mysteries of Wisdom) to Naftali Bacharach's *Emek ha-Melekh* (Valley of the King) and culminating in Menasseh ben Israel's 1651 *Nishmat Hayyim* (Soul of Life).[32] This last work contained many accounts of spirit possession among Jews, a number of which were said to have taken place in Safed. In the works published in the latter half of the seventeenth century and beyond containing possession accounts, these early narratives would be reprinted time and again.[33]

In summary, we have a number of cases that were mentioned in contemporary sources:[34] the Karo exorcism in Hallewa's work and the famous Falcon case of 1571. The possession of the young man first published in the *Ma'aseh Buch* cannot with certainty be located in Safed, as that identification depends solely upon Sambari's late-seventeenth-century text, other versions[35] not stating specifically that the case took place in Safed. At the same time, Sambari's work contains the *best* text of the Falcon case, copied as it was from Falcon's manuscript.[36] The major accounts of spirit possession involving R. Hayyim Vital were not printed until the efflorescence of Hebrew hagiographic literature in the mid-seventeenth century,[37] though they were at least mentioned in Vital's own manuscripts, if not recounted at length. Let us now focus on these accounts and explore the ways in which they suggest something about Safed's particular environment, its society of the living and the dead.

Falcon's A Great Event in Safed

Elijah Falcon, in the aftermath of a dramatic possession case that began on 16 February 1571, penned what was to become one of the best-known accounts of spirit possession in Jewish history: *The Great Event in Safed*.[38] Falcon's account, signed by three other prominent rabbis of Safed who, like himself were eyewitnesses and participants in the affair, was circulated in the Diaspora as a broadsheet by the late 1570s.[39] R. Eliezer Ashkenazi, writing in Poland after having departed from Italy, wrote that he had heard "in this, our own time" of cases of spirit possession, and that only "this year, in 5340" (1579–80) had he become familiar with the phenomenon, when he received a broadsheet from Safed that described such a case. Gedalia ibn Yahia, in his *Shalshelet ha-Kabbalah* (Venice, 1586), mentions having seen this signed broadsheet as well.[40] Falcon, it would seem, was an early publicist in Safed's bid for acknowledged centrality and preeminence in the Jewish world.[41] Falcon's didactic and dramatic broadsheet is less hagiographically oriented that we might have expected and asserts Safed's aspirations for leadership on the basis of its being the center of Jewish values and their instruction as well as a locus of ongoing divine incursion into the historical process. In this case, the divine incursion came in the form of the return of the dead to the society of the living, constituting a dramatic reification of traditional Jewish values in a period of transition and crisis.[42]

Falcon opens his account with an exhortative prologue in which he laments that human nature leads people to indulge themselves in the sensory pleasures of the body. This inclination leads to the impoverishment of the soul and to the abandonment of the Torah and its directives. Falcon bemoans the fact that even "believers and the punctiliously observant" generally fail to overcome this inclination. Their inability to champion the cause of their soul and the holy Torah, writes Falcon, is chiefly due to the inability of the spirit to impress itself sufficiently upon the flesh. The most sublime elements of the soul make but faint traces alongside the powerful desires of the body. Few have the capacity to recognize the folly of their material pursuits, so long as the claims of the spirit fail to compete with the those of the flesh. In Falcon's view, there is only one conceivable way for people to overcome the hedonism and epicureanism that naturally vanquish the still, small voice of the spirit in the contest for the shaping of human will: for the spirit to become flesh. Nothing in the Torah, he writes, can possibly make a strong enough impression upon a person to enable him "to separate himself from any aspect of evil and wrongdoing, whether in speech, thought, or action." The opportunity to meet a soul who has passed over into the realm of the dead is incomparably effective in inducing one to accept that the soul lives on after the death of the body, that reward and *especially* punishment await the sinning soul upon its departure from its short stay in the corrupting body.

And verily, it is known to him from one who came from that World, and told to him by one who has crossed over there. For perhaps the Holy One, Blessed be He, sent him so that they might fear Him, as the Sages of blessed memory said, " 'And God does it, so that men should fear him' [Eccles. 3:14]—this is a bad dream" [BT Berakhot 55a]. And this is not a dream but while awake, before the eyes of all.[43]

While a nightmare might have sufficed in former good days to inculcate fear of the Lord, such phantasms pale before the persuasiveness of a face-to-face meeting with a denizen of the world of the dead. Here and throughout his account, Falcon emphasizes the embodied presence of the dead before the living, who gathered in large numbers to see the evil dead *with their own eyes*. He is only one eyewitness among many, and his broadsheet begins and ends with this repeated refrain. "I was there, and my eyes saw and my ears heard all this and more—he who sees shall testify," signed Shlomo Alkabetz.[44] "I too was summoned to see this matter, and my eyes have seen, and my ears have heard," added Abraham Aruety.[45] Lest the reader have any doubts, we are told that some one hundred people attended the exorcism, including many sages and dignitaries.[46]

Before this "great assembly," the dead began to appear through the lifeless body of the possessed woman. Responding to the adjurations of the exorcists, a voice erupted from the woman's throat, unformed by any movement of her tongue or lips. This inchoate growl was like the roar of a lion rather than any human voice. Gradually, the exorcists forcefully imposed the standards of human language upon this rumble, and the voice became "like the voice of men." Such a development cannot but bring to mind de Certeau's analysis of the role of exorcists in reinstating within established language that which "manifests itself as speech, but as an uncertain speech inseparable from fits, gestures, and cries."[47] Tempting as it may be to assume that the human speech emerging from the woman's mouth— as we have it in the account—was entirely a projection of the anonymous exorcists or Falcon himself, its content would seem to belie such an interpretation. While we do well to recall that our sources were written by rabbinic figures rather than by the possessed, possession accounts often include statements by the possessed that suggest themselves as faithful renderings of the possessed's speech. In his analysis of the demonic possession of a Silesian girl in 1605, H. C. E. Midelfort notes this phenomenon. On the one hand, possession accounts were written by learned writers and were crafted accordingly, as apparent in the theologically learned arguments that the devil pursued with Tobias Seiler, the exorcist in the case. As Midelfort writes, these arguments were so complex that "any reader is bound to conclude that Seiler was composing not only his own lines, but the Devil's, too." On the other hand, threats to defecate in the pastor's throat until he became hoarse "have the ring of spontaneous reporting." Thus, Midelfort suggests, "if we can take the shape and color of the lens into account, we may yet be able to say something of what demon possession was like to the demon-possessed, and, more generally, what ordinary people in the German-speaking lands thought of the Devil."[48] If we try to listen for the voice of the possessed in these accounts, we also stand to restore some degree of agency to these victims—agency denied to them originally on theological grounds and more recently by historiographic trends that emphasize political and ecclesiastical circumstances, psychoanalytic readings that analyze the self the possessed could not herself know, or, as with de Certeau, interpretations stressing the semantic aggression of the exorcists.[49]

And what does the woman in the Falcon case actually say? What can we find out about her and her relationship to the soul possessing her? Here, Sambari's text is invaluable—for it alone preserves all the proper nouns found in Falcon's manuscript. Menasseh ben Israel's version and subsequent works dependent upon it have simply "so-and-so" where the identities of the spirit and the victim's in-laws are mentioned.[50] According to Sambari, the victim is the young daughter-in-law of "the venerable Joseph Zarfati."[51] We learn neither the name of the girl herself nor anything else about her. We can offer only something of a wild conjecture about the girl's origins, that she may have been from a *converso* family. Slender clues points in that direction: the usage of an expression from Esther 4:16 ("What can I do, if I perish, I perish") which, if not a literary embellishment of Falcon's, may disclose the special identification with Esther known to have existed among *conversos*.[52] Neither do we learn anything about her husband, Joseph's son, other than that at the time of the episode, he was away from Safed in Salonika. The spirit, however, declares himself to be Samuel Zarfati. This Samuel Zarfati explains that he died in Tripoli, leaving one son, two divorcees, and a widow.[53] The third wife was now married to a certain Tuvia Deleiria.[54] Samuel seems to have been well known in the community, as Falcon mentions a number of times that the spirit's words accorded with what people remembered about the deceased. While it is hard to understand why, if these details were known to many in the crowd in attendance, they should have been considered unknowable to the young possessed woman, Falcon indicates that these details were considered validating marks of the authenticity of the possession. "Then we recognized, all of us present, that the spirit was the speaker," he writes after hearing the spirit recount his family tree (sec. 7). In addition to this description of his family, other details considered convincing were the spirit's identification of his profession—money changer (sec. 20)—and his synagogue, the local prayer hall of the Castilian exiles, *Bet Ya'akov* (sec. 15).[55] Many in attendance also confirmed that the spirit's admission of his most egregious sin was known to them: the assertion that all religions were the same.[56] "Many testified before us that he would say such things while still alive," notes Falcon (sec. 8).[57] Samuel was also known for taking oaths and breaking them (sec. 18). If Samuel was no particular champion of the Torah, his son seems to have been no better. When asked by the exorcists if his son should recite the mourner's prayer *kaddish* or learn Torah on behalf of his soul, Samuel replies that such a notion was untenable and that his son was wholly unsuited to learn Torah (sec. 12). Still, some doubts as to the authenticity of the possession seem to have lingered, and the exorcists decided to test the spirit's ability to speak the languages he was known to have spoken when still alive. The spirit's successful display of his linguistic prowess in Hebrew, Arabic, and Turkish—coupled with his inability to understand Yiddish—must have been especially convincing, as "the woman did not know any of these languages."[58]

Clearly an important question is whether this Samuel Zarfati had a relationship with Joseph Zarfati's daughter-in-law, within whom he had lodged himself. A recent cultural history of ghosts found that in over three-quarters of the cases studied, percipients of early modern apparitions knew the identity of the apparition before them; possession cases in which the spirit was viewed as a disembodied soul seem to have worked similarly.[59] Simply the fact that the possessed woman was married into the Zarfati family would suggest the possibility of familiarity. Many of those present knew Samuel, who would have probably been an older contemporary of hers (his widow had recently remarried), perhaps even her brother-in-law.

Samuel seems to have been quite a cad—married three times and an irreligious skeptic. As a spirit he relates to the adulterous intimations of his presence with urbane humor. In an exchange deleted from Menasseh ben Israel's version, the exorcists ask the spirit pointedly: "And if she is a married woman, have you no reservations about copulating with her?" The spirit responded, "And what of it? Her husband isn't here, but in Salonika!"[60] Shortly after this remark, the exorcists worked diligently to expel Samuel from her tortured body, and she began to writhe and kick violently. In the process, she exposed herself immodestly.[61]

> [Samuel] raised her legs and lowered them one after the other, with great speed, time and again. And with those movements, which he made with great strength, the blanket that was upon her fell off her feet and thighs,

and she uncovered and humiliated herself before everyone's eyes. They came close to her to cover her thighs; but she had no self-consciousness in the course of any of this. Those who were acquainted with her knew of her great modesty, but now her modesty was lost. (sec. 21)

This image seems to amplify the exorcists' concern, and the spirit's admission, that some sort of intercourse was taking place between Samuel and the woman.[62] The possibility that women could have intercourse with spirits was discussed in the rabbinic literature of the period, and rabbis were called upon to determine whether women who had engaged in such forms of deviant sexual behavior were classifiable as adulteresses, prohibited to their husbands—precisely the concern voiced by the exorcists in this case.[63] The final detail suggesting the sexual nature of the relationship between the woman and Samuel—at least in this young woman's mind—was the spirit's chosen point of departure from her body, her vagina. The account is discreet about this point, but the woman seems to have maintained that blood flow from her vagina was due to his departure and sufficed to demonstrate that he had left.[64] Unfortunately for her, however, he soon returned, and only eight days later she died.[65] Given the amount of smoke to which she was subjected in the course of the exorcism, it seems likely that irresponsibility on the exorcists' part may have brought about her death—attributed in the account to "choking" at the hands of the spirit.

Untangling what we have learned about this case, we may distinguish a meaning that this event may have had for the young woman possessed and perhaps for her family and others who gathered around her during those difficult days out of concern and curiosity. Another meaning may be discerned in Falcon's *use* of the event in his constructed narrative, printed as a broadsheet for circulation throughout the Jewish world. What was Jewry at large to learn from the suffering and death of this innocent woman?

Whatever the etiology of the affliction that brought so much suffering upon this young woman, the disclosure of a network of filiations between the possessed and her possessor certainly suggests that the episode was a meaningful struggle between familiar parties. A psychodynamic reading would highlight the sexual anxiety felt by this woman, left behind by her husband—perhaps away on business—and some lurking feelings of guilt over improper feelings for Samuel. The "other" that has displaced her "self" has confessed his lust for her and his utter disregard for her husband; he has also given voice to sentiments at odds with the pietistic standards that climaxed in the years around the possession. Perhaps struggling with a *converso* legacy, her "other" spoke the voice of Esther, the hidden one, risking transgression in the hope of eliciting the King's compassion.[66] And only the degenerate who was Samuel could utter the guilelessly heretical words of a popular *philosophia perennis*: all religions are equal.

For those who witnessed this incursion of the dead into the land of the living, several points therefore emerged with palpable clarity:[67]

1. Life persists after death. Few could have imagined otherwise then, but the appearance of the dead made the conclusion inescapable. In a later period, when this tenet became contentious, Falcon's account, along with others, was called upon to prove decisively what had once been obvious.[68]
2. The wicked are punished after death. Judging from Falcon's introduction alone, this tenet was all too imaginable. During the case itself, Falcon did not miss the opportunity to ask the spirit to describe the punishments he suffered after death (sec. 13).
3. The dead are in close proximity, still embedded in networks of association with the living.[69] Not only in the graveyard a few paces away, they are in and about the synagogue, blocking Samuel's path as he seeks respite within its walls (sec. 15). New associations with the living may also be formed, as with the exorcists who were called in to rectify the spirit's soul even as they ejected it from the victim's body. A certain dependence of the dead upon the living is thus apparent.
4. The dead cast social and ethical ideals into relief by articulating their transgression.[70] Sexual propriety is encouraged by the spirit's flagrancy, yet for Falcon at least, there is no more serious violation of communal codes than the subverting of Judaism's exclusive authority. The spirit, in denying this exclusivity and the traditional claim of Judaism's singular truth and in disregarding the most solemn oaths of the Torah, had placed himself beyond redemption. His inability to enter *Gehinnom* signifies this unredeemability—rectifiable only through the intercession of the living saints, the kabbalists. These latter do not, however, always succeed. "One can search in vain," wrote Midelfort, " . . . for Catholic accounts of unsuccessful exorcisms."[71] Not so in the Jewish literature of the period, which begins with failures and is thereafter regularly punctuated with them. The didactic punch of these early accounts might even have been weakened by success, for in becoming a hagiographic genre, the fear of heaven inculcated by the spirit's travails might be supplanted by the benign hope of miraculous, salvific intercession regardless of one's sins. For writers like Falcon, religious authority could be strengthened no less by the didactic inculcating

of its values (through fear) than by the hagiographic amplification of its leading personalities.

The Young Man in Safed

Sambari's text conjoins another possession episode with the Falcon account. This second case does not seem to have been part of the original broadsheet, as the signatories on the latter appear immediately after the recounting of the woman's death. The case, as we have noted, is said to have taken place contemporaneously in Safed by Sambari, where other versions omit its location. It certainly pairs well with the Falcon account, in any case, with which it has much in common. This time, the victim was a young man, into whom the spirit of another dead young man entered. The spirit's greatest lament was not his own cruel fate but that of his young widow. Because he had died at sea, his young bride was trapped in *agunah* status. Such a status applies to the wife of a man who has disappeared without granting her a divorce, who is thus forbidden from remarrying unless reliable news of his death arrives.[72] While we are given no details, the account relates that the spirit argued assiduously with the assembled rabbis to permit her to remarry, even "invoking rabbinic teachings" in defense of his position (sec. 2).

Then come the disclosures and revelations: the woman, unable to remarry, is engaged in illicit sexual relationships; the spirit's bitter fate is also a punishment for his having had intercourse with a married woman in Constantinople, a transgression punishable by death in classical Jewish sources beginning in the Bible (Lev. 20:10). His death by drowning thus fulfilled the requirement that one guilty of adultery die by choking, a neat fact that may bespeak the learned construction of the whole account.[73] When a group of young men comes in to examine the possessed, the spirit is quick to reveal clairvoyantly that they too were guilty of adulterous activities, which they immediately confess. Like the Falcon case, then, the case of the possession of the young man in Safed suggests a network of sexual intrigue on the part of the victim, his spirit, and his family—here his wife. If the account is at all factual, it is hard to allay the suspicion that the possessed man was somehow involved sexually with the widow. Psychodynamically, the emergence of the dead on the scene facilitated the dramatic demand for her release from the accursed *agunah* status while allowing for the transference of the possessed's feelings of guilt at his involvement with a married woman upon her husband and all the young men who come to see their peer. The ability of the spirit to argue with the sages bespeaks a degree of learning that would prompt guilt over adultery, if not its avoidance.[74]

While sexual transgression may be most prominent in this account, the Torah is also championed: by the dead who would still abide by its rules and by the implementation of its statutes even when lack of evidence, let alone judicial autonomy, prevented ordained penalties from being carried out. The Torah called for the choking of the adulterer, and choke he did. Thus the dead man continued to live; he was punished; he made claims of, and was dependent upon, the living; and his sins, manner of death, and ongoing participation in learned dialectical modes of argumentation reestablish core values of the religious tradition and its overall cogency.

The Luria Cases

1571: The Spirit in the Widow/Woman of Safed

Although they were already in Safed, neither Luria nor Vital participated in the exorcism documented by Falcon. They did, however, participate in other exorcisms in 1571, including one or two[75] involving a possessed woman, and another involving a possessed young man. The reports of these cases became standard inclusions in seventeenth-century hagiographic works dedicated to Luria and his circle. The case of the possessed widow of Safed was even printed twice in Naftali Bacharach's *Emek ha-Melekh* (Amsterdam, 1648).[76] The other oft-published case involving a woman is quite similar to the account of the widow and may simply be a reworking of the same material; the two cases were not printed alongside one another until 1720, when a collector of these accounts, Shlomo Gabbai of Constantinople, failed to note their essential similarity. In addition to these widely circulated accounts, Vital's "private" diary, *Sefer ha-Hezyonot*, provides some external corroboration of this case.[77] Indeed, while the report of the possession of the widow is presented by an anonymous narrator, the other reports purport to be first-person accounts written by Vital himself.

The possession of the young nephew of R. Yehoshua Bin Nun is itself preserved in two distinct forms, one reported by an anonymous narrator, the other ostensibly by Vital. The two versions have much in common: a young man, suffering for years from a recurring illness, is diagnosed by Luria as a victim of spirit possession. In each, the spirit explains at Luria's command that he has possessed the nephew to avenge the wrong committed against him by the young man in his previous incarnation.[78] Luria prevails upon the spirit to abandon his quest for vengeance and to leave the young man voluntarily. The spirit agrees, but on the condition that the young man be isolated from any contact with females for a full week. Luria, while recognizing the difficulty of these terms, accepts them. At this point, the spirit departs, and Luria establishes a watch over the boy.[79] According to both accounts, the young man was left alone mistakenly in the course of the watch; during that time, his aunt arrived to celebrate his recovery. Finding the young man, she kissed him with joy. At that moment, the spirit returned and choked the lad to death.[80] Having been associated with the episode, Luria quickly departs from Safed to escape punishment from the Turkish authorities in connection with the young man's demise.[81] This short, simple account focuses on the dramatic consequences of sin, exemplifying the indefatigable relentlessness of what we might call transmigrational *lex talionis*. While blessed with magical gifts and extraordinary powers, even Luria is ultimately unable to rescue this poor young man from his deceased avenger. It may be no accident that this account is the only one in which Luria plays the role of exorcist actively; in other cases, Luria provided others with the requisite instruction to expel unwelcome spirits as we will see below.

With the account of the possession of the widow of Safed, we return to a case of Falcon-like proportions. Unlike the Falcon report, this account opens without any didactic introduction.[82] In this case, we are confronted immediately by the penetration of the spirit into the poor widow, a penetration that caused her great suffering. Her suffering notwithstanding, however, we are told that the immediate consequence of this affliction was her transformation into a public attraction in Safed. She was visited by many people, answering their questions and revealing their innermost troubles and desires. Two of the three major versions of the account portray the scene in terms that seem to normalize her newfound clairvoyant powers and relation to her community, while the third adheres more strictly to a problematized portrayal of the situation.[83] In the latter, the visitors never cease imploring the spirit to leave the poor widow in peace so that she may support herself and her children, while the spirit's clairvoyance is devoted to the exposure of the visitor's sins, to their public embarrassment. When a sage finally visits the woman, the spirit declares himself to be this rabbi's former student.[84] Again, the same sources that normalized the woman's interactions with her previous visitors leave us here with a picture of the spirit as at least a formerly learned rabbinical student, while the third supplements the encounter with the spirit's admission that while a student of the sage, he was often rebuked for his foul behavior.[85]

Finally, according to all accounts, the woman's sufferings became so unbearable that her family sought out the services of R. Isaac Luria, whom they hoped would exorcise the spirit. Unable or unwilling to attend to the matter personally, Luria sent Vital to the woman after empowering him through the laying of hands and furnishing him with mystical intentions and threats that had the capacity to evict the spirit against its will.[86] Thus prepared, Vital made his way to the widow's house. Vital never forgot this first meeting with the woman and included a description of the encounter in his diary decades later. This private journal entry is very similar to the versions presented in the three "popular" accounts.

> The year 5331 [1571]. When I was in Safed, my teacher of blessed memory taught me to expel evil spirits by the power of the unification that he taught me. When I went to him, the woman was lying on the bed. I sat beside her, and he turned his face away from me to the other side. I told him to turn his face to me to speak with me, that he depart, though he was unwilling. I then squeezed his face with my hand, at which point he said to me, "Is not turning my face towards you a reason to strike me? I did not do this out of evil, but because your face is alight with a great burning fire and my soul is incinerated if I look at you from the extent of your holiness."[87]

While clearly afflicted, and indeed bedridden, the woman's clairvoyant powers are unabated. Her avoidance of face-to-face contact with Vital, the spirit explains, was due to Vital's sublime holiness, a quality of Vital's that seems to have been appreciated primarily by men and women gifted with clairvoyant powers.[88] For Vital, this meeting was recalled as an encounter with yet another visionary who was able to assess his spiritual stature. While quite willing to accept the testimony of visionary women to this effect,[89] this short entry exhibits, through its evident confusion of gendered pronouns, the acute cognitive dissonance felt by Vital in encountering a visionary of this kind—demonic/clairvoyant/female/male.[90] The *woman* was lying on the bed; he sat beside *her*. Yet *he* turned *his* face away. Vital did not hesitate to use physical force to respond to this perceived insolence, and "squeezed *his* face" with his hand to bring about the face-to-face encounter.[91]

Here we might note the small but telling differences between the accounts of this meeting in *Sefer ha-Hezyonot* and in the three other accounts. The popular accounts fail to mention that the woman was in bed when Vital arrived; they also claim that Vital used a "decree" to force the spirit to face him. Finally, it is the sinfulness of the spirit that, in the popular accounts, explains the spirit's inability to face Vital rather than the spirit's visionary insight of Vital's spiritual grandeur. From these differences, we may see precisely the areas in which accounts that have some factual basis are reported quite accurately but with omissions and additions that bowdlerize the texts where they might prove embarrassing or insufficiently didactic. Apparently a portrait of Vital grabbing a visionary woman in her bedchamber was not what the writers and redactors of these accounts had in mind.[92]

Sexual transgression is at the heart of this case, the spirit's sin being the fathering of bastards in an adulterous affair with a married woman. In his conversation with Vital, the spirit recounts his sins and (at greater length) the travails he has undergone since his death by drowning.[93] After having been refused entry into *Gehinnom* by ten thousand sinners more worthy than he, the spirit attempted to find refuge in a Jewish inhabitant of the city of Ormuz, near India.[94] To his misfortune, not a single Jew in that city could provide him with an inhabitable body. Here again, sexual transgression figures prominently. Owing to their "fornication with menstruating and Gentile women," the bodies of these Jews are filled and surrounded with the forces of defilement. The account of this case, perhaps more than any other, is indeed rife with images of bodies filled—filled with these forces of defilement, with souls of the living and the dead, and even with fetuses.[95] As the spirit could not enter these Jewish bodies in Ormuz, so polluted as to have done injury even to his reprobate soul, in desperation he entered a doe in the wilderness of Gaza.[96] This doe, however, was itself an unsuitable container—"for the soul of a human being and the soul of a beast are not equal, for one walks upright and the other bent. Also, the soul of the beast is full of filth and is repulsive, its smell foul before the soul of a human being. And its food is not human food." To make matters worse, the doe was pregnant, and therefore already quite full—painfully so for the spirit as well as the doe, for "three souls cannot dwell together" in a single body. The doe, in agony, ran wildly in the hills and through rocky terrain, her belly swollen, until it split open, pouring out the three occupants with her death.[97]

The next bodily container for the spirit was to be a Kohen (a Jew of the priestly caste) in the city of Nablus. This gentleman, apparently realizing that he was possessed, called in the local expert exorcists for assistance. In this case, the spirit tells us, not kabbalists but Muslim clerics were summoned. This detail accords well with what we know about Jewish life in mid-sixteenth-century Nablus. Unlike the Jews in Safed, who lived in a separate Jewish quarter, the Jews of Nablus lived in mixed Jewish-Muslim neighborhoods.[98] It also reminds us of the acceptance of non-Jewish magical healers in Jewish society.[99] The Islamic holy men, using incantations, adjurations, and amulets, do, in fact, succeed in exorcizing the spirit from the Kohen. Here again, it is the bodily vessel and its contents that determine the matter. Responding to Vital's astonishment that the Muslims' magio-mystical arsenal was capable of effecting the exorcism, the spirit explains that the techniques employed by the Muslims infused the Kohen's body with so many defiling spirits that he had to leave to avoid the kind of contamination he had feared contracting from the impure contents of the bodies of the Jews of Ormuz.[100]

Now to the question of the motivation underlying the spirit's possession of the widow. Early modern Christian attitudes regarding demonic motivations underlying possession reflected theological premises quite remote from Jewish conceptions. In his *Traicté des Energumènes* of 1599, Pierre de Bérulle (Léon D'Alexis) explained the devil's motives in a manner that reveals how broad the gulf could be between Jewish and Christian views. The devil, he argued, being "the ape of God,"[101] is dedicated to incarnating himself in men, as did Christ himself. This, he suggested, accounts for the proliferation of possession since the birth of Christ.[102] Most Catholic theologians of the sixteenth century indeed assumed that demonic possession was most likely to occur as a punishment for the sins of the possessed, while popular accounts most commonly portray victims of possession as "pious young Christians."[103] Is there a similar disparity between learned and popular views of this issue in Jewish culture? R. Moses Cordovero stated in his *Drishot be-Inyane ha-Malakhim* (Inquiries concerning Angels) that "the types of *ibbur* depend on a man's moral and spiritual state, whether his soul is entered by a good soul—because he has done a *mitzvah*—or an evil soul—*because he has committed some sin.*"[104] While we have few sources that can directly provide a "popular" Jewish conception of the typical victim of spirit possession, we may be able to infer a disparity of this kind from the degree of inner confusion on this point displayed in Jewish sources. Early modern Jewish possession accounts shift inconsistently between affirmations of the innocence and even piety of the victim and ascriptions of blame—often of the same person. When the exorcists in the Falcon case asked the spirit of Samuel Zarfati what allowed him to possess a "kosher" woman, he replies that the woman had inadvertently cast some mud upon him as he was hovering in her midst.[105] In the case currently under consideration, we know that the most egregious sin of the spirit was sexual, but what of the widow? The sin that allows for the possession to take place seems not much less trivial, though "justifiable" on the basis of the positions staked out in the contemporary Jewish demonological literature. As Vital himself wrote in his treatise on transmigration, "it sometimes happens that notwithstanding the presence in a person of a pure and sublime soul, he may come at some point to anger. Then, [that soul] will depart from him, and in its place will enter another, inferior soul."[106] Before concluding his exorcism of the widow (and the woman in case 4), Vital asks the spirit how he obtained permission to enter his victim's body:

> The spirit responded: "I spent one night in her house. At dawn, this woman arose from her bed and wanted to light a fire from the stone and iron, but the burnt rag did not catch the sparks. She persisted stubbornly, but did not succeed. She then became intensely angry, and cast the iron and the stone and the burnt rag—everything—from her hand to the ground, and angrily said, 'to Satan with you!' Immediately I was given permission to enter her body."[107]

What appears to us as a small matter, a casual curse out of frustration, was evidently taken quite seriously. This severe approach to cursing had its basis in the strict enforcement of the third commandment, and traditional Jewish law prescribed penalties for such verbal crimes that paralleled those meted out to witches and idolators.[108] Sixteenth-century Jews were not alone in regarding the consequences of cursing most gravely; Christian tales of possession often dealt with the consequences of the curse "the devil take you."[109] M. Flynn has recently noted that "blasphemy was the most frequently censured religious offence of the Spanish people in the early modern period, far outnumbering convictions on charges of Judaism, Lutheranism, Illuminism, sexual immorality or witchcraft."[110] Moreover, J.-P. Dedieu's work has shown that, as in the expression by the woman in the possession case under our consideration, the Spanish Inquisitors were concerned with "petty crimes . . . of the word . . . that never attained the status of formal heresy, much less of unbelief."[111] These types of verbal offenses, known in Spain as *palabras*, seem to have been particularly prevalent in the mid-sixteenth century. In addition to her angrily spoken words, the woman had thrown down the stone and rag in frustration. Such an act, like cursing, was traditionally considered an invitation to the demonic forces to act, as we read, for example, in zoharic passages.[112] Nevertheless, according to our account, Vital could not accept the idea that a woman could be possessed for letting an ill-chosen word, rock, or rag slip on that cold morning. The spirit, for his part, was forthcoming with a more serious transgression that indeed justified his siege. Here, we return again to the issue of skepticism; the curse was merely the outward expression of a deeper heretical posture.

"Know," the spirit tells Vital, "that this woman's inside is not like her outside." While participating in the religious observances of Safed's Jewish community, the widow had her doubts.

> For she does not believe in the miracles that the Holy One, Blessed be He, did for Israel, and in particular in the Exodus from Egypt. Every Passover night, when all of Israel are rejoicing and good hearted, reciting the great *Hallel*[113] and telling of the Exodus from Egypt, it is vanity in her eyes, a mockery and a farce. And she thinks in her heart that there was never a miracle such as this.[114]

At this point, Vital turns his attention away from the spirit and focuses upon the widow.

> Immediately the Rav said to the woman, "Do you believe with perfect belief that the Holy One, Blessed be He is One and Unique, and that He created the heavens and the earth, and that He has the power and capacity to do anything that He desires, and that there is no one who can tell him what to do?" She responded to him and said, "Yes, I believe in it all in perfect faith." The Rav, may his memory be a blessing, further said to her, "Do you believe in perfect faith that the Holy One, blessed be He, took us out of Egypt from the house of slavery, and split the sea for us, and accomplished many miracles for us?" She responded, "Yes, master, I believe in it all with perfect faith, and if I had at times a different view, I regret it." And she began to cry.

This confrontation concluded, Vital speedily exorcises the spirit with little difficulty.[115]

Finally, in an epilogue that again raises the issue of the woman's skepticism and religious identification with the traditional community, we are told that the spirit continued to threaten the woman after its exorcism from her body. Concerned, her relatives returned to Luria for help, and he again sent Vital as his emissary. This time, Vital was to check the integrity of the mezuzah of her home to insure that she was adequately protected from evil.[116] Upon inspection, however, Vital discovered that the woman had no mezuzah whatsoever upon her doorpost.

Once again, then, we are confronted with an account that presents a possessed woman who, by virtue of her possession, is able to function as type of clairvoyant figure in the community, providing "services" not far removed from those provided by figures such as Luria.[117] She attracts substantial numbers of people and is able to discern their hidden sins and desires. Her visionary ability also results in a caustic encounter with Vital, recorded by him in his journal years later. By comparing the various versions of the story that have survived, we note apparent evidence of discomfort with aspects of this scenario—bowdlerization of unsavory details and the heightening of didactic elements signifying later redactions of an account that may have originally been penned by Vital himself. Moreover, the spirit's presence in the woman fulfills the functions considered above: his appearance before and among the living demonstrates the persistence of life after death, while his suffering dramatizes and embodies the doctrine of punishment for the wicked. While there is little that suggests a relationship between the spirit and the widow, he is not unknown in the community and soon establishes himself as a former student of a leading rabbinic figure in Safed. Finally, the sins of the spirit, and those of the widow no less, by stark transgression cast in bold relief the values and aspirations of the rabbinic writers who crafted the account, if not broader sectors of the cultural environment. Sexual licentiousness and popular skepticism emerge in this account, as in others we have examined, as fundamental threats to communal leadership struggling to establish a community on the basis of pietistic ideals.

In seeking to understand the apparent proliferation of the phenomenon of spirit possession in sixteenth-century Safed, these efforts to forge a pietistic community cannot be forgotten. In addition to the Iberian cultural influences on these developments,[118] Safed constituted a pressure cooker uniquely capable of stimulating apparitional contact with its dead through the idiom of possession. We ought to recall that in northern Germany, Midelfort discovered twice as many cases of demon possession in this period than in southern Germany, with the greatest frequency "among nunneries and among the most gnesio-Lutheran areas." In his estimation, this concentration was due to the fact that "in both situations the attempt to live an ever more perfect life may have led to stronger temptations [manifested as demonic possession] than those felt in other parts of Germany."[119] It would be difficult not to notice how aptly this observation applies to the religious environment of sixteenth-century Safed, the epicenter of the possession phenomenon in Jewish culture. As Scholem described it, "Ascetic piety reigned supreme in Safed. At first the religious ideal of a mystical elite only, asceticism now allied itself to an individual and public morality based on the new kabbalism; it struck deep roots in the collective consciousness."[120] Joseph Dan has also commented upon the "megalomaniacal" posture that reigned in Safed in this period:

> The very pretension of Safed to be a spiritual center and the epicenter of ordination in the Jewish world after the destruction of the center in Spain has within it something of megalomania: a remote village, which even

in its apex of development had a population smaller than scores of Jewish communities in Europe—and which lacked the vitality of a large and crowded assembly of Jews, with a high level of culture and organization—dared to aspire to serve as a replacement for the tremendous center that was destroyed in Spain, and to carry the miracle of redemption to the whole community of Israel.[121]

In short, every element was present in the culture of mid-sixteenth-century Safed to make it a conducive environment for a substantial increase in the incidence of spirit possession. Situated in an Islamic world with active traditions of *jinn* possession and exorcism, on more than one occasion rabbis called on Arab sorcerers for assistance in the difficult task of expelling the spirits.[122] Moreover, substantial number of Spanish and Portuguese immigrants, carrying with them stories, memories, theory, and praxis as well as inner conflicts and turmoil, elation and despair, faith and doubt, had made Safed their new home. Rabbinic leadership in Safed was also leading a campaign to make of this newly developed community a new spiritual center for world Jewry, producing didactic texts designed to inculcate its values and discipline its people. Finally, embracing the cemetery at its very heart, the people of Safed were living with their dead in exceedingly close proximity. With visionary mystics beholding apparitions of the dead at every turn, with farm animals being disclosed as deceased relatives, and with the quotidian brushes with death faced by a society still beleaguered by plagues and the tragic mortality of the young, possession by the dead could be regarded as "normal." Its etiology was certainly familiar to all; if each possession case required careful diagnosis and inquiry to be established as authentic, no doubts were voiced as to its fundamental plausibility. The men and women who were thus possessed were full somatic participants in the ferment that charactcrized their cultural environment. Their experience and its diffusion through the accounts carefully drafted by leading Safedian figures was to resonate for centuries in Jewish communities around the world for whom Safed, itself long since in decline, had come to represent pietistic aspiration and achievement.[123]

Notes

This essay is a revision of chapter 5 of my doctoral dissertation, "Spirit Possession and the Construction of Early Modern Jewish Religiosity," (Ph.D. diss., Yale University, 1999). Another version of the essay will appear in my book, *His-*

tories of the Spirits: Dybbuk Possession, Magical Exorcism and Early Modern Judaism (Philadelphia: University of Pennsylvania Press, forthcoming.)

1. H. Vital, *Sha'ar ha-Gilgulim*, vol. 10, *Kitve Rabbenu ha-Ari ZT"L*, ed. Y. Z. Brandwein (Jerusalem: n.p., 1988), chap. 24, 59a.

2. See, for example, the material in *Toledot ha-Ari, Studies and Texts*, ed. M. Benayahu (in Hebrew) (Jerusalem: Ben-Zvi Institute, 1967), 236–37.

3. Vital emphasizes the positive role played by the sacred imagination in cultivating mystical experience. See *Sha'are Kedushah* (Jerusalem: Eshkol, 1985), 3:gate 5, 89–90. Nevertheless, here he emphasizes the nonimaginary nature of Luria's visions. Compare *Sha'ar ha-Gilgulim*, 117b.

4. See M. Benayahu, "Devotional Practices of the Kabbalists of Safed in Meron" (in Hebrew), in *Sefer Zfat [Sefunot 6]*, ed. M. Benayahu and Y. B. Zvi (Jerusalem: Ben-Zvi Institute, 1962), 10–40; P. Giller, "Recovering the Sanctity of the Galilee: the Veneration of Sacred Relics in Classical Kabbalah," *Journal of Jewish Thought and Philosophy* 4 (1994): 147–69; M. Ish Shalom, *Kivre Avot* (Jerusalem: Mosad Bialik, 1948); A. Yaari, "History of the Pilgrimage to Meron" (in Hebrew), *Tarbiz* 31 (1961): 72–101. A. David treats the location of the Jewish quarter of sixteenth-century Safed in *To Come to the Land: Immigration and Settlement in Sixteenth-Century Eretz-Israel*, trans. D. Ordan (Tuscaloosa: University of Alabama Press, 1999), 95–97.

Sha'ar ha-Gilgulim concludes with a kind of traveler's guide to the tombs of Safed and its environs, including examples of tombs identified (or reidentified) by Luria. See 181a–185b.

5. C. M. N. Eire, *From Madrid to Purgatory: The Art and Craft of Dying in Sixteenth-Century Spain* (Cambridge: Cambridge University Press, 1995), 518–19.

6. Alsheikh (c. 1507, Adrianople or Salonika–1597, Damascus) ordained Vital in 1590. Notwithstanding his desire to study Kabbalah with Luria nearly twenty years earlier, Alsheikh—like his own teacher, R. Joseph Karo—was not accepted as a student by the master. On this matter, see Vital's account in *Sefer ha-Hezyonot*, ed. A. Z. Aescoly (Jerusalem: Mosad Bialik, 1954), 8; and D. Tamar's discussion in "On the Book *Toledot ha-Ari*" (in Hebrew), in his *Mehkarim be-Toldot ha-Yehudim be-Eretz Yisrael u'be-Italia* (Jerusalem: Rubin Mass, 1986), 166–93, esp. 176–77. Tamar established the date of Alsheikh's death in "Towards the Clarification of the Years of the Deaths of the Great Sages of the Land of Israel and Turkey" (in Hebrew), in his *Mehkarim be-Toldot ha-Yehudim be-Eretz Yisrael u've-Artzot ha-Mizrah* (Jerusalem: Mosad ha-Rav Kook, 1981), 94–106; he posited the existence of a second "Moshe Alsheikh" in "Gleanings regarding *Sefer ha-Hezyonot*" (in Hebrew), *Sinai* 46.91 (1982): 92–96. See also the lengthy treatment of Alsheikh in M. Benayahu, *Yosef Behiri: Maran Rabi Yosef Karo* (Joseph, My Chosen: Our Master Rabbi Joseph Karo) (Jerusalem: Yad Harav Nisim, 1991), esp. 233–55. On the *hatzer* (literally, court) in which Alsheikh and Vital studied, see M. Benayahu, "R. Hayyim Vital in Jerusalem" (in Hebrew), *Sinai* 30 (1952): 65–75; and Chajes, "Spirit Possession," chap. 6.

7. Cited from the critical edition prepared by M. Pachter, " 'Terrible Vision,'

by R. Moses Alsheikh" (in Hebrew), in his *From Safed's Hidden Treasures: Studies and Texts concerning the History of Safed and Its Sages in the Sixteenth Century* (Jerusalem: Shazar Center, 1994), 69–117; citation from 112–13.

8. Safed's numerical value is 21 if one drops the zeros from each of its letters (*mispar katan*). Thus צ=90, פ=80, ת=400 gives us 9+8+4=21. Adding the entire word itself (the *kollel*) brings us to 22.

9. תקע Now simply 90+80+400=570. Azulai explains earlier in this chapter the significance of the word תקע (literally "pitch," as in Gen. 31:25) as alluding to the Cave of Machepelah, the passageway to the Garden of Eden given its numerical equivalence to עובר לסוחר (literally, current money with the merchant). This latter phrase was mystically interpreted in earlier kabbalistic literature as "passage to the supernal worlds." See, for example, Zohar 1:123b and 141a; 3: 128b.

10. The Cave of Makhpelah, the first and foremost grave in the Bible (Gen. 23), was the resting place of the Patriarchs and Matriarchs. Located in Hebron, this cave was held by mystical tradition as the entrance to the Garden of Eden. See, for example, Zohar 1:127a, 219a, 248b.

11. A. Azulai, *Hesed le-Avraham* (1685; reprint, Jerusalem: Ben-Yishai Hotza'ah le-Or, [1996]), 115–16.

12. On the especially intense link between spiritual ecstasy and death in early modern Spain, see Eire, *From Madrid to Purgatory*, 6–7, 396–98, 411–12.

13. A longing for death is also apparent in Safedian mystical literature, from R. Joseph Karo's wishes to be burned at the stake—inspired by the martyrdom of Shlomo Molkho—to the frequent meditations on death and martyrdom in the prayer intentions of Luria. On Karo's death wish, see J. Karo, *Maggid Mesharim* (Amsterdam, 1708), 65a; and R. J. Z. Werblowsky, *Joseph Karo: Lawyer and Mystic*, 2nd ed. (Philadephia: Jewish Publication Society, 1977), 98–99. On "martyrological devotion during prayer" from the thirteenth to the nineteenth century, see M. Fishbane, "The Imagination of Death in Jewish Spirituality," in *Death, Ecstasy, and Other-Worldly Journeys*, ed. J. Collins and M. Fishbane (Albany: State University of New York Press, 1995), 183–208. Luria's "daring" amplification of death meditations in worship is discussed on 199–202. Fishbane's full treatment of the subject may be found in his *The Kiss of God: Spiritual and Mystical Death in Judaism* (Seattle: University of Washington Press, 1993). See also E. R. Wolfson's contribution to the *Death, Ecstasy and Other-Worldly Journeys* volume, "Weeping, Death, and Spiritual Ascent in Sixteenth-Century Jewish Mysticism," esp. 230–31.

On the phenomenon of apparitions, see W. A. Christian Jr., *Apparitions in Late Medieval and Renaissance Spain* (Princeton: Princeton University Press, 1981); C. M. Staehlin, *Apariciones* (Madrid: Razón y Fe, 1954).

14. Another Safedian who was associated with frequent contact with the dead was R. Lapidot Ashkenazi. See *Sefer ha-Hezyonot*, 5. On this figure and the stories associated with him, see M. Idel, "R. Yehudah Hallewa and His *Tzafnat Pa'aneah*" (in Hebrew), *Shalem: Studies in the History of the Jews in Eretz-Israel* 4 (1984): 119–48, esp. 145–48; R. Meroz, "From the Compilation of Ephraim Penzieri: The Ari's Homily in Jerusalem and the Intentions for Eating" (in Hebrew), in *Jerusalem*

Studies in Jewish Thought, vol. 10, *Kabbalat ha-Ari*, ed. R. Elior and Y. Liebes (Jerusalem: Hebrew University, 1992), 235; D. B. Ruderman, *A Valley of Vision: The Heavenly Journey of Abraham ben Hananiah Yagel* (Philadelphia: University of Pennsylvania Press, 1990), 220–21; idem, *Kabbalah, Magic, and Science: The Cultural Universe of a Sixteenth-Century Jewish Physician* (Cambridge, Mass.: Harvard University Press, 1988), 125–26.

15. See S. Avizur, "Safed—Center of the Manufacture of Woven Woolens in the Fifteenth Century" (in Hebrew), *Sefunot* 6 (1962): 43–69.

16. For a poetic introduction to the superabundance of rabbinic talent that gathered in sixteenth-century Safed, see the classic essay by S. Schechter, "Safed in the Sixteenth Century: A City of Legists and Mystics," in idem, *Studies in Judaism*, 2nd ser. (Philadelphia: Jewish Publication Society of America, 1908), 202–328.

17. See B. Lewis, *Notes and Documents from the Turkish Archives: A Contribution to the History of the Jews in the Ottoman Empire* (Jerusalem: Israel Oriental Society, 1952), 5–7; A. David, "Demographic Changes in the Safed Jewish Community of the 16th Century," *Occident and Orient: A Tribute to the Memory of Alexander Scheiber*, ed. R. Dan (Budapest: Akademiai Kiado, 1988), 83–93.

18. See A. David, "Safed, foyer de retour au judaïsme de 'conversos' au XVIe siècle," *Revue des études juives* 146.1–2 (1986): 63–83.

19. See, for example, B. Bennassar, *The Spanish Character: Attitudes and Mentalities from the Sixteenth to the Nineteenth Century*, trans. B. Keen (Berkeley: University of California Press,1979), esp. chap. 9.

20. Giller, "Recovering the Sanctity," 155.

21. See appendix A, case 3, sec. 4. Visitations of the dead in dreams were not unknown. See, for example, E. de Vidas, *Reshit Hokhmah ha-Shalem*, ed. C. Waldman (Jerusalem: Or Hamussar, 1984), 1:238, 471 (Gate of Fear 12:49; Gate of Love 6:35).

22. See M. Sluhovsky, "A Divine Apparition or Demonic Possession? Female Agency and Church Authority in Demonic Possession in Sixteenth-Century France" *Sixteenth Century Journal* 27.4 (1995): 1036–52. In all of the cases discussed here by Sluhovsky, the possessed initially "identified their possessing agency as a messenger who reappeared from the dead to demand stricter obedience by family members of religious precepts."

23. See the discussion in J.-C. Schmitt, *Ghosts in the Middle Ages: The Living and the Dead in Medieval Society*, trans. T. L. Fagan (Chicago: University of Chicago Press, 1998).

24. See P.-A. Sigal, "La possession démoniaque dans la région de Florence au XVe siècle d'après les miracles de Saint Jean Gualbert," in *Histoire et société: Mélanges offerts à Georges Duby*, vol. 3 (Aix-en-Provence: Publications de l'Universite de Provence, 1992); Schmitt, *Ghosts in the Middle Ages*; Christian, *Apparitions*; N. Caciola, "Discerning Spirits: Sanctity and Possession in the Later Middle Ages" (Ph.D. diss., University of Michigan, 1994), part 2. The Islamic parallel must also be noted. See E. Zbinden, *Die Djinn des Islam und der altorientalische geisterglaube* (Bern: Paul Haupt, 1953). On the tension between Islamic teachings and

popular beliefs with regard to the evil dead and their ability to harm the living, see p. 94.

25. See my "Judgments Sweetened: Possession and Exorcism in Early Modern Jewish Culture," *Journal of Early Modern History* 1.2 (1997): 124–69.

26. See, for example, the excellent recent discussion and bibliography in P. J. Geary, "Saints, Scholars, and Society: The Elusive Goal," in idem, *Living with the Dead in the Middle Ages* (Ithaca: Cornell University Press, 1994), 9–29. See also Eire, *From Madrid to Purgatory*, 371–76.

27. See my *Histories of the Spirits*.

28. MS. B.5.27, Trinity College, Dublin. This work and its author have been treated by M. Idel in two articles: "Inquiries into the Doctrine of *Sefer ha-Meshiv*" (in Hebrew), *Sefunot* 2.17 (1983): 185–266; and "R. Yehudah Hallewa and His *Zafnat Pa'aneah*" (in Hebrew), *Shalem: Studies in the History of the Jews in Eretz-Israel* 4 (1984): 119–48.

29. I treat the Damascus case at length in a forthcoming article, "Off the Kabbalistic [Accepted] Path: Jewish Mystical Women in Light of R. Hayyim Vital's *Sefer ha-Hezyonot*," (in Hebrew) *Zion* (forthcoming). Vital's *Sefer ha-Hezyonot* is now available in an English translation in *Jewish Mystical Autobiographies*, trans. and ed. M. Faierstein (Mahwah, N.J.: Paulist Press, 1999).

30. There is little to suggest that the case of *dybbuk* possession in ibn Yahia's *Shalshelet ha-Kabbalah* resulted from Safedian influence. *Shalshelet ha-Kabbalah* was published in 1586, decades before the Safedian cases were published for the first time. J. Dan posits such influence in "The Case of the Spirit and the She-Demon" (in Hebrew), *Ha-Sifrut* 18–19 (1974): 74–84, esp. 75.

31. See M. Gaster, ed., *Maaseh Book* (Philadelphia: Jewish Publication Society of America, 1934), 301–03.

32. On Menasseh ben Israel (1604–57), see *Menasseh ben Israel and His World*, ed. Y. Kaplan, H. Méchoulan, and R. H. Popkin (Leiden: E.J. Brill, 1989). For further bibliographic information, see J. H. Coppenhagen, *Menasseh ben Israel: Manuel Dias Soeiro, 1604–1657: A Bibliography* (Jerusalem: Misgav Yerushalayim, 1990).

33. A list of these works and the accounts they contain may be found in appendix 1 of Chajes, "Spirit Possession."

34. If we include the evil *ibburim* suffered by mystics in Luria's circle (including Vital and Yehudah Mishan), the number of cases would grow. We might also note that Vital writes that it was Luria's practice to send him to perform exorcisms, indicating that he did so on a somewhat regular basis. See *"Ma'aseh Nissim shel ha-Ari Z"L (Shivhe ha-Ari,)"* in *Me'irat 'Ainayim*, ed. S. b. D. Gabbai (Constantinople: n.p., 1666), 17a–17b (misprinted as 16a–b).

35. For example, the Yiddish version in the *Ma'aseh Buch*, and the version in Menasseh ben Israel's *Nishmat Hayyim*.

36. Sambari prefaces his reproduction of this account with the phrase, "as I found written in the autograph of the great tamarisk, our teacher the rabbi, R. Elijah Falcon, his memory for life everlasting." *Sefer Divre Yosef by Yosef ben*

Yitzhak Sambari, ed. S. Shtober (Jerusalem: Ben-Zvi Institute, 1994), 319. Compare Benayahu, *Toledoth ha-Ari*, 104, n. 6. Sambari's text contains a number of details missing from other versions, all of which indicate its greater accuracy and freedom from the bowdlerization that plagues all printed versions of these cases. See below.

37. See J. Dan, "Toward the History of Hagiographic Literature" (in Hebrew), *Jerusalem Studies in Jewish Folklore* 1 (1981): 82–100; and idem, "Hagiographic Literature: East and West" (in Hebrew), *Pe'amim* 26 (1986): 77–86.

38. On Falcon, see Chajes, "Spirit Possession," chap. 2, n. 135.

39. On the publication of this story as a broadsheet, see Benayahu, *Toledoth ha-Ari*, 47 and 104, n. 6. It is possible, though unlikely, that the printing could have been accomplished in Safed, as the earliest printing press in Safed—and in the entire region—was founded in 1577. See A. Yaari, *Ha-Defus ha-Ivri be-Artzot ha-Mizrah* (Hebrew Printing in the East) (Jerusalem: Hebrew University Press, 1936), 1:10.

40. See *Shalshelet ha-Kabbalah* (Jerusalem: Ha-Dorot ha-Rishonim ve-Koratam, 1962), 204.

41. This centrality was indeed acknowledged by world Jewry. As Pachter notes, "the recognition of the centrality of Safed became one of the unquestioned givens of the period." See his "'Terrible Vision,'" 76, n. 36, and below. On the contemporary propagandistic writing of R. Shlomo Alkabetz (c. 1505, Salonica–1584, Safed) on behalf of Safed, see Pachter's "The Parting Sermon of R. Shlomo Alkabetz in Salonika" (in Hebrew), in idem, *From Safed's Hidden Treasures*, 17–38. On Alkabetz generally, see B. Sack, "The Secret Teaching of R. Shlomo haLevi Alkabetz" (Ph.D. diss., Brandeis University, 1977).

42. Many anthropologists have identified possession as a response to "lack of structure and socio-political indeterminacy" or "as an attempt to enrich the spiritual armoury of a community beset by chronic environmental uncertainty, or rapid and inexplicable social change." See M. Douglas, *Natural Symbols: Explorations in Cosmology* (London: Barrie and Rockcliff, 1970); This is the approach generally advocated by I. M. Lewis as well, in his *Ecstatic Religion: A Study of Shamanism and Spirit Possession* 2nd ed. (London: Routledge, 1989).

43. Ben Israel, *Nishmat Hayyim*, book 3, chap. 10, 109a–11a. Compare Shtober, *Divrei Yosef*, 319–24.

44. See n. 40.

45. Another sage of Safed (from a well-known Spanish-Portuguese family) whose name also appears alongside those of Joseph Karo and Moses Trani in a halakhic responsum from 1560.

46. Sambari's version has "more than one hundred," while the version in *Nishmat Hayyim* has "nearly one hundred." Accounts of the other Safed exorcisms of the early 1570s also stress the large numbers of people who assembled to observe the proceedings. See, for example, the account published in *Emek ha-Melekh*, 16b–17a.

47. M. de Certeau, "Discourse Disturbed," in idem, *The Writing of History* (New York: Columbia University Press, 1988), 244–68 (citation 255–56).

48. H. C. E. Midelfort, "The Devil and the German People: Reflections on the Popularity of Demon Possession in Sixteenth-Century Germany," *Religion and Culture in the Renaissance and Reformation, Sixteenth Century Essays and Studies* 11 (1989): 99–119 (citation 119).

49. The problem of agency in demonic possession is an intractable one. It is no less a distortion to suggest that the possessed *sought* or desired their possession than that they were helpless victims of circumstances beyond their control. Sluhovsky's article, "A Divine Apparition or Demonic Possession?" includes a thoughtful discussion of this problem.

50. *Nishmat Hayyim*, book 3, chap. 10, 109a–11a. See appendix 1 of Chajes, "Spirit Possession," for later works incorporating this account, all of which seem to have found it in Menasseh ben Israel's work. On such bowdlerization by editors seeking to remove "objectionable or offensive references to living or revered personalities," see the remarks of Werblowsky in *Joseph Karo*, 31.

51. Zarfati is a surname given to Jews of French origin. Well-known families by this name lived in Italy and Morocco beginning in the late fifteenth century. The Italian branch included a number of figures by the name of Joseph and Samuel, the names that figure in this possession case. On conversions to Christianity in the Italian Zarfati family in the mid-sixteenth century, see R. Segre, "Sephardic Refugees in Ferrara: Two Notable Families," in *Crisis and Creativity in the Sephardic World, 1391–1648*, ed. B. R. Gampel (New York: Columbia University Press, 1997), 164–85, esp. 167.

Joseph Zarfati (Sarfati), a rabbi in Fez in the early sixteenth century, converted to Christianity and actively preached against Jews and Judaism under the auspices of his godfather, Pope Julius III (1550–55). This Joseph Zarfati, whose vehemently anti-Jewish sermons were heard by Michel de Montaigne, was an instigator of the condemnation of the Talmud and its subsequent burning in Rome in 1553. See *Encyclopedia Judaica*, s.v. "Sarfati (Zarefati, Sarfatti)," by R. Spiegel. See also K. Stow, *The Jews in Rome*, 2 vols. (Leiden: E.J. Brill, 1997).

52. See C. Roth, "The Religion of the Marranos," in idem, *A History of the Marranos* (New York: Sefer-Hermon Press, 1992), 168–94; and the doctoral dissertation in preparation by D. Siegman of Columbia University. The spirit's pronouncement of his worst sin also carries a *converso* scent and might be read as a transference of an issue particularly acute for the woman to the spirit within her. See below.

53. This according to Menasseh ben Israel's version, which reads three *wives* rather than *daughters*, as in Sambari. This reading accords better with the expression "from the third one, he passed away," which seems to express that he left her a widow, rather than a divorcee, and makes little sense if referring to his daughter. It also makes the spirit's mention of her current husband more intelligible. Then again, *lexio difficilis* could give Sambari's text the nod.

54. I have not been able to find any information about a figure by this name, spelled די לירייאה in Sambari. The name indicates that the man's family was of Portuguese origin, from the town of Leiria.

55. This synagogue was founded around 1525, and led by R. Moses Trani for some fifty years.

56. שכל הדתות שוות, according to Sambari. Menasseh ben Israel's version has the somewhat more generic "he would speak against the Torah of Moses our teacher, of blessed memory." See sec. 8.

The spirit's statement that "all religions are the same" bespeaks a type of popular skepticism that has not been studied sufficiently. Treatments of skepticism in this period have been primarily devoted to the elite, neo-Pyrrhonist skepticism of figures such as Zarfati's contemporary, Michel de Montaigne. The most significant studies of this high skepticism of the sixteenth century are R. H. Popkin, *The History of Scepticism from Erasmus to Spinoza*, rev. and enl. ed. (Berkeley: University of California Press, 1979); and *The Skeptical Tradition*, ed. M. Burnyeat (Berkeley: University of California Press, 1983). Also worthy of mention among the foremost works treating sixteenth-century skepticism is L. Febvre, *The Problem of Unbelief in the Sixteenth Century: The Religion of Rabelais*, trans. B. Gottlieb (Cambridge, Mass.:Harvard University Press, 1982). See also the suggestive treatment of J. L. Sánchez Lora, *Mujeres, conventos y formas de la religiosidad barroca* (Madrid: Fundacion Universitaria Española, 1988), esp. 217. A trailblazing study of popular skepticism in the early modern period is C. Ginzburg, *The Cheese and the Worms*, trans. J. and A. Tedeschi (Baltimore: Johns Hopkins University Press, 1980).

Skepticism among *conversos* has been studied by a number of scholars, though generally they concentrate on the seventeenth century. See Y. Yovel, *Spinoza and Other Heretics: The Marrano of Reason* (Princeton: Princeton University Press, 1989). Dr. Juan de Prado allegedly made the claim in 1643 that all religions were equal, according to inquisitorial testimony discussed by Yovel, 62. See also the recent contributions of D. B. Ruderman in *Jewish Thought and Scientific Discovery in Early Modern Europe* (New Haven: Yale University Press, 1995), esp. 153–84, 276–80; and the many studies of Y. Kaplan, including his *From Christianity to Judaism: The Story of Isaac Orobio de Castro*, trans. R. Loewe (Oxford: Oxford University Press, 1989), esp. 319–22. See also J. Faur, *In the Shadow of History: Jews and Conversos at the Dawn of Modernity* (Albany: State University of New York Press, 1992).

57. I will return to this admission and its meaning in my discussion of skepticism in these accounts below.

58. This example of xenoglossia was examined by Raphael Patai in his article "Exorcism and Xenoglossia among the Safed Kabbalists," *Journal of American Folklore* 91 (1978): 823–35. Patai writes that given the skeptical frame of mind of the exorcists as the identity of the spirit, one must assume that the spirit's display of mastery of the three languages was sufficient to convince them that it was indeed the spirit who was speaking because it exceeded by far any rudimentary knowledge

the woman could have had. That is to say, the account as it stands must be taken as prima facie evidence of an authentic multiple xenoglossia (827–28.)

59. R. C. Finucane, *Appearances of the Dead: A Cultural History of Ghosts* (London: Junction Books, 1982), 84.

60. השיב הרוח מה בכך ובעלה אינו בכאן אלא בשאלוניקי. R. Lamdan has argued that adultery became quite widespread in the Jewish communities of Palestine and Egypt of the sixteenth century. See her "Deviations from Norms of Moral Behavior in the Jewish Society of Eretz Israel and Egypt in the Sixteenth Century" (in Hebrew), in *Sexuality and the Family in History*, ed. I. Bartal and I. Gafni (Jerusalem: Shazar Center, 1998), 119–30.

61. Underwear had not yet been invented. See E. Muir, *Ritual in Early Modern Europe* (Cambridge: Cambridge University Press, 1997), 37.

62. For an anthropological study arguing that possession is a means for sexually deprived women to find some measure of sexual satisfaction, see M. E. Spiro, *Burmese Supernaturalism* (Englewood Cliffs, N.J.: Prentice Hall, 1967).

63. See, for example, the responsum by R. Haim Joseph David Azulai (the Hida) (1724–1806), *She'elot u'Teshuvot Hayyim Sha'al*, 1:sec. 53. The Hida cites responsum sec. 117 of the *Maharam mi-Lublin* to the same question. These responsa also treat male intercourse with female spirits, which is a less halakhically problematic phenomenon. See H. J. Zimmels, *Magicians, Theologicans, and Doctors: Studies in Folk-Medicine and Folk-Lore as Reflected in Rabbinical Responsa (12th-19th Centuries)* (New York: Feldheim, 1952), 82.

Jewish mystical literature is replete with discussions and stories of incubi and succubi. See, for example, Zohar 3:276a; R. Hayyim Vital, *Arba Me'ot Shekel Kesef*, Kitve Rabbenu ha-AR"I zt"l ed. Y. Z. Brandwein, (15 vols.) vol. 12 (Jerusalem: n.p., 1998) 252; Ibn Yahia, *Shalshelet ha-Kabbalah*, 195; "Shivhe ha-Ari," in *Sefer ha-Kavanot u-Ma'aseh Nissim*, ed. S. b. M. Gabbai (Constantinople, 1720), 3b. See also Menasseh ben Israel's extended treatment of the problem in *Nishmat Hayyim*, book 3, chap. 16.

64. While she may simply have been menstruating, it is also possible that the woman hemorrhaged vaginally in the course of her violent seizures. St. Teresa of Avila hemorrhaged vaginally shortly before her death, leading some to suspect that she may have had epilepsy. See M. B. Barton, "Saint Teresa of Avila: Did She Have Epilepsy?" *Catholic Historical Review* 68 (1982): 581–98; Eire, *From Madrid to Purgatory*, 404, n. 17.

65. Rapid repossession was a common phenomenon. Barthélemy Perdoux, an early seventeenth-century French doctor, described it in his *De Morbis Animi* of 1639. His explanations are discussed in S. Ferber, "The Demonic Possession of Marthe Brossier, France 1598–1600," in *No Gods Except Me: Orthodoxy and Religious Practice in Europe, 1200–1600*, ed. C. Zika (Melbourne: University of Melbourne, History Department, 1991), 59–83, esp. 63.

66. The expression of resignation to the possibility of destruction from Esther 4:16 follows her declaration of determination to come before the king in violation of the law.

67. This analysis of the cultural functioning of spirit possession is based on Finucane, *Appearances of the Dead*, 85–86. Eire has made use of Finucane's categories in his analysis of St. Teresa's apparitions. See *From Madrid to Purgatory*, 475.

68. See chapter 7 of Chajes, "Spirit Possession."

69. The reciprocity between the living and the dead in Ashkenazic Jewish culture is examined by C. Weissler in "The Living and the Dead: Ashkenazic Family Relations in Light of Hebrew and Yiddish Cemetery Prayers," in idem, *Voices of the Matriarchs: Listening to the Prayers of Early Modern Jewish Women* (Boston: Beacon Press, 1998). Early modern Catholic views and Protestant critiques of those views are discussed in N. Z. Davis, "Ghosts, Kin, and Progeny: Some Features of Family Life in Early Modern France," in *The Family*, ed. A. Rossi, J. Kagan, and T. Hareven (New York: W.W. Norton, 1978), 87–114.

70. These transgressions emerge in the course of the revelations made by the spirit, including the sins that brought him to his insufferable limbo state as well as his disclosure of the sins of many in attendance (in other cases).

71. Midelfort, "The Devil and the German People," 118.

72. The status of the *agunah* and the requirement to rule legally on her behalf are discussed in Maimonides, *Mishnah Torah*, Laws of Divorce, chap. 13, sec. 28. Earlier rabbinic discussions of the status may be found in the Jerusalem Talmud, *Gittin* 20a and BT Babba Kamma 80a and Rashi and Tosaphot there. On the *agunah* problem and young brides in sixteenth-century Egypt, Syria, and Palestine, see R. Lamdan, "Child Marriage in Jewish Society in the Eastern Mediterranean during the Sixteenth Century," *Mediterranean Historical Review* 11 (1996): 37–59, esp. 49–50.

73. See appendix A, case 2, sec. 2 and note 47 above. Compare Rashi on Lev. 20:10: " 'The adulterer and the adulteress shall surely be put to death': All death [penalties] mentioned without specification in the Torah are carried out by strangulation." See also BT Ketubot 30a–b; BT Sanhedrin 37b; *Numbers Rabbah* 14.6.

74. See Lamdan, "Deviations from Norms of Moral Behavior."

75. There is some question as to whether one account is merely an adaptation of the other rather than a separate case.

76. On this work, see Y. Liebes, "Toward a Study of the Author of *Emek ha-Melekh*: His Personality, Writings, and Kabbalah" (in Hebrew), *Jerusalem Studies in Jewish Thought* 11 (1993): 101–37; and chapter 7 of Chajes, "Spirit Possession."

77. Vital, see below. M. Oron argues that Vital's autobiographical journal was intended to remain private in "Dream, Vision, and Reality in Hayyim Vital's *Sefer ha-Hezyonot*" (in Hebrew), *Jerusalem Studies in Jewish Thought* 10 (1992): 299–309. Compare Benayahu, *Toledoth ha-Ari*, 99.

78. See appendix A, case 5, sec. 1.

79. See ibid., case 5, sec. 2.

80. See ibid., case 5, sec. 3.

81. See ibid., case 5, sec. 4. According to the accounts, Luria's speedy departure was accomplished through a magical technique known as *kefitzat ha-derekh*.

On this technique, see M. M. Verman and S. H. Adler, "Path Jumping in the Jewish Magical Tradition," *Jewish Studies Quarterly* 1 (1993–1994): 131–48. The technique is also part of the Islamic magical tradition. See the references in G. Bos, "Moshe Mizrachi on Popular Science in 17th Century Syria-Palestine," *Jewish Studies Quarterly* 3 (1996): 250–79, esp. 261, n. 68.

82. A didactic prologue introduces the account in Bacharach's *Emek ha-Melekh*, but not the accounts in the earlier *Ta'alumot Hokhmah* or in Sambari's manuscript. For a synoptic edition of this account see appendix 2, case 5, sec. 1 of Chajes, "Spirit Possession."

83. *Emek ha-Melekh* and *Ta'alumot Hokhmah* on the one hand and Sambari on the other. See appendix A, case 5, sec. 3–4.

84. Our sources differ as to the identity of this sage, owing to the probability that the earliest written source of the account provided no more than his initials, ר״א. As it would happen, these initials were shared by a number of leading rabbinic figures in Safed in 1571: Isaac Luria (Ashkenazi), Joseph Ashkenazi, Joseph Arzin, Isaac Arha, Joseph Alton, Jacob Altaraz, Israel Auri, Judah Ashkenazi, and others. Here again we come to an issue that has been smouldering for thirty years in the prodigious—and contentious—output of M. Benayahu and D. Tamar. According to Benayahu, Joseph Ashkenazi is correct here, while Tamar argues for Joseph Arzin. See, for example, Benayahu, *Toledot ha-Ari*, 46; D. Tamar,"On the Book *Toledot ha-Ari*," 191.

85. See appendix A, case 3, sec. 1.

86. A comparative morphological analysis of Lurianic exorcism technique may be found in chapter 3 of Chajes, "Spirit Possession." See appendix A, case 3, sec. 2.

87. *Sefer ha-Hezyonot*, p. 36. Compare appendix A, case 3, sec. 3. There are a number of parallels to this incident in *Sefer ha-Hezyonot*. When Vital consulted with sorcerers who engaged in divinatory practices involving the adjuration of demons, the sorcerers were unable to proceed due to the reluctance of the demons to appear in Vital's presence. See, for example, sec. 19, sec. 21.

88. While Vital's spiritual stature was recognized by Karo's *maggid*, Luria, R. Lapidot Ashkenazi, the shamanic kabbalists Avraham Avshalom of Morocco and Shealtiel Alsheikh of Persia, palm readers, Arab seers, and a number of visionary women in Safed and Damascus, he appears to have been underappreciated by those lacking visionary powers. See *Sefer ha-Hezyonot*, 1–13.

89. See Chajes, "Off the Kabbalistic [Accepted] Path."

90. Vital's discussions of the problems associated with the "normal" transmigration of male souls into female bodies also suggest just how complex and troubled was his construction of gender. Vital believed, for example, that his wife Hannah had a male soul, the reincarnation of Rabbi Akiva's father-in-law. See *Sha'ar ha-Gilgulim*, 139b–140b. He discusses the complications of male-souled females in pregnancy and birth in *Sha'ar ha-Gilgulim*, introduction 9, 33a–35b.

91. Vital seems to have had an inclination to violence, stemming, according to Luria, from his transmigratory origin as Cain. Luria required Vital to be especially careful to keep this tendency in check, ordering him to avoid killing even the most insignificant of creatures such as fleas or lice (Luria himself, Vital reports, killed no creatures intentionally), to remove knives from the table before reciting grace after meals, and never to function as a *mohel* (circumciser) or slaughterer-butcher (or even to observe them at work). See *Sha'ar ha-Gilgulim*, 128b, 132b, 133b. Compare *Sha'ar ha-Gilgulim* (Radomsk ed., Przemysl, 1875), 33c; *Sefer ha-Hezyonot*, 238. In the case of the possessed *woman* of Safed (case 7), Vital writes that Luria sent him to perform exorcisms specifically because of his Cainic descent. See Chajes, "Spirit Possession," appendix 2, case 7, sec. 3.

92. In the parallel case, the spirit anticipates Vital's arrival prophetically and questions Vital's capacity to evict him from his abode in the woman's body, but then greets Vital with great respect upon his entry. See appendix A, case 4, sec. 2.

93. The circumstances of the spirit's death are presented after a dialogue between Vital and the spirit over the meaning a rabbinic passage (*Eduyot* 2,10). See n. 47 above. See appendix A, case 3, sec. 3. This close parallel with the account of the young man discussed above probably, though not necessarily, indicates literary dependence of one account on the other.

94. Until 1622, Ormuz was a Portuguese outpost at the mouth of the Persian Gulf. My thanks to Prof. Geoffrey Parker for providing me with this identification.

95. L. Roper has written on sixteenth-century notions of the body as a container. In the literature of excess, the body is imagined as a container for a series of processes: defecation, sexual pollution, vomiting. Fluids course about within the body, erupting out of it, leaving their mark on the world outside. The body is not so much a collection of joints and limbs or a skeletal structure as a container of fluids, bursting out in every direction to impact the environment. See *Oedipus and the Devil: Witchcraft, Sexuality, and Religion in Early Modern Europe* (London: Routledge, 1994), 24.

96. Benayahu located a reference to this episode in Abraham Galante's commentary on the Zohar, *Yerah Yakar* (MS. Jerusalem, Jewish National and University Library, 8§ 493, p. 263b). See *Toledot ha-Ari*, 101.

97. See appendix A, case , sec. 6.

98. See Lewis, *Notes and Documents*, 8.

99. See the recent comments of M. Rosman in *Founder of Hasidism: A Quest for the Historical Ba'al Shem Tov* (Berkeley: University of California Press, 1996), 57. I also discuss this issue in chapter 4 of "Spirit Possession."

100. Given what we know of Vital's own frequenting of Muslim wonder-workers, this astonishment seems either disingenuous or a literary embellishment by someone unfamiliar (or uncomfortable) with Vital's openness in these matters. The entire passage of the account relating to the possession of the Kohen in Nablus is absent from Sambari's version, which has the doe wandering "crazily" until arriving in Safed, and the spirit vacating the doe for the widow,

who was among a crowd of people observing the strange behavior of the suffering doe.

101. On the history and significance of this image, see R. J. Z. Werblowsky. "Ape and Essence," in *Ex Orde Religionum (Geo Widengren Festschrift)* (Leiden: E.J. Brill, 1972), 318–25. My thanks to Prof. M. Idel for this reference.

102. See Léon D'Alexis [Pierre de Bérulle]. *Traicté des Energumènes, suivy d'un Discours sur la possession de Marthe Brossier, contre les calomnies d'un Médecin de Paris* (Troyes, 1599), 38–39. Cited by H. C. Lea, *Materials toward a History of Witchcraft*, ed. A. C. Howland (Philadelphia: University of Pennsylvania Press, 1939), 3:1062.

103. See Midelfort, "The Devil and the German People," 112.

104. M. Cordovero, "*Derishot be-Inyane ha-Malakhim me-ha-RM"K*," in *Malakhe Elyon*, ed. R. Margalioth (Jerusalem: Mosad Bialik, 1945), 64–114, citation 64–65 (now in *Or Yakar*, vol. 17 [Jerusalem: Hevrat Ahuzat Yisra'el, 1989]). Translation from Werblowsky, *Joseph Karo*, 81. Compare G. Scholem, "The *Maggid* of R. Yosef Taitatzak [Taytaczack] and the Revelations Attributed to Him" (in Hebrew), *Sefunot* 13 (1971–77): 69–112, esp. 71–72.

105. See appendix A, case 1, sec. 9.

106. *Sha'ar ha-Gilgulim*, 24b.

107. See appendix A, case 3, sec. 7. The early sixteenth-century kabbalistic work *Galya Raza* maintained that Satan and the *Sitra Ahra* oversaw the entire realm of transmigration. See R. Elior, "The Doctrine of Transmigration in *Galya Raza*," in *Essential Papers on Kabbalah*, ed. L. Fine (New York: New York University Press, 1995), 243–69.

108. See, for example, the discussions in BT Sanhedrin 45b ff., where the death penalty applied to blasphemers, witches, and idolators is discussed in a single Mishnaic passage. See also the remarks by I. Ta-Shma, "Notes to 'Hymns from Qumran'" (in Hebrew), *Tarbiz* 55.3 (1986): 440–42; J. Trachtenberg, *Jewish Magic and Superstition: A Study in Folk Religion* (New York: Behrman's Jewish Book House, 1939), 58–59; E. Yasif, *Sippur ha-Am ha-Ivri* (Jerusalem: Mosad Bialik, 1994), 394.

109. See D. D. Hall, "A World of Wonders: The Mentality of the Supernatural in Seventeenth-Century New England," in *Seventeenth-Century New England*, ed. D. D. Hall and D. G. Allen (Charlottesville: University Press of Virginia, 1984), 246.

110. M. Flynn, "Blasphemy and the Play of Anger in Sixteenth-Century Spain," *Past & Present* 149 (November 1995): 29–57.

111. J.-P. Dedieu, "Les causes de foi de l'Inquisition de Tolede (1483–1820)," *Melanges de la Casa de Velazquez* 14 (1978): 148ff. (cited by Flynn, "Blasphemy and the Play of Anger").

112. See, for example, Zohar 2:267b; Compare Menasseh ben Israel's discussion of this matter in *Nishmat Hayyim*, book 3, chap. 27, esp. p. 268.

113. *Hallel* designates the Psalms 113–18, which are included in the liturgy on special occasions to express thanksgiving and joy.

114. See appendix A, case 3, sec. 7. On Passover night and its rituals, see *The Passover Haggadah: Its Source and History*, ed. E.D. Goldschmidt (Jerusalem, n.p., 1969).

115. While managing to bring about the spirit's expulsion, Vital was unable to rectify the spirit, who was consigned to his torments until the last of the bastards whom he had fathered had died (appendix A, case 3, sec. 7) The irrevocability of the spirit's punishment and Vital's inability to assist in his rectification brought "the many assembled" to tears and repentance (appendix A, case 3, sec. 7).

116. The mezuzah, a parchment-based phylactery, must be written properly and in good condition to be "kosher," fulfilling the biblical command (based on Deut. 6:9). While earnest efforts were made by some rabbinic authorities to mitigate the widespread perception of the mezuzah as affording amulitic protection to those within the houses bearing them, this perception remained dominant. Indeed, the inscription on the outside of the parchment, *SD"I*, normally translated as the divine name "Almighty," was taken as an acrostic for "Keeper of the Doors of Israel."

117. See Tzvi Mark's essay in this volume for a study of this phenomenon in Hasidic eastern Europe.

118. See above and chapter 2 of Chajes, "Spirit Possession."

119. Midelfort, "The Devil and the German People," 118.

120. G. Scholem, *Sabbatai Sevi: The Mystical Messiah, 1626–1676*, trans. R. J. Zwi Werblowsky, (Princeton: Princeton University Press, 1973), 19.

121. J. Dan, "Rabbi Joseph Karo: Halakhist and Mystic" (in Hebrew), *Tarbiz* 33 (1964): 89–96, citation 93. Dan is here summarizing the argument made in J. Katz, "The Ordination Controversy between R. Jacob Berab and R. Levi b. Habib" (in Hebrew), *Zion* 16 (1951): 28–45 (English version: "The Dispute between Jacob Berab and Levi ben Habib over Renewing Ordination," *Binah: Studies in Jewish History, Thought and Culture* 1 [1989]: 119–41). In the lines that follow those quoted, Dan notes that even more astounding than the audacity of the megalomaniacal aspirations of individuals (for example, Karo and Vital) is the fact that their aspirations—nonmessianic, at least—were realized! Safed and its rabbis indeed became the font of legal and mystical teaching for the entire Jewish world.

M. Pachter's studies also provide generous evidence of Safed's pietistic aspirations while asserting the relative marginality of the circle of Luria on the larger Jewish population. See, for example, the large number of synagogues and study halls noted in Pachter, "'Terrible Vision,'" 76–77. On Luria and the larger community of Safed, see his "The Eulogy of R. Samuel Uzeda upon the Death of the AR"I" (in Hebrew), in *From Safed's Hidden Treasures*, 39–68.

122. Cultural historical studies of Islamic magic in the early modern period are a clear desideratum and will ease the task of studying Jewish magic in this period comparatively. For now, recent anthropological studies of spirit possession in the Islamic world are helpful, if problematic. See esp. J. Boddy, *Wombs and Alien Spirits* (Madison: University of Wisconsin, 1989).

123. While the Kabbalah of Safed may have had little impact on popular Jewish culture in the decades following Isaac Luria's death (1572), the pietistic message seems to have spread quite effectively. With it, we may suppose, the plausibility of demonic possession in Jewish communities around the world certainly increased. See Z. Gries, *Sifrut ha-Hanhagot: Toldoteha u'Mekomah be-Haye Haside R' Yisrael Ba'al Shem Tov* (Conduct Literature [Regimen Vitae]: Its History and Place in the Lives of Beshtian Hasidim) (Jerusalem: Mosad Bialik, 1989); M. Idel, " 'One from a Town, Two from a Clan'—The Diffusion of Lurianic Kabbala and Sabbateanism: A Re-Examination," *Jewish History* 7.2 (1993): 79–104.

Pneumatic Mystical Possession and the Eschatology of the Soul in Lurianic Kabbalah

MENACHEM KALLUS

Recent research has pointed out the fact that at the forefront of interests in the circle of R. Isaac Luria (the AR"I) were types of mystical speculation and practice that focused on discovering and connecting with the soul roots of its members.[1] This pursuit was even more central for Luria and his associates than the cosmogonic theories that so much interested an earlier generation of Kabbalah scholars,[2] though the two issues cannot in fact be separated.

Evidence for this can be found in the diary of R. Hayyim Vital, Luria's chief disciple, wherein one finds that the issue of soul roots continued to occupy the minds and dreams of Vital's circle long after the passing of the AR"I in 1572.[3] For example, in a 1608 entry Vital records the dream of a disciple in Damascus, one of many such dreams experienced in his circle.[4] The student dreams he is with Vital visiting the graves of the righteous around Safed, an important Lurianic practice.[5] While immersed in this apocalyptic dream atmosphere, he discusses the relationships of the souls of Mishnaic sages and biblical personages to the soul of Adam.[6]

Interest in the issue of soul roots can be found especially in the literature on theurgic practices for achieving higher levels of soul manifestation in order to expedite the soul's attainment of eschatological fulfillment.[7] This literature discusses soul roots and soul families[8] as well as the different types of "new" souls and the cosmic ecology underlying the theurgy that produces them.[9] There is thus a major distinction in these writings between new and reincarnated souls.[10] The texts consider differences between reincarnated souls and "soul impregnation" (*ibbur*) and their implications for moral responsibilities between souls sharing the same root.[11]

The following discussion of these issues presents a schematic topology of possession and soul impregnation phenomena along with a discussion of their implications in Lurianic Kabbalah. This material is then applied to the personal diary of R. Hayyim Vital to outline Vital's soul pattern as well as differences in the approaches of Luria and Vital to the use of these ideas. The entire range of issues concerning the eschatology of the soul mentioned above are considered as they arise.

Possession and Soul Impregnation in Lurianic Kabbalah

Various relationships between the souls of the living and the dead are discussed in the Lurianic literature. No terminological distinction is made between possession and impregnation of the living by the dead, but R. Hayyim Vital posits the following distinction between *gilgul* (reincarnation) and *ibbur* (impregnation).[12] *Gilgul* refers to the entrance of a soul into a human body at birth for the sake of the soul's self-rectification, while *ibbur* refers to the various possibilities of influence between related souls— that is, souls whose spiritual sparks share a given root or root pathway.[13] The hierarchy of such influences is described below.

The term "soul roots" refers to the 613 spiritual limbs of the original Great Adam, who contained all future souls within himself.[14] Each limb of the Great Adam corresponds with one of the Torah's 613 commandments, on the one hand,[15] and with particular biblical personages on the other.[16] These latter include Cain,[17] Abel,[18] Abraham,[19] Sarah,[20] and others, each representing certain particular soul roots. Thus there are 613 original soul roots. It is important to note, however, that in the extant Lurianic literature, the lists of these correspondences are far from complete.[21]

According to Lurianic theory, souls from a common root have responsibilities toward each other in enacting their part of the cosmic *tikkun* (repair of the world).[22] Each individual soul spark is given three or four lifetimes in which to repent of its sins,[23] and the other souls from the same root, whether alive or dead, are responsible for helping that soul achieve atonement and rectification. Only if a soul becomes detached from its root through the continual transgression of a Torah commandment punishable by *Karet* (severance from the totality of souls in this world and the next) does the responsibility of other souls for that root cease.[24] The general result of *Karet* in such cases is that the souls of saints no longer "impregnate" the sinner with thoughts of remorse and repentance.[25] Instead, another soul from that root that has itself been punished with *Karet* is sent by Providence with the soul of a *tzaddik* (righteous person) from the same root to separate the little good left in the sinner so it can be transferred to other souls from that root. The evil core, now bereft of any holy sparks, then self-destructs.²⁶ This, in a nutshell, is the rather cruel economy of negative *ibbur* and constitutes the realm of *dybbuk* tales.

There are, however, *tzaddikim* (alive or dead) possessing such a degree of selflessness that instead of seizing the merits of these lost souls, they hold that merit in safekeeping and continue trying to influence the wayward spark toward repentance.²⁷ Generally, at the end of each of the soul's three lifetimes of opportunity to repent,²⁸ any unrepentant, cutoff soul spark loses its individual connection to its accumulated merits. The only exception is one who is cared for by one of these selfless *tzaddikim*. In such a case, when the soul spark finally does repent, its previous merits from each life are retroactively returned to it. In the Lurianic *Kavvanot* (intentions) of the Silent Prayer, one begs to be aligned with this type of selfless *tzaddik*.²⁹

It should be emphasized that when the soul of the *tzaddik* impregnates the soul of the sinner with thoughts of repentance, the *tzaddik* is under no obligation to actually be attached to the sinner's soul if the sinner goes on to fail the tests. The impregnation (*ibbur*) of the *tzaddik* exits at that point, though it may return to try again. Thus the *tzaddik* stands only to gain by rectifying a soul with which it shares a soul root.³⁰ The departed *tzaddik* or the living *tzaddik*'s soul emanation³¹ is under no *personal* obligation to help the sinner—it is merely under the general obligation devolving upon confreres of the same soul root. The *tzaddik* does not need to make its presence known to the one being impregnated on this level.

A higher level of relationship between souls from a common root is the following. There are times when a departed *tzaddik* had transgressed a certain law in its past life requiring atonement and rectification, but not to the degree that the soul needs a full reincarnation to rectify itself. Instead what this soul must do is find a living person from the same soul root, impregnate that person temporarily with its soul, enter a test situation involving its unrectified sin, and pass it.³² When this occurs, both the impregnating soul and the one impregnated prosper: the latter by helping a departed soul perfect itself (the departed soul being now in the debt of the living soul, as it were), the former by becoming perfected.³³ If the departed soul does *not* pass the test, however, it has caused the living soul to sin, and this sin may bring another and another in its wake. Should this occur, the living soul inherits the portion of the departed *tzaddik* in the "Edenic" way station before the eternal afterlife.³⁴

A higher level yet of relationship between souls from a common root occurs when a living person performs a commandment in a manner similar to the way it was previously performed by a certain *tzaddik* sharing the same root, whether living or dead.³⁵ This type of action attracts a positive impregnation by a higher-level soul than that of the person who performed the commandment—the soul of the *tzaddik* he or she imitated, in fact. Depending on the nature of the commandment and the level of devotion, enthusiasm, and contemplative attention with which it was performed, the corresponding level of the *tzaddik*'s soul impregnates the person.[36] This effect illustrates the Lurianic principle of *Reshimu* (trace impression), referring to the impact of the imprint of previous manifestations of holiness, the effect of which is everlasting.[37] The principle of *Reshimu* is, I believe, the most important pneumatic image used in Lurianic spirituality.[38] The subject is often unaware of this type of impregnation as well. R. Luria often told his disciples of the impregnations they were carrying with them as a result of special commandments or *Kavvanot* they had performed.[39] This appears to have been a means of positive reinforcement.

The impregnations acquired in this manner can be compounded. R. Hayyim Vital speculates in one of his writings on the subject about a vertical chain of ten souls over a given soul that connects it to its ultimate root.[40] Some of the ten may be souls of *tzaddikim* whose ultimate roots are of a higher level than the ultimate root of the particular soul that is related to them,[41] thus enabling a soul to rise to levels beyond those accessible to it in accord with its original ultimate root. At any given moment, a soul may also have as many as three impregnating souls working simultaneously within it.[42] If the soul is worthy, it attains a single impregnation, then a second and a third; it proceeds vertically along this chain of impregnating souls. Since there can be no more than three of these at a time, the lowest one falls away each time a higher one is appended until the soul finally reaches its ultimate root.[43] The reason for the limit of three impregnating souls has to do with the schema of soul levels,[44] to which we will now turn.

Soul Levels

The lowest level of the soul in Lurianic Kabbalah is the *nefesh*—the soul that animates the physical body—associated with the World of *Assi'ah* (the material World of Action). Above this is the *ru'ah*, the animator of the emotional realm, associated with the World of *Yetzirah* (Energy-Formation). Above *ru'ah* is *neshamah*, the individual mental-conceptual consciousness originating in the World of *Beri'ah* (Creation), from the Divine Throne. Above these are two transpersonal levels, as it were: *Hayah*, associated with the World of *Atzilut* (Divine Emanation), and *Yehidah*, associated with the *Keter* (Crown; the transcendent element) of *Atzilut*.[45] Since only the first three levels of soul are embodied, the individual is limited to the direct aid of only three impregnating souls at any given time. The impregnation remains with the person for as long as he or she does not transgress the commandments, or for as long as he or she does not merit a higher level of impregnation, as explained above.[46]

The highest possible level of contact with the souls of *tzaddikim* connects one directly with the realm of the greatest *tzaddikim*. This is accomplished through performing *yihudim*—unifications of the Divine Names relating to various Divine Attributes, brought together in the consciousness of the practitioner by intentional acts of devotional invocation.[47] The performance of *yihudim* allows one to transcend the hierarchy of particular soul roots, so that one "unifies the part with the whole."[48] One thereby connects directly with the souls of *tzaddikim* who had performed *yihudim* all their lives (as the Zohar explains),[49] so that after their departure they were permanently joined to Divinity, and they are automatically present when any *yihud* is performed.[50] Indeed, the Divine relation to the process of *tikkun* is said never to be without the presence of these particular souls.[51] One need not share a root with such *tzaddikim* in order to become connected with them during *yihudim*;[52] but if one does happen to share a root with one of them, one may transcend the level of one's particular root, that is, the immediate source of the individual spark that gives life to one's soul.[53] One thus becomes so aligned with this righteous soul during one's lifetime that after death one actually inherits the portion of that *tzaddik* in the World to Come.[54] This occurs because one's union with such an exalted soul during one's lifetime brings one into direct union with the higher manifestation of one's own root by participating with the *tzaddik* in union within the Divine realm upon one's demise. One thus attains far more than merely one's own limited portion in the World to Come.[55] The relationship to the *tzaddik* is created consciously through the Lurianic practices of *Kavvanot* in daily prayer and special *Kavvanot* for connecting with these specific *tzaddikim*, who were determined by R. Luria to be such souls through his examination of their soul roots.[56]

A Case Study: The Soul of R. Hayyim Vital

To understand what has been discussed so far it will be useful to examine a composite portrait of the actual and potential incarnations and impregnations of R. Hayyim Vital. R. Hayyim explains in his *Sefer ha-Hezyonot* (Book of Visions) and *Sha'ar ha-Gilgulim* (Gate of Reincarnations) that these were taught to him by his teacher, R. Isaac Luria.

Vital's soul is exceedingly complex. One of its sparks is entirely "new,"[57] having only recently been purified from the *kelippot* (evil husks) and taking its first residence inside a human body. "New" souls have advantages and disadvantages. This is understood in the context of Lurianic eschatology, where it is said that each of the five levels of the soul contains all of the five levels. Thus, in order to perfect the *nefesh*, for example, one needs to have manifested all the five levels of the aspect of the soul with which one was born.[58] The "new soul," however, can reach the level of Divine Emanation (the *nefesh* of the *Hayah*) in one lifetime.[59] On the other hand, the "new soul" spark must begin its development from the very bottom, at the level of the *nefesh* of the *nefesh* (of the realm of the World of *Assi'ah*), close to the realm of the *kelippot*.[60]

Three other soul sparks in R. Hayyim were from a common group. According to Luria, an unredeemed soul spark can only become incarnated anew if it becomes an activated part of the *Tzelem* (form)—the spiritual mechanism of the interface of consciousness between the human and Divine—of three souls originating from the same root.[61] The meritorious actions and prayers of these three souls (who are not necessarily *tzaddikim*)[62] bring about this effect, which then allows the unredeemed spark to begin its process of redemption and become incarnate for the first time. The spark of R. Hayyim's soul was activated within the *Tzelamim* of three souls, which were incarnated together with the three inner aspects of his *nefesh* (the *nefesh*, *ru'ah*, and *neshamah* aspects of his *nefesh*.)[63] All these souls needed to be reincarnated in order to atone for transgressions in past lives.[64] Some were souls from recent generations, and some were known authors (including a famous commentator on Maimonides).[65] These souls themselves had the potential to be impregnated with the souls of Talmudic sages,[66] and these, in turn, had the potential to be impregnated with the souls of zoharic heroes[67] and central biblical characters.[68] This is one level of soul hierarchy.

Superimposed on this level is an additional hierarchic structure. Each of the souls mentioned also manifests the fivefold soul structure,[69] and these also have potential impregnations connected with them. R. Hayyim's soul was said to be connected to that of Rabbi Akiva, the great Mishnaic sage, whose soul is of the highest level. The connection, however, was only on the *nefesh* level.[70] However, on the highest root level of his connection with R. Akiva, R. Hayyim was connected with King Hezekiah, a messianic figure, which may explain R. Hayyim's own doomed messianic pretensions.[71] This web of connections forms a soul tree, as it were. R. Hayyim writes about a weekly regimen of *Kavvanot* received from his teacher for connecting his soul to some sixteen *tzaddikim*; these varied by day, prayer, and *tzaddik*.[72]

R. Isaac Luria himself possessed a soul root different from that of R. Hayyim, but he would never divulge his previous incarnations except to mention relations with the souls of Moses, R. Hamnuna Sabba (a zoharic hero), and R. Simeon bar Yohai (purported author of the Zohar).[73] He also stated that he himself did not need to enter his present incarnation to rectify any transgression; rather, he entered into bodily incarnation only in order to teach his student R. Hayyim. In the course of their eighteen months of direct association, R. Isaac Luria said he had "become a near-constant impregnation," presumably as a result of R. Hayyim's practice of Lurianic *yihudim*.[74]

At thirteen years of age, R. Hayyim had received an impregnation from the *nefesh* of R. Eliezer ben Arakh,[75] a disciple of the Mishnaic sage R. Yohanan ben Zakkai, who was himself designated as a potential impregnation of R. Hayyim at the *ru'ah* level.[76] At the age of twenty, he received an impregnation from the *nefesh* of R. Elazar ben Shamu'a,[77] a disciple of R. Akiva; and at age twenty-nine (when he had started to study with the AR"I), the *ru'ah* of R. Akiva had begun "to hover over [him] so as to be available as an impregnation."[78] Indeed, the *nefesh* of R. Akiva was connected with the soul of the commentator on Maimonides, one of the souls responsible for R. Hayyim's incarnation, which R. Hayyim was attempting to rectify. R. Hayyim came to all these because of the commandments he performed, which attracted their respective *Reshimu* on the one hand,[79] and in order to bring them to greater perfection on the other.[80]

R. Hayyim had begun to study with the AR"I in March of 1571.[81] Two months later, in virtue of this association and the practices he learned to follow, R. Isaac told him of a new power his soul had achieved. The *ru'ah* level of the Sabbath-Additional-Soul of the *neshamah* component in R. Hayyim's soul had been activated. He was thus able on the Sabbath to awaken the *nefesh-ru'ah-neshamah* aspects of the *Sefirah Malkhut*, the lowest *sefirah* within the realm of Emanation.[82] If this level of achievement could be maintained for two and a half years, R. Isaac told him, the *ru'ah* level of his soul would be complete, and he would have a complete grasp of the Torah and a stable apprehension or participation in permanent *Ru'ah ha-Kodesh* (holy spirit; that is, prophecy).[83] Four months passed, during which the AR"I instructed R. Hayyim in great detail concerning the makeup of his soul and its impregnations[84] as well as imparting to him the *Commentary on the Idra Zutta*[85] and related prayer *Kavvanot*.[86] At that point, the AR"I told R. Hayyim that he was still not ready to engage in the special *yihudim* that would pneumatically enhance his kabbalistic understanding. R. Hayyim insisted that he be given a *yihud* to practice, and the AR"I relented.[87] (This appears to have been a pattern in their relationship.)[88] R. Hayyim began practicing the *yihud* but felt that he was becoming mad; he also lost control of his facial muscles. R. Isaac told him that indeed, had he not been connected with the soul of R. Akiva he would in fact have gone mad.[89]

Two months after this, on Tuesday, the eve of the new month of Elul 5331 (31 August 1571), the AR"I deemed his disciple ready.[90] There is a fascinating sequence of two entries in R. Hayyim's diary, covering four pages of text,[91] in which he details the highlights of the following week's psychic activity. Briefly, after what was apparently a sleepless night,[92] R. Hayyim went to the grave of the Talmudic sage Abayye, with whom he had a particularly auspicious potential bond of impregnation, and who was connected with another of R. Hayyim's transcendent potential impregnations, the zoharic figure R. Yeiva Sabba.[93] There he performed a cosmic (as opposed to a personal) *yihud*[94] for the purpose of establishing a connection between the lower levels of the most recondite Divine Crown and the levels below. This accomplished, he followed his teacher's bidding and carried out the AR"I's *yihud* for the activation and embodiment of the souls of *tzaddikim* for the purpose of communicating with them. With the ensuing combination of autosuggestive and spontaneous elements, R. Hayyim was actually successful in contacting Abaye.[95]

When the AR"I next saw R. Hayyim, he expressed strong approval of the order in which R. Hayyim carried out his practice, saying that the soul of King David's general, the transcendent *tzaddik* Benayahu ben Yehoyada,[96] had entered with R. Hayyim. R. Isaac also told R. Hayyim that if he should succeed in contacting the soul of R. Yeiva Sabba during his Sabbath repose it would be most fortunate. After the Sabbath R. Hayyim returned to Abaye's gravesite and succeeded in connecting directly with the soul of R. Yeiva Sabba. The latter requested that R. Hayyim tell his teacher, the AR"I, to contact R. Yeiva in order to learn from him a novel application of certain Lurianic *Kavvanot* for Vital's benefit. The AR"I did as he was asked, and indeed taught R. Hayyim the new application.[97] Over the next forty-eight years R. Hayyim attempted to reconnect with R. Yeiva Sabba with varying degrees of success, but without any sustained communication.[98]

A certain combination of factors suggests an insight into R. Hayyim's personality. One is his own perception of the newness of his soul spark.[99] Another is the disappointment in R. Isaac's evaluation of him. The AR"I had told R. Hayyim that in order to "attain spirituality in a wholly complete way," so his impregnations would remain in unbroken contact with him, R. Hayyim must fully acquire all the spiritual levels of his *ru'ah*.[100] But a week before his own sudden passing,[101] the AR"I also told R. Hayyim that R. Hayyim had succeeded in effecting a *tikkun* only up to the middle aspect of the *ru'ah* level of *nefesh* in the world of *Assi'ah*, in the Feminine passive manifestation of the realm of the *Sefirah Gevurah* (*Gevurah* of the *Malkhut* of *Malkhut* of the *nefesh*.)[102] This meant that R. Hayyim was working on the level of the *ru'ah* of the *nefesh*,[103] a much lower plane than the level that the AR"I told him he must attain in order to be in constant contact with the *Ru'ah ha-Kodesh*. It is therefore no surprise that R. Hayyim had difficulty with confidence issues for the remainder of his life. This, of course, does not detract from the depth of his understanding and the magnitude of his achievement—the organized writing and preservation of the teachings that constitute the Lurianic corpus.[104]

With all this in mind, it is interesting to contrast R. Hayyim's unassured self-image in matters of the soul with the total self-confidence about this matter displayed by his teacher, R. Isaac, both in Egypt and during his short teaching period in Safed.[105] R. Hayyim suffered from tremendous doubt about his possibility of success in maintaining consistent contact with his impregnations. He was also plagued by deeper doubts about his entire enterprise, even questioning the veracity of his psychic experiences and whether they were really more than the effects of autosuggestion.[106] The contrast between these two personalities may be due to the following difference. The AR"I had firsthand experience of these psychic processes, mediated only by his own original understanding and his novel reconstruction of various previous mystical materials.[107] Vital's experience, on the other hand, was largely derived from—and affected by—his teacher's imputations regarding him and his use of R. Isaac's meditative techniques of mystical autosuggestion,[108] which only occasionally rose to the level of spontaneous revelation.

Conclusion

Taking into consideration the material treated above, one may conclude that the following combination of factors was considered necessary for success in the Lurianic scheme of impregnation mysticism:

1. Knowing one's "tree of impregnations," generally by means of revelation.[109]
2. Attaining a clear picture of how the system of soul evolution works.
3. Practicing cosmic *yihudim* in conjunction with personal *yihudim*.
4. Possessing a self-image that enables absolute self-confidence.
5. Wholehearted devotion in practicing the Lurianic pneumatic techniques.

This appears to be what is meant by "the full acquisition of all the levels of the *Ru'ah*," which the AR"I told R. Hayyim he must acquire.

Appendix 1: On the Discovery of Past Lives

It seems that R. Isaac Luria revealed information to members of his circle concerning their past lives based on his own pneumatic revelations. They accepted them because of his authority as one who had attained the "holy spirit" (*Ru'ah ha-Kodesh*); but he did not pass to his disciples the *techniques* by which they might achieve such knowledge themselves. Scholem discusses the existence of such techniques and adduces sources from R. Naphtali Bacharach's neo-Lurianic work *Emek ha-Melekh*.[110] These passages mention oaths administered to angels in order to obtain such information in dreams, though they supply no instruction or formulae. Luria would probably have rejected such methods because he opposed the adjuration of angels.[111]

Scholem fails to mention a "psychological" technique found in *Emek ha-Melekh* (94a), which aims at discovering the personal reason for one's present *gilgul* by examining which commandments require one's particular vigilance. One arrives at this knowledge by analyzing one's temptations and counteracts them by performing certain commandments that neutralize them. Indeed, the author of *Emek ha-Melekh* writes explicitly that the best way to discover information about one's past lives is through an authority like the AR"I. In the absence of such a person, however, one may ask a dream question; or, if one is not proficient in this, one may resort to psychological devices. In this connection *Emek ha-Melekh* mentions the *Sefer ha-Haredim* (another Safedian work) for the relationship between the limbs of the body and particular commandments. An examination of the *Sefer ha-Haredim*, however, reveals that there is no systematic correlation of this type but only a general type of association. For example, certain commandments are connected with the ears, eyes, and so on. The well-known correspondence between the 248 positive commandments and the equal number of bones or "limbs" in the body[112] has thus never been specifically illustrated.

The recently published *Me'orot Natan* contains the glosses of the seventeenth-century Lurianic kabbalists R. Nathan Shapira and R. Moshe Zacuto on the Lurianic corpus. There we find a psychological method for determining whether one is from the soul root of Cain or Abel.[113] They say, ostensibly quoting from an anonymous interpolation in an early *Etz Hayyim* manuscript, that those deriving from the root of Cain are agoraphobic, since their souls are rooted in the element of fire. Furthermore, they are overly afraid of demons, which represent the unrectified aspect of Cain's soul sparks, and they prefer handcrafts to the craft of oratory, which is in Abel's domain.[114]

Scholem further mentions a work called *Minhat Ya'akov Solet*,[115] which he claims contains "another procedure" for discovering one's previous incarnations. In my opinion, the practice contained there, consisting of a two-day fast and a dream question based on oaths administered to angels and demons, is probably the same as the one found in *Emek ha-Melekh*. I base this conclusion on the fact that the practice is found word for word in *Sefer Mif'alot Elohim*.[116] There it is quoting from a manuscript of the editor's grandfather, R. Joel Ba'al Shem of Zamosc, a younger contemporary of R. Naphtali Bacharach, author of *Emek ha-Melekh*.

This fascinating practice prepares one for a dream revelation of one's earlier incarnations by means of a two-day process involving isolated retreat, fasting, ablutions based on Lurianic contemplations, the donning of white garments, and the adjuration of angels and demons. This represents a return to magical techniques that were repudiated in Lurianic Kabbalah.[117] At a recent conference devoted to R. Moses Zacuto held at the Ben-Gurion University in Be'er Sheva, my friend the very reverend Dr. J. H. Chajes pointed out a similar phenomenon—a return to magical practices in the absence of successful Lurianic alternatives—in the magical works of Zacuto.[118] I was, however, unable to find any practices for discovering one's earlier incarnations in Zacuto's works.

In *Sefer ha-Goralot*, a work attributed to R. Hayyim Vital (though Scholem rightly questioned its authenticity), we find prayers and mantic practices intended to reveal information about one's soul roots and previous incarnations.[119] On p. 107, however, there appears to be clear evidence of the Sabbatean provenance of this work: it refers to the *telat kishre de-mihemnuta*, a technical Sabbatean term.[120] In the same section of *Sefer ha-Goralot* (pp. 106–7), we find interesting material that sheds light on the theurgic orientations given by some Sabbatean schools to the Lurianic *Kavvanot*, though this is beyond the scope of the present essay. The Sabbateans' interest in matters concerning soul roots is well known.[121]

Appendix 2: Undecided Issues

There are many undecided issues in Lurianic Kabbalah, some of which arise from the fact that when we apply a critical method to a set of texts, even if we remain within the terminology of its "system," we often ask questions of this "system" that were apparently not posed to its founders. In the case of the Lurianic corpus, we must also include the consideration of the extremely short period of time that constituted the association between R. Hayyim Vital and the AR"I, during which both of them were in the midst of their own accelerated creative personal (and interpersonal) development. Certainly an enormous amount of kabbalistically innovative discourse took place between them in this period that was abruptly cut short by the AR"I's untimely demise.

One essential question posed by classical Lurianic theologians and by an earlier generation of researchers concerns its theoretical-phenomenological ur-assumptions: is this Kabbalah "realist" or "nominalist"? We find numerous statements that support the nominalist position.[122] These nominalist and panentheistic orientations have yet to receive the attention due them from the researchers of Lurianic Kabbalah.[123] In fact, in the most recent of R. Meroz's articles on Lurianic Kabbalah, this time focusing on the Sarugian recensions, she indeed acknowledges nominalist panentheism in these recensions. However, although she is of the opinion that Sarug was a genuine disciple of the AR"I, she still repeats the going theistic dogma vis-à-vis the formulations of R. Hayyim Vital.[124] She states quite clearly that according to Sarug, from the Divine point of view there is no "change," and that the distinction between the functioning of the various Divine Attributes is merely from the human point of view. However, the basic style of exposition of the Lurianic Kabbalah and its dynamic theurgical instructions in particular, suggests a "realist" orientation.

With regard to some ultimate questions of eschatology: on the one hand we find that all souls are rooted in one great all-inclusive soul, which before its "fall" inhabited a higher ontological state than at present—the midpoint between the Worlds *Assi'ah* and *Beri'ah*, a station one and a half "worlds" higher than the world inhabited by us today.[125] Yet after the fall, there are always no fewer than six hundred thousand souls, deriving from that one soul, differentiated according to "root." First they are divided into two general souls—Cain and Abel (plus the souls that fell into the *kelippot*, which are under the general rubric of Seth); and then further differentiated into the souls of the Patriarchs; and then into the Souls of the Seventy who descended into Egypt; and then to 613 "limbs" that are not ostensibly differentiated within the Lurianic literature; to six hundred thousand souls[126] present in each generation in the "fallen world." A question that suggests itself is this: when the "general soul of Adam" is finally rectified, do all souls "telescope" back (albeit differentiated) into one soul? Do they revert to the ontic station of before the fall—that is, to the level where the World of Action is on the level of what is presently *Tif'eret* of the World of Formation, but in a state of *tikkun*? Or does the *tikkun* also extend to the World of Action, the (former) "domain of the *kelippot*"? This crucial question is nowhere discussed in the Lurianic corpus.

In this connection, considering that the names of the personages of the 613 primal roots corresponding to the "limbs" of *Adam* (and of the Primordial *Adam*) are not stated, we may ask: are there actually heads for each root of the 613, or are they subsumed within the earlier differentiations (70–12–3–2-l), meaning that the "heads" of the "limb-roots" are nominal? Alternatively, are their "real" designations based on their actual level of purification so that, for instance, at any given time, for any number of people who are associated with a given "limb" or "sinew," is the one who is the most developed at that time the "head" of that limb? Perhaps the 248 limbs, associated with the "positive commandments," are thus the realm of *Hesed* (Grace), which is connected with Abel; whereas the 365 sinews, associated with the "negative commandments" and the realm of *Din* (severity), is connected with Cain. Alternatively, since a person or soul root is not considered "complete" until it attains to the level of *Yehidah* of *Arikh Anpin* of *Atzilut*[127]—a level not yet attained even by the divine *partzuf* of *Ze'ir Anpin*[128]—perhaps the *essential* Divine Body is completely primordially rooted, whereas the *emanated* body is "rooted" only at the end of the process of *tikkun*, when the "head sparks" of all the 613 roots attain to the level of *Yehidah* of *Arikh Anpin* of *Atzilut*. This would explain why there is no "list of names" for the heads of the roots.

It seems to me that we may arrive at some satisfaction when we address the question of ultimate soul roots in Lurianic Kabbalah within the context of its ideas regarding the transition between the "present" World to Come and the next stage within this ontological category (which is apparently equivalent to the stage of the final resurrection.)[129] In the texts where these are construed as equivalent designations, each entity returns to its essential root, and the dynamic intradeical process apparently comes to an end or, alternatively, there are texts asserting that it attains a presently unimaginable new level. This new level requires a "new *Zivvug*" within *Arikh Anpin* in order to finally equalize the lower Divine Masculine and Feminine levels (the "Sun" and the "Moon") by means of returning the higher Divine Masculine and Feminine levels (*Hokhmah* and *Binah*) to the womb of *Arikh Anpin* for the first time since the creation. And for this, a new "raising of Feminine Waters" arising from the merit of the *tzaddikim* is required.[130] But only a few *tzaddikim* are able to accomplish this. They are called "those who are invited to the World to Come,"[131] whereas the lesser *tzaddikim*, who can affect lesser "new *Zivvugim*," are regarded as either "being assured" of the World to Come or being a "Son of the

World to Come" (if such a person is on the level to raise the "Feminine Waters" sufficiently to cause a new *Zivvug* between *Hokhmah* and *Binah* as they are presently constituted). A person might alternatively be described as "having a portion in the World to Come," if he or she is on the level to raise the "Feminine Waters" only in conjunction with a *tzaddik* who is on a higher level. I would suggest that those first-order *tzaddikim*, those who can raise *Hokhmah* and *Binah* to the new level of gestation into *Arikh Anpin*,[132] are those who (will) stand at the head of the 613 limbs having attained the level of *Yehidah* of *Arikh Anpin* of *Atzilut*. The second level of people, who have not yet fully developed themselves (for example, Samuel and Hezekiah, who apparently will attain this through *ibbur*[133]), are the potential "heads of the 613 limbs." The level below this enables the lower *Zivvug* of *Atzilut*. The lowest level are those righteous who have not yet attained the level of *Atzilut*. It seems to me that upon the enactment of the new *Zivvug* of *Arikh Anpin*, the higher-level *tzaddikim* will influence those below and so on. This formal orientation enables us to examine another question.

How are we to understand the appearance of *Kelippah* in the seed of *Adam Kadmon* as indicated in *Likkute Torah* (43b)? (I will not here enter the rather unpleasant, albeit important, discussion regarding the Lurianic dualist doctrine vis-à-vis the "souls of the gentiles.") For in most of the Lurianic writings the *kelippot* begin in the World of *Beri'ah*. And yet, *Adam Kadmon* (which denotes a higher level than the [relative] World of Emanation, which exists within *Adam Kadmon*) is called *Adam* of *Beri'ah*.[134] I suggest that perhaps the *partzufim* may be seen as primordial prefigurations that work in both directions—in the preemanative and on the postemanative realms. Thus the *Iggulim* (Circular Light) and *Yosher* (Straight Light) of the reentry of the Divine Light after the *Tzimtzum* constitute the Cosmic *nefesh* and *ru'ah* (that is, the two lower worlds) of *Adam Kadmon*, who is himself *neshamah*, and from *Beri'ah* or *Binah* (which is the first revelation of the autogenesis—the Self-Created-Creator-God). With reference to this we read[135] that all levels of *neshamah*, even those of the lowest world, are the direct manifestation of the realm of the Divinity, although this level of Divinity may become obscured by the *kelippot*. We also read[136] that the essence of all the five levels of even the lowest manifestation of soul, the *nefesh*, even in the lowest world, is considered "Absolute Divinity." This nominalism seems to be suggested as well from *Etz Hayyim*, gate 3, chapter 3, regarding the universal process of gestation-suckling-maturity of the two lowest *partzufim* of all worlds, including *Adam Kadmon*.[137]

Here we find a conflation between *Adam Kadmon* and *Adam ha-Rishon*. Thus, we may suggest that when the AR"I states that the *Tzimtzum* was "in the middle of His Infinity," he means this in the context of the (bidirectional prefigurative) five-partite division of the Cosmic-Soul, and the *Tzimtzum* taking place "in His middle" refers to the level of *neshamah*, that is, *Adam Kadmon*. Thus, there are levels beyond: the two top *partzufim* are fixed in a prefigured way according to their innate natures, and the relative nature of the *partzufim* remains constant within each "world," so that the general *Beri'ah* aspect of *Adam Kadmon* has the potential for *Kelippah*, but the two higher *partzufim*, *Hokhmah* and *Keter*, which are the realm of the Infinite *En-Sof*, do not. These two aspects of the inner light of *Adam Kadmon* may be understood as the agency of repair and the primordially perfect. One possible proof-text (in addition to the AR"I's own Zohar commentaries regarding the unchanging nature of *Arikh Anpin*,[138]) can be found in the *Ta'ame ha-Mitzvot* of *Likkute Torah* (90a–b, *Pinhas*, and parallels) regarding the Seven Kings, that is, the "broken vessels," which are called there the two lower *partzufim*. (This is similar to the *Iggulim* and *Yosher* after the *Tzimtzum*, the prefigurations of the *nefesh* and *ru'ah* that need to become realized on the level of *neshamah* through the process of gestation-suckling-maturity, where these levels become reconnected to the "agency of repair"—*Hokhmah*.)

According to the Lurianic Kabbalah, the ultimate purpose of the process of *tikkun* is the raising of all the sparks to the level of *neshamah*, which is the return of the fallen sparks to the level of emanated Divinity—the "ensouling divinization" of the entire creation.[139] Within the human realm, this is exemplified when the individual soul becomes united with, and incorporated within, the transcendent soul of a saint who succeeded in "uniting the part to the whole."[140] This indeed may have been the AR"I's ultimate intention in his explanation of the rabbinic statement "he takes his portion and his neighbor's portion in Eden."[141] Thus, the cosmic *Arikh Anpin* refers to the primordially perfect changeless realm, and any change taking place vis-à-vis this level is only with reference to its reincorporation of the lower levels into itself. From the timeless point of view, there is no change, for reincorporation is assured; but from our perspective this process is all that matters.

Notes

1. Y. Liebes, "The Messiah of the Zohar: On R. Shimeon bar Yohai as a Messianic Figure" (in Hebrew), in *The Messianic Idea in Jewish Thought* (Jerusalem: Israel Academy of Sciences and Humanities, 1982), 109. This section is missing in the English version published in Liebes, *Studies in the Zohar* (New York: State

University of New York Press Press, 1993). See also Liebes, "New Trends in Kabbalah Research," (in Hebrew), *Pe'amim* 50 (1991): 150–70; P. Giller, "Recovering the Sanctity of the Galilee: The Veneration of Sacred Relics in the Classical Kabbalah," *Journal of Jewish Thought and Philosophy* 4 (1994): 145–69.

2. See Gershom Scholem, *Major Trends in Jewish Mysticism* (New York: Schocken, 1941), 244–86. Most of his discussion centers on Lurianic cosmogonic theories and his historiosophic assertion that these resulted from Luria's speculations arising from the trauma of the Jews' expulsion from Spain. He devotes pp. 279–83 to a general discussion of *gilgul* but does not discuss the soteriological side of *ibbur* or the personal soul issues of the members of the Lurianic circle. In his seminal article, "The Transmigration of Souls," in *On the Mystic Shape of the Godhead* (New York: Schocken, 1991), 197–251, he discusses the historical development of the distinction between *gilgul* and *ibbur* in general. In his section on the Lurianic doctrines concerning transmigration (228–41), there are a few brief comments on *ibbur* and soul roots (234), but no discussion of the central role of *ibbur* in Lurianic soteriology; nor is there an investigation of issues directly related to the members of the Lurianic circle. Isaiah Tishby, *The Doctrine of Evil and "Kelippah" in Lurianic Kabbalism* (in Hebrew) (Jerusalem: Magnes Press, 1984), contains no discussion of these matters.

3. See appendix 1 below; *Sefer ha-Gilgulim* (1886; reprint, Jerusalem, n.d.), chap. 35; *Sha'ar ha-Gilgulim, im Perush b'ne Aharon*, by R. Shimon Agassi, 2nd ed. (Jerusalem: Keren Hotza'at Sifre Rabbane Bavel, 1981), chap. 39; R. Hayyim Vital, *Sefer ha-Hezyonot*, ed. A. Z. Aescoly (Jerusalem: Mosad ha-Rav Kook, 1954), esp. app. 1, 250–53; and see next note.

4. *Sefer ha-Hezyonot*, 89–91, sec. 13, a dream of R. Elijah Amiel; and also 98–99, sec. 24 (ca. 1608), a dream of R. Isaac Al'Atif; 132–33, sec. 70 (ca. 1610), a dream of R. Elijah Najjar. Note that R. Samuel Vital regarded himself as a successful practitioner of this technique. See *Sha'ar ha-Gilgulim*, end of sec. 39, p. 385.

5. See *Sha'ar Ru'ah ha-Kodesh* (1912; reprint, Jerusalem, 1983), 27b–28a, 43a–b, where the principle texts of these practices are found. Essentially, it is as if the higher attributes, Wisdom (*Hokhmah*) and Understanding (*Binah*) and the Divine Names associated with them, as well as the lower attributes Harmony (*Tif'eret*) and Kingship (*Malkhut*) and the Names associated with them are seen as discrete entities identifiable within the practitioner. These also have a contiguous connection to both the life energy of the deceased *tzaddik* and the manifestation of these attributes within the Divinity. The person may attempt to enliven and unite these attributes within him- or herself for the sake of activating them within their other two fields of sentience—the deceased *tzaddik* and the Divinity. He or she is successful if his or her intentions are proper, and the person then achieves the ability to commune with the deceased *tzaddik* and learn from it. For alternative kabbalistic views on the nature of theurgic symbolism, see Boaz Huss, "R. Joseph Gikatilla's Definition of Symbols and Its Influence on Kabbalistic Literature" (in Hebrew), *Jerusalem Studies in Jewish Thought* 12 (1996): 157–76; and the first four

chapters of my dissertation, containing extensive discussions of the nature of Lurianic symbolism.

6. For the dream atmosphere of such activities, see *Sefer ha-Hezyonot*, 90, where the colleagues go to the Holy Temple and read from an ancient Torah scroll the words "The Lord will do battle for you" (Exod. 14:14); and see appendix 2 below.

7. These states are attained by means of three theurgic practices, one performed in the day and two at night. First is falling on the face (*Nefilat Apayim*) in the morning prayer. Through this form of theurgic union one may attain the higher levels of the root of one's soul through the emanated level or, if the root of one's soul is from the World of Action (*Olam ha-Asi'ah*), one can attain to levels higher than one's root by having the higher levels incarnate within someone else, such as one's son. See *Etz Hayyim*, Mekor Hayyim edition (Jerusalem, n.d.), gate 39, chap. 4; *Sha'ar ha-Kavvanot*, Mekor Hayyim edition (Jerusalem, n.d.), "Sha'ar Nefilat Apayim," chap. 3, fol. 47c; *Sha'ar ha-Gilgulim*, sec. 3, 19. Second is the reading of the *Shema* prayer before sleep. Herein one with a "low [spiritual] birth" may attain to levels higher than the root of one's soul by performing a *yihud* based on the verse "In Your hand do I entrust my spirit" (Ps. 31:6). See *Sha'ar ha-Kavvanot, Sha'ar Derushe ha-Laylah*, chap. 10. This operates separately from the possibility of attaining to levels above one's root based on *ibbur*, on which see below. Third is a *yihud* made at night with the verse "My soul longs for Thee" (Isa. 26:9), designed particularly for those whose higher functions were repaired in earlier lifetimes or for the accelerated development of first-time souls. See *Sha'ar ha-Kavvanot*, "Sha'ar Nefilat Apayim," chap. 3, fol. 47c; *Sha'ar ha-Gilgulim*, sec. 3, 7. A long fragment that may have been written by the AR"I himself concerning this last practice has escaped the attention of scholars. See *Zohar ha-Raki'a* (1875; reprint, Jerusalem: n.p., 1985), 107d–108c. I will expand upon this in my dissertation.

8. See Scholem, "Transmigration of Souls," 215–18, for an earlier kabbalistic doctrine of "soul sparks" from *Tikkune ha-Zohar*, and 231ff. for the Lurianic formulation. According to Scholem, the term "soul family" originates with R. Solomon Alkabetz and was used by his disciple and brother-in-law, R. Moses Cordovero. It apparently occurs only once in the Lurianic corpus, in *Sha'ar ha-Pesukim* (1912; reprint, Jerusalem, n.d.), 31r. But as Scholem points out, the AR"I preferred the term "soul root." See Scholem, "Transmigration of Souls," 224–25.

9. The idea that there are "new souls" being created as a result of the merit of the generation goes back to the earliest period of the Kabbalah, the time of the *Bahir* and Rabbi Isaac the Blind. See Scholem, "Transmigration of Souls," 204–5, 207. Concerning Lurianic Kabbalah, where this is a central motif, Scholem says nothing. I will discuss this extensively in my dissertation, but for now see *Sha'ar ha-Gilgulim*, sec. 6, 7, 12, 16. There the AR"I distinguishes between three levels of "new souls"; *Sha'ar Ma'amare Haza"l* (1898; reprint, Jerusalem, 1978), 5a–b, where a fascinating allegorical interpretation of BT Babba Kamma 21a is presented. Merit in the context of the creation of "new souls" is described as the result

of reciprocity. There is also a discussion of the cosmic Union (*Zivvug*) effected by the *tzaddikim* during the period of exile. See more on these matters below.

10. See above, note 7, the third practice.

11. See appendix C below.

12. See *Sha'ar ha-Gilgulim*, sec. 2, pp. 21–25.

13. The term "root pathway" does not actually appear in the Lurianic corpus, but the idea is very much present. If the "soul root" refers to one of the spiritual limbs of the Great Adam, a "root pathway" refers to what might be called the root of the root: that is, the more primal souls—those closer to the original Adam, meaning Cain and Abel. See below on Vital's root pathway and appendix 2 below.

14. See Scholem, "Transmigration of Souls," 229–31.

15. See Scholem, "Transmigration of Souls," 231 and 220 for an earlier kabbalistic version from the *Tikkune Zohar*; and appendix 1.

16. It is important to stress that most of the biblical personages are *not* actually classified in the authentic Lurianic writings. In *Sefer Gilgule Neshamot [Im Perush Me'ir Ayin]* (1908; reprint, Brooklyn, 1985) by the Italian Lurianic kabbalist R. Menahem Azariah de Fano, there is a much larger number of biblical personages than one finds in the Lurianic writings of R. Hayyim Vital, though not all are mentioned. Some of de Fano's information came from R. Israel Sarug, about whose authenticity as a direct student of Luria a scholarly controversy exists. Perhaps there were other avenues of genuine Lurianic Kabbalah that reached de Fano, or perhaps he derived this knowledge from his own pneumatic sources. See appendix 2.

17. See Scholem, "Transmigration of Souls," 236, where he rightly expresses surprise and consternation regarding the elevation of the status of Cain. In virtually all pre-Lurianic Kabbalah, Cain is regarded as being the expression of the evil side of the Tree of Knowledge, but in Lurianic Kabbalah he is elevated to the status of one of the highest "new root souls." See also appendix B below for further discussion.

18. Cain and Abel are considered the roots for second-level "new souls." See *Sha'ar ha-Gilgulim*, sec. 6, pp. 66–73 and passim.

19. Abraham and the other Patriarchs are considered one configuration of the primal souls that is part of all souls as well as part of the Divine Face (*partzuf*) Ze'ir Anpin. See *Sha'ar ha-Gilgulim*, 89–90; *Sefer ha-Gilgulim*, chap. 14, fol. 22b; and see *Sha'ar ha-Kavvanot*, Drushe Rosh ha-Shanah, chap. 8, fol. 98c.

20. See *Etz Hayyim*, gate 50, end of chap. 4. Regarding the roots of Rachel and Leah in connection with souls, see gate 32, chaps. 1, 2. In general, however, women do not undergo *gilgul* according to Lurianic Kabbalah, because they are exempt from studying Torah. See *Sha'ar ha-Gilgulim*, sec. 9, p. 79, and compare sec. 20, pp. 140–41. Here it implies that the feminine soul is distinct from the masculine soul. Yet there is a long discussion in *Sha'ar ha-Pesukim, Parashat Vayerah*, about the nature of the feminine soul that is incarnated in a masculine body.

21. See appendix 1 and appendix 2 below.

22. See *Sefer ha-Gilgulim*, chap. 4, fols. 6b–7a.

23. See *Sha'ar ha-Gilgulim*, sec. 4, p. 46, where the three and four are associated with the verse in Exod. 20:5. Compare also with Exod. 34:7; and see appendix B, n. 20. See also *Sefer ha-Gilgulim*, chap. 6, fol. 10b, where it states explicitly three incarnations, not counting the first kind.

24. See note 23; and *Sefer ha-Gilgulim*, chap. 6, fol. 11a. See also *Sha'ar ha-Gilgulim*, sec. 4, pp. 46–47, where we find a distinction between the spark of the *nefesh*, which suffers *Karet* for certain transgressions committed over four lifetimes with no improvement at all, and the spark of the *ru'ah* and *neshamah*, which are potentially associated with this soul spark that does not suffer this punishment. See also appendix B.

25. See *Sha'ar ha-Pesukim*, 39c; *Sha'ar ha-Gilgulim*, sec. 4, p. 46 and sec. 22, p. 159. This entire section deals with the wicked who are not destroyed after four incarnations but instead undergo expiatory incarnations into lower forms of sentience such as stones, plants, or animals. These may refer to the souls of the wicked discussed in the previous note. See also p. 153 concerning the *Kaf ha-Kela*—the incarcerating sling of the void out of which the spirits attempt to escape by becoming *dybbuks*. See also *Ma'ase Shel ha-Ru'ah*, where the exorcism by R. Hayyim Vital is discussed. This appears as an appendix after chap. 40 in most editions of *Sha'ar ha-Gilgulim* but is missing in the edition used in this essay. Although the idea of *Kaf ha-Kela* appears only twice in the entire Lurianic corpus, it played a central role in *dybbuk* stories. Apparently these are the wicked ones referred to in the previous note. See esp. R. Judah Petaiah, *Minhat Yehudah: Ha-Ru'hot Mesaprot* (Jerusalem, 1995); the author was a great kabbalist and exorcist of the first half of the twentieth century. This fascinating document details the expiatory incarnations and *dybbuk* activities of the Jewish villains of the Shabbatai Zvi movement and deserves a separate treatment, particularly in connection to its use of both Lurianic and folk materials. See J. H. Chajes, "Spirit Possession and the Construction of Early Modern Jewish Religiosity," (Ph.D. diss., Yale University, 1999) on Jewish exorcism in the early modern period for a more extensive discussion of many of these issues; and see text appendix B below.

26. See appendix B.

27. See *Sha'ar ha-Kavvanot*, Sha'ar Kavvanot ha-Amidah, chap. 6, on the blessing *Al ha-Tzaddikim*, 36d. This passage is translated below, appendix B, sec. 6. See also ibid., "Sha'ar Nefilat Apayim", chap. 2, fols. 47a–b. It is highly significant that in the Lurianic system there are *tzaddikim* who transcend the "normal" operations of the justice of Divine Providence, functioning in the realm of duality (*partzuf Ze'ir Anpin*). For the theurgic background and implications of this idea, see references in appendix C below.

28. See *Sha'ar ha-Gilgulim*, sec. 4, p. 46.

29. See above, note 27.

30. See *Sha'ar ha-Gilgulim*, sec. 2, p. 22.

31. See *Sha'ar ha-Gilgulim*, sec. 3, p. 26; *Sefer ha-Hezyonot*, 148. There he quotes the AR"I as saying that his soul is "almost as if it is an impregnation" within the soul of R. Hayyim Vital. This idea, an impregnation by a teacher within the

disciple while both are alive, is found in the writings of the AR"I's teacher in Egypt, R. David ben Zimra (RiDBa"Z). See his *Responsa*, vol. 3, #910:

> It is also recounted in books of wisdom that when a person concentrates on the presence of his teacher and places his heart therein, then his soul becomes bound up with the soul of his teacher so that there shall be imparted upon such a one the emanated abundance which would constitute an "extra soul," and this is called by [the Sages] the secret of soul-impregnation during the lifetime of both of them [the disciple and the master]. This accords with what is written: "And your eyes shall behold your Master" (Isaiah 30:20); and it is implied in the verse "And they shall stand there with you [Moses], and I shall emanate [upon them] from the spirit [that is upon you] . . ." (Numbers 11:17).

My thanks to Dr. Melila Eshed-Helner for calling my attention to this source.
32. See *Sha'ar ha-Gilgulim*, sec. 5, pp. 49–52, and esp. sec. 11, p. 100.
33. See appendix C.
34. This is described in the AR"I's own commentary on the *Aggadot* of the Talmud, translated in appendix C.
35. See *Sha'ar ha-Gilgulim*, sec. 3, p. 26.
36. Ibid.
37. See *Etz Hayyim*, gate 6, chap. 5 (new version), gate 19, chap. 1; *Sha'ar ha-Kavvanot*, Sha'ar Rosh ha-Shanah, chap. 1; Sha'ar Tefilin, chap. 5; *Sha'ar Ru'ah ha-Kodesh*, esp. 1a–2a.
38. See my dissertation, where I describe this at length as the activated embodiment of the idea of continuity from the original Divine autogenesis; and I discuss the role of *Reshimu* in this process, as the impetus for the effect of the theurgic activity of the righteous. The *Reshimu* are implicit on the higher level and are differentiated and consciously active in the emanated and created stages through sacred contemplative activity. I also discuss how, in the course of practicing *Kavvanot* during the daily Lurianic regimen, voluntarist elements (which create new *Reshimu*) and "theurgically automatic" elements resulting from earlier *Reshimu* are intermixed.
39. See appendix D, sec. 6; *Sha'ar ha-Gilgulim*, sec. 17, p. 130; *Sefer Toledoth ha-AR"I*, ed. Meir Benayahu (Jerusalem: Ben-Zvi Institute, 1967), 175–77.
40. See *Sha'ar ha-Gilgulim*, sec. 5, pp. 53–54.
41. See *Sha'ar ha-Gilgulim*, sec. 2, pp. 20, 22.
42. Ibid.
43. Ibid.
44. This is my surmise, based on my explanation below concerning the five-part division of the soul. This itself is based on Lurianic sources, such as those adduced in the next note. Two of these are "surrounding" lights, which are not "enclothed" in it.

45. See *Etz Hayyim*, gate 6, chap. 2 (2nd ed.) and gate 40, chap. 10 and elsewhere.

46. See *Sha'ar ha-Gilgulim*, sec. 2, p. 22 and sec. 5, p. 54.

47. See appendix D, end of sec. 6. This is the meaning of "raising the Feminine Waters"; see *Etz Hayyim*, gate 39, chap. 1; and my dissertation.

48. That is, it unites one's individual soul with the entirety of the "field" of the Divine. One thereby connects directly with the souls of the *tzaddikim* who had practiced these all-encompassing *yihudim* all their lives, and, as the Zohar explained (see next note), after their departure from this world, these *tzaddikim* are permanently joined to Divinity. See *Olat Tamid* (1907; reprint, Jerusalem, n.d.), 46b, where the Torah is called the "restorer of the soul," for "She restores [the soul] to be in its proper place, so that the part cleaves to the whole." See also *Sha'ar Ru'ah ha-Kodesh*, 13a, 27b–28a, with regard to one who performs a *yihud* at "a time of favor." It states that such a person is able to "unify all the Supernal roots," and not merely to bind oneself to one's own essential root. See also *Sha'ar ha-Gilgulim*, sec. 38, p. 330 for some of the times of the day considered "times of favor."

49. See *Zohar* 1:6a regarding R. Hamnuna Sabba; *Sha'ar Ma'amare RaShB"I* (Jerusalem: n.p., 1988): 12b–d.

50. See *Sha'ar Ru'ah ha-Kodesh*, 27b–28a and sources in the previous note.

51. Ibid.

52. See *Sha'ar Ru'ah ha-Kodesh*, 28a.

53. For example, if one's soul spark is on the level of an aspect of the Cosmic Adam manifesting on the level of the *nefesh* or the *ru'ah* of the lower realms, *Beri'ah*, *Yetzirah*, or *Assi'ah*, whereas the ultimate root of all soul sparks is on the *neshamah* level of *Atzilut*, then if one's individual soul spark becomes connected with a *tzaddik* of the same root but who manifests this root on the level of *Atzilut*, one's soul may become entirely identified with this *tzaddik* through the practice of cosmic *yihudim*.

54. See *Sha'ar ha-Gilgulim*, sec. 2, pp. 21–22.

55. Ibid. There are phenomenological parallels to this in various religious traditions, such as the *Guruyoga* and saint veneration in their various religious forms. The Buddhas, such as Amitabah or Avelokateshvara, and the devotees who share his paradise with them, are an example. This area requires careful study to draw out the circumstantial and phenomenological parallels in a cross-cultural context.

56. It is indeed the goal of Lurianic saint veneration to attain conscious union. See *Sha'ar Ru'ah ha-Kodesh*, 28a, 42bff., 62a, and passim; appendix D below. The importance of these practices has long been recognized by scholars such as Lawrence Fine. See esp. Fine, "The Contemplative Practice of *Yichudim* in Lurianic Kabbalah," *Jewish Spirituality: From the Sixteenth Century Revival to the Present*, ed. A. Green (New York: Crossroad, 1986).

57. See *Sefer ha-Hezyonot*, 154, 192, 202, sec. 51. The following is a somewhat synthetic portrait attempting to bring out a coherent picture from the many

inconsistencies of the *Sefer ha-Hezyonot* and to resolve some of them. It may well be that an exhaustive study of this work would turn up another reconstruction or would present compelling reasons to conclude that no reconstruction is possible. But insofar as my reconstruction is rather loosely based on the primary sources, I present it as a reasonable conjecture.

58. See *Sha'ar ha-Gilgulim*, sec. 2, p. 21.

59. See ibid., sec. 7, p. 67.

60. See ibid., sec. 27, pp. 199–201 and sec. 38, pp. 367, 369; *Sefer ha-Hezyonot* 202, sec. 50.

61. See *Sha'ar ha-Gilgulim*, sec. 27, pp. 200–1, 369; *Sefer ha-Hezyonot*, 202, sec. 51.

62. See *Sefer ha-Hezyonot*, 134–35, sec. 2 and 151, sec. 16. I surmise this given the fact that some of these were sinners. See esp. *Sha'ar ha-Gilgulim*, sec. 38, p. 326.

63. This is my surmise, based on the structure described in *Sha'ar ha-Gilgulim*, sec. 11, p. 90. All soul roots contain Torah scholars at their center; immediately surrounding these in a separate sphere are business people; and surrounding these in the outer sphere are ignorant peasants. Vital's soul emerged on the *Tzelamim* of three people in exactly this pattern: one wrote a commentary on Maimonides' legal work *Mishneh Torah*; one was a business man; and one passed away at the age of fourteen.

64. See *Sefer ha-Hezyonot*, 140–41; and see 323, sec. 38; *Sefer ha-Hezyonot*, 137, sec. 5 shows where we read that this information was imparted to Vital by the AR"I on the first of the intermediate days of Passover, 1571. It is implied there that the same *nefesh* incarnated in all of the above. We may, however, wish to conclude that he is referring there to the levels of the *nefesh*, *ru'ah*, and *neshamah* of the same *nefesh*, and that he is using the terms "activate" and "incarnate" with reference to the *Tzelem* interchangeably.

65. *Sefer ha-Hezyonot*, 134, sec. 2. This was indicated to the AR"I by the phonetic similarity between their respective names: R. Hayyim *Vital* and R. *Vidal* of Toulouse. Elsewhere (*Sha'ar ha-Gilgulim*, sec. 38, p. 327).

66. *Sefer ha-Hezyonot*, 135, sec. 3; 144–45.

67. Ibid., 151, sec. 16.

68. Ibid., 144; 135, sec. 3; 144–45; 151., sec. 16.

69. See *Sefer ha-Gilgulim*, 64a, "Gilgulim Melukatim"; *Sha'ar ha-Gilgulim*, sec. 1, beginning.

70. See *Sefer ha-Hezyonot*, 135, sec. 3; 161–62, sec. 24.

71. See *Sha'ar ha-Gilgulim*, sec. 38, p. 327. This has not been sufficiently stressed by earlier researches. See David Tamar, "The AR"I and R. Chaim Vital as the Messiah of the House of Yosef" (in Hebrew), *Sefunot* 7 [=*Sefer Zfat*] (1963): 167–79; idem, "The Messianic Dreams and Visions of R. Chaim Vital" (in Hebrew), *Shalem* 4 (1984): 211–29. It is interesting to find (*Sha'ar ha-Gilgulim*, sec. 38, p. 353) that the AR"I told R. Hayyim that Samuel the Prophet stands at the head of the root of Cain. Elsewhere (p. 339) he tells him that King Hezekiah is at the head of this root. I would speculate that neither Samuel nor Hezekiah had

as yet attained the ultimate level of his root, but that Samuel was the "current" head whereas Hezekiah was the destined head. See appendix 2 below for more on this.

72. See *Sha'ar ha-Gilgulim*, sec. 38, pp. 343–44 for this fascinating, complex practice of *Guruyoga*.

73. The AR"I is associated with various souls from the root of Abel. See *Sefer ha-Hezyonot*, 54, sec. 11; *Sefer ha-Gilgulim*, 64b, 65a–b.

74. *Sefer ha-Hezyonot*, 134, sec. 1; 148, sec. 12; 239, sec. 13; and esp. 17, 25, sec. 27.

75. Ibid., 135, sec. 3.

76. Ibid., 135, sec. 3; 227, sec. 63.

77. Ibid., 135, sec. 3.

78. See *Sha'ar ha-Gilgulim*, sec. 38, p. 323; *Sefer ha-Hezyonot*, 135, sec. 3.

79. See *Sha'ar ha-Gilgulim*, sec. 39, p. 384.

80. Ibid., sec. 38, pp. 323–24.

81. See *Sefer ha-Hezyonot*, 134, sec. 1.

82. Ibid., 161, sec. 24.

83. Ibid., 150, sec. 14; 161, sec. 24. This, as he explained in this second source, is because R. Hayyim Vital's *ru'ah* was developing in conjunction with its embodiment of the *ru'ah* of Rabbi Akiva. Apparently he was referring to all the five levels of the *ru'ah* as also incorporating the *ru'ah* level of Emanation.

84. See *Sefer ha-Hezyonot*, 134–50 and elsewhere.

85. See *Sefer ha-Derashim* (Jerusalem, 1996), 215–36. It is clear that this work was written by R. Hayyim while the AR"I was still alive, based on his teacher's lectures about the central zoharic *Idrot* treatises as well as the Lurianic system of Divine Faces (*partzufim*). On p. 233 (middle) is a specific reference to the AR"I being alive at the time. This dating is also established by the similarity of this work to *Sha'ar ha-Kelalim* of R. Moses Jonah, universally regarded by researchers as the earliest stratum of the AR"I's teaching in Safed. See Ronit Meroz, *Ge'ulah be-Torat ha-AR"I* (Ph.D. diss., Hebrew University of Jerusalem, 1987), 36; Y. Avivi, *Binyan Ariel* (Jerusalem, 1987), 36. See my dissertation, chap. 3, for additional discussion.

86. These would include the *yihud* of the "Thirteen Reparations of the Beard" (*Sha'ar Ru'ah ha-Kodesh*, 50a–53a; *Sefer ha-Derushim*, 216b, 217b, 218b), the practice of the recitation of the *Shema* prayer before sleeping, and the *Kavvanot* of the phylacteries (*Sefer Sha'ar ha-Derushim*, 228ff.).

87. *Sha'ar ha-Gilgulim*, sec. 38, p. 363.

88. See *Sha'ar ha-Kavvanot*, Inyan Sefirat ha-Omer, chap. 12, fol. 86b; *Sefer ha-Hezyonot*, 188–89; Y. Liebes, "'Two Roes of a Doe': The Secret Sermon of Isaac Luria before His Death" (in Hebrew), *Jerusalem Studies in Jewish Thought* 10 (1992): 113ff.

89. *Sha'ar ha-Gilgulim*, sec. 38, p. 363.

90. See *Sefer ha-Hezyonot*, 170, sec. 32; and compare *Sha'ar ha-Gilgulim*, sec. 38, p. 363.

91. This can be found in translation below as appendix D: R. Hayyim Vital and his Psychical Experience.

92. See *Sha'ar Ru'ah ha-Kodesh*, 11a, where we read that if one stays awake and studies all through the night, one is expiated from *Karet*. One of the earlier incarnations of an aspect of R. Hayyim Vital's soul was liable for *Karet* (see *Sha'ar ha-Gilgulim*, sec. 38, p. 325), and we know (see appendix D below) that R. Hayyim fell asleep at the beginning of the practice. I consider this a distinct possibility. It would help to further explain the functioning of R. Hayyim's associative mind.

93. See *Sefer ha-Hezyonot*, 162, sec. 25, p. 193.

94. See *Sha'ar Ru'ah ha-Kodesh*, 43a–45a, esp. *yihud*, #3; *Sefer ha-Hezyonot*, 170, sec. 32.

95. See appendix D below.

96. He is one of those *tzaddikim*, like R. Hamnuna Sabba or R. Yeiva Sabba, alluded to above near note 49. See *Sha'ar Ru'ah ha-Kodesh*, 28a; and *Sha'ar ha-Kavvanot*, derush 6 of Drushe Keri'at Shema, 23c.

97. See *Sefer ha-Hezyonot*, 171–73; R. Meroz, "Faithful Transmission versus Innovation: Luria and His Disciples," *Gershom Scholem's "Major Trends": 50 Years After* (Tübingen: Mohr-Siebeck, 1995). On the association between the Sabbath afternoon nap and the possibility of conducting a positive *ibbur*, see *Sha'ar ha-Kavvanot*, 74d, "Sanctification of the Sabbath, Excursus 1: Concerning the Morning Meal."

98. On R. Hayyim's self-doubt, see *Sefer ha-Hezyonot*, 16–17, 25. I do not, however, see any reason for attributing this self-doubt to the phenomenon of "early modernism." In my opinion, sixteenth-century Safed spirituality and R. Hayyim's place therein were still cultural phenomena of the premodern world.

99. See *Sefer ha-Hezyonot*, 154, sec. 19; 163, sec. 26; and, regarding great souls emerging from the *kelippot*, 191.

100. See ibid., 161, sec. 24.

101. Ibid., 56, 190. A plague hit Safed on Tuesday, 27 Tammuz 5332 (18 June 1572). The AR"I fell ill on Friday of that week and passed away the following Tuesday, 5 Menahem Av. See appendix 2 below.

102. Ibid., 203, sec. 51: "The *nefesh* [the soul that animates the material body; the lowest level of soul] of [the realm of] *Assi'ah* [Action], to the extent of the left arm [*Gevurah*, but not yet the full level of *Da'at*] of the Feminine [that is, passive] aspect of *Assi'ah* alone." In other words, he had access to only the five levels of the Soul on the level of the *ru'ah* of the *nefesh*. His ultimate root is described in *Sha'ar ha-Gilgulim*, sec. 38, p. 366, as follows:

> To summarize, my *nefesh* is of the aspect of "Power" [*Gevurah*], which refers to the level of the *neshamah* of the level of *Immah* [Mother; Understanding], from Her *Gevurot*, which are in the *Sefirah* of *Da'at* [Intimate Knowledge; the union of *Hokhmah* (Wisdom), with *Binah* (Understanding)] of the Lesser Countenance [*Ze'ir Anpin*] within the *Hod* [Glory—of the three lower

Sefirot—That Unites] within the *Da'at* of *Malkhut* of the *Keter* [Crown] of *Da'at*, as this is manifested in each of the five *partzufim* [faces] in each of the four worlds: Emanation, Creation, Formation and Action. And within Adam himself, [I am of his] Cain aspect and higher, within the three Supernal *Sefirot*: *Keter*, *Hokhmah* and *Binah* within the *Malkhut* of all the Crowns of the Ten Sefirot of the *Lesser Countenance*.

In other words, he derived from the highest aspect of the three supernals of the second level of New Souls that can attain to *Malkhut* of *Atzilut* within one lifetime. See note 18 above. The "Feminine [passive] aspect of *Assi'ah*" implies *Malkhut* in our passage. On the other hand, as explained above, being a "new soul," R. Hayyim Vital had to begin at the very lowest level.

103. This is because he was working on the realm of *Gevurah*, which strictly speaking is above the three lowest levels of the *Nefesh Malkhut* of *Malkhut* (that is, the *Netzah-Hod-Yesod*); whereas the three middle levels (*Hesed-Gevurah-Tif'eret*) are at the *ru'ah* level.

104. In addition to the twenty-five years between 1572 and 1597 when R Hayyim was writing and editing no fewer than three recensions of the Lurianic corpus, he also reedited and expanded the first recension sometime after moving to Damascus. This conclusion was the result of a philological comparison I conducted between the early precis of a first edition recently published as *Sefer ha-Derushim* and the standard *Sha'ar ha-Hakdamot*.

105. See appendix D, sec. 7–9. From his commentaries on the Zohar and his *Commentary on the Sifra de-Tzne'uta*, written in Egypt and published in *Sha'ar Ma'amare RaShB"I*, it seems quite clear that the AR"I saw himself as approaching levels of prophecy nearly on par with the biblical prophets. See there fols. 3d, 4d, 5a, 24a, 25d, 26b, 30b, and elsewhere. He says, for example, that "until a spirit from on high shall dawn and bestow wisdom," and "until He shall kiss me with the kisses of His mouth . . ." The association between Luria and Vital lasted about one and one half years, from 1 Adar 5331 (6 February 1571) until 5 Menahem Av 5332 (25 July 1572).

106. See *Sefer ha-Hezyonot*, 16–17, 25.

107. He used a wide variety of sources, which he synthesized in a novel way. His principal sources were the zoharic literature. See Pinchas Giller, *Reading the Zohar: The Sacred Text of the Kabbalah* (Oxford: Oxford University Press, 2001).

108. This, in short, is how I would describe the experiential base of the practice of *yihudim* in phenomenological terms. I would, however, reject Michel de Certeau's privileging of apophatic mysticism (*The Mystic Fable*, vol. 1, *The Sixteenth and Seventeenth Centuries*, trans. Michael B. Smith [Chicago: University of Chicago Press, 1992], 5). There he criticizes a type of mystical technique similar to that used in Lurianic theurgy, as follows:

> In multiplying the mental and physical techniques that fixed the conditions of possibility of an encounter or dialogue with the

Other (methods of prayer, meditation, concentration, etc.), they end up, in spite of having laid down the principle of an absolute gratuitousness, producing an ersatz presence. That preoccupation with technique is already the effect of what it opposes. Unbeknownst even to some of its promoters, the creation of mental constructs (imaginary compositions, mental void, etc.) takes the place of attention to the advent of the Unpredictable.

To this I ask: How does one distinguish a theurgically induced "real presence" from an "ersatz presence"? This is especially problematic when we bear in mind that these techniques were quite successful when employed by the AR"I in bringing him to an altered state of consciousness in which he had creative concourse with "the Presence." See below, at the end of this essay, and in appendix D, where I attempt to begin distinguishing the "real presence" from a self-induced, nearly self-conscious "ersatz presence."

109. See appendix 1 below.

110. Scholem, "Gilgul," 310, n. 100; *Emek ha-Melekh* (1648; reprint, B'ne Berak, n.p., 1973), 63a, 94a.

111. See *Sha'ar Ru'ah ha-Kodesh*, 13b, *tikkun* 3, for the repair of souls engaged in magic practices of this type.

112. See, for example, *Midrash on Psalms* (Jerusalem: n.p., 1966), chap. 32; *Tikkune Zohar* (Brody: n.p., 1885), 74a.

113. *Me'orot Natan* (Jerusalem, n.d.), 57, #12.

114. It is interesting that this "manuscript interpolation" (see appendix B at the end of my remarks on sec. 5) originated in *Sha'ar ha-Gilgulim*, sec. 38, p. 33. Here one finds the vast majority of section 4 of R. Hayyim Vital's diary, later published in *Sefer ha-Hezyonot*, 134–229 (and see p. 157 there).

115. *Minhat Ya'akov Solet* (Williamsdorf, 1731), 41a–b.

116. *Sefer Mif'alot Elohim* (1725; reprint, Jerusalem, 1994), 135–36 (and see p. 43 for the provenance of this material).

117. See *Sha'ar Ru'ah ha-Kodesh*, 13b, *tikkun* 3, performed in order to repair the soul of one who engaged in such magical practices and adjurations such as those advocated above.

118. This paper will appear in the conference proceedings, being edited by Dr. David Malkiel (Jerusalem: Ben-Zvi Institute, forthcoming).

119. *Sefer ha-Goralot* (1899; reprint, Jerusalem, 1997), esp. 4–6, 55–61, 76; Gershom Scholem, *Kabbalah* (Jerusalem: Keter, 1974), 447.

120. See Gershom Scholem, *Researches in Sabbateanism* (in Hebrew), ed. Y. Liebes (Tel-Aviv: Am Oved, 1991), 109, 128, 346, 354, and passim.

121. See Gershom Scholem, *Sabbatai Ṣevi: The Mystical Messiah* (Princeton: Princeton University Press, 1973), index s.v. "Soul; soul-sparks, roots doctrine."

122. In all, I have collected eighteen such statements. See Menachem Kallus, "A Prolegomenon to a Critical Edition of the Authentic Writings and Direct Quotes of the AR"I Himself" (in Hebrew), in *Proceedings of the Thirteenth Interna-*

tional Conference of Jewish Studies in Jerusalem: Kabbalah Section (Jerusalem: World Congress of Jewish Studies, 1998) as well as my forthcoming article, "Rabbi Moshe Cordovero and the AR"I: Similarities and Differences," in *Proceedings of the Conference of Safedian Kabbalah Held in Safed, May 2000.*

123. I have elaborated on this in my dissertation, where I compare the AR"I's ontology with that of R. Moses Cordovero.

124. See her otherwise quite interesting "An Anonymous Commentary on the *Idra Rabba* Deriving from the Saruqian School; or, What Is the Connection between Saruq and His Circle, and Ergas, Spinoza, and Others?" (in Hebrew) *Jerusalem Studies in Jewish Thought* 12 (1996): 307–78.

125. See *Sha'ar Ma'amare RaShB"I*, 35d–38b, "Parshat Kedoshim"; and see the fine schematic maps constructed by R. Sasson Mizrahi in his *Ba'ati le-Gani* (Jerusalem, 1995), 4:11–12. The latter is a commentary on the Lurianic *Kavvanot* on the Sabbath liturgy according to the tradition of R. Shalom Shar'abi.

126. See *Sha'ar ha-Gilgulim*, 89–90.

127. See ibid., sec. 11, p. 94.

128. See section 3 of Kallus, "Prolegomenon to a Critical Edition."

129. See above, appendix B, sec. 10; and see *Sha'ar ha-Gilgulim*, sec. 10, p. 83.

130. See *Sha'ar ha-Gilgulim*, sec. 24, pp. 176–79, and compare the parallel text in *Sha'ar Ma'amare Raza"l* (Jerusalem: n.p., 1988), 6a–b on BT Sanhedrin 90a.

131. Samuel the Prophet was uncertain as to whether he attained that level. See *Sefer ha-Gilgulim*, 64a, Gilgulim Melukatim; *Sha'ar ha-Gilgulim*, sec. 1, beginning.

132. *Sha'ar ha-Gilgulim*, 178–79.

133. See *Sefer ha-Gilgulim*, 64a, Gilgulim Melukatim; *Sha'ar ha-Gilgulim*, sec. 1, beginning.

134. *Etz Hayyim*, gate 3, chap. 1.

135. *Etz Hayyim*, gate 43, introduction; and *Sha'ar ha-Hakdamot* (Tel-Aviv: n.p., 1961), 49a.

136. *Mavo She'arim* (1904; reprint, 1974), gate 6, sec. 2, chap. 2, fol. 56a.

137. See esp. *Adam Yashar* (Jerusalem, 1994), 17a–b; and see *Sha'ar ha-Kavvanot*, derush 3 of Inyan Arvit Layl Shabbat, 68a–b, where we read "a principle of inestimable value" regarding the "rising of the worlds" as a result of theurgic contemplation. There he states that the Essence is One and is always the same; it is only the rising of the relative vessels, that rise vis-à-vis the Essence, that produces the effect of the "rising of the worlds."

138. See *Sefer ha-Derushim* (Jerusalem: Ahavat Shalom, 1996), 251a; and *Etz Hayyim*, gate 3, chap. 4; and the unchanging Divine essence referred to in *Mavo She'arim* (Jerusalem: n.p., 1988).

139. See Zohar 3:141b; and the Lurianic commentary by R. Jacob Tzemah in *Kol be-Ramah* (1785; reprint, Tel-Aviv, 1970), 97a–b; as well as *Etz Hayyim*, gate 39, chaps. 1–2 and elsewhere.

140. See material around n. 54 above.

141. See appendix B.

Maggidim, Spirits, and Women in Rabbi Hayyim Vital's *Book of Visions*

MORRIS M. FAIERSTEIN

Spirit possession[1] is a concept associated with Lurianic Kabbalah in sixteenth-century Safed. Two recent articles have studied the relationship of women to this phenomenon.[2] Y. Bilu concludes that women were the primary "victims" of spirit possession. J. H. Chajes arrives at more far-reaching conclusions in his study, in which he compares the stories of spirit possession in the Lurianic hagiographic literature and other sources to the European witch craze in its historical importance. In this study I wish to deal with two basic questions. First, how widespread and how significant was this phenomenon? Second, is the characterization of women as the primary "victims" of possession by evil spirits accurate?

Possession and exorcism are first encountered as a significant motif in the kabbalistic literature of the sixteenth century and, most importantly, in the hagiographic literature about Rabbi Isaac Luria and his disciples in Safed.[3] When one ventures into the literature beyond the stories emanating from the circle of Luria on this motif, the methodological and historical problems multiply exponentially.[4] For this reason I will concentrate on the stories relating to kabbalists associated with Safed and the Lurianic circle.[5] There are two types of possession: *gilgul* (transmigration) and *ibbur* (impregnation).[6] The first, *gilgul*, is associated with the more typical type of spirit possession, that of a malevolent spirit. The second, *ibbur*, refers to a positive form of possession, where a soul adheres to the person for a particular reason. Normally, this type of "possession" does not manifest itself publicly. I have identified a total of eleven episodes of spirit possession in Safed; seven are negative possessions and four are positive possessions.[7]

The incidents of negative spirit possessions are these:

1. In R. Judah Hallewa's *Sefer Tzafnat Pane'ah*, we read that R. Joseph Karo was able to exorcise the spirit of a deceased Jew who had entered the body of a young boy in Safed in 1545.[8]
2. In 1571 the spirit of a deceased Jew entered the body of a woman in Safed. The attempts at exorcism failed, and the woman died. The letter describing this event was signed by R. Elijah Falcon[9] and a number of other witnesses, the most prominent of whom was R. Solomon Alkabetz.[10]
3. The spirit of a deceased Jew entered the body of a young boy in Safed. In this case, too, the possessed boy died. The unidentified sages who were present were powerless to exorcise the spirit.[11]
4. In 1571 the spirit of a deceased Jew entered the body of a widow in Safed. R. Isaac Luria was not able to go and exorcise the spirit, so he taught his disciple, R. Hayyim Vital, how to do so. Vital was able to successfully force the spirit to leave the woman's body after a long interrogation.[12]
5. During R. Isaac Luria's tenure in Safed, the eighteen-year-old nephew of R. Joshua ben Nun, one of Luria's disciples, was possessed by the spirit of a deceased Jew. Luria attempted to exorcise the spirit, which finally agreed to leave if certain conditions were met. In the end, the primary condition was not fulfilled and the young man died.[13]
6. Vital mentions in passing that the daughter of Daniel Romano came to his house and was possessed by an evil spirit and that he healed her. Vital devotes only one sentence to this story and provides no details.[14] It will be discussed below.
7. The most unusual story of possession is that of Vital's own possession by an evil spirit, of which his teacher, R. Isaac Luria, healed him. This story is not discussed in the literature on possession. It will be discussed below.

There are two other reports that have been mentioned in the literature that I have not included in this list. The first is the story of the migration of the soul of R. Joseph della Reina into the body of a gentile maidservant.[15] This story is more related to the cycle of stories about della Reina and his unsuccessful attempt to bring the Messiah than to the stories of possession and exorcism.[16] There is no reference to any attempt to exorcise him. Rather, it relates to the punishment imposed on him for his failed attempt to bring the Messiah by magical and mystical means. The second report is a fragmentary story by R. Gedalia ibn Yahia (1515–87) in his *Shalshelet ha-Kabbalah*.[17] It reports that someone was possessed in Italy in 1575. He says about it, "The truth is, it would seem or appear to be one of the wonders of our time and exceedingly strange."[18] This comment apparently reflects the attitudes of his contemporaries in Italy during this period toward various oddities of nature.[19] Neither of these stories contributes to our understanding of this phenomenon in Safed, which is universally considered the locus classicus of this literary topos.

The larger claims that have been made about the significance of these stories must await much more detailed studies of their historical reliability and their purpose in the works in which they appear. Their role in the propagation of the legend of R. Isaac Luria and his teachings must also be considered. One aspect of this legend, that of the kabbalist as magician, deserves more consideration in light of Moshe Idel's studies, which have demonstrated the importance of magic during this period.[20]

However, the claim that the majority of those possessed were women, and young women in particular, and that those doing the possessing were evil spirits, can be readily disproved.[21] Those possessed in these stories are almost equally divided between men and women. In most cases the age is not specified; nor should conclusions be drawn from terms like "widow" or "daughter" of someone. Thus we can conclude that possession by malevolent spirits is not a female phenomenon but can occur in a person of any age or gender.

A second broad generalization is that women were possessed only by evil spirits and did not have access to other forms of positive contact with divine beings such as *maggidim*,[22] angels, and visitations from the prophet Elijah.[23]

An examination of the role played by women in R. Hayyim Vital's mystical diary, *Book of Visions* (Sefer ha-Hezyonot), will dispel this misconception as well. The *Book of Visions* is a very unusual work. It was written for Vital's own purposes and was not intended for publication. As a result, Vital's testimony concerning this subject was probably more honest and less tainted by external considerations than works intended for public consumption.

The *Book of Visions* contains two accounts of women who were "possessed" by *maggidim*. The most famous story of "possession" in this work is that of Raphael Anav's daughter. Even a cursory examination of the details of this story presents a picture completely different from the conventional stereotypes of possession. The spirit that "possessed" Raphael Anav's daughter was not malevolent but rather the soul of a pious scholar, R. Jacob Piso, who was sent from heaven to bring a message to Vital. A week after the initial possession, R. Joshua al-Boom[24] contacted an angel, one of the servants of the angel Tzadkiel, so that Vital could ask a number of questions. This angel told Vital the following regarding the spirit of R. Jacob Piso and his mission in entering the body of Raphael Anav's daughter:

> God only sent this spirit into the daughter of Raphael Anav to cause the people of Damascus to repent. The spirit was very pious and in his place in Paradise. Because of a small sin which he still had to repair he was sent to accept his punishment in a river where he was embodied in a fish which Raphael bought. When his daughter ate the head, he entered her and remained there for twelve days. On Sunday, the first day of *Ab*, the time for his ascent came and he ascended of his own will, not by means of any person's actions. On the previous Sabbath, he sent for you in the morning. You went there, but did not return again until Sunday, when the time for his ascent had already come. He had wanted to reveal divine secrets to you. His whole intent was that the world should repent. Several souls and angels descended with him on the Sabbath eve and they were all waiting to speak to you about this. However, you did not believe their words, and you lost all those secrets. God only sent them so that the people will hear about the awesome deeds of the Lord and through this they would repent.[25]

The career of Raphael Anav's daughter as a clairvoyant did not end with this episode. Vital reports that she had further visitations from the spirit of R. Jacob Piso. In addition, she had visions of angels and even visits from Elijah, who had a message for Vital. Vital even consulted her about the refusal of his teacher, R. Isaac Luria, to visit him in his dreams or in other visions. Luria transmitted an answer through her, which Vital did not understand. A few days later she had another dream, wherein Luria asked for Vital's response. Luria was not happy that Vital did not understand his message. Several months later, Luria again appeared to her with another message for Vital.

R. Jacob Abulafia,[26] Vital's nemesis in Damascus, was also the subject of a visit from the spirit of R. Jacob Piso. In this case, the spirit voluntarily embodied himself in the girl so that he could deliver a message to Abulafia. The details of this incident are quite informative but would take us too far afield. The central point is that Raphael Anav's daughter was not a "helpless victim of an evil spirit" but a medium for divine messengers whose messages were taken seriously by Vital and even by his archenemy in Damascus, R. Jacob Abulafia.[27]

Another woman to whom Vital attributed possession by a heavenly messenger was Francisa Sarah. Vital calls her "a pious woman, who saw visions in a waking dream and heard a voice speaking to her, and most of her words were true."[28] Joseph Sambari, in his chronicle *Divre Yosef*, says about her: "In those days in Safed, in the upper Galilee, there was a woman who was wise and great in her deeds whose name was Francisa. She had a *maggid* who told her what would happen in the world. The sages of Safed tested her several times to see if there was substance in her words, and everything she said never failed to occur."[29] Sambari goes on to describe several incidents in which she predicted events that later occurred as she had foretold, and how the sages of Safed heeded her admonitions.[30] She was the only woman to whom a *maggid* was attributed.

Raphael Anav's daughter and Francisa Sarah were not the only woman credited by Vital with the ability to see divine beings. Vital reports:

> 5338 [1578] I was preaching publicly in Jerusalem one Saturday morning. Rachel, the sister of R. Judah Mashan[31] was there and she told me that the whole time I was preaching she saw a pillar of fire over my head[32] and Elijah z"l to my right supporting me. They both disappeared when I finished preaching.
>
> She also saw a pillar of fire over my head when I led the *Mussaf* service on Yom Kippur in the synagogue of the Sicilian community in Damascus, in 5362 [1601]. The above mentioned woman was used to seeing visions, demons, spirits and angels, and most of what she said was correct from the time of her youth and through adulthood.[33]

Rachel was also not the only female to see the pillar of fire over Vital's head. In 1568 Sa'adat, the wife of Jacob Nasar, saw a heavenly pillar of fire on Vital's head when he served as a *sandek* at a circumcision.[34] Many years later, in 1610, Simhah, the wife of Cuencas, saw a pillar of light brighter than the sun over Vital as he left the synagogue.[35] What is important for our discussion is that this sign of divine grace was seen by ordinary women rather than by great rabbis or scholars. It is significant that Vital had no problem attributing this phenomenon to women and did not feel the need to attribute it to men. He did not find it problematic or inconceivable that women would have these visions.

While she was in a coma, Vital's wife, Hannah, had a vision of Heaven and described at length the glories of the place that had been prepared for Vital.[36] Vital describes having a similar experience when he too was extremely ill and in a coma.[37] We see here as well that Vital had no problem in ascribing an experience to his wife that he also underwent and to which he attributed significance.

Vital cites only two instances of "evil spirit possession" in his *Book of Visions*. In both cases the possession is incidental to another point that Vital wishes to illustrate. In the first case, Vital mentions that R. Isaac Luria taught him how to exorcise evil spirits with the power of a Unification (*yiḥud*).[38] The only aspect of the exorcism that Vital finds significant enough to mention is the incidental fact that the spirit turned his face away from Vital when the latter entered the room, whereupon Vital slapped his face. The spirit, upset by this, told Vital that he did not turn his face maliciously but did so because Vital's face burned like a great flame as a result of his tremendous holiness, and he feared that his soul would be burned if he looked at Vital. Vital does not bother recording the final outcome of the exorcism. We hear about it only in other sources.[39]

The second incident is related to a dream Vital had. Judah Gano, a wealthy man who had died a year before in Damascus, came to Vital in a dream and begged him to repair his soul because nobody else could do it. Gano said that he would come the next day to be repaired. Vital reports that the next day the daughter of Daniel Romano came to him to be relieved of an evil spirit who had possessed her. He says that he healed her. What is significant here is that Vital devotes only one sentence to the possession and exorcism aspect of this story.

In this case and in the previous one, Vital's emphasis is on his own greatness and importance, a motif central to the whole work.[40] One is struck by how little weight Vital attaches to the actual exorcism. If exorcizing evil spirits was a significant concept in Vital's worldview, he would certainly have devoted more space to his exorcisms. We must conclude that this was not seen by Vital as especially noteworthy or important. The spirit's recognition of Vital's holiness, or the fact that he had a dream where a deceased person recognized his greatness, were more important to him than his ability to exorcise these spirits. Vital's indifference to the details of the possession, then, is eloquent testimony to the relative lack of weight attached to the phenomenon of spirit possession in the worldview of the Safed mystics.

The third part of Vital's *Book of Visions* is devoted to dreams that others had about him. Of the seventy dreams he reports, seventeen, or approximately a quarter of the total, were dreams by women.[41] This, I would suggest, is a significant percentage; it shows that Vital valued the dreams of women and considered them as significant as those of men. A careful reading of this part of the *Book of Visions* reinforces the conclusion that Vital made no distinction between the dreams of men and women and valued both equally.

The last story in the *Book of Visions* I will consider is that which Vital tells of his own possession. Ironically, of all the events reported by Vital, this story conforms most closely to the "classic" possession tale. In this case, however, the one possessed is not some "young girl" but rather an eminent kabbalist. It is also the only first-person account of a possession. This episode is quoted in full in appendix E at the end of the book. It is noteworthy that this incident appears in the fifth part of the *Book of Visions*, which is a collection of miscellaneous additions tacked onto the end. There is an indirect reference to this incident in the main body of the book. When R. Isaac Luria appeared to Raphael Anav's daughter, he asked if Vital had understood his response to Vital's earlier question about why Luria did not appear to him in his dreams. Vital reports:

> The night of the twelfth of *Ab*: In a dream, she saw my teacher z''l in a cave and he said to her: What did R. Hayyim reply to you? She said to him: He told me that he did not understand the three words. He said to her: Such an easy thing. Has his intellect been so retarded that he did not understand? Where is the wisdom that I taught him?!
>
> Remind him of the evil spirit that I expelled from him. It has been four years that he has not seen me in a dream. Now I planned to return to him, but since he does not understand my response, I do not want to return to him.
>
> In my humble opinion, the meaning of the above mentioned evil spirit, concerns the resurrection of the dead. He revived me on our journey to Kfar Akhbara because the spirit who was in the grave of the gentile injured me; or perhaps it is related to what twisted my mouth with the first Unification that I taught myself.[42]

In this case it might be argued that Vital "forgot" about this incident because he was embarrassed by it rather than because it was insignificant. However, if that was the case, why even mention it at all?

Although it is premature to reach any final conclusions about the significance and importance of the motif of possession and exorcism in the world of the Safed kabbalists, some preliminary conclusions are possible at this stage of research. The starting point of the "conventional wisdom," that this motif is about the possession and exorcism of young women by evil spirits and everything that flows from this basic assumption, is plainly wrong. There were as many men possessed as women; and the "evil spirits" were, for the most part, deceased Jews who became wandering spirits for a variety of reasons.

On the other hand, the fact that women participated in the positive aspects of this phenomenon needs to be addressed. It would be difficult to draw any significant conclusions about the place of women in the kabbalistic tradition solely on the basis of this evidence. In some respects, these women are not unique. Earlier examples do exist of women who were prophets and visionaries in medieval Judaism.[43] The role of women in the Jewish tradition is more complex than older scholarship would have us believe. The sources must be studied in greater depth and breadth before reliable conclusions can be drawn.

A related question remaining to be studied is how significant these stories are in the broader world of Safed kabbalists and later Jewish literature. The evidence of Vital's *Book of Visions* would tend toward the conclusion that it was not significant during the sixteenth and seventeenth centuries. The number of stories of possession in later centuries is relatively small, and a significant percentage of them do not represent actual cases of possession—they are merely retellings of earlier "famous" cases. In some instances the author alludes to the original case and in others tries to "sell" it as an actual event.[44] It is quite possible that the late-twentieth-century interest in this subject is more influenced by the great success of S. Anski's early-twentieth-century play, *The Dybbuk*, than anything stemming from sixteenth-century Safed. Much work remains to be done before any definitive statements can be made about this subject.

Notes

1. It is inappropriate to use the term "*dybbuk*" since it did not come into use until the seventeenth century in central and eastern Europe. See *Encyclopedia Judaica*, s.v. "Dibbuk," by G. Scholem.

2. The two recent studies are Yoram Bilu, "*Dybbuk* and *Maggid*: Two Cultural Patterns of Altered Consciousness in Judaism," *AJS Review* 21.2 (1996): 341–66; J. H. Chajes, "Judgments Sweetened: Possession and Exorcism in Early Modern Jewish Culture," *Journal of Early Modern History* 1.2 (1997): 124–69.

3. Stories of possession and exorcism can be found as early as the writings of Josephus. See G. Nigal, *Dybbuk Tales in Jewish Literature* (in Hebrew) (Jerusalem: Rubin Mass, 1984), 265; and in rabbinic literature. See *Pesikta de-Rav Kahana*, ed. B. Mandelbaum (New York: Jewish Theological Seminary, 1962), 1:74; *Bamidbar Rabbah* 19.8; *Tanhuma, Hukat*, 8. There is also a story of possession in M. Gaster, ed. *Ma'ase Buch* (Philadephia: Jewish Publication Society, 1934), 1:301–03 (and see Nigal, *Dybbuk Tales*, 66f.). My thanks to Prof. Ze'ev Gries for these references.

4. Two studies by Sara Zfatman-Biller illustrate the problems one encounters when dealing with the post-Safed stories. See "Exorcisms in Prague in the

17th Century: The Question of the Historical Authenticity of a Folk Genre" (in Hebrew), *Jerusalem Studies in Jewish Folklore* 3 (1982): 7–33; idem, "Tale of an Exorcism in Koretz—A New Stage in the Development of a Folk Literary Genre" (in Hebrew), *Jerusalem Studies in Jewish Folklore* 2 (1982): 17–65. J. H. Chajes, in his review of the revised edition of Nigal's *Dybbuk Tales*, which is the most complete collection of these tales to date, discusses a number of additional issues and methodological problems relating to this work. His review appears in *Kabbalah—Journal for the Study of Jewish Mystical Texts* 1 (1996): 288–93. I did not have access to the second edition of this work and all my citations are from the first edition of 1984.

5. The common thread is the Lurianic circle rather than the physical space of Safed. Thus I have included stories that take place outside of Safed, as in the case of the Damascus incidents relating to R. Hayyim Vital.

6. The classic discussion of *gilgul* and *ibbur* is found in Hayyim Vital, "Preface" 2–5, *Sha'ar ha-Gilgulim* (Jerusalem: n.p., 1963), 12–25. Vital discusses the specific issue of "negative possession" in ibid., preface 22, 58–63.

7. Two of the positive possession stories are the famous *maggid* of Rabbi Joseph Karo and the less well-known one of Rabbi Joseph Taitatzak. On Karo's *maggid*, see R. J. Z. Werblowsky, *Joseph Karo: Lawyer and Mystic*, 2d ed. (Philadelphia: Jewish Publication Society, 1977). Taitatzak's *maggid* is discussed in G. Scholem, "The Maggid of Rabbi Joseph Taitatzak and the Revelations Attributed to Him" (in Hebrew), *Sefunot* 11 (1971–77): 76–112.

8. This story was first described and discussed in M. Idel, "Inquiries into the Doctrine of the *Sefer ha-Meshiv*" (in Hebrew), *Sefunot*, n.s., 17 (1983): 224.

9. Falcon (also called Falco in some sources) was a disciple of R. Isaac Luria. According to Vital (*Jewish Mystical Autobiographies: "Book of Visions" and "Book of Secrets*," ed. and trans. M. M. Faierstein, Classics of Western Spirituality Series [New York: Paulist Press, 1999]: 4.59 [hereafter cited as "Book of Visions"]), Luria expelled Falcon from the fraternity of his disciples.

10. Alkabetz (1505–84) was an important kabbalist in Safed. He was the teacher of R. Moses Cordovero and author of the well-known hymn "Lekhah Dodi." The story is found in Nigal, *Dybbuk Tales*, 61–66, where full details are given on the various sources that contain this story. It is also found in the chronicle of Joseph Sambari, *Divre Yoseph*, ed. S. Shtober (Jerusalem: Ben-Zvi Institute, 1994), 319–24. An English translation of this story, based on the version found in *Sefer ha-Gilgulim* (Przemysl: n.p., 1875), is found in Raphael Patai, "Exorcism and Xenoglossia among the Safed Kabbalists," *Journal of American Folklore* 91 (1978): 823–33 and reprinted in idem, *On Jewish Folklore* (Detroit: Wayne State University Press, 1983), 314–25.

11. Nigal, *Dybbuk Tales*, 65–66 and 66–67. Nigal presents two versions of the same story.

12. Ibid., 67–70 (70–72 gives a variant of this story); Sambari, *Divre Yosef*, 351; "Book of Visions," 1.25 has a brief reference to this incident. All references to the *Book of Visions* are to this translation, which is based on the Hebrew edition of

A. Z. Aescoli (Jerusalem: Mosad ha-Rav Kook, 1954). The chapter and paragraph numbering is the same as the Aescoli edition.

13. Nigal, *Dybbuk Tales*, 72; Sambari, *Divre Yosef*, 350.

14. *Book of Visions*, 2.35.

15. Idel, "Inquiries," 229–30.

16. Some of the important studies of the della Reina legend are: Joseph Dan, "The Story of Joseph della Reina" (in Hebrew), in *Studies in Jewish Religious and Intellectual History in Honor of Alexander Altmann*, ed. R. Loewe and S. Stein (University: University of Alabama Press, 1979), 101–8; Michal Oron, "Waiting for Salvation: History and Literature in the Metamorphosis of the Legend of R. Joseph della Reina" (in Hebrew), in *Between History and Literature: Jubilee Volume in Honor of Isaac Barzilai*, ed. S. Nash (Tel-Aviv: Ha-Kibbutz ha-Me'uhad, 1997), 79–90.

17. Gedalia ibn Yahia, *Shalshelet ha-Kabbalah* (Venice, 1586), 86b.

18. Quoted in Chajes, "Judgments Sweetened," 129.

19. His contemporary, Abraham Yagel, displays a similar attitude. See D. Ruderman, "Unicorns, Great Beasts, and the Marvelous Variety of Things in Nature in the Thought of Abraham B. Hananiah Yagel," in *Jewish Thought in the Seventeenth Century*, ed. I. Twersky and B. Septimus (Cambridge, Mass.: Harvard University Press, 1987), 343–64.

20. Idel has written a number of studies on this theme. Among them are: "Inquiries"; "The Magical and Neoplatonic Interpretation of the Kabbalah in the Renaissance," in *Jewish Thought in the Sixteenth Century*, ed. B. Cooperman (Cambridge, Mass.: Harvard University Press, 1983), 186–242 (reprinted in *Essential Papers on Jewish Culture in Renaissance and Baroque Italy*, ed. D. B. Ruderman [New York: New York University Press, 1992], 107–69); "Solomon Molkho as Magician" (in Hebrew), *Sefunot*, n.s., 3 (1985): 193–219.

21. Both Bilu and Chajes make this claim.

22. A *maggid* is a divine messenger, usually an angel, but it can also be something else. The most famous *maggid* is the one that visited R. Joseph Karo. He believed that it was the personification of the Mishnah.

23. I would also question the use of the term "possession" for these experiences. However, arguing this point would take us too far afield into methodological and philosophical issues that are beyond the province of the present discussion.

24. Joshua al-Boom was a kabbalist in Damascus who was expert in the magical aspects of Kabbalah. He owned an ancient manuscript that taught him how to expel demons and spirits from persons who were possessed. He taught these practices to Vital. See *Sefer Toledoth ha-Ari*, ed. Meir Benayahu (Jerusalem: Ben-Zvi Institute, 1967), 291–95.

25. *Book of Visions*, 1.23. For more of this story, see appendix G.

26. (1550?-1622?) Rabbi of the Spanish congregation in Damascus. He is mentioned often in the *Book of Visions*. Abulafia had also spent time in Safed and studied with many of the important figures there.

27. *Book of Visions*, 1.24.

28. Ibid., 1.18.

29. Sambari, *Divre Yosef*, 364. This chronicle was written in the second half of the seventeenth century.

30. Ibid., 364–66.

31. A colleague of R. Hayyim Vital and student of R. Isaac Luria.

32. There is a tradition that R. Moses Cordovero said before he died that whoever would see the pillar of fire that would precede his coffin would be his successor. The only one who saw it was R. Isaac Luria. See D. Tamar, "The Greatness and Wisdom of Rabbi Hayyim Vital" (in Hebrew), in *Rabbi Joseph B. Soloveitchik Jubilee Volume*, ed. S. Yisra'eli, N. Lamm, and Y. Raphael (Jerusalem: Mosad ha-Rav Kook, 1984), 2:1300. The pillar of fire seen over Vital undoubtedly was meant to validate that he was Luria's successor.

33. *Book of Visions*, 1.12.

34. Ibid., 1.26.

35. Ibid., 1.27.

36. Ibid., 1.17.

37. Ibid., 1.19.

38. A description of this procedure is found in *Sha'ar Ru'ah ha-Kodesh* (Jerusalem: n.p., 1963), 88ff.

39. See above, episode number 4.

40. For a more extended discussion of Vital's obsession with his own importance, see the introduction to *Book of Visions*.

41. The dreams by women are found in *Book of Visions*, 3.3, 3.7, 3.8, 3.10, 3.12, 3.15, 3.18, 3.19, 3.20, 3.28(27), 3.37(37), 3.45(44), 3.46, 3.47, 3.49, 3.50, and 3.66.

42. *Book of Visions*, 1.24.

43. I deal with several examples in my article "Women as Prophets and Visionaries in Medieval and Early Modern Judaism," in *Women and Judaism* (Studies in Jewish Civilization, vol. 14), ed. L. J. Greenspoon, R. A. Simkins, and J. Cahan (Omaha: Creighton University Press, forthcoming).

44. See note 4 above for sources that discuss this issue at greater length.

A Spirit Possession Tale as an Account of the Equivocal Insertion of Rabbi Hayyim Vital into the Role of Messiah

HARRIS LENOWITZ

The account of the spirit possession of the daughter of Rafael Anav and its aftermath in the *Sefer ha-Hezyonot* (The Book of Visions, Vital's spiritual journal) sheds light on several important matters. These include the role of women in the time and place of the account and the ways in which that role surfaces in accounts of heavenly-earthly communication, including spirit possession events and messiah events. It also helps us understand the matter of spirit possession in general.[1] I intend to touch briefly on the topos of women as it appears in the earliest accounts of the Jewish messiah, Isaac Luria, and his disciple and successor, Hayyim Vital (Calabrese). But I will connect my thoughts to the genres of the spirit possession account and the messiah account and to one particular sort of messiah account: the one that serves to insert the messiah into his community of followers and antagonists.

The accounts of Luria and Vital differ from each other as they touch on the role women play in advancing or retarding the messiahship of these two personalities, and the difference between them has to do with the authorship and purposes of such messiah accounts themselves. A complete description of the role of women in the primary narratives of these two messiahs—those narratives related by the messiah or his protagonists/antagonists—is desirable but not practical here. Rather, I will bring forward the exposition of Vital's ambivalent feelings about being the messiah, the most distinctive feature in his autobiography, in the presentation and consideration of the tale of a single woman, the daughter of Rafael Anav,[2] her possession by a spirit, and the aftermath.

Two Genres Combined: Accounts of Spirit Possession Events and of Messiah Events

R. Hayyim Vital's autobiography, *Sefer ha-Hezyonot* (Book of Visions),[3] part 1, sections 22 and 24,[4] relates this messiah's experiences with "Rafael

Anav's daughter," whom Vital first encounters, apparently, when she is possessed by a spirit from the divine realms.[5] These narratives represent two distinct literary genres—messiah accounts and accounts of spirit possession—that have some common features. As I have shown elsewhere, messiah accounts, accounts of messiah events, are the third most important active element in the time of such a possession event.[6] They are responsible for attracting followers, inciting opponents, pulling in money, and the like. The accounts are the most important constituent remaining from a past messiah event—the sine qua non, in fact—for the messiah events that lie in their future and for the accounts of those events. Spirit possession accounts are, likewise, activated literature. They have the same relationship to ongoing spirit possession events as do the messiah accounts to ongoing messiah events and the same independent authority and power in relation to those that lie in their future. Some writers see these events as manifestations of the employment of particular lexical items and phrases: "messiah" (*mashiah*); "a spirit enters him/her" (*nikhneset bo/a ru'ah*), "[evil] spirit" (*ru'ah* [*ra'ah*]), "added [soul]" (*tzeruf*), "psychic impregnation" (*ibbur*) and, ultimately, "adherent," (*dybbuk*). I think that the analysis of these accounts as literature contains that perspective and is admittedly dependent on it,but goes beyond it, in the same way that the accounts have a certain dependency on events but go beyond them and enrich them.

These two genres—the messiah account and the spirit possession account—are closely wound together as they emerge in and define these passages from Vital's autohagiography. The most important theme they have in common is their representation of the interrelated worlds of the divine and the human. The most important characteristic these two genres have in common is their active engagement in the contemporary and developing events they narrate, followed closely by their overwhelming significance in later messiah events and spirit possession events and in the accounts of these. The motility the combination provides serves Vital well as he formulates and reformulates his self-doubt and his ambivalence about being the messiah as circumstances change. Since it is Vital who authors these accounts, the genre of spirit possession account is subordinated to that motive. (Other famous motifs in messiah accounts include the name of the messiah, the date of the event, the exchange of family members for followers, new economic structures, the conquest of death and illness. These all relate to the way in which a messiah event lives its future in its present moment.)

This spirit possession account is then only a motif in a messiah account, one of many available to this messiah in the ongoing creation of his identity. But it is a very rich one, a megamotif, since it too contains or sets out selections made from the motif-menu of its own, independent genre. (These include the details of the site of the events that take place in the accounts, the persons present and their roles, the gender of the speaker, the unmoving lips of the speaker, the speaker's voice, the exchange of questions and answers between the exorcist and the speaker, the ongoing and ultimate impact of the messages conveyed, and so on.) While the spirit account comes to be a component of certain messiah accounts, these latter are not, on the other hand, generally subordinated components in spirit possession accounts (though the very first account of spirit possession, the tale of Joseph della Reina, oddly does eventually bring the two sorts together in those versions where he attempts to bring the messiah or hasten the redemption and is forced into the body of a black dog).[7]

This remains true even after the "Safed experience," where the two sorts of literature are often found embedded in a single narrative peculiar to that experience, one that brings together an immediate interest in messiahs and a uniquely fruitful period in the history of the genre of the spirit account. The divine world and the human world were uncommonly close together in sixteenth-century Safed,[8] and the people and literature of Safed exported this propinquity to the whole Jewish world.

There are six cases of spirit possession joined to Safed and the pillars of its community in the days of its greatness. One is related to R. Joseph Karo; one to R. Eliyahu Falcon and several witnesses, including R. Solomon Alkabetz; one to a group of unnamed *hakhamim*; one to Luria alone; two to Luria and Vital.[9] Two other cases narrate the experience of Vital alone in Damascus. Issues concerning the status of Luria and Vital as messiahs are found only in the last five of these, and all five of them differ in important ways from the others. None but the second conforms to the ritual of exorcism as Patai described it in the introduction to his presentation of the narrative in which Falcon takes the role of exorcist.[10]

The narrative of Luria's failure to rescue the nephew of Yehoshua Bin-Nun from an *ibbur* (psychic impregnation) that has lasted twelve years is a "variant" of some importance here. It lacks the feature of rigorous interrogation as to the identity of the spirit; the spirit is not that of a sinner but of one sinned against; no fumigation takes place nor blowing of shofars; the promise made by the spirit to leave the boy is freely made, and the spirit places a condition upon the "exorcists" rather than the reverse. The most significant difference between this narrative and all the others is that Luria becomes aware of the presence of the second soul in the young man without the victim presenting any of the symptoms that lead to an exorcism. Luria makes his diagnosis in another way entirely, basing it on his own access to the world of the divine as it emerges through his scrutinizing the roots of the soul, its past history and sefirotic location. This narrative is then most like others that make their appearance in the hagiographa of the AR"I, relating his vision to his status as prophet and messiah.

The Recognition Accounts of Two Messiahs

From the first century B.C.E. to the present, Jewish messiahs have tended to appear in sporadic clusters. Within a cluster, one messiah tends to be linked with his immediate or most important predecessor as the inheritor of his messiahship.[11] Perhaps the messiahs seek to maintain the adherence of a previous messiah's following; perhaps the following seeks to find someone who will inherit the central role; or perhaps, more generally, the social conditions that obtained in the case of the first messiah of a cluster are extenuated. The accounts of the messiahs reflect this tendency toward clustering whether they are written by proponents or antagonists. Nevertheless, a good deal of information about the personal characteristics of the individual messiah is always to be found in the accounts as well. We see this, for example, in the cases of the bevy of messiahs mentioned in Josephus leading up to the Jesus movement; in the lineage of Persian messiahs—Abu-Isa, Yudeghan, and Mushka—in the ninth century; with David Reubeni and Shlomo Molkho in the early sixteenth century and Isaac Luria and Hayyim Vital in the middle of that same century; in the long series of messiahs who inherit the role of Shabbatai Zvi (Ya'akov Querido, Barukhia Russo, Heshel Tzoref, Hayyim Malakh, and Ya'akov Frank, to mention some of the more important ones) after 1666; in Frank himself and his daughter Ewa, who follows him in the role after his death in 1791; in the Yemenite messiahs of the nineteenth century, Shukr Kuhayl and Shukr Kuhayl II.

Hayyim Vital became first Isaac Luria's student, then his best student, then his only student, then his heir presumptive and, at last, his heir. The two met in Safed when Luria came from Egypt to reside in what was the most important city in Ottoman Palestine in late 1569 or early 1570. Vital became Luria's disciple in 1570 when his former teacher, Moses Cordovero, died. Cordovero was the preeminent commentator and authority on the central text of the Kabbalah, the Zohar. A central story in the sacred biography of Luria tells of the deathbed prophecy of Cordovero, that at his funeral the one who saw the pillar of cloud going before his coffin would be the one chosen to replace him and carry his teaching forward to redemption.[12] Luria alone saw the pillar.

The Equivocal Messiah

Luria lived about two and a half years in Safed before he died there. Tales in his sacred biography narrate his teaching of Vital, his preferring Vital to the exclusion of others, and finally his recognition of Vital as the messiah when he understood that he himself would not survive to complete the Repair (of the cosmos) and would have no heirs from his own children.[13] The passing of the leadership from Luria to Vital—whether the latter's role be that of prophet, granted permission to write down Luria's teachings, or that of messiah, ordained as teacher in his own right—is shrouded in tragedy. Luria, it is told, died as a result of being forced to reveal a certain secret, that of the necessary death of the messiah, by Vital. The vision of the pillar of cloud at Cordovero's funeral established Luria as successor. Given the function of the symbol in that account, visions of a pillar or pillars in Vital's autobiography carry the heavy weight of acknowledging his candidacy to be the messiah. The changes the symbol undergoes from the tale of Luria to those of Vital bring to light Vital's characteristic concern.

The pillar that Luria saw at Cordovero's funeral appears in a variant form in two recensions. In the version known as *The Book of the History of the ARI*, it is a pillar of cloud; as the tale appears in the memoirs of one of the contemporary residents of Safed, David Conforté, it is a pillar of fire.[14] Meir Benayahu, who edited these texts, notes that the history of the sign (which begins with the pillars that lead the tribes of Israel through the wilderness from Egypt to Canaan, Exod. 13:22) calls for it to be a pillar of cloud, since the funeral took place during the day. If we recall the kabbalistic structure within which the symbol might likely be read, the descent of the righteous man into the grave that takes place in the realm of darkness, the realm of the other side, the *sitra ahra*, wherein the sparks lie captive, the appropriate pillar might equally be that of fire, which served as a guide for Israel during the night. The variant readings lead us into indecision. The more famous text might easily have been amended itself on just the grounds Benayahu suggests; his inference makes more sense against the biblical background. (Since the case is of the appearance of but a single pillar, one must consider as well the column in the center of the Garden of Eden, the one that moves and sings and "links the lower Paradise to other levels of reality."[15]) Yet the pillars in Vital's autobiography are all of fire.

A more interesting characteristic of his pillar narratives is not the material of the pillars as this is observed but rather the matter of the one that observes the pillars in his record and what that signifies. In brief, I read the pillar or column as identifying the person with whom it is associated as both divine and mortal. While one art critic[16] has referred to the floating cloud as "a hinge onto eternity," when clouds are vertical, swirling pillars they make an even more dynamic connection between the worlds. The placid suspension and its potential movement is replaced by a wind with a gravitational function, lowering Heaven to Earth and at the same time raising Earth to Heaven. Here the column serves to move the person identified with it up and down, inserting him into both the society of Heaven and that of his own community on Earth where the supernatural sign is observed. At the upper end, Heaven acknowledges the entry into its society of the personage—Luria, Vital, Moses—found at the lower end. At the lower end, as the sign is seen it grants extraordinary social status to the same person, entering him into the society of humans as a divinely radiant being in their midst. Yet since the single sign makes two evaluations it remains ambivalent and subject to the volition of its interpreters beneath (as well as to the desire of its "senders," appearing or not at their pleasure).

(A group of texts from Vital's autobiography concerning the pillars, which should be consulted at this point, appears in appendix F at the end of the book.)

Vital's autobiography brings to the front his doubts concerning his role and his transhuman status, perhaps simply because he writes it himself. Luria's life, per contra, is written by others. We might speculate that Luria had doubts, too, but we find no support for that speculation in the narratives written by his adherents. From the material in appendix F, one notices first Vital's concern to retell accounts that involve the motif of the cloud pillar. Thereafter, with the exception of his own observation of the pillar(s), he relates the observations of women. The circumstances of all these observations are public and, incidentally, the pillars in them are of fire rather than cloud. It is less important, I believe, to remark on the peculiarities of one versus two pillars, of fire versus cloud, or of green or white fire versus red, than to note that the observation of the signal marks Vital's certification as the "righteous one of the generation, the messiah of the lineage of Joseph" (as it was most succinctly asserted by R. Hayyim ha-Kohen[17]) and to observe the manner in which he records the observation.

The ambivalent assessment of the meaning of the sign reflects Vital's own doubts about being the messiah. Ambivalence is itself a standard motif in the literature of messiah events: in Judaism (to except doctrines of a sort like the *parousia*) the accounts ascribe the failure of a messiah to bring on redemption to his being the messiah of the lineage of Joseph/Ephraim, preparing the way through his own failure for the coming of the messiah of the lineage of David. The promotion of this aspect of the motif is in the hands of the following.

Another aspect, the reticence of the messiah to declare himself, lies on the other side of the negotiations between the messiah and his followers/opponents, actual or potential. In the two most influential sets of messiah accounts, Bar Kokhba refuses to say he is the messiah and insists on the title *Nasi*. Perhaps R. Akiba makes the claim for him or without his knowledge,[18] though that tale may have more to do with Bar Kokhba's account contemporary, Jesus. The latter never admits his status himself in the early accounts and only urges others to make the claim for him by instructing them not to mention it, thereby assuring that they will not only mention the claim but elaborate upon it by including the motif of modesty or unworthiness as the messiah plays it in their recountings. In this connection, relative to ambivalence and ambiguity as they appear in the pillar accounts, the most meaningful points to note are the public circumstance and the identity of the observers themselves (women). I will suspend an explanation of the significance of these two points until the end of this essay and present now the matter of the possession of the daughter of Rafael Anav, the exorcism (1.22), and its aftermath (1.24). I will summarize the account of the possession and the exorcism and then turn to the account of the aftermath.

Heaven Comes Calling

In Damascus in the summer month of Tammuz, the daughter of Rafael Anav is stricken with pains and fainting. No magic avails her and eventually, over the Sabbath of the New Moon of Av, a spirit, that of one R. Ya'akov Piso, speaks through her mouth. He tells the bystanders that he has almost completed the expiation of all his sins and is therefore all but admitted to Paradise. But, on account of the fact that he had restrained others from studying the ways of repentance, this otherwise righteous man had been sent back to this world from the upper reaches of the Other World to ask Vital to gather a group for prayer and to pray for his acceptance, and thereby to match in this world the deeds of Vital's master, who is praying on his behalf in the Upper World. Vital comes (sec. 15) and hesitates to act (sec. 20). The spirit interprets a dream Vital has had the previous night; the spirit makes it clear to him that he has come to teach Vital those secrets he has not yet been taught that are necessary in order for him to become the messiah (sec. 15–17; cp. sec. 19).

Vital hesitates, goes to pray, spends the next night away, and, when he returns in the morning, the spirit speaks to R. Ya'akov Ashkenazi and others at the Anav house once more to say that he must depart. He names

Vital's own failings—his pride and his having ceased to preach repentance out of fear. The spirit says that the reason for Vital's ceasing to preach repentance and to bring on redemption thereby is the jealousy of R. Ya'akov Abulafia,[19] an opponent in Damascus, and Vital's fear of him. Abulafia ridicules Vital in public for preaching repentance and fasting in order to bring the messiah, who, Abulafia says, will not come in this generation—that is, will not be Hayyim Vital (sec. 21ff.).

With the dawn, the spirit emerges and returns to the Other World. In the dream Vital dreamed, the one that served to bring him to the interview with the spirit, he failed to save a diligent student of the law (*talmid hakham*). The spirit provides the interpretation: that the *talmid hakham* Vital has failed to save is he, the spirit, and that he is returning to his former place before the gates and not inside them. By the same token, the *talmid hakham* is Vital, who has left off preaching repentance, perhaps of his own choice, perhaps forced to do so by antagonists. His parallel in this is Piso himself who, while alive, prevented others from studying repentance. If Vital fails to save himself he can save no other; if he fails to save Piso, can he save himself? Vital did not work the exorcism. That was done by R. Yehoshua Al-Boom, employing the "classic" ritual and relying on a book and training, mentioned by the spirit, that he had received from one David Hamograbi (the Moroccan).

Many themes have been set in motion by this episode. The mere presence of the detailed knowledge of what happened in his absence—presumably gathered by Vital's later investigation and inquiry—along with the length and particularity of the account he sets down, indicates that more is to come. Or, to revert to the order of events rather than to their appearance in the *Book of Visions*, more has already come. In section 23 motifs from the theme of equivocation—Vital's inability to trust what he has heard from the Other World, inconsistency in attention to the message of the spirit of Piso, vacillation in his preaching of repentance, fear of public contempt—are all brought to his attention by an angelic visitor lowered into the world through the agency of the exorcist, Al-Boom, and mirror-magic.

The daughter of Anav returns in section 24. This is itself quite unusual in spirit possession accounts since the "victim" of the possession once cured holds no further interest for the possession account. The narrative hereafter may as well be considered as a messiah account alone. One can be sure, since the stories continue to be told, that their central figures continue to hold a special claim on the interest of their neighbors and a special status in the community.[20] (This interest appears only infrequently in accounts of any sort.) In agreement with the convention that a successful exorcism frees both the spirit and the possessed, the daughter of Anav continued to speak and be heard in several roles and did not cease to serve as a conduit between the Upper and Lower Worlds with the departure of the spirit of Ya'akov Piso. Instead she took up her place among a number of figures, most of them marginal in the society of the time and place, to whom Vital—and one presumes others as well—turned for information and communications. She has her own interests at heart: Piso's hunger during the possession (sec. 13) is in fact her own, and she argues for its satisfaction. She makes us aware of her feelings of importance—the importance of the message she brings in the name of the spirit—particularly when Vital fails to return to the house (see the complaint of Piso, sec. 21).

Her interests coincide with Vital's. Speaking at first in the voice of the spirit, she condemns Vital's enemies, the poet Israel Najjara (sec. 20) and R. Ya'akov Abulafia (sec. 21), and approves his role and message. Later she reports on what the spirit of Piso, angels, and other spirits, including those of Luria and Elijah, have said to her in visions and on visits to Heaven, reinstituting the attacks on these contemporaries whom Vital sees as his competitors for power and charisma. From section 34 through the end of the account she moves Abulafia from place to place, keeping him outside the chamber looking in, just as she and Vital have been shoved to the fringes of the society by him (sec. 35). She voices her disdain for his learning (sec. 35f.), calls him a sinner, and assails him for his arrogance and the disrespect he shows Vital.

Then, after she has broken him to the point of tears, she allows Abulafia into the chamber— forces him to enter, actually—as she enlarges her offensive, naming names and laying waste many figures associated with wealth and power in the community,[21] including Najjara again (sec. 38). And at last she returns to her description of Abulafia as a sinner (sec. 40), a fool for taking her to be one, and a hypocrite, catching him in his casuistry. She concludes by denying him the pulpit he has denied Vital. In a coda, Vital describes how Abulafia sought to protect himself and his associates (I presume that some, at least, of the people whose sexual misconduct is revealed in the message she brings from the spirit are Abulafia's supporters) and cover things up. We hear once more from Anav's daughter, from far-off Tripoli in Lebanon, as she lets Abulafia (and Vital) know that the spirit he had tried to shut up now pronounces excommunications upon him and his co-conspirators daily in Heaven.

What we have here is a war for voice in the community. Abulafia, the preacher, and Najjara, the singer, have stolen Vital's voice. The male community, especially those with power, have stolen the voice of the daughter of Anav, debasing women and depriving them of honor and protection—identity—by their own sexual malfeasance. (It seems possible that some women have themselves contributed to their own loss of standing.) At first taking the voice of a male spirit, a Torah scholar, within her, and then in her own voice as a seer and prophetess, Anav's daughter strikes back. She is knowledgeable in Torah matters and in community affairs, and she will make her voice, and Vital's, heard.

Vital consents to this to some degree, but he is also threatened by it. The nameless daughter is making a name for herself, but Vital keeps it out of his journal. He too has a secret name that he cannot expose: messiah. Vital has great self-doubts and seeks repeatedly to verify what his teacher has told him about his role. He goes to seers, asks dream questions, and has visions. He asks the figures in the visions about his place in the cosmic scheme so often that his teacher, Luria, and the daughter of Anav get sick and tired of it, as it were, and tell him so. Vital asks the question concerning his role in the redemption on many, many occasions in part 1 of the *Book of Visions* and throughout the remainder of the journal in his own dreams. Part 3 consists mostly of other dreamers telling him that they have dreamt that he is in fact the destined one. Vital repeatedly asked Luria while he was yet alive to reassure him of his worth and place in the scheme of salvation. The daughter of Rafael Anav, having been asked the question more than once, speaks for Luria (sec. 30). She wearies of his hesitations and of his unwillingness to accept her testimony and that of other supporters, chiefly women, who have common cause with him.

The similarity between women in the society, and particularly the learned and vigorous prophetess, and Vital, is twofold: they seek power and they cannot quite attain it. Vital keeps it from her in his account; and Abulafia and the others, in person and through the medium of the daughter of Rafael Anav, keeps it from Vital. As he acts out his role of Vital's enemy, Abulafia expresses Vital's self-doubts. But, as is seen in the words of Vital's reflective self, the daughter of Rafael Anav, she conveys the words of Vital's master: "At first [Luria] was angered with him because he would not listen to the words of that spirit and waited until R. Ya'akov Abulafia came from Safed. And thereby the matter became confused, for when the spirit spoke to him, then was the proper time and thereafter the moment had passed."[22] Abulafia stands for Luria as well. Vital finds approval for his self-doubt in Abulafia and depends on him to regenerate his own self-doubt. He keeps his role from himself by seeking to have it verified again and again—but never authoritatively—by turning to witnesses that he and tradition define as alien and dreadful: magic-working Moslem sheiks and, particularly, women.

We may recall that Luria himself observes the pillar that invests him in the mantle of his predecessor and then reports it to another male. Though there is not time to present an investigation of women in the hagiographa of Luria, it may be said that they are entirely passive. Women appear as neutralized features on his cosmic plain, only important when they are his suppliants and his patients, providing him the opportunity to diagnose their ailments and doctor their spirits. They are potential sources of great danger (as with Vital), and in one case, through simply appearing in the sickroom of a child, his own mother and aunt cause his death. But, enclosed in the environment of assurance and certainty that characterizes the accounts of Luria, the women are unambiguous and less capable of endangering Luria than he is capable of endangering himself.

Just as Vital's self-doubt—his fear of others and of being the messiah himself, and perhaps of meeting the doom of such a one—has stopped him from saving the spirit of Ya'akov Piso, it has stopped him from saving the world. In fact, the former stands for the latter. I believe that Vital feels that his inconsistency, his repeated turns away from the teaching of his master concerning the joining of this world to the next through repentance and devotion to the task, has stopped him. Like Lot's wife, he has turned back toward Sodom, back toward alchemy and acts of magic, away from the Kabbalah of his master, away from a future that would depend on him alone. Ya'akov Abulafia of Damascus, his enemy, reflects Vital's feelings of self-doubt and his accusations back to him, as Vital tells it.

Vital and the Spiritual Power of Women

In these two episodes—that of the pillars and that of the spirit—Vital presents women as authorities who testify to his doubts. (In part 1 of the *Book of Visions*, women read lights, mirrors, and oil for him. One to whom he turns, a *soñadora*, tells him his dreams and their meanings.) How does Vital think of women? What powers and limitations placed upon them by others bring him to employ them as witnesses to his own turmoil? What are his own needs?

Two constraints on women's status come to mind. The first is a matter of the legal standing of women in Jewish law as concerns witness: they are legally incompetent to serve in that role. Vital's attention to the recitation of the circumstances of the women's testimonies in both matters, his careful naming of these informants as the wives, daughters, and sisters of legally competent witnesses, display his awareness of the legal inadmissibility of their testimonies, as does the public circumstance. The public is there to witness that what the women have to say is not from the world of Torah. (In contrast, Luria, not knowing Cordovero's prophecy, did not know the meaning of his own vision and was therefore, by dint of his impartiality [*me-si'ah lefi tumo*], a qualified witness to his own legitimacy.) The women speak from the spirit world. But this is the Other side of the community's existence—invested with tremendous authority for the determination of daily conduct by Lurianic teachings—and the authority of the performer and the performance flashes back and forth between these extremes. This points toward the second reason Vital has to enlist women. In the Kabbalah of the Zohar and of Luria, women have two aspects: they are the avatar of ultimate benignity— the female aspect of the manifestations of God, the Shekhinah, the Bride of the Crown of Creation—and they are the embodiment of blackest evil, the *nuqba ditehom rabba* in the language of the Zohar, the Female of the Great Depth. What they are depends on how they are perceived. As has been said, in the Kabbalah, particularly in that of the school of Luria, the awareness of the significance of deed and word determines its consequence.

What does Vital himself need that he can gain through the possession event as he presents it to himself, and perhaps to others, in his spiritual journal? Vital relies on this woman in particular in her social role as the spirit-possessed woman, a role that involves certain acts and characterizations on her part and requires an audience.[23] Vital, who apparently has some difficulty in gathering an audience of his own at this period of his life (because of his self-doubts and because of the opposition of others), cannot participate as the exorcist in this event. He and the daughter of Rafael Anav, as well as the spirit of Piso, are all bound together, symbols of marginality and instability in the societies of both Heaven and Earth. But he needs the audience to reflect and ratify his ambivalence.

In the end, the doubts Vital has about himself and about the Kabbalah of his master prevent him from becoming the messiah and leave the world where it is: on hold. He turns away from the Kabbalah and the teachings of his master to find assurance in the world of alchemy and magic—science, as it were. In the same way, he looks to women, not to reassure himself of his capacity to carry out his cosmic role, but through their witness, as he turns toward them and registers what they say, to see to it that he not believe in himself. Vital can inherit the messiahship from Luria, who is legitimated by his vision, but his own vision of ambivalence and self-doubt makes it impossible for Vital to take it up or hand it on.

Notes

1. Since the appearance of A. Braude's *Radical Spirits: Spiritualism and Women's Rights in Nineteenth Century America* (Boston: Beacon Press, 1989), there have been a number of attempts to extend her thesis. Braude connects mediumistic acts in which women serve as mediums with the process by which a greater degree of power is gained by women. Others try to connect this thesis with other women's issues and other times and places. The case examined here will show that such extensions of Braude's case are not generally applicable to the involvement of women in spiritual roles within male-dominated societies, nor even to cases of female spirit possession in such societies. An observation made about the general nature of *dybbuk* cases—to exclude the accounts presented here—is Y. Bilu, "*Dybbuk* and *Maggid*: Two Cultural Patterns of Altered Consciousness in Judaism," *AJS Review* 21.2 (1966): 365: "The extreme passivity of the possessed was a convenient guise for rebellious acting out. . . . But [through exorcism] the rebellious spirits were transformed into conservative agents of the social order." A similar opinion, anthropological in its emphasis rather than psychological, is brought forward by J. H. Chajes, "Judgments Sweetened: Possession and Exorcism in Early Modern Jewish Culture," *Journal of Early Modern History* 1.2 (1997): 161ff. and n. 127 (see further literature there). Both authors speak of exorcisms, but the episode discussed here is not an exorcism at its beginning, or for most of its duration, and not in its aftermath. Whereas Bilu and Chajes write about the exorcism performance, it would seem that observing details of public performances in the community (including prayers, and the like) and the onset of exorcism and its epilogue—or postscript, as it were—yields information that supports a public presence *throughout* incidences of spirit possession. Attention to the interplay of gender roles would also demonstrate the crucial participation of males in what would appear to be a fully personed social ritual encountering gender identity and power concerns rather than "female acting-out" or "the assumption of male roles by women." Faierstein's essay in this volume provides an important corrective to the facile supposition of an automatic connection between women and spirit possession. While the modern accounts may commonly present this feature, such is not the case for the genre from the first accounts in the first century through the seventeenth century. More care is called for as well in regard to the terminology for the spirit as this relates to the divine-earthly axis of communication. The terminology cannot be generated to present the spirit as malign in every case.

2. Her personal name is not mentioned in the journal. The *Book of Visions* is generally quite restrained in referring to women by their personal names. *The Toledoth ha-ARI* (in Hebrew), ed. M. Benayahu (Jerusalem: Ben-Zvi Institute, 1967), 191–97, contains the tale of the possession of "a widow" and goes so far to avoid her name as to write, "Then the rabbi addressed the widow, '*plonit*,' [Mrs. Anonymous] . . ." See the history of the transmission of this tale in ibid., 191, n. 1; and note 20 below.

3. *Sefer ha-Hezyonot*, ed. A. Z. Aescoly (Jerusalem: Mosad ha-Rav Kook, 1954),

from which I have made my translations. And see now M. Faierstein, *Jewish Mystical Autobiographies* (New York: Paulist Press, 1999), which contains a translation of the whole work.

4. The full texts are to be found in appendixes F and G at the end of this volume. References to the appendix are by section number.

5. How these two figures came together, why Anav's daughter wanted to bring Vital to her in the context of her possession, and later, why Vital came to visit her and write extensively of his contacts with her—direct and indirect—is quite an interesting matter. The two share a concern with the critique of social behavior as it is associated with both spirit possessions, many of them at least, and the role of messiah. This critique—called variously "summoning the people to repentance" and "returning the people to righteousness"—is presented as the revelation of behavior that would be ostracized if made public and would result in a temporary reduction in the social status of the miscreants. The long list of evildoers in the revelations made in section 24 includes names that crop up as members of leading families in the society of Jerusalem/Safed/Damascus-Aleppo. One powerful figure who is depicted as an opponent of claims made by and on behalf of Luria and Vital in Safed and thereafter, Ya'akov Abulafia, is severely chastised. See notes 19 and 21 below.

6. H. Lenowitz, *The Jewish Messiahs* (New York: Oxford University Press, 1998).

7. See M. Idel, "Inquiries into the Doctrine of the *Sefer ha-Meshiv*" (in Hebrew), *Sefunot*, n.s. 2 [17] (1985): 183–266 and notes there on the earlier literature about this tale.

8. This atmosphere was present before the coming of the ARI. See Idel, "Inquiries," 255; D. Tamar, *Studies in the History of the Jewish People in Eretz Israel and in Italy* (in Hebrew) (Jerusalem: Rubin Mass, 1986), 69–80.

9. See a lengthier description of these accounts in the chapter by M. Faierstein.

10. R. Patai, *On Jewish Folklore* (Detroit: Wayne State University Press, 1983), 314–25.

11. A lineage or inheritance is common enough in the histories of Jewish messiahs. Exceptions to this are of three sorts: when the messiah is spectacularly unsuccessful, no other may ascend to follow him, as in the case of Simeon Bar-Kokhba; when the role becomes institutionalized, as in the case of Jesus Christ, there may be no opportunity for some time for a follower to rise into the role; and as in the case of the Hasidic messiahs of some dynasties, the role may become multilocal so that matrilineal and patrilineal descent and locality confuse the issue. A fuller discussion of the genre of messiah accounts may be found in Lenowitz, *Jewish Messiahs*, 14–17.

12. There are several versions of the sacred biography of Luria. All are collected and studied in Benayahu, *Toledoth ha-ARI*. (But see the extensive critique of Benayahu in Tamar, *Studies*, 166–93.) This tale appears in Benayahu, *Toledoth ha-ARI*, 159, and see the discussions on 89, 107, and 159, n. 1. It appears in the most

famous of the collections, the title of which is the same as the title of Benayahu's work: *Sefer Toledoth ha-ARI* (Book of the History of the ARI). The tale appears as well in the Yemenite version known as The Praises of the ARI (Benayahu, *Toledoth ha-ARI*, 263). In the Yemenite version of the tale the point is made that Luria is the reincarnation (mutatis mutandis) of R. Simeon bar Yohai. In the legend of the Zohar, the latter is both its author and the messiah of which the work speaks. Luria is the messiah of his own narrative of the Kabbalah. See Y. Liebes, "The Messiah of the Zohar," in *The Messianic Idea in Israel* (in Hebrew), ed. Sh. Re'em (Jerusalem: Israel Academy of Sciences and Humanities, 1982), 134–45 (republished in a shorter English version in Liebes, *Studies in the Zohar* [Albany: State University of New York Press, 1993], chap. 1); idem, "'Two Young Roes of a Doe': The Secret Sermon of Isaac Luria before His Death" (in Hebrew), in *Proceedings of the Fourth International Conference on the History of Jewish Mysticism* (Jerusalem: World Congress of Jewish Studies, 1992), 113–70.

13. See Benayahu, *Toledoth ha-ARI*, 161, 164, 167, 170, 191–97f., 200, 202–5, 261–62.

14. See R. David Conforté, *Kore ha-Dorot*, ed. D. Cassel (1846; reprint, Jerusalem: n.p., 1969), 36b. See also Benayahu, *Toledoth ha-ARI*, 107, n. 1 on the history of the variant.

15. Moshe Idel *Kabbalah: New Perspectives* (New Haven: Yale University Press, 1988), esp. 321, n. 133, notes the significance of the pillar in a slightly different context and singles out *Seder Gan Eden ve-Gehinnom* in *Otsar Midrashim*, ed. J. D. Eisenstein (New York: n.p., 1915), 85–86 (the moving, singing column appears in Zohar 2:271a–b). The symbol of the column receives many and various readings in the Zohar literature. Zohar 1:176b connects it with the Shekhinah and with the column of smoke rising from the incense offering. The two pillars/columns are counterposed, representing the two tendencies, the left and the right, fire and water, while Ya'akov appears as a middle column in Zohar 1:252b–253. A different reading, based on the same principles, is found in Zohar 2:46b. The *amud* is associated with Moses in 2:149a, and in 3:103b the *amud he-anan* is associated with the *Sefirah* of *Hesed* and with Aaron.

16. Hubert Damisch, *Theorie du Nuage: Pour une histoire de la peinture* (Paris: Editions du Seuil, 1972).

17. *Torat Hakham* (Venice: n.p., 1654). See the extensive discussion in D. Tamar, "The AR"I and R. Hayyim Vital as the Messiah of the Lineage of Joseph" (in Hebrew), in idem, *Studies*, 115–23.

18. See Lenowitz, *Jewish Messiahs*, 51, n. 22, 57.

19. Vital is not the only labile personality among the dramatis personae of his life and circumstances. Tamar (*Studies*, 188ff.) points out that Vital's enemy in Damascus was occasionally his enemy and his master's in Safed and occasionally not, seeking amulets and witnessing the truth of Luria's prophecy. By the end of the tale of the daughter of Rafael Anav, Abulafia has humbled himself before Vital and the daughter. It is no less the case in matters of spiritual commerce than in the marketplace that individuals change their positions as they feel the need to.

20. I do not share the opinion that the function of the effacement of the names of the spirit-possessed in an exorcism (several cases are brought by Chajes ["Judgments Sweetened," 136, 142, 150, 165ff.] from both Jewish and Christian accounts) was to return the possessed person to the community in the case of renormalization. I think rather that the effacement is related to the account, as opposed to the incident itself.

21. Abulafia himself, along with R. Moses Galanté, was among those who received ordination from the ones who were themselves ordained by R. Ya'akov Berab. (It is not this Galanté but his son who is the target of one of Anav's revelations.) If Vital takes these two to task, it might be that one reason for their resistance to him as messiah resembles what John (4:44 and cp. Matt. 13:57) writes that Jesus said, about how difficult it is to convince one's fellows of one's mastery.

22. See appendix G, sec. 33.

23. See Bilu, "*Dybbuk* and *Maggid*," 353; Chajes, "Judgments Sweetened," 161ff. and n. 128 there.

Section III
The Seventeenth and Eighteenth Centuries

Prologue

Spirit possession cases and accounts tend to appear in clusters in all societies that experience them. After the large grouping in the later sixteenth century, there was a period of approximately half a century with only a few scattered accounts of *maggid* and *dybbuk* events. Then, with the advent of the messianic movement surrounding Shabbatai Zvi of Smyrna in 1665–66, a new and even larger wave of possessions (essentially all "positive") appears. The patterns these follow are largely those established in the Lurianic context but often appear now in a popular mode. The relationship between possession and messianism was previously articulated by Harris Lenowitz in connection with Rabbi Hayyim Vital but with the Sabbateans (among whom was Vital's son, Samuel), this relationship was taken to new heights.

After the apostasy of Shabbatai Zvi to Islam in 1666, the Sabbatean movement continued underground and with it the widespread occurrence of spirit possessions. At the same time, however, both "positive" and "negative" possessions, and exorcisms connected with the latter, were taking place in some number without any known connection to Sabbateanism. A particularly detailed account is found in the writings of Rabbi Moses Zacuto, a native of the Amsterdam Portuguese community, who spent much of his life in Italy spreading the doctrine and practice of Lurianic Kabbalah. The Zacuto material mainly concerns the methods of exorcism and some details of one specific case. The example of Zacuto, probably the foremost Lurianic propagandist of the seventeenth century (with the possible exception of Nathan of Gaza, Shabbatai Zvi's prophet), exposes the error of those who assume Sabbateanism ruined the reputation of the Kabbalah for an extended period. Here the mystical techniques he teaches help restore harmony and spiritual health to a suffering Jew.

The relationship between prophetic possessions and the Sabbatean debacle remained in the Jewish consciousness for many generations, however. In the century between Shabbatai Zvi and the flowering of the Hasidic movement in the late eighteenth century, one finds prophetic *maggidim* in the scholarly circles of figures like Abraham Miguel Cardoso, a Sabbatean leader, and Rabbi Moses Hayyim Luzzatto, a famous Italian rabbinic scholar who was apparently not a Sabbatean but was a reader of Nathan of Gaza's treatises. There were also *dybbuk* possessions in this period. But when the Ba'al Shem Tov, founder of the Hasidic movement, showed signs of spiritual "madness," there was some struggle to determine whether these possession-like occurrences would be interpreted as a holy or a profane phenomenon.

There are three papers in this section. First, Matt Goldish draws a strong connection between the *maggid* possession of Nathan of Gaza at the dawn of the Sabbatean movement and the possession traditions from Safed, suggesting that neither situation fits the accepted scholarly models of spirit possessions. Roni Weinstein places the material of Rabbi Moses Zacuto in its Italian cultural context and points out the differences between possession accounts from Italy and those from Palestine and the Ottoman Empire. Zvi Mark brings out the complex relationship between madness and prophecy as represented by the concepts of *dybbuk* and *devekut*. The possession brought on by an evil *dybbuk* and the trance state of spiritual elevation called *devekut* among the Hasidim have similar symptoms, and both suggest a connection with upper worlds; but the former is anathema and the latter a sign of divine favor.

Vision and Possession: Nathan of Gaza's Earliest Prophecies in Historical Context

MATT GOLDISH

The *maggid*, a type of benevolent heavenly spirit whose prophetic presence possesses worthy individuals, was little known before the late fifteenth century. In the sixteenth century the phenomenon became known through several famous discussions and accounts, dealing principally with manifestations in Safed. The first half of the seventeenth century saw a few cases, particularly among Lurianic kabbalists, but with the advent of the messianic movement surrounding Shabbatai Zvi beginning in 1665–66, a virtual explosion of maggidim appeared, along with a plethora of other prophetic phenomena.[1]

The immediate question I wish to address here is, what caused this rash of maggidim under the impact of Shabbatai Zvi? While I have written elsewhere of the mass possessions at the height of the movement and will soon deal with the range of prophetic phenomena after Shabbatai's conversion,[2] I believe that a great deal of the answer lies in the impact of the *first* Sabbatean possession, that of Nathan of Gaza, during Shavu'ot night in 1665.

Maggidim

Little evidence exists for the phenomenon of *maggidim* before the Spanish Expulsion, though Professor Pines has traced its roots through the late medieval mystical work *Sefer ha-Tamar* back to Muslim origins.[3] In the late fifteenth century *maggidim* appeared in the circle of mystics associated with the radically prophetic and messianic *Sefer ha-Meshiv*. Rabbi Joseph Taitatzak, apparently a member of this circle, appears to have brought the concept of the *maggid* with him when he left Spain to settle in Saloniki and Constantinople—he was himself known to have had a *maggid*.[4] Rabbi

Joseph Karo, the great legal scholar and author of the *Bet Yosef* and *Shulhan Arukh*, was associated with members of the Taitatzak circle. It was apparently while he was still in Greece that Karo first experienced his own *maggid*, a matter that will be discussed more below.

Karo's *maggid* became famous though a widely disseminated epistle describing it. Meanwhile, he and several of his close associates settled in Safed, where persons close to him, including R. Moses Cordovero, appear to have experienced maggidic possessions as well.[5] Later in the century, when Rabbi Isaac Luria (the AR"I) came to Safed, he too was reported to have a *maggid*, as did a number of persons described in the writing of Rabbi Hayim Vital, the AR"I's chief pupil.[6] Maggidic prophecy was co-opted and incorporated into Luria's mystical system; Vital's *Sha'ar Ru'ah ha-Kodesh* and other writings explain the nature of *maggidim* and methods of soliciting their presence.[7] Lawrence Fine sums up this discussion by stating that *maggidim* are "angelic creations whose existence is brought about by the sounds of a man's voice uttered in the course of religious devotion such as prayer or study."[8]

Over the forty-five years between the death of Vital (1620) and the rise of Sabbateanism (1665), there were scattered reports of maggidic possessions among kabbalists, all but one of them adherents of the Lurianic doctrine. The known cases are Rabbis Menahem Azariah of Fano, Aaron Berakhiah of Modena (a student of Fano), David Habillio, Moses Zacuto, and Samson of Ostropol. The latter was not a Lurianist per se, though he certainly had access to some Lurianic writings and teachers; he was also the only Ashkenazi *ba'al maggid* known in the period and a complicated case in many ways.[9]

In general, then, *maggidim* would have been familiar to mystical scholars from a tradition going back to Spanish mystical messianism, continuing through its influence on R. Karo to the Safed context in which it became widespread, and from there into the Lurianic stream. Most Jews, however, would have been familiar only with the *maggid* of Karo because of the widespread publicity it received.

An enormous recrudescence of maggidim and related phenomena occurred in the Sabbatean movement. I have counted literally dozens of cases among Sabbateans, far more than all the previous accounts combined. While there is undoubtedly some question about whether preserved accounts can be said to reflect correct numbers of events, we can reasonably speak about two major clusters of maggidic possessions: the first in the circles of Karo and Luria in the sixteenth century and the second, much larger, wave among the Sabbateans.

I will argue that the central key to understanding Sabbatean maggidim lies in the *maggid* possession experienced by Nathan of Gaza, chief theologian and propagandist for the Sabbatean movement, on Shavu'ot night 1665. This event sent certain very specific signals to those present and the many others who were later apprised of it. The significance of all this for the direction of the movement can hardly be overstated.

The original meaning of Nathan's possession must be understood in connection with an earlier prophecy, a day-long vision that Nathan experienced a few months before the *maggid*'s revelation on Shavu'ot. This vision will therefore be treated briefly, followed by a discussion of the maggidic possession, its significance in the Sabbatean movement, and its meaning as an instance of benevolent possession.

Nathan's Prophetic Vision

Nathan of Gaza's first major prophecy about the messianic mission of Shabbatai Zvi came in the spring of 1665 in the form of a prophetic vision that lasted a full twenty-four hours. The stories of this vision indicate that it was not a spontaneous event, as tended to be the case with Christian mystical visions (at least by their accounts), but rather a prophecy Nathan induced and for which he deliberately prepared himself. While this vision is not the main subject of the current discussion, it is significant to note that: (1) the techniques used by Nathan were quite clearly drawn from Abulafian instruction manuals well known in the Land of Israel during the preceding century; and (2) there are many specifically Safedian and Lurianic elements in both the preparation and the experience.[10] Generally speaking, the practice of deliberately fomenting prophetic experiences in this way was widespread among the Sufis and kabbalists but little practiced among Christians.

Examining one text concerning this earlier prophecy will shed light on Nathan's spiritual biography in a way that helps to understand his Shavu'ot possession.

> Rabbi Moses Pinheiro examined Rabbi Nathan concerning the latter's prophecies when he was in Livorno. [He answered that] in his early life he spent all his time in talmudic study, served [God] much, and knew three orders [of Mishnah] by heart. Eventually a certain soul commenced coming to speak with him and began to teach him all the introductions to [hidden] wisdom. [Pinheiro] asked him what it was like. He answered that he would sometimes see an image like a pillar of fire standing before him with which he would speak; other times he would see the image of a man's face. [Pinheiro] asked him if he would know whose soul it was that spoke with him. He answered that each time he knew the spiritual identity of

the soul, but he did not wish to reveal them so as not to seem arrogant. This continued for a long period, until he knew all the Kabbalah, all the books of Rabbi Isaac Luria of blessed memory.

One day he determined to concentrate the whole day so as to receive a revelation of the great light, and that is what he did. While he was wrapped in his prayer mantle and phylacteries, all his senses were extinguished, though his eyes remained open. His mind was more clear than on any previous day, and he saw all things [of the Creation] in order, the *merkabah* [Ezekiel's chariot; this word is missing in Freimann] and the face of AMIRA"H [Shabbatai Zvi]. [Pinheiro] asked him how long he stayed in this state, and he replied, for twenty-four hours.

[Pinheiro] then asked him how things appeared: as in a dream? as if from far away or from close up? or just like a man learning? He answered that [he saw] by the light God made on the first day, which permits a man to see from one end of the world to the other, each thing in its appropriate place in heaven; then above [heaven] in the ascending order of levels.[11]

While there are several texts recounting this vision, each with different details and emphases, this version is particularly reliable, and it is most revealing. Not only did Nathan of Gaza have mystical experiences before either of his Sabbatean prophecies of 1665, but some of these experiences were specifically maggidic. In the description above we find the spirit of a dead sage coming to teach Nathan, not necessarily by possessing him but in a manner closely resembling some conditions of possession. Nathan's deep attachment to Lurianism is also clear. His definition of complete mastery of Kabbalah is knowing "all the books of Rabbi Isaac Luria." Finally, this is a vision whose noetic (or prophetic) content adumbrates that which would afterward be communicated on Shavu'ot night. The particular text cited offers little detail of Nathan's preparations for his great vision, but in other versions many specifics are recorded, whose basis in the methods of the Abulafians and Sufis is undeniable. These, like the possession induction techniques analyzed in the next section, were particularly associated with the mystical circles of Jerusalem and Safed in the sixteenth century.

With all this in mind, the Shavu'ot night possession can be understood in its essential contexts.

Nathan's Spirit Possession

If Nathan's first prophecy was a mystical event of a type well known among the adepts of Jewish and Muslim spirituality, his second vision, on the night of the Shavu'ot festival in 1665, falls into that twilight of experience at the frontiers of mysticism, shamanism, magic, and theater: he was publicly possessed by an auditory *maggid*. The full account of this event is given in Baruch of Arezzo's chronicle *Zikkaron Li-vne Yisra'el*:

> When the holiday of Shavu'ot arrived, Rabbi Nathan called to the scholars of Gaza to study Torah with him the entire night. And it occurred that in the middle of the night a great sleep fell on R. Nathan; and he stood on his feet and walked back and forth in the room, and said over the entire tractate *Ketubot* by heart. He next told one of the scholars to sing a certain hymn, then he asked another of the scholars [to sing]. Meanwhile, all those scholars heard [sic] a wonderful and very fragrant smell, as the smell of a field which the Lord has blessed. They therefore investigated the neighboring streets and houses to find out whence this fragrant odor came, but could discover nothing. Meanwhile, he [Nathan] leaped and danced in the room, shedding one piece of clothing after another until his underclothes alone remained. He then took a great leap and fell flat on the ground. When the rabbis saw this they wished to help him and to stand him up, but they found that he was like a dead man. There was present the scholar Rabbi Me'ir ha-Rofe, who felt his hand in the manner of the doctors and pronounced that he had no life at all. They therefore placed a cloth over his face, as is done to the deceased, far be it from us.
>
> Presently a very low voice was heard, and they removed the cloth from his face; and behold, a voice emitted from his mouth, but his lips did not move. And he said, "Take care concerning my beloved son, my messiah Shabbatai Zvi"; and it said further, "Take care concerning my beloved son, Nathan the Prophet." In this way it became known to those sages that the source of that wonderful odor they had smelled was in the holy spiritual spark which came into Rabbi Nathan and spoke all these things.
>
> Afterwards he rested a great rest and began to move himself. His colleagues helped him to stand up on his feet, and asked him how it had happened and what he had spoken; he replied that he didn't know anything. The sages told him everything that had happened, at which he was very amazed.[12]

This account is remarkable in itself, but there are several literary and historical particulars that deserve special attention. The matter of the special odor is particularly noteworthy. In Genesis, the patriarch Isaac precedes his blessing to Jacob, who wears the clothes of Esau, by comparing his smell to that of a field the Lord has blessed (Gen. 27:27). But the Zohar further associates a special odor, the fragrance of the Garden of Eden, with the prophet Elisha (Zohar 2:44r) and, most significantly, this same fragrance is attributed to Rabbi Isaac Luria.[13] On the other hand, such an odor is noted as well in the case of an ordinary Jewish woman who was possessed not long before these events and went on to offer messianic prophecies.[14]

The description of Nathan's wild dancing is also worthy of attention because it serves a polemical purpose. The wording is taken from 2 Sam. 6:16, a passage describing King David's religious ecstasy as he danced before the Ark of the Lord. David's wife, Michal, daughter of King Saul, who had established ideas of appropriate royal behavior, found this conduct offensive. She was particularly concerned with the fact that David disrobed, at least partially, during the performance, an act imitated by Nathan. When Michal reproached David, his response was: "Before the Lord who chose me above thy father, and above all his house, to appoint me prince over the people of the Lord, over Israel, before the Lord will I make merry" (2 Sam. 6:21). Michal is ultimately punished for her criticism, and David is vindicated. The author of our account is clearly responding to those who found Nathan's behavior inappropriate. The association with King David, who was also messiah and father of the messianic line, can hardly be accidental.

Benevolent possessions similar to Nathan's *maggid* were a well-known phenomenon among Muslims and Jews. The most important feature of the maggidic experience (aside from simply having one) was the noetic content, what contemporaries would call prophecy, with which the subject or perhaps the witnesses were left. In this case that prophecy was a confirmation that Shabbatai Zvi was the messiah and Nathan his prophet.

In order to understand the cultural and religious valences of Nathan's possession that gave it such significance for the movement, I will discuss what I believe was the most important single influence on this prophecy: Nathan's relationship with the sixteenth-century maggidic experiences of Rabbi Joseph Karo.

Nathan's Possession and the *Maggid* of Rabbi Joseph Karo

Few Jews could have failed to notice the similarities between Nathan's maggidic experience and that of Rabbi Joseph Karo, the most famous possession in Judaism. Rabbi Karo, who was born in Spain and left with the exiles as a child, lived and studied in Constantinople and Adrianople, settling finally in Safed. There he not only wrote the *Bet Yosef* and *Shulhan Arukh* but was an active member in the circle of mystics around Rabbis

Moses Cordovero and Isaac Luria. Most important for our purposes is the fact that Rabbi Karo experienced possessions of a *maggid* throughout a long period of his life.[15]

These possessions began on a Shavu'ot night, probably while Karo was still in Greece, in an event recorded in a very famous letter by Rabbi Solomon Alkabetz:

> Know that the saint [Karo] and I his and your [the readers'] humble servant, belonging to our company, agreed to stay up all night in order to banish sleep from our eyes on Shavu'ot. We succeeded, thank God, so that, as you will hear, we ceased not from study for even a moment. This is the order I arranged for that night. [Alkabetz describes the reading of portions from the Torah and prophets.] All this we did in dread and awe, with quite unbelievable melody and tunefulness. We studied the whole of the Order *Zera'im* in the Mishnah and then we studied in the way of truth [the Kabbalah].
>
> No sooner had we studied two tractates of the Mishnah than our Creator smote us so that we heard a voice speaking out of the mouth of the saint, may his light shine. It was a loud voice with letters clearly enunciated. All the companions heard the voice but were unable to understand what was said. It was an exceedingly pleasant voice, becoming increasingly strong. We all fell upon our faces and none of us had any spirit left in him because of our great dread and awe. The voice began to address us, saying: "Friends, choicest of the choice, peace to you, beloved companions. Happy are you and happy those that bore you. Happy are you in this world and happy in the next that you resolved to adorn Me on this night. For these many years had My head been fallen with none to comfort me. . . . Behold, I am the Mishnah, the mother who chastises her children and I have come to converse with you.[16]

Gershom Scholem took note of the parallels between the possessions of Nathan and Karo. He says that "Solomon Alkabes' description of a similar manifestation—also in the night of Pentecost—when the voice spoke through the mouth of R. Joseph Karo in the presence of many brethren, provides a perfect analogy [*makbil*] to the case of Nathan."[17] In his monograph Scholem does not develop the significance of the parallel, but the similarities cannot be a coincidence. Karo's possession by the spirit of the Mishnah was a famous event in the Jewish world. The specifics of the possessions are also too similar to occur by chance. Both took place late on Shavu'ot night in an atmosphere of scholarly group study and music. Both experienced xenoglossia. Both men were mystics who appear to have prepared for a spiritual experience quite deliberately.

Nathan had a special connection with the *maggid* of Rabbi Karo. Nathan's father, the Palestine emissary Elisha Ashkenazi, owned part of the manuscript (perhaps an autograph) of *Maggid Mesharim*, the work in which Karo's experiences with his *maggid* are recorded. R. Elisha brought this portion of the *Maggid Mesharim* to press for the first time in 1649.[18] Karo's original maggidic possession apparently occurred in Nicopolos in the first half of the sixteenth century. Karo had been studying with members of the circle of Rabbi Joseph Taitatzak, an exiled Spanish kabbalist. Others in the group included Alkabetz and the messianic prophet Solomon Molkho, whose martyrdom deeply affected Karo. Taitatzak was tied to the *Sefer ha-Meshiv* circle and was well known as a *ba'al maggid*, as we have seen. As it happens, Elisha Ashkenazi owned a prophetic manuscript of R. Joseph Taitatzak as well: a work containing revelations Taitatzak received while still in Spain. Scholem notes that Nathan may or may not have seen this manuscript,[19] but it is surely from there that Nathan quotes a passage concerning the messiah so critical to his later thought: "It is furthermore found in the manuscript work of the words of the *maggid* of our teacher Rabbi Taitatzak of blessed memory that when the Sages say 'The Son of David [the messiah] will not come until the kingdom turns to heresy,' they refer to the Kingdom of Heaven. In the future the Shekhinah will dress in the clothes of an Ishmaelite."[20]

Finally, the most famous story emanating from the *Sefer ha-Meshiv* circle was the legend of Rabbi Joseph della Reina, who tried to bring the messiah by incapacitating Satan according to prophetic instructions he had received. This tale became known through a work of Rabbi Solomon Navarro, Elisha Ashkenazi's partner in his long fund-collecting mission through Europe.[21] Nathan thus grew up with an atmosphere steeped in these sixteenth-century remembrances.

Around the time Solomon Alkabetz reported Karo's maggidic possession in the epistle quoted above, Alkabetz himself left for Palestine, and in 1536 the *maggid* told Karo to join his friend there. Having arrived in Safed, Karo was involved in another messianic enterprise, the attempt of Rabbi Jacob Berab to reintroduce *semikhah*. This was the form of ordination passed down from Moses to the generations of biblical leaders and long since lost by Karo's day. A way was found to artificially renew the tradition, which would allow the formation of a Sanhedrin, a Jewish supreme court that could anoint the messiah. Karo was one of four rabbis ordained with *semikhah* before the enterprise collapsed under heavy criticism.[22] He remained associated with Alkabetz and was later active in the circles of

Rabbis Moses Cordovero and Isaac Luria. Not only were *maggidim* and possessions of various types common in these groups, but the mystical theology explaining their meaning (much of it closely related to Sufi thought) was developed there.[23]

R. Karo's writings are not imbued with acute messianic sentiments, but it will be clear by now that his legacy in Jewish hagiography is permanently associated with messianic persons and enterprises: the Taitatzak circle, prophetic maggidim, the messianically charged *semikhah* controversy, and the Luria period in Safed. Nathan clearly felt a deep personal tie with both R. Karo and the whole atmosphere of prophetic Kabbalah he brought to Safed.

The Impact of Nathan's Possession: The Medium Is the Message

What, then, can we learn from Nathan's prophetic vision and his maggidic possession? Nathan, with this initial public Sabbatean prophecy, inserted himself (to use Harris Lenowitz's phrase) directly into the hereditary line of a powerful tradition: the messianically charged spirituality of sixteenth-century Safed.[24] Safed prophecy was itself heir to a tradition of apocalyptic prophetic Kabbalah connected with Spain on the one hand and the Land of Israel on the other. These associations created a profoundly resonant first image for Nathan's message, whose propaganda value was critical in the rise of Sabbateanism. As one examines Nathan's career one finds that his desire to be seen as the Safedian heir is a running theme. The Lurianic doctrine of metempsychosis, which stood at the root of *ibbur* possession ideas, lent itself to his purposes particularly well—among other things, it actually allowed him to identify himself with the messianic souls of the AR"I and Vital.[25]

Gershom Scholem claims that in the 1660s, at the time of Shabbatai's peak, Jews in Europe and the Ottoman Empire were familiar with Lurianism, and it was Nathan's Lurianic writings that attracted them to Sabbateanism. This thesis has been systematically criticized.[26] Nevertheless, it is certain that Jews in all these lands, whether or not they knew Kabbalah of any kind, were familiar with the *hagiography* connected with Karo and the Safed mystical circle. Scholem states that "Luria's name was freely used because the Lurianic legend as well as the popular hagiography *Shivhe ha-ARI* was widely known by that time, whereas Lurianic theories were still unknown to the majority of kabbalists."[27] And while modern scholarship is attuned to controversies within the coterie of Safed kabbalists (including some friction between R. Karo and the Luria circle), the image of that community stood in the seventeenth century as a harmonious monolith of righteous mystics with their eyes turned toward the future.[28]

Certainly in Italy, a center of Sabbatean activity, there is evidence that the fame of the AR"I and his mystical abilities was well established in the seventeenth century, partly through the enthusiasm of Rabbi Menahem Azariah of Fano. A student of R. Menahem, Rabbi Shlomiel Dreznitz, was so inspired by the stories that he went to Safed in 1602 and thence wrote a series of letters describing Safed and its scholars, particularly the late Rabbi Luria (and not omitting Karo and his *maggid*). These letters were published in Rabbi Joseph Solomon Delmedigo's *Ta'alumot Hokhmah* (Basel, 1629–31). A fascinating story is preserved from 1613, when the Lurianist R. Jedidiah Galante was in Italy as an emissary for Safed's Jewish community. As the *converso* physician Elijah Montalto lay ill in bed, Galante came with a group of rabbis and began to regale everyone with stories of the AR"I's wonders. Montalto became increasingly agitated, until he sat up in bed and shouted at Galante that such prophecy no longer occurs, and it is all lies. Needless to say, the Lurianic mystique made better headway with less skeptical audiences.[29] Other stories of the AR"I's greatness and events in his circle were known from the *Toledot ha-Ari*, *Shene Luhot ha-Brit*, and ethical classics like R. Eliezer Azikri's *Sefer Haredim* and R. Elijah de Vidas's *Reshit Hokhmah*.

Thus, by the time Nathan of Gaza underwent his prophetic vision and spirit possession, the association of these particular types of prophetic experience with the Safed mystical circle of the later sixteenth century was widespread. There may have been few Lurianic kabbalists, but there were also few who didn't know about the holy AR"I and his circle or about the *maggid* of Rabbi Joseph Karo. There is abundant evidence of the manifold relationships Nathan sought to establish between himself and the Luria-Vital circle, not only through his theology but through numerous more exoteric expressions as well.[30] The possession episode was simply the first public indication of these relationships. It played on the moving emotional and religious image and messianic associations of Safed.

Since the demise of the AR"I's circle, half a century had elapsed. This was a period in which the creative genius of the Safedian kabbalists was discussed and expounded in works such as Naphtali Bacharach's *Emek ha-Melekh* and Isaiah Horowitz's *Shene Luhot ha-Brit*.[31] Meanwhile, Jews, Christians, and Muslims in Europe and the Mediterranean were gripped by escalating messianic expectations as the seventeenth century progressed. Yet there were almost no Jewish messianic pretenders from Vital's passing until the rise of Shabbatai Zvi.[32] The Safed kabbalists had proffered both messianic personalities and writings thick with inherent messianic themes, fueling expectations of redemption.[33] When the members of the circle died out, it was as if the dynamite had been left undetonated but with a live cap—there remained a sort of messianic *tehiru* awaiting a catalyst. Indeed, many understood that the role of Messiah son of Joseph had been claimed by Luria and Vital, but the greater crown, Messiah son of David, remained unclaimed.[34] The prophetic and messianic tools were in place, and Nathan simply picked them up and used them, beginning with two explosive prophecies in the Lurianic style.

The medium, then, was a very large part of the message. Wherever Jews heard of Nathan's prophetic experiences they understood the meaning clearly: *the prophetic messianism of the great kabbalists had returned.* This recognition opened the door for the acceptance of Nathan's prophecies about Shabbatai Zvi; it also prepared the minds of scholars to accept the radical new kabbalistic system introduced by Nathan. Finally, Nathan's possession by a *maggid* inspired an unprecedented outbreak of spirit possessions among the Sabbateans.

Soon after Nathan's Shavu'ot night experience, spontaneous possession outbreaks began in various Mediterranean cities; scores of Jewish men, women, and children were reported to be prophesying the messiahship of Shabbatai. It is noteworthy that among these prophets were several scholars as well as common folk. Following the conversion of Shabbatai to Islam in 1666 and after his death in 1676, circles of Sabbateans in Italy, Greece, and Turkey continued to be inspired with Sabbatean prophecy, including spirit possessions. The most noteworthy of these was the group surrounding Abraham Miguel Cardoso, in which possessions occurred on a scale unprecedented in Jewish, Christian, and Muslim literature. The issues discussed below of scholars and laymen, prepared and unprepared for the experience, are important in those instances. In any case, the trace of Nathan's influence is discernible throughout all of this in the physical symptoms and noetic message of those possessed.

The Cultural Interpretation of Sabbatean Possessions

This history and major theories concerning early modern spirit possession are discussed at length elsewhere in this volume, so I will not go back over them extensively, but I will comment on the application of general scholarship to the Sabbatean cases.

Certain distinctions are generally used by both social scientists and historians in the attempt to impose categories and seek the causes or significance of possessions. These include:

> good versus evil possession ("positive" and "negative" or "benevolent" and "malevolent")
>
> male versus female subjects
>
> scholarly versus untutored subjects
>
> fomented versus spontaneous possessions
>
> altered states of conscience versus unaltered states
>
> possession phenomena in different cultures
>
> possession versus nonpossession states[35]

Most of these distinctions appear to run aground, or at least lose much clarity, in an examination of Nathan and the Sabbatean phenomena.

The gender distinction fails not only in the Sabbatean cases but in their predecessors, the possessions among the Luria-Vital circle as well. Both clusters of possessions included both women and men, and among women, both those from educated backgrounds and those from ordinary homes.[36]

If malevolent possessions are to be distinguished from benevolent possessions, scholarly possessions from lay possessions, Jewish possessions from those of other cultures, spontaneous possessions from solicited ones, and altered states of conscience from unaltered states, one would expect to find *some* differentiation between the symptoms, both physical and mental. Such a difference is essentially impossible to detect when one compares the various Sabbatean possession accounts with each other and with cases from other contexts. The actual "symptoms" of possesion—appearance in geographic and temporal clusters, suddenly falling down in a dead faint, exuding a strong odor, xenoglossia, seemingly impossible mental or physical feats and subsequent amnesia—are widespread in all types of possession. Many of these manifestations can be found in numerous cultures' possession accounts, both malevolent and benevolent. For instance, they are common in the descriptions of "witches" in New England, who were supposed to be possessed by the devil.[37]

The relationship between the possessions of the untutored and those of someone like Nathan offers additional complications. On the one hand, one may wish to see a benevolent, solicited possession of this type as entirely different from that of lay prophets—it is an essentially trained mystical experience. On the other hand, one might attempt to consider Nathan's experience and those like it as spirit possessions similar to those of unlettered subjects, which are not mystical despite the fact that subjects like Nathan were in fact mystics. One might be driven toward the latter conception by the opinions expressed by scholars like Underhill, who essentially claim that possession is a phenomenon not comprehended within mysticism.³⁸ This view is supported by the fact that the possessions of Nathan and Karo bear striking similarities to "popular" possession cases.

To concretize the point, here are some accounts of "popular" possessions among the Sabbateans that illustrate the problem of differentiation by "scholarly" versus "lay," male versus female, or solicited versus spontaneous experiences.

> I saw with my eyes a young student in particular on Rosh Hodesh of this past *Adar*. He recited biblical passages, and while speaking he lost use of his limbs and was almost without pulse. Then he said, "Shabbatai Zvi is our king and our savior." . . . And when he returned to his senses, he remembered nothing. A person may lie about all things, but with a pulse nobody can deceive.³⁹

> And this is an account of the prophecy as it befell in those days. A deep sleep fell upon them, and they fell to the ground as the dead in whom there is no more spirit. After about half an hour a spirit would sound from their mouth, though their lips did not move, and they would utter [scriptural] verses of praise and consolation, and all would say "Shabbatai Zvi, the anointed of the God of Jacob." Thereafter they would arise without remembering what they had done or said.⁴⁰

> For thus far had God permitted the Devil to delude this people, that their very children were for a time possessed, and voices heard to sound from their stomacks, and intrails: those of riper years fell first into a trance, foamed at the mouth, and recounted the future prosperity, and deliverance of the Israelites, their visions of the Lyon of Judah, and the triumphs of Sabatai, all which were certainly true, being effects of Diabolical delusions: as the Jews themselves since have confessed unto me.⁴¹

This last case is particularly instructive because it illustrates not only the similarity between lay and scholarly possessions among the Sabbateans but also the ability of an onlooker from Christian Europe to take what was a benevolent possession by a Godly spirit for the Jews as a malevolent possession by the Devil. These eyewitness accounts all report details of the popular possessions, which accord in almost every particular with that of Nathan and other learned Sabbateans and with possession experiences in numerous other cultures, both malevolent and benevolent. In comparing Nathan's case with those quoted here, then, we have the basis for real questions about many category distinctions that scholars have attempted to make in this field.

Finally, despite the danger of undermining the entire enterprise of this volume, I would like to suggest that the very isolation of spirit possession—"positive" possession in this case—as an independent category is hard to sustain in the case of Sabbatean manifestations. We have seen that, in general, "positive" and "negative" possessions share many of the same symptoms; yet "positive" possessions seem to be part of a different prophetic category as well. Bilu notes that maggidic experiences can come in various forms other than (apparent) possession, especially dreams.[42] Sabbatean revelations bearing the same prophetic message, the messiahship of Shabbatai Zvi, come in possession states, trances, dreams, and other media, often in the same person. Nathan, for example, prophesied Shabbatai's messiahship in a trance and a maggidic possession and later in other states. Popular Sabbatean prophets experienced dreams, possessions, visions, automatic writing, and other prophetic forms, but again, the messages were all essentially identical at this early stage.

One is thus left with the question of whether the common distinctions made by social scientists between possession and nonpossession states, between types of possessions, and between types of possession subjects can be sustained in the light of the Sabbatean examples. Later Sabbatean contexts, particularly those is the Cardoso circle (with which I will deal elsewhere), confuse the picture even further.

The Mimetic Model

Despite the difficulties of placing Sabbatean possessions in the categories of the social scientists and psychologists, it is clear that the work those scholars have done in the field is useful for understanding our cases as well. While the Sabbatean (and some Safedian) possessions largely defy theories so far produced, ideas like behavior models, crowd psychology, and variant states of consciousness can certainly be used by historians in creative new ways in conjunction with historical data about the social, religious, political, geographic, and temporal contexts of particular possessions.

For now, I would like to bring another approach to possession to bear: the work of Jean-Michel Oughourlian.[43] Oughourlian, a psychiatrist from the circle of René Girard in Paris, has described hysteria, possession, and hypnosis (which he considers identical phenomena) as functions of "interdividual psychology," the result of "universal mimesis," the unwitting imitation of others' desires. Oughourlian's thesis is that the human personality is shaped exclusively by mimesis, the most basic and universal relationship between people. In considering causes and effects in the Sabbatean movement, I have found this mimetic theory to be a very powerful tool. It is productive to look at the experiences of individuals like Nathan and see how they mimed and were mimed by others. This approach has the potential to teach a great deal about the way the belief in Shabbatai and the activities of his prophets were stimulated and communicated.

Mimesis is by nature a contextual phenomenon, and for that reason it works well in the explanatory paradigms of historians as well as social scientists. What contexts can help explain the mimetic models of Sabbatean possessions?

First, there was a tradition of "positive" Jewish possessions from at least the time of the *Sefer ha-Tamar*, which, as Professor Pines has shown, was based on Muslim texts. This Jewish tradition of *maggidim* was presumably passed along among the tiny cells of kabbalists until the Expulsion from Spain. In the sixteenth century, when Kabbalah in general was becoming far more exoteric, this tradition made its way from the remnant of Spanish kabbalists, represented by Rabbi Joseph Taitatzak, to his circle in the Ottoman Empire, where Karo appears to have come in contact with it. Karo and members of his circle, including Moses Cordovero, experienced maggidic possessions, but this was also the moment at which those experiences (like so much else in Jewish mysticism) was revealed to a wider public, in this case through the letter of Rabbi Solomon Alkabetz. From the Karo circle, and perhaps from some texts, *maggidim* became known to the Luria circle, who institutionalized it in their writings. This was also the time, in the mid- to late sixteenth century, when unwanted possessions by evil souls appeared in Safed and Italy with many of the same symptoms as maggidic possessions. In the hagiography of Luria and writings of Vital, especially *Sha'ar Ru'ah ha-Kodesh* and *Sha'ar ha-Gilgulim* (which also deals with unwanted or "negative" possession), as well as the Alkabetz letter, Jewish possessions became known to a wider public.

External influences were also at work in the mimetic background. As a result of humanism and the Reformation, large numbers of people had access to the Bible, where they would find much material about possessions by devils and evil spirits in the New Testament. Jews were in much contact with their Christian neighbors during this period and could well have absorbed influences in this way. This was also the Age of Exploration, when Europeans traveled down the coast of Africa and westward to the Americas. Many of the cultures they encountered in these regions had possession traditions. Similarly, the era witnessed greatly increased contact between European Christians and Ottoman Muslims, who had Sufi traditions similar to maggidic revelation. New England witchcraft events (in which possessions played an important part) probably owed a great debt to the presence of slaves raised in Afro-Carribean culture, with its rich traditions of possession. Tituba and John Indian are of course the best-known examples of this relationship. The spread of print undoubtedly facilitated the effects of mimesis greatly by disseminating details of cases widely among both the literate and illiterate. By the late seventeenth century, when Sabbatean possessions broke out in large numbers, any or all of these sources could have been known and influenced events.

In addition to these various contacts between heretofore little-known possession traditions and European culture, J. H. Chajes has suggested another element that must have come into play as well. Chajes explains that the same social and religious conditions that created the stresses underlying outbreaks of possession among European Christians were at work among Jews as well.[44] Nevertheless, I want to stress that without mimetic models of communication, it is highly unlikely that these stresses would have caused possession idioms specifically.

Thus, while there were various contexts of possession with completely different cultural meanings in the early modern world, because the nature of the possession event was communicated mimetically, there is little puzzle in the fact that possessions from different contexts often had strikingly similar features. Fainting, xenoglossia, and amnesia, for example, could occur with Nathan, with the "popular" Sabbatean prophets, and with New England witches because all absorbed their familiarity with possession mimetically.

The maggidic possession of Nathan of Gaza, then, was itself a message. In its blatant similarity to the possession of R. Joseph Karo a century earlier, it brought an automatic association between Nathan and the Safed mystics, whose powerful hagiographa had strong messianic associations. The message found an eager audience in the acute messianic atmosphere of 1665. Nathan's possession, in turn, was the model for a wave of popular Sabbatean possessions on the one hand, and a long series of rabbinic Sabbatean *maggidim* on the other. For various reasons connected with Jewish thought and the larger seventeenth-century context, Jews were prepared to listen to well-qualified prophecies, so that these possessions became a major force in the rise of the Sabbatean movement. While many of the well-known theories about possession from the social sciences do not throw much light on Sabbatean prophecy, their methods, combined with historical background information, may yield helpful results. The theories of Oughourlian concerning the effects of mimesis appear to show particular promise in this respect.

Notes

1. The literature on possession is very large. In general, see: T. K. Oesterreich, *Possession: Demoniacal and Other, among Primitive Races, in Antiquity, the Middle Ages, and Modern Times* (London: Kegan Paul, 1930); I. M. Lewis, *Ecstatic Religion: An Anthropological Study of Spirit Possession and Shamanism* (Middlesex, Eng.: Penguin, 1971); D. P. Walker, *Unclean Spirits* (Philadelphia: University of Pennsylvania Press, 1981); Clarke Garrett, *Spirit Possession and Popular Religion from the Camisards to the Shakers* (Baltimore: Johns Hopkins University Press, 1987). Several of the articles in *Religious Ecstasy*, ed. N. G. Holm (Stockholm: Almquist and Wiksell, 1982) also deal with this topic. For the specifically Jewish aspects, the essays in this volume and their bibliographies supply the most recent views. See also Gedalyah Nigal, *Magic, Mysticism, and Hasidism: The Supernatural in Jewish Thought* (Northvale, N.J.: Jason Aronson, 1994); idem, *Dybbuk Tales in Jewish Literature*, 2d ed. (in Hebrew) (Jerusalem: Rubin Mass, 1994); Yoram Bilu, "The Taming of the Deviants and Beyond: An Analysis of *Dybbuk* Possession and Exorcism in Judaism," *Psychoanalytic Study of Society* 11 (1985): 1–30 (and reprinted in this volume); idem and Benjamin Beit-Hallahmi, "*Dybbuk*-Possession as a Hysterical Symptom: Psychodynamic and Socio-Cultural Factors," *Israel Journal of Psychiatry and Related Sciences* 26 (1989): 138–49; Howard Schwartz, "Spirit Possessions in Judaism," *Parabola* 19.4 (winter 1994): 72–77.

2. For now, see Gershom Scholem, *Sabbatai Ṣevi: The Mystical Messiah* (Princeton: Princeton University Press, 1973), 6:6 and passim; Isaiah Tishby, "The First Sabbatean 'Maggid' in the Study Hall of Rabbi Abraham Rovigo," in idem, *Paths of Faith and Heresy* (in Hebrew) (Jerusalem: Magnes Press, 1982), 81–107. On mass prophecy see my "Rabbi Jacob Sasportas: Defender of Torah Authority in an Age of Change" (M.A. thesis, Hebrew University of Jerusalem, 1991), Ch. 5. There I enumerate over two dozen Sabbateans with *maggidim*.

3. See S. Pines, "Le *Sefer ha-Tamar* et les *Maggidim* des kabbalistes," in *Hommage à Georges Vajda*, ed. G. Nahon and C. Touati (Louvain: Editions Peeters, 1980), 333–63.

4. See Gershom Scholem, "The 'Magid' of R. Yosef Taitazak and the Revelations Attributed to Him" (in Hebrew), *Sefunot* 11 (*Sefer Yavan* 1), (1971–77): 67–112; Moshe Idel, "Inquiries into the Doctrine of *Sefer ha-Meshiv*" (in Hebrew), *Sefunot* 17 (n.s., 2), (1983): 185–266.

5. See R. J. Z. Werblowsky, *Joseph Karo: Lawyer and Mystic* revised ed. (Philadelphia: Jewish Publication Society, 1977).

6. See Werblowsky, *Joseph Karo*, 14; Vital's *Sefer ha-Hezyonot*, now available in translation in Morris J. Faierstein, *Jewish Mystical Autobiographies: "Book of Visions" and "Book of Secrets"* (New York: Paulist Press, 2000); and Harris Lenowitz's essay in this volume.

7. See Werblowsky, *Joseph Karo*, chaps. 4 and 12; Lawrence Fine, "Maggidic Revelation in the Teachings of Isaac Luria," in *Mystics, Philosophers, and Politicians: Essays in Jewish Intellectual History in Honor of Alexander Altmann*, ed. J. Reinharz,

D. Swetschinski, and K. Bland (Durham, N.C.: Duke University Press, 1982), 141–57; Menachem Kallus's contribution to this volume; and appendix I at the end of this volume.

8. Fine, "Maggidic Revelation," 143. Part of the text of R. Hayyim Vital, *Sha'ar Ru'ah ha-Kodesh* containing this description is found in appendix H.

9. On R. Samson Ostropoler's *maggid*, see Yehuda Liebes, "Mysticism and Reality: Towards a Portrait of the Martyr and Kabbalist, R. Samson Ostropoler," in *Jewish Thought in the Seventeenth Century*, ed. I. Twersky and B. Septimus (Cambridge: Harvard University Center for Jewish Studies, 1987), 221–55. Oddly enough, there is a possible connection between R. Samson's *maggid* and the original Sabbatean circle in the Land of Israel as well (24–25 and notes there).

10. I discuss this event at more length in the second chapter of the monograph I am currently writing on Sabbatean prophecy.

11. This version of the story dates to ca. 1668. It comes from a London Rabbinical College MS, formerly in the possession of H. Graetz, reproduced in A. Freimann, *Injane Sabbatai Zewi* (1912; reprint, Jerusalem: n.p., 1968), 95–96. Excerpts are corrected and reproduced in G. Scholem, *Shabbatai Zvi ve-ha-Tenu'ah ha-Shabta'it be-Yeme Hayyav* (in Hebrew)(Tel-Aviv: Am Oved, 1957), 1:167–9, and idem, *Sabbatai Ṣevi*, 205–6. The text given is translated from Freimann with some corrections based on Scholem's Hebrew quotations.

12. Freimann, *Injane Sabbatai Zewi*, 47.

13. See Harris Lenowitz, *The Jewish Messiahs* (Oxford: Oxford University Press, 1998), 132–33.

14. See A. Z. Aescoly, *Jewish Messianic Movements* (in Hebrew), 2d ed. (Jerusalem: Mosad Bialik, 1987), 286–89.

15. On Karo and his *maggid*, see Werblowsky, *Joseph Karo*. For Karo in general, see Meir Benayahu, *Yosef Behiri* (Jerusalem: Yad ha-Rav Nissim, 1991).

16. Louis Jacobs, *The Schocken Book of Jewish Mystical Testimonies* (New York: Schocken, 1996), 123–26.

17. Scholem, *Sabbatai Ṣevi*, 218.

18. Werblowsky, *Joseph Karo*, vii, 26; Avraham Ya'ari, *Shluhe Eretz Yisra'el* (Jerusalem: Mosad ha-Rav Kook, 1977), 154–55, 157–58, 281–82. Ya'ari notes the influence of the *Maggid Mesharim* on the maggidic manifestations in the later Sabbatean R. Mordecai Ashkenazi and the Sabbatean-influenced R. Moses Hayim Luzzatto. I hope to discuss the prophecy of these later figures elsewhere.

19. See Scholem, *Sabbatai Sevi*, 203.

20. Quoted in Chaim Wirszubski, "The Sabbatean Ideology of the Messiah's Apostasy according to Nathan of Gaza and the *Iggeret Magen Avraham*," in idem, *Between the Lines: Kabbalah, Christian Kabbalah, and Sabbatianism*, (in Hebrew), ed. M. Idel (Jerusalem: Magnes Press, 1990), 232 (originally in *Zion* 3 [1938]: 232).

21. See Scholem, *Ṣabbatai Ṣevi*, 75–76.

22. Werblowsky, *Joseph Karo*, 122–24.

23. See note 5 above. On aspects of Safed mysticism in the sixteenth century, see the essays in this volume and literature in their notes. On the particular Sufi-

kabbalistic relationships, see Moshe Idel, "R. Yehudah Hallewa and his 'Zafenat Paane'ah' " (in Hebrew), *Shalem* 4 (1984): 119–48 and n. 75 there.

24. Scholars are well aware that there was not one Safed mystical tradition but rather many variegated approaches that often clashed. R. Karo, for example, was in a certain amount of tension with the Luria circle, and Cordovero and Alkabetz taught different approaches than the AR"I. This, however, is of no consequence concerning the *image* of Safed, the hagiographic halo that surrounded these figures in the middle of the seventeenth century, and was in no way concerned with their differences or fallings out.

25. See, for example, Scholem, *Sabbatai Ṣevi*, 280.

26. See, most recently, Moshe Idel, " 'One from a Town, Two from a Clan'— The Diffusion of Lurianic Kabbala and Sabbateanism: A Re-Examination," *Jewish History* 7 (fall 1993): 79–104.

27. Scholem, *Sabbatai Ṣevi*, 84.

28. Werblowsky, *Joseph Karo*, 15–19, correctly points out that in the letters of R. Shlomiel Dreznitz, one of the best-known sources on Karo's *maggid* and mysticism in the Luria circle, the Lurianists tend to deprecate the mysticism of the Karo-Alkabetz-Cordovero group. He astutely comments, however, that the style of criticism is to fully embrace these older kabbalists but to say that their great spiritual achievements were not quite as great as those of Luria and Vital. I do not know if premodern readers operating without a critical historical sense would have noticed the tension inherent in passages of this type. This general view may be borne out by the tendency of later kabbalists to include elements of Cordoverian Kabbalah in their Lurianic treatises or even fuse the two traditions. See, for example, Bracha Sack, "The Influence of Cordovero on Seventeenth-Century Jewish Thought," in Twersky and Septimus, *Jewish Thought*, 365–79; *Encyclopedia Judaica*, s.v. "Fano, Menahem Azariah da (1548–1620)."

29. See Howard E. Adelman, "Success and Failure in the Seventeenth Century Ghetto of Venice: The Life and Thought of Leon Modena, 1571–1648," part 1 (Ph.D. diss., Brandeis University, 1985), 469–78.

30. For now, see the many references in Scholem, *Sabbatai Ṣevi*; and Avraham Elqayam, *The Mystery of Faith in the Writings of Nathan of Gaza*, part B (in Hebrew),(Ph.D. diss., Hebrew University of Jersusalem, 1993).

31. See Gershom Scholem, *Kabbalah* (New York: Quadrangle, 1974), 394–95.

32. Jacques Basnage speaks of a pretender named Ziegler who was active in western Europe around 1650, but he clearly made little impression. See A. Z. Aescoly, *Jewish Messianic Movements*, 2nd ed. (Jerusalem: Mosad Bialik, 1987), 438–39.

33. See Scholem, *Sabbatai Ṣevi*, chap. 1; Moshe Idel, *Messianic Mystics* (New Haven: Yale University Press, 1999), chap. 5; David Tamar, "The [Messianic] Expectations in Italy for the Year of Redemption in 1575," in idem, *Studies in the History of the Jewish People in Eretz Israel and in Italy* (in Hebrew) (Jerusalem: Rubin Mass, 1986); idem, "The AR"I and R. Hayyim Vital and Messiah the Son of Joseph," in ibid., 115–23; Yoram Jacobson, *Along the Paths of Exile and Redemp-*

tion: *The Doctrine of Redemption of Rabbi Mordecai Dato* (in Hebrew) (Jerusalem: Bialik Institute, 1996), chap. 4. Dato may not be thinking of Luria and Vital in messianic roles, but his writings exemplify the acute messianism of the period. Idel downplays the messianic aspects of Safed mysticism, perhaps somewhat more than necessary, but he makes the important distinction between "many rumors and legends that link Luria himself to a messianic role, and his Kabbalistic theoretical doctrines [which] include some messianic elements" (165). It will be clear by now that I am interested more in the hagiographic and legendary aspects of Safed messianism, which I believe actually grew in importance rather than fading in the seventeenth century.

34. For a far deeper and broader perspective on this issue, see Avraham Elqayam, "The Hidden Messiah: On Messiah Son of Joseph according to Nathan of Gaza, Shabbatai Zvi, and A. M. Cardoso" (in Hebrew), *Da'at* 38 (1997): 33–82. See also Tamar in the previous note.

35. Yoram Bilu claims that the "popular" Sabbatean prophets were in a state of possession trance, while the scholarly prophets like Nathan were in a nonpossession trance state, and that generally, "phenomenologically the maggid is closer to nonpossession trance than to possession trance" In Sabbateanism (to which Bilu makes extensive reference) these categories are either unworkable or viable only with excessively tendentious delineations. See Yoram Bilu, "*Dybbuk* and *Maggid*: Two Cultural Patterns of Altered Consciousness in Judaism," *Association for Jewish Studies Review* 21.2 (1996): 341–66.

36. See Morris Faierstein's essay in this volume.

37. See, for example, *Witch-Hunting in Seventeenth-Century New England: A Documentary History*, ed. D. D. Hall (Boston: Northeastern University Press, 1991), 208–9; Rossell Hope Robbins, *Encyclopedia of Witchcraft and Demonology* (1959; reprint, New York: Bonanza Books, 1983), 392–93.

38. Evelyn Underhill, *Mysticism* (New York: Meridian, 1974), chaps. 5, 8.

39. Jacob Sasportas, *Tzizat Novel Tzvi*, ed. I. Tishbi (Jerusalem: Mosad Bialik, 1956), 73 (my translation).

40. Baruch of Arezzo, *Zikkaron le-vne Yisra'el*, in Freimann, *Injane Sabbatai Zewi*, 49. Most of this is according to the translated citation in Scholem, *Sabbatai Ṣevi*, 420.

41. This is the account of the English merchant Paul Ricaut, reproduced in *Two Journeys to Jerusalem . . . with an Account of the Wonderful Delusion of the Jews, by a Counterfeit Messiah or False Christ at Smyrna, in 1666. and the Event Thereof . . .*, ed. Nathaniel Crouch (London, 1685), 143–44.

42. Bilu, "*Dybbuk* and *Maggid*," 357–58.

43. Jean-Michel Oughourlian, *The Puppet of Desire: The Psychology of Hysteria, Possession, and Hypnosis* (Stanford: Stanford University Press, 1991).

44. J. H. Chajes, "Judgments Sweetened: Possession and Exorcism in Early Modern Jewish Culture," *Journal of Early Modern History* 1.2 (1997): 124–69.

Kabbalah and Jewish Exorcism in Seventeenth-Century Italian Jewish Communities: The Case of Rabbi Moses Zacuto

RONI WEINSTEIN

An anonymous memorial poem from an Italian manuscript of the late seventeenth century was dedicated to two persons with the same surname: Zacut (Zacuto). The first was Abraham Zacut, author of the *Book of Genealogy* from the mid-sixteenth century, and the second was Rabbi Moses Zacut (known as ha-Ramaz), an Italian rabbi of the seventeenth century. Beyond the same patronymic these two had little in common; they lived in different centuries and their cultural activity was of very different types. The shared memory of these two different men seemed possible because the poem did not center upon their personal characteristics but upon the process of mourning. Not the dead persons but the emotional reaction of the mourners is its central focus. The opening lines include exaggerated expressions of grief. The writer then pulls himself together and tries to console himself and his readers with the thought that life must by nature end, that every composite entity must decompose, and that every element will eventually return to its source, since death awaits living creatures from their very moment of birth. Between the exaggerated grief at the start and the terminating sobriety before death stand the following lines:

> But what is this bad spirit that would force me
> to mourn and wail, to cry and weep?
> A bad sickness, a delusive idea crossing my mind!
> Never did I see such an evil;
> You [the delusive idea] are too despairing—leave me in peace.[1]

Mourning becomes a threat once the personal grief is out of control and turns into a lasting sorrow. In the Jewish Italian society of the late seventeenth century, men, especially educated men, did not approve of exaggerated, long, and extroverted expressions of sorrow ("to mourn and wail, to cry and weep"). In Christian urban society in Italy at that time, mourning patterns had changed radically; externalized expressions of grief were disfavored by men and relegated to women.[2] The poem is another testimony of the growing suspicion of and hostility to "overreacting" expressions of grief, considered not much different from "a bad sickness" and "delusive idea." Those moments of sadness, unless one controls them and shows restraint, might overcome one ("enough, enough my sadness, let go of me / you lasted too much, leave me in peace") and might permanently change one's character—the momentary excitement might lead to melancholy (*melinconia*).[3]

This mourning poem, then, mediocre and routine in its content and literary quality, exposes certain dichotomies: men versus women, restraint and self-control versus madness and sickness, and the individual versus the menacing powers. The unsuspected slide toward "delusive ideas," overreacting sentimentality, and the malaise of melancholy might annihilate one's own identity in favor of another identity ("this bad spirit that would force me"). In other words, the ultimate fear of the mourner is not death, but *possession*, that is, being under the control of an external spirit. Death rituals, melancholy, possession, and gender issues seem to be closely interrelated.

In what follows I will describe the growing interest in possession among Italian Jewish communities during the early modern period, its "diagnosis" as a culturally significant event, and its treatment or cure by exorcism ritual. I would claim that Kabbalah played a central role in constructing possession as a coherent phenomenon—not as a derivative of theological positions about reincarnation, whether of Lurianic, or Cordoverian origins, but due to the ability of Kabbalah to create new cultural and ritualistic patterns canalizing social needs and responding to fears and anxieties typical of this period. I will also allude to some issues requiring further discussion: the growing interest in body deportment, public rituals, and redefining gender relations. Possession seems to be the tip of an iceberg, indicative of increasing magical praxis. Finally, I will present R. Moses Zacuto as a main figure in the introduction of possession into the Jewish Italian cultural milieu.

Possession in Italy

The presence of demons in the vicinity of human living space was a basic belief in the Greek world, and according to Dodds it was not necessarily regarded as a menacing factor.[4] The demon, or *Daimon* in Greek, threatened the integrity of the human being, but at the same time it was a source of religious and philosophical inspiration. A person benefiting from such a contact was more esteemed.[5]

The encounter with unfamiliar powers and the immersion in their influence have attracted much interest in students of anthropology and religious studies. "Altered states of consciousness" might be considered a source of religious renovation, or they might be seen as a subject for medical care. Ecstasies, trances, mystical experiences, or shamanistic voyages are no longer regarded as marginal domains but as basic components in various religious experiences. Possession can thus be deemed another aspect of religious activity, aiming to intensify close contact with those powers-of-beyond and leading to purposeful changes of consciousness.[6] Such encounters might change the social identity of a person and his or her life. He or she could acquire a new role (shamanic healer) or join a group/fraternity of men or women who share this experience. Possession is neither a single experience nor a brief encounter. Usually it does *not* enable the participants (the possessed) to return to their former lives or to reacquire their former personal and social identities.[7]

Attempts to gain divine inspiration, so common at the beginning of Christianity, were mitigated in inverse proportion to the degree that the church—once an organized and influential institution—gained power. Whenever the church did not succeed in institutionalizing these phenomena or absorbing them, it tended to label them as heresies, demonic relations, or acts of witchcraft.[8] But in places where religious competition and polemics between Catholics and various Protestant denominations still persisted, there was a marked increase in cases of possession and exorcism rituals. In the case of Augsburg, studied meticulously by Lindal Roper, the Catholic church used these rituals in order to combat the local Lutherans and was not deterred by the disparaging attitude of its opponents. Not only the Catholic Church but even the Protestants made use of such performances as a propaganda tool.[9] Possession, along with prophecy and inspired lay preaching, became almost a plague in the Camisard movement, founded in southern France by Swiss Calvinist refugees.[10] According to Roper, possession became historically significant in situations where the basic cultural assumptions stood trial. We may conclude that possession has remained a permanent component in the religious repertoire since the early days of the church. The increase in its dimensions and the shift in its cultural functions are related to historical context.

The Catholic Church in Italy was ambivalent in respect to exorcism.[11] The battle against "superstitions" during the sixteenth century included attacks on the uncontrolled activity of exorcists. Those considered too daring in their techniques or their relations with patients were sometimes summoned to the Inquisition.[12] At the same time, the church itself could not forego such an important medium of contact and influence over believers, especially in times of their personal crisis. The *Ritualum Romanum* of 1614 even contained the "orthodox" instructions to churchmen about this matter. The publication of semiofficial guiding tracts to exorcists—particularly those of Gerolamo Menghi—contributed to the significant increase of such activity during the last third of the seventeenth century. Italian church exorcism was much different from French or German versions because it lacked propagandistic use, incorporated healing techniques, and developed in a different cultural setting.[13]

According to Gedalya Nigal, who conducted seminal research in this field, possession in Jewish society became a phenomenon significant enough to stir social reaction (and hence written documentation) only during the second half of the sixteenth century.[14] Contemporary sources document cases of marginal deportment labeled as possession (*dybbuk* in Hebrew) for the first time in that period. In other words, such effects were not relegated to anonymity for lack of cultural or collective significance nor stamped as insanity or personal idiosyncrasy. On the contrary, they aroused heated reaction by central community figures who practiced techniques of exorcism.

Labeling an exceptional behavior as possession by devils presupposes some basic social and cultural assumptions. Similar behavior could have been analyzed in other circumstances either as insanity (that is, a state of personal distress and hence of no interest to the community), or as some kind of cooperation with demonic forces (and hence a direct threat to collective life), or as magical occupation. But possession is of utmost importance to the social historian because it was regarded as neither the one nor the other. It was, rather, given an intermediate status: contact with malign forces with no clear responsibility of the possessed person. Nigal further claims that kabbalists of the small Galilean town of Safed (Tzfat) during the sixteenth century had to a large extant set the norms for diagnosing the state of possession, contacting the alien spirit, and eventually expelling it out of the human body.[15] Later possession cases would follow the ritual and narrative patterns set by the kabbalists of Safed and the eastern Mediterranean.

The earliest story relates a case from 1571 containing the main elements of the Jewish version of exorcism:

> I have agreed to print, in order to benefit others, what has passed in front of my own eyes today, the eleventh of the month of First Adar, 5331

years from the creation of the world [1571], about a woman into whom entered a spirit of a Jewish man, as I will immediately relate. The truth is that whoever was present at that time and heard what the spirit said and discovered, or heard from people present, should surrender his heart to heaven, and fear and awe the day of Judgment, because everything is taken into account.... I found myself in a large assembly, about a hundred persons, among whom were some great Torah scholars[16] and community leaders. Two men approached the woman, men knowledgeable of conjurations and many matters, to speak to the spirit inside that woman. And by putting smoke and sulphur inside her nostrils, she became null and void [that is, lost consciousness], and she didn't try to distance herself, or even her head, from the fire or the smoke. Following the conjurations a voice was heard, a thick voice; these two aforementioned men were forcing themselves and warming themselves up, diligently and hastily, to do what they did. And they would quarrel and speak against him [the foreign spirit], saying: "You evil, speak and clearly say who are you." And then the voice would be revealed to everybody as a human voice ... and they asked him for what sin was he incarnated and returned to "The World Of Incarnations," and he said that he committed many sins during his lifetime.[17]

The significance of the story requires some elaboration, since it served as an archetypical pattern for later narratives in Safed and the eastern Mediterranean (in contrast to the unique Italian Jewish pattern, which will be discussed below). The story starts with the description of exceptional signs in the woman's behavior: fainting, xenoglossia, swelling of different body zones, speaking in foreign languages. It moves on to the negotiations with the spirit about terms for leaving the woman's body and the attempt to heal or reshape (*letakken*) the foreign spirit. The final phase includes conjurations, use of holy names and prayers, blowing of the sacred horn (shofar), and application of sulphur smoke. The Safed story does not end well. A short while after leaving the woman's body, the spirit returns and causes her death.

Possession stories in Safed, and the Land of Israel (Eretz-Israel) versions more generally, carry a clear didactic message: the story consciously intends to reinforce the legal norms of halakhah and the fulfilling of religious commandments (*Kiyum Mitzvot*). Hence the spirit had a well-defined personality (a Jewish personality, of course) and acknowledged its past moral-religious sins. The dialogue with the spirit does not seem to be significantly different from one with any other living person of the local community.

Italian communities were the main way station for the spread of interest in possessions from Safed and the eastern Mediterranean generally to western Europe and later on to eastern Europe. This is sufficient impetus to undertake an analysis of possession in the Italian Jewish context, including its modes of acceptance in the cultural atmosphere of the sixteenth and seventeenth centuries and the role of Kabbalah in this historical change.[18] It is here that possession is defined for the first time in Europe as a cultural phenomenon of independent significance (sui generis) and here that healing techniques are first institutionalized. Furthermore, every possession event bears unique traits and does not repeat thematic or narrative formulae. During the seventeenth and eighteenth centuries, possession stories in the eastern Mediterranean and eastern Europe tended to blur the specific details of each case or the uniqueness of local traditions. This trend naturally bears a phenomenological resemblance to stories of saints' lives (*vitae sanctorum*), increasingly crystallized in semantic and narrative formulae. Possession testimonies in Italian Jewish communities, then, are a fresh and direct testimony of reception and commentary, less "contaminated" by the thematic and linguistic tradition of Safed and the eastern Mediterranean.

The Jewish Tradition of Possession in Italy

Several years after the first Safed narrative of 1571, the first testimonies of possession in Italy had already began to appear. The book *Chain of Tradition* (*Shalshelet ha-Kabbalah*) tells of a young woman into whose body the spirit of a local Christian criminal, recently executed, entered. The author does *not* regard this exceptional case as another proof of the verity of the sacred law or as evidence of the obligation to fulfill religious commandments. His main interest is theoretical, philosophical, not particularly "Jewish." The possession presented a unique opportunity to probe for knowledge about death and the existence of the soul in the world to come. But to the author's dismay, his questions failed to receive any significant response, since the spirit that had taken over this woman had been ignorant and uneducated in the earthly life and apparently incapable of any greater shrewdness after death. The attempt to exorcise the spirit is conducted and narrated in a calm tone, unlike the agonized stories coming from Safed. The combat between the spirit and the Jewish exorcist was replaced by a dialogue, a polite and civilized exchange. The author—who is involved for the moment not only as eyewitness but as exorcist—asks the spirit to leave the woman's body, receives a negative answer, and does not insist further. Gedalia ibn Yahya, the book's author, does not even bother to tell his readers the outcome of this scene. There is no suspense, and the resolution appears in a literary but sober report.

Had the story in the book *Chain of Tradition* been read by a contemporary Christian reader, he or she might have considered it no less significant and familiar than would a Jewish reader. The narrative contains elements of popular culture common to both Jews and Christians in Italy at that time. For example, both held the belief that bodies of executed persons "contain" magical powers. For this reason people (especially men) used to steal parts from these corpses for use in magical rituals.[19] In our case, the magical power of a man who suffered violent death by execution remained an independent entity and later penetrated another body.

Another element relates well to the local Christian milieu. The woman is in her bed, lying down (*Aprakdan*),[20] probably for long periods of time. This situation is exceptional in a double sense: she suspends her normal functions as adult and housewife, and she is also exposed to masculine gaze inside her own house, lying in her bed. For reasons of honor—men's honor and family honor—such a situation would be unthinkable in normal life.[21] This prohibition is temporarily suspended to allow the presence of men around her, for only they are in a position to define the feminine *Aprakdan* as an external sign of contact with spiritual powers. This specific reaction of the Jewish men fits well in an urban society that partially legitimizes feminine passivity—lying in bed—for long periods of time. It is this passivity in particular that may serve as a claim for spiritual distinction.

Gabriella Zarri and others described the lives of women belonging to the Third Order (the Tertiaries), conducting their activity according to monastic-like regulation but still living in the family's home and keeping their unmarried lay status.[22] Some of the most famous women saints belonged to this tradition. Some of them spent days and even months lying in their beds, continuing their activity of preaching, healing, or other religious activity. The legitimization of feminine religious tradition and the construction of separate institutions to respond to the mental needs of urban women are well known in Italian Catholic society. Hardly anything of the sort, however, is known in the Italian Jewish context. The possession story might be a partial Jewish response to this semiformal path of female religiosity.

Thus, the local Jewish tradition concerning exorcism during the second half of the sixteenth century is closer to the local Christian conception than it is to the Safedian ideas, which center on reincarnation and Kabbalah. The story in the book *Chain of Tradition* connects a Jewish woman's body not only to the spirit of an executed Christian male but to a whole substratum of local popular culture common to Jewish and Christian urban populations during the early modern period.

While the first Italian case (1575) remained unique in the sixteenth century, one cannot ignore the increasing attention to both the documentation of possession and the healing potential associated with it a century later. The central figure in this reawakening was the rabbi-cum-kabbalist Moses Zacuto. The main testimony about his activity in this area is found in his collected letters.[23] The exchange of correspondence was very common among Italian Jews,[24] and the thousands of private letters they left behind may serve as invaluable source for social and religious history. The art of letter writing (*ars letteras scribendi*) formed part of local educational curriculum, and special manuals (*Igronim*) were composed for young students or adults wishing to express themselves in high rhetorical fashion. There were various subgenres of letters among the Jews, and in Zacuto's case we are dealing not with a two-sided epistolary dialogue but with small tracts sent by Zacuto to his disciples. These included religious instructions, personal guidance, and kabbalistic exegesis of the commandments (*Perush ha-Mitzvot*). The second letter instructs one on how to react in the case of a possessed woman:

> What He[25] told me about the evil spirit entering that woman in Turin: His Honor notified me of this matter and that he already followed the rabbi's instruction, but to no avail. . . . He did not notify me about what the signs are that it is spirit possession and not a case of madness. For the typical sign of a spirit is that its voice is heard, but not through the mouth, and its presence is felt in a swollen bodily part, such as the throat or the breast etc. Some of the spirits predict the future. In any case they [the exorcists] should try to light sulphur and direct the smoke into the nostrils, and if the spirit becomes angry they should add more and more [sulphur smoke], and say a biblical verse. And if this does not force it to identify itself by name, ten religious scholars should gather, including righteous persons, and the senior amongst them should take a ritual bath beforehand. All of them carry phylacteries on their heads. . . . I recall having given to Raba"kh [Rabbi Benjamin ha-Cohen, a disciple of Zacuto] an amulet of the aforementioned rabbi. They should write it while in a purified state, and hang it on her [the suffering woman] to benefit her. And if she does not heal after all this, let His Honor notify me if she had those specific signs [of possession, mentioned earlier] or if she tears her clothes, or her shape changes, or if one can detect red stripes in her eyes. Send all the details that can be delivered, and then I will know how to treat her . . . written in the month of Tammuz 1672.

The letter contains all the elements of the Safed version: the way to recognize the possession, the manner of ritual healing, the detection of an evil spirit by swelling of body parts, and xenoglossia. The ritual of exorcism includes reiteration of sacred formulae, the use of the magical power of the written and oral word, sulphur smoke, and the gathering of men around the woman's bed. Apparently this is a testimony to the transference of the Safedian and eastern Mediterranean traditions to the Italian Jewish context through the intermediary of kabbalists. This case therefore tends to confirm the claim of Gershom Scholem and those who followed him that Lurianic reincarnation theology laid the foundations for the acceptance of possession within Jewish culture as a phenomenon of distinct cultural significance.[26]

This is but a "local" or partial claim that fits into a comprehensive historiographic thesis proposed by Scholem. He says that Lurianic Kabbalah spread from Safed to major communities of the Jewish diaspora. This shift caused significant changes in ritual life and social reality. The Kabbalah was no longer an esoteric tradition, limited to small number of experts, but a source of social change.[27] The messianic movement of Shabbatai Zvi, which swept through the Jewish world, is of course the most blatant illustration. Lurianic theology presented God in terms of a crisis that could be healed and overcome by human religious activity. Sooner or later this theological activism was bound to get channeled into a politico-messianic phenomenon. One could ascribe a parallel phenomenological dynamic to the idea of reincarnation as a means of personalized relationship with the heavenly world and its eventual ritualistic transference to possession events.

This overarching claim does not stand to test for several reasons. The research of Idel has demonstrated that the writings of Rabbi Luria and his disciples were much less widely disseminated than was previously thought.[28] These texts are extremely complex and require long study before any practical implications can be drawn from them. It is doubtful to what extent they were accessible or available to the public. The kabbalists of Safed were very strict about keeping their secrets in esoteric circles and prevented the copying of the masters' manuscripts. Furthermore, the possessed persons described in Zacuto's letters were all women, as was true in most other cases as well. In a society where the accessibility of even basic holy texts to women was highly limited, it is very questionable to what extent the complex Lurianic theological constructions—and their derivative concepts of reincarnation—could be relevant to female possession.

The spread of Kabbalah in Italy during the sixteenth century, in the Cordoverian rather then the Lurianic variation, does not provide a sufficient motive for the growing interest in possession. The first Italian case (1575), described in the book *Chain of Tradition*, was roughly contemporary to similar stories in Safed (1571 and onward) and the eastern Mediterranean. But a century would pass before the important Italian kabbalist rabbis showed interest or involvement in possession and its cure. How are we to reckon the passage of these four generations, a hundred years during which Lurianic theology was increasingly taught and studied yet produced no activity in either staging or documenting exorcisms? Is it not an act of historiographic arbitrariness to suggest a direct line of influence between Safed and Italy? Should the local context not be more significant for understanding the process of reception and legitimation of the exorcism ritual?

On further examination, Zacuto's letters demonstrate even more about the gap between the Safedian and Italian possession traditions in the matter of diagnosis and treatment and the cultural significance they carry. The basic distinction to be made in cases of improper female deportment is: Is this possession or insanity? ("He did not notify me about what the signs are that it is a spirit possession and not a case of madness.") This distinction is shared by both physicians and churchmen practicing exorcism.[29] The debate in seventeenth-century Italian Christian society about this issue clearly illustrates how blurred the border between insanity (as understood by contemporaries) and possession was. One could easily turn into the other. But insanity leads to improper deportment of the private or personal character, and therefore the public interest in it decreased. Possession, on the other hand, blurs the border between human identity and divine powers, and hence might serve as a source of personal inspiration and religious propaganda for the entire community.

The fear of its uncontrolled use enlivened the debates about the validity of verbal expressions made during possession or the ability of the religious establishments—Catholic or Protestant—to use possessions as a reliable source for propaganda. Physicians (males, of course), who strengthened their professional monopoly at the expense of women healers, claimed to have authority in this issue. They are the ones who should distinguish between possession, a phenomenon of the sacred domain, and illness or insanity, which would fall within their professional capacity. Church exorcists in Italy often described their activities in terms of cure and healing. They treated the soul the same way a physician treats the human body. Since the distinctions between body and soul were so unclear, physicians and exorcists competed at times over the same patients.

The letters of Zacuto mention similar suspicions about the cultural value of these bizarre acts. Unlike contemporaneous eastern Mediterranean possession stories, there is little interest here in any didactic message behind the scene. The woman mentions no sins or infractions of religious commandments, nor does she repent of her behavior. The narrative is prosaic and accurate. Rabbi Benjamin ha-Cohen asks for the advice of his mentor and receives a sober answer. Possession is not a revelation or an apparition from above.

In another letter from the same year, dealing again with a female possession, the gap between the Italian tradition and the Safed model is clear. The description focuses on the external deportment of the woman and the modes of treatment:

> Moreover I pity this distinguished lady, whose unclearness of mind and confusion of thought you mentioned. I am afraid it is to be ascribed to some hidden spirit inside her. For the time being I can not expand on this matter, but as a start you should order an examination of all the mezuzot[30] on her doors. Warn her strongly against being in a state of anger. When her time of ritual bath comes, let her go to synagogue after her purification and pray and confess, and then let others open a scroll of the Holy Law[31] for her. She should look with great care and concentration at the holy Names in the Scripture, and she should exert herself to incise these names [in her memory] as she saw them in the Holy Scripture. If any case of confusion of thoughts should occur, she should say the verse "Satan, God will rebuke you," and in mentioning God she will concentrate on the Most Holy Name.[32] If all these methods fail to help her, order [Rabbi Benjamin ha-Cohen, the addressee of the letter] to examine her with sulphur over fire, as I have already informed you, and thus we shall know if a spirit is inside her. May God have compassion on her.[33]

Zacuto alludes to well-known methods of possession treatment: the use of holy names and examination with sulphur smoke to assure that the woman is not an impostor. But these are the most extreme methods, to be implemented only when more basic ones are found ineffective. One of them—looking intensely at holy names and inscribing their visual pattern on the memory—is a well-known mystical technique among Jewish men. Here it is transferred from the masculine to the feminine realm. This woman, who in normal circumstances would have no access to the Torah scroll and whose skill in reading the Hebrew language was probably more limited than that of most men, is placed before the most sacred object in Jewish tradition. In this situation she is supposed to practice a visual technique reserved until this very moment for a limited number of men, viz., the inscription of holy names in the memory. The visual praxis is the basic mode of healing, and only after its failure ("If all these methods fail to help her . . .") is it advisable to revert to other, more drastic physical means known from the Safed tradition ("order to examine her with sulphur over fire").

The focus of the healing process, then, was transferred from the physical to the psychological realm. Again, this fits well into the Italian Christian milieu. Baroque religiosity during the time of the Counter-Reformation placed much emphasis on the visual, whether in such popular religious contexts as pious brotherhoods or in home rituals.[34] The "Spiritual Exercises" of Ignatius of Loyola are but one illustration of the way every believing Christian was to visualize a familiar surrounding where he would find himself next to Christ, sharing his suffering, and consequently improve his faith and religious consciousness. Artistic works and architectural constructions were specifically created to enable believers to implement this mystical technique.[35] The visualization of holy names recommended by Zacuto may relate to this baroque religious atmosphere.

I mentioned before that the acceptance of possession as a meaningful phenomenon and its establishment as part of the cultural network, and similarly the increase in cases of exorcism, are typical developments during states of crisis regarding basic beliefs and conceptions. If this is so, in response to what crisis or historical challenge should we attribute the growing interest in possession among Italian Jewish communities? These are very murky waters. Might it be that the transition to life within ghetto walls, and the consequent creation of an overcrowded society, bred a need for emotional liberation? It seems again that this can only partially explain the phenomenon, since the earliest documented cases occur in Ferrara in 1575 and 1577, before the establishment of the local ghetto. Most of the other cases occurred in the last third of the seventeenth century, when the majority of Jewish communities had already lived in ghettos for a long period.

I would like to suggest that the increasing interest in possession relates to three essential elements: (1) conceptions of the body and the attempt to stabilize normality by bodily means; (2) the power of ritual; and (3) the gender issue. These three aspects are indistinguishably interwoven in the theatrical scene of exorcism. Possession in Italian Jewish communities during the early modern period turns out to function as a key to perspective on basic aspects of collective life.

The body is the hidden, yet central, "hero" of possession. Signs of the entrance of alien spirits are all manifested on the physical plane: swelling of body parts, xenoglossia, and "strange acts." The healing ritual, as it is described in detail in Italian Christian cases and in Zacuto's letters, occurred in a theatrical arena of dialogue between the exorcist and the alien spirit. This dialogue turned increasingly into a confrontation as the moment of expulsion was approaching. In the middle lay the patient's body, upon which the active and at times violent means of healing were used in front of growing number of spectators. From the Italian Jewish versions it is unclear weather the ritual took place in the patient's home or elsewhere (perhaps the synagogue).

The body and its reshaping became one of the central issues of interest in Italy starting from the mid-sixteenth century.[36] Since external behavior was thought to reflect inner "movements of the soul" or to project personal characteristics, the body turned out to be a major target or object of edification. This was part of a comprehensive "civilizing process" taking place in Europe, in which Italian Jewish society had a unique role as well. Civility meant first and foremost a reworking of everyday acts (walking, sitting, talking), common gestures, and social activities (praying, eating). The refinements of the body and its outer manifestations would consequently cause the ennoblement of the spirit. Hence, daily comportment was increasingly subject to attention, control, and manipulation.[37] Zacuto's letters and his literary activity are only one further aspect of the increasingly intense inspection of the private domain, including bodily deportment.

Rituals—both the creation of new ones and the interpretation of old ones—attracted most of Zacuto's attention. The reader of his works, particularly those still in manuscript, will readily notice that they are little occupied with classical theological issues and mostly deal with the interpretation of practical religious commandments. Zacuto himself was one of the central contributors to the re-creation of ritual frameworks of the pietistic confraternities, the invention of penitential prayers concerning the sin of masturbation (*Tikkun Shovavim*), and the development of other, similar prayers. Indeed, the Kabbalah, according to Robert Bonfil, was a central agent of change and modernization in Italian Jewish communities, not because of its theological or theosophical novelties, but rather because of the ritual restructuring and renovation it caused.[38]

Gender issues were essential to possession. In contemporary Christian society most of the patients were women, children, and bachelors, or recently married people. Their inferior status in the public domain and family life fueled the possession crisis. In the Jewish context as well, possession put at women's disposal a legitimate mechanism for the expression of personal distress, typically represented by a strange voice and an alien identity. This mechanism is all the more important because, as mentioned earlier, the Jewish context did not offer any formal institutions for the expression of unique feminine religious needs in the same way that the Catholic Church did; women like St. Catherine or Humiliana dei Cerchi could enjoy a certain religious status in urban Christian neighborhoods.[39] At the same time, Jewish society exposed the inferiority of Italian Jewish women in public space with respect to men. Whether the exorcism was conducted in the synagogue, at home, or some other place, the woman was surrounded by a masculine circle, inspecting and touching her body. Women's supposed virtue and modesty (*Tzniut*)—such central values in their identity and status—had to be suspended during long exorcism rituals. The boundaries crossed for the sake of therapeutic needs were clearly gender boundaries.

One of the preparations required before the confrontation with the possessing spirit is personal confession ("let her go to synagogue . . . and pray and confess, and then let others open a scroll of the Holy Law for her"). I have demonstrated elsewhere the significance of the spread of confession and its institutionalization in Italian Jewish communities during the seventeenth century.[40] Giovanni Romeo, in his recent and detailed study, has illustrated the convergence of confession and exorcism functions.[41] The ability to heal possessed women was intimately related to their confidence and acquaintance with their confessors-cum-exorcists. Confession on a regular basis, entailing intimate exposure of events and sentiments, was to a great extent a feminine matter. As in the Christian context, the Jewish woman was probably required to deliver a detailed and personal confession, after which her body would be exposed to physical manipulations.

Exorcism stories of the Safedian type were shaped in didactic form, very much like the Exemplary Literature in Europe. Thus they tended to evolve in the fashion of popular stories: distress/challenge, confrontation, solution. The solution, or the "happy ending," returns the hero to his previous state of life and erases the stressful situations from his (or better, her) consciousness. The alien spirit is not completely alien—it carries a name and personal identity, and it has a defined place in the Jewish cultural milieu. Male values are reconfirmed and legitimized, since the patient and the spirit eventually accept the exorcist's authority.

Possession cases in Italy are not presented as narratives but as "particular cases." Therefore the didactic element is only secondary. The confrontation between the patient and the exorcist exudes a constant tension—still unresolved after the exorcism—between men and women, between husbands and wives. The cases do not terminate in happy endings but always remain pending, waiting to be resolved. The reader of these stories remains in doubt whether the spirit was indeed exorcised once and for all.

It is not unlikely that the encounter with alien spirits diverted the woman from the direction of her former life, never to return to her previous social identity.[42] Anthropologists have occupied themselves little with the question of what happens to possessed women after the public rituals of healing are terminated and the collective interest in their eccentric acts subsides. The comparative evidence provided by Lewis suggest that return to previous "normal" life is the exception. In a like manner, we may well ponder whether possession in Jewish communities was a semiformal attempt to carve out some religious independence and identity for women.

Zacuto's letters clearly testify to the central role of kabbalists in legitimizing possession within Italian Jewish communities. The first letter describes a futile attempt to heal a possessed woman by holy verses and meditation: "he already followed the rabbi's instruction, but to no avail." The rabbi in question, according to a later part of the same epistle, is Samson Bacchi.[43] Zacuto adopts some of the practices of this rabbi and passes them on to his disciple ha-Rabakh, Rabbi Benjamin ben Eliezer ha-Cohen.[44] The latter was the master of the famous rabbi and kabbalist Moses Hayyim Luzzatto (known as ha-Ramhal). Luzzatto and his disciples cultivated visionary activity using a technique of holy incarnations (*maggidim*), that is, angelic figures who would disclose heavenly secrets. The contact with these figures was described in erotic metaphors of infiltration into the human body.[45] The *maggid* is similar to the alien spirit in the act of penetration, obfuscating the lines between the human and the divine. We detect, then, a chain of four generations—that is, about hundred years—of occupation with possession or para-possession behavior, by persons who placed Kabbalah at the heart of their work and life.

Conclusion

Some questions have been left unresolved or in need of further discussion. They might well change the perspective offered here. Functional theories tend to explain, or explain away, religious phenomena in terms of social roles. They might underestimate the sacral dimensions of possession. Possession is above all a scene of contact with the world above, the sacred world, a source of inspiration-healing very much like other altered states of consciousness (ecstasies, trances, or shamanic voyages). The attempt to understand the introduction of possession into Jewish culture during the sixteenth century could not ignore this component, nor the unique kabbalistic contribution.

Legitimizing possession is one expression of the growing visibility and presence of magic in Jewish society during the early modern period.[46] The interest in magical practices was not limited to marginal figures but included central personalities as well, such as Zacuto. The role of Kabbalah in spreading magical practices, including conjurations, amulets, and bewitchment, is a little-studied phenomenon. It should be noted that while magic and "superstitions" were relegated to marginality by "enlightened" and church circles in Europe, in the Jewish milieu they held an increasingly respectable place.

The entrance of alien spirits into the body remained a numerically insignificant phenomenon.[47] Its importance lies not on the statistical plane, but in the mere acceptance of such a new cultural mechanism, and one connected with marginal deportment. It is a mechanism that deals dialectically with the exceptional by placing it at the center of collective interest. The marginal marks the new borders of social distinction. Possession enables a society to redefine basic territories of life in a way that verbal expression would fail to do, or would fail to find an audience for. The theatrical show—and the act of exorcism undoubtedly is a show—attracts many spectators, and visually represents the limits in dichotomization of sacred versus lay, authority versus submissiveness, and men versus women.

Notes

1. My gratitude goes to Dr. Yoni Garb for his beneficial remarks, and especially to Dr. Matt Goldish for his literary and editorial emendations. A manuscript containing this "Collection of Poems for Various Occasions," dating from the eighteenth century, is located in Moscow—Lenin Library, MS 654:254a.

2. On the change in mourning rituals in sixteenth-century Italy, see D. Owen Hughes, "Mourning Rites, Memory, and Civilization in Premodern Italy," in *Riti e rituali nelle società medievali*, ed. J. Chiffoleau, L. Martines, and A. Paravicini Bagliani (Spoleto: Centro Italiano di Studi Sull'alto Medioevo, 1994), 23–38.

3. For the apprehension that religious excitement or any lack of emotional restraint might lead to states of melancholy, or are derivative of this state, see M. Heyd, *'Be Sober and Reasonable': The Critique of Enthusiasm in the Seventeenth and Early Eighteenth Centuries* (Leiden: Brill, 1995).

4. E. R. Dodds, *The Greeks and the Irrational* (Berkeley: University of California Press, 1968).

5. The inspirational benefit of madness recurs in Plato. See the *Phaidros* and the *Apologia*.

6. See I. M. Lewis, *Ecstatic Religion: A Study of Shamanism and Spirit Possession* (London: Routledge, 1989); *Religion, Altered States of Consciousness, and Social Change*, ed. E. Bourguignon (Columbus: Ohio State University Press, 1973); *Altered States of Consciousness and Mental Health: A Cross-Cultural Perspective*, ed. C. Ward (Beverly Hills: SAGE Publications, 1989).

7. On the change in the social identity of shamans, see, for example, G. Samuel, *Civilized Shamans: Buddhism in Tibetan Societies* (Washington, D.C.: Smithsonian Institute Press, 1993).

8. For the church's position in regard to possession during the early modern period, see L. Roper, "Exorcism and the Theology of the Body," in idem, *Oedipus and the Devil: Witchcraft, Sexuality, and Religion in Early Modern Europe* (London: Routledge, 1994), 171–98; M. Sluhovsky, "A Divine Apparition or Demonic Possession? Female Agency and Church Authority in Demonic Possession in Sixteenth-Century France," *Sixteenth Century Journal* 27.4(1996): 1039–55. Both references include elaborate and recent bibliographies. See also S. Ferber, "The Demonic Possession of Marthe Brossier, France, 1598–1600," in *No Gods Except Me: Orthodoxy and Religious Practice in Europe, 1200–1600*, ed. Ch. Zika (Melbourne: University of Melbourne, History Department, 1991), 59–83.

9. See Roper, "Exorcism and the Theology of the Body," 174–80.

10. Clarke Garrett, *Spirit Possession and Popular Religion from the Camisards to the Shakers* (Baltimore: Johns Hopkins University Press, 1987), 2–34.

11. Giovanni Romeo, *Esorcisti, confessori e sessualità nell'Italia della Controriforma: A proposito di due casi modenesi del primo Seicento* (Florence: Sansoni, 1998); idem, *Inquisitori, esorcisti e streghe nell'Italia della Controriforma*, (Florence: Sansoni, 1990).

12. G. Levi, *Inheriting Power: The Story of an Exorcist* (Chicago: University of Chicago Press, 1988).

13. Romeo, "Confessori, donne e sessualità femminile," in *Esorcisti, confessori e sessualità*, 163–97.

14. G. Nigal, *Dybbuk Tales in Jewish Literature* (in Hebrew) (Jerusalem: Rubin Mass, 1984), 12–16. For a useful review of this book, see that by J. H. Chajes in *Kabbalah: Journal for the Study of Jewish Mystical Texts* 1(1996): 288–93. For the most recent and comprehensive study on Jewish possessions, see J. H. Chajes, "Spirit Possession and the Construction of Early Modern Jewish Religiosity" (Ph.D. diss., Yale University, 1999).

15. See Nigal, *Dybbuk Tales*, 12. Compare his findings with Ferber, "Possession of Marthe Brossier," 63–65; Sluhovsky, "Divine Apparition," 1045–46.

16. *Talmide Hakhamim* in Hebrew, that is, those who make the study of Jewish tradition their profession and personal commitment.

17. Nigal, *Dybbuk Tales*, 62–66. See also 67–72.

18. For a comprehensive perspective on the role of Italian Jewish communities in shaping early modern Jewish culture, see R. Bonfil, "The Jews of Venice: A Cultural Profile," in *The Jews of Early Modern Venice*, ed. R. C. Davis and B. Ravid (Baltimore: Johns Hopkins University Press, 2001), 169–90. There Bonfil states (169):

> The role of Italian Jewry in the making of the cultural profile of Early Modern European Jewry should not be underestimated in the light of the twentieth century tendency to be-

little its achievements. One should rather constantly keep in mind that at the dawn of the modern era, Italy was the home of the most numerous Jewish population in Christian Europe. Italy then played an active role of many faceted bridging between East and West. The harbor of Venice was the standard embarking and disembarking place for Jewish travelers between Western Christian Europe and the Eastern Ottoman Empire, which included the Land of Israel. This was of course the case not only for business trading between the two areas, but also for intellectual exchanges carried out by scholars seeking a satisfactory living and much more by the reputation of the Italian printing art which attracted authors and entrepreneurs to print their books in Venice, and from there to enter Jewish book-markets along the same itineraries followed by dealers trading in other kinds of goods.

19. On the belief in the magical powers of corpses of those who suffered a violent death, see Roper, "Exorcism and the Theology of the Body," 189–90.

20. On the Aramaic expression *Aprakdan*, see BT Berakhot 13b; Pesahim 108a (and Rashi there, s.v. "*ve-shema yakdim*"); Niddah 71a.

21. R. Weinstein, "'The Honorable Death Is Better than a Shameful Death': Honor Ethos, Family Life, and Community Control in Italian Jewish Society during the Late Middle Ages and the Early Modern Period" (in Hebrew), *Proceedings of the World Congress of Jewish Studies* 12.B(2000): 111–25.

22. On feminine religious activity in Italy during the sixteenth and seventeenth centuries, see G. Zarri, *Le sante vive: Profezie di corte e devozione femminile tra '400 e '500* (Turin: Rosenberg & Sellier, 1992); idem, "Dalla profezia alla disciplina (1450–1650)," in *Donne e fede: Santità e vita religiosa in Italia*, ed. L. Scarraffia and Ga. Zarri (Rome: Bari, 1994), 177–225; A. Jacobson Schutte, "'Piccole Donne,' 'Grandi Eroine': Santità femminile 'simulata' e 'vera' nell'Italia della prima età moderna," in ibid., 277–301. For a more comprehensive European context, see C. W. Bynum, "Corpo femminile e pratica religiosa nel tardo Medioevo," in ibid., 115–56; idem, *Fragmentation and Redemption: Essays on Gender and the Human Body in Medieval Religion* (New York: Zone Books, 1991); idem, *Holy Fast, Holy Feast* (Berkeley: University of California Press, 1987).

23. *Igrot ha-Ramaz* (Letters of Moses Zacuto) (Livorno, 1780). These letters were later printed in a book of central position in Lurrianic tradition, *Sha'ar ha-Gilgulim* of Rabbi Hayyim Vital (Premisl: n.p., 1875). See Nigal, *Dybbuk Tales*, 23, n. 117.

24. On epistolary activity in Italy, see R. Bonfil, *A Shining Speculum: Jewish Life in Italy during the Renaissance* (in Hebrew) (Jerusalem: Magnes Press, 1994), 183–84; R. Weinstein, "Marriage Ritual among the Italian Jews: A Chapter in Social History and History of Mentalities" (in Hebrew) (Ph.D. diss., Hebrew University of Jerusalem, 1996), 19–21 (forthcoming in Brill's Series in Jewish Studies).

25. "He" is a respectable mode of third-person address, much like the Italian "Lei."

26. *Hebrew Encyclopedia* (in Hebrew), s.v. "Dibbuk," by G. Scholem; Nigal, *Dybbuk Tales*, 16.

27. G. Scholem, *Sabbatai Ṣevi: The Mystical Messiah, 1626–1676* (Princeton: Princeton University Press, 1973).

28. M. Idel, "The Expansion of Lurianic Kabbalah," (in Hebrew), *Peamim* 44 (1990): 5–30.

29. On the distinction between possession and insanity, see the books of G. Romeo cited above; D. P. Walker, *Unclean Spirits: Possession and Exorcism in France and England in the Late Sixteenth and Early Seventeenth Centuries* (Philadelphia: University of Pennsylvania Press, 1981), 10–11.

30. Mezuzah (mezuzot in plural) is a small container attached to the entrance of every room containing certain biblical verses written on a small scroll.

31. Torah scroll (*Sefer Torah* in Hebrew), that is, the Pentateuch written on a large scroll from which the biblical text is read in synagogue during certain ritual events.

32. The Tetragrammaton, known as the "Name of Being."

33. *Igrot ha-Ramaz*, 24b, a letter to Benjamin ha-Cohen dating from 1672.

34. On the visual element in baroque religion, see Ch. Poletto, *Art et pouvoir à l'âge Baroque: Crise mystique et crise esthétique aux xvie et xviie siècles* (Paris: L'Harmattan, 1990); M. Praz, *Studies in Seventeenth-Century Imagery* (Rome: Ed. di Storia e Letteratura, 1964); N. Bryson, *Word and Image: French Painting of the Ancien Regime* (Cambridge: Cambridge University Press, 1981), 1–28. In contemporary philosophical discourse the visual element was sometimes perceived as more significant than the verbal for the understanding of reality. See A.-El. Spica, *Symbolique humaniste et emblématique: L'évolution et les genres (1580–1700)* (Paris: H. Champion,1996).

35. D. Freedberg, *The Power of Images: Studies in the History and Theory of Response* (Chicago: University of Chicago Press, 1989), 192–99.

36. On the control of body and sexuality in Italian Jewish communities, see Weinstein, "Marriage Ritual," 306–25. I am currently devoting a comprehensive research to these issues, supported by the Israeli National Academy for Sciences and Humanities. The matter has some repercussions in the work of Ramaz. See *Igrot ha-Ramaz*, letters 9, 12, 13, and 27; and idem, *Tofta Aruch* (Hell in Order) (Josepef: n.p., 1882), cantos 145–46, 172.

37. R. Weinstein, "What Did Little Samuel Read in His Notebook? Jewish Education in Italy during the Catholic Reformation Period" (in Hebrew), *Italia: Studi e ricerche sulla storia la cultura e la letteratura degli Ebrei* (forthcoming).

38. R. Bonfil, "Changing Mentalities of Italian Jews between the Periods of the Renaissance and the Baroque," *Italia: Studi e ricerche sulla storia e la cultura e la letteratura degli Ebrei* 11(1994): 61–79. For a recent debate, see idem, "A Cultural Profile." He states that:

the resulting restructuring of the references to talmudism engendered a revisiting of the entire structure through compound mediations in which kabbalah would be particularly instrumental. The story of this peculiar development has already been told in some detail elsewhere.... Suffice it to say that the entire range of the devotional ritual was deeply reformed—this was indeed the first radical reform of Judaism in Modern Times. It affected the prayer book, the customary way of performing age old religious precepts, interpreting the Biblical text and exposing it in public preaching, and so on and so forth.... The confraternities' activities, such as coffee breaks during midnight gatherings, solving intricate enigmas in which erudition, not just confined to the traditional talmudism but also to any other kind of profane knowledge, provided the tool for sociocultural prominence, staging theater shows, listening to music, and so on and so forth.

39. On possession as a feminine phenomenon, see Sluhovsky, "Divine Apparition," 1050–55 and references there.

40. R. Weinstein, "'Segregatos non autem eiectos' (Segregated Yet Not Ejected): Jews and Christians in Italian Cities during the Catholic Reformation" (in Hebrew), in *Being Different: Minorities, Aliens, and Outsiders in History*, ed. Shulamit Volkov (Jerusalem: Shazar Center, 2000), 93–132, esp. 119–23.

41. Romeo, "Per la storia della confessione dei peccati nell'Italia della Controfirorma: La svolta del tardo Cinquecento," in *Esorcisti, confessori e sessualità*, 127–61.

42. Lewis, *Ecstatic Religion*, 36–37, 50–52, 61–69, 83–84, 141–42.

43. On Rabbi Samson Bacchi, see M. Mortara, *Indice alfabetico dei rabbini e scrittori israeliti di cose giudaiche in Italia* (Padua: F. Sacchetto, 1886), 5.

44. On Rabbi Benjamin ha-Cohen (Rabakh), see idem, 14.

45. On *maggidim* in Ramhal's circle and their usage of erotic metaphors, see I. Tishbi, "Ecstatic Notes of Rabbi Moses David Valle, the Messiah in Ramhal's Circle" (in Hebrew), in *Shlomo Pines Jubilee Volume* (Jerusalem: Hebrew University/Jewish National and University Library, 1990), 2:441–72.

46. On the growing extent of magic in European Jewish society during the early modern period, see M. Idel, "Judaism, Mysticism, and Magic" (in Hebrew) *Mada'e ha-Yahadut* 36(1996): 25–40. For the case of Italian Jewish communities, see R. Weinstein, "Medicina popolare e magia nella società ebraica in Italia (Ferrara 1641)," *Rassegna mensile di Israel* (forthcoming).

47. For other cases of possession in late-seventeenth-century Italy, see Nigal, *Dybbuk Tales*, 74, 88–89, 267; *Igrot ha-Ramaz*, letter 25.

Dybbuk and *Devekut* in the *Shivhe ha-Besht*: Toward a Phenomenology of Madness in Early Hasidism

ZVI MARK

One of the widespread explanations given in seventeenth- and eighteenth-century Jewish society for certain varieties of madness was the demonic account. Madness was understood as the result of a person's bodily possession by a spirit, shade, or departed soul. Phenomena that are today termed hysteria, schizophrenia, epilepsy, possessions of various sorts, or flagrant transgressions of social and religious norms all were considered well explained by demonic interpretations of spirit possession.[1] This understanding of madness is merely one aspect of a complete picture of reality in which demons play a central role. Physical diseases and numerous nonphysical occurrences were explained through the activities and presence of spirits.

This worldview had a direct effect on the thoughts and actions of people.[2] A belief in spirits and the use of magical means with which to manage them were not simply matters for common people, and it would be erroneous to describe them as folk beliefs that held sway solely among the lower classes. Rather, this was a view of reality that pervaded the thought of broad sectors among both the popular classes and the social and religious elites. Furthermore, the echoes of antagonism toward magical practice and the voices raised against *ba'ale shem* (wonder-workers; literally, "Masters of the Name") did not necessarily derive from a lack of belief in demons or from incredulity in the effectivity of the essential powers of magic. They rather came from other sources, including the suspicion of charlatans parading as *ba'ale shem* or negative moral attitudes toward the use of magical media, despite their possible effectiveness. The essential fact that demons exist was an obvious point, part of their picture and experience of reality.[3]

The understanding of madness as an evil spirit is not new to this period, nor is it unique to Jewish society. In the days of the Second Temple and the Talmud, we already find a concept of madness as a spirit inhering in people.[4] This view continues constantly, with different variations, throughout history.[5] Nonetheless, it seems that we may view the increase in reports of Jewish spirit possessions and exorcisms in eastern European writings from the seventeenth and eighteenth centuries, which occurred in the atmosphere of Hasidism,[6] to be evidence of the dominance this subject had in the Hasidic world. It is noteworthy that some claim these discussions are only a tiny fraction of "the historical reality of thousands of *dybbuk* [possessive spirit] cases which were brought before the Hasidic masters in each generation."[7]

The founder of Hasidism, too, Rabbi Israel Ba'al Shem Tov (the Besht), was, as his name indicates, a practicing *ba'al shem*. This affected his image of himself, his image in the eyes of others, and the formative image of Hasidic leadership in future generations.[8] The comprehension of madness as the effect of a *dybbuk* caused the *ba'al shem* (who is occupied with the manipulation of divine names) to view spells and exorcisms as the central means for treating the insane. The Ba'al Shem Tov, like other *ba'ale shem*, dedicated a considerable amount of effort and skill to the struggle against demonic activity and the defense against fiendish spirits, since madness was one of the most common problems he had to deal with as a *ba'al shem*.[9] We find masters among future generations of Hasidism, as well, who follow the Besht both in their understanding of the spiritual cause of madness and in their methods of treating mad individuals.[10]

The connection between *dybbuk* and *devekut* (spiritual attachment to God) is a matter of particular interest in Hasidism. Clarification of the relationship between these two phenomena necessitates the examination of further background concerning the place of *devekut* in early Hasidism. I will demonstrate in the following discussion that the central place occupied by *devekut* in the world of the Besht derives not only from his mystical universe but also from his methods as a magician, so that any description of *devekut* that does not touch upon its integral part in the magical cosmos of the Besht is incomplete.

I must emphasize at this point that in what follows I am not attempting to offer a full treatment of the place and nature of *devekut* in Hasidism or the world of the Besht. I wish rather to stress a particular aspect within this broad subject. I will focus on the place of madness and the *dybbuk* in the work *Shivhe ha-Besht* (In Praise of the Ba'al Shem Tov). It will be my assumption that the attitude toward madness found in these stories reflects and confirms widely held views among the Hasidim, and that at the same time, this book was itself instrumental in forming the relationship found in Hasidism between madness, *dybbuks*, and prophecy.[11] I believe that studying the place of madness in *Shivhe ha-Besht* and in Hasidism can serve as an outstanding benchmark for the history of madness in Jewish culture.

This examination of *Shivhe ha-Besht* is undertaken with an awareness of the various layers and sources integrated in the makeup of the work, its many variants, and the problems involved in using *Shivhe ha-Besht* as a historical source.[12] At the same time, however, it must be remembered that such care ought not to detract from its importance as a reflection of the image of the Besht in the eyes of Hasidim in the period when it was composed and printed and as a formative force in creating his image for Hasidim in subsequent generations.

Madness in the *Shivhe ha-Besht*

The Author's Introduction to Shivhe ha-Besht *and* Shivhe ha-Besht *as a Substitute for the Insane*

In the author's preface to *Shivhe ha-Besht*, the author, R. Dov Baer of Linits, explains his purpose in composing the book.

> I said to myself, Let me explain *with the roll of a book which is prescribed for me* [Ps. 40:8] so that the reader will not question my decision or wonder what brought me to write meaningless narratives. . . . And to the scholars of my nation I reveal only a small part. . . . I myself have noticed as well that in the time between my youth and my old age every day miracles have become fewer and marvels have begun to disappear. This happens because of our many sins. In earlier days when people revived after lying in a coma, called a *"hiner bet,"* close to death, they used to tell about the awesome things they had seen in the upper world. . . . In his days there were also the insane who injured themselves with stones during the reading of the Torah, and who used to reveal people's sins to them and to tell them which of their sins would cause their soul to wander restlessly. I know that in my youth in the village where I studied with a teacher, poor people once came to the *heder* [elementary school room] and were given a meal. Among them there was a woman possessed by an evil spirit, but they did not realize it. The teacher began to study the portion of the Torah with the children, but when he had recited two or three verses the evil spirit threw the woman down, and her husband came and asked the teacher to stop his instruction because the contaminated spirit could not stand anything holy. When he stopped teaching she rose and sat at her

place. Because of all these things, many repented and the faith in the heart of each Jew was strengthened. Now, because of our many sins, the number of pious people is lessened. Therefore, I was careful to write down all the awesome things that I heard from truthful people. . . . I wrote it down as a remembrance for my children and their children, so that it would be a reminder for them and for all who cling to God, blessed be He and His Torah, to strengthen their faith in God and His Torah and in the *Tzaddikim* [righteous ones], and so they would see how His Torah purifies the souls of its students so that a man can reach higher stages. . . . *Telling the praises of the Lord, and His strength, and His wondrous works that He [hath done]. (For He established a testimony in Jacob, and appointed a law in Israel, which He commanded our fathers, that they should make them known to their children; that the generation to come might know them.) A watcher and a holy one came down from heaven* [Ps. 78:4–6; Dan. 4:10]. . . . The souls of the pious ones, who together are the soul of the light of the world, the holy light. They are Rabbi Israel Besht and his companions.[13]

According to the statement of the author, the purpose of writing *Shivhe ha-Besht* was not to attract people to Hasidism by glorifying the image of its founder, nor was it intended as a tool for polemics and explanation on the background of arguments with *mitnaggedim* (opponents of Hasidism) or *maskilim* (adherents of the Jewish Enlightenment). Its avowed intent was rather to give succor among the difficulties that had arisen in his generation but had not existed in earlier generations.

In the past there were phenomena that strengthened the faith in people's hearts. There had been the insane into whom spirits entered so that they knew with astounding clarity matters that were hidden from the eyes of ordinary people. These mad ones were able to recount the transgressions that had been committed unbeknownst to any, or the sins of people committed during previous manifestations of their souls. A further phenomenon that strengthened their credibility was the *hiner bet*, a type of trance or clinical death in which the soul of the living dead rises upward, and afterward, upon its return to this world, relates what it has seen in the upper regions.

These phenomena served to corroborate the existing religious norms and to strengthen faith. "And as a result of all these things, many people repented and the faith increased in the hearts of all the Jewish people."[14] It is noteworthy that the strengthening of faith was not a result of the success righteous men had in exorcisms or healing the insane but rather of the effect caused by encountering the insane themselves. The prophecies of the insane and the visions of the entranced were a sign and miracle confirming the existence of a supernal world as well as an example proving the workings of a system of reward and punishment. Mad people functioned as prophets with knowledge of the Higher Wisdom who publicly reproved transgressors.

However, "in our multitude of sins," as the author puts it, these phenomena have disappeared and the need arises for an alternative method to strengthen people's faith. That method is the writing of *Shivhe ha-Besht*. This being the case, the role of telling stories recounting the wonders of the Besht is presented as a replacement for certain cultural and religious functions formerly fulfilled by the insane.

In the first edition of *Shivhe ha-Besht* (Kapust, 1815), R. Dov Baer of Linits does not offer a single example, among all the cases of faith-strengthening events that have ceased to occur, that features a miracle performed by a righteous person or any description of a person possessing marvelous knowledge. Instead, all the stories concern either possessions by *dybbuks* and evil spirits or mad and entranced individuals who went to the upper worlds and returned. It is true that in the later Berditchev edition the following was added: "And now, because of our many sins, these phenomena have ceased, though indeed we have had righteous men in our generation who revealed secrets of the future, thereby strengthening belief in the Lord and the Torah. But now the numbers of the righteous too are dwindling."[15] This formulation also preserves the analogy between righteous people and the insane—and even strengthens it. The righteous man and the madman both know hidden things, and both help strengthen faith. This version, however, also presents the righteous as a mere appendix to the phenomena of the insane and *hiner bet*, the replacement for which R. Dov Baer of Linits intends to present in *Shivhe ha-Besht*.[16]

Additional "Praises"—Madness and Prophecy

A complete examination of Shivhe ha-Besht permits and even supports the thesis I presented concerning the analogy between the Besht and madmen, as well as the image of the Besht as a substitute figure for the specific role formerly filled by the insane. In the stories recounted in *Shivhe ha-Besht* we find the Besht described and characterized with the precise properties of the insane and *hiner bet*, by whose merit faith had previously been increased and many had repented. As a parallel to the insane we find in the Besht the quality called "amazing knowledge" (*ha-yedi'ah ha-mufla'ah*); and as a parallel to the pheomenon of the *hiner bet* we find heavenward journeys of the Ba'al Shem Tov's soul, along with his ability to see things in the upper world and receive messages during the soul's ascent. The implication is that revelations from the upper world, which had previously descended through the medium of the insane and those returned from the dead, would now come by way of the Besht. I will present a few tales through which this point will be clarified.

The relationship between madness and prophecy already emerges in the first tale concerning the early revelations of the Besht, which is cited in the "Writings."[17] Great importance is attached to the appearance of madness in this story, because the tales concerning his revelation are intended to present the unique qualities of the Besht, those by which he was revealed.

The First Tale of Revelation: The Story of a Madwoman

And now I will tell you the great events of which I heard from my father-in-law about how [the Besht] was revealed. He was then living in the town of _____. One time he came to a town where there was a madwoman who revealed to everyone his virtues and vices. When the Besht, may God bless his holy memory, came to the town, Rabbi Gershon asked the righteous rabbi, the head of the court of the holy community of Kuty, the righteous rabbi, the great light, our master and teacher, Moses, to take the Besht to this woman. Perhaps he would take to heart her reproaches and return to the proper path. And all of them went to her.

When the rabbi of the holy community of Kuty entered, she said: "Welcome to you who are holy and pure." She greeted each one according to his merits. The Besht came in last and when she saw him she said: "Welcome, Rabbi Israel," although he was still a young man. "Do you suppose that I am afraid of you?" she said to him. "Not in the least, since I know that you have been warned from heaven not to practice with holy names until you are thirty-six years old."

The Besht was very modest. And the people asked her: "What did you say?"

She repeated her words to them until the Besht chided her and said: "Be quiet. If not, I will appoint a court to release me from my vow of secrecy, and I shall exorcise you from this woman." She began to implore him, "I will be quiet." The Hasidim who accompanied him said that they would permit him to break his vow and urged him to exorcise the spirit from the woman. The Besht asked them not to grant him permission since the spirit was very dangerous, but they insisted. Then the Besht said to the spirit: "Look what you have done. My advice to you is to leave this woman without causing any difficulty and all of us will study on your behalf." And he asked the spirit for his name.

He answered: "I cannot reveal it before the others. Let the people leave here and I will reveal it to you." Otherwise, it would have shamed his children who were living in the town. When the people left, he revealed his name to the Besht. My father-in-law, blessed be his memory, also knew him. He had become a spirit only because he had mocked the Hasidim of that community. Then the spirit released himself from that woman without causing any trouble.

From that time on they did not let the Besht stay in that village.[18]

The madwoman in this story corresponds with the description of the insane in my introduction. She has exceptional knowledge, and it would appear that her words indeed aroused people to improve themselves, whether because of the content of her statements or the very fact that she had this astounding power to know things. The phenomenon of madness as it is represented in this story served to confirm preexisting religious values and to strengthen moral norms.

The ability of the Besht to know people's transgressions in the way that the madwoman knows them already appears in this story as a subtext—only the Besht, who heard the spirit's name, is able to know its sins. "He had become a spirit only because he had mocked the Hasidim of that community." This theme is more explicit in other tales from *Shivhe ha-Besht*. Despite the "similarity" between the Besht and the madwoman, or perhaps as a result of it, tension is created between them, which peaks when the Besht is asked to exorcise the spirit from within her—and thereby also to remove her special powers. The "positive" abilities of the madwoman are not represented as deriving from her closeness to God qua madwoman, but rather from "negative" powers. The spirit of a man who died in his transgressions has entered her, and it is this spirit that has turned her into both madwoman and prophet.

Neither Rabbi Moses nor Rabbi Gershon has any compunction about taking advantage of the madwoman's supernatural powers, despite the fact that their source is negative and their basis is in transgression.[19] The tale describes an organized procession of the chief rabbinical judge of Kuty, the judge Rabbi Gershon, his problematic brother-in-law, and an entourage of Hasidim who accompany them on their way to get help from the madwoman. However, because of the suffering experienced by one possessed, society attempts to help him or her be rid of the evil spirit that has entered, despite the advantages to be gained by having a spirit available.

With the author's preface framing the *Shivhe ha-Besht* as a sort of replacement for the insane in mind, the fact that the madwoman was the first to recognize the greatness of the Besht assumes special significance.

The story builds an image of the Besht as an individual with supernatural powers on the basis of his recognition as such by a figure already known to have special abilities. The tale can be interpreted as a passage of the crown of supernatural powers from the the insane to the Besht. This is accomplished through the device of an antipathy between the Besht and the prophetic madwoman—a confrontation that concludes with the victory of the Besht, wherein his supernatural powers are exposed, her powers are annulled, and she admits his superiority.

A comparison between this story and the first tale of revelation, as edited by the printer R. Israel Jaffe, offers further testimony to this view. In the first revelation tale according to Jaffe's version, R. Gershon brings the Besht to R. Moses of Kuty, rabbi of the community, in order "that he give him words of reproof. . . . And the rabbi was a very righteous man." The Besht comes to the rabbi, and the rabbi sees "a great light and rises before him"—he understands that the man standing in front of him is holy, and the Besht requests that he not reveal this. The structure of this tale of revelation parallels that which occurs before the madwoman. In both stories R. Gershon searches for some way to reprove his son-in-law, and in the end the individual before whom the Besht is brought comprehends his greatness, rather than any deficiency in him. In our story, the first tale of revelation as it appears in the arrangement of R. Dov Baer of Linits, R. Gershon and R. Moses of Kuty are unable to reprove the Besht, and they therefore bring him before the madwoman, who alone would be able to give him reproof. As it turns out, it is only she, and not the righteous rabbi, who is able to grasp the true nature of the Besht. On the other hand, R. Israel Jaffe places the righteous rabbi of Kuty in place of the madwoman, so that it is not the madwoman offering reproof but rather the rabbi. Nor is it the madwoman who exposes the true qualities of the Besht—it is again R. Moses, the "very righteous and great man," who is able to see the great light of the Besht and perceive his real character.

It would appear that R. Israel Jaffe was uncomfortable with the idea that the Besht should receive his first imprimatur as a great man at the hands of a prophetic madwoman; it must rather be from a righteous leader such as "the rabbi of our community." R. Jaffe's approach in this story corresponds to his overall method of editing *Shivhe ha-Besht*. His editing style clearly reveals an agenda: to shape the image of the Besht as a learned leader, expert in both exoteric and esoteric knowledge, while minimizing his persona as a magician and *ba'al shem*. Starkly opposed to this is the approach of Rabbi Dov Baer of Linits in the "Writings," which is to present the Besht as a *ba'al shem*, a powerful expert in the field of healing and one knowledgeable in the wisdom of practical Kabbalah.[20] This is the context of the first revelation tale according to the "Author": the greatness of the Besht is confirmed by a madwoman with supernatural powers; while in the version added by R. Israel Jaffe, the approval and crowning come through a righteous and scholarly figure, R. Moses of Kuty. Further aspects of Jaffe's aims in shaping a different image of the Besht will be discussed below.

The parallel between the madwoman's ability to discern each person's sins and the story of R. Nahman of Kosov, who would communicate each disciple's transgressions and his penance, has already been pointed out by A. Rubenstein.[21] This parallel does more than strengthen the analogy between the image of the madwoman and the righteous individual—it also shows the superiority of the madwoman over the rabbi.[22] While the madwoman's prophecies are received willingly and people are even brought to her especially to be reproved, R. Nahman's reproofs elicit anger and criticism. "They were very annoyed with his prophecies because they had an agreement among them not to prophesy."[23] Later he is asked, "Why is it that you make prophecies?" R. Nahman answers these criticisms as follows: " 'I was no prophet, neither was I a prophet's son' " (Amos 7:14). R. Nahman goes on to explain at length that his "prophecy" is not a regular prophecy, but its source is rather a *kelippah* (husk), an evil spirit of a transgressor who comes to him in dreams and reveals the sins of the group of disciples. Thus R. Nahman of Kosov, like the madwoman, prophesies not from the power of a holy spirit but through an evil spirit appearing before him, just as the madwoman's knowledge comes from the evil spirit that possesses her. In this case, then, we do not find the righteous rabbi and the madwoman presented in contrast with each other, holy prophecy against prophecy from the evil side; rather, they are two prophets whose knowledge comes from the power of a transgressor's soul. Both use this sinning soul with the intention of provoking repentance and offering erring individuals a program of atonement for their sins. The story implies a paradox, whereby prophecy whose source is the spirit of holiness is "forbidden," while prophecy deriving from the evil power of the *kelippot* is "permitted," perhaps even desirable. Indeed, it would appear from the explanation of R. Nahman that before the group of disciples agreed (to ban prophecy), there were apparently some of them who prophesied through a holy spirit. Now, however, they have accepted upon themselves not to prophecy through the spirit of holiness; but prophecy through the power of evil *kelippot* is still "permissible." From this point of view, the prophecy of the insane is preferable to that of the righteous unless the rabbi too is prophesying through the power of the *kelippot*. This may help us to understand why R. Nahman thought his colleagues would be appeased by his explanation that his prophecies came through an (evil) spirit—it would otherwise appear that he had violated the agreement against prophesying. R. Nahman's defense, then, was that prophecy through the medium of the *kelippot* is not the same as ordinary prophecy vouchsafed by the holy spirit. The latter type necessarily infers a special closeness between the prophet and God, thereby implying his status is exalted over the other colleagues of the society. Certainly the instructions R. Nahman sent to each person recommending atonement for his particular sins strengthened the suspicion that he wished to raise himself and lead them on the basis of his prophetic powers. It was for this reason that R. Nahman explains that his amazing knowledge comes by means of a transgressing man's spirit, a *kelippah*. This type of prophecy was normally found among the insane and demoniacs, so there is no need to fear either an attempt to grab power or a violation of the agreement made between them. It is no honor or cause for haughtiness to prophecy in the manner of a mad person, nor is there any breach in the pact of the fellowship.

Dybbuk, Devekut, and Madness

From Madman to Saint

In addition to the structural parallel between the Besht and the insane, we discover that before his "revelation" the Besht was himself often described as or called a madman and a person lacking comprehension (*she-eno bar da'at*). We will see that these epithets were not mere insults; those who used them truly viewed him as mad. Moreover, the mad actions of the Besht were not a ruse designed to cover up his true greatness; they rather derived in an authentic way from his unique world, particularly when he was given over to a condition of *devekut*.

The brother-in-law of the Besht, R. Gershon of Kuty, urges his sister to divorce the Besht, explaining that he observes the Besht performing the acts of a madman.[24]

Even in the tale of the Besht's self-revelation to R. Moses of Kuty before his public revelation, as it appears in the Yiddish version of Koretz-Ostrog, R. Gershon is presented as one who views the Besht as a madman.[25] It is for this reason that he brings the Besht to R. Moses of Kuty, who, after speaking with the Besht, informs him that "in my opinion nothing improper [*hutz la-shitah*] will be done."[26] Elsewhere in the *Shivhe ha-Besht* Rabbi Jacob Joseph is quoted as saying that during a certain period the Besht indeed "spoke improperly [*hutz la-shitah*]," not as part of his disguise but rather from within a state of *devekut*.

> I heard from the rabbi of the holy community of Polonnoye [Rabbi Jacob Joseph] that because of his devotion [*devekuto*] the Besht could not communicate with people. His words lacked order [*mi-hutz la-shitah*; they were inappropriate]. His well-known rabbi had taught him to recite each day the chapter of *Happy are they that are upright in the way* [Ps. 119] and other special psalms. He revealed to him a way by which he would talk with people and continue his devotion. He used to recite these psalms every day.[27]

Thus the claims of R. Gershon and his concern that the Besht would act "improperly" were not unfounded. They were not leveled out of mockery of his boorish brother-in-law, nor even as a reaction to the disguise of the Besht. They came rather in response to the odd actions, a result of the *devekut* in which the Besht was immersed—a *devekut* that drove the Besht to act "improperly."

An additional example of this phenomenon can be found in the tale of R. Gershon's attempt to help the Besht by employing him as his wagon driver. When R. Gershon fell asleep in the wagon, the Besht was unable to keep control of the horses, and he "drove the horses into a marsh filled with mud and mire from which it was impossible to pull them free." R. Gershon feared to send his brother-in-law to the town for help lest "he wander wherever he pleased, since he did not account him a rational creature [*bar da'at*]."[28] In the Koretz-Ostrog version this lack of rationality is understood to be the result of the Ba'al Shem Tov's involvement in his pure thoughts.[29] The Besht, immersed in *devekut*, was unable at the same time to function as a normal human whose mind is on what he is doing. His brother-in-law observed him in this condition without an understanding of its cause and concluded that he was a madman incapable of rational thought.

On the basis of this story concerning the improper speech of the Besht, we can see that the difference between his earlier "mad" actions and his "normal" condition later derived not from his removal of the madman's mask he wore, but rather from the lesson he learned from his teacher about how to remain in a state of *devekut* without it being accompanied by improper behavior.

It may not be out of place here to note that this passage from possessed madman to holy man possessed of the holy spirit has a precedent in the biographical confession of R. Abraham Abulafia. There R. Abulafia reveals that in his youth he had visions and dreams from Satan, "And I went mad from what my eyes saw." Only after many years did he merit true visions. This is to say that R. Abulafia passed from an early period, in which he was "mad" and saw satanic visions, to a second period, in which he merited true revelations from the Holy Chamber. Here are his own words:

> When I was thirty-one years old, in the city of Barcelona, God woke me from my sleep and I studied Sefer Yetzirah with its commentaries, and the hand of God [rested] upon me, and I wrote some books of wisdom and wondrous books of prophecies. And my spirit was quickened within me, and the spirit of God came into my mouth, and a spirit of holiness moved about me, and I saw many awesome sights and wonders by means of these wonders and signs. And among them, there gathered around me jealous spirits, and I saw imaginary things and errors, and my thoughts were confused because I did not find which of my people would teach me the way by which I ought to go. Therefore I was like a blind man groping at noon for fifteen years, and the Satan [stood] by my right hand to accuse me. And I was crazy from the vision of my eyes which I saw, to fulfill the words of the Torah and to finish the second curse [of] the fifteen years in which God had graced me with some little knowledge, and God was with me to help me from the year [5000] to the year [50]45, to save me from every trouble. And at the beginning of the year "Elijah the Prophet" [5046, or 1286 C.E.), God favored me and brought me to his holy tabernacle.[30]

This comparison also raises the possibility that the Besht, too, early in his mystical journey, had not yet achieved complete control in his work with spirits and was thus "mad" at the time of his *devekut*. Only afterward, when he had learned from his teacher, did he return to normal behavior.

Other tales indicate that it was the revelation of the Besht that gave rise to a new *interpretation* of his mad actions rather than any change in his behavior itself. In the revelation tale that concludes the "Order of Geneology" in the name of "Our master and teacher, whose soul rests in the heavenly treasure-house," it is told that when the Hasidic community of the town of Kuty heard of the great light found in their midst, "they remembered all the times they had wondered at him, and that all was now good and straight."[31] In the Koretz-Ostrog Yiddish version it states that "Rabbi Israel used to make himself seem like a fool, and other things as well, and [now] all is well and straight."[32] In the printed version of Koretz-Ostrog, the Besht's revelation to Rabbi Judah Leib, "the Rebuker" of Polonnoye, is recounted.

> The Rebuker used to think him a madman, never paying attention to the movements he made in the manner of madmen. Then, however, the

time for his revelation had arrived. . . . When this occurred the Rebuker stood astounded and taken aback, greatly regretting that he had heretofore thought [the Besht] a madman. . . . "It is clear that he possessed the holy spirit [that is, divine inspiration], and I could therefore have learned from him."[33]

These tales reiterate the phenomenon we observed previously with reference to Rabbi Gershon. The Besht performed mad actions, and so long as his real value was not recognized it was assumed that his conduct was the result of madness. When his true greatness was recognized, however, it was understood that his actions, "which he made in the manner of madmen," were generated by his state of *devekut*, that "he possessed the holy spirit" rather than an evil one.

This image shift of the Besht, from madman to master of the holy spirit experiencing *devekut*, was possible only because of a preexisting belief that the external manifestations of *dybbuk* and *devekut* states are identical, since the phenomena themselves are similar.[34]

Devekut and Madness

In the various tales we have seen, there has been no specific attempt to explain the combination of madness and *devekut*; nor is there reference to the question of whether the apparent combination derives from strictly external symptoms or if these symptoms rather signify a more essential relationship as well. Indeed, a possessed person acts mad whether the spirit within is evil or holy. In works of Hasidic theory both before and after the *Shivhe ha-Besht*, we find mention of the affinity between *devekut* and madness. Among these is an explanation based on the understanding of madness in general as the result of *dybbuk* possession and the understanding of *devekut* as a situation in which the spirit (the holy spirit, or Shekhinah) rests on a person, turning the person into its mouthpiece by speaking from his or her throat. This approach had a profound impact on the nature of Hasidic prayer.[35]

This assumption suggests a substantive comparison between the condition of *devekut* and that of madness fomented by a *dybbuk*. In both cases the subject loses control and is taken over by a foreign existence that invades or resides within him or her, determining the person's actions. Both conditions are characterized by a disconnectedness from the surrounding environment, and in both situations descriptions repeatedly stress that it is the spirit rather than the person that speaks. This was at times determined not only from the content of the speech but also by the strange voice or style of locution issuing from the subject's throat.

> Occasionally, when the holy spark of the Shekhinah in the soul spreads, it actually speaks that which issues from [the subject's] mouth. It thus appears that he [the subject] is not speaking at all, but that the words exit his mouth of their own accord. This is a very high spiritual level. On the other hand, we see the opposite effect from the "Other [Evil] Side" among madmen.[36]

This adds another aspect to the analogy between the Besht and the insane, not with reference to the social functions they fulfill, but in the phenomenological resemblance between *devekut* and madness.

Let us return to *Shivhe ha-Besht*. Beyond the claim that the Besht's image was formed on the background of the phenomenon of the insane possessed by evil spirits, I wish to argue that this image was affected further by the polemical desire to fashion and exemplify an alternative to the Sabbatean prophets and as a reaction to the mass popular prophecies that occurred during the Sabbatean period. Many anti-Sabbateans did not deny the reality of Sabbatean prophecy, but rather saw these visionaries and popular prophets as people possessed by evil spirits or as mad. The presentation of the Besht as an alternative to the insane and other forms of prophecy incorporates his image as the *proper* example of spirit inspiration and prophecy—that which come out of *devekut* with the holy spirit, not out of *devekut* with evil spirits or madness, like that of Shabbatai Zvi and commonly in the Sabbatean period (see below). I will open with a description of Shabbatai Zvi's madness and the prophetical phenomena connected with Sabbateanism.

The Madness of Shabbatai Zvi and His Prophets

In *Shivhe ha-Besht* we saw the process undergone by the founder of Hasidism: from being taken as an insane fool who does bizarre and improper things to being an esteemed religious figure possessing inspiration and the holy spirit. We further observed that the selfsame actions that had previously been taken as evidence of his madness turned, after the Besht's revelation, into proof of the holy spirit present in him. A parallel process is found in the image of Shabbatai Zvi. He too began with the reputation of a madman, ill and foolish, who acted outlandishly. Only after his revelation was a new interpretation given to his mad behavior and mood swings. These were still considered "strange actions," and the reasons for his depression remained unclear, but they were nevertheless cast as proof of his exalted soul and messianic identity, becoming an important factor in the theology and development of the Sabbatean movement. Similarly, the tension between the two alternatives, holy spirit versus evil spirit or *devekut* versus *dybbuk*, remains clearly visible throughout the annals of the Sabbatean movement, both in attitudes toward Shabbatai Zvi himself and his major prophets and in views of popular Sabbatean prophecy. It appears that this precedent had a certain influence on the acceptance and image of the Besht, which will be explored below. I will first offer a basis for what has been said thus far.

The First Period: Shabbatai Zvi as Madman

Many sources indicate that those of Shabbatai Zvi's generation "spoke of him as of a madman, a fool, or an idiot; even his followers admitted that his actions since adolescence caused him to be called thus."[37] Comments about Shabbatai such as "the man who was known his entire life as a fool and a madman"[38] are widespread in the literature of the period. The compass of Shabbatai's madness was broad and varied. It extended from problematic behavior in his relationships with women to individual acts distinguished by their peculiarity. His first and second marriages failed because he would not touch his wives, and after suits were filed against him in the rabbinical court he was forced to divorce them.[39] "One day he purchased an enormous fish, decorated it, and placed it in a cradle like a baby. The rabbis who heard of this incident were flabbergasted, and saddened about his obvious dementia."[40]

Shabbatai Zvi's Madness as Seen by Himself, His Circle, and His Believers

Gershom Scholem insisted that his picture of Shabbatai Zvi as a madman derived not only from the statements of his detractors but also from those of Shabbatai himself, members of his circle, and of some of the believers, who were aware of his madness and the "sickness" that came upon him. Scholem even expands on the decisive role Shabbatai's madness played in shaping the nature of the Sabbatean movement, with all its paradoxical tendencies.[41]

Scholem claims conclusively that Shabbatai's coming to Nathan of Gaza was the act of "a sick man to the doctor of souls, who knew the hidden roots of every soul and who could prescribe to each its appropriate *tikkun*. . . . Now, like the Hasidic devout of a later generation, he besought the doctor of souls to cure him. But the cure was a surprise. Nathan announced to him that his was a soul of a very high order which needed no *tiqqun*; he was, in fact, the messiah."[42]

At first Shabbatai objected and mocked this claim about his own messiahship. But Nathan would not relent, explaining and convincing Shabbatai that the depressions and euphorias that overcame him were not simply indicators of madness or bad spirits, but were rather evidence of the upheaval within his mind and great messianic soul. Eventually, Shabbatai adopted Nathan's explanation of his strange actions and assumed the role of messiah upon himself.[43] Thus, Nathan's announcement of Shabbatai as messiah did not occur *despite* the latter's bizarre and mad behavior, but *because* of it, as an explanation both for these acts and for his obviously odd personality, which swung between extreme depression and ecstatic states. It was exactly this mad behavior that brought Shabbatai to Nathan of Gaza, and it was Nathan's interpretation of these actions that constituted Shabbatai's first "coronation" as messiah.

An examination of Nathan's theological discourses similarly leads to the conclusion that he did not see Shabbatai's strange actions as a source of doubt or a difficulty for his acceptance as messiah, but rather as a corroborative element that would awaken people's awareness of Shabbatai's messianic and prophetic identity.[44]

The Planet Saturn, Madness, and Prophecy

Moshe Idel, in his article "Saturn the Planet and Shabbatai Zvi: A New Approach to Sabbateanism,"[45] argues that among the factors that contributed to Shabbatai's acceptance as prophet and messiah were certain kabbalistic and astrological conceptions concerning the planet Saturn (*Shabbatai*) that preceded the Sabbatean movement. In these sources Saturn is associated with a "prophetic faculty" and "the secret of the messiah." The connection between Saturn, spirit possession, and the messiah could bolster the claims of one whose name was Shabbatai to place himself in the role of messiah and prophet. For our purposes, it is important to examine other qualities perceived in the planet Saturn that are mentioned in these sources. Rabbi Joseph Shalom Ashkenazi writes that this planet

> emits the controlling power of evil spirits which paralyze people's limbs as in the case of epileptics, victims of the smaller and greater plague, and the mentally handicapped. The issue of the mentally handicapped is understood to refer to this world; but they have an added prophetic power, and the Sages of blessed memory state, "From the day the Temple was

destroyed prophecy has been granted to fools and small boys and girls," for which see Tractate Babba Batra.[46]

In another version, cited in *Sefer ha-Peli'ah*, we read:

> From Saturn comes power of those angels [*sarim*] which paralyze people's limbs as in the case of the deaf, the blind, the lame, the sightless [sic] and the mentally handicapped. He [who taught this] was asked: Master! Saturn receives [influence] from *AB"G YT"Tz* who is appointed over wisdom. How, then, can the mentally handicapped come from it? It is rather wise men who should come from it! He replied: They are mentally handicapped from matters of this world like him [Shabbatai Zvi], but they have an added prophetic power, and are wise in understanding the knowledge which is not of this world. This is the meaning of that which the Sages, of blessed memory, said: "Since the destruction of the Temple prophecy has been granted to fools and children."[47]

It is similarly stated in connection with Saturn, "With it are associated those who have become mad because of the loss of their mental faculty."[48] These qualities are brought together with the established relationship between Saturn and melancholy.[49]

Shabbatai Zvi's madness, his bizarre behavior and the "melancholy" that engulfed him, correspond perfectly with the qualities of Saturn, which controls fools and the insane, on the one hand, and prophets, on the other. Through this direction of inquiry as well, madness is revealed as a factor that does not detract from the prophet's status but rather augments it as further evidence of his prophetic and messianic identity. The process of transition from a madman to a prophet turns out to be consistent and logical, with roots to be found in kabbalistic sources.[50]

Tobias the physician, describing what is known to him about Shabbatai Zvi, writes:

> He was accomplished in all Torah wisdom, especially the knowledge of Kabbalah, in which he was extremely proficient. Despite all his wisdom and learning, however, he performed childish acts from the time of his youth, and people said that a spirit of foolishness entered him which caused boorish behavior. Ultimately people spoke ill of him, calling him a lunatic and a fool.[51]

This paradoxical image of Shabbatai Zvi, the learned scholar who is also a fool and madman, corresponds perfectly with the paradoxical duality of foolery and wisdom, idiocy and prophecy, associated with the powers of

Saturn. On the background of these sources, Shabbatai's madness could be understood as a natural component of his image as messiah and possessor of the holy spirit.

Shabbatai Zvi's Prophets in the Eyes of Believers and Opponents

The assumption that Shabbatai Zvi and his prophets were genuinely prophesying with a divine spirit upon them, and that this was not simply lies and trickery, can be found among his opponents as well. The argument was about how to understand this prophecy and, based on this, how to relate to it.

R. Jacob Emden (an opponent) describes Rabbi Tzadok, a Sabbatean prophet, according to what he had heard from his father, the Hakham Zvi.

> A certain man came from Lithuania called R. Tzadok, an unlearned lout, and prophesied that the messiah would come in the year 1695. He would let on with deceitful hints and secrets, and he was certainly possessed by a profane *dybbuk* like all his mad companions. . . . Testimony was given that he drank heavily and was unlearned, but this fool suddenly became a prophet and spiritual man, and he would tell *gematriot* [numerological interpretations] regarding kabbalistic matters.[52]

The epithet "mad" does not serve Shabbatai's detractors simply as an insult; it rather serves also as an explanation of how R. Tzadok and his companions were indeed able to prophesy. Similarly, the Hakham Zvi and his son, staunch opponents of Sabbateanism and its prophets, do not deny that the spirit of prophecy rested upon R. Tzadok, in the sense that he would utter words not of his own formation but rather from the power of a spirit that had entered him. Otherwise, how are we to understand that an ignorant commoner was suddenly able to utter "*gematriot* regarding kabbalistic matters"? A spirit must therefore rest on him, but it is a "spirit from the external realms." This explanation accounts for the other Sabbatean prophets as well, who would also become "mad" because of a *dybbuk* that entered them and caused them to prophesy.

Similar approaches were taken toward the Frankists and Dönmeh, which reveal the close similarity and the difficulty in distinguishing between evil spirits and *dybbuks*, on the one hand, and *devekut* through a holy spirit and prophecy, on the other. In this case, again, even the most vehement opponents did not deny the fact that a spirit rested on the person involved and revealed secrets to him. They claimed, however, that this spirit derived from the powers of evil: shades or ghosts. In the words of M. Balaban:

The Polish Jews used to say that the members of the Dönmeh sect were experts in magic; and that they were epileptics, who would fall to the ground and tell secrets and heresies, dressing themselves up in the words of Kabbalah and the language of the Zohar because they wanted to multiply signs and wonders. In a similar manner "shades and spirits" would appear to Frank as well, so that the empty vessel [ignoramus] suddenly turned into "a scholar who would tell secrets and Torah mysteries, but in the manner of an ignoramus. . . . And an evil spirit came upon him suddenly one night when he was standing with them [the disciples], and he was seized by an epileptic fit. He fell to the ground and revealed Torah secrets and mysteries. It was thus that he misled the heretics in Podolia."[53]

When we encounter the traces of indecision among the believers in Shabbatai Zvi concerning prophets, we learn that they too understood there to be two possibilities about how to perceive the phenomenon: either it was an evil spirit or shade, or it was a holy spirit and genuine prophecy. In a letter from R. Abraham ben Amram to R. Benjamin Duran, the former offers his impressions of a visit to the Sabbatean prophet Joseph ben Tzur:

> He answered me: "I do not know who speaks with me, neither do I myself see or speak. Rather, my lips move and the speech comes out of them, which produces the sounds I hear." I said to him: "With all this [power] are you not able to ask [questions of the spirit]?" He answered: "All my senses are extinguished, and I do not even know whether I am in heaven or on earth." He [said he] wished to open his eyes but was unable, as if there was lead upon them. . . . In short, I left there happy and well pleased because *it was clear to us that neither an evil spirit nor a shade was involved (may they remain far from us!)*, since he was in excellent possession of his senses, and all his words concerned God's unity, and he fasted constantly.[54]

In the eyes of both believers and opponents, the symptoms of *dybbuk* possession and prophecy were deemed similar. The distinction had to be established based on additional factors, such as the content of their words[55] and the righteousness of the speaker. The possibility of no prophecy at all is never raised here.

This attitude appears again in the letter fabricated by the Adrianople rabbis during their fight against Shabbatai Zvi, in which the latter is made to confess to his error, as follows.

> Whatever has befallen me in this matter, whether through myself or through those that prophesied about me, was nothing but a spirit of utter

folly or a spirit of some other kind, and the world will continue as usual until the true Redeemer will arise. Accordingly, everyone should remain in his house and engage in his affairs and should no longer be deceived by the words of the *sar*.[56]

Again, one finds in the epistle from the Venetian rabbis of 28 Iyar 5428 (12 April 1668) as follows:

> He suffered from a disease which affected his imagination. . . . He lost his faculties of imagination and description . . . claiming that they saw what they did not in fact see. . . . An evil spirit frightened him and a foolish spirit misled him to imagine to himself and to tell [others] of things which never occurred and never were. . . . It was neither a matter of rebellion nor betrayal [against rabbinic authority], but a loss of [proper] imagination with which this disaster was effected by him.[57]

We will conclude these examples with the description offered by R. Leib ben Oyzer of the Sabbatean prophet R. Moses, a story that offers an example of the qualities of the insane and prophets during the generations preceding Hasidism, and to which the author's introduction to *Shivhe ha-Besht* refers.

> Meanwhile R. Moses would begin to dance like a young man. In the middle of the dance he would fall to the ground like one who is stricken (God protect us!) with epilepsy. He would twitch for a moment and then begin to speak. . . . And all the prophecies of this R. Moses Saravel were proved true. And just as he was able to predict the future, so too did he know what had occurred in the past. I spoke with great men of the world [rabbis] who testified concerning this prophet R. Moses, that he had told them of their youthful transgressions of which they were indeed guilty, and gave them a *tikkun* [remedy] as well.[58]

Sabbateanism in the Author's Preface

With this background, when we return to the author's preface to *Shivhe ha-Besht*, his purposes in composing the work take on additional meaning; they now fit into a larger picture. In his preface, R. Dov Baer of Linits cites an incident that served as a buttress to faith:

> [There was] a man who had been lying in a coma [*hiner bet*] in the holy community of Bershad. It was in the time when the sect of Shabbatai Zvi,

may his name be blotted out, was stirring. That man was shown several places in the books in which some rabbis had erred and were almost led astray by that sect. He was ordered to tell them the exact meaning of those passages. In his days there were also the insane who injured themselves with stones during the reading of the Torah, and who used to reveal people's sins to them.[59]

This indicates that the days of the insane prophesying and the days of *hiner bet* were in fact the period of the rise of Sabbateanism. This specific example offered by the author teaches that the phenomenon of prophecy that flourished in the Sabbatean period included not only Sabbatean advocates but even opponents of the movement. R. Dov Baer notes that other incidents of the insane prophesying also occurred "in his days," that is, "in the time when the sect of Shabbatai Zvi . . . was stirring."[60] The author's negative attitude toward Sabbateanism is certain; nonetheless, we cannot ignore the clear fact that the phenomenon of mass prophecy, whether due to the *hiner bet*, madness, or epilepsy, occurred under the impact of Sabbateanism and the mass prophesying it aroused.[61]

Although the example of prophecy cited by the author was anti-Sabbatean, this is still an instance of prophecy based in negative sources. It is to offset this that the author presents the Besht, as the correct alternative to a prophesying madman seized by a *dybbuk*. It is this image of the Besht—the man of God whose soul rises in holiness to the upper worlds, who also knows the messiah's answer to the question "When will you come?", who knows secrets and hears heavenly decrees because he is in a state of *devekut* with his God—this is the image offered as an alternative to the outbreak of prophecy in the period of Sabbateanism. R. Dov Baer never says explicitly that the Besht is a substitute for Sabbatean prophecy. He does state outright, however, that the Besht can be an alternative for the bolstering of faith and fear of heaven, which was formerly available from the prophetic madmen and fainters of Sabbatean times who exposed the falsehood of Sabbatean claims. I am not arguing that R. Dov Baer saw the Besht primarily as a charismatic figure who entered this world in order to function as an alternative to the Sabbatean leadership. I would maintain, however, that the Besht did fill this function as well.

The personality of the Besht communicated in the writings of R. Dov Baer follows these lines, formulating his image as a *ba'al shem* and wonder-worker who fathoms past and future, serving as a proper example of an exalted character and possessor of the holy spirit. His image, then, stands in contradistinction to other figures who indeed have amazing knowledge and supernatural powers that, however, derive from the evil side and the realm of the *kelippot*. These individuals are possessed by an evil spirit rather than a holy one, and are therefore now under the power of a *dybbuk*, the ghost of a dead sinner, rather than in a state of *devekut* with God.

An additional aspect pointing to the presence of Sabbateanism in the background of *Shivhe ha-Besht* and the world of the printer R. Israel Jaffe can be found through an examination of the work *Me'oreot Zvi*.

Me'oreot Zvi

Me'oreot Zvi (A Story of Dreams and End of Wonders) was the first historical romance written in Hebrew about Shabbatai Zvi. The work seems to have been composed by an anonymous *maskil* (advocate of the Jewish Enlightenment) in Galicia or Volhynia, and it was first published in 1814 by the Hasidic printer R. Israel Jaffe. It was published a second time by R. Israel Jaffe a year later in 1815—the same year he edited and printed *Shivhe ha-Besht*.[62] The book unfolds the life story of Shabbatai Zvi from a hostile point of view, denigrating him and his adherents. It makes no pretense of offering an accurate historical record; the author freely invents names, figures, and events as the literary need arises. Nevertheless, it is clear that there is some attempt to follow the actual historical occurrences. Despite the highly questionable value of the book as a historical source,[63] it is nevertheless a fascinating literary document from which it is possible to learn much about the image of the Sabbateans and other matters.

The book assumes new dimensions of importance when discussing *Shivhe ha-Besht*, particularly the impact of Sabbateanism on the manner in which *Shivhe ha-Besht* was edited. It appears that in R. Israel Jaffe's editorial considerations regarding *Shivhe ha-Besht*, the work *Me'oreot Zvi* occupied a significant place, so that a close examination of the latter can shed light on the editing of the former. In appendix 1, "Shabbatai Zvi as a Spark of the Messiah," I will illustrate how *Me'oreot Zvi* may have served as a factor in R. Israel Jaffe's editorial decisions when printing the writings of R. Dov Baer of Linits.[64]

Dybbuk and *Devekut* in *Me'oreot Zvi*

The book *Me'oreot Zvi* is composed as a demonological commentary on the personalities of Shabbatai Zvi and his followers. Shabbatai is not presented as an ordinary charlatan, nor was his an ordinary attempt to extort power, honor, and money. Shabbatai was a magician with formidable spiritual powers who mobilized both pure and impure Names to rise into the upper worlds, where he became entangled with the powers of evil.[65] A precursor to this image of Shabbatai is mentioned in the book: R. Joseph della Reina, who had also become embroiled with the evil powers.[66] The success of Shabbatai and the Sabbatean movement depended first on prophecy, spirit possession, fainting fits, and other supernatural revelatory phenomena that indicated the messianic reality of Shabbatai and his prophets,[67] and second on the tremendous desire of the people to be redeemed.[68]

The book is based on the essential kabbalistic assumption that God created the world in such a way that the forces of good and evil stand in a dialectic of parallel counterposition to each other. So, too, in the realm of prophecy: opposite every level of holy prophecy exists a parallel level of impure prophecy. The author places in the mouth of R. Jacob Hagiz an explanation of the prophecy of his student, Nathan of Gaza, that systematically explains all the existing types of prophecy in a clear structure of dialectical parallels.

> Know that the matter of prophecy itself can be divided into three categories. The first is the prophecy of all the [biblical] prophets . . . from the mouth of the Holy One, blessed be He, Himself, all of whose words are upheld and true. . . . The second is from the side of impurity . . . the words of whose prophets sometimes come true. These two sorts of prophecy do not require the extinguishing of the senses in their prophesying. . . . The third comes as a result of a holy or impure spirit enveloping a person. At the moment that the holy spirit comes upon him he faints, just as epileptics faint with their bodies bereft of sense; and it is heavy upon them like a weighty load. Following its indwelling, the spirit will speak from within him of past and future events in a prophetic manner. This, however, is no prophecy—it is rather a simple statement about some spiritual matter, since every spirit knows simple matters of the past and future. However, one should not depend on them concerning major issues of the past or future, since they sometimes lie and sometimes tell the truth. . . . Another matter which is called "appearance" [*hofa'ah*; *erleichtig*] occurs when a person closes his eyes and sees the soul within someone through his heart, by the light of God. He sees everything done in secret, all which occurred in the past along with all that will occur in the future, as if it occurred before him with his eyes open. This type, then, is divided into two categories: one is called appearance through the holy spirit . . . the other is through an impure chariot, which is what the priests of idolatry used. . . . There is another matter here, which is called "miracle working" by the masses. It is not in fact miraculous, but rather the invention of a person who knows the servants of the upper world

and their qualities, and adjures them to do some action on earth. This matter too can be divided into two categories: first, the sort done from the holy side; . . . second, from the impure side; i.e. he adjures a shade or false god or dangerous being or impure spirit to do something for him on earth. . . . And all those adjurations, both holy and impure, compel those forces to act against their will.[69]

In light of this understanding, one who stands before Shabbatai Zvi, Nathan of Gaza, and the other Sabbatean prophets must discern whether each of them is steeped in a holy or an impure spirit. The great difficulty lies in the fact that the multiplicity of prophetic phenomena exists both in the holy and profane realms.

In the terms central for our study, a person must decide: Is the prophet before him or her attached to a holy or an impure spirit? Is he experiencing *devekut*, or is he possessed by a *dybbuk*? External symptoms that the person is genuinely prophetic, that a spirit rests on him, will not suffice to decide. Supernatural powers, magical abilities, signs of ecstasy, and a heavenly spiritual presence are not decisive concerning the matters before him, since they are identical to the indications of ecstasy and prophecy fomented by impure spirits.

The Influence of *Me'oreot Zvi* on the Editing of *Shivhe ha-Besht*

R. Israel Jaffe, then, faced a very serious problem with the image of the Besht as it emerged from the writings of R. Dov Baer of Linits that he had before him and wished to publish. The Besht appears from the very beginning of the book as a powerful magician whose sanction is given him by a *dybbuk*-possessed madwoman and who is worryingly reminiscent of the popular Sabbatean prophets. As a *ba'al shem*, the Besht was in constant contact with demons, shades, and other dangerous spirits. Even in his great moments, in an ecstasy of soul elevation and *devekut* as they are described in *Shivhe ha-Besht*, there is much resemblance to the images of ecstasy of Sabbatean prophets as they are depicted in *Me'oreot Zvi*. For example, one finds in the *Me'oreot Zvi*: "In this year they prophesied, . . . and the manner was as follows. First the spirit in them would faint, and they would look like one attacked by epilepsy. They fell to the ground, sang some psalms, and then prophesied." Elsewhere it is reported: "And in the city of Gallipoli there were twenty-two tables full of his [Shabbatai's] prophets with him, eating of his largesse and constantly fainting to the ground, twitching with their hands and feet like epileptics, prophesying of him that he is their king, messiah, and redeemer."[70] In *Shivhe ha-Besht* it is revealed that at the time his soul would ascend on the eve of Yom Kippur,

> [The Besht] began to make terrible gestures, and he bent backwards until his head came close to his knees, and everyone feared that he would fall down. They wanted to hold and support him, but they were afraid to. They told it to Rabbi Ze'ev Kotses, of blessed memory, who came and looked at [the Besht's] face and motioned that they were not to touch him. His eyes bulged and he sounded like a slaughtered bull. He kept this up for about two hours.

Regarding the prayer of the Besht at another time it is related:

> The Besht trembled greatly as he always did while praying. Everyone who looked at the Besht while he was praying noticed this trembling. When Rabbi Abraham finished the repetition of the prayer, the Besht was still standing at his place and he did not go to the podium. Rabbi Wolf Kotses, the Hasid, looked at his face. He saw that it was burning like a torch. The eyes of the Besht were bulging and fixed straight ahead like those of someone dying, God forbid. Rabbi Ze'ev [Wolf] motioned to Rabbi Abraham and each gave his hand to the Besht and led him to the ark. He went with them and stood before the ark. He trembled for a long time and they had to postpone the reading of the Torah until he stopped trembling.[71]

In addition to all this, the Besht announces that Shabbatai Zvi possessed a messianic spark (see below, appendix 1).

What, then, differentiates between the Besht, as he appears in *Shivhe ha-Besht*, and the Sabbatean characters of *Me'oreot Zvi*? The tales of the Besht's revelation with which R. Dov Baer opens his writings could as well have been related of Nathan of Gaza or other Sabbatean prophets. His image as an ignoramus in the eyes of all who saw him, until the day he revealed himself as a master of supernatural powers, is a most problematic description for anyone who would read *Me'oreot Zvi* and *Shivhe ha-Besht* one after the other—it is identical with the descriptions of many Sabbatean prophets. The depiction of the powers and greatness of the Besht as a *ba'al shem* and magician is no answer to the question of what differentiates him from the Sabbateans. They, too, were magicians, and their leader, Shabbatai Zvi, was an archmagus. Even the emphasis on the Besht as an orphan raised grave doubts: whence did this foundling come? The question put forward about Shabbatai in *Me'oreot Zvi* is just as applicable here: how do we know he was holy from the time he was conceived?[72]

The juxtaposition of these books forced R. Israel Jaffe to edit *Shivhe ha-Besht* anew, organizing the opening in such a way that it would answer the difficulties raised by a comparison of *Shivhe ha-Besht* with events in *Me'oreot Zvi*. Indeed, R. Israel could be certain that a large number of his customers who would read the one had already read the other, which he himself had published the previous year. If not, they might well read the second edition of *Me'oreot Zvi*, which appeared the same year as *Shivhe ha-Besht*.

It is for this reason that the opening of *Shivhei ha-Besht*, as edited by R. Israel, presents the Besht as a child of righteous parents and the pupil of a faithful teacher who initiated him into the mystical secrets. The Besht is above all a scholar, a holy leader, one recognized by sages the likes of R. Moses of Kuty for the holy spirit within him and the light shining upon him. It is only after acquaintance is made with the positive persona of the Besht and the benign nature of his connections with the upper worlds that his power as a *ba'al shem*, knower of secrets, and master of supernatural abilities is extolled. R. Israel Jaffe had no intention of minimizing the image of the Besht as a magician and *ba'al shem*; rather, he hoped to lay down a foundation based on which these abilities would be understood to derive from his connection with the holy rather than the impure. His *devekut* must be perceived as *devekut* with God rather than with impure Names, and his connections with the upper worlds as one with the holy side rather than with the other, evil side.

A comparison between the method for achieving the holy spirit and prophecy among the righteous and the method used by Shabbatai Zvi and his prophets is cited by R. Zvi Hirsch of Zidechov in the name of his teacher as well as in the name of the Besht himself. He says:

> Thus I heard from my teacher of blessed memory. He said this about those students connected to the episode which occurred, the known sect which profaned the name of God in the days of the Rabbi Ta"Z [*Ture Zahav*; that is, R. David b. Samuel ha-Levi, author of the *Ture Zahav* (1586–1667)]. It occurred because he wanted to achieve an understanding of God and prophecy and the holy spirit through the unification of Names, but they did not evaluate their own moral condition, nor did they overcome their physical [desires]; thus they were not meritorious, and they did not safeguard themselves. They went with the wonders they achieved and stood by the knowledge of their uniqueness (the ass came and knocked down the lamp [BT Shabbat 116b]), without purifying their

physical selves. They drew supernal images before them which exist under the divine Chariot, and thereby the images overcame them; they had adulterous thoughts, God save them, and the known result occurred, mercy be upon us! Thus far were the words of my teacher. He also said in the name of the Besht, whose spirit rests in the uppermost hidden place, that these fools learned this wisdom without perspiring over it from the great awe and fear of heaven involved. For this reason they were overcome by the physical and this is how they came out.[73]

The descriptions of ecstasy and prophecy and the amazing powers of the Besht were a double-edged sword. Just as they could testify to his high spiritual level, so could they be understood as testimony of his attachment to the impure, as readers of R. Israel's recent edition of *Me'oreot Zvi* would well remember. It was therefore important and pressing to reedit *Shivhe ha-Besht* so as to set the matters in their proper order.

Implications of the *Devekut* Issue

Devekut, a central value in Hasidism and a key to understanding its uniqueness,[74] is generally studied as a peak in the world of the mystic, without addressing its magical context. The literature has usually regarded *devekut* as a mystical experience belonging to a value system and purposes far distant from the world of magic, and has thus caused a bifurcation between these realms, leaving the discussion of *devekut* only in its mystical context. The fact that the Besht himself was both a great mystic and a *ba'al shem* who supported himself by engaging in magic throughout his entire public life, has never shaken this assumption. It was merely cited as evidence of his complex character that such different worlds existed juxtaposed within him.[75] Moshe Idel's approach has been different. He describes Hasidic mysticism and the mystical life of the Besht as a composite of mystical experience and magical praxis, so that the magical and mystical ingredients intertwine to the point that Hasidic mysticism can not be considered independently of its magical elements.[76]

An examination of *Shivhe ha-Besht* yields a picture of the Ba'al Shem Tov's religious life that integrates the desire for and the ability to achieve *devekut* with the holy spirit. This capability is directly connected to abilities and methods used by him in his practice of healing and the exorcism of shades and *dybbuks*. *Devekut* and the holy spirit, as they are presented in *Shivhe ha-Besht* and elsewhere, are directly connected with the phenomena of the *dybbuk*, evil spirits, and madness. *Devekut* arises from the same sources as *dybbuks*, under the same view of reality that perceives direct contact with spiritual forces as a simple fact of existence. In this reality there are instances in which such spiritual forces, positive or negative, bond themselves to humans or possess them.[77]

This worldview corresponds with the reality depicted in the Lurianic Kabbalah. It is a picture in which a sharp dualism inheres between the forces of good and evil, with good and evil represented by parallel structures "one opposite the other."[78] The argument that in the Hasidic perception "the dualistic division between God and the world is entirely neutralized, and the battle between good and evil is confined strictly to the realm of human psychology,"[79] if it refers to the Beshtian view as well,[80] ignores the war of the Besht against evil, shades, and dangerous spirits by means of magic, as described fully in *Shivhe ha-Besht* and elsewhere. It would be difficult to explain this war as being "confined strictly to the realm of human psychology." It is similarly difficult to understand the claim that the Besht "rejected the existence of evil as an independent demonic being,"[81] once we are clearly aware of his activities as a *ba'al shem*.

Parallel to *devekut* with holiness, then, is a *devekut* with impurity; and parallel to the holy spirit that speaks through the throat of a person are evil spirits that possess a person and speak through him or her.[82] This parallel structure and dynamics yield a parallel for dealing with the phenomena of good and evil. The Besht, as a *ba'al shem* specializing in spells, Names, and charms, who used these to battle shades and exorcise *dybbuks*, was the same person who could mobilize the identical techniques for uplifting the soul and achieving mystical experience.[83] The outstanding document in this connection is the Ba'al Shem Tov's letter to his brother-in-law, R. Gershon of Kuty: "On Rosh Hashanah 5507 [autumn 1746] I cast a spell for uplifting the soul . . . strictly from what I learned there: three methods [connected with] charms and three divine Names. . . . And I thought that thereby the people of my age could arrive at my level and insights, that is, that they could uplift souls."[84] The use of Names and spells and the manipulation of their applied power—this is the practice of both magic and mysticism. Mystical and magical praxis are intertwined to build a unique mystical-magical world, whose most important characteristic is the very amalgamation of these two elements in one cosmos.[85]

It is no coincidence that in Hasidism, which puts *devekut* at the head of its value system,[86] we find the vast majority of *dybbuk* tales.[87] The Besht could have seen *devekut* as an immediate and achievable goal and raised it to the head of his list of values, not only out of adherence to immanent theological positions asserting that "no place is empty of Him [God]" but also based on the common view and sense of reality that a person encounters spiritual entities, both positive and negative, on a daily basis. In other words, the ability to come in contact with spirits, and their strong presence in this world, was more than a theological view—it was a reality of life experienced every day and highly familiar to the Besht in his role as a *ba'al shem*.[88]

States of consciousness similar to that of *dybbuk* possession, such as prophecy, ecstatic states, and the like, which occurred in Hasidism and are also ingredients in the composition called "Hasidic *devekut*," conjoined naturally with the contemporary worldview that recognized the frequency of possessive conditions in which the spirit speaks out of the throat of the victim. There was no reason why good spirits, the holy spirit, or the Shekhinah (Divine Presence) should not similarly be able to speak out of a person's throat. The phenomenological similarity depicted here between *dybbuk* and *devekut*, in the particular hues of the latter, undermines the widely accepted theory that "in 'pure' phenomenology magic and mysticism are found on opposite ends of the spectrum of religious events."[89] It rather places the two experiences on a common phenomenological base whose branches extend to various types of mystical-magical practice.

It should be clear that *devekut* in Hasidism and in the world of the Besht cannot be described only in terms of its relationship to magic; nor would I maintain that *devekut* in Hasidism is necessarily connected with possession states. On the other hand, I do argue that a full picture of the role played by *devekut* is early Hasidism and the world of the Besht would not be complete without an understanding of the close connection between *devekut* and *dybbuk*. Furthermore, the many types of *devekut* in Hasidism are not properly comprehended without taking into account the varieties of *devekut* connected with possession states.

On Madness—A Final Note

I noted above the special status of the insane in *Shivhe ha-Besht* and other sources, a status deriving from the phenomenological similarity between possession states and the trances typical of certain mystical experiences. Along with a recognition of the problematic standing of the insane and the need to try rescuing them from madness, the insane also merited honorary treatment as those who acted as mediums for spirits that adhered in them. The spirit was not merely an evil to battle and attempt to expel; it was also a representative of the upper world. The insane person acted perforce as a prophet and rebuker, as well as living proof to the truth of faith and the existence of a system of reward and punishment.

A number of important characteristics distinguishing states of madness from *devekut* states can be derived from the material cited. While the mystic, whether good or bad, brings upon himself trance or possession states the nature of which he willfully determines, the insane person and *dybbuk*-possessed neither cause nor desire their condition.[90] Possessions and trances[91] assail the insane and other victims against their will.[92] We find the most vehemently positive and negative evaluations in relation to those states people have brought upon themselves, whereas in unwilling possession cases evaluations tend to be less extreme, more ambivalent. The insane and those with *dybbuks* are possessed by spirits against their will— they are forced participants. The fact that the spirit inhering in them is evil, or the ghost of a dead sinner, does not necessarily mean that the *dybbuk*-possessed themselves are sinners or criminals. Although the very possibility that a spirit was able to enter them indicates some imperfection, this could be very minor and marginal, not casting any aspersions on their personalities overall.

Even if entry into a certain state of consciousness is willful, and even if this state is described as *devekut* with the holy spirit or inspiration by God's presence, in some cases, after entering this state, people would lose control of events inside themselves and would be given over to spirits speaking through their throats and controlling their actions and movements.

I disagree with Yoram Bilu's claim that "in Judaism, a positive aspect to possession trances[93] is totally absent,"[94] as well as his later moderated version of this position, that the only positive spirit trances in Judaism were in the Sabbatean movement.[95] It is true that "the *dybbuk* is the outstanding exemplar of the first type, i.e. possession trance as an illness that must be cured with an exorcism of the negative entity, the spirit which has entered the body."[96] However, there are many examples of possessions where the positive evaluation given them is undeniable. The phenomenon of *maggidim* speaking through people's throats is an obvious example of this, and the *maggid* of R. Joseph Karo is only one of many of this type.[97] But possession as a positive prophetic state is already found in Scripture, in the *Hekhalot* literature, Rabbinic literature, and the Kabbalah from its beginnings through Hasidism.[98]

In this essay I have sought to show that even in Hasidism, certain manifestations of "*devekut*" that merited very positive evaluations, and whose subjects were taken as holy and exalted men, were quite definitely possession states. Even "*devekut* with the holy spirit" is a type of "*dybbuk*" in the sense that it is explained as a spirit entering the body of a person and speaking through his or her throat. This is the manner in which many Hasidic sources describe the level of "prophecy" in the process of *devekut*.[99] Thus, in Jewish culture as in other cultures, there is no lack of positive spirit possessions accompanied by altered consciousness. This is borne out by one of the most important descriptions of prophetic states in Hasidism, found in *Ma'or va-Shemesh*:

> This is well known. I saw among great *tzaddikim*, that when they attached themselves to the upper worlds and shed their physical coverings, and the Shekhinah came upon them and spoke through their throats, their mouths would speak prophecies of the future. Those very same *tzaddikim* knew not afterward what they had said because they were attached to the upper worlds and it was the Shekhinah which spoke through their throats.[100]

We learn from this that the state of *devekut* would induce unconscious automatic speech, which could not be remembered by the prophet himself. This disproves Y. Bilu's claim that amnesia, which characterizes possession trance states, does not exist in "positive" prophetic occurrences in Judaism, except in Sabbateanism.[101]

It appears that the existence of possessions that were positively valuated, and even viewed as a religious achievement or ideal, was reflected as well in positive attitudes toward the insane, to the point that a mad person could act as a prophet or spiritual reformer. It also served to raise the great importance of stories regarding the esteemed image of the Besht, since they served as a replacement for the positive function in society formerly filled by the insane. The place of the insane in the early days of Hasidism, as it appears in *Shivhe ha-Besht* and elsewhere, is a fascinating chapter in the history of madness in Jewish society.

Appendix 1: Shabbatai Zvi as a Spark of the Messiah

In the manuscript version of *Shivhe ha-Besht* preserved in the Habad Library, a version earlier than the one printed by R. Israel Jaffe,[102] in the context of the story concerning the Besht's efforts to repair the soul of Shabbatai Zvi, the following passage is found: "He said that the Besht declared that he [Shabbatai Zvi] had a spark of the messiah in him, but the Evil One [ס״מ] ensnared him, mercy upon us."[103] R. Israel Jaffe "slightly" modified this reading and wrote "that the Besht said he [Shabbatai] had a holy spark in him, but the Evil One ensnared him."[104]

A. Rubenstein and Y. Liebes have argued that for R. Israel Jaffe, the attribution of a messianic spark to Shabbatai Zvi by the Besht was too bold a matter, and he therefore saw fit to moderate it by writing "holy spark." Even the term "holy spark" is radical, but at least it makes no messianic reference to Shabbatai Zvi.[105] Y. Mondshine, on the other hand, claims that it is hard to know for certain whether this change really had any significance, because if R. Israel Jaffe was worried about giving any legitimacy at all, even potentially, to Shabbatai Zvi, he would not have left the words "holy spark"—even in them there is some slight approbation of Shabbatai.[106] In this context it is most instructive to note that in the book *Me'oreot Zvi*, one finds the explicit possibility that Shabbatai Zvi was not indeed the actual messiah but did have "a spark of the messiah." This possibility is raised in the claims of Shabbatai's detractors, who assert that Nathan and his group prophesied falsely but add:

> "We even question whether he could be a spark of the true messiah, since his father Mordecai was a spice merchant who traveled occasionally by sea to Egypt and elsewhere to buy or sell something, and his [Mordecai's] wife was beautiful, and sailors and mariners from our lands came regularly to do business with him, from Portugal, Spain, France, Holland, and England. Who can attest for us that he was holy from conception in his mother's womb? This is our estimation, based on his great prophet Nathan and the sons of prophets [that is, lesser Sabbatean prophets]." Many things of this type were spoken by the unbelievers to the princes [of the Jews] and the common people.[107]

It is clear from here that a problem faced R. Israel Jaffe: how to publicize a book in which Nathan of Gaza and other Sabbateans claim that Shabbatai had a "spark of the messiah" with the Sabbatean opponents struggling to refute this claim and simultaneously to publish that the Besht, the founder of Hasidism, also maintains Shabbatai Zvi "had a spark of the messiah in him."[108] It therefore appears that R. Israel Jaffe decided to slightly modify the manuscript version of R. Dov Baer in his possession, changing the "spark of the messiah" into a "spark of holiness" in order not to publish in the same year both the story of Shabbatai Zvi's detractors, who argued against the claim that Shabbatai had a spark of the messiah, and the words of the Besht, who accepted that claim.

Appendix 2: A Note on Mystical Ecstasy, Mystical Quietism, and Magic

It appears that the tendency to differentiate between magic and mysticism in research on Hasidism became more pronounced in the wake of the description of Hasidic mysticism as a quietistic mysticism, which seeks the nullification of the will and discounts any human activism. According to this view, the Hasidic mystic is called upon to develop an absolute indifference toward this world and all human existential desires.[109] This understanding of the mystic's goals places him in distinct opposition to the magician—an activist whose goals concern this world, whose business is to aid human desires and alleviate suffering.[110]

Viewing the goal of the Ba'al Shem Tov's mysticism as ecstatic experience[111] facilitates our understanding of the synthesis of mystical efforts and magical praxis in his world. His descriptions of what occurs during the elevation of the soul reveal the existence of a self-consciousness in him that is active even at the height of mystical experience.[112] Some of the ways the Besht teaches for reaching mystical states are distinctly magical, involving activities that by their nature require activity and initiative, such as the use of spells and Names. These stand in contradistinction to other paths, such as the "annihilation of the self," the "attribute of *hishtarut*" (positive indifference), or methods of negation, from which the passage to mystical states is passive, natural, and apparent.[113]

The physiological phenomena accompanying mystical experiences, as they are described in *Shivhe ha-Besht*, are characterized by constant movement and bodily activity.[114] It is difficult to regard these phenomena as an expression of the attempt to extinguish the faculties or of passivity. All this testifies to the active facet in some mystical experiences of the Besht as well as the phenomenological gap between these experiences and quietist mysticism. In ecstatic mystical experience of this type, in which the subject retains an active self-consciousness,[115] it is easier to synthesize magical activity, reducing the phenomenological gap between magic and mysticism.

Notes

This essay is part of my doctoral dissertation, "Madness and Knowledge in the Work of R. Nahman of Bratslav" (Hebrew University of Jerusalem, 2000), written under the direction of Professor Moshe Idel. A Hebrew version of this paper appeared in *Within Hasidic Circles: Studies in Hasidism in Memory of Mordecai Wilensky*, ed. I. Etkes, D. Assaf, I. Bartal, and E. Reiner (in Hebrew) (Jerusalem: Bialik Institute et al., 1999), 247–286. I wish to thank Professor Idel for his willingness to open the storehouses of his knowledge for me and for his generosity in spending time with me in advising and discussion. I would also like to thank Professor Immanuel Etkes, Dr. David Assaf, and Dr. Elhanan Reiner for their insightful comments; the Shalom Hartman Institute for Advanced Studies, whose support made the writing of this essay possible; and, last but not least, Dr. Matt Goldish for translating and helping edit this work for an English readership. My debt to him is enormous.

1. *Encyclopedia Judaica*, s.v. "Dibbuk," by G. Scholem; G. Nigal, "The *Dybbuk* in Jewish Mysticism" (in Hebrew), *Da'at* 4 (winter 1980): 76, 80, and n. 28; Y. Bilu, "The *Dybbuk* in Judaism: Mental Disorder as Cultural Resource" (in Hebrew), *Jerusalem Studies in Jewish Thought* 2 (1983): 529–63; S. Zfatman-Biller, "Exorcism of Spirits in Prague in the Seventeenth Century" (in Hebrew), *Jerusalem Studies in Jewish Folklore* 3 (1982): 7–32, esp. 9–10, n. 18, which touches on the identity of madness and *dybbuk* in the texts themselves. See also Y. Bilu, "*Dybbuk* and *Maggid*: Two Cultural Patterns of Altered Consciousness in Judaism," *AJS Review* 21 (1996): 341–66; J. H. Chajes, "Judgments Sweetened: Possession and Exorcism in Early Modern Jewish Culture," *Journal of Early Modern History* 1 (1997): 124–169. On the phenomenon in general, see E. Bourguignon, *Possession* (Corta Madera, Calif.: Chandler & Sharp, 1976); I. M. Lewis, *Ecstatic Religion: A Study of Spirit Possession* (London: Routledge, 1988); S. Clark, *Thinking with Demons: The Idea of Witchcraft in Early Modern Europe* (Oxford: Clarendon Press, 1997), 389–422. On the problem of transferring our contemporary concepts of madness as an explanation for possessions in earlier cultures, see ibid., 393–94. In my interpretation of the types of madness, I have no intention of offering a precise psychological diagnosis; I only point out the general similarity between *dybbuk* and certain varieties of madness as they are referred to by the larger society.

2. I. Etkes, "The Role of Magic and Ba'alei-shem in Ashkenazi Society in the Late Seventeenth and Early Eighteenth Centuries" (in Hebrew), *Zion* 60 (1995): 71–77. In note 10 is a bibliography of magic in Christian and Jewish society.

3. M. Piekarz, *The Beginning of Hasidism* (in Hebrew) (Jerusalem: Bialik Institute, 1978), 137; I. Etkes, "Role of Magic," 69–104; G. Nigal, *Magic and Mysticism in Hasidism* (in Hebrew) (Tel-Aviv: Yaron Golan, 1992), 13–15; M. Idel, "Jewish Magic from the Renaissance Period to Early Hasidism," in *Religion, Science, and Magic in Concert and in Conflict*, ed. J. Neusner, E. S. Frerichs, and P. V. M. Flesher (New York: Oxford University Press, 1989), 82–117; M. Rosman, *Founder of Hasidism: A Quest for the Historical Baal Shem Tov* (Berkeley: University of California Press, 1996),13–26.

4. BT Rosh ha-Shanah 28r; and see below. In *Sefer ha-Razim* we find the connection between Names and exorcism spells (*"Sefer ha-Razim": A Newly Recovered Book of Magic from the Talmudic Period* (in Hebrew), ed. M. Margoliot (Tel-Aviv: Yedi'ot Ahronot, 1966), 88.

5. G. Nigal, *Dybbuk Tales in Jewish Literature* (Jerusalem: Rubin Mass, 1983), 11–60; Scholem, "Dibbuk," 19–20.

6. G. Nigal, "*Dybbuk* Spirits in Hassidic Tales" (in Hebrew), *Bar-Ilan Annual* 24–25 (1989): 52; A. H. Fisch, "Doubles and *Dybbuks*" (in Hebrew), in *Atid Zakhur: On Literature, Myth, and History* (Jerusalem: Bialik Institute, 1996), 62.

7. Nigal, *Magic and Mysticism*, 77.

8. On the Besht as a *ba'al shem*, see G. Scholem, "The Historic Figure of

R. Israel Ba'al Shem Tov" (in Hebrew), in *Explications and Implications* (Tel-Aviv: Am Oved, 1974), 287–324; Etkes, "Role of Magic," no. 9 in *Poland*, 69 (in Hebrew) (Tel-Aviv: Open University, n.d.), 15–29; Nigal, *Magic and Mysticism*, 13–32; Rosman, *Founder of Hasidism*, 173–86.

9. "What was the occupation of a ba'al shem? He would visit the barren and heal the sick, especially illnesses of the spirit and madness" (Scholem, "Historic Figure," 337). "An important activity of every ba'al shem, if not his primary function, was to heal the ill who were called in Eastern Europe simply 'madmen'" (Nigal, *Magic and Mysticism*, 30). See also *Shivhe ha-Besht* (in Hebrew), ed. A. Rubenstein (Jerusalem: Rubin Mass, 1992), 60–61, 64–65, 67, 209–10. References through the rest of the essay will be to this edition unless otherwise noted.

10. On exorcism as a method for healing madness in Hasidism, see Nigal, "*Dybbuk* Spirits," 55–56, 58; idem, *Dybbuk Tales*, 50–54.

11. For a similar approach to legendary-hagiographic sources that do not represent objective historical truth, see David Assaf, *The Regal Way: The Life and Times of R. Israel of Ruzhin* (in Hebrew) (Jerusalem: Shazar Center, 1997), 44.

12. See A. Yaari, "Two Basic Editions of the *Shivhei ha-Besht*" (in Hebrew), *Kiryat Sefer* 39 (1964); Z. Gries, "Between Literature and History: An Introduction to the Debate and Discussion of *Shivhei ha-Besht*" (in Hebrew), *Tura* 3 (1994), esp. 153–60 and 171–72; E. Reiner, "In Praise of the Ba'al Shem Tov: Transmission, Editing, Printing" (in Hebrew), *Proceedings of the Eleventh World Congress of Jewish Studies*, vol. 11, *Jewish Thought, Kabbalah and Hasidism* (Jerusalem: World Congress of Jewish Studies, 1994): 145–52; Y. Mondshine, *Shivhe ha-Ba'al Shem Tov: A Facsimile of a Unique Manuscript; Variant Versions and Appendices* (in Hebrew) (Jerusalem, 1982), 71–75; M. Rosman, "The History of an Historical Source: On the Editing of *Shivhei ha-Besht*" (in Hebrew), *Zion* 58 (1993): 175–214. In n. 1 there other studies are mentioned that deal with the issue of reliance on *Shivhe ha-Besht* as a historical source. M. Rosman, *Founder of Hasidism*, 97–99, 143–58.

13. *Shivhe ha-Besht*, 29–32, with omissions; *In Praise of the Baal Shem Tov [Shivhei ha-Besht]*, ed. D. Ben-Amos and J. R. Mintz (Bloomington: Indiana University Press, 1970), 3–5, with omissions and minor editing. All further sizeable quotations from *Shivhe ha-Besht* in English are from this edition, with minor editing.

14. On the *dybbuk* and exorcism ceremonies for it as a confirmation of religious values, see Nigal, *Dybbuk Tales*, 7–13; Bilu, "*Dybbuk* in Judaism," 529–63.

15. *Shivhe ha-Besht*, 31, n. 39.

16. I refer to the author's preface of R. Dov Baer of Linits, as opposed to the printer's preface of R. Israel Jaffe. In the beginning of the book, according to its new editing of the writings, a new purpose appears, which I shall discuss presently. On the purposes of the printer R. Israel Jaffe, see A. Rubenstein, "The Appearance of the Besht in the *Shivhei ha-Besht*"(in Hebrew), *Alei Sefer* 6–7 (1979): esp. 182–84; Rosman, "History of an Historical Source"; Reiner, *In Praise of the Ba'al Shem Tov*.

17. In the order in the "Writings," not the edition of R. Israel Jaffe. On this see the sources cited in the previous note.

18. *Shivhe ha-Besht*, 64–65; *In Praise*, 34–35.

19. Both the sin of the possessing spirit and that of the possessed person are intended. The assumption was that the possessed had also transgressed some law, even the most minor, and it was this transgression that allowed the *dybbuk* to possess him or her specifically. Scholem, "Dibbuk," 19–20; Nigal, *Dybbuk Tales*, 33–35.

20. Rubinstein, "Appearance of the Besht"; Rosman, "History of an Historical Source."

21. The story is found in *Shivhe ha-Besht*, 264–66. Rubinstein points out the parallel in "Appearance of the Besht," 167–68.

22. R. Nahman is referred to in this story as "the crazy Nahman [*meshugenner* Nahman]," but this appellation is not associated with R. Nahman's prophecies, as Rubinstein hints ("Appearance of the Besht," 168). Rather, it is connected with the question of why R. Nahman insists on loading the produce himself instead of giving this difficult task to a servant.

23. *Shivhe ha-Besht*, Mondshine ed., 219; *In Praise*, 208. In Rubinstein's edition is written *yitga'eh* (he shall be proud) rather than *yitna'beh* (he shall prophesy), but this is not how it appears in the *princeps* (Kapust) nor in the Haba"d manuscript published by Mondshine. My thanks to Dr. David Assaf, who directed my attention to this point.

24. "*Warum alle tage hat er gesehen von ihm zein shiga'on un prostatzki zachen*," Koretz-Ostrog ed., chap. 12; and see Rubinstein, "Appearance of the Besht," 163. On the Yiddish versions of *Shivhe ha-Besht* and their relationship to the Kapust edition of R. Israel Jaffe, see Mondshine, *Shivhe ha-Besht*, 12–13.

25. "*Iber dem hat er im gehalten fer ein meshuga*," *Shivhe ha-Besht*, 55, n. 7.

26. *Shivhe ha-Besht*, 56 and n. 20. See also Rubinstein, "Appearance of the Besht," 161.

27. *Shivhe ha-Besht*, 174; *In Praise*, 129.

28. *Shivhe ha-Besht*, 54; *In Praise*, 26.

29. "*Iber mahashavto ha-tehorah*," *Shivhe ha-Besht*, 54 and n. 21.

30. From "Otzar Eden Ganuz," Oxford MS 1580, folio 165v–166r,; according to the translation in M. Idel, *The Mystical Experience in Abraham Abulafia* (Albany: State University of New York Press Press, 1988), 144–45. Published in Adolph Jellinek, *Beit ha-Midrash* vol. 3 (Jerusalem: Vahrmann, 1967 [reprint]), introduction; again in G. Scholem, *The Kabbalah of Sefer ha-Temunah and R. Abraham Abulafia* (in Hebrew), ed. Y. Ben-Shlomo (Jerusalem: Akademon, 1987), 195. For more on demonic revelation in Abulafia, see Scholem, ibid., 103–04, 166–68, 172–74; Idel, *Studies in Ecstatic Kabbalah* (in Hebrew) (Jerusalem: Akademon, 1990), 121–22.

31. *Shivhe ha-Besht*, 58.

32. "*Was der Rabbi Yisra'el hat gitten was hat sich gidacht wie nit kein bar da'as un andere sachen was er hat gitten is als tov ve-yashar*," *Shivhe ha-Besht*, 58, n. 43.

33. From the Hebrew translation by A. Rubinstein, *Shivhei ha-Besht*, app. 28, p. 363.

34. This is probably the manner in which to understand some of the descriptions of the Besht as a madman, applied by the *mitnaggedim* (opponents of the Hasidim). For example, the booklet *Shever Posh'im* quotes the following in a letter pertaining to the Besht: "And we have found . . . that he is a drunken prophet [*navi shikur hu*] who becomes mad" (M. Wilensky, *Hasidim and Mitnaggedim* [in Hebrew][Jerusalem: Bialik Institute, 1990], 125–26. See also S. Dubnow, *History of Hasidism* [in Hebrew] [Tel-Aviv: Dvir, 1967], 65–66; Scholem, "Historic Figure," 350–51).

35. On prophetic prayer in Hasidism, see J. Weiss, "*Via Passiva* in Early Hasidism," in idem, *Studies in Eastern European Jewish Mysticism* (Oxford: Littman Library, 1985), 69–83; R. Schatz, *Hasidism as Mysticism: Quietistic Elements in Eighteenth Century Hasidic Thought* (in Hebrew) (Jerusalem: Magnes Press, 1968), 118–21. On *devekut* states as possession in early Kabbalah, see H. Padaya, " 'Possessed by Speech': Toward an Understanding of the Prophetic-Ecstatic Pattern among Early Kabbalists" (in Hebrew), *Tarbiz* 65 (1996): 565–636, esp. 579, n. 27. On prophecy during prayer in the Mishnah and Talmud, see Sh. Naeh, " 'Creates the Fruit of Lips': A Phenomenological Study of Prayer according to Mishnah Berakhot 4:3, 5:5" (in Hebrew), *Tarbiz* 63 (1994): 185–218; A. Walfish, "Response to S. Naeh, 'Creates the Fruit of Lips' " (in Hebrew), *Tarbiz* 65 (1996): 301–14.

36. *Likute Yekarim* 12c. In R. Azriel the words of Meisels are the following: "And for this reason we find that the prophet was called a madman: because the spirit of God resonates in him like a bell, causing him to dance and sing for the presence of God within him" (*Tif'eret Uziel*, 53, cols. 2–3). See also R. Moses Teitelbaum, *Yismah Moshe* (1859; reprint, Jerusalem, 1976), 2:107r; Moses Hayyim Ephraim of Sudylkow, *Degel Mahaneh Ephraim* (Jerusalem: n.p., 1994), *Yitro*, 101. An analysis of this last source, showing that it is describing an ecstatic, unwilled mystical experience, can be found in I. Etkes, "The Besht as a Mystic" (in Hebrew), *Zion* 61 (1996): 434–35.

37. G. Scholem, *Shabbatai Zvi* (Tel-Aviv: Dviri, 1957), 100.
38. Ibid.
39. Ibid., 99.
40. Ibid., 129.
41. Ibid., 100–10.
42. Ibid., 175–76; in English, idem, *Sabbatai Ṣevi: The Mystical Messiah (1626–1676)* (Princeton: Princeton University Press, 1973), 43.
43. A different view of this chain of events is presented by I. Tishbi, *Paths of Faith and Heresy* (in Hebrew) (Jerusalem: Magnes Press, 1982), 247–58, 268–75.
44. "His strange actions do not nullify his messianic standing; they rather confirm it" (Scholem, *Shabbatai Zvi*, 251). Scholem further shows that the roots of the description of sinking into depression for no apparent reason as typical of, and indicating specifically very exalted souls connected to King David, already exist in R. Hayim Vital: "Know too that this man . . . though his soul will be very exalted, because this is the beginning of his purification from the husks . . . and for the reason mentioned, it is certain that this man will be very sad all his life,

and will always worry within himself baselessly. . . . This is sufficient reason for King David, of blessed memory" (R. Hayim Vital, introduction 27, in *Sha'ar ha-Gilgulim* [Jerusalem: Kol Yehudah, 1995], 75; Scholem, *Shabbatai Zvi*, 249). Thus, from here too the baseless fits of depression in which Shabbatai Zvi was steeped become a proof and sign that he possessed an exalted soul connected to the secret (*sod*) of King David.

45. (In Hebrew) *Jewish Studies* 37 (1997): 161–84.

46. R. Joseph b. Shalom Ashkenazi, in his commentary on *Sefer Yezirah*, quoted by H. Padaya, "Shabbat, Shabbatai, and the Reduction of the Moon—The Holy Connection: Letters and Pictures"(in Hebrew), in *Eshel Be'er Sheva*, vol. 4, *Myth in Judaism* (1996), 151.

47. 57 a–b. This text was apparently one of the main sources on which R. Nahman drew in his story "Tale of the Seven Beggars." Concerning this and the influence of *Sefer ha-Peli'ah* on R. Nahman, I hope to write elsewhere.

48. *Sefer ha-Peli'ah*, 58a.

49. *Sefer ha-Peli'ah*, 57c.

50. Since we know that Shabbatai learned and taught *Sefer ha-Kanah* and *Sefer ha-Peli'ah*, it is difficult to claim that he and his students were ignorant of these texts (see Scholem, *Shabbatai Zvi*, 93–94, 130; *Ha-Entziklopedyah ha-Ivrit*, 1st ed., s.v. "Shabbatai Zvi"; Idel, "Planet," 176–77).

51. *Ma'ase Tuviah* (Venice, 1707), 1:6:3, p. 18v.

52. R. Jacob Emden, *Torat ha-Kana'ot*, 56. On him see G. Scholem, *Studies and Texts concerning the History of Sabbatianism and Its Metamorphoses* (in Hebrew) (Jerusalem: Bialik Institute, 1974), 93–95.

53. M. Balaban, *Toward a History of the Frankist Movement* (in Hebrew) (Tel-Aviv: Dvir, 1934), 112. The quotation he cites is taken from *Sefer ha-Shimush*, by R. Jacob Emden: R. Jacob Emden, *Sefer Shimush: Facsimile Edition of the First Printing, 1758–1762* (Jerusalem: Shazar Center, 1975), 83.

54. A. Freimann, *Injane Sabbatai Zewi* (Berlin: Mekize Nirdamim, 1912), 74–75; my emphasis.

55. A parallel to the determination of the essential nature of prophecy and automatic speech, whether they derive from a foolish spirit or prophecy and a wise spirit, according to the content of the words spoken, is to be found in the following passage by Abulafia's student, the author of *Sha'are Tzedek*: "And as the image of speech exits my heart and arrives at my lips, it determines their movement. I said, Perhaps this is a foolish spirit, God forbid, which has entered me! But when I saw that it spoke wise things I said, It is without doubt a spirit of wisdom" (*Sha'are Tzedek*, MS 148 8§, 65r, Jewish National and University Library, Jerusalem). Cited in M. Idel, "Inquiries into the Doctrine of *Sefer ha-Meshiv*" (in Hebrew), *Sefunot*, n.s. 2 (1983): 221.

56. Scholem, *Shabbatai Zvi*, no. 622; idem, *Sabbatai Ṣevi*, 733.

57. Scholem, *Shabbatai Zvi*, 2:650; idem, *Sabbatai Ṣevi*, 766 [the English translation here is mine since it is paraphrased in Scholem's version. —ed.]. R. Jacob Sasportas, *Sefer Tzizat Novel Tzvi*, ed. I. Tishbi (Jerusalem: Bialik Institute, 1954), 263–67.

58. Leyb b. Oyzer, *Beshraybung fun Shabsai Zvi*, trans. Zalman Shazar (Jerusalem: Shazar Center, 1978), 59–60. A similar account of his prophecy is found in de la Croix; see Scholem, *Shabbatai Zvi*, 357–59.

59. *Shivhe ha-Besht*, 30–31; *In Praise*, 4.

60. An additional testimony concerning people who "struck their chests with stones and threw themselves to the ground in front of synagogues during the Torah reading" in the sixteenth century can be found in *Divre Binah*, by R. Dov Baer of Bolechow; see A. J. Brauwer, *Galicia and Its Jews* (in Hebrew) (Jerusalem: Bialik Institute, 1965), 203.

61. J. Weiss posited the unlikely claim that the phrase *naf'lah ha-emunah* refers to the Sabbatean faith, whose loss is mourned by the author of *Shivhe ha-Besht*. The expression "may his name be blotted out" that the author appends to the name of Shabbatai Zvi is understood by Weiss as nothing more that a formulaic expression. He ignores the fact that the story discusses an opponent of the Sabbateans and rebukes their errors. Nevertheless, it seems appropriate to accept his claim that there is a phenomenological affinity between the prophecy of R. Nahman of Kosov and his circle, on the one hand, and that of Sabbatean prophecy on the other; Weiss, *Studies*, 27–42, esp. 40.

62. On *Me'oreot Zvi*, see C. B. Friedberg, *Bet Eked Sepharim* (in Hebrew) (Tel-Aviv: Bar Yudah, 1954), 762. The work was printed in Lvov in 1824, but the date was falsified as 1804. See A. Ya'ari, "Miscellaneous Bibliographical Notes: Judith Rosanes' Hebrew Press at Lwow" (in Hebrew), *Kirjath Sefer* 17 (1940): 95–108; Scholem, *Shabbatai Zvi*, 643. S. Werses refers to 1804 as the actual date of the first publication. See Werses, *Haskalah and Sabbateanism: The Story of a Controversy* (in Hebrew) (Jerusalem: Shazar Center, 1988), 220–26. In n. 165 he refers the reader to p. 108 in A. Ya'ari's article, where the date of publication printed on the title page, 1804, is indeed cited. However, on p. 97 of the same article, Ya'ari claims that the printed date is falsified; and to this G. Scholem assents. Scholem attests that he personally saw the edition of R. Israel Jaffe from 1814 and apparently thought R. Israel printed only this one edition. He therefore claimed that Friedberg's dating of the Kapust edition, 1815, was erroneous, and should be corrected to 1814. He seems not to have investigated closely enough to discover that the book was printed a second time by R. Israel Jaffe in 1815. The 1815 dating is therefore not erroneous, but the 1814 edition should be added to the list. A copy of the 1815 edition can be found today in the G. Scholem collection at the Jewish National and University Library in Jerusalem. On the title page the printer mentions the previous printing in Kapust and the demand for another printing:

> Since its printing a short time ago here in the holy community of Kapust, its great importance and usefulness have become known among the Jews. Many say, "Who will show us these letters and read them to our ears, in order to strengthen the fear of God in our hearts so we turn not away from His commandments all the days of our lives?" It will be searched for and not found, sought out but unavailable. We have therefore decided to print it anew,

and we have been assisted in the new printing with increased stamina and strength.

Y. Vinograd notes in his book that there were indeed two printings of the book in Kapust. See Vinograd, *Thesaurus of the Hebrew Book* (in Hebrew) (Jerusalem: Institute for Computerized Bibliography, 1995), 630–31.

63. Scholem, *Shabbatai Zvi*, 100, 643. For more on this book and its views, see Werses, *Haskalah*, 220–26.

64. No claim can be made for the influence of *Me'oreot Zvi* on R. Dov Baer of Linits himself, because he died before either it or *Shivhe ha-Besht* was published. See *Shivhe ha-Besht*, 9.

65. *Me'oreot Zvi*, 6, 7, 10–11, 16, 30–31, 45, 48–49, and elsewhere.

66. Ibid., 13–14.

67. "And all the rabbis and leaders of each city listened to him because he used his spells there. They praised him as a wonder-worker from heaven, and they believed in him and his messiah" (*Me'oreot Zvi*, 4); "All this is verily true and correct; more than four hundred men from the select of Macedon testify and prophecy to it, with a great prophet at their head, Nathan of Gaza" (ibid., 26); "Some have turned to them and been pulled in . . . and the greatest of them are caused to faint by a spirit which speaks lies from inside them" (ibid., 49). See also ibid., 15, 27, 32, 38–39, and elsewhere.

68. "Out of their great desire to be redeemed" (ibid., 19, 30, 36, and elsewhere).

69. Ibid., 13–14. This type of perception and even more extreme ones concerning the messianic status of Shabbatai Zvi are found in R. Jacob Emden as well. He saw Shabbatai as a messiah from the "other [evil] side," parallel to the true messiah, because "it is known that God created 'one opposite the other': the 'other side' vs. the holy" (*Torat ha-Kana'ut*, 70v). The (biblical) allusions and Names interpreted by the Sabbateans to refer to Shabbatai are genuine, but they must be understood as impure Names, standing opposite the holy Names. See Y. Liebes, "The Messianism of R. Jacob Emden and His Attitude towards Sabbateanism," in idem, *On Sabbateanism and Its Kabbalah: Collected Essays* (Jerusalem: Bialik Institute, 1995), 198–203. On the other hand, unlike *Me'oreot Zvi*, R. Jacob Emden does not stress the magical aspects or external manifestations.

70. *Me'oreot Zvi*, 15 and 39, respectively.

71. *Shivhe ha-Besht*, 92 and 85–86, respectively; *In Praise*, 55 and 50, respectively. On the ecstatic aspect of the Besht's mystical experience, see Etkes, "Besht as a Mystic," 427–35.

72. *Me'oreot Zvi*, 19.

73. R. Zvi Hirsch of Zidechov, *Sur me-Ra ve-Aseh Tov* (Lublin, 1928), 55. On the relationship of this passage to Sabbateanism, see R. Elior, "Between Existence and Nothingness: A Study in the Doctrine of the *Tzaddik* according to R. Jacob Isaac, the Seer of Lublin" (in Hebrew), in *Hasidism in Poland* (in Hebrew), ed. R. Elior, Y. Bartal, and C. Shmeruk (Jerusalem: Bialik Institute, 1994), 187. "The

Sabbatean failure was not a matter of methods and techniques, nor did it lie in the essential ability to connect with higher worlds. Rather, it failed on the moral level, in ethics and fear of God, which are a precondition for achieving *devekut* and the holy spirit. If one does not have this, 'The [good] spirit will turn for you, Heaven forbid, into another kind of spirit' " (*Sur me-Ra*, 56).

74. On *devekut* in Hasidism, see G. Scholem, "Devekut, or Intimate Contact with God in Early Hasidism: Rules and Activities" (in Hebrew), in idem, *Explications and Implications*, 325–50; R. Schatz, *Hasidism as Mysticism*; *Ha-Entziklopedyah ha-Ivrit*, 1st edition, s.v. "Hasidism and Its Literature," by I. Tishbi and J. Dan; Y. Jacobson, *From Lurianic Kabbalism to the Psychological Theosophy* (in Hebrew) (Tel-Aviv: Ministry of Defense Press, 1984), 89–97; idem, *Hasidic Thought* (in Hebrew) (Tel-Aviv: Ministry of Defense Press, 1985), 44–75, 95–106. A differing view can be found in M. Piekarz, "Devekuth as Reflecting the Socio-Religious Character of the Hasidic Movement" (in Hebrew), *Da'at* 25 (1990): 127–44. See also M. Pachter, "The Theory of Devekut in the Writings of the Sages of Safed in the Sixteenth Century" (in Hebrew), *Jerusalem Studies in Jewish Thought* 3 (1982): 51–121; Etkes, "Besht as a Mystic," 421–54; R. Elior, "R. Joseph Karo and R. Israel Ba'al Shem Tov—Mystical Metamorphosis, Kabbalistic Inspiration, and Spiritual Internalization" (in Hebrew), *Tarbiz* 65 (1996): 671–709; G. Nigal, "Sources of 'Devekut' in Early Hasidic Literature" (in Hebrew), *Kirjath Sefer* 41 (1971): 343–48.

75. Scholem, "Devekut"; idem, *Major Trends in Jewish Mysticism* (New York: Schocken, 1961), 348–49; idem, "Historic Figure," 287–324. Despite Scholem's claim that the Ba'al Shem Tov's life cannot be properly divided into periods in which he engaged in magic and periods in which he engaged in the spread of his mystical teachings, Scholem himself preserves a division between the Besht's charismatic and mystical identity and his activities as a *ba'al shem*. Scholem even offers a value judgement distinguishing between earning a living by the practice of magic, which has more legitimacy in his eyes, and the "exploitation" of charismatic talents and prayer, which he sees as improper. "The expenses of his home were met by his professional activities as a ba'al shem, a popular healer (an idolatrous doctor, if you will); but not on the convenient conception that a spiritual person who prays for his community should be supplied with his physical needs" (*Explications and Implications*, 312). According to Scholem, the Besht "knew that 'charisma' must not be exploited, as occurred frequently thereafter" (313). I. Etkes also participates in this bifurcational approach (Etkes, *Poland*). He describes the Besht as a *ba'al shem* and the Besht as a mystic as two different and separate phenomena in the Besht's persona. In his recent article, as well, "The Besht as Mystic," the *devekut* and mystical path of the Besht are treated separately from his magical universe. R. Elior ("R. Joseph Karo") also treats mystical aspects of the Besht and R. Karo separately from their magical personae, despite the fact that several of the interesting common elements between the two figures hinge on exactly these aspects. Both the Besht and R. Karo engaged in exorcisms. A detailed testimony of an exorcism carried out by R. Karo is cited in M. Idel from the *Zafnat Pane'ah*

of R. Judah Hallewa, in Idel, "Doctrine of *Sefer ha-Meshiv*," 224. It is likely that R. Karo, like the Besht, used magical media to achieve mystical states. On this, see ibid., 223–s4, and concerning the Besht, below. See also the next note.

76. Idel, "Jewish Magic," 100–6; idem, *Hasidism: Between Ecstasy and Magic* (Albany: State University of New York Press Press, 1995); idem, "Judaism, Jewish Mysticism, and Magic" (in Hebrew), *Jewish Studies* 36 (1996): 25–40; A. Green, "Idel on Hasidism, Ecstasy, and Magic" (in Hebrew), *Jewish Studies* 36 (1996): 279–81; G. Nigal, *Magic and Mysticism*; R. Elior, "The Ba'al Shem Tov and the Beginnings of the Hasidic Movement" (typescript prepared for publication by the Open University), 11, claims there is an intertwining of magic and mysticism in the thought of the Besht, though she does not go into detail. In her article "Between 'Being' and 'Nothingness,'" she goes into some depth describing a model that depicts the synthesis of magic and mysticism in the thought of the Seer of Lublin. Elior sees this synthesis as a paradoxical combination of two foci that contradict each other. Concerning the synthesis of magic and mysticism among the earliest kabbalists, see Padaya, "'Possessed by Speech,'" 609–10.

77. R. Joseph Ashkenazi, "the Tanna of Safed," already describes the phenomena of *dybbuk* and madness as parallels to the appearance of the holy spirit and prophecy. The difference is that a *dybbuk* is the attachment of the spirit of an evil or mad person, whereas the holy spirit is attached to the spirit of a pure and holy person. This doctrine found its way into the *Otzarot Hayyim*, by R. Hayyim Vital, as well as *Sha'ar ha-Gilgulim*. On this, see G. Scholem, "New Information on R. Joseph Ashkenazi, the Tanna of Safed" (in Hebrew), *Tarbiz* 28 (1969): 61–62. On the concept of maggidism as the other face of the *dybbuk*, see Scholem, *Shabbatai Zvi*, 65. See also R. J. Z. Werblowsky, *Joseph Karo: Lawyer and Mystic*, trans. Y. Zuran [Hebrew] (Jerusalem: Magnes Press, 1996), 262; Idel, "Jewish Magic," 106–8. For the psychological interpretation of this phenomenon, see Werblowsky, *Joseph Karo*, 259–64; Scholem, *Shabbatai Zvi*, 171, n. 3.

78. On the powers of good and evil in the Zohar and teachings of R. Isaac Luria, see I. Tishbi, *Mishnat ha-Zohar* (in Hebrew) (Jerusalem: Bialik Institute, 1949–61), 1:285–359; idem, *The Doctrine of Evil and Kelippah in the Kabbalah of R. Isaac Luria* (in Hebrew) (Jerusalem: Magnes Press, 1992); G. Scholem, *Elements of the Kabbalah and Its Symbolism* (in Hebrew) (Jerusalem: Magnes Press, 1976), 167–212.

79. Tishbi and Dan, "Hasidism"; R. Elior, "The Relationship of Kabbalah to Hasidism—Continuity and Change," in *Proceedings of the Ninth World Congress of Jewish Studies, Division 3* (Jerusalem: World Congress of Jewish Studies, 1986), 109.

80. Etkes, "Besht as a Mystic," 440–43.

81. Ibid., 454.

82. A basis for the double use of the term *devekut* as referring both to attachment to the holy side and to the other (evil) side can be found in the Zohar's assertion that a man will certainly be in a state of *devekut*—the question is whether it will be with the good or the evil forces (Zohar 1:54a; 3:41b, 62a, 53b).

On this parallel, Y. Liebes states: "The author of the Zohar writes explicitly and repeatedly concerning the resemblance in method. In absolutely parallel contrast to the kabbalist is the sorcerer, who is also 'sequestered by the impure spirit' and 'absorbed' into it. It pulls an impure soul over itself and holds fast to the 'other side.'" (Liebes, "The Messiah of the Zohar," in *The Messianic Idea In Israel* (in Hebrew), ed. Sh. Re'em (Jerusalem: Israel Academy of Sciences and Humanities, 1990), 180). From the generalization by the Zohar it would appear that it is not attempting to describe a *dybbuk* episode with noticeable external symptoms such as one finds in ecstatic *devekut*, like what the Besht experienced, or like *devekut* with an evil spirit like the madman with a *dybbuk*. Rather, we are dealing with a widespread phenomenon whereby any person could experience *devekut*. Nevertheless, the zoharic model offers both a linguistic basis for the terminology of *dybbuk* and *devekut* and a basis for the parallel between the two types of *devekut* that stand "one opposite the other." For more on the terminology of "*dybbuk*," see G. Scholem, "'Golem' and 'Dybbuk' in the Hebrew Dictionary" (in Hebrew), *Leshonenu* 6 (1934–35): 40–41.

83. On the use of magical methods to achieve revelation and mystical experiences in the sixteenth century, see Werblowsky, *Joseph Karo*, 50–89; Idel, "Jewish Magic," 106–8; idem, "Judaism Mysticism and Magic," 33 and n. 32 there; idem, "*Sefer ha-Meshiv*," 223–24. On mystical states of consciousness used for the achievement of magical ends before Hasidism, see M. Idel, *Golem* (in Hebrew) (Tel-Aviv: Schocken, 1996), 231–33.

84. *Epistle on Elevation of the Soul*, according to the Karlitz version, in Mondshine, *Shivhe ha-Besht*, 235. On the letter of the Besht in its different versions and its authenticity, see ibid., 229–42; Rosman, *Founder of Hasidism*, 99–113 and references to earlier studies on the subject there.

85. See Elior, "Ba'al Shem Tov," 11; Green, "Idel on Hasidism," 279–81.

86. Scholem, "Devekut, or Intimate Contact," 325–50; Tishbi and Dan, "Hasidism"; Jacobson, *From Lurianic Kabbalism*, 89–97; idem, *Hasidic Thought*, 44–75, 95–106; Etkes, "Besht as a Mystic," 421–54; Elior, "R. Joseph Karo," esp. 689–98.

87. See above, note 6.

88. See Etkes, "Role of Magic," 71–77.

89. "On the Kavvanot of the Eighteen Benedictions according to R. Isaac the Blind" (in Hebrew), *Masu'ot* (1997): 25. Idel himself claims there that "it was not actually thus in the reality of religious life," yet he still accepts the phenomenological gap between these events. See also E. Underhill, *Mysticism: A Study in the Nature and Development of Man's Spiritual Consciousness* (New York: Noonday Press, 1955), 149–64. In appendix 2 below I have added some details on this point.

90. On the manner of differentiating between mystical states and madness based on the criterion of the subject's control over his condition, see B. Scharfstein, *The Mystical Experience* (in Hebrew) (Tel-Aviv: Am Oved, 1972), 177–80; J. Campbell, *Myths to Live By* (New York: Bantam Books, 1978), 215.

91. In "possessions," a spirit or other power comes into the subject and speaks through his or her throat or speaks with him or her. On the other hand, in "trance"

states the soul leaves the body of the subject and rises to another world. On possession and trance states, see the editor's introduction to *Religion, Altered States of Consciousness, and Social Change* ed. E. Bourguignon (Columbus: Ohio State University Press, 1973); Bilu, "*Dybbuk* in Judaism," 530–33. Bilu, following Bourguignon and others, differentiates between possessions that do not involve altered states of consciousness, such as *dybbuks*, which express themselves only through pains and inflated limbs, and possession trances (PT), which involve altered states of consciousness.

92. An example of an involuntary trance is the state of *hiner flot* or *hiner bet*, in which the subject falls unconscious and his or her soul rises upward, having certain experiences, and remains able to relate what it experienced in the upper worlds when it returns to the body. See *Shivhe ha-Besht*, 30, 313–15.

93. See note 90 above.

94. Bilu, "*Dybbuk* in Judaism," 533.

95. See Bilu's recent essay, "*Dybbuk* and *Maggid*"; Bourguignon, *Altered States*.

96. Bilu, "*Dybbuk* in Judaism," 533.

97. Werblowsky, *Joseph Karo*, 50–89. Bilu, in "*Dybbuk* and *Maggid*," claims that the phenomenon of maggidism is not in the category of PT.

98. On possession states in Scripture and the *Hekhalot* literature, see H. Pedaya, "Vision, Falling, Song, Cravings, Visions of God and the Spiritual Basis in Early Jewish Mysticism" (in Hebrew), *Asufot* 9 (1995): 237–77, esp. 263. On prophesying during prayer in the Mishnah and Talmud, see Naeh, " 'Creates the Fruit of Lips';" Walfish, "Response to S. Naeh." On *devekut* states during possession in early Kabbalah, see Pedaya, " 'Possessed by Speech,' " 565–636, esp. 579, n. 27; Idel, "*Sefer ha-Meshiv*," 220–26; idem, "Jewish Magic," 107. On these issues in Safed Kabbalah, see Werblowsky, *Joseph Karo*, 50–89.

99. See the sources cited above, note 73; see also the discussion in R. Schatz concerning prophesying in the style of "the Shekhinah speaks from their throats" (Schatz, *Hasidism as Mysticism*, 110–21); Etkes, "Besht as a Mystic," 431–35; Elior, "R. Joseph Karo," 697–98.

100. R. Kalonymous Kalman Epstein, *Ma'or va-Shemesh* (Breslau: Rubinstein, 1842), *Parashat Va-Yigash*, 51r.

101. See Bilu, "*Dybbuk* and *Maggid*," 362–64. Another claim made there as well, that convulsions do not exist in "positive" Jewish possession cases outside of Sabbateansim, is disproved by the testimony concerning the convulsions that seized the Besht during his mystical experience (*Shivhe ha-Besht*, 85–86).

102. Mondshine, introduction to *Shivhe ha-Besht*, 5–22; Rosman, "History of an Historical Source," esp. 183–86.

103. Mondshine, *Shivhe ha-Besht*, 98 (in MS 24 [11]).

104. *Shivhe ha-Besht*, 133. See also Mondshine, *Shivhe ha-Besht*, 16, 172.

105. A. Rubenstein, "Concerning Three Stories in the *Shivhe ha-Besht*" (in Hebrew), *Sinai* 90 (1982): 277–79; Y. Liebes, "New Light on the Matter of the Ba'al Shem Tov and Shabbatai Zevi" (in Hebrew), *Jerusalem Studies in Jewish Thought* 11 (1982): 564–69.

106. Mondshine, introduction to *Shivhe ha-Besht*, 16.

107. *Me'oreot Zvi*, ed. Israel Elimelekh Stund (Lemberg: n.p., 1871), 19 according to my numbering, and so below.

108. The possibility that in the soul of a given person a spark of the messiah exists, despite the fact that ultimately he is not the true messiah, can be found already in the writings of R. Hayyim Vital. He claims that the soul of Bar Kokhba contained a spark from the soul of the messiah son of David (Vital, *Sefer ha-Likkutim* [Jerusalem: Kol Yehudah, 1995], *Vayehi be-kheziv*, 111). These matters were apparently at the root of Nathan of Gaza's claim that Shabbatai Zvi was a reincarnation of Bar Kokhba and that Shabbatai would perform a *tikkun* for the soul of Jesus (this is in *Treatise on the Dragons*; see Scholem, *Shabbatai Zvi*, 231). In other words, Shabbatai Zvi would make a *tikkun* for all the messianic attempts that had not borne fruit in the past. This would be accomplished by a *tikkun* of the unsuccessful figures at the center of these failed movements, since in them too there was a messianic spark. It is on this background that we can understand the story in *Shivhe ha-Besht* concerning the Ba'al Shem Tov's attempt to repair the soul of Shabbatai Zvi, as well as the mention of Jesus in the story. This was not simply an attempt to raise Shabbatai Zvi from Gehennom or the like, but a messianically charged exercise involving the *tikkun* of all those previous messianic pretenders. Despite their failure, they indeed had a messianic spark in them, and this had to be raised up.

109. Schatz, *Hasidism as Mysticism*; Jacobson, *From Lurianic Kabbalism*, 89–97; idem, *Hasidic Thought*, 44–75, 95–106.

110. On magic as an active approach, see Werblowsky, *Joseph Karo*, 59; H. N. Altmann, "The *Golem* and Modern Science," trans. A. Kaplan, in Idel, *Golem*, 11–28.

111. See Scholem, *Major Trends*, 335; Tishbi and Dan, "Hasidism"; Etkes, "Besht as a Mystic," 429–39.

112. *Shivhe ha-Besht*, 91–94, 117–18; *Epistle on the Elevation of the Soul*, 235.

113. Ibid.

114. *Shivhe ha-Besht*, 85–86, 92.

115. These attempts are more likely in the realm of trance states than possession, and it would be useful to compare them with techniques and trances in Kabbalah. See Y. Garb, "Trance Techniques in the Kabbalah of Jerusalem" (in Hebrew), *Pe'amim* 70 (1997): 47–67.

Section IV
The Nineteenth and Twentieth Centuries

Prologue

With the onset of modernity there has been a marked decline in the accounts of *maggidim*, and spirit possessions have been almost exclusively *dybbuk* events, following the Christian model of negative possessions. The rabbinic elite has thus mainly discontinued its practice of fomenting "positive" possessions, but it has maintained its role as a body of spiritual experts and potential exorcists.

On the other hand, the artistic and scientific interests of the modern world have had a profound impact both on spirit possession as a phenomenon and, of course, on the understanding of its meaning. One of the most significant events in the field was the publication of a play by the Russian and Yiddish author An-Ski in the late 1910s called *The Dybbuk*, or *Between Two Worlds*. This became one of the most famous Jewish theater pieces of the twentieth century. It tells the tale of a *dybbuk* possession in the pattern of a love story, thereby preserving the form of possession narratives but radically altering their content and cultural meaning. It is remarkable that some of the recent *dybbuk* cases show signs of having been influenced by An-Ski, a case of life imitating art imitating life. Our understanding of possession has been greatly enhanced, meanwhile, by the extensive research conducted in the twentieth century about possession in general, and Jewish possessions in particular. The tools of the historian, anthropologist, and psychologist have been brought to bear on possession research, opening new vistas of insight.

The arrival of Jews from around the world to the new State of Israel in the mid-twentieth century allowed scholars a closer look at popular possession modes from a variety of communities, but at the same time it helped cause the near extinction of most traditional forms. Yet new and hybrid variations on the established tropes of possession crop up and sometimes flourish in Israel.

This section contains two essays. The first, by Tamar Alexander, offers a unique opportunity to glimpse the inner workings of a possession and to have its significance explicated from the point of view of folklore and cultural studies. Alexander was privy to the development of an exorcism event in the court of a young Israeli kabbalist. She interviewed all the participants and has placed their narratives in a larger cultural and historical framework. Yoram Bilu's study examines three culturally determined possession states found among twentieth-century Jews from various regions of the world. He uses anthropological tools to develop the significance of each.

Love and Death in a Contemporary *Dybbuk* Story: Personal Narrative and the Female Voice

TAMAR ALEXANDER

ybbuk tales are found throughout the Jewish diaspora, in both West and East, over the course of four centuries. They are known in locations as diverse as Safed, Ferrara, Damascus, Seville, Tetuan, Prague, Korets, Egypt, Nikolsburg, Baghdad, Jerusalem, and Netivot. These stories have been examined by various researchers from different points of view. I will first review some of these approaches, then discuss the development and structure of *dybbuk* tales before speaking about the very rich contemporary case that I was personally able to witness and study.

Approaches to the *Dybbuk* Tale

The most complete description and analysis of these is provided by Gedalya Nigal, who has collected more than sixty texts describing *dybbuk* possessions spanning some four hundred years. His book provides the main corpus of *dybbuk* tales, covering cases from the appearance of *dybbuk* narratives during the period of R. Isaac Luria in the sixteenth century through episodes occurring in the early twentieth century.[1]

On the basis of this corpus, Yoram Bilu has proposed a psychological/anthropological analysis of *dybbuk* episodes.[2] He treats the communal and personal characterizations creating the conditions for employing the aberration of a *dybbuk* as a social lever for the promotion of conformity in the community, defining it as "a culturally dependent syndrome."

Sarah Zfatman-Biller offers an analysis proceeding from the treatment of two texts through a literary/folkloric analysis, emphasizing that even among such stories that purport to be true, one finds that some tend more toward imaginative and fictive literature than others.[3]

In his article "Ma'ase ha-Ru'ah veha-Ishah ha-Shedah," Joseph Dan deals with an elaborated literary adaptation of a *dybbuk* tale as it was written by Avraham ibn Susan in his work *Ma'ase Tzaddikim* (Jerusalem, 1889).[4] Dan sees the publication of this book as part of a stream of creative literary work written in the Land of Israel in the nineteenth century but not yet investigated.

J. H. Chajes contributes perspectives from history and comparative religion to this research.[5] Chajes focuses on theological texts that treat the *dybbuk* phenomenon and the modes of its exorcism. He presents the act of exorcism in Judaism against the background of parallel phenomena in Christianity but also considers matters that are unique to Jewish culture, such as the kabbalistic concept of the *ibbur* (soul impregnation). He emphasizes the nature of the *dybbuk* as the spirit of one who has died, rather than being the devil, as most possessing spirits are in Christianity.

All this research deals with written texts. Nevertheless, as in the case of every folktale, the tradition of oral narration coexists with that of the written tradition. In every exorcism ritual an audience attends, and it is reasonable to assume that, paralleling the work of the composer of the written account, everyone in attendance at the occasion told the tale to acquaintances. Thus the tale became widespread, as each narration told it newly and differently, in accord with the purposes of the narrator and his or her relationship with the audience at the various times and places the tale was told.

The folklorist Richard Bauman distinguishes between the narrative event and the narrated event in tales that are related as having happened in reality.[6] He sees the narrative as a verbal icon of the event it describes.

The description of the narrated event—the exorcism of a *dybbuk*—reaches us as a written text expressing the perspective of the author and his aims. In this essay, however, I will directly examine a *dybbuk* narrative that was related orally. The point of departure here is that an oral narrative is a communicative performance event that mutually relates the narrator and the audience, as well as a cultural communicative event that relates the individual to the surrounding society.

The Transformation of the *Dybbuk* Narrative

In the popular understanding in folklore and Jewish culture up to the present, the *dybbuk* is taken to be the spirit of a dead person that enters into the body of a human being, through which it acts. The term itself, whose Hebrew meaning is "to stick" or "to cleave," appears for the first time in a Yiddish pamphlet published in Volhynia about 1680,[7] though the phenomenon preceded this coinage by over a century. Generally, as Bakhtin has pointed out, the labeling of a phenomenon occurs *after* it has already made its appearance in that culture.[8] In this instance the term itself underwent a metamorphosis over the years, acquiring a certain added specificity. The original, kabbalistic term was *ibbur*, which could signify either a beneficent or maleficent spirit. "*Dybbuk*" carries a strictly negative connotation.

As a consequence of the popularity of the Yiddish drama written by S. An-Ski at the beginning of the twentieth century, *The Dybbuk*, and its Hebrew translation by H. N. Bialik,[9] both the term and the phenomenon became popular and widely disseminated, along with the Hebrew idiom, "A *dybbuk* has possessed him/her."

Before the sixteenth century, particularly in the periods of the Second Jewish Commonwealth and Talmud, possession meant penetration of demons into the bodies of living humans. Demons are incorporeal creatures, created on the eve of the Sabbath (*Abot* 5.6), and they at once possess characteristics of both humans and angels (BT Haggigah 16a). Since they have no body they can clothe themselves in any one they choose; they can even enter into the body of a human and take up residence.[10]

This concept of demonic possession continues to exist in oral folk traditions to the present day. I will offer an example here, the story told by Yefet Shvili, a Yemenite immigrant to Israel who engaged in the expulsion of a demon.[11]

Yefet's tale is presented as testimony of an event that really occurred, testimony that the narrator heard from his father. He opens his tale with a sentence intended to strengthen the claim of fidelity to the truth: "This my father saw, truly," he begins; he quotes his father as a source of authentification, adding the word "truly" as further support for his claim. This sentence closes the account as well as opening it, thus locating the story within a frame of persuasive conviction: "My father was there and saw this."

The tale itself depicts a magician, a witch, whose servant's body is entered by a she-demon. The servant goes to wash in a river, a site appointed for catastrophe since demons dwell near water. The entry of the she-demon into the servant's body causes him to act wildly—he tears his clothes, shrieks, and runs wild. The community diagnoses this behavior as "madness." The people say to the magician, "Your servant has gone mad."

The magician, in his professional capacity, determines that an incidence of magic has occurred and asks that the servant be brought before him in bonds, in order to subdue him.

Following the opening episode, the tale concentrates on the exorcism of the she-demon. The ritual of exorcism is divided into three episodes, a structure commonly encountered in folktales,[12] in each of which the magician intensifies his magical activity until the she-demon departs. The deeds of magic include lighting a fire, writing magical formulae, and burning them in the fire. This a very common technique in magical rituals.

The act of burning serves as a work of imitative magic "like to like" (compare pouring out water in order to bring rain), so that the incineration of the chit causes the she-demon inside the body of the servant to feel that she herself is being set on fire. At each occasion, she cries out "It hurts! It burns!" but refuses to depart, and each time the magician heightens the intensity of the magic act. Finally, at the third attempt, the she-demon does exit, as is customary in spirit tales, from the little toe of the servant, knocking over a glass of water on her way out as proof that she has gone.

In this tale there is neither evidence of a system of reward and punishment nor of the conflict between holiness (the exorcising *tzaddik*) and impurity (the sinning spirit), as one often finds in possession narratives. The cause of the affliction is the servant's entry into a demon-ridden locale. The explanation the she-demon gives is one that is customary in magic-folkloric systems: the she-demon became enamored of a human male and desired him for herself.[13] Generally, however, a love of this sort does not entail introgression into the body of the male; rather, the she-demon clothes herself in the body of a human woman and seduces the man in order to bear children from him.

This tale joins the motif of marriage between a human male and a she-demon with the narrative structure typical of demonic tales, including motifs common to these tales: the dialogue between the exorcist and the spirit and the egress of the spirit. The execution of the magic act outside the body of the afflicted is atypical of such tales. In this tale, however, the exorcist neither flogs nor beats the victim in order to force the she-demon out but kindles a fire nearby. Another highly unusual element in this spirit tale, atypical of the genre, is the division of gender roles. Generally one finds a male spirit penetrating the body of a woman, but in this case it is a she-demon possessing the body of a man.

Dybbuk and *Ibbur*

The understanding of a *dybbuk* as a spirit, the soul of a deceased person that has entered into the body of a living human, is associated with the mystical conceptions that developed principally in Safed in the sixteenth century in connection with kabbalistic doctrines of metempsychosis.[14]

The kabbalistic term for the phenomenon is not "reincarnation" (*gilgul*) but "impregnation" (*ibbur*). R. Hayyim Vital distinguishes the two conceptions and terms as follows:

> *Gilgul* takes place at the moment of birth. A soul [not that of the child being born] enters into the body of the one being born and suffers all the pain and tortures that befall the body from the moment it comes forth into the atmosphere until it dies, and it has no right to depart the body until then. But an *ibbur* occurs in a situation where the human has already been born and matured. At that time a different soul enters into the body, so that the person is similar to an impregnated female carrying a baby within her; thus it is called a pregnancy [*ibbur*].[15]

The underlying assumption supporting the doctrine of *gilgul* is that souls are generally recurrent, reborn to enter the body of a new person or other creature after the demise of their former habitation. This is how the *Bahir* interprets the biblical verse "one generation passes away and another appears" (Eccles. 1:4), as if the verse speaks of the identical "generation" disappearing and reappearing.[16]

An *ibbur*, on the other hand, takes place when an additional soul joins itself to one already present in a living human body. The *ibbur* may be benign, an additional soul that has descended in order to help a human being, to strengthen his or her ability to carry out a particular religious injunction (*mitzvah*). Thus, for example, the collectanea *Shivhe ha-Ari* (In Praise of Rabbi Isaac Luria) tells how the soul of R. Pinhas ben Ya'ir descended and impregnated the body of R. Shmu'el Uceda in order to assist him in carrying out the *mitzvah* of charity (*tzedakah*).[17] The individual who merits such an *ibbur* is normally one of the righteous (*tzaddikim*).

But a malign *ibbur* may occur as well. Such cases involve the impregnation of one sinner by another, in order to punish the former. In most cases the sin involves transgression of one of the sexual taboos. The victim is punished by the entry into his or her body of the impregnating soul that refuses to depart from its new residence, since it finds surcease therein from its own restless wandering and punishments.[18] The residence of the spirit brings the guilty party to engage in a series of bizarre practices not sanctioned by the community, such as deviations from religious norms, acts of abandon, the utterance of insults and curses. The afflicted individual may also speak in strange voices, sometimes those of animals or of the opposite gender, or evince an inexplicable knowledge, such as the sudden possession of facility in a foreign language. At this stage the afflicted individual is brought to the attention of a folk healer (a *ba'al shem*) or a well-known mystical rabbi, a holy man, who will exorcise the spirit in a public ceremony in accord with established principles.

Sacred Theater: The Structure of Exorcism

The accounts possess a fixed structure that ranges from the descriptive to the iconic and monoepisodic and sometimes appear as a complex and highly developed work of prose narrative. The elements are generally these.

1. An appeal to a holy man (specifically a kabbalist) for help. This frequently occurs following unsuccessful attempts made by other exorcists or conventional doctors.
2. The conflict between the kabbalist and the spirit. This is the central episode of the tale, containing several verbal ceremonial components. First is the *identification* of the spirit. The rabbi forces the spirit to identify itself by its full name, that is, its own name and those of its father and mother.

    Second is the *biography* of the spirit. At the rabbi's demand the spirit recites its history: how it sinned, how it has been punished (generally by destructive angels), and what made it possible for the spirit to enter into the body of the victim (a particular transgression on the part of the victim).[19]

    Third is the spirit's *refusal to depart*. The rabbi uses adjurations, including excommunication and other bans, to force its departure, as well as other practices, such as sounding the shofar, fumigation, whipping, and promises to pray on behalf of the spirit and its release from punishment.
3. The spirit leaves the body. The departure of the spirit may cause *injury* to the limb through which it departs. Therefore, in general, the rabbi requires the spirit to depart through that limb least likely to cause real harm to the victim, such as through the space between the toenail and the flesh of the little toe.

    There must be *proof* that the spirit has left. The egress of the spirit is accompanied by the physical evidence of its departure, such as the appearance of a hole in a window pane or waves in the surface of a liquid-filled bowl, prepared beforehand.

    Restoration is achieved. The victim's physical health is restored and the victim returns to his/her place in society.

Every tale also contains at least five participants, each with a different role: the Victim, the Spirit, the Exorcist, the Community, and the Narrator.[20]

The Victim

In most cases the victim is a female (forty-one out of the sixty-three known accounts are women and twenty-two are young boys).[21] The act of penetration by the *dybbuk*, usually a male, is described in terms of rape. Indeed, the transgressions of both the dead soul and the living victim are generally connected with sexuality, such as adultery or incest. The sin of the possessing spirit is usually serious, while that of the female victim may be mild—a single forbidden kiss, for example. The victim is generally passive; it is not her place to recount what has happened to her. If she has sinned it is the role of the spirit to present that as part of its narrative about how it came to enter the victim's body. The victim performs a double function, both passive and active: she becomes the vessel for the spirit, the conduit for the spirit's narration; but she is at the same time an instigating force who manifests her personality through those powers.

It is not always the case that the victim has committed a sin. Like encounters with demons, the encounter with a spirit can be accidental. Circumstances such as ill-temper, anger, injuries, and fear make it possible for the spirit, like the demon, to assault the victim.[22] Proximity to such places as graveyards or sewers and other sources of foul water, where demons and evil spirits linger, also enables a spirit to enter into a human being, even though he or she may have committed no sin.

Yoram Bilu, in his anthropological/psychological analysis of *dybbuk* cases, emphasizes that these constitute an articulation of women's sexual urges.[23] I would like to point out a further dimension of these episodes. A woman in traditional Jewish society who was possessed by a *dybbuk*, that is, her entire being was taken over by a male spirit, was now empowered to express her own repressed voice through the *dybbuk*—sexual needs, cursing, or transgressing any number of other social and religious mores. The victim literally spoke in a male voice. Her own voice deepened to male tones and took on a strange, otherworldly quality (xenoglossia).

The price she paid for her few moments of freedom, however, was high. As a perceived victim of spirit possession she was compelled to undergo the public rigors of the exorcism ritual, which might involve whipping, blows, and inhaling the smoke of a malodorous, sometimes toxic incense. In a very few cases the ritual even resulted in the victim's death. However, it usually concluded with her return to the straight and narrow path as a newly reformed deviant.

The Spirit

The main event in these narratives is the spirit's story. This actually functions as a story within a story, and it too has a fixed structure.

1. Identification. The spirit identifies itself as a dead man by name, family, and location.
2. Sins. The spirit confesses all its sins in detail, including names of those with whom it sinned.
3. Punishment. The spirit tells of the tortures it has endured after death.
4. Penetration. The spirit recounts the circumstances that enabled it to penetrate the victim's body, including her sin, if this was involved.

In most cases the spirit was that of a dead male Jew, though in rare cases gentile spirits appear. Sinning gentiles were not of great interest to the Jewish community, which sought to use *dybbuk* tales as a means to strengthen its religious norms for the preservation of Jewish life.

Sometimes the spirit was some famous historical personality from the past, such as the messianic pretender Shabbatai Zvi. Cases like this served the purposes of the Jewish community at large in its anti-Sabbatean stance, aiding its attempt to condemn Shabbatai as a false messiah. His fate after death constituted proof of the intense punishments his activities had incurred. This raises a further interesting question that has not yet been investigated: which personalities among those taken to be famous sinners in the annals of the Jews have come back as *dybbuks*, and in what contexts?

Often the spirit is a man well known to the community present at the exorcism, and some of those attending can actually remember him and his deeds.[24] This type of situation presents an opportunity for a theodicy, because the witnesses can confirm what the spirit says and recall his sins, or, if these were done in secret, express their astonishment and reprove the spirit with the admonition that nothing is concealed before God and every evildoer is punished for his sins.

Spirits of men who have died in the recent past may connect themselves to relatives with whom they had contact in their lifetime, or a particularly close relationship. This is what occurred in the recent case of Judith Seegautekar, wherein the spirit was that of her late husband returning to her three years after his passing. In this case those present testified that they could even identify the voice of the spirit as that of the man when he was alive, as well as his mannerisms and lifestyle.[25]

The Exorcist

The exorcist is a famous kabbalist, a rabbi or a folk healer. The first known narrative concerns a case from 1563 in which the exorcist was R. Joseph Karo. Exorcisms were carried out in the sixteenth and seventeenth centuries by R. Isaac Luria, creator of a great kabbalistic school, and his disciple, R. Hayyim Vital, both of whom were alleged to be the messiah. Twentieth-century exorcists include R. Abraham Isaac Kook and R. David Basri, who was called in to the recent Dimona case.

The victim is brought to the exorcist by her family, often after previous exorcists have failed to remedy the situation. These previous failures function as part of the hagiography around the powerful, miracle-performing rabbi who succeeds. These failures can also serve the purpose of the narrator, showing that *this* rabbi succeeded where physicians, or non-kabbalists, or non-Hasidic rabbis failed. In one tale the Sephardi rabbi succeeds after the failure of Ashkenazi rabbis.[26]

The exorcist and the spirit play the two central and most active roles in the plot of the tale. Their conflict is described in increasingly intense stages. The rabbi begins by asking terse questions of a fundamental nature: Who are you? What is your name? Where did you live? What did you do? What are your sins? What happened to you after you died? How did you enter this body? Why did you enter this body? What do you want? Have you repented? The answers at this stage are lengthy and detailed.

In the following stage the rabbi negotiates with the spirit to secure its departure, which the spirit does not wish to undertake. The spirit, for its part, negotiates favorable terms for its departure, such as a promise from the rabbi to achieve a cosmic repair (*tikkun*) of the spirit's circumstances. Thus the encounter with the exorcist is beneficial from the spirit's perspective, for it offers the opportunity to gain the aid of a powerful rabbi in ameliorating the spirit's condition.

In the third stage the dialogue is acerbic and again terse, constituting the dramatic apex of the tale. Each response is constituted of a single word or two, such as: "Go out!" and "I won't." When words are not effective the rabbi resorts to rituals, for some of which he requires the assistance of the congregation: for example, praying, reciting Psalms, opening the holy ark, giving charity, or putting on white prayer shawls (*tallitot*). If this too is not sufficient the rabbi threatens the spirit and begins to torture it, working on all the senses: he burns incense (olfactory), lights candles (vision, touch), and whips it (touch). Finally, if all else has failed, the rabbi will impose the most extreme torture: excommunication. The spirit is expelled from all the worlds and from the Jewish community. This again requires the agreement and participation of the community as the exorcist speaks the words and those present all blow ram's horns (*shofarot*). No spirit can stand up to this.

The Community

The role of the community, the collective, is no less important. The exorcist cannot perform without its help and consent. The exorcism occurs in a public space, usually a holy place such as a synagogue. The ritual itself serves as a stimulus for acts of repentance, disclosures of transgression, expressions of regret, and religious revival. For the audience, the *dybbuk* exorcism confirms that sinners indeed undergo bitter suffering, the present victim as well as the spirit; and that even if one is not punished for sinning in this world, the punishment will inevitably be imposed after death. The spirit's story proves that sin cannot be hidden, for it may not be only God who sees everything and forgets nothing—the whole community might come to know of one's sins in a public setting. Those present will be driven not only to a sense of fear, but to shame as well.

The appearance of the spirit answers the eternal human question, What happens to the human being after death? The impact is the same whether the spirit is from those recently deceased, so that people still remember him and can verify the details themselves, or whether it belongs to the distant past, in which case he would be a very famous personality, part of the collective historical memory.

The Narrator

The written tales are for the most part related from the perspective of a narrator who was present at the event and is now describing it. The narrator may play a number of different roles. First, he may be a part of the audience within the story; that is, he himself was present at the time of the event and describes it in the first person as a witness. A tale of this sort is connected to the genre of folk literature known as a *memorate*. A second possibility is that the narrator relates what he has heard from someone else who was himself present or who has heard what happened from a third person. This sort of tale is called a *fabulate*.[27] The farther along the chain of transmission the testimony goes, the less faithful it is to the tale as a report of what actually transpired. A third possible role for the narrator is to function in a more active role than that of a mere spectator; he may assist the exorcist in performing the ritual of excommunication. A fourth possibility is that the narrator is himself the exorcist, describing events in the first person. In such a case the authority of the exorcist, as the chief representative of heavenly forces telling his own tale, augments the validity of a firsthand report.

As in all personal narratives, the narrator wants to convince his present audience or reader that he is imparting a true account. He therefore takes care to give many accurate details, such as names of people involved, names of places, and dates. If he is not himself the exorcist, he will usually give the names of the transmitters or add sentences such as, "I myself was there and saw it with my very own eyes." Sometimes a negative sentence, such as "You know that I do not believe in such things, but there is no other explanation," is part of the narrator's rhetorical arsenal. He may describe the reactions of the audience present at the exorcism in order to create the same reactions in the reading or listening audience, using language like, "And the whole community was amazed."

The Narrative Function

Exorcism narratives function at multiple levels to reinforce normative communal values. The greater the name of the rabbi involved, the more convincing the story will be. The greater the power of the spirit the rabbi overcomes, the more distinct the hagiographic intent of the tale glorifying the godly man. The more painful the punishments of the victim and spirit, the stronger the ethical-social lesson of the story as a moral tale, and the more potent for one straying, or intending to stray, from the norms of social-religious behavior. The shorter the chain of the testimony's transmission, the greater its credibility as a report of what actually happened.

Dybbuk tales are taken to be true accounts, descriptions of a deed that actually transpired, by those belonging to the reference group. They base their position on the belief that the soul continues to exist after the body dies and that the soul has the capacity to roam our world, ceaselessly seeking the opportunity to take up a dwelling among living human beings. The written texts as well as the Hasidic tales are based on this kabbalistic doctrine and emphasize tales of the exorcism of spirits. In every case, these are malign spirits, or what is termed in kabbalistic literature "an evil *ibbur*." Descriptions of a "benign *ibbur*," like those that appear in tales from the period of R. Isaac Luria himself, are relatively few, and failed to develop a literary tradition in succeeding periods.

Perhaps due to the fact that the negative occurrences are more dramatic, they make possible literary expansions that engage the theme of the victim's suffering and that of the spirit, and possess a greater capacity to awaken their audience to spiritual renewal. Moreover, while the "good *ibbur*" is restricted to great *tzaddikim*, the "bad *ibbur*" can happen to anybody. In the oral tradition of folk tales, such stories continue to be told up to the present and follow both narrative tracks: that of the expulsion of demons that have entered into the body of a human (especially common among Moroccan Jews) and that of the exorcism of spirits of deceased individuals. The rituals of expulsion in both cases continue to be found to the present in Israel.

An interesting mixture of both elements occurs in the creative literary work of Avraham ibn Susan. In his story "The Spirit and the She-Demon" ("Ma'ase ha-Ru'ah ve-ha-Ishah ha-Shedah"), a spirit enters into a young boy of Damascus and forces him to have intercourse with a she-demon. The two Sephardic rabbis of Tiberias, R. Shlomo Abulafia and R. David de la Reina, succeed in carrying out the exorcism and expel both the spirit and the she-demon.

Ibn Susan's tale is a polished literary retelling of a *dybbuk* narrative, which Joseph Dan has quite correctly placed in the context of a trend in nineteenth-century writing from the Land of Israel.[28] It is probable that he based his story on an actual incident about which he knew or heard through an oral tradition, particularly since he mentions the specific names of the Tiberias rabbis, but this has no bearing on the process of stylistic crafting the tale underwent.

Ibn Susan's work is different from An-Ski's play, *The Dybbuk*, in that the latter was not a reworking of oral tales but rather a literary invention. An-Ski did base his story on known literary *dybbuk* traditions, but he departed sharply from these early sources. An-Ski presents a story of love rather than a theological tale of reward and punishment. The emphasis is on the romantic plane—the uniting of lovers after death. Leah begs the spirit of her lover, Hanan, which has possessed her body, not to abandon her. Despite a successful exorcism she chooses to die and thus remain united with him.

At the extreme opposite end of the literary spectrum, both in terms of reworking and new creativity, is the documentary: the precise cataloguing of these tales (in recordings or images) as they are told over by the heroes of the story themselves. This documentation is generally undertaken in a research context, but such records can only be made concerning contemporary cases narrated orally, where the recorder is an investigator with no specific ideological expectations from the resulting documents.

The majority of *dybbuk* tales that have reached us over the past several hundred years have been mediated, having been passed along as written accounts. Some are transmitted in reports that attempt to include precise details in order to impart to the reader the impression of believability and accuracy; others tend more toward an imaginative and creative style.[29] In most instances, however, the impression imparted is directed toward a goal: to enhance the image of a rabbi and to strengthen the foundations of faith and religious norms of the reprimanding community by means of the ceremony.

I would also include in this category the most recent exorcism of which I am aware, the expulsion of a spirit from the body of Judith Seegautekar, performed by Rabbi David Basri in Jerusalem in 1999. While the ceremony was videotaped, a seemingly precise documentation of events, the video recording later sold to the public was a version edited by the rabbi's proponents,[30] consisting of only one and a quarter hours from an event that lasted over six hours. I therefore take this recording as an exemplar of the same type of text as all those written texts that have reached us from previous centuries. The obvious aim in the video recording is to inspire repentance among its viewers, a fact that is actually stated outright by Judah Basri, the son and spokesman of the rabbi.[31] In the middle of the exorcism Rabbi Basri was highly aware of the cameras and the fact that the ceremony was being broadcast live on radio. Together with his repeated remonstrations for the repentance of the assembled crowd, he also appealed directly to the radio audience and those who would watch the video later.

Menuhah's *Dybbuk*

The event on which I will focus below is one I recorded myself in Jerusalem in 1994.[32] In contrast to the written tales from the past, this is an orally communicated narrative. It therefore presents the opportunity for the feminine voice to be heard, since the young woman who was the victim speaks, as well as others. In all prior written sources, the *dybbuk*'s female victim never speaks; rather, the male spirit speaks through her body. The exorcist is always a male rabbi, as is the narrator of events.

I recorded three different versions of the story myself: one told by the victim, a seventeen-year-old girl; one told by her father, who witnessed the events; and one told by the exorcist, who in this very unusual case was also a woman, the wife of the rabbi involved. In each version the narrator portrays himself or herself as the hero of the story, but in the women's version the father is never mentioned, while in his versions he is central. In yet another unusual twist, the spirit itself in this case was that of a young woman, and she pointedly does *not* speak. Furthermore, no transgression of hers is mentioned. The spirit's story, the reasons for its return to this world, the reason it chose to enter this specific young woman, all were understood by the rabbi through his powers of insight, as he claimed. The rabbi's words were passed along through the victim, who quotes him.

The event itself occurred in a private setting, the house of the rabbi, in the presence only of those directly connected with the matter, with none of the public communal aspect that generally accompanies *dybbuk* exorcisms. The settings of the narrations were also intimate: discussions between myself and the victim, between myself and the wife of the rabbi, and between myself and the father. The feminine context gave the first two the opportunity to tell their story freely and to include intimate details. The young woman was not prepared to speak in the presence of anyone, even her father, who had been at the exorcism. Each of the women communicated a degree of rebellion against negative male figures in her life: the young woman against her father, the rabbi's wife against her husband. The father himself, when first interviewed, spoke in a highly abbreviated manner and with clear unwillingness. The second time he was more prepared to expand the discussion, and he created a much "smoother" version of events in which he avoided details he didn't like and apparently did not wish to share with me.

All this stands in stark contrast to Judith Seegautekar, whose narrative was broadcast to every radio and television in Israel and who granted interviews to various newspapers during both the phase when she was working with Rabbi Basri and the phase when she denied the whole story. The present case is instead the personal experience of a suffering woman—there is no publicity or tendentious intent. The victim's declaration of repentance is bereft of dramatic purposes and certainly of documentary ones. The reason the participants requested that I withhold their real names is clear.

The Victim's Story

The girl, Menuhah,[33] opens her story with a declaration and a confession that define her religious situation: "I was then attempting to strengthen my Jewishness. I am not so very strong [in my faith]."

Menuhah, a young woman of seventeen, was a new immigrant from Russia whose father decided to renew his faith and move to Israel with his family. She found herself in a new land without her consent, forced to learn a new language and conform to a whole structure of ordinances and inhibitions with which she had been unfamiliar. She was sent to a women's religious boarding school in Jerusalem in which close attention was paid to her religious and social conduct. Her decision to begin her story of the event with this opening statement attests to her feelings of guilt and her perception that what occurred was a punishment for her spiritual weakness.

In order to strengthen her faith she set herself additional tasks that are not, strictly speaking, required by Jewish law: "Whenever a transport belonging to the *hevrah kadishah* [the "holy society" that attends to the care of the Jewish deceased] passes, I read psalms to aid the departed soul in the next world."

Menuhah chooses here to relate a deed that is conventionally defined as one of true charity (*hesed shel emet*) since its performance carries no socioreligious recompense. She prays on behalf of the soul of deceased people with whom she is unacquainted and no one takes note of her deed. Her choice to perform a religious act that is associated with death, as she relates it, forebodes what will occur in the event.

This constitutes the opening episode of the tale, a general opening related in the present continuous tense—that is, an activity that repeats itself.

The plot begins its forward movement as it abandons that which commonly occurs for that which is extraordinary. The depiction of the time is now "one day." On that day a transport of the *hevrah kadishah* passed by with a loudspeaker on top, blaring the name of the deceased. But Menuha failed to discern the name in order to read those passages appropriate to him or her, the psalms whose first word begins with the same letter as the name of the dead, as is customary. She decided to carry out the tradition by reading random psalms and, in place of a fixed prayer, to turn to God in direct speech, appealing to his mercy. "I said, 'God, I will read the chapters. You already know what the correct letters are and which soul to help.'"

The style of her address is that of the simpleton's prayer, said by one who is not acquainted with the customary forms of prayer but whose supplication is likely to be granted due to pure intent and the direct connection with God. For example, in a Hasidic tale, a villager turns to God and says, "Master of the World! What can I do? I do not know how to pray, but I do know the alphabet. . . . I will just repeat the letters and you, Master of the World, join them together as they should be."[34]

In ironic contrast to the prayer of the villager, which meets with favor in heaven and enables the prayers of the other members of the community to ascend, what happened to Menuhah is entirely different. The transport made an additional circuit and Menuhah saw in this a response to her prayer. She hurried to the window this time to decipher the name of the deceased.

Instead, what Menuhah witnessed through the window was a fatal traffic accident: a white automobile collided with a girl riding a motorcycle. Menuhah recites the horror with precision: "I saw the girl crawling slowly beneath the wheels of the car, powerless. She tried to raise her head but she fell. She had no strength left. She lay there on the road."

It appears that this took place on Friday afternoon, almost a holy time. It was on a weekend that Menuhah stayed in the boarding school awaiting the visit of her sister, according to the practice of what was termed in the school a "sisters' Shabbat." Menuhah called out to her sister and came down with her to show her where the accident had taken place. The victims had already been removed, but the road was "still full of spilled blood." Menuhah was attentive to the power of blood and careful not to approach. "I didn't want to point at the blood with my finger, so I pointed at it with my foot. My foot touched the blood."

Menuhah, who was apparently aware of the structure of folk beliefs connected with blood,[35] reached the conclusion at once that she had done something terrible that would have severe consequences. "Blood is the soul" is a concept that appears in the Bible (Deut. 12:23). "Blood is the principle of life in human beings" (*Avot de-Rabbi Natan* 31), and Jews are forbidden to eat blood (Lev. 7:26f.) but are required to cover the blood of animals and birds with dust (Lev. 17:13).

Touching blood, then, is the same as touching a soul. Touching this spilled blood conveyed the soul of the slain girl to the body of Menuhah.

This point is connected to a whole system of folk beliefs concerning blood. Among certain tribal societies, drinking blood is understood to occasion the incorporation of the soul of the possessor of the blood. When a person sells his or her soul to the devil, he or she signs the contract with blood because the soul is corporealized in the blood. When the death of a young person is concerned, especially a violent death, the soul is left to wander restlessly until it finds revenge or is otherwise satiated. At the time of death the soul of the deceased remains near the body or its environs. (Thus one covers the mirrors in the house with dark cloths during the seven days of mourning, so that the soul, which is yet present in the home, may not be seen in them.)

Bereshit Rabbah (22.9) explicates the verse, "Your brother's [Abel's] blood cries out to me from the earth" (Gen. 4:10) as follows: "Since no soul had yet risen to Heaven [Abel's] could not ascend; and since no human had yet been interred in the earth [Abel's] soul could not remain below. His blood was hurled out upon the trees and stones." The blood of the young victim Menuhah saw was yet spilled out on the street; her soul was yet nearby.

From that day, Menuhah began to suffer from pains in her stomach and head and from what she termed "confusion." "Every time I stepped on the foot that had touched the blood, I got a terrible headache." Menuhah certainly saw her suffering as directly and causally connected to what she had done. This situation persisted for three months. During this period several incidents and behaviors occurred in connection with what had happened that were completely at odds with those appropriate for a young woman in her position—raised in a family governed by an authoritarian and powerful father and living in a boarding school under a religious administration. These included radical alterations of conduct such as cursing, using obscenities and coarse gestures, spending whole days on the sofa, failing to get out of bed in the morning, sleeplessness, long uninterrupted stretches listening to her Walkman, and wild laughter.

Menuhah, caged in her home, was connected to the world outside by her radio. This was the way she learned the name of the girl killed in the accident. On one of the programs she heard a woman request a song to be played in memory of her daughter, who had been killed in an auto accident. The mother related the details of the accident, and thus Menuhah acquired a name and an identity to attach to the slain girl: Miri.

"I knew it was her," Menuhah describes her reaction; "I trembled very hard."

Another dramatic turn of events occurred in Menuhah's life: she fell in love with a soldier. The temporal sequence in which the alterations in her behavior, the identification of the dead girl, and the meeting with the soldier took place is not clear. The meeting itself was an abnormal and forbidden act, an insult to the social and communal norms of the society in the conduct of a modest young religious girl. Menuhah met the soldier on Mt. Herzl in Jerusalem near the military cemetery there, not far from her boarding school. The most serious consequences followed upon the relations that began to develop between Menuhah and the soldier: the director of the school questioned her and screamed at her, shaming her in front of all the other girls. Her mother suspected her of having become pregnant; her father brought her schooling to an end, removed her from the school, and locked her up in the house.

Menuhah was aware that her acts were shameful. "I did other things," she said to me. "I'm ashamed to tell you." Nevertheless, she defended herself, employing the same sentence with which she opened her account, "I am very religious, but my faith is not strong enough."

The motif of death dominates the tale. Of all the commandments, Menuhah chooses that of reading psalms for the benefit of the dead. She witnesses the death of a young girl, touches her blood, and finally falls in love with a soldier near a graveyard. Her proximity to death mounts step by step, from that of an anonymous corpse whose name she fails to hear to that of a young girl who dies before her eyes to that of a dead soul that enters into her body. This brings to an end the first movement of the tale, in which a sequence of events is described taking place in the real world. But Menuhah's situation was becoming more complex.

In the second part of the tale, the resolution emerges—both the solution to the riddle of the connection among the events and the physical resolution of Menuhah's condition. This resolution is brought about only through the involvement of a supernal power. Menuhah's father takes her to a person who represents the realm of holiness, the rabbi.

The rabbi is R. Daniel, a young kabbalist about forty years of age, of Moroccan background, a spiritually reawakened Jew (*hozer biteshuva*). He has the reputation of someone with the power to resolve difficulties and relieve distress, an aid to the sick, and a person who can work cures through the employment of kabbalistic treatments. Dozens of people, including very well-known politicians, visit him at home from morning to night seeking his aid, though it is difficult to see him or gain an audience. He effects his labors in mystery, disappears for days at a time or for months on end, and may vanish suddenly, leaving a number of people waiting for hours while he departs and returns. Menuhah's father, Evgeni, works as the rabbi's beadle, conducting people into his presence and making appointments. Under the rabbi's influence, Evgeni and his entire family became spiritually reawakened.

It was in this context that I became acquainted with Evgeni and Menuhah. I was doing research, gathering miracle tales and spending many day and nights in R. Daniel's home.

R. Daniel connected the diverse details and, by means of his unique vision, perceived the cause behind the way they had developed. Menuhah says, "The rabbi said that this girl, Miri, was the girlfriend of the boy I was dating. He loved her very much. She came back to him through my body."

R. Daniel's explanation considerably reduced Menuhah's guilt. Her aberrant conduct was explained as unintentional, since she was being forced to behave as she did by the deceased girl, Miri. But, on the level of reality, the same supernatural resolution established an emotional conflict with the complex of causative factors. The tale of the romance between Menuhah and the soldier shifts to one of a love triangle. Menuhah becomes two people, herself and the deceased Miri, the soldier's previous beloved. How does this affect Menuhah? Will her confidence not be shaken by the possibility that the soldier is not at all involved with her but still longs for the deceased Miri? This emotive configuration, a common one in relationships in which one or the other partner is still attached to a previous but now deceased lover, acquires concrete dimensions in this tale: the dead lover continues to exist in the body of the current, living partner.

Menuhah did not express such fears openly. She continued to be close to the soldier, carrying on their relationship in secret in complete defiance of her father's wishes. The soldier called her on the telephone and wrote her; Menuhah hid the letters. She showed me the soldier's picture while her sister, her accomplice, kept watch for her father at the door. The romance with a soldier in particular represents an attachment to the secular world from which Menuhah has been segregated. The world of an Israel in whose armed forces citizens serve is one into which Menuhah is prevented from entering by her religion.

After R. Daniel establishes the diagnosis, the stage of treatment and cure follows. Contrary to other *dybbuk* tales in the narrative tradition, R. Daniel does not require an interview with the spirit to establish its identity. By dint of his power he is able to identify the spirit before the exorcism begins.

What leads the spirit to invest the body of Menuhah is not a sin that the spirit committed and for which she seeks remission from the angels of destruction, but her love for the boy. She clothes herself in a living body in order to draw close to him once more. Menuhah's "sin" is explicated on two different levels: on the religious level, as a sin of neglect and weak faith, and on the magical level, as the act of touching blood. Thus, a parapraxis, Menuhah's accidental contact with the blood of the slain girl, is necessarily added to the magic level of the narrative structure.

The ritual framework within which the spirit is exorcised is referred to by R. Daniel as an *aliyah*, an ascent. This is a term he employs in dealing with anyone who comes to him for help. The supplicant seeks to know what will happen or what position a third person takes. The rabbi joins himself to the soul of the third person, has a discussion with him, and reports the results to the petitioner. Occasionally, R. Daniel joins himself to the soul of some great deceased personage and transmits advice to the petitioner. Such an "ascent" is termed a "minor ascent, "*aliyah ketanah*. A major ascent, *aliyah gedolah*, occurs infrequently and involves many preparations. I myself was present at one such "ascent."

These are the components of the ritual:

1. Time. It is not possible to establish the time for an *aliyah* beforehand. The rabbi and his wife, who also takes part in the ceremony, must be in the proper spiritual and psychic mood. Thus, someone seeking an *aliyah* may have to wait for months for the anticipated

telephone summons, "Come tomorrow night." Once the excited seeker arrives he or she must be aware that the *aliyah* may be canceled on account of various sorts of changes or complications that have taken place. One of the rabbi's seven children may have fallen ill, the rabbi's wife—given to mood alterations—is not willing to participate, or the rabbi has left on a more urgent errand.

2. Duration. Once the appointed time has arrived, the *aliyah* commences at some point after midnight and may go on until dawn.
3. Preparations. The electric lights are turned off, candles are lit, incense is kindled; that is, the efficacy of the sensual apparatus—hearing, smell, and vision—is suspended.
4. Participants. The rabbi, his wife, the supplicant, and additional onlookers are all seated in a circle.
5. Stages of the ceremony. The rabbi introduces his wife into the ritual in a slow speech spoken in a low monotone appropriate to the situation of mystical involvement. She enters a state of lowered affect, closes her eyes, and speaks in a ponderous voice.

The rabbi begins to pray, seeking to aid the supplicant. He asks his wife to begin "raising her soul." At every stage, he asks his wife whom she sees and where she is situated. His wife begins her "ascent," passing through the upper palaces. Often she encounters a "guide." The rabbi is frequently able to identify him: R. Akiva, the prophet Elijah, or a well-known rabbi who has died recently. With the assistance of the guide, the rabbi's wife moves from palace to palace and sees pictures, visions that she describes aloud. These are thought to be responses to the problem the supplicant has presented. At times, the rabbi's wife sees disturbing visions or encounters a difficulty, and, unable to continue, asks the rabbi at once to pray. He, in accord with the situation, repeats biblical verses that are suited to the problem by reason of their vocabulary or their content. (This technique of associating the proper verses with the problem is similar to that employed in the interpretation of dreams.[36]) For example, if the problem is associated with a male child, he might say, "Your children are like olive seedlings" (Ps. 128:3). Or, for a matter connected to barrenness, "Your wife is like a fruitful vine" (ibid.).

This particular night the rabbi was away, but an *aliyah* was performed nevertheless! Menuhah describes this event.

> We were sitting in the salon when suddenly the kitchen faucet began pouring water by itself. I got up to turn it off and we heard a loud "boom"

in the room. The lights went out and we couldn't see anything. Dina [the wife of the rabbi] called to me and said, "Someone is here. A girl. She is sitting on your chair. She has curly hair and she is dark. She is wearing a t-shirt and jeans. She has had an accident." I sat down in my chair again, and Dina said "Now she is in your belly. She is lying there like a fetus." Dina asked the spirit, "Who are you? What is your name? What is your mother's name? Get out!"

Menuhah's description makes no mention of the preparations; she begins at once to describe the critical moment. The signal of a supernatural occurrence is the faucet beginning to pour on its own. When Menuhah gets up to turn it off, the rabbi's wife sees the soul of the slain girl, which remains seated on Menuhah's chair. In a symbolic magical reckoning, the water contrasts with blood; as the expression says, "blood is not water." The activity of the water neutralizes the act of coming in contact with blood. Contact with her blood is what caused the soul of the slain girl to enter Menuhah's body; the contact with water causes her to leave it. When Menuhah gets up to turn off the faucet, the soul of the slain girl remains on the chair.

In contrast to the literary traditions relating tales of exorcism, no conflict between the rabbi's wife and the spirit takes place, nor any conversation between them, including negotiations for the spirit's departure. The wife of the rabbi simply orders the spirit out and perceives its departure from the body. Just as its entry had been accidental, so was its egress. Menuhah responds physically at once, understanding well the meaning of the release: "I began to tremble violently. I felt hot, as if I had a high fever. My feet burned . . . I shook. My hands shook. But I got up and tried to walk on my feet. My head didn't ache."

Her release from the spirit freed Menuhah from her physical sufferings. "I'm O.K. now. I feel fine."

When I asked her whether she had forgotten the young man, Menuhah answered, "It isn't so simple. In spite of [her leaving], she still left me harmed. I cannot be completely cured."

I expected that her return to the good graces of the religious community would be followed by her exposure to a proper suitor through her father's selection and the arrangement of a marriage in accord with the norms of such a community, completing the narrative cycle. However, the relationship with the soldier continues, in spite of Menuhah's own description of this as "harm"—something that she was unable to overcome, notwithstanding the *aliyah*.

The Witness's Story

Evgeni, Menuhah's father, told me what happened to his daughter on two different occasions. I was surprised that he agreed to speak with me, and even more, that he permitted me to interview his daughter. It is possible that my status as a person marginally associated with the rabbi's household led him to desire that I participate in the event. Still, while I was a member of the household and not part of the normal group of supplicants, I was also a researcher and reporter, a representative of the intellectual and academic world. From one point of view, he had a desire to boast of his rabbi and his own position at his court. I had also established a relationship of trust with him during the many long hours of my stay in the rabbi's house, which similarly served his purpose. Nevertheless, his discomfort at being exposed can be felt throughout his account.

His first narration took place in the morning after the *aliyah*. He spoke laconically: "My daughter was very confused. A lot of disturbances for several months. She was completely off track. We arranged an *aliyah*. Dina saw a *dybbuk*, someone in [my daughter's] stomach. It was a soul. My daughter had stepped on the blood of a girl who was killed."

Evgeni defines his daughter's condition in three descriptions, progressing from "confusion" to "disturbances" to "completely off track." At that point he turns to the description of the *aliyah*, that is, to the stage of remediation, and this too he describes dryly and with great concision. The last sentence explains the cause for the soul's entry into Menuhah: she "stepped on the blood of a girl who was killed." Prompted by my inquiries, he added, unwillingly, a few more sentences about her physical symptoms—stomach pains and headaches—and closed the conversation decisively, "I don't want to tell you any more, though there are many other details I haven't told you, that I don't want you to know. What Menuhah will tell you is up to her."

In comparison with Menuhah's tale, her father Evgeni did not, in fact, relate many details. He did not tell about his daughter's religious perplexity, about her attempts to strengthen her belief. He did not mention her relationship with the soldier—a detail that certainly embarrassed him and in which he saw his own failure as her instructor. He did not say that he had removed his daughter from the school, nor did he mention that he had imprisoned her at home. He must have thought that any of this would naturally have diminished his figure in my perception, and that I would certainly not be able to understand or find justice in his actions. Nevertheless, he left the door open for me in his last sentence; he gave me permission to talk with his daughter. I did meet with

Menuhah in her house, where she was still shut up in punishment for her conduct.

After I spoke with Menuhah, Evgeni agreed to talk with me again. This time the manner of his narration was completely different: very excited and emotional. In the description he presented this time he attributed to himself the central role in the affair, becoming the hero of the tale. From the role of a witness he shifted into the role of the exorcist's assistant, if not the exorcist himself.

"What happened on the night following the Sabbath was just wonders and miracles," he says. He turns to me several times to emphasize how much I'd lost by not acceding to his invitation to come. (I was, in fact, very sorry I hadn't, though I was invited.) He summarizes his description with the double repetition of the idiom, "What events, what events; wonders and miracles!" He apparently had no way to describe and define further what had taken place than the banal term, "events."

In the second part of the story, Evgeni becomes the hero. According to his version, the soul agreed to exit the daughter's body on condition that she enter his. "At first I agreed, for my daughter's sake." Evgeni presents himself as a devoted father; "I was prepared to sacrifice myself for my daughter." This statement seemed to me to be in complete contradiction to his hard-hearted figure as the father who imprisoned his daughter and prevented her from meeting her heart's desire. He was aware that I'd already met Menuhah and heard her story. No wonder, then, that he wanted the opportunity to present himself in a better light.

"But I reconsidered. Why do that? Let's get rid of [the *dybbuk*] altogether. We made her go into the body of a dog," he continues. Evgeni passes here from a description of the event in the third person to one in the first person, something he does frequently, presenting himself as an active participant in the exorcism. He says, "Let's get rid of her." He finds the solution that will benefit his daughter as well as himself. "We made her go into the body of a dog." Transmigration into the body of an animal is a severe punishment for the soul, and in *dybbuk* tales it generally represents the stage of punishment immediately preceding the soul's entry into the body of a human. In this case we don't even know if the dead girl sinned at all; but in Evgeni's tale the process is reversed. He elaborates his part and magnifies himself into the equivalent of the rabbi. "I too did something. *Kavvanot* and *tikkunim* [acts of spiritual purpose and cosmic effect]." But he immediately becomes frightened at what he has said and disclaims it. "I did only that which the rabbi taught me and told me to do."

This sentence is to be understood against the background of the relations between Evgeni, who was an employee of the rabbi, and the rabbi himself. Evgeni was paid a wage as the rabbi's beadle. His duty was to make appointments for supplicants and to conduct relations between the rabbi and the outside world. During the long hours that the supplicants in attendance waited there to be received by the rabbi, tense and emotional, people would turn to Evgeni with a multitude of questions. Prior to their audience they would ask him all about the rabbi, and afterward they would ask him to explain what the rabbi had said. While waiting they spoke freely of their sufferings with Evgeni, and thus he found himself giving advice—at first in the rabbi's name and eventually independently. Given this background, a certain tension came to exist between him and the rabbi that reached its conclusion with Evgeni's dismissal.

In the description of the event that happened to his own daughter, Evgeni felt very involved emotionally and was not able to restrain himself from describing the part he played in the success of the exorcism.

Of the three narrators, the father alone used the traditional term "*dybbuk*" and described the ritual of the *aliyah* as "the exorcism of a *dybbuk*." Within the framework of his newfound faith, Evgeni read many collections of Hasidic tales and was acquainted with those *dybbuk* tales found in the written tradition.

The Exorcist's Story

In contrast to the great self-confidence Evgeni presents, the tale of the rabbi's wife, who found herself in the actual role of exorcist rather than that of the exorcist's assistant, overflows with hesitancy and expressions of doubt and uncertainty. The single feature that distinguishes this *aliyah* from others is the decisive fact that the rabbi is absent. (This is also the reason I hadn't bothered coming on this occasion. When Evgeni telephoned to invite me and I heard that the rabbi was away from the city, I decided to remain home. I had, moreover, been the victim of dozens of previous disappointments, cancellations at the last moment.)

Dina begins with the apology that "I had no intention of making an *aliyah* for Menuhah. All at once, I saw this transparent figure. I saw it in Menuhah's stomach, curled up like a fetus. A curly-haired girl, wearing jeans and a black tricot blouse."

The description is precise and detailed: the clothing of the dead girl, including the color and material of the blouse, and the visual description of the way in which the girl is lying in the stomach of the afflicted Menuhah, a sort of pregnancy. As mentioned, Menuhah's mother suspected that Menuhah had become pregnant by the soldier. Menuhah was in fact pregnant mystically. The soul of the deceased girl had become an embryo in her belly.

The rabbi's wife begins her tale at the first stage of a traditional *dybbuk* exorcism: the identification of the *dybbuk*. "I asked her, 'Who are you and who are your parents and why have you entered?'" She skips over the spirit's response and turns immediately, in her next sentence, to what she did next: "I asked her to go away. She went away . . ."—and she adds "apparently." The rabbi's wife doesn't mention the water running from the faucet as Menuhah did in her tale. She doesn't mention Menuhah's father, Evgeni, at all, or his involvement in the occurrence. In her own story she is the heroine, though she sets herself up rather as an antiheroine. She is uncertain whether the spirit really did depart, and if it did, she doesn't know where it went. "And this frightens me. . . . The rabbi was not present. When he's there one sees where the spirit goes."

She adds:

I did not intend to do it alone. I just suddenly saw the dead girl inside Menuhah so clearly. But I did not see where she went when she left. The rabbi always makes sure the spirit will leave and never come back. He knows where to send it. That night I was very sick. I had a severe stomachache. I had to go to the hospital, leave my children alone. Yes, there is a connection, I am sure. Maybe she penetrated into me.

Not only is there no mention of a dog, as in Evgeni's tale, there is also the fact that the rabbi's wife feels an utter lack of confidence, perhaps because of her having invaded her husband's territory. As I mentioned, normally she only assists the rabbi in the function of a medium and does not herself oversee *aliyot*. The result was immediate: the rabbi's wife felt severe stomach pains, though examinations at the hospital found nothing. "All night long I heard footsteps, as if people were walking around." The rabbi's wife suspects that the spirit entered into her and that she absorbed Menuhah's suffering; as she puts it, she "certainly connects the events."

She expresses her fears again at the conclusion of her tale. "It troubles me that I did not see where the spirit went. Who knows? Menuhah is still not normal." In order to convince herself and those listening, however, the wife of the rabbi adds proofs of the efficacy of her unique powers by mentioning how she had predicted the Six-Day War before it began.

The rabbi's wife explicates the *aliyah* as one that was marred on her account, because she took the role of the rabbi on herself. This explains why Menuhah had not been completely cured and remained attached to the soldier. Menuhah explains this as remaining "damage" done her by the spirit. The father disregards the whole matter and says, "My daughter, thank God, is now completely normal."

Paralleling the interpretation on the mystic level, the rabbi's wife adds an interpretation on the level of emotional reality. "Her father is too strict with her. Before it's over with, she'll run away. Her boyfriend is in fact a good boy and he ought to be brought closer to the family. The rabbi spoke with him." At this point I recalled that Dina herself had become a *hozeret be-teshuvah* (a penitent or, more correctly, a newly observant Jew) in order to marry the rabbi when she was seventeen years old—the same age as Menuhah. Perhaps Dina was comparing the present situation with her own, which ended happily in marriage to the rabbi and no conflict with her parents.

In addition to the mystical explanation (the imperfect *aliyah*) and the emotional interpretation, the rabbi's wife adds an educational interpretation. "Too much pressure will cause the opposite result. The father will lose his daughter completely. It would be better to reach out to the boy." This way of doing things is typical of R. Daniel, who operates in general on two parallel tracks, the mystical and the emotive/realistic.

Menuhah's Tale as a Narrated Event

The three versions of the tale examined here are those of a single *narrated* event told in three different voices, that is, separate *narrative* events. Together they constitute one tale. The tale emerges and engages its audience in several different dimensions at once: the religious, the magical, the social, the romantic, the gender, and the genre.

The Religious Dimension

On this level, the tale is one of a young woman whose religious life is reawakened as the result of a decision made by her father in spite of her doubts and hesitations. She takes upon herself an additional religious duty in order to strengthen her weak faith, but it turns out that this religious duty is insufficient to its task. Ironically, it is precisely the attempt to carry out this duty that leads to the chain of negative events.

Within this system, figures representing the power of holiness are employed: the rabbi, the wife of the rabbi, and the father. In this type of story it is usually only male characters who represent holy powers, but our tale contains an unusual exception: the rabbi's wife, who is also a figure of holiness. Nevertheless, the story functions as a laudatory tale only for the male characters. The figure of the rabbi delineates the hagiographic aim of the tale. It is a tale of praise, one of many told about R. Daniel—how his wondrous mystic power brings him to know how to diagnose a problem at once and to see the supernatural causation of the events that occur. The figure of the rabbi is set up in direct opposition to the figure of the father, who interprets Jewish faith harshly, rigidly, and uncompromisingly but praises himself as the exorcist in the event. The rabbi, graced with a supernatural perspective, seeks to bring the boy nearer and even has a conversation with him. The wife of the rabbi serves as a mediator between the two males, the rabbi and the father, and as a medium between worlds—that of the girl and that of the *dybbuk* that has entered her. In this dimension, the entry of the spirit into the girl's body is to be understood as punishment for the weakness of her faith.

The Magical Dimension

On this level, the spilled blood is set at the center of the tale. The young woman's error is not a religious offense but rather the breaking of a taboo—touching the blood of a slain person whose life has been brought to an untimely end. Blood and water are polarized in this dimension—the two serve as symbols with opposite meanings. Touching the blood caused the spirit to enter; touching the water made it possible to expel the spirit.

According to magical systems of thought, women are considered closer to the demonic and supernatural world than men because of their connection with the sources of impurity. The author of the kabbalistic *Emek ha-Melekh* (Valley of the King), for example, explains that "the impurity from the serpent still abounds in them." This impurity is also connected with menstrual blood, which was used for various purposes in black magic and witchcraft. Both menstrual blood and the blood of the dead are considered *tamé* (impure) in Jewish law. From this point of view the magical dimension of the tale stands in opposition to the holy or religious dimension. The symbol of water preserves the connection between them. In magical folk customs water is used against the evil eye, which dries everything. One spits against the evil eye to prove that the body still contains water, representing the power to fight against evil. In religious terms water is a metaphor for the holy Torah and God: for example, "For My people have done a twofold wrong: They have forsaken Me, the Fount of living waters" (Jer. 2:13).

The Social Dimension

On this level, the story focuses on a young woman upon whom weighty social pressures are set in motion: settling in a new country, learning a new language, studying in a cloistered boarding school, striving for a new level of religiosity imposed on her by her father, being estranged from the world of young men and love. She is in effect suddenly catapulted into a closed feminine existence.

In this system, the girl is set up in diametric opposition to society and her family—her father, mother, the principal of the school, and her companions in the boarding school. The entry of the *dybbuk* enables her to break through these containments: to conduct herself in a an irregular fashion, to leave her school, to fall in love, to curse, and to dedicate her days and nights to listening to the radio. The *dybbuk* enables her to neutralize all the social pressures, to disobey her father, and to express her response, as it were, by means of another—the "spirit" of the dead girl, who is the kind of girl she would like to be. The penetration of the *dybbuk* fills her and allows her to feel impenetrable by the people who surround her, particularly by the older women (her mother and the director of the school) who seek to intrude on her intimate life by their inquiries. Touching the blood of the dead empowers her not to answer when asked whether she is pregnant, that is, if her menstrual blood had ceased to appear.

I am not a psychologist, so I will not attempt a psychological analysis, but it is clear that this is another dimension at which the tale functions as well. This much is clear, in any case: Menuhah is an adolescent girl, deprived of men's company and required to suppress her sexual desires. It is no wonder that when she is penetrated by the spirit she allows herself to use obscene language and gestures. Another aspect of this issue concerns her relationships with her two "fathers": the biological father, Evgeni, and the spiritual father, the rabbi. These men compete for her thoughts and her education, and the two experience strained relations between themselves. The mother is hardly mentioned in this story, and the sister vacillates between Menuhah and the father. On the one hand she is attracted by the new femininity of her sister, but on the other hand she will not break faith with her father.

The Romantic Dimension

On this level, a triangle of relationship is set at the center: the soldier, his dead lover, and his current one. The dead girl and the live one are polarized in this system, each representing the other's opposite. Miri, dark and curly-haired, wearing jeans and a tight tricot blouse, and the bike she rides like a man, represent the secular life, freedom, and equality. The love story of Miri and the soldier is an open book. Menuhah, shut up in a girls' boarding school, clothed in long skirts and loose blouses with sleeves down to the wrists, is hidden from the sun and her skin untanned. Her hair is pinned up tightly. She will obviously never ride a motorcycle. Her love for the soldier is a secret, and in order to realize it she has to pay the high price of conflict with all the social systems in which she lives.

In this dimension, the story does not offer a clear and simple resolution to the choice between good and evil. Miri's way leads to her death; Menuhah's, to madness and social ostracism.

Here, the figures of the father and the soldier are set against each other. The father imprisons his daughter and prevents her from meeting with her chosen, who is not to the father's taste or liking. In this explication of the tale the story of the *dybbuk* becomes a story of fate, known in folk literature as Type no. 930.[37] It is impossible to prevent the association of the lovers; their connection is one written in the world of the dead. The tale thus joins the story type of a tale of fate, like "Solomon's daughter in the tower" (*Midrash Tanhuma*, ed. S. Buber, 31), in which King Solomon imprisons his daughter in a tower to prevent her marrying. The subtext of the imprisonment is interpreted as the father's desire to keep his daughter for himself.[38]

The adult women in the story, the mother and the principal of the school, represent the social norms of the religious community, the authority of the family and the educational framework. Both of them permit themselves to intrude into the girl's privacy, to investigate the nature of her relationship with the soldier and the extent of her intimacy with him. The mediating figures in this dimension are Menuhah's sister and the wife of the rabbi. Menuhah's sister is connected to the family but is Menuhah's confidante. She helps hide the continuing connections with the soldier, keeping watch at the door to Menuhah's room in order to warn her of her father's approach. The door represents the dangerous liminal line between the social public and the forbidden private, the outside and the inside.[39] At the same time, however, the sister conducts herself in accord with the norms of the society. She even connects the home with the school, coming there to visit and to pass the time of the "sisters' Shabbat" with Menuhah there. She accompanies Menuhah to see the blood spilled on the road; she does not refuse to come down. And, though she fails to warn Menuhah off, she herself does not come in contact with the blood.

The wife of the rabbi, Dina, understands the youthful love of Menuhah. She suggests that the boy be brought near the family, which can then influence him to be an observant Jew. It is possible that Dina identifies (in a reverse way) with Menuhah. When Dina was seventeen years old, she fell in love with R. Daniel. She changed her lifestyle for him, became very observant and married him. Now she is herself considered a righteous woman, a *tzaddikah*. Dina hopes that as the romantic aspect of Menuhah's life becomes merged with the religious one, the same will happen to her. For the moment, the romantic facet of Menuhah's life stands in opposition to the religious and social facets.

The romantic aspect of the *dybbuk* is the main motif in An-Ski's play *The Dybbuk*. It is never mentioned in any traditional *dybbuk* accounts with which I am familiar. However, the play had an enormous social impact in the Jewish world and was very widely known. It has been produced in Russia, Israel, and the United States, even withstanding a mock trial in Israel in 1926. In Israel today the very term "*dybbuk*" is associated most with An-Ski's play. Menuhah's father, who came from Russia, knew these stories and was familiar with An-Ski's play. He was the only figure in this story who uses the term "*dybbuk*." I see this fact as an example of how literary works influence reality and reshape it. An-Ski himself based his play on traditional accounts but augmented them with a tale of love and death. The uniqueness of our story, its romantic dimension, might actually derive from the impact of the play. Thus the literary invention is returned to the world of real events.

The Gender Dimension

In the dimension of gender, this is a story about women, told by women to another woman (myself), in which the main active characters are women, related in a female context. The rabbi's wife told me her story while she was cooking dinner in her kitchen, and the story was written down by another woman, me.

In most of the witness tales in the written tradition, which are composed by men, the victim, generally a woman, has no active role. In fact, the descriptions almost convey an impression that she has been raped. The voice of the female victim is audible only as that of the *dybbuk*—a male spirit. He tells his story at length and also tells what transgression the young woman has committed (if any) that enabled him to enter into her body. The only possibility the woman has to make herself heard is by absorbing a *dybbuk*—by becoming a man.

In the story under discussion, the voice of the injured girl is presented directly. The circumstances of the narrative event are female ones. The young woman told her tale in the intimacy of another woman's presence, mine, where I represented for her the life of experience (an older woman), the secular life, the life outside her circle for which she perhaps yearned, and the possibility of pursuing an independent career. These circumstances permitted her to make her own voice heard freely and to allow me to participate in her intimacy—an intimacy that had found no attentive mother's ear. From this perspective, perhaps I served as a replacement for her mother just as the rabbi served as a replacement for her father.

This story differs from most of those in the literary tradition, in which a male spirit penetrates the body of a woman, in that a woman here penetrates another woman. This is the reverse of the relationship between a male *dybbuk* and a female victim, though the framework of the heterosexual system is maintained. Here the *dybbuk* is a dead female who realizes her love for a living male by way of another woman's body.

From this perspective, our tale closely resembles An-Ski's literary adaptation, in which the soul of Hanan returns to take up residence in the body of his beloved, who had been denied him while he lived. It is less similar to the traditional literary renditions of the *dybbuk* tale.

Even the role of the exorcist is taken in this story by a woman, the rabbi's wife—a most unusual circumstance for such stories. In the tales told by the two women, the father, who was a witness and took part in the exorcism in his own account, goes unmentioned. The *dybbuk*'s entry is the means for the daughter's rebellion against her father's authority as a male. The expulsion of the *dybbuk* throws off the balance of power between the rabbi's wife and the rabbi in regard to his authority as a male. Both of the women are punished with stomach pains, associated with the feminine role of motherhood.

The *dybbuk* lies in the belly of the girl like a fetus. The wife of the rabbi makes a point of the fact that she normally sleeps well at night as a result of the many labors required of her as a mother and her early rising, but that at present stomach pains kept her awake. They have brought her to neglect the care of her own children and even to become hospitalized for several days.

Through the agency of the *dybbuk*, both the women play parts that they are generally denied. The girl seeks love and freedom; the woman seeks authority on a par with that of a rabbi.

The Genre Dimension

Each version is told orally in first person as a personal experience. Only recently has folklore research included this form among the legitimate classical genres such as legend, folktale, and fairy tale. Obviously, personal narratives are told by both men and women, but this genre offers a particular opportunity for the voices of women to be heard. Rosan Jordan and Susan Kalcik emphasize this position in the introduction to the collection of papers they edited dealing exclusively with women, *Women's Folklore, Women's Culture*.[40] This is a genre that flourishes mainly in the privacy of the domestic sphere or as part of ordinary conversation. "A tendency to see the world in male terms has influenced what kind of data folklorists have looked for and from whom, and also what data they have collected and from whom" (xi).

Margaret Yocom, as an example, describes the phenomenon in terms of public and family conditions.[41] Her father would take the center of attention in the various stories, while the father's wife would always just sit and smile. When Yocom wanted to interview the grandmother, she refused, claiming she had nothing to relate. However, when Yocom asked that she tell about her life, her memories, and various events from her past, it became clear she was an excellent storyteller. The attention of the researcher, the conditions of the telling, privacy, and the granting of genre legitimization to the personal story, all enabled the unveiling of the grandmother's talent as a fine teller of tales.

I had a similar experience in my own fieldwork, when I asked Sephardic Jewish women of Jerusalem to tell their personal stories: women who thought they "had nothing to relate" or to tell revealed themselves and the value of their stories, centering mainly on unfulfilled love that brought lovers to the grave. This was similarly the central subject in the relation of the *dybbuk* story through the women who told it in our case.

In considering these three versions of events, it is clear that the stories of the two women agree with each other, while that of the father goes far beyond them. The distinctive feature of the oral narrative is that it is created as it is narrated. On this occasion I chanced to be offered the opportunity to hear their stories directly from the people involved, each according to his or her own perspective and personal experience. Each told his or her tale making certain choices and presenting himself or herself as the hero of the story. This tale is based on a personal experience or an event that happened to the narrator herself. The event was the same event, but each narrator played a different part in the different versions.

In order for an event to become a story, several conditions must be met:

1. It must deal with a dramatic incident.
2. It must contain a continuous flow of components that constructs a

plot, though this may be a single episode that exhibits a complication and its resolution.
3. The story must exhibit itself as a true account, as something that really happened to the narrator.

The degree to which the audience is attentive and the success of the narration depend on the performative talents of the narrator. For the fidelity of the events to reality to be convincing, the narrator employs such rhetorical devices as the cataloging of precise and multiple details. If the matter of time is brought up, the narrator will be specific as to the date and hour; if place, exact locations. The same is true of details of clothing and of the description of the exact situation as the narrator portrays it. Additionally, the narrator makes use of others' voices and words, quoting particularly those who are regarded as authoritative by the audience: the rabbi, a teacher, or even public communications (radio, television, newspapers). The narrator turns frequently to the audience, engaging it with verbal annotations to matters lying outside the tale and with rhetorical questions.

Sandra Dolby-Stahl distinguishes between a memorate and a personal narrative.[42] The memorate is a personal tale constructed in accord with belief, whether popular or religious.[43] This sort of tale is connected to an experience of the supernatural, whether this be constructed by an individual's religion or involve an encounter with an alien being. In the tale of a memorate some departure from reality takes place, even if the departure be only on the level of the interpretation of the tale by its teller, that is, in the way results and causes are connected in a succession that is not perceived as accidental. In contrast to the memorate, the personal narrative contains no supernatural experience and does not deviate from reality. It might be a story about an entertaining occurrence taken from daily life, such as an anecdote, or an exaggerated account—a tall tale, a *chizbat* or a tale of courtship, acquaintance, and love.[44]

The narration of the personal narrative or of the memorate is an invitation to enter the intimate world of the narrator, a glimpse into his or her personal biography that satisfies curiosity and sometimes enables an escape from the vicious circle of loneliness and alienation of modern times. The memorate engages awe, wonder, and the attraction to mystery toward the un-understandable and the abnormal. It fulfills the wish for a miraculous solution to distress, whether personal or general. Both the personal narrative and the memorate form an open channel for communication and identification between the narrator and his or her audience.

All these dimensions are interrelated, and the story, assembled from three different narratives, is transformed into a single complex unity in which the details complement each other.

In spite of its uniqueness, I conceive this story as a component in a traditional literary genre, the *dybbuk* tale, with a long history in Jewish culture. The present story is based on the same spiritual concept as all its predecessors in the genre: the spirit of a deceased person enters the body of a living person. This story, again like others in the same literary tradition, retains the literary structure consisting of the entry of the spirit, the revelation of the circumstances of the entry, and the expulsion of the spirit. Both Menuhah's father and the wife of the rabbi are acquainted with this tradition. The father terms the event a "*dybbuk* exorcism." The rabbi's wife begins her negotiations with the *dybbuk* by repeating the formulaic, "Who are you and whose daughter are you?"

The hand of the editor is visible in the written versions of such stories, rearranging reality to construct a coherent plot development and to accord with a particular orientation. The personal narrative, on the other hand, related orally and documented by a researcher, seeks to transmit the narrator's affective experience to the listener and to convince the listener of the factuality of the incident. It is this last aim in particular that forces the narrator to employ descriptions that are so precise, so faithful to reality, that the unity and structure of the story suffer. Every narrator presents that fragment of reality that is of importance to him or her and in which he or she plays the central part.

The text of the tale performed orally remains one single, complete narrative text. The narrated event, the *dybbuk* expulsion, is told in three different narrative events that include and relate the narrator and the audience. In each narrative event the narrator and the audience are different. I am the only constant, the only person who heard all three accounts. Moreover, the factors of time and place change with each narration. Menuhah told her story in her room in her house; her father told his story in the waiting room at the rabbi's house; the rabbi's wife told her story in her kitchen.

In each narrative event the narrator constructed the narrated event in a different way, suited to his or her aim and to the different relationships between the narrator and those being addressed. Each narrative event represented a different sort of communication. The communications between two women—one adult and the other young in the case of my audition of Menuhah's tale, contemporaries in the case of my audition of the tale of the rabbi's wife—were similar in that I was the only audience from outside their community. One was also Orthodox and the other traditional, as in the case of the communication between a man and a woman, that is, between the father and me. In all three cases, the communication between the interviewer and the one being interviewed was called into play as well. In each of the three narrations, the narrator chose a different way to represent himself or herself, varying in the employment of justification, self-justification, amazement, and excitement. In all three narrative events, the narration functioned as a channel of communication between the individual and the surrounding society. Each narrative event was told separately; writing the three of them here together, of course, creates a literary communication among the three of them.

The text treated is that of an actual, contemporary tale, precisely situated in time and place: Jerusalem, 1994, in a girls' boarding school in the neighborhood of Bayit ve-Gan and in a meeting on Mt. Herzl near the cemetery there. Modern means of communication were also employed in the initial identification of the *dybbuk*. The mother of the slain girl requested a particular song to be played on a popular radio program in memory of her daughter.

The time gap between the exorcism and the documentation was one night. The original penetration of the *dybbuk* had taken place a few months previous. Thus, from all standpoints this is a very immediate story. The recording, analysis, and publication of it have taken four years.

The existence of this story indirectly confirms the vitality of the written, literary tradition that treats of encounters between the spirits of the dead and living human beings. The tale retains the same literary structure that was created in Safed in the sixteenth century and the same thematic motifs, though they have been recast in terms of contemporary Israeli circumstances. As long as the mystical belief in the continuing life of the soul or spirit after death remains potent (a belief that modern science is unable to overcome), stories will continue to be created that connect the worlds of the living and the dead—stories that enable the living to express what they would not otherwise dare to express.

Another, more recent proof that this phenomenon continues is the *dybbuk* exorcism performed by Rabbi Basri in Jerusalem in 1999. In addition to this rather famous episode, however, other such events have occurred over the years that have never been researched. Judith Seegautekar herself testified that she went to Rabbi Harshish two years before she arrived at Rabbi Basri's door. I myself have been given the names of popular healers who deal with *dybbuk* exorcisms, though I have not yet had the opportunity to meet them.

These tales are to be understood as a genuine and true part of the reality of the community to which they are referred. The fixed literary structure, the same motifs, the repetitions, and even the fixed oral formulae in the dialogue between the spirit and the exorcist, do not tilt the story, as far as the members of the community are concerned, toward literary fiction, nor toward a recognition of borrowed elements. To the contrary, these features reinforce the understanding of the narrators that, even though they are aware of the literary tradition themselves, the existence of literary analogs over many generations is an additional proof of the reality of the matters they relate, and that there has been no alteration in the apprehension or belief in the possibility of *dybbuk* possession to the present.

By taking the story down as a personal tale, executed orally, my method has permitted us to attend to the feminine voice, muted in traditional *dybbuk* tales written by males, and to grasp the meaning of the story and its aims as a genre of interfeminine communication, in which women possess an active function no less than men. The women direct the ritual as well as the narration of the tale.

And yet there remains a gap between the centrality of the women's role in the narrated event and in the narrative event—in our case, the expulsion of the *dybbuk* and its retelling—and their role in the society of their actual world. In the description of events that preceded the ritual and the chain of events following the ritual, the daughter permits her father to hold the authoritative role as master of her life. The wife of the rabbi once again endows the rabbi with the fourfold authority of father, husband, male, and rabbi. Nevertheless, the uniqueness of the episode under consideration here is to be found in its being described by women as a completely female ritual, in which a woman exorcises a female *dybbuk* infesting another woman, as retold by women to another woman.

Notes

I am grateful to my friend, Professor Harris Lenowitz, who translated this paper from Hebrew and made many helpful suggestions. I would also like to thank Professor Matt Goldish for reediting the material following many changes and improvements.

1. G. Nigal, *Dybbuk Tales in Jewish Literature*, 2d ed. (in Hebrew) (Jerusalem: Rubin Mass, 1994); idem, "The *Dybbuk* in Jewish Mysticism" (in Hebrew), *Da'at* 4 (1981): 75–100. Several additional *dybbuk* tales were published by Aryeh Malakhi and Ya'akov Bazak; the latter describes the exorcism of an evil spirit by Rabbi Kook

in Jerusalem. See A. Malakhi, "*Dybbuks* in Beirut and Jerusalem in the Nineteenth Century" (in Hebrew), *Studies of the Folklore Research Center* 1 (1970): 183–91; Y. Bazak, "Rabbi Kook as Freer of an Ill Person from an Evil Spirit" (in Hebrew), *Shana be-Shanah* (1976): 387–91.

2. Y. Bilu, "The *Dybbuk* in Judaism: Mental Disorder as Cultural Resource" (in Hebrew) *Jerusalem Studies in Jewish Thought* 2.4 (1982): 529–63; idem, "The Taming of the Deviants and Beyond: An Analysis of *Dybbuk* Possession and Exorcism in Judaism," *Psychoanalytic Study of Society* 11 (1985): 1–32 (reprinted in the present volume).

3. S. Zfatman-Biller, " 'Tale of an Exorcism in Koretz'—A New Stage in the Development of a Folk-Literary Genre" (in Hebrew), *Jerusalem Studies in Jewish Folklore* 2 (1982): 17–65; idem, "Exorcism in Prague in the Seventeenth Century: The Question of the Historical Authenticity of a Folk Genre" (in Hebrew), *Jerusalem Studies in Jewish Folklore* 3 (1982): 7–35.

4. J. Dan, "The Story of the Spirit and the She-Demon" (in Hebrew), *Hasifrut* 18–19 (1974): 74–84.

5. "Judgments Sweetened: Possession and Exorcism in Early Modern Jewish Culture," *Journal of Early Modern History* 1.2 (1997): 124–69.

6. R. Bauman, *Story, Performance, and Event* (Cambridge: Cambridge University Press, 1968), 1–10.

7. G. Scholem, *Elements of the Kabbalah and Its Symbolism* (in Hebrew) (Jerusalem: Mosad Bialik, 1977), 332.

8. M. Bakhtin, introduction to *Rabelais and His World* (Cambridge: Cambridge University Press, 1968). I am grateful to Professor Dan Ben-Amos for this reference.

9. Published in *Ha-Tekufa* 1 (1918): 223–96. The play has been presented a number of times in Yiddish and Hebrew by the Ha-Bima theater in Moscow, Tel-Aviv, and the United States. A new production by Hanan Senir was presented on the stage of the Ha-Bima theater in 1998. It was translated into English by Joachim Neugroschel for the Theater Communications Group (New York, 1998) and produced in New York by Tony Kusher the same year. It was also adapted for opera by the Italian composer Lee Rocca and elaborated for the Israeli cinema, first by Pieter Prye and later by Yossi Zomer (1997).

10. For demon tales, see T. Alexander, "Theme and Genre Relationships between Man and She-Demon in Jewish Folklore," *Folklore and Ethnographic Review* 14.1–2 (1992): 56–61; idem, The Woman Demon in Jewish Customs and Folktales," *Dappim: Research in Literature* (1992): 203–22. Further bibliography on the subject can be found there.

11. Israeli Folklore Archive, no. 902, University of Haifa, Israel.

12. See A. Olrik, "Epic Laws of Folk Narrative," in *The Study of Folklore*, ed. A. Dundes (Englewood Cliffs, N.J.: Prentice-Hall, 1965),129–42.

13. See Y. Zfatman, *The Marriage of a Mortal Man and a She-Demon* (in Hebrew) (Jerusalem: Akademon, 1988).

14. Concerning the doctrine of metempsychosis (*gilgul*), see among others, G. Scholem, "*Ha-Gilgul,*" in *Elements of the Kabbalah,* 308–57; M. Hallamish, "The Doctrine of Transmigration," in *An Introduction to the Kabbalah* (Albany: State University of New York Press Press, 1999), 281–310.

15. R. Hayyim Vital, *Sefer ha-Gilgulim* (Vilnius: n.p., 1886), chap. 5, fol. 8b; Hallamish, *Introduction to the Kabbalah,* 312.

16. Scholem, "*Ha-Gilgul,*" 312.

17. *The Toledoth ha-ARI,* ed. M. Benayahu (in Hebrew) (Jerusalem: Ben-Zvi Institute, 1967), 175–76.

18. M. Ben-Israel, *Nishmat Hayyim* (1862; reprint, Jerusalem: n.p., 1968) 3:10; Benayahu, *Toledoth ha-'Ari,* 252–56.

19. Concerning the spirit's inclinations, see Chajes, "Judgments Sweetened," 147–48.

20. Zfatman-Biller proposes four roles: victim, spirit, exorcist, and reporter. See Zfatman-Biller, "'Tale of an Exorcism in Koretz,'" 20.

21. I refer to the cases cited in Nigal, *Dybbuk Tales.*

22. See Y. Bilu, "The Moroccan Demon in Israel: The Case of 'Evil Spirit Disease'" (in Hebrew), *Jerusalem Studies in Jewish Folklore* 2 (1982): 108–23.

23. Bilu, "Taming of the Deviants."

24. See the case brought by Zfatman-Biller, "Tale of an Exorcism in Koretz."

25. A carefully edited video recording of the exorcism was produced by the Ihud Levavot (Uniting the Hearts) religious organization in Israel, 1999.

26. See the case told by ibn Shoshan in Dan, "The Spirit and the She-Demon."

27. Concerning the memorate and fabulate, see, for example, S. Dolby-Stahl, *Literary Folkloristics and the Personal Narrative* (Bloomington: Indiana University Press, 1989). See also L. Degh and A. Vazsonyi, "The Crack on the Red Goblet, or Truth and Modern Legend," in *Folklore in the Modern World,* ed. R. M. Dorson (Paris: Mouton, 1978), 253–72.

28. Dan, "The Spirit and the She-Demon."

29. See Zfatman-Biller, "'Tale of an Exorcism in Koretz.'"

30. Ihud Levavot.

31. See the interview with Isaac Basri in the Israeli daily newspaper *Ha-Aretz,* 24 December 1999.

32. Elsewhere I have categorized the various systems of writing folktales: documentation, stylization, elaboration, re-creation, fusion. See T. Alexander, *The Beloved Friend-and-a Half: Studies in Sephardic Folk Literature* (in Hebrew) (Jerusalem: Magnes Press, 1999), 30–45.

33. I have honored the wish of those interviewed and changed their names, with the exception of the rabbi, R. Daniel Ben-Lulu, who granted permission for the use of his real name. The others agreed to the publication of their story only with pseudonyms. I would like to thank all the participants for permitting me to publish this material.

34. See D. Noy, "The Prayer of the Simple Brings Down Rain" (in Hebrew), *Mahanayim* 51.49–50 (Heshvan 1960): 34–45; T. Alexander, " 'God Loves the Heart': Toward the Study of the Hispano-Jewish Tale" (in Hebrew), in *The Sephardi and Oriental Jewish Heritage*, ed. Issachar Ben-Ami (Jerusalem: Magnes Press, 1982), 293–305; A. Sheiber, "Two Legends with the Motif: God Wants the Heart" (in Hebrew), *Yeda Am: Journal of the Israeli Folklore Society* 4.1–2 (September 1965): 60.

35. The power of a victim's blood to expose his or her murderer is explored in G. A. Kohut, "Blood Test and Proof of Kinship in Jewish Folklore," *Journal of the American Oriental Society* 24 (1903): 129–45; T. Alexander, *The Pious Sinner: Ethics and Aesthetics in the Medieval Hasidic Narrative* (Tübingen: J.C.B. Mohr, 1991), 39–55.

36. See T. Alexander, introduction to *Dream Encounters [Mifgashim ba-Halom]*, by M. Reymond (Hod ha-Sharon: Astrolog, 1995), 5–50.

37. See A. Aarme and S. Thompson, *The Types of the Folktale: Classification and Bibliography*, 2d ed. (Helsinki: Folklore Fellows Communications, 1973).

38. On this tale type, see, for example, T. Alexander, "The Cinderella Tale: The Dress of Gold, of Silver, and of Stars—A Motifeme Viewed within its Cultural Context" (in Hebrew), *Criticism and Interpretation: Journal for Literature, Linguistics, History, and Aesthetics (Bikoret u-Farshnut)* 30 (1994): 157–75; A. Dundes, "The Maiden without Hands," in idem, *Folklore Matters* (Knoxville: University of Tennessee Press, 1989), 112–50; idem, "To Love My Father All: A Psychoanalytic Study of the Folktale Source of King Lear," in idem, *Cinderella: A Folklore Case Book* (New York: Wildman Press, 1983), 229–45.

39. On liminality, see V. Turner, *The Forest of Symbols* (Ithaca: Cornell University Press, 1967); idem, *Dramas, Fields, and Metaphors: Symbolic Action in Human Society* (Ithaca: Cornell University Press, 1974).

40. R. A. Jordan and S. J. Kalcik, eds., *Women's Folklore, Women's Culture* (Philadelphia: University of Pennsylvania Press, 1985).

41. M. Yocom, "Woman to Woman: Fieldwork and the Private Sphere," In *Women's Folklore, Women's Culture*, ed. Rosan A. Jordan and Susan J. Kalcik, (Philadelphia: University of Pennsylvania Press), 45–53.

42. S. Dolby-Stahl, *Literary Folkloristics and the Personal Narrative* (Bloomington: Indiana University Press, 1989).

43. L. Honko, "Memorates and the Study of Folk Beliefs," *Journal of the Folklore Institutte* 1 (1964): 5–19.

44. For the analysis of personal narratives of this sort, see Bauman, *Story, Performance, and Event*. Bauman analyzes anecdotes related by fisherman and merchants in markets who utilize the personal narrative to make sales and also deals with tall tales related in summer.

Dybbuk, Aslai, Zar: The Cultural Distinctiveness and Historical Situatedness of Possession Illnesses in Three Jewish Milieus

YORAM BILU

Spirit possession refers to the notion that external entities with special ontological status are capable of taking control of humans by temporarily inhabiting their bodies and putting their ordinary selves in abeyance. Possession is a cultural option known in many societies, from Asia, Africa, and Mediterranean Europe to America and Oceania.[1] Even though it subsumes a dazzling diversity of cultural phenomena, from a naturalist perspective possession is viewed as an independent category of behavior, couched in panhuman (precultural) psychophysiological structures, that constitutes a "natural" field of study. Students of possession in this tradition, while not indifferent to local epistemologies, etiologies, and idioms, have sought to make sense of possession "by reducing it to behavior explicable in . . . universal and substantially medical terms, to discover its presumed logical basis as folk psychiatry or status compensation."[2] Research methodologies designed in this vein have mapped, systematized, and compared the variety of possession experiences using generalized typologies and dichotomies, while theoretically and analytically emphasizing its instrumental aspects, the biopsychological mechanisms underlying it, and the personal and social functions it serves.[3]

As against this naturalist approach (also designated essentialist, universalist, or rationalist), context-sensitive anthropologists have critiqued the cross-cultural endeavor to distill regularities and uniformities from culturally heterogeneous phenomena.[4] Alerting us to the fact that possession transcends "natural" oppositions such as self and other, spirit and matter, seriousness and comedy, and reality and illusion, they make a plea "to examine possession on its own terms in the societies where it is found."[5]

The two paradigms spawn contrasting views on various aspects of possession. Since some of these aspects are pertinent to my own work, I will review them in brief before staking a claim in the Jewish section of this contested territory.

The first aspect concerns the very conceptualization of the phenomenon. At the heart of the naturalizing paradigm lies the analytic distinction between "trance" and "possession"[6] implied in Erika Bourguignon's two-tier designation, "possession trance."[7] Trance is viewed as the natural matrix, the universal human capacity for altered consciousness, on which the cultural category of possession is superimposed. This conceptualization resonates with the classic "layer-cake" or "stratification" model in anthropology.[8] The inchoate and diffuse behavioral options granted by the panhuman potentials for dissociation are molded and embellished in line with the cultural category or native theory of possession. This analytic bifurcation makes it possible to distinguish "possession trance" from other cultural constructions of altered consciousness where the dissociative state is not articulated through the possession idiom ("nonpossession trance"). Shamanic trance, for example, may take the form of a culturally constituted dissociation diametrically opposed to possession. Shamans ordinarily do not summon the spirits by letting them into their bodies, but by launching their own souls outside the body to meet with the spirits in nether land. Note also that "possession" may be used just as an explanation, for example, to account for bodily distress such as pain or dizziness, without the "trance" component of altered consciousness.

Critics of the "possession trance" conceptualization challenge the analytic separation of behavior (trance) and theory (possession) it implies and its universalizing penchant that bolsters the facile imposition of these monothetic decontextualized categories upon a wide range of otherwise diverse cultural phenomena.[9] They suggest forsaking general theories of trance and possession, with their grid of preconceived categories, for richly nuanced, context-sensitive ethnographies that seek to capture the cultural phenomena of possession as life forms inseparable from other spheres of social reality and grounded in local epistemologies.

A related bone of contention concerns the issue of medicalization. Anthropologists in the naturalist, rationalizing tradition tend to translate various manifestations of possession into clinical language, particularly (though not exclusively) when the possessive spirits are negative and, at least initially, the trance experience is not willfully sought. Lewis's distinction between *central* and *peripheral* possession cults is a noted example.[10] Whereas in the former the spirits uphold the moral order and the possessed, mostly men, are locally viewed as partaking of religiously endorsed rituals, possession by amoral spirits, which is usually the share of women, is locally understood as a form of illness. Participation in a peripheral possession cult is viewed as a form of group therapy that enables the afflicted, under the protective cover of the possessing agent, to give voice to their distress and to achieve some redress.[11]

Again, culture-sensitive anthropologists criticize this pathological view of possession as reductive. While not denying the fact the possession may be indigenously labeled as aberrance entailing some sort of intervention, they assert that in many non-Western settings possession illness, and medicine at large, are subtly interwoven with religion and other cultural spheres.[12] They alert us to other meanings of possession, which transcend the pathological model and the relative deprivation view attached to it. Lambek contends that possession can be broadly viewed as a system of communication or metalanguage that constitutes an idiom for articulating a wide range of experiences.[13] Within these "semantic" horizons, the rhetorical force of possession is emphasized, and the internal and external discourses it produces are brought to the fore. Rather than a symbolic expression of an unconscious conflict, the internal dialogue with the spirits, though recalled only piecemeal, may be viewed as facilitating the growth of the self and the dialogue with otherness. As a textual or discursive production, with its own levels of constraints, grammars of interpretations, modes of representations, specific genres, and repository of images and metaphors, possession opens new avenues of creativity and expansion of self boundaries.[14] In this capacity it allows for a greater acceptance of ambiguity and a novel expression of paradox, parody, and subversive themes. This broader perspective also alerts us to the performative and aesthetic qualities of possession eschewed by the pathological model.

Finally, the two paradigms propose different accounts for the preponderance of women in possession. The rationalists situate their explanation within the instrumental model, emphasizing women's life problems and role stresses in male-dominated societies that may find voice and some redress through possession. This motivational accent is augmented by a metaphoric one: the symbolism in possession is clearly more resonant with female sexual experiences of being intruded and impregnated. Culture-sensitive anthropologists elaborate on the metaphoric and idiomatic dimensions of possession beyond explicit sexual symbolism. They emphasize the scope given to women via possession to expand and regenerate their sense of self through their more permeable physical boundaries and more flexible attachment style and to resist male-dominated religious, text-based versions of morality and history.[15]

The analysis that follows concerns three variants of spirit possession that appeared among Jews in different cultural milieus. Starting with the classic case of the *dybbuk*, I deploy it against *aslai*, a possession illness I encountered during fieldwork among Israeli Jews of Moroccan extraction, on the one hand, and against *zar* possession found among Ethiopian Jews, on the other hand. It is undertaken according to the context-sensitive approach, using possession also as a marker of the degree of cultural distinctiveness in three Jewish communities.

Admittedly, most of the points raised against the naturalist paradigm in the study of possession apply to my own analysis, given its comparative thrust. Assuming that the three variants of possession are commensurate, I extract them from their wider sociocultural contexts, despite the fact that historically they evolved under very different conditions. Moreover, the comparison is perforce selective and, aside from the Jewish Moroccan case, is based on secondary sources that are a far cry from a reliable ethnography. These drawbacks notwithstanding, I still believe that the comparison proposed is worth pursuing since it may produce theoretical insights that a single case ethnography, richly nuanced as it may be, cannot provide.

In defense of the comparative stance it should be noted that all three cases unequivocally comply with Bourguignon's definition of "possession trance" (that is, some cultural notion of a spirit invading a human host that involves a special state of consciousness). In all of them, the possession episodes occur or are elicited in the context of illness (stemming from a local model of pathology); and in all three females by far outnumber males among the possessed, whereas males outnumber females among the spirits. Note also that most arguments against the naturalist paradigm were elicited in the context of a possession *cult*—something that hardly exists in the cases of *dybbuk* and *aslai* and plays a minor role in *zar* manifestations in Israel.[16] As I said before, culture-sensitive anthropologists would no doubt question the validity of comparing cultural phenomena that evolved in different times and different places. But this methodological predicament could become a virtue if the differences in cultural setting and in historical trajectory are problematized on a more substantive level and placed as the major variables for examination.

Indeed, the two theoretical issues that inform the proposed comparison concern these differences. The first issue has to do with *cultural distinctiveness*. It involves the notion of illness as a marker or index of cultural distance in a multiethnic setting. The focal question is to what extent were the possession experiences in each case articulated in specifically Jewish religious idioms or in idioms bespeaking a "common universe of discourse" with the indigenous, non-Jewish surrounding culture. The second issue involves *historical situatedness*. It deals with the significance of the different historical trajectories of the three Jewish possession ailments. I argue that the differential attenuation of these cultural phenomena as viable idioms of distress is related to successive waves of modernization and secularization that have swept various Jewish communities in different times since the nineteenth century.[17]

Manifestations of Possession in the Jewish World

My analysis of *dybbuk* possession is based on records that have appeared in Jewish sources over the last four hundred years. Most of these cases appeared in an anthology of *dybbuk* stories compiled by Gedalia Nigal.[18] I collected the material on *aslai* during fieldwork in Israeli *moshavim* (cooperative agricultural villages) inhabited in the 1950s and 1960s by Jews from southern Morocco. The data on *zar* possession is based on interviews with and written material by Israeli mental health practitioners. I will start with short depictions of the three possession types.

Dybbuk

The first documented cases of possession by spirits of the dead are from sixteenth-century Sephardi communities in the Circum-Mediterranean.[19] The term *dybbuk*[20] was not conferred on the phenomenon until two centuries later, in Ashkenazi circles.[21] Only toward the end of the seventeenth century did the first European cases appear, but in the eighteenth and nineteenth centuries mystically oriented Hasidic communities in eastern Europe supplied most of the cases. Throughout this period cases from the Mideast continued to appear in print. The last cases to be documented appeared in Lithuania, Palestine (Jaffa and Jerusalem), and Baghdad in the beginning of the twentieth century. Core notions in Jewish mysticism, related to *gilgul*, the transmigration of souls, and *ibbur* (impregnation), had informed the behavioral manifestations of *dybbuk* possession. The doctrine of *gilgulim* (pl.), which emerged in Jewish mysticism in the twelfth century, asserted that the spirit of a deceased person might transmigrate into a newborn human (and also, although rarely, into animal and inanimate forms) as retribution for certain transgressions committed during the person's lifetime. Although considered a severe punishment, transmigration signified a divine mercy as well, since it was meant to rehabilitate and purify the sinner's spirit by virtue of his or her reformed behavior in the new lifetime. In sixteenth-century Kabbalah, the idea of the transmigration of souls became a universal law.

The doctrine of *ibbur*, more specifically relevant for possession, was developed in the second half of the thirteenth century. It expanded the notion of *gilgul* to include the entry of a spirit into a living person after he or she was born. According to this doctrine, not only wicked spirits but also righteous ones took possession of people (themselves innocent and just) in order to complete their quota of good deeds required for entry to Paradise. But the designation "*dybbuk*" was reserved for the spirits of the wicked who penetrated humans to find refuge from persecution. As spirits of arch-sinners, they were doomed by the celestial court to remain in limbo, wandering between the two worlds,[22] without even being allowed to enter Hell. In this liminal state, the spirits were exposed to ruthless persecutions by angelic and demonic beings. Thus the inhabitation of humans gave the spirit a temporary shelter as well as a unique opportunity for initial rectification. Minor transgressions committed by the victims-to-be constituted the moral trigger for possession.[23]

As with other forms of possession in Judaism and elsewhere, the typical gender pattern is of a male spirit penetrating a female victim, with a significant minority of male-in-male possession. The obverse pattern of female-in-male hardly ever existed.

While *dybbuk* possession was characterized by a wide plethora of symptoms, those behavioral manifestations through which the presence of the possessing agent was palpably visible drew most of the attention in the case reports. These behaviors, which included convulsions, speaking in a strange voice (congruent with the spirit's gender), verbal and physical aggression, and other impulsive acts with blatantly amoral character, as befits the wicked spirit, were most often evidenced in the exorcistic ritual. The presence of the spirits was also noted through spectacular feats of xenoglossia and divination. The possession episode was marked by dissociation and ordinarily followed by amnesia.

Exorcism was typically a public ritual, conducted by a revered rabbi who confronted the spirit with various religiously informed measures used in a fixed graded order. Often the exorcism was performed in the synagogue and involved the active employment of Jewish sacred paraphernalia by the congregants. During the ritual, the spirit was compelled to betray its identity, to confess its sins in its lifetime and punishment in the afterlife, to specify the terms of departure, to give its consent to leave through a minor organ (usually one of the big toes), and then to depart for good.[24] The exorcist's arsenal included prayers, incantations, and mystical formulae from a variety of Jewish sources. A particularly effective intercession involved the burning of a piece of linen, with or without written formula, under the nostrils of the patient, in order to choke or scorch the evil spirit.[25]

Aslai

"Evil spirit illness" (in Hebrew) or *aslai* (in a Moroccan Berber dialect) was a possession ailment that immigrants from southern Morocco, mostly females, brought with them to Israel during the 1950s and 1960s. Unlike *dybbuk* cases, in which spirits of the dead haunted the possessed, the penetrating agents in the case of *aslai* were demons (Arabic: *jnun*, Hebrew: *shedim*). The demonic hegemony in possession was but one manifestation of the central role that *jnun* occupied in Jewish Moroccan cosmology. Demons are invisible spiritual creatures with supernatural powers that may assume animal or even human guises at will. Their universe, juxtaposed to the human world, is also symmetrical to it in many respects, with the same basic divisions according to sex, age, race, religion, and social hierarchy, and antithetical in terms of space and time. Thus, the demons ordinarily inhabit the zone below ground, and the night is their natural realm. The parallelism between the worlds is extended to the personal sphere, as each human being is believed to have a demonic double who accompanies him or her throughout the entire life cycle. Demons are considered extremely dangerous, even though they attack humans only in response to an assault on themselves or their offspring. Ruthless, capricious, and arbitrary, they make no allowances for the fact that their invisibility makes them vulnerable to accidental injury by humans. Their assault can take one of two forms: either an external blow involving the sudden onset of disturbances to physical and mental health, or else the penetration and taking possession of the victim's body.[26]

In the *moshavim* I studied, a possession episode was usually precipitated in an emotionally loaded context of intrafamily or interneighbor dispute. The attack often commenced with an abrupt loss of consciousness followed by disorganized and agitated behaviors that were dominated by verbal and physical aggression. Male adults were often called upon to restrain the victim's indiscriminate aggression—taken as clear evidence of the demonic presence inside her. As with the *dybbuk*, the demonic presence endowed the possessed with powers of diagnosing and divining and with special lingual skills (xenoglossia). When the possession episode ended, either through the healer's exorcistic intervention or spontaneously, it was usually marked by massive amnesia. The exorcistic ritual was performed by a rabbi-healer, erudite in *kabbalah ma'asit*, "applied" (magical) forms of Jewish mysticism. While involving the same series of steps as in *dybbuk* exorcism, the expulsion of the demon usually took place in the victim's house rather than in the synagogue.[27]

Zar

In Ethiopian cosmology, *zar* is a category of personified spirits that occupy a stratified universe of their own alongside humans and are distinguished from other categories of potentially injurious beings.[28] These categories include entities like *seitan, aganent, ganel, ganian*—more akin to the *jnun*— that lack a developed personal identity, and *buda*, hyena-like spirits, cannibalistic personifications of the evil eye, imposed by certain categories of people like craftsmen, particularly blacksmiths.[29] Jews serving as blacksmiths and other artisans were often accused as *buda* by their non-Jewish neighbors. As in the case of the Moroccan *jinn*, a local Maghrebi variant of a wider demonic category spread in many Muslim societies, the distribution of the *zar* spirits includes Egypt, Sudan, and East Africa, with some presence in the Persian Gulf. *Zar* spirits are believed to cause a wide variety of ailments, from pain and other somatic problems to depression, eating problems, and hysterical symptoms. The gender pattern typical of *dybbuk* and *aslai* possession—a male spirit inhabiting a female—is no less represented in the *zar* case, and the motivation of the spirit to possess its victim is often presented as explicitly sexual. Male and female victims may embrace cross-sexual behavior in accord with the gender identity of their *zar*. *Zar* spirits are often transmitted in the family, from mother to daughter.

The *zar* specialist, *balazar*, is typically an ex-patient who obtained his or her healing skills from an association with and control over high-rank *zar* family. Unlike the former cases, healing here is not exorcistic but symbiotic:[30] attempts are made to placate the spirit so that the host is able to maintain a stable, ongoing relationship with it. While in *dybbuk* and *aslai* the possession episodes constitute the illness, *zar*-caused symptoms do not ordinarily crystallize into full-blown possession trance before the healing phase. Only then the patient is induced into possession trance by the *balazar* in order to communicate with the injurious spirit and to transform it from adversary into ally. This is done in the course of a public ritual in which the presence of the *zar* is made clear through stylized head-swinging and torso-bending dances. The "domestication" of the *zar* puts its host under certain daily ritual obligations. Aside from these domestic rituals (which include roasting coffee for the *buna* ceremony, lighting incenses, and sacrificing a fowl), public rituals that are conducted periodically in concert with other patients include ceremonial performances of "invited" possession that constitute the "*zar* society." In Ethiopia the *zar* coterie has been an important source of social support, particularly for single women devoid of family protection who are indeed overrepresented among the possessed.

Possession Illness as an Index of Cultural Distance

The first comparison examines the *cultural distinctiveness* of the three forms of possession. Starting with the *dybbuk*, it appears that in the Hasidic communities of eastern Europe, where the cultural overlap with the Christian world was relatively small and religion all-encompassing, certain forms of illness were among the many life-forms that were specifically grounded in Jewish meaning systems and articulated through Jewish idioms.[31] The discourse of the *dybbuk* germinated in a peculiar Jewish mystical semantic field. The possessing agents were always spirits of the dead, doomed to pay for sins committed in their lifetime, as entailed from the Jewish mystical doctrines of *gilgul* and *ibbur* that provided the rationale for possession and shaped its manifestations. In contrast, episodes of possession among Christians in Europe were as a rule attributed to the devil and its demonic allies. This difference in the intruding agents launched Jewish and Christian victims of possession into entirely different orbits. The Jewish character of the *dybbuk* was particularly salient in the exorcistic ritual. Exorcism was often conducted in the Jewish sacred territory of the synagogue by a rabbi-healer amply using Jewish paraphenalia that included candles, ram's horns, Torah scrolls, and other ritual objects. Magical formulae and other curing devices derived from Kabbalah also formed an institutionalized part of the exorcistic project.

The specifically Jewish character of the *dybbuk* need not blind us to significant historical and structural similarities between Jewish and Christian possessions and exorcisms.[32] The onset of the *dybbuk* coincides with the "age of the demoniac" in Europe in the sixteenth and seventeenth centuries. Moreover, the general behavioral attributes of the possession episode, and particularly the structured stages of the exorcistic ritual, appear the same in the two milieus. Yet from this common syntax or "deep structure," a specific Jewish idiom of possession evolved with a cultural vocabulary that could not make much sense outside Jewish mystically oriented circles. As to the theory of possession, the Jewishness of the *dybbuk* was twofold. Not only was the rationale for the intrusion of the spirit shaped by Jewish mystical doctrines, but the personal identity of the spirits was predominantly Jewish (though gentile spirits do appear in the reports).

The human origin of the spirits perforce made *dybbuk* possession a *past-oriented* endeavor, the embodiment of former lives, and thus an exercise in memory. This *diachronic* tenor of the *dybbuk* was quite far-reaching. The memory of the spirits in the community often was personal and direct, relating to figures from recent history known in the family and social circles of the possessed. But it also could be collective and indirect, relating to notorious historical sinners from more remote periods, like the seventeenth-century false messiah Sabbatai Zvi, who haunted a Baghdadi Jew in the beginning of the twentieth century.[33] Sometimes this elicited memory took metahistorical or mythical dimensions and encompassed sinners from the biblical period, such as the first man to throw a stone at the prophet Zacharia at the time of the first Temple.[34] Due to the Jewish identity of the spirits, the *dybbuk* was not only past-oriented but also inner-oriented. The record was set when noted sinners from even a biblical past were made to pay their dues in a dramatic performance that pushed the stunned spectators toward stronger religious conformity. In contrast to the "temporally oriented" *dybbukim*, demons and *zar* spirits, occupying universes parallel to the human world, seem to be more locus-bound.

Far removed from the *dybbuk* in terms of cultural distinctiveness, *zar* possession appears to be devoid of uniquely Jewish characteristics. While in Ethiopian society the boundaries between different ethnic and religious groups where quite sharply delineated, *zar* possession clearly transcended these boundaries. In Lewis's terms, the *zar* coterie promoted a peripheral cult related to amoral entities that were not part of the moral-religious social code.[35] Therefore, *zar* possession was similarly alienated from the church, the mosque, and the synagogue. As noted by Young, the *zar* society was characterized by the blurring of social boundaries and hierarchies, as patients from different ethnic groups, socioeconomic status, and religious affiliations participated in the cult.[36] The religious affiliation of the *balazar* entered the scene only marginally (for example, in addressing different divinities in praying for the possessed), and the ethnoreligious identity of the possessing spirit, although occasionally mentioned, did not play any significant role in the management and treatment of the distress. Thus, the commonalities in form *and* contents of *zar* manifestations enacted by Jews and non-Jews in Ethiopia bespeak a common universe of discourse in regard to possession illness. It might well be that other forms of possession attributed to the aforementioned *seitan* or *ganians*, for which exorcism by a religious specialist was deemed the intervention of choice, were more differentiated in terms of religion and ethnicity, but I do not have data on this issue.

Aslai occupies an intermediate position between *dybbuk* and *zar* in terms of the cultural distinctiveness of the possession idioms. Even though Moroccan Jewry has been steeped in Jewish mysticism,[37] the typical form of possession did not involve the spirits of deceased sinners, as the kabbalistic doctrine of the transmigration of souls would prescribe. In all the narratives of possession from southern Morocco I collected and the actual cases I encountered and documented in Israel, the intruding agents were demons, not human spirits. "The triumph of the demonic" resonates with the central role given to *jnun* in Muslim Maghrebi cosmology as against the relatively minor role assigned to the spirits of the dead.[38] Thus, the resort to the same agents of afflictions in the two traditions is another indication of the noticeable cultural overlap between Jews and Muslims in the Maghreb. It should be noted that *shedim* were basic givens in ancient Jewish cosmology as well, as amply indicated by various Jewish classical sources.[39] But according to Jewish Moroccan healers and their books of healing that I consulted in Israel,[40] the identity of the possessing demons was clearly more *jinn*-like then *shed*-like. The seven demons believed to dominate each day of the week (and thus assumed to be the principal agents of affliction on that day) were of a Muslim stock.[41] More pertinent to possession, the six demonic camps responsible for subdivisions of *aslai* also had a Muslim identity.[42] As I have shown elsewhere,[43] there were some attempts on the part of Moroccan Jews to "Judaize" the Maghrebi *jnun* by identifying famous individual *jnun* with famous *shedim* in Jewish classical traditions. Along these lines, the monstrous and libidinal Aisha Qandisha[44] was identified with Ma'hlat Bat Agrat, and the demon-king Shamharush with Ashmedai; but these attempts were pale and inconsistent. The term *aslai* in itself is a Berber idiom designating a *jnun*-caused possession illness. As a folk diagnosis in the local ethnopsychiatry, it is devoid of any particularly Jewish connotations. This makes *aslai* akin to the *zar*, but significantly different from the *dybbuk*, a specific Jewish designation, derived from Hebrew, which does not transcend ethnoreligious boundaries. It should be noted that my informants used also the Hebrew designation *mahalat ru'ah ra'ah* (evil spirit illness) in referring to possession syndromes, but I suspect that this term was not much in use back in southern Morocco. Interestingly, the same designation—though connoting spirits of the dead rather than demons—was used in Sephardi communities to refer to the Jewish possession syndrome designated "*dybbuk*" in Ashkenazi circles.

In terms of cultural distinctiveness, however, *aslai* is a hybrid case, merging an indigenous non-Jewish theory of possession (like the *zar*) with a healing ritual based on Jewish mystical curative devices (like the *dybbuk*). Note that in the Maghreb the cultural distance between Jews and non-Jews was much smaller than in Europe,⁴⁵ but the religious boundaries between the groups were still sharply delineated. In this context, it was the impure agents of afflictions that were shared with the Muslims, while the healing ritual, based on mystico-religious premises that highlighted holy names as divine panacea, remained strictly Jewish and was, therefore, quite similar to *dybbuk* exorcism.

Despite the similarities in the ritual steps, the Jewish ambiance of *dybbuk* exorcism was much denser than in *aslai*. One aspect of this difference concerns the Jewish identity of most of the possessing spirits as opposed to the non-Jewish background of most of the demons.⁴⁶ Thus, the sins of the possessed in the case of the *dybbuk* were often transgressions of various religious laws defined by clear moral criteria.⁴⁷ *Aslai* possession, on the other hand, was ordinarily explained as a demonic retaliation following a physical injury unknowingly inflicted upon the demon by the possessed-to-be. These transgressions, situated in a different order of morality, were typically place-related, occurring in areas haunted by demons (like slaughterhouses, caves, springs, and sewage canals) devoid of specifically Jewish content. Second, in *aslai*, unlike the *dybbuk*, the sacred space of the synagogue was not the preferred arena for exorcism. The mundane settings for exorcism and the resultant paucity in the use of Jewish paraphernalia during the healing ritual also detracted from its Jewish distinctiveness.

The similarity in the exorcistic rituals of *dybbuk* and *aslai* possessions accentuates their difference from the symbiotic healing in the *zar* case. Interestingly, in Morocco coteries or confraternities based on symbiotic relations with the *jnun* solidified by periodic ceremonial possessions existed among Muslims.⁴⁸ But in contrast with the Ethiopian scene, this pattern of long-term association with the demons, compatible with I. M. Lewis's definition of peripheral cults, the Jews hardly embraced. It is possible that the Sufi-religious basis of these societies with their Muslim saints was too high a barrier for the Jews to cross. In Europe, neither Jews nor Christians were involved in coteries like the *zar* society or the Muslim Maghrebi *Hamadsha*. Hence, the deployment of the three cases in terms of symbiotic relations with the possessing entities in a group setting replicates the cultural distinctiveness continuum. With exclusively Muslim groups of this kind, the Maghreb again is an intermediary case between Europe, where such coteries hardly existed, and Ethiopia, where the *zar* society encompassed Christians as well as Jews.

I discussed before the vertical diachronic cosmology of *dybbuk* possession. Note that *zar* and other possessing spirits in Africa were often described as agents of oppositional (counterhegemonic) historical scripts that served also as female-embodied protest against male dominance.⁴⁹ But the cases of *aslai* and *zar* that I directly or indirectly came to know were primarily informed by a synchronic ("horizontal") cosmology of a demonic world juxtaposed to the human world, without a significant carryover of past memories. Therefore, it also lacked the strong tenor of moral agency and religious reawakening that the confessions of the spirits regarding their vices in their lifetime and persecutions in the hereafter stirred in the community. In situating the spirits under the canopy of core religious tenets, subject to God's judgment, the *dybbuk* was accommodated to the flow of the Jewish master commemorative narrative, while *zar* and *aslai* were not.

The Historical Trajectories of Possession Illness

The *historical situatedness* of the three possession illnesses is correlated with the variable of cultural distinctiveness. The differential dispersion of the "life spans" of the three cases stresses the need to view even psychiatric ailments, particularly those designated culture-bound syndromes, as historical events influenced by social and political factors.[50] Cases of *dybbuk* possession that thrived in Ashkenazi and Sephardi communities in former centuries became a rarity in the first decades of the twentieth century. With the advent of secularization and enlightenment in Jewish Europe, *dybbukim* were viewed by rationalists and *maskilim* (secularized modernists) as an emblem of religious ignorance and superstitions and soon became a fierce battlefront between them and the Hasidim. The former published satirical pieces that mocked and parodied *dybbuk* possession and reframed it as mental illness or sheer fraud. The latter fought back vehemently but had to resort to abstruse arguments in their attempts to cope with the empirical attenuation of the phenomenon.[51] By and large, it appears that possession illnesses, like other "participational" manifestations of metaphysical cultural identities—that is, events in which these beings become visible, audible, or otherwise tangibly experienced as "real"—are amenable to attenuation in times of rapid social change.[52] This vulnerability is related to the fact that cultural phenomena of the "participational" type are articulated through idioms deeply ingrained in local epistemologies and cosmologies. When the latter are being forsaken, attenuation is inevitable. In this vein, the unparalleled success of the play *Ha-Dybbuk* by An-Ski, which became the trademark of the Hebrew National Theater, may be taken as an indication of the immense gulf formed between the traditional past, now exoticized, and the modern, secular, and disenchanted present. A viable culture-bound syndrome with strong moral implications that tormented many individuals in Sephardi and Ashkenazi communities throughout the centuries was relegated to the domain of the imaginary and became a theatrical performance. The psychological grip of the possession ailment on its victims and the moral grip on the community were supplanted by the aesthetic impact of the play on its audience.

While the Jewish traditional centers of eastern Europe were already corroded by modernization in the nineteenth century, the Jewish communities in the Muslim orbit maintained their traditional contours well into the twentieth. Of the North African countries under French rule, Morocco was the last to be taken over (1912). In the remote southern regions of the country, where *aslai* possession was a frequent event, modernization was slow and piecemeal. In the early 1970s, when I did my fieldwork among immigrants from southern Morocco, I was witnessing the last reverberations of that possession type.[53] The possessed were all middle-aged women who contracted their illnesses in Morocco and were subsequently subject to recurrent possession episodes there. As some of my informants would put it, "they brought their demons with them (from Morocco)." I have never heard of a case of full-blown *aslai* possession that started anew (not as a reappearing episode) in Israel. Moreover, the possession episodes were systematically declining in intensity and frequency—so much so that in some cases my informants had long debates whether or not one or another woman in this group should be described as suffering from *aslai*. My own follow-up showed that most of the women were symptom-free for long periods of time. For all practical purposes, the Jewish-Moroccan version of demonic possession was an extinct illness in the 1980s. Like the *dybbuk*, it is now being mainly represented in the domain of the arts, in the form of stories, novels, and films.

Zar possession is alive and well in Israel, although the possessed manage to stay hidden from the public eye. Unfortunately, ethnographic accounts of this cultural phenomenon are yet to be produced, and we have to rely on psychiatric reports dealing with people who were referred to mental health centers in Beer-Sheva[54] and Natanya.[55] In all of the cases discussed, the first onset of the ailment and the following symbiotic alliance with the spirit had been established in Ethiopia. While these reports dwell on the individual dimensions of the affliction, particularly on symptomatology and the daily domestic rituals conducted to appease the spirits, there is some scant evidence that sporadic group rituals, headed by *zar* specialists, are also conducted in Israel from time to time. Most of the *kessoch*, the religious leaders of the Ethiopian Jewish community in Israel, disapprove of the *zar* cult.

Summary and Conclusions

In this essay I undertook to compare three possession clusters, *dybbuk*, *aslai*, and *zar*, which waxed and waned in different Jewish milieus. I sought to discuss these forms of distress as cultural phenomena, molded by local meaning systems that were differentially susceptible to non-Jewish traditions in the multiethnic settings where they emerged. Contrary to the biomedical model of illness as a robust, stable, and universal entity,[56] the possession syndromes under discussion may be viewed as fragile cultural edifices, liable to attenuation and extinction in times of massive social change. Admittedly, my strong cultural bias does not spare me the vices of generalized comparisons as portrayed from a context-sensitive, phenomenological perspective. Two of these vices are particularly problematic: the heterogeneity of my data, mostly based on secondary sources that were promulgated from a definite moral viewpoint (be it traditional-Jewish or modern-psychiatric), and the wide cultural variability in the case of the *dybbuk*.

While the first issue cannot be much rectified, given that two of the cultural phenomena under discussion are near extinct (see epilogue), the second one poses a real threat to the sharpness of the comparisons. Unlike *aslai* and *zar* that appeared among Jews in culturally circumscribed areas—southern Morocco and northern Ethiopia respectively—the distribution of the *dybbuk* was much wider, haunting individuals in Sephardi and Ashkenazi mystically oriented communities in the Middle East and Europe. Needless to say, my arguments regarding the cultural distance between Jews and non-Jews in eastern Europe are less applicable to the Middle East; and yet reports on possession by spirits of the dead in the mold of the *dybbuk* (though under different appellation) were coming also from Jerusalem, Safed, and Baghdad. It might be argued that *dybbuk* possession was more salient in the eastern European shtetls than in the Muslim orbit, but this cannot be ascertained since we do not have epidemiological studies comparing the incidence of spirit possession among Jews in different territories. Nevertheless, I would like to stick to my comparison by stating the cultural distinctiveness variable in *relative* terms. While the cultural boundaries between Jews and non-Jews in the Middle East were more permeable than in Europe, it might be argued that in southern Morocco, and more so in northern Ethiopia, the interethnic cultural overlap was more encompassing than in both areas.

In dealing with the first variable for comparison—possession illness as a marker of social distance in a multiethnic setting—I thought to evaluate the extent to which specifically Jewish idioms were part of the behavioral manifestations of the possessing entities and the therapeutic interventions against them. This notion may be viewed as an extension of Sharot's macroanalysis of the differential cultural distinctiveness of Jews in different part of the world, even though the world areas he discussed are not identical with the locales of the three forms of possession.

Turning to the second variable, it should be noted that Israeli society is built of stratified layers of immigrant groups. The ideology of the ingathering of the exiles (*kibbutz galuyot*) formalized by the Law of Return is in a certain way the raison d'etre of the Zionist nation-state. Yet this ideological openness to the Jews of the Diaspora has not spared many of the newcomers from enormous predicaments. Following my discussion of possession illness as a historically bounded phenomenon, I would like to argue that the "migrant illnesses" of the incoming groups have fared no better than the immigrants themselves, as they were among the first casualties of the *kulturkrieg* in the new country. Will *zar* possession, the culture-bound syndrome of the most traditional Jewish group ever to stake a claim in the Zionist dream, follow the track of its predecessors, *dybbuk* and *aslai*, and evaporate in the inhospitable ambiance of modern Israel? And if so, could it be taken as a crude measure of the first steps toward "assimilation"? It might be conjectured that the symbiotic nature of *zar* possession, bespeaking a lasting (albeit strained) coexistence with the spirit world—as against the intolerant exorcistic mode dominant in *dybbuk* and *aslai*—constitutes a more congenial ground for a longer "life span" in the new country.

Epilogue: The Return of the *Dybbuk*

In seeking an ending that will epitomize my major arguments, I thought to emphasize the distance in contemporary Israel between the *dybbuk* as a theatrical performance and *zar* possession as a cluster of actual behavioral manifestations. Whereas the former is an artistic creation that reflects a nostalgic ambivalence toward the exoticized "world of yesterday," the latter is an exotic syndrome treated by western-trained psychiatrists in mental health settings. I considered presenting this difference as indicative of the enormous gap between mainstream Israeli society and its margins. But the recent emergence of a new case of *dybbuk*, exorcised in Jerusalem by a known kabbalist under the limelight of the Israeli mass media, seems to suggest questions about this line of reasoning.[57] A cultural phenomenon dormant since the first decades of the twentieth century resurfaced at the end of the millennium. Does this comeback not cast doubt on the historical boundedness of a cultural phenomenon described before as fragile and amenable to attenuation in times of rapid change?

It is still premature to determine whether the new case is the harbinger of a new wave of *dybbukim*. But even if it were, I would like to argue that, when evaluated against the changing faces of contemporary Israeli society, the return of the *dybbuk*, no less than its earlier disappearance, lends support to the notion of the *dybbuk* as culturally constituted. In recent years Israel has witnessed an astonishing revival of folk religious, mystical, and esoteric beliefs and practices[58] that in the formative years of the state were denigrated and suppressed. Without going into the reasons for this revival, it is clear that it constitutes a spiritual ecology conducive to the return of the spirits. An elaborate and effective system of communication, aided by sophisticated technology—from audiocassettes and videocassettes to ultraorthodox radio channels and Internet Web sites—propagates mystical doctrines like *gilgul* and *ibbur*. Popular preachers, seeking to bring secular Jews back to the fold, conjure large audiences with detailed descriptions of the horrible persecutions awaiting the souls of the wicked in the afterlife. Autistic children, aided by facilitators to communicate otherworldly messages, present themselves in public performances as reincarnations of sinners from former generations and justify their suffering as rectification. Is it far-fetched to assume that this mystical matrix germinates palpable idioms like possession that people in distress will use to articulate their suffering and misery? From a social science perspective, opposed to a unilinear and "progressive" conception of history and a biomedical view of dissociation, it is exactly the historical vicissitudes in the social zeitgeist and religious sensibilities that we should explore to account for the ebbs and flows of possession.

Notes

1. See Erika Bourguignon, ed., *Religion, Altered States of Consciousness, and Social Change* (Columbus: Ohio State University Press, 1993); idem, *Possession* (San Francisco: Chandler & Sharp, 1976). Note, however, that possession is not a "cultural universal" since there have been human societies where it did not exist (see Bourguignon, *Possession*).

2. Janice Boddy, "Spirit Possession Revisited: Beyond Instrumentality," *Annual Review of Anthropology* 23 (1994): 414.

3. See Luc de Heusch, *Why Marry Her? Society and Symbolic Structures* (Cambridge: Cambridge University Press, 1971); F. Kramer, *The Red Fez: Art and Spirit Possession in Africa* (London: Verso, 1993); I. M. Lewis, *Ecstatic Religion: A Study of Spirit Possession and Shamanism* (London: Routledge, 1989).

4. See Janice Boddy, *Wombs and Alien Spirits: Women, Men, and the Zar Cult in Northern Sudan* (Madison: University of Wisconsin Press, 1989); idem, "Spirit Possession Revisited"; Bruce Kapferer, *A Celebration of Demons: Exorcism and Healing in Sri Lanka* (Washington, D.C.: Smithsonian Institute Press, 1991); Michael Lambek, *Knowledge and Practice in Mayotte: Local Discourses on Islam, Sorcery, and Spirit Possession* (Toronto: University of Toronto Press, 1993).

5. Boddy, "Spirit Possession Revisited," 408.

6. Michael Lambek, "From Disease to Discourse: Remarks on the Conceptualization of Trance and Spirit Possession," in *Altered States of Consciousness and Mental Health: A Cross-Cultural Perspective*, ed. C. A. Ward (Newbury Park, Calif.: Sage, 1989), 38.

7. Bourguignon, *Psychological Anthropology: An Introduction to Human Nature and Cultural Differences* (New York: Holt, Rinehart, and Winston, 1979).

8. See Clifford Geerz, *The Interpretation of Cultures* (New York: Basic Books, 1973).

9. See, for example, Lambek, "From Disease to Discourse."

10. Lewis, *Ecstatic Religion*.

11. See E. Cardena, "Trance and Possession as Dissociative Disorders," *Transcultural Psychiatric Research Review* 29.4 (1992): 284–300; Ward, *Altered States*.

12. See Boddy, "Spirit Possession Revisited," 411.

13. Lambek, "From Disease to Discourse." See also Vincent Crapanzano, *The Hamadsha: A Study in Moroccan Ethnopsychiatry* (Berkeley: University of California Press, 1973); Gannanath Obeysekere, "The Idiom of Demonic Possession," *Social Science and Medicine* 4 (1970): 97–111.

14. See Lambek, "From Disease to Discourse."

15. See Boddy, *Wombs and Alien Spirits*; idem, "Spirit Possession Revisited."

16. This holds particularly true for Boddy (*Wombs and Alien Spirits*; "Spirit Possession Revisited"), who studied the *zar* cult in northern Sudan; Lambek ("From Disease to Discourse"; *Knowledge and Practice*), who studied spirit possession in Mayotte in the Comoro Archipelago, and Stoller (Paul Stoller, *Fusion of the Worlds: An Ethnography of Possession among the Songhay of Niger* [Chicago: University of Chicago Press, 1989]), who studied Songhay possession in Niger.

17. The two variables are separated for analytic reasons, but they are highly correlated. After all, culture is the organization of the current situation in the terms of the past.

18. *Dybbuk Tales in Jewish Literature* (in Hebrew) (Jerusalem: Rubin Mass, 1983).

19. The exorcist in the first documented case from Safed (1545) is none other than Rabbi Joseph Karo. See Moshe Idel, "Jewish Magic from the Early Renaissance Period to Early Hasidism," in *Religion, Science, and Magic*, ed. J. Neusner, E. S. Frerichs, and P. V. M. Flesher (Oxford: Oxford University Press, 1989): 82–117.

20. From *davok*, to cleave or to stick in Hebrew. The noun *dybbuk* (pl. *dybbukim*) refers to an external agent "clinging" to a person.

21. The first to use the term was Rabbi Jacob Emden in the context of his

fierce war against the Sabbatean movement. See Yoram Bilu, "*Dybbuk* and *Maggid*: Two Cultural Patterns of Altered Consciousness in Judaism," *Association for Jewish Studies Review* 21 (1996): 340–66.

22. Note that An-ski's classic play, *The Dybbuk* (New York: Liveright, 1926), was subtitled "Between Two Worlds."

23. See *Encyclopedia Judaica*, s.v. "Gilgul," by Gershom Scholem; reprinted in Gershom Scholem, *Kabbalah* (Jerusalem: Keter, 1988), 344–50.

24. For detailed descriptions of *dybbuk* exorcism, see Yoram Bilu, "The Taming of the Deviants and Beyond: An Analysis of *Dybbuk* Possession and Exorcism in Judaism," *Psychoanalytic Study of Society* 11 (1985): 1–32, reprinted in this volume; Nigal, *Dybbuk Tales*.

25. See Bilu, "Taming of the Deviants"; Nigal, *Dybbuk Tales*.

26. See Yoram Bilu, "Demonic Explanations of Illness among Moroccan Jews in Israel," *Culture, Medicine, and Psychiatry* 3 (1979): 363–80; idem, "The Moroccan Demon in Israel: The Case of 'Evil Spirit Diseases,'" *Ethos* 8.1 (1980): 24–38; Crapanzano, *The Hamadsha*; Edward A. Westermarck, *Ritual and Belief in Morocco* (London: Macmillan, 1926).

27. Bilu, "Moroccan Demon in Israel."

28. See R. Giel, Y. Gezahegn, and J. N. van Luijk, "Faith Healing and Spirit Possession in Ghion, Ethiopia," *Social Science and Medicine* 2 (1968): 63–79; Yael Kahana, "The Zar Spirits: A Category of Magic in the System of Mental Health in Ethiopia," *International Journal of Social Psychiatry* 31 (1985): 135–43; Simon D. Messing, "Group Therapy and Social Status in the Zar Cult in Ethiopia," *American Anthropologist* 60 (1959): 1120–26; Allan Young, "Why Amahara Get Kureynya: Sickness and Possession in an Ethiopian Zar Cult," *American Ethnologist* 2 (1975): 567–86.

29. See Young, "Why Amahara."

30. See Crapanzano, *The Hamadsha*, as well as the similar differentiation between exorcism and adorcism in De Heusch, *Why Marry Her?*

31. I later address the problematic fact that *dybbuk*-like possessions continued to appear outside Europe.

32. See J. H. Chajes, "Judgments Sweetened: Possession and Exorcism in Early Modern Jewish Culture," *Journal of Early Modern History* 1.2 (1997): 124–69.

33. See Nigal, *Dybbuk Tales*, 201–3.

34. Ibid., 234.

35. Lewis, *Ecstatic Religion*.

36. Young, "Why Amahara."

37. See Harvey E. Goldberg, "The Zohar in Southern Morocco: A Study in Ethnography of Texts," *History of Religions* 29.3 (1990): 233–58; Avraham Shtahl, "Ritual Reading of the Zohar" (in Hebrew), *Pe'amim* 5 (1980): 77–86.

38. See Westermarck, *Ritual and Belief*.

39. On demons in the Jewish lore see, for example, Joshua Trachtenberg, *Jewish Magic and Superstition: A Study in Folk Religion* (New York: Atheneum, 1974); Sara Zfatman, *Human-Demon Intermarriage* (Jerusalem: Academon, 1988).

40. Yoram Bilu, "Traditional Psychiatry in Israel" (Ph.D. diss., Hebrew University of Jerusalem, 1978).

41. Their names, according to a Jewish book of healing, are Modav, Murat, El-Khmar, Shamharush, Borkan, Mimun el-Biad, and Mimun Swed. The same list appears with little variations in Muslim sources. See Westermarck, *Ritual and Belief*, 391.

42. These camps appear in a Jewish healing book as Damdama, Hatifa, Askara, Kavkava, Saita, and Sahaba. See Bilu, "Moroccan Demon in Israel," 26.

43. Bilu, "Traditional Psychiatry," 114.

44. See Crapanzano, *The Hamadsha*; idem, *Tuhami: Portrait of a Moroccan* (Chicago: University of Chicago Press, 1980).

45. See Stephen Sharot, *Judaism: A Sociology* (New York: Holmes & Meier, 1976).

46. While demons could have various religious identities, including Jewish, most of the possessing agents were non-Jewish.

47. Nigal, *Dybbuk Tales*, 33–35.

48. See Crapanzano, *The Hamadsha*; Westermarck, *Ritual and Belief*.

49. See Boddy, *Wombs and Alien Spirits*; Lambek, *Knowledge and Practice*; Stoller, *Fusion of the Worlds*.

50. See Arthur Kleinman, *Rethinking Psychiatry* (New York: Free Press, 1988).

51. Nigal, *Dybbuk Tales*, 14.

52. See Bilu, "Moroccan Demon in Israel."

53. Ibid.

54. Eliezer Witztum, Nimrod Grisaru, and Danny Budowski, "The 'Zar' Possession Syndrome among Ethiopian Immigrants to Israel: Cultural and Clinical Aspects," *British Journal of Medical Psychology* 69 (1996): 207–25.

55. A. Arieli and S. Aycheh, "Mental Illnesses Connected to the Belief in Possession by the 'Zar'" (in Hebrew), *Ha-Refu'ah* 126 (1994): 636–42.

56. See Kleinman, *Rethinking Psychiatry*.

57. See Yoram Bilu and Yehuda Goodman, "What Does the Soul Say? Metaphysical Uses of Facilitated Communication in the Jewish Ultraorthodox Community," *Ethos* 25.4 (1997): 375–407.

58. See Benjamin Beit-Hallahmi, *Despair and Deliverance: Private Salvation in Contemporary Israel* (New York: State University of New York Press, 1992).

APPENDIX A

Texts concerning Spirit Possession in Sixteenth-Century Safed

Translations by J. H. CHAJES

Case 1: A Great Event in Safed

[Translated from *Divre Yosef,* by Joseph Sambari, ed. S. Shtober (Jerusalem: Ben-Zri Institute, 1994), 319–24.]

1. A Great Event in the Holy Community of Safed, *may it be rebuilt and reestablished speedily and in our days* [hereafter *tvb"b*]. For man is more attracted to the pleasure of his body for his sensory pleasure than he is inclined to follow the advice of his soul and the direction of the Torah—even believers and those most punctilious in all things. For the matters of the World to Come are not felt; thus who can establish them in his heart so that they might make an impression upon him to separate from any aspect of evil or wrongdoing—whether in speech, thought, or action? Not every person merits this. Therefore, in order to bestow merit upon others, I concluded to commit to writing that which transpired before me today, 11 Adar I 5331 [16 February 1571]: the case of a woman, the daughter-in-law of the venerable Joseph Zarfati, into whom entered a spirit of a man of Israel, as I will describe below. In truth, whoever was there at the time and heard from the spirit what he said and what he revealed, and whoever heard it from him, ought to subdue their hearts to heaven and have fear and dread of the Day of Judgment on account of their actions. For all comes to account, and there is no House of Refuge in Sheol [Avot 4:29]. And this is known to us from one who came from that World, and told to us by one who has crossed over there. Perhaps the Holy One, Blessed be He, sent him so that they might fear Him, as the Sages of blessed memory said, "'And God does it, so that men should fear him' [Eccles. 3:14]—this

is a bad dream." And this is not a dream but while awake, before the eyes of all.

2. I was amidst a great gathering, for there were over one hundred people there, Torah scholars and heads of communities. Two men, who knew the adjurations and many matters, approached the woman so that the spirit within the woman would speak, by means of the smoke of fire and sulfur that they would make enter her nostrils. She was like naught, for she would not push herself away—not even her head—from the fire, nor from the smoke. By means of the adjurers the voice would begin to be heard, "like the voice of the Almighty," drawn out like "the roar of a lion and the howl of a fierce lion" [Job 4:10] without any movement of the tongue or opening of the lips. When this voice began to be heard, the two aforementioned men would strengthen and intensify themselves quickly and diligently so as to do that which they would do rapidly. They would quarrel with him with a loud voice, and say to him: "Evil one, speak and say who you are in a clear tongue!" Then the voice would reveal itself and show itself to all that it was like the voice of men.

3. And they again spoke to him in a great voice and by means of all the aforementioned: "What is your name, evil one?" He would respond, "Samuel Zarfati." They asked him, "How can we be sure that your name is Samuel Zarfati?" He responded that he had died in Tripoli, and that he had left one son, whose name is so-and-so; that he had had three daughters, the name of the first being so-and-so, the name of the second so-and-so, and the name of the third so-and-so; and from the third he died, and she is now married to Tuvia Deleiria. And on all of the signs that he said, [his] word [was] correct and veracious, a word of truth. Then we recognized, all those present, that the spirit was the speaker.

4. They asked him, "For which matter do you reincarnate in the world in reincarnations such as these?" He responded, "for many sins that I have committed during my life." In turn, they demanded, "Be explicit about them." He said that he did not want to, for what purpose would be served? They then compelled him to state at least the greatest transgression of them all, and he answered and said that he had been a type of *apikorus* [heretic], and that he had said that all religions are the same. Regarding this, many testified before us that he had spoken in such a way during his lifetime. And they asked him, "And now of what mind are you regarding this?" And he responded like one groaning with a voice crying and raging, and said: "I recognize that I sinned, transgressed, and wronged." And he asked for forgiveness from the Holy One, Blessed be He, and of His Perfect Torah for his many transgressions.

5. And then the aforementioned two men began to entreat him and compel him by means of the ban to depart from within her and to go to a

place of barren wilderness, by means of the techniques mentioned above. They also [promised that they] would petition for mercy upon him, and pray for him, and blow the shofar. He said, "What I wouldn't give for that!" They asked him, "Who should blow the shofar?" He said, "The sage, his honor the rabbi Solomon Alkabetz." The aforementioned sage responded that he was unable. They again said to him, "Request another." The spirit said, "Let it be the sage, his honor the rabbi Avraham Lahmi." They asked him, "Who should request [mercy] for you?" The spirit responded, "Let it be the rabbi Elijah Falcon."

6. And then we said "*El melekh*" and "*Va-ya'avor*" [Exod. 34:6] thrice with the blast of the shofar. And all was done according to the revelation of his will. Then they said to him once again that he must depart, since they did for him according to his will. The spirit responded, "Let a little time pass; then I will depart." They asked him, "Do you want your son to say *kaddish* for you or learn Torah?" He said that it would not help it at all, and that his son was unsuited to learn Torah.

7. They asked him about the matter of "the beating of the grave." And one of those seated there responded, "This one never entered the grave!" Then the spirit said—and refuted his words, "I entered on the day of my burial, and on that same night they removed me, and I did not enter again. And from that very time, which was nearly three years ago, I have gone from mountain to mountain, and from hill to hill. I did not find rest in any place, except that for a period of time I was in Shekhem, where I entered into one woman, and they removed me through the aforementioned and placed amulets upon her so that I was unable to return upon her further." And all this is true from what we knew from the mouths of others that such had transpired. "After that I was roving through the city to enter synagogues [thinking that] perhaps I would find rest and comfort there for my soul, but they did not allow me to enter any synagogue." And they asked him, "Who prevented you?" The spirit said, "The sages." They asked him again, "Were they alive, or were they dead?" He said, "Dead. And they trampled me and said to me, 'Depart from here, wicked one!'" The questioner asked further, "To which synagogue did you go first?" He said, "To my own congregation." They said to him, "Which is it?" He responded, "Bet Ya'akov." They asked him further, "Your seat: who sits upon it?" He responded, "If they did not allow me to enter, how am I supposed to know who sits in my place?" They asked him further, "Who sat by your side when you were alive?" He responded, "So-and-so." And all that he said was true.

8. Then they said to him, "And how did you enter this woman? Is she not forbidden for you?" He said, "What can I do, for I found no rest anywhere other than inside her, for she is a kosher woman." "And if she is

a married woman, have you no reservations about copulating with her? The spirit responded, "And what of it? Her husband isn't here, but in Salonika!"

9. The two first men asked further, "How did you enter this house, which has a mezuzah?" He answered, "I came in via a lower entrance which did not have a mezuzah." And they asked him, "And how was it that you entered her, being that she was kosher?" He said, "There was a difficult time and she threw a little mud on her [sic] head, and for that, I was able to enter inside her." And all this was on Thursday of last week in the evening. All this the spirit himself said, and thus it was that from that moment she had felt it herself. While still compelling him to depart, they said to him, "And why have you not feared the *herem* that you received yesterday, to depart and not to return again inside her? How could you transgress it?" He responded, "I did depart, but did not find rest in any other place, until I saw that they did not put amulets upon her; then I was able to enter her another time." Then they strengthened themselves and said to him, "Depart, evil one! If not, we will decree upon you the *herem Kol Bo* that you depart in any case." And they cast the *herem Kol Bo* since he had been adjured by the Ten Commandments to depart after one hour. Many testified that such was his custom while alive, to take this oath. And they delayed among themselves for a short time and reproached him and spoke harshly against him: "Is it that you do not fear from any man, nor even from your vow, and not from the *herem Kol Bo*?" And the spirit would say, "What can I do, if I perish, I perish" [cf. Esther 4:16].

10. After this, they wanted to test whether this speech was spoken by the spirit. They spoke with him in the Holy Tongue, and in the Arabic tongue, and in the tongue of Ishmael, called *Moorish*. To each and every language, he responded in a clear tongue, as he did while alive, as his acquaintances said of him. The woman did not know any of these languages. Thus, when they spoke with him in the Ashkenazic language, he would not respond to them in it, as he did not know or understand that language.

11. They asked him, "Who am I?" To each he responded with their names. They also asked him, "What was your trade when you were alive?" "Money changing," he answered. And so it was. They also asked him about ibn Musa, whether he had seen him, and the course of his transmigration. He responded that he had not seen him at all.

12. They pressed him with the aforementioned adjurations, and with the aforementioned smoke, and with the Names, that the spirit should depart through the big nail of one of her feet. He then tried to deceive them into believing that he had departed the way that they told him; he raised her legs and lowered them one after the other, with great speed,

time and again. And with those movements, which he made with great strength, the cover that was upon her fell off her feet and thighs, and she revealed and humiliated herself for all to see. They came close to her to cover her thighs; neither did she feel herself in this at all. And those who were acquainted with her knew of her great modesty; now her modesty was lost to her. All this because she was like dead and naught, as we said above.

13. They said to him, "The sign and demonstration by which we shall know that you indeed went out completely is that when you go out you should extinguish the candle hanging on the wall at a distance of roughly three cubits from him." And by those movements that we mentioned he wanted to extinguish the candle. But although he strengthened himself and hurried and warmed himself to show us that he was going out through the aforementioned nail to extinguish the candle that hung on the wall, nevertheless he did not go out. For he did not want to go out, but wanted to mock us. Many times he said, "Bring the candle nearer, to the place where it was yesterday," so as to extinguish it there. And they said to him, "If you extinguish the candle where it is, we shall know with certainty that you departed; but if not, then you are mocking us." He again strengthened himself to make movements and shakings with the legs until he blew the air with those movements. As [he did not] want to depart and abandon his dwelling there, he was unable to extinguish the candle from there. Had the candle been nearer, he could have extinguished it, for the spirit was on top of her feet, as he said. The two adjurers and we saw the spirit going out, close to her feet. They again adjured him and gave him smoke, fire, and sulfur into her nostrils, so that he should go out completely through the aforementioned nail, and should uproot himself with a total uprooting and extinguish the aforementioned candle, which was at a distance of three cubits, on his way out from there while going to the desolate desert place. He said many times, "Let this poor Jewish woman be, and do not hurt her!" And they said to him, "It is you who hurts her; depart if you have pity on her." And he answered, "Do not continue to force me, for if you force me to go out I shall take out her soul with me." Nevertheless the aforementioned adjurers decreed upon him that he should go out unfailingly. But he did not go out. They said to him, "Sit up on the bed and then go out, and if you do not want to, then we will force you with all the things mentioned." He sat up on the bed without any help. Then, when he was seated, they said to him with a great voice, "Go out, you evil one, quickly, without her soul."

14. Then he himself touched the feet with the fingers as if he was pushing the spirit that was in the flesh through the nail by means of that

touching. And then suddenly she began to speak. She was sitting and saying, "He has already left." And they did not believe her, for they suspected that perhaps the spirit himself was speaking. For they saw that he did not extinguish the candle. And she said that he forgot to extinguish the candle because of the great confusion and the great hurry to go out. Nevertheless, they still did not believe her, and they wanted to do again as they had done before, and she cried to her father-in-law and her grandmother, "Why do you let them burn me, for he has already left, and they do not leave me alone!" And she said, "I know that it is true that he indeed has left." And they said to her, "What is the truth?" And she answered, "I cannot tell you." And then they understood that it was a matter that cannot be told in public, and they said to a woman, "Go to her and she will reveal the matter to you." And so it was done, and it became known that the spirit went out through that place and drew blood as he went out. And all this cogent evidence made all of them accept that there was truth in her words. And they placed the amulets upon her that were ready in the house, and she was assumed to have recovered.

15. An hour later the sages came to her, when the cry went out in the city: "Behold, the spirit of a man from Israel speaks in a woman." And when they saw her, they said, "He certainly did not leave, and if he left he again returned." [They said so] because of the signs they saw, such as glazed eyes and labored breathing. And from these signs they knew that he was still in her. And then the voice [in the city] told about the ruination, a voice that did not cease, that the spirit was still in her. But the two adjurers said that he surely had gone out, but thereafter he returned, because, for one thing, the amulets that they put on her were not written for her name, and for another, because of the confusion, since the whole city, Jews and Turks, were coming one after the other to her, to see the terrible thing that was astonishing to the eyes of every man. They hushed up the matter because of the danger on the part of the nations that would have wanted to burn her, until it should be forgotten in a few days, then the matter could be corrected. And eight days later the poor woman died because of the spirit that did not leave her, and they say that he choked her and went out with her soul.

16. Everything I wrote above, every detail is written precisely as it was. One must not doubt anything in it, because it is written accurately, and there is no addition in it nor any deletion, for I wrote exactly what I saw and heard. I further request the sages who were there that they, too, should put their signatures on this, for by their mouths we live, that they verify my words through their signatures. And the eye that sees this writing of mine and the ear that hears it should believe with a complete faith as if

he had heard it from the mouth of the spirit, and should fear and be afraid and believe everything written in the Torah and in the words of our rabbis of blessed memory, and then he will rest on his couch in peace and three groups of ministering angels will go out before him, one will say, "Peace, etc. . . . ," and no plague will go near his tent, and his soul will cleave to God and will return to the place whence it was hewn. Thus says the writer, the young and the poor among the thousands, the devoted servant of the fearers of the Lord, and those who think of His name, Elijah Falcon.

17. I was there, and my eyes saw and my ears heard to instruct all this and more—he who sees shall testify, your servant SHLOMO LEVI BEN ALKABETZ (author of the book *Shoresh Yishai* on Ruth)

These words are words of truth, which have no measure so that every man should know about this event and leave his evil ways, and every man [should give up] the wrong of his thoughts before he goes and is not, and he who knows will return, and repent, and come back, and will be healed. The youth ABRAHAM HA-LAHMI

SHMUEL BUENO

I too was called to see this matter and my eyes have seen and my ears have heard, and it is a miraculous thing, to teach us that we should turn back in repentance. Says ABRAHAM ARUETY.

Case 2: The Possession and Death of the Young Man in Safed

[Translated from *Divre Yosef*, 324–25. Rounded parentheses indicate passages that appear in Menasseh ben Israel's *Nishmat Hayyim* version only (Amsterdam, 1651), 111a–b.]

1. Again a similar event happened a second time in Safed. Once a spirit entered a young man, and they adjured him by all the conditions mentioned above, and he too recalled his name and the name of his city and the name of his wife.

2. (Every time he recalled his wife, he would weep and say that his wife remained an *agunah* after him, since he drowned at sea. The sages are unable to permit her to marry, and she whores. He would beg of the sages who were standing there to permit her [to remarry], and he gave many signs [attesting to the truth] of what he said. They said to him that, all of that notwithstanding, she was still forbidden. He debated with them over this, invoking rabbinic teachings.) They asked him what his sin had been.

He said that he had relations with a married woman in Constantinople. (And that the statement of the Sages to the effect that the four manners of execution had not been nullified, had been the case for him. They said to him, "What was the name of that woman?" He did not want to expose her, for she too had already died, and there was no purpose in exposing her.)

3. In the midst of all of this he stood up on his feet. They said to him, "Why did you arise?" He said to them, "Because the Sage so-and-so has now come." (And so it was, for immediately after this he came, as he had said.) After that a group of young men entered his midst. He said, "Why are these coming here to see me? The cup shall also pass over to them as well! [See Lamentations 4:21–22.] For we all share the same transgression. I am shocked by these, for matters of common knowledge need no proof! But I am astounded by this man, who makes himself appear as though he were a pietist, dressed in white, and he is blanched by the evil: he commits the acts of Zimri and requests the reward of Pinhas! Did he not have relations with a married woman in Constantinople?" And all those present expressed their shock to one another. The one dressed in white clothes began to weep with great weeping, and all admitted and confessed their actions. Then one of the sages there asked him, "How do you know?" He said to him, "And does the verse not say 'he places a seal upon the hand of every man'[Job 37:7]? And I know even what is in the innermost chambers." (One of the sages standing there said to him, "Tell me my actions." He said to him, "Regarding our master we have no permission to say anything." And they asked that same young man inside whom was the spirit, "Why does this spirit speak with your mouth and lips as if you were the speaker? Let him speak for himself." He again began to laugh and said, "And did not the Sages say in [BT] *Babba Kamma* 'the agent of the person is like him, etc. . . . .' ")

4. They then asked him to tell them in what way he entered into this young man. He answered that he drowned at sea at a particular place, and fish ate his flesh. His spirit wandered in the land, (hiding and concealing itself from the eye of every creature, for all would torment him with all types of suffering). He finally entered a cow. The cow then went mad. When the owner of the cow saw its actions, he sold her to a Jew, and that Jew slaughtered her. When he slaughtered her, the young man was there; he left the cow and entered into him. Many testified that such was the case, (and that immediately after the slaughtering of the cow, the young man felt the spirit that was tormenting him).

5. Within eight days this young man passed away. Thus one fearing the word of the Lord should return and regret the sins he has committed

and plead with his maker; perhaps the Lord will hear and return and heal him.

Case 3: The Spirit in the Widow of Safed

[Translated from *Kitve Shevah Yakar u'Gedulat ha-Ari Z"L*, in *Ta'alumot Hokhmah*, ed. Joseph Delmedigo (Basle, 1628), 49b–50b.]

1. There occurred an event at the time that the holy and pure Rav, the divine kabbalist Isaac Luria Ashkenazi *z"l* (his memory for a blessing) was in Safed, *may it be rebuilt and reestablished speedily in our days*. A spirit entered one woman, a widow, and made her suffer very great and enormous suffering. Many people assembled about her and spoke with her, and the spirit replied to each and every one, making known the wounds of his heart, and all of his needs for that which he lacks. And among those who came one sage entered his midst, and his name was *mvhr"r* [our teacher, the rabbi R.] Joseph Ashkenazi [or Arzin] *zt"l*. Immediately the spirit said to him, "Blessed is he who comes, my master, my teacher and my rabbi! I recall my master, for I was his student in Egypt for a long time, and my name is so-and-so, and my father's name so-and-so.

2. Now, when the relatives of the woman saw her suffering and her pain, that it was very great, they went to the Holy Rav, *mvhr"r* Isaac Luria, *zt"l*, to beg him to go with them to the woman and to remove this spirit from the woman. Being that the Rav *zt"l* was not free to go himself, he sent his student, *mhr"r* Hayyim Calabrese *zt"l*, and laid his hands upon him and transmitted to him *Kavvanot* [plural of *kavvanah*, in this context a magico-mystical meditative intention] with Names. He also commanded him to decree upon him bans and excommunications, and to remove him against his will.

3. As soon our teacher the *mhr"r* Hayyim Vital *z"l* entered her midst, the woman immediately turned her face away to the wall. The Rav *z"l* said to her, "Evildoer, why did you turn your face away from me?" The spirit replied to him and said, "I am unable to gaze upon your face, for the wicked are unable to gaze upon the face of the *Shekhinah*!" Immediately our teacher the *mhr"r* Hayyim *z"l* decreed upon him that he turn his face, and he then immediately turned his face. He said to him, "What is your sin and your transgression for which they have punished you with this severe punishment?" The spirit replied to him and said, "I sinned with a married woman and fathered bastards. It has now been twenty-five years for me that I go wandering in the land, and they have given me no respite, even for an hour or for a minute. For three angels of destruction go with me to all

the places to which I go, and punish me and beat me with exceedingly hard blows, and declare before me: 'Such will be done to one who multiplied bastards among Israel.' And these three angels of destruction are alluded to in the verse: 'Appoint over him a wicked man, and may Satan stand at his right'" [Ps. 109:7–8]. And the spirit also said to the Rav z"l, "Do you not see one angel of the angels who stands on my right, and one on my left, and they declare, and the third strikes me death blows?" The Rav asked him, and said to him, "Did not our sages z"l say: 'The sentence of the wicked in Gehinnom is twelve months'?" [*Eduyot* 2:10]. The spirit responded to him and said to him, "My master was not precise in this statement, for when our sages z"l said that 'the sentence of the wicked in Gehinnom is twelve months,' it was after they have suffered the punishments outside of Gehinnom, in reincarnations and though other hard judgments. Then they are admitted to Gehinnom, and there they spend twelve months. They whiten and wash them in order to remove from them the stains of the soul, in order for them to be invited and prepared to enter Gan Eden [the Garden of Eden]. This is like an expert doctor who first administers hard and sharp substances upon the wound, which consume the living flesh, and afterward he puts on the wound good salves and bandages in order to cool and grow the flesh back to its former state. So is the matter of Gehinnom, for the suffering of Gehinnom is not one fiftieth part that the soul endures before it enters Gehinnom.

4. The Rav z"l then asked him, "How did you die?" He responded and said to him, "My death was by choking, for although the four manners of death of the *Bet Din* [Supreme Rabbinical Court] have been abrogated, the four types of death have not been abrogated. When I left from Alexandria in a boat to go to Egypt, my boat was sunk in the Nile delta region, where the Nile enters the sea. We drowned, other Jews who were with me on the boat and I." Mhr"r Hayyim z"l then asked him, "Why did you not say the confession at the hour of the departure of your soul from your body; perhaps it would have helped you." "The spirit responded to him, "I did not manage to confess, for immediately the water choked me in my throat. Also immediately in the drowning in the sea my mind became confused, and I was not in my right mind to confess."

5. The Rav then asked him, "Tell me what happened to you after you drowned in the sea and after the departure of your soul from your body?" The spirit responded and said, "Know that when the matter of the sunk boat became known in Egypt, immediately the Jews of Egypt went into the sea and took all of us out of the sea and buried us. Immediately thereafter, when the Jews left the cemetery, a cruel angel came, with a staff of fire in his hand, and he roughly struck my grave with that staff. Immediately the

grave split in two from the strike, which was so very great and strong. That angel said to me, 'Evil one, evil one, arise in judgment!' Immediately he took me and put me in the hollow of the sling and slung me in one shot from Egypt to before the opening of Gehinnom in the wilderness. And as I fell there before the opening of Gehinnom, there immediately came out of Gehinnom one million souls of evildoers who are being judged in Gehinnom, and all of them shouted against me and said to me, 'Depart, depart, man of blood, depart from here evildoer, tormentor of Israel!' And they cursed me with vehement curses and said to me, 'You are still unworthy of entering here, and you still have no permission to enter Gehinnom.' Then they slung me from mountain to mountain, and from hill to hill, and those three angels of destruction go with me always and decree before me and strike me always. And at each and every moment other angels of destruction, evil spirits, demons, and she-devils injure me. And upon hearing the decree that they decree before me, they beat me with great and difficult blows as well. These pull me here, and that one pulls me there, until all the knots of my soul are unwound.

6. "In this way, I went wandering to and fro in the land, until reaching the city of Ormuz, a large city close to the land of India. My intention was to enter into the body of some Jew, perhaps to be saved from those blows, sufferings, and torments. Now, since those Jews who are evil and sinning to the Lord exceedingly, fornicating with gentile women and other transgressions, I was unable to enter even one of them due to the many spirits of impurity that dwell in them and around them. Had I entered into the body of one of them, I would have added defilement to my defilement and injury to my own injury. For that reason I returned, and went from mountain to hill and from hill to mountain, until I came to the wilderness of Gaza. There I found a pregnant doe; due to my great suffering and pain I entered her body. This was after seven years during which I went through many terrible troubles. When I entered the body of this doe, it was tremendously painful for me, for the soul of a human being and the soul of a beast are not equal, for one walks upright and the other bent. Also, the soul of the beast is full of filth and is repulsive, its smell foul before the soul of a human being. And its food is not human food. I also had great pain from the fetus in her belly. The doe also had great pain because of me; her belly swelled, and she ran in the mountains and in the rocks until her abdomen split and she died. From there I left and I came to the city Shekhem, where I entered the body of a Jew, a Kohen. And that Kohen immediately sent after the holy men and clerics of the Ishmaelites, and from the number of their incantations and adjurations of impure names and also the amulets of unholy names that they hung from his neck, I was

unable to bear it and to remain in his body. I immediately left there and fled from there." Immediately the Rav said to him, "Is it really the case that there is something to the forces of impurity to injure and to ameliorate by themselves?" He said to him, "No, but because the clerics, through their adjurations, infused so many spirits of impurity into the body of that Kohen-Jew that I saw that if I continued to stay there all those spirits would cling to me. Thus I was unable to stay with them.

7. "I then came to Safed, *tvb"b*, and I entered the body of this woman. For me, as of today, it has been twenty-five years that my suffering persists." The Rav said to him "For how long will you have this suffering, for have you no recovery forever?" The spirit responded to him, "Until all the bastards die that I fathered, for as long as they live and exist I have no reparation." Then all those who were there, a very great multitude, all of them cried many cries, for fear of judgment fell upon them. A great awakening took place throughout the region from that very occurrence. The Rav then asked him, "Who gave you permission to enter the body of this woman?" The spirit responded, "I spent one night in her house; at dawn this woman arose from her bed and wanted to light a fire from the stone and iron, but the burnt rag did not catch the sparks. She persisted stubbornly, but did not succeed. She then became intensely angry, and cast the iron and the stone and the burnt rag—everything—from her hand to the ground, and angrily said, 'to Satan with you!' Immediately I was given permission to enter her body." The Rav *z"l* asked him and said, "And for a minor transgression such as this they gave you permission to enter her body?" The spirit responded and said, "Know, my master the sage, that this woman's inside is not like her outside, for she does not believe in the miracles that the Holy One, Blessed be He, did for Israel, and in particular in the Exodus from Egypt. Every Passover night, when all of Israel are rejoicing and good-hearted, saying the great Hallel and telling of the Exodus from Egypt, it is vanity in her eyes, a mockery and a farce. And she thinks in her heart that there was never a miracle such as this."

8. Immediately the Rav said to the woman so-and-so, "Do you believe with perfect belief that the Holy One, Blessed be He, is One and Unique, and that He created the heavens and the earth, and that He has the power and capacity to do anything that He desires, and that there is no one who can tell him what to do?" She responded to him and said, "Yes, I believe in it all in perfect faith." The Rav *z"l* further said to her, "Do you believe in perfect faith that the Holy One, blessed be He, took us out of Egypt from the house of slavery, and split the sea for us, and accomplished many

miracles for us?" She responded, "Yes, master, I believe in it all with perfect faith, and if I had at times a different view, I regret it." And she began to cry.

9. Immediately the Rav decreed a ban on the spirit to depart, and he decreed upon him that he not depart by way of any limb other than via the little toe of the left foot, because the reason is that from the limb that it departs, that limb is ruined and destroyed utterly. And the Rav intended the Names that his teacher *z"l* had transmitted to him, and immediately the little toe swelled and became like a turnip, and [the spirit] left by that way. After that, on a number of nights the spirit came to the windows of the house and to the entryway and terrorized the woman, [threatening] to return and to enter her body. The relatives of the woman returned to the kabbalist the AR"I *zt"l*. The Rav sent his student *mhr"r* Hayyim *z"l* to check the mezuzah, and he found the entryway without any mezuzah. Immediately the Rav commanded that a kosher mezuzah be affixed to the entryway, and so they did. And from them on, the spirit did not return.

Case 4: The Possessed Woman of Safed

[Translated from *Ma'aseh Nissim shel ha-Ari z"l (Shivhe ha-Ari)*, in *Me'irat Ainayim*, ed. Shlomo ben Mordechai Gabbai (Constantinople, 1666), 17b–18b.]

1. One day, when we were in the study hall of my teacher [the AR"I], they brought one woman before him to know whether she was ill, or if some spirit had enclothed himself in her. They said to my teacher, *zlh"h*, that she had been free of any sickness or pain, and that suddenly she was transformed to this state. Her whole body shook. My teacher, *zlh"h*, checked her pulse and said that it was a spirit who enclothed himself in her. He sent her to her home and told me to go there in the evening to remove the spirit from her. He also told me to be particularly wary of that spirit because he is a great deceiver, and when asked his name, lies up to three times; he also gave me *Kavvanot* to remove him. For it was my teacher's custom to send me to carry out this kind of mission, the reason he would give me being that I am from the soul root [*behinat*, or "aspect"] of Cain, the left side of the Primordial Adam, which is severity, and judgments are only sweetened at their source. For this reason I have this power.

2. Now, I only left at dusk on Thursday night. Before I went in to the house of that woman, the spirit said to those standing there, "See that the Sage Rabbi Hayyim Vital has come here to remove me from here. We

will see what his power is, and what he is able to do. I am not afraid of him; what power has he to remove me from here?" When I entered and the spirit saw my face and I greeted them, the spirit paid me great respect. And half his body arose, and he began to quake. I asked him who he was, and he responded, "I am so-and-so." I said to him, "Lies you speak; that is not your name." And thus he lied three times, and on the fourth time he said his true name, as my teacher, *zlh"h*, had said he would. Then I drew close to his ear and I said a few *Kavvanot*, and the spirit panicked very much and spoke abusively, and wanted to depart until I thoroughly rebuked him and he gave me a sign that he wanted to depart by way of the little toe of the foot. This was a lie, for I saw that he was standing entirely in the throat, and that he wanted to depart and extinguish the candles and to harm those standing there. Seeing this, I decreed upon him a *niddui* that he not depart from there. I left things in this state, and went to pray the evening prayer in the home of my teacher, *zlh"h*.

3. After we prayed and the comrades left, I told my teacher, *zlh"h*, the entire episode. He said, "I am surprised at you; for I told you to go in the evening and you went at night, which is the time when all the spirits and *kelippot* [demonic "husks"] have dominion. It is no time to act upon them anything, for then is their time." In the meantime, it had become very late and rain was falling. My teacher, *zlh"h*, told me, "Go in peace," and he walked with me a little, which he never did any other time. And he said to me, "You need to protect yourself from that spirit very well, for he is extremely angry with you for wanting to remove him from his place. And I want to reveal to you one thing, and do not allow it to make your soul grow haughty: See the power that is yours, and how many *kelippot* flee and fear you; for even if all the *kelippot* in the world came, they would be unable to harm you. If you shake the corners of your garment, all will flee from you and be unable to stand before you."

4. After this, I went to my house by way of the Jewish market, for that is my path. It was then already one o'clock at night. When I wanted to go up to the market, a dog came before me at close range, black and huge as a mule. I was shocked before him, and could not recall any *Kavvanah*, for upon seeing him I forgot everything. I walked with great fear. I was close to him in a narrow place, fenced in on both sides; it was night, dark and raining, and I could not turn back from fear of the Turkish sergeants and also because the *kelippot* are *ahorayim* [literally "rear-beings"] and adhere to and harm the back more than they do the front. I passed across from the dog and, behold, he cried out in a great voice. I was startled, and I fell upon the ground, and my hand touched the hand of the dog. When I arose,

the corners of my garment were full of mud and I shook them—without the intention of one performing a *Kavvanah*—and behold, the dog fled immediately and did not stand before me any longer. I walked to my home. The hand that touched the hand of the dog was withered. In the morning, I walked to the house of my teacher, *zlh"h*, and he said to me, "Did I not tell you to shake the corners of your garment? I also accompanied you and did not enter my house until I saw that you had already entered your house, and my heart was with you." Then my teacher, *zlh"h*, held my hand and it returned to its original state.

5. After this my teacher gave me different *Kavvanot* and I went and spoke into the ear of the woman within whom was the spirit. The spirit did not want to leave. I went to my teacher, *zlh"h*, and told him this, and he said to me, "The spirit did just as you decreed upon him—not to depart." He also gave me different *Kavvanot*, and they are written in their place. I went to the woman, and the spirit started to quake and I recited those *Kavvanot* into the ear of the woman. I then asked the spirit through which place he entered the house. He responded that there was a small hole in the wall, and from there he entered, because he was unable to enter from the entrance, upon which there was a kosher mezuzah, nor by way of the windows, for they are not for the comings and goings of men and do not require a mezuzah. I also asked him in what way he entered this woman. He said that he had been in that same house for three days before he entered that woman, and was seeking some opportunity to enter her. Finally, on Thursday night, that woman wanted to arise early and to busy herself with her labor. When she was striking the steel and stone to release the fire, the spirit was sitting upon the stone, and the woman would strike and no sparks would emerge. After she troubled herself greatly and there was no fire, she threw the steel from her hand in anger, and then he entered her—for he found an opening to enter her. Afterward I asked him what he did during those three days that he was in the house and in what place he dwelled. He responded that he was hiding in a beam from which candles are hung; he entered the beam because the guards appointed over him came and he entered there and they did not find him. I said to him, "Give me a sign that this is true." He responded to me that the sign was that on such-and-such a day you all ate such-and-such, and that on such-and-such a day the woman said such-and-such to her husband, and he responded to her such-and-such. And they acknowledged that such had been the case. Afterward I released him from the *niddui* that I had decreed upon him. Then I caused him to go out and he went away by means of the *Kavvanot* that my teacher, *zlh"h*, had given me.

Case 5: The Nephew of R. Yehoshua bin Nun

[Translated from "Ranu le-Ya'akov," MS Bodleian 1870, 164A, Institute for Hebrew Microfilmed Manuscripts, no. 18805, University of Oxford, England; cf. *Divre Yosef,* 350–51.]

    1. An event in Safed, *tvb"h,* in the time of my teacher, *zlh"h.* There was a young man, the son of the sister of Rav Yehoshua bin Nun, *z"l,* and he was a young man of eighteen years of age, in the yeshivah. My teacher, *zlh"h,* saw him and said to his father, "Your son—a spirit is in him; do not waste your money on doctors." The father of the young man answered and said to him, "Do not say that, master, for he only has occasional heart pain. He has had this pain for twelve years, and he is healed by the doctors; this heart pain then returns." My teacher, *zlh"h,* answered him, "Now you will see that it is a spirit." And he decreed upon him, and the spirit spoke and said to him that he had been impregnated within this young man for twelve years. The Rav *zlh"h* said to him, "And why have you been here for twelve years?" The spirit responded, "I was a pauper in Rome and supported myself on charity in that incarnation. This young man was also there, and he was a charity warden in that incarnation. I cried out to him, 'Give me some support!' and he did not want to; I died of hunger. Now the Supernal Court has decreed that just as he killed me in that incarnation, I too will now kill him."

    2. Then the Rav *zlh"h* decreed upon him that he not do him any harm. The spirit said, "If you want me to leave here, agree with me to one condition—that after I depart from here, this young man not see the face of a woman for three days; if he transgresses this condition I will kill him." The father asked the son if he had heart pain, and he said no. The Rav *zlh"h* ordered that there be a watch over the young man, and not to allow him to depart from the House of Study, nor [to allow] women to come to him. The spirit, he said, was a scoundrel, for he demanded of him a condition difficult to fulfill.

    3. And the first day was Rosh Hodesh [New Moon] and I, Hayyim, went to make a feast. I left the Rav Rabbi Yehoshua Bin Nun in my place for the watch. He too left afterward, and left the young man in the House of Study. His mother and aunt then came to see the young man, saw his face, and kissed him. At that same moment the spirit returned, entered him, and strangled him.

    4. And out of fear of the nations of the world—that they would say that we killed him—the Rav *zlh"h* made a magical jump over two reeds and traveled to Tiberias in one second, this being dusk. In Tiberias the Rav *zlh"h* made a prayer that the matter not spread among the nations,

and that there be no informing against the Jews. And thus it was. After eight days we returned to Safed, *tv"bb*.

Notes

This appendix is related to J. H. Chajes's essay in this volume, "City of the Dead."

Appendix B

Lurianic Texts concerning "His Portion and His Neighbor's Portion"—A Moral Problem

Translations and commentary by MENACHEM KALLUS; sources as noted

The idea that a person may receive "His portion and his neighbor's portion" in the afterlife derives from the Babylonian Talmud (*Hagigah* 15r). An interesting introduction to kabbalistic approaches can be gained from examining the comments on this issue in *Sefer Avodat ha-Kodesh* of R. Me'ir ibn Gabbai.[1] The author was among the Jews exiled from Spain in 1492, and his work is a classic of Jewish mysticism. The following is my own translation. My comments and interpolations are added in square brackets or notes.

1. The first Adam was created in the Image of God, and he transgressed because the serpent led him astray. And if he had not contained within himself any part of the *Kelippah*, [the serpent] would not have had the power to cause him to sin. It is indeed within the choice of all people to either repair or to ruin; and although all are drawn after the animating soul [*nefesh*] and [each] *nefesh* is drawn according to its root; yet, with learning and habituation, one may either improve or deteriorate. And, it is possible for a person to change [one's predisposed *nefesh*] with regard to its attachment to the inner and outer attributes. One has the ability to increase wickedness and evil. So too with regard to the good. As our sages [*Hagigah* 15r] have commented on the verse, "God made one as well as [that is, in parallel contrast to] the other" [Eccles. 7:14]. He created *tzaddikim* and created the wicked. He created the Garden of Eden and created Gehenna. Each and every person possess two portions: one in Eden and one in Gehenna. If one merits and is a *tzaddik*, one takes his portion and

385

the portion of his neighbor [who is wicked] in Eden. If one is culpable and is wicked, he takes his portion and the portion of his neighbor [who is righteous] in Gehenna.

All this is in accordance with [the direction to which] one is drawn, be it after the good or after evil, in conjunction with the portions that caused their influence to be felt in him. For certainly the higher levels and their Celestial Halls and "branches" and "wings," as well as their *kelippot*, are bound to us through our Forms, which are effused by the Tree of Knowledge of Good and Evil, by the One who begins and ends all things, and [the one whose] name is included within Him [that is, the angel Metatron], who fastens diadems for his Master.

> Here we find expressed an essentially voluntarist position concerning the destiny of the soul after death. Its fate depends on one's actions in this world, without regard to issues that would arise as a result of a doctrine of "soul roots." Indeed, I have not found a kabbalistic discussion on the application of this principle, "his portion and his neighbor's portion," to the doctrine of soul roots prior to the Lurianic Kabbalah. Questions do, however, arise about which body or bodies of the *same* incarnated soul attain resurrection.[2]
>
> One context in which the concept of "his portion and his neighbor's portion" is explicated concerns the interrelationships between the cosmological structures of the Divine *Partzufim* (personage-configurations) in the realm of *Atzilut* (Divine emanation) in the Lurianic Kabbalah. There we find situations described in which those higher levels of *Atzilut* that are able to descend to the lower *Partzufim* are held "in safekeeping" until such time as the lower *Partzufim* are ready to receive them. In this sense the usage is similar to the phenomenon of the "inscribed *tzaddik*," which I have discussed elsewhere.[3]
>
> Another context in which "his portion and his neighbor's portion" arises is in some of the personal eschatological doctrines in Lurianic Kabbalah, where ethical issues are at stake. I would like to suggest, however, that the objectionable versions of this doctrine presented below were discussed by Luria in a state of delirium brought about by his final illness (typhoid fever or black plague), to which he succumbed two days after he taught them. As we shall see below, these objectionable doctrines and their eschatological consequences are contradicted in at least four other teachings from the AR"I.
>
> The following text is taken from *Sha'ar ha-Gilgulim*, sec. 39, pp. 380–82 (and compare with *Sefer ha-Hezyonot*, 220–22).

2A. Two days before my teacher o.b.m. passed away, he told me that even those colleagues who were of the first tier [among his disciples], studying together with me, need to undergo a sifting process. Others would be brought in to replace some of them. The secret meaning of this is based on what we explained with regard to the verse, "If your enemy is hungry feed him bread" (Prov. 25:21). For these colleagues are not whole [that is, wholly good]. There are those who possess merely a small portion of that exalted [soul] garment mentioned above [*Sha'ar ha-Gilgulim*, 372–73, 379] who are constituted from the seed drops of [the Divine union] after midnight, though not all of them are equal in this. There are those who are mostly good with a minor part of evil, and those who are mostly evil with some good. There are also those who are evenly balanced in this, and in these there are many levels. And he said to me that those who are mostly good will remain so, but the others who are mostly evil, with some good, will take on the evil of those [who were mostly good] and give them their goodness, so that all of them would end up either all good or all evil.

2B. And my teacher o.b.m. told me that this was his intention in gathering them together. For through their camaraderie and love they would draw one to another, and the good would go to the one who is mostly good, whereby he will become whole. The minor part of evil will go over to join with the one who is mostly evil; then, those who are completely evil will leave, and the others, who are wholly good, will remain.

2C. And my teacher o.b.m. said that it is for this reason that a person needs to become exceedingly friendly with the wicked who are mostly evil and have a minor part of good [in them]: in order to make them repent. By this means he will take the good that is in them. This is particularly so if one encounters someone who is of his own soul root, who possesses a good quality that he himself is missing. In this way, he would take it and become complete through it. Therefore my teacher told me to be very vigilant in this; to love the colleagues and to teach them. For through this I will sift out my good portion that is in them and take it, and become whole. . . .[4]

2D. And my teacher o.b.m. told me that I am obligated to make the blameworthy meritorious even more than other people, because all the wicked of this generation are of the "Mixed Multitude," and most—nearly all—are from the root of Cain, whose good sparks were mixed with evil ones, leaving most of them evil.[5] Therefore I need to rectify them because they are of my root.[6]

Not only this, but even with regard to the wicked of the previous generations of old who are in hell, I am able to rectify them through my deeds so as to raise them from hell, so that they may enter into human bodies in this world and become rectified.

The reason for this is because my soul is of the primary essence of Cain,[7] and also because I have become incarnate in the last generation [the generation of the redemption]. And furthermore, it is because I came from the highest drops that are from the actual Mind of *Da'at* [the union of *Hokhmah* and *Binah*],[8] not merely of the six directions [the six lower Sephirot] that are drawn into the body. Therefore I have the power to accomplish this if I desire to better my deeds.

And he said that for the aforementioned reason, if I were to attempt to make the blameworthy of the generation meritorious, they would really listen to me, and my words would enter their ears.[9] And during that very week that he passed away,[10] my teacher o.b.m. taught me a certain *yihud* for raising the seventy sparks that remain in hell among the *kelippot*, which are of Cain's root and of the root of my *nefesh*....[11]

> Is this "exchange of good and evil" between souls, a kabbalistic example of a vindictive and parsimonious point of view on behalf of the Divine regarding human fate? Is it like that of the Christian myth of Revelation, chapter 7, where a mere 144,000 will be "saved" on the Day of Judgment? (In the Lurianic Kabbalah, perhaps the Divine parsimoniousness would extend to at least 600,000 at the End of Days!) See appendix E on this as well.
>
> My interpretation of this passage is that it indicates a self-justifying, manipulative absconding by a "higher soul" with the holy sparks of a person who succeeds in repenting as a result of the influence of such a higher soul. This is borne out by another passage found in *Sha'ar ha-Gilgulim*, most likely based on the Lurianic principle just quoted, that was passed on to Vital a few days before Luria's death, probably for the first time, and further applied by R. Hayim Vital. There (sec. 20, pp. 143–44) we read the following.

3A. Know also that through the sin of the First Adam, good became mixed with evil. Therefore at times it may be the case that a bit of good became mixed into [the soul of] a wicked person and a bit of the evil of the wicked one became mixed within [the soul of] the *tzaddik*. Through this you will understand the verse "... that there are just men to whom it happens in accordance with the deeds of the wicked ..." [Eccles. 8:14]. For there are various *tzaddikim* who commit particular transgressions, and [with regard to them] fail in ways that even the wicked would not. And so too in reverse. There are many completely wicked people who fulfill particular commandments perfectly and are careful with these throughout their lives! Also through this we will understand what is meant by the terms "a complete *tzaddik*" and "a complete *rasha* [wicked one] and a *"Benoni"* [a middling or average person]. These designations are dependent on the number of good and evil sparks that they possess. In addition, the types of wrongdoing or positive acts one performs are in accordance with the quality of one's sparks and the quality of the "limb" and root from which they derive, whether good or bad. According to this will they desire and long for good or bad deeds, more so than others, and they will constantly strive after them.[12]

3B. For this reason did the Zohar[13] insist that one must "strive to make the blameworthy meritorious with the same zeal as one who strives after one's livelihood." The meaning of this is that when the *tzaddik* goes after the wicked person in order to make him worthy, it may be that this wicked one contains those good sparks that were lost to him [the *tzaddik*], and he [the *tzaddik*] will give to him [the wicked one] his evil sparks. And by their uniting together with desire and love, the good within him [the wicked] will be removed from him and be given to you, so that you will be completely good and he will be wholly evil.

This is the secret of "if he merits, he takes his portion and the portion of his neighbor in the Garden of Eden, and the wicked takes his portion and the portion of his neighbor in Gehenna" [BT Hagigah 15r]. This is as the verse states: "If your enemy be hungry feed him bread" [Prov. 25:21], and as was said [in BT Pesahim 113b] on the verse "If you shall see the donkey of your enemy . . ." [Exod. 23:8]. This verse refers to a wicked person, whom one is commanded to hate, as the verse states: "Do I not hate those whom You hate?" [Ps. 139:21]. And it is said: "If your enemy be hungry feed him bread" [Prov. 25:21]. All of these are due to the good spark within him on which account he is hungry and desirous to do good. "Feed him bread" [means] the bread of the Torah and commandments, so as to make him meritorious, because through this, "you shall heap coals of fire" [Prov. 25:21], referring to the evil sparks that are within you. Heap "upon his head" so that they unite with him and are removed from you. This is as the verse states: "And the goat shall bear upon itself all of their sins to a barren land" [Lev. 16:22]. The good sparks that are in him shall be removed from him, "and god [whose god?] will make them whole for you," so that it will come out that you are whole in the good and he is whole in evil. This accords with what is said: "Read not 'he shall pay' [*yishalem*], but 'he shall make you whole' [*yashlim*]" [BT Sukkah 52a]. And because the good and blessed Name does not place His Name on evil, the verse states "you shall heap coals of fire upon his head"; whereas He does place His Name upon the good, as the verse states [Prov. 25:22], "and God shall repay you" [or "make you whole"], as was stated before. For it is He [God] who bestows this goodness.

I believe this passage preserves Vital's original reworking of the Lurianic teaching just quoted.[14] Indeed, we will see below,[15] where we adduce genuine teachings from the AR"I presenting analogous cases, that this cruel exchange between souls does not take place.

It is also important to note that when this teaching of the "karmic exchange" between the good and the wicked is discussed in the Beshtian Hasidic literature, the exchange takes place only if the wicked persist in their wickedness after the *tzaddik* tries to help them to repent.[16] On the other hand, in later Hasidism we find notions such as threats by Rebbes toward their disciples that they would "*avek nemen zayere madreiges*" (take away their "higher levels") in case of insubordination.[17] The stipulation mentioned above, limiting the karmic exchange to instances of persisting wickedness, seems to hold as well in a teaching attributed to the AR"I. In *Sha'ar ha-Pesukim, Parshat Yitro*, 29d, we read:

4. Through the sin of Adam, all of the souls became intermixed as regards good and evil, as discussed above,[18] and subsequently, each person [was born] according to his level. There are those who are mostly evil and whose lesser part is good, and some for whom the opposite is true. In this there are various degrees. However, there is no *tzaddik* who will do [only] good and will not transgress [Eccles. 7:20], because all are mixed, containing both good and bad as mentioned. And one who is mostly evil is called a *Rasha* [wicked person] and the opposite one is called a *tzaddik*. Now the wicked person, with each new reincarnation that he enters in order to purify himself, heaps more evil upon his soul. Therefore [if he persists in evil], his [potentially] purifying incarnations end after four times, and the good left in the evil person is given to another of his soul root who is worthy of it, as is stated [BT Hagigah 15r]. "If he merits he takes his portion and the portion of his neighbor"; and the absolute evil remains with him, and he goes to perdition and has no further hope, because he has no good spark at all.

But for one who is mostly good and is one of the *tzaddikim*, quite the contrary is true. Each time they incarnate they become more rectified than before; but necessarily in each incarnation they transgress in an area other than their earlier incarnations.[19] Therefore they incarnate until they become whole in all the 613 *Mitzvot*, and until they rectify all the wrongdoings of their past incarnations. Thus their incarnations can go on thousands of times! This is as the verse states: "Visiting the iniquity of the fathers on the children to the third and fourth generations" [Exod. 34:7]—that is, He brings them back for up to four incarnations, and in their second incarnation they are called "sons" with reference to their first incarnation;

and more [than four times], they have no repair at all. But this is only with regard to those who hate Him—that is, those who are completely evil. But all of this notwithstanding, [if one begins the process of repentance] the blessed Holy One bestows a great boon, which is, that they may incarnate for up to two thousand "generations."[20]

In contrast to this nuanced passage, we find a passage in *Likkute ha-Shas me-ha-AR"I z"l*[21] attributed to R. Hayyim Vital where this merit-exchange takes place after a lifetime of accumulation of meritorious and wicked deeds, albeit when the *tzaddik* ends up being wicked. There we read:

5. "It was said [BT Avodah Zarah 17a] about R. Eliezer [Elazar] ben Durdaya, etc. [that he acquired his portion in the world to come in one instant.]" You know what is stated in *Sefer ha-Gilgulim*, that one who is reincarnated and becomes whole takes his portion and the portion of his friend, in accordance with the secret meaning of "The wicked will prepare, but the *tzaddik* shall wear" [BT Babba Metzia 61a, after Job 27:17]. For that very garment that the wicked person made by his meager accumulation of righteousness in performing a few good deeds, but did not merit to wear after having completed this garment, is given the *tzaddik* to wear.

Now, R. Yohanan the High Priest served in this capacity for eighty years, and it is certain that through his service he accumulated a great many precious garments. Only afterward, when he became a Sadducee, he lost all of these good portions. And in the same manner of this Yohanan, who in his earlier days was a *tzaddik* but at the end transgressed (his transgression having been committed in his last days), there came another: R. Elazar ben Durdaya, who was blemished for most of his early days, and in his last days he repented. Thus, we have many rectified days and many blemished days. So the evil aspects of these days were taken by Yohanan, whereas the good aspects of those days were taken by R. Elazar ben Durdaya. This corresponds to what was explained in *Etz Hayim* regarding the verse [Ps. 7:10] "Oh let the wickedness of the wicked come to an end," and the verse [Prov. 25:21] "If your enemy be hungry feed him bread."—From R. Hayyim Vital o.b.m.[22]

An additional clear contrast to the extreme teachings of R. Hayim Vital with regard to the phenomenon of the "exchange of merit for demerit" is to be found in the *Sha'ar ha-Kavvanot*, in the sixth chapter of *Drushe Kavvanot ha-Amidah*, 36d, where we read:

6. *On behalf of the tzaddikim* [the thirteenth blessing of the Eighteen Benedictions, or *Amidah* prayer]: from here on, and further, [in the *Amidah* Prayer, the theurgic principle of the *Amidah* Prayer operates according to] a different order. The meaning [of this] is that until now we referred to the Ten *Sefirot*, which were constructed and repaired from the Feminine side. But from here on, the construction [of the *Sefirot*] is in the *Netzah-Hod-Yesod* and the [lower] two-thirds of *Tif'eret* of the [Masculine] Small Face [*Ze'ir Anpin*] which illuminate [and effluence] within Her Ten *Sefirot*, as mentioned. Thus, the order [of invocation within the blessings] is from below to above. [And the blessing] *On behalf of the tzaddikim* is in *Yesod* [of *Ze'ir*], applying the invocation of [the Divine Attribute of *Ze'ir*] "The *tzaddik* is the Foundation [*Yesod*] of the World" [Prov. 10:25]; for the *tzaddik* is called *Yesod*. Thus we need to invoke [*likavven*] the Tetragrammaton within this blessing, as it is punctuated by the vowel *Shuruk*.[23]

Now, when you recite the words "and may You place our portion with them [the *tzaddikim*]," we need to consider the meaning of these words, for indeed it would seem that this is a vain prayer, and a wasted request! Because if the human being has free will, how can one pray that the blessed Name place one's portion with the *tzaddikim* as if there is no free choice? For as our rabbis have said, [although many aspects of our life are predetermined by Divine Providence], whether one is to be a *tzaddik* or a wicked person is not predetermined.[24] So if we think that our intention [in saying "and may You place our portion with them"] obtains even if one sins—that we are praying [to be regarded as *tzaddikim* even if we do not deserve to be]—then the difficulty is compounded! For "the work of the Rock [that is, God; see Deut. 32:4] is with integrity," so as to bestow unto each according to his way, be it good or bad.

However, the real intention [of these words] is as follows: When a person transgresses occasionally and commits sins that extinguish [the light of] commandments performed, this person impedes the reward of the commandment from reaching him. Thus, in the meantime, for as long as such a person does not return [to God] in repentance, those lights and angels and defending spirits that are formed by means of the commandments that the person performed[25] are given to a *tzaddik* who is deemed appropriate by the decree of the blessed Divine Wisdom, as indicated by the secret meaning of [BT Babba Metzia 61a, following Job 27: 17]: "the wicked will prepare, but the *tzaddik* shall wear." All of this notwithstanding, there are some highly exalted *tzaddikim* who do not want to derive benefit from others [in this way], but [rely] only from their own [merit]; so that when they take the above-mentioned illuminations [resulting from the observance of the commandments by the transgressor] they are in the possession of such a *tzaddik* merely for trustworthy safekeeping. And when the original owners [of the merit] repent, the *tzaddik* will return to them the illuminations taken from them.

Therefore we pray before Him, may He be blessed; since "There is no *tzaddik* in the land who shall do good and not transgress" [Eccles. 7:20], so that it is almost as if it is inevitable—one is forced to sin. Therefore, those illuminations that are of our portion and are our lot, that we have earned by the *Mitzvot* that we performed in this world, but [whose illuminations, etc.] are not given to us on account of our transgressions, may He place them with those great *tzaddikim* who are inscribed.[26] Thus those illuminations would continue to subsist; and when we return [to God] in repentance, they [those *tzaddikim*] would return them to us; and [we pray] that He not place [our merits] with other *tzaddikim*[27]—that is, those who would not return them to us.

> In addition, in *Sha'ar Ma'amare RaZ"al*, 2d–3a, on BT Eruvin 59b, we read about one particular soul root with a decidedly nonparsimonious destiny situation, and which seems to beg the question of determinism raised in the previous passage:

7. "R. Pereda had a disciple to whom he taught [the same teaching] four hundred times. . . . So a heavenly Voice issued forth and declared to him: '[R. Pereda], Would it be pleasing to you if they [the Heavenly Court] add four hundred years to your life, or would you prefer that we find both you and your entire generation meritorious so as to attain the World to Come?' He said, 'Would that I and my generation merit the World to Come.' Said the blessed Holy One, 'Give him both this boon and that.'" This is awesomely wondrous, for we have not encountered reward as great as this—even with regard to our teacher Moses, peace be upon him, all his praiseworthiness notwithstanding—that one's entire generation (and there is no generation with fewer than six hundred thousand souls) attains to the World to Come. Indeed BT Sanhedrin has already stated [BT Sanhedrin 108a] that the generation of the desert, the generation of Moses, has no portion in the World to Come! The meaning of this [the case of R. Pereda] is as I have informed you: that all of the souls are subdivided into six hundred thousand distinct roots, and in each there are six hundred thousand soul-sparks. Now, all of the sparks whose roots depend upon the root of R. Pereda are referred to as "members of the same generation," although they are not incarnated together with him at the same time. Rather, [the "generation" is constituted from these souls] from the day of the creation of the world until the ultimate future; and each one incarnates

at the time most appropriate for it until it becomes whole through being repaired. Now, regarding some roots, it may come to pass that one spark of one particular soul would be lost at the time when [the whole root] has reached the ultimate end of purification and the last dross is expelled; yet [this one spark] cannot purify itself on account of its own great subtlety and the abundance of dross that covers it. Regarding this it is said, "And they shall go out and see the corpses of those people . . ."[Isa. 66:24]. Therefore did the blessed Holy One vouchsafe R. Pereda, that with regard to all of the sparks of the root of his soul—all of them will be set right by means of reincarnations and not even one of them will be wasted, Heaven forfend. Because if the root is good then all of its branches become rectified.

> The fact that R. Pereda is not mentioned elsewhere in the Lurianic corpus, and particularly the fact that it is not in Vital's *Gilgul* texts, may indicate that the AR"I explained this only once and there was no follow-up. Indeed, this paradigm of destiny brings to mind the *Kavvanah* referred to above in passage 6 as a further example of an orientation other than the parsimonious one, which, as was mentioned above, is the prevailing attitude obtaining in the Divine realm of *Atzilut*, with reference to the relation between the lower and the higher Divine *Partzufim*.
>
> The question as to how there can be a root in which no sparks—even those mostly evil ones—fail to fulfill the beginning of their purification within four incarnations, is elliptically addressed by the words "each one incarnates at the time most appropriate for it." This was God's gift to R. Pereda: a universally positive, semideterministic outcome. This is in contrast to the infelicitous situation of most souls at the beginning of their process of *tikkun*.[28] This is related to the *Tikla*, the "scales of deceit," referring to incarnations in inopportune circumstances, discussed in the Zohar.[29] This work is crucially important as the background for Lurianic eschatology.[30] It must be noted that in the Lurianic *Zohar ha-Raki'a* we have a fifty-folio commentary on this text, with no fewer than twenty-five fragments from the AR"I himself, some of them quite long (although it seems that some of these are from the AR"I only in a nominative way; that is, he is most likely the "ultimate" author of these ideas.[31] I will elaborate on these issues further in my dissertation. But it may also indicate the ideal of conscientious safekeeping associated with the "inscribed" *tzaddikim*, just as this Divine reward came as a result of the transcendent patience shown by R. Pereda to one of his charges.
>
> One possible distinction vis-à-vis the competitive paradigm of the "exchange of merit, etc." and the paradigm of "safekeeping" may be related to the degree that the higher of the two souls has attained. In *Sha'ar*

Ru'ah ha-Kodesh, 43b, we read from the *Yihud* written by the AR"I to attain contact with deceased *tzaddikim:*

8. Know, that although we learned in the Zohar [1:225b–226b] that the *nefesh* of the *tzaddik* resides in the grave, and his *ru'ah* is in the Garden of Eden, and his *neshamah* is under the Throne of Glory, this is so with regard to those who have not merited to more than the *nefesh, ru'ah, neshamah* of [the three lower worlds]: Creation, Formation, and Action. As for those who merited the *nefesh, ru'ah, neshamah* of *Atzilut* [Emanation], however, there is no doubt that the *nefesh* would ascend to *Malkhut*, and his *ru'ah* would ascend to *Tif'eret*, and his *neshamah* to *Binah*, because all things return to their root.[32]

Given the distinction between these two general grades of soul, R. Hayim Vital's view about souls that have not yet entered the (unified Divine) realm of *Atzilut*, where only goodness obtains,[33] may be correct: that in these lower realms the spiritual politics of parsimonious scarcity prevails. Thus, Vital would be able to include the *Kavvanah* regarding the "inscribed *tzaddikim*" while presenting much less morally savory (I daresay, unacceptable) options. See also in the AR"I's own commentary on the *Sifra de-Tzene'uta*[34] regarding the status of certain souls being called "free" (*bene horin*). This means they derive from such a high root that they transcend the dualistic realm of (Metatron and) *Ze'ir Anpin*, where the dichotomy of Grace and Judgment prevails, and are instead effluenced by *Hokhmah* and *Binah*. This is apparently a gloss on Zohar.[35] It is interesting to note in this connection that the passage from R. Me'ir ibn Gabbai with which we began this discussion associated the phenomenon of taking "his portion and his neighbor's portion [in Eden]" with souls that are within the realm of the "Tree of Knowledge of Good and Evil" and Metatron. Here, however, we may speculate that since this "free soul" is not within this dualistic (competitive) category, it does not need to participate in the accumulation of the merit of others and is able to be one of those *tzaddikim* who hold others' merit in safekeeping.

There is an additional Lurianic perspective on the relative "reality" (and otherwise) of other human beings, which further complicates the situation of reconstructing a complete picture of Lurianic eschatology. It has its roots in the later strata of zoharic literature and echoes in Beshtian Hasidism.[36] BT Ta'anit 11a states: "At the time one departs from the world, all of one's *ma'asim* [deeds or "makings"] depart before him." About this we read:

9. We know that while alive, a person in this world commits both *Mitzvot* and transgressions, and the [essential] reward for *Mitzvot* is in the World to Come.[37] So too regarding transgressions: the main retribution takes place in Gehenna. If so, it comes about that [as for the performer of] the *Mitzvah* for which the reward is conferred in the World to Come, [the *Mitzvah*] is regarded as death in this world, because its reward is hidden for the World to Come. However, with regard to transgressions, the situation is the opposite: in this world he [the transgressor] is called alive because such a one does not receive retribution in this world, whereas in the next world he is called dead, for it is there that he is punished. But there, [in the World to Come] the *Mitzvah* is called "alive."[38]

This is the meaning of "his 'deeds' depart": because [from] those transgressions that he committed there were created the sons of man, the "outsiders," and these die with him as well. Thus it is written "that all men shall know his works" [Job 37:6]; that is, the people who were made [or "created"] by his actions, and were made into wicked people. This is what is meant by "his works": the actual work of his hands—[his "creations"] as a result of his sins. —From the Rav [the AR"I], his remembrance is for life eternal.

> It seems to me that these "manufactured" people may refer to those souls forced to take the route of the *Tikla* as a result of this person's transgressions.[39]
>
> Regarding the larger issue, the instruction of the AR"I in his last days to R. Hayyim Vital, Lurianic eschatology may hold that there is an optimal number for each soul root. This, however, is not stated explicitly with regard to the 613 primal root souls, each of which can potentially yield 600,000 x 600,000 souls (as implied in the R. Pereda passage and as stated explicitly in *Sefer ha-Gilgulim*, 6a). Furthermore, since the number of good sparks from the (potentially aggressive) soul of Cain is extremely small,[40] so too the optimal number of rectified souls is also small. This may perhaps be borne out when we consider the possible implications of the fact that the AR"I had practiced the *yihud* discussed at the end of text 2 (perhaps even as a standard practice) a number of times in the course of his life. It would also seem to imply that the generation of Luria and Vital was seen by them as the "last generation," the generation of the coming of the Messiah, and also as the generation in which most of the souls of the root of Cain then incarnate were in their fourth evil incarnation, with no hope for a future incarnative *tikkun* process. Here we witness the moral tension inherent in the conceptual combination of reincarnation and acute messianic eschatology.

On the other hand, the various counterexamples, particularly those implying that the "merit-exchange" takes place only when one of the souls remains wicked and unrepentant, would mitigate this. Also, the above-mentioned consideration vis-à-vis the survival of the sparks refers to the resurrection, whereas the "merit-transfer" refers to "his portion and that of his neighbor in Eden" (and regarding the important distinction between Eden and the resurrection, see below, appendix C).

Regarding the relationship between the Edenic after-death state, the World to Come, and the Resurrection, we find in *Likkute ha-Shas* on BT Berakhot 66a, an unattributed passage on the difference between the World to Come (which clearly also would include the after-death Edenic state). This passage has a conceptual parallel in *Sha'ar ha-Gilgulim*, sec. 10, p. 83. It reads as follows:

> 10. "Scholarly sages (*Talmide Hakhamim*) have no rest, neither in this world nor in the World to Come." This is because in the after-death world, *Talmide Hakhamim* are engaged in Torah study and ascend from level to level and from Academy to Academy. For even our teacher Moses, peace be upon him, ascends and attains to higher levels each and every day. For just as the blessed Name has no limit, so too does His Torah have no end. This is the secret [of Ps. 104:23]: "Man goes forth to his work ... ," that is, to involve himself in Torah study, in [those areas in] which he toiled in this world. For when a person leaves this world he first "goes forth to his work," that is, to study those areas in which he toiled while in this world,[41] and then [he goes] "to his labor" in which he toils "until the night" [Ps. 104:23]; that is, until this world, which is like the night, comes to an end. This is because in the [ultimate] future, after the resurrection [which is the stage above the lower aspect of the World to Come], they [the *Talmide Hakhamim*] will attain to rest and "The land shall be filled with knowledge ... "[Isa. 11:9], each according to his level. Now there is [the level of] the Torah of *Atzilut* [Emanation], and so too [the Torah of the worlds of] Creation, Formation, and Action, as well as the Essence [of the Torah, which on each of those levels] contains the fourfold hermeneutic levels: PaRDeS [*Peshat*, the plain meaning; *Remez*, allusions; *Drush*, homily; *Sod*, secret]. And the Torah contains 248 positive commandments and 365 negative commandments, which correspond to the limbs and sinews of Man. Thus, each *Partzuf* [configuration of *Sefirot* modeled after the Divine realm] comprises all 613 commandments. Understand this.

> It may thus be the case that in the Edenic state, or Lower World to Come of R. Hayyim Vital, certain *tzaddikim* are enriched by their repentant soul

root colleagues—to their detriment—whereas at the time of the resurrection these latter ones receive their reward.

In addition, it is interesting that in most instances in Lurianic Kabbalah and in the Zohar, the "Mixed Multitude" are associated with the soul of Moses, to which the AR"I is connected.[42] Note also that the majority of the sparks of the root of Cain are evil, but the few "good" sparks are "very good";[43] whereas only once, other than in the above-mentioned text 2, is it said that the "Mixed Multitude" is associated with Cain. In *Sha'ar ha-Pesukim*[44] this soul root also appears as the origin of the nation of Amalek, which will ultimately be destroyed. Thus, it may be that at certain junctures of the AR"I's thought (or perhaps only in R. Hayyim Vital's thought), Cain's root was seen as constituting a special case, which R. Hayyim Vital misapplied to other cases as a general principle. On the other hand, lest we forget, besides the places in the corpus where R. Hayyim Vital acknowledges that any improvement within the *nefesh* of the incarnate sinner during his first four incarnations puts him in another category,[45] we must also recognize that we have preserved the Lurianic counterexamples to parsimoniousness only due to the editorship of R. Hayyim Vital.

Furthermore, as mentioned before, regarding the AR"I himself, I would speculate that the extreme examples of what could only (it seems to me) be characterized as vindictive and paranoid parsimoniousness in texts 2 and 3 may have been the result of delirium, or the combination of general weakness and extreme pessimism. Luria may have suffered from these conditions as a result of high fever, after having contracted either the black plague or typhoid fever, that claimed him before his time, five days after he fell ill.[46] This is especially likely considering that text 2 was quoted from the AR"I a mere two days before his demise. R. Hayyim Vital, out of reverence for his teacher, took his words at face value and applied them as a general principle, despite the fact that they were contradicted by other statements of the AR"I, as was seen above. Clearly, this type of thinking regarding the moral and eschatological nature of the soul exemplifies an ultimately monistic, but provisionally dualist, essentialism. And see above appendix 2.

Notes

This appendix is related to the section entitled "Possession and Soul Impregnation" in M. Kallus's essay in this volume, "Pneumatic Mystical Possession and the Eschatology of the Soul in Lurianic Kabbalah."

1. (Jerusalem: n.p., 1973), 1:19, fol. 19a.

2. See Scholem, "Gilgul," 216.

3. A related document appears in translation below (text 6). For examples of this usage as a cosmological-theurgic priniciple in the Lurianic Kabbalah, see *Etz Hayyim*, gate 20, chap. 9; gate 29, chap. 4; gate 34, chap. 2 (final version); and so on. Regarding its application in the matter of *Kavvanot*, see *Sha'ar ha-Kavvanot*, *Inyan Rosh ha-Shanah*. The chapter of my dissertation devoted to summarizing the daily *Kavvanot* of the *Shema* will cite additional sources on this matter.

4. See, however, *Sefer ha-Hezyonot*, 251–52, where this assessment that the roots of the other disciples were the same as R. Hayyim's root is not borne out, based on what the AR"I said about them at another time.

5. Whereas in most of the Lurianic corpus and the Zohar, the Mixed Multitude are associated with Moses (for example, 2:191a, 195a, 197a), there is one place (1:28b) where they are associated with Cain.

6. Indeed, the attempts of R. Hayyim Vital to urge the members of his generation to repentence were singularly unsuccessful. See *Sefer ha-Hezyonot*, 14, 16, 25, 28, and so on. With the attitude advocated here this is hardly surprising.

7. See *Sha'ar ha-Gilgulim*, 89–90.

8. See also note 102 in my essay above; and *Etz Hayyim* 39:11, principle 19.

9. See the following set of citations, texts 3A–B, for the possible ramifications of this "rectification."

10. He passed away on Tuesday, whereas this transaction took place on Sunday. See note 96 above.

11. See *Sha'ar ha-Gilgulim*, 382–83; and more elaborately, in *Sha'ar Ru'ah ha-Kodesh*, 32b–33a, where it is implied that the AR"I himself had practiced this *yihud* in the course of his life, and thus that it was not a recently invented *yihud*. The *yihud* combines seven aspects into a transformational chain: human personages—both good and evil—of both biblical and rabbinic literature; the numbers of holy sparks associated with each of them; tranformative Divine Names and Attributes; behavioral strictures; and Archangelic elements. It seems to me that given the fact that the AR"I was not of the root of Cain but nevertheless practiced this *yihud* implies that he saw himself as operating within the unified realm of *Atzilut*, which transcends the dichotomy of disparate roots.

12. Here we find an uncharacteristically clear deterministic view, which is contradicted by quotation 6 below, containing an argument against determinism.

13. 2:129a

14. It seems that this "teaching" was found by R. Samuel Vital in the miscellaneous writings of his father, R. Hayyim Vital, and was placed by the various editors of the Lurianic corpus in the appropriate places (*Sha'ar ha-Gilgulim* and in both *Likkute Torah* and *Sefer ha-Likkutim*, on Proverbs, chap. 25). See the end of *Sha'ar Ma'amare Raza"l*, 17a, "Likkute mo[renu]ha-Rav Hayyim Vital ZLH"H," which begins with R. Samuel Vital [?] introducing it, saying: "Thus says the writer: I will copy here some of the novellae of R. Hayyim Vital, may he be remembered for eternal life, as I have found in his writings."

15. See quotation 4, the segment quoted in my comments at the end of my translation of quotation 5, and quotations 6 and 7, and below in appendix C.

16. See R. Jacob Joseph of Polonnoye, *Ben Porat Yosef* (1884; reprint, New York: n.p., 1953),. 53c

17. I learned this through a personal communication from Rivka Schatz, although I have not come across this expression in my own searches.

18. This is found in the Lurianic discussion of this topic earlier in that work, on *Parshat Bereshit*.

19. This implies that they shed their evil sparks in the process of purification.

20. This implies that even if they have mostly evil sparks, they may be able to begin their process of repentance during the four lifetimes and therefore begin to reverse the process and "shed their evil sparks." See also *Sha'ar ha-Gilgulim*, 73–74; and see note 24 in my essay above, where I paraphrase from ibid., sec. 4, p. 46. There R. Hayyim Vital also says as much.

21. (1897; reprint, Jerusalem: n.p., 1976), 20b.

22. This is not in *Etz Hayyim*, in fact, but toward the end of the seventh section of *Sha'ar ha-Gilgulim*. And see there, 73–74, where, significantly, regarding the verse (Ps. 7:10) "Oh let the wickedness of the wicked come to an end," R. Hayyim Vital says that he did not understand what his teacher said. There we also read: (1) that the "merit-transaction" takes place only if one of them remains (or becomes) evil (p. 73); and (2) "At times, if one has a majority of evil and a minority of good, etc., one needs to purify all the evil within one until he remains entirely good" (p. 74). The implication is that there is no inevitability regarding one who is born with a majority of evil sparks. Perhaps the designation *Etz Hayim* refers to the original recensions of R. Hayim Vital, to which the editor of *Likkute ha-Shas* referred. See Y. Avivi, "Kitve R. Hayyim Vital be-Kabbalat ha-AR"I, *Moriah* (Sivan 5741 [1981]).

Regarding the bibliographic problems with reference to the attributions contained in this work, see my discussion in "A Prolegomenon to a Critical Edition of the Authentic Writings and Direct Quotes of the AR"I Himself" (in Hebrew), in *Proceedings of the Thirteenth International Conference of Jewish Studies in Jerusalem: Kabbalah Section* (Jerusalem: World Congress of Jewish Studies, 1998), n. 22.

23. This vowel, in the tradition of the *Tikkune ha-Zohar* 7b, refers to that Sefirah.

24. See BT Niddah 30b; and *Mo'ed Katan* 18b.

25. See *Sha'ar Ru'ah ha-Kodesh*, 1a–b.

26. The adverb "who are inscribed" calls to mind the reference [see above, section 1 near note 49] to the *tzaddikim* who are "inscribed on the Throne, and never depart from It, and without whom the Throne is never found." See *Sha'ar Ma'amare RaShB"I*, 12a–d; and see appendix D, quotation 6 below. And it seems to me that these *tzaddikim* are those described as having attained the level of *Atzilut* (Emanation), and who throughout their lives "perform *yihudim* which unite all of the Divine roots within the realm of *Atzilut*." On this see below, quotation 8 from *Sha'ar Ru'ah ha-Kodesh*, 43b, and see in particular ibid., 27b–28a, which uses similar language and refers to the same referents as the passage from *Sha'ar Ma'amare RaShB"I*.

27. He refers, perhaps, to the type of *tzaddik* apparently suggested by the AR"I that R. Hayyim Vital become two days before the former's unfortunate demise. And yet, this passage does seem to imply a sanction, albeit not a clear interdiction of this kind of *tzaddik*. Yet we must bear in mind that if not for R. Hayyim Vital, this passage would not have been preserved!

28. See what the AR"I says about this, in *Sha'ar Ma'amare RaShB"I*, 9a–b.

29. See 1:109b; and the *Sabba de-Mishpatim*, in ibid., 2:95b, 96b, and 99b.

30. See there also fol. 97a and elsewhere.

31. Isaac Luria, *Sefer Zohar ha-Raki'a* (Sighet: 1874 or 1875; reprint, Jerusalem: Mekhon "Sha'are ziv" she-a. y. Yeshivat ha-mekubalim "Sha'ar-ha-shamayim," 1983). An example is that regarding the *Tikla* on fols. 73c–d, from *Etz Hayyim*, gate 49, chap. 7.

32. Compare to *Sha'ar ha-Pesukim*, 1 Sam. 5, fols. 42c–d.

33. This includes R. Hayyim's own soul. See the discussion in the section "Possession and Soul Impregnation" of my essay above concerning this matter.

34. *Sha'ar Ma'amare RaShB"I*, 29b; and compare statements attributed to him in *Likkute Torah* on *Parshat Mishpatim*, 64a; and *Sefer ha-Likkutim* in ibid., 36d.

35. Zohar 2 *Parshat Mishpatim*, 94a; and in the *Sabba de-Mishpatim*, 96b–97a.

36. See *Likkute ha-Shas*, 9a-b, on BT Ta'anit, where we find a teaching attributed to the AR"I that seems to take an extremely mythomagical view regarding the existence of some human beings. Also see *Toledoth Ya'akov Yosef*, Parshat Metzorah, 96b (*Sefer Besh"t*, Metzorah #24).

37. Although neither the AR"I nor R. Hayyim Vital addressed the issue, it seems to me that here the designation "World to Come" is equivalent to the Garden of Eden and not to the Resurrection. See also below, text 10.

38. I find it quite curious that twice here, the transgression is associated with the one who commits it, whereas twice, the *Mitzvah* is not!

39. See *Sha'ar ha-Kavvanot, Drushe ha-Laylah*, drush 7.

40. See *Sha'ar ha-Gilgulim*, sec. 29, p. 209.

41. See *Midrash Mishle*, beginning.

42. For the sources on Moses in the Zohar, see above, text 2, sec. D. For the Lurianic sources, see *Etz Hayyim*, gate 32, chaps. 1–2, *Sha'ar ha-Gilgulim*, sec. 2 and 20 and elsewhere. On the connection of the AR"I to Moses' soul, see *Sefer ha-Gilgulim*, 64b.

43. See *Sha'ar ha-Gilgulim*, sec. 29 and 38.

44. See *Sha'ar ha-Pesukkim* on *Balak* 36a..

45. See above toward the end of text 4.

46. See August Hirsch, *Handbook of Geographical and Historical Pathology* (London: New Sydenham Society, 1883), 1:500 regarding the occurrence of the black plague in the Middle East of the sixteenth century, and 1:548–49 regarding the appearance of typhus in the Mediterranean in 1572. My thanks to Professor Samuel Kottek of the Hebrew University and Hadassah Hospital, Ein Kerem, for this important citation.

Appendix C

Lurianic Texts concerning the Hazards of the Self-Rectification of the Incomplete *Tzaddik*

Translations and commentary by MENACHEM KALLUS; sources as noted

This in an important exposition, both because it contains many of the principles discussed in my paper, and because it is a teaching directly attributed to the AR"I, as recorded by his disciples.[1] It probably represents one genuine, uninterrupted discourse rather than a later synthetic reconstruction, which is the nature of the vast majority of R. Hayyim Vital's writings. I therefore decided to provide a full translation of it. This is an allegorical explanation of the second Mishnah of the tractate *Babba Kamma*.

[The Mishnah (*Babba Kamma*, chap. 1, m. 2, fol. 9a) states: "All that I am obligated to guard, I am also liable for the payment of the damages that may incur. If I obligated myself for partial payment of damages, I am liable to pay as if I obligated myself for full damages."]

The *tzaddikim* who are already deceased return to watch over those living in this world; [and they watch over] those who are of the same root as their own souls. For [originally] all the souls within the first Adam were of one *Partzuf* [level of the Divine Countenance], and all the souls that came into the world were included in him alone. This is implied in what God inquired of Job: "Where were you when I founded the earth . . ." [Job 38:2; that is, where in this Great Adam are you rooted]? Afterward [that is, after "the fall"], the souls, as well as all that exists in this world, were differentiated. And the *tzaddikim* are close to those who derive from the roots of their souls, so if the living person is a "limb" of the soul of the *tzaddik*, then the *tzaddik* toils on his behalf to guard him from sin, and so that he rectify himself. This will be beneficial for the *tzaddik*, for one of his limbs is being repaired.[2] And our sages have stated [BT Shabbat 104a], "As for one who comes to be purified, we help him." And it is said that the souls of the *tzaddikim* help such a person. . . . Furthermore, [the Talmud says] "All that I am obligated to guard . . . ," that is, that they not sin, "I am also liable for the payment of the damages that may incur . . . ," that is, I will make him fit, that he not be harmed and not transgress.

Now these *tzaddikim* sometimes impregnate themselves [*mit'abrim*] within the person [that is, not merely guarding from the outside, but also "within" the person] as an *ibbur*. For there is "*gilgul*" [incarnation], and there is "*ibbur*" [impregnation]. And regarding "*ibbur*" there are two possibilities: (1) when the *tzaddik* comes to rectify the person; and (2) [when] sometimes the soul of a *tzaddik* impregnates the person in order to rectify himself. For example, he [may need to rectify the fact that in a past life the *tzaddik*] ate forbidden fat, or something similar [in its level of stringency—for example, incurring *Karet* if done intentionally]. Since [in this second instance] the *tzaddik* is impregnated in order to rectify himself, he needs to have freedom of choice.[3] Therefore there is a possibility that [the *tzaddik*] would make things worse rather than better. And since one transgression carries in its wake another, it is possible that the [living] person [who is impregnated by the *tzaddik*] would not have transgressed by eating forbidden fat. The *tzaddik* who impregnated in him [may have] caused him to fail; and he stumbled and ate the forbidden fat, and thus was liable for *Karet*, and died [before his time and before repenting]. Thus, the *tzaddik* killed him!

Regarding this [did the Talmud state] "If I obligated myself for partial payment of damages. . . ." For sometimes I only partially caused him [to] damage [himself] because he [the impregnated] also transgressed [of his own free will, though he may not have faced the test had he not been impregnated] because [it was] two souls and one body [that] derived pleasure from this transgression of eating forbidden fat. And I [the *tzaddik*] obligated myself to pay damages on his behalf, as if I obligated myself for all his damage—[that is, that it be regarded] as if I did it all. For it is possible that he [the impregnated, even if he did face the "test" by himself without the impregnation of the *tzaddik* with its predisposition toward forbidden fat] would not have transgressed, and I [the *tzaddik*] caused the whole thing! Therefore, am I [the *tzaddik*] obligated to pay him [the impregnated] with "the best of my land," that is, with the *tzaddik*'s portion in the Garden of Eden?[4] This is similar to what is stated [in BT Hagigah 15a]: "He takes his portion and the portion of his neighbor in the Garden of Eden." Now, this body has two souls: one is his, and one belongs to the *tzaddik* who was impregnated in him. And we know that if the soul would not hover over the bones they would rot and would not rise in resurrection, as implied in the verse: "And when you rest he will watch over you" [Prov. 6:22]; and "God shall cause you to always be at ease . . ." [Isa. 58:11]. And every Sabbath eve the soul rises on high and takes light and effluence [from on high], and brings it to the bones, as it is stated: "And your bones will be made strong" [Isa. 58:11].

[The question may be asked], Which one of the two souls is obligated to watch over the dead body [of the impregnated]? It is the one to whom the damage was caused [the one impregnated]. This is as it is said: " . . . [liable for] the payment of *damages*. . . ." The implication is that the one who causes the damage, that is, the soul of the *tzaddik* who comes as an impregnation, is obligated only to make whole the soul [*nefesh*] of the one who was damaged, insofar as his portion in Eden is concerned. But as for the [resurrection of the] body of the original owner, it is the responsibility of the damaged one to deal with the dead body. . . . [The soul of the *tzaddik* thus attends his own dead body.] But this [conjunction] is something that happens only rarely—that [the *tzaddik*] comes to rectify but causes damage instead. . . . With regard to all of these [soul relations], it is said that the [original] owner [of the body] is responsible for the corpse, whether the case is one of direct damage [caused by the *tzaddik*], or indirect causation; or if [the *tzaddik*] is merely appointed [that is, hovering close but not impregnating]. Regarding all, the owner [of the body] deals with the corpse and not the soul of the *tzaddik*. This is as it is stated, "the dead body belongs to [the one who suffered the damages]" [Exod. 21:36]. We may think that it belongs to the one who incurred [and paid for] the damages, for he is the direct cause of death. But this is not the case. For when the person came into this world, [the *tzaddik*] was not in the body; he impregnated it only later. —This too is by the Rav [the AR"I], his memory a blessing of eternal life.

Notes

This appendix is related to the section entitled "Soul Levels" in M. Kallus's essay in this volume, "Pneumatic Mystical Possession and the Eschatology of the Soul in Lurianic Kabbalah."

    1. See *Likkute ha-Shas*, 13b–14a.
    2. See in my essay in the main text near note 33.
    3. Does this imply that the *tzaddik* is rectifying an intentional transgression punishable by *Karet*, of which the *tzaddik* had repented in a past life, since he

is still called a *tzaddik*? Or does the fact that he derived pleasure from an albeit unintentional transgression imply a predisposition that needs to be overcome by free choice?

4. The Garden of Eden is the station of reward between the after-death state and the state of resurrection.

Appendix D

Lurianic Texts concerning Rabbi Hayyim Vital and His Psychical Experience

Translations and commentary by MENACHEM KALLUS; sources as noted

Below, I present my translation of the only full-length report by R. Hayyim Vital of his psychic experience. It occurred on Monday, 30 August 1571 (Erev Rosh Hodesh Elul, 5331). Rosh Hodesh Elul is always two days, and he was instructed to perform the long and complex *yihud* of the "Thirteen Reparations of the Beard" in order to invoke unconditional Divine compassion.[1] Following those two days, Thursday and Friday, he was told to fast and perform a *yihud* over the course of forty-eight hours, in order to conduct the energy of the above-mentioned compassion into all the months of the year.[2]

Then, on Sabbath, he was to connect with the soul of R. Yeiva Sabba during his afternoon nap. These practices give one an idea of the level of sophistication in the learning of the Lurianic theurgic nomenclature attained by R. Hayyim Vital over the first seven months of his association with his teacher. Needless to say, the fact that this was his first successful experience of pneumatic *yihud* leaves open the possibility for improvement in later attempts. But the fact that no other experiences of this type are recorded by him in his private diary seems to me to mitigate this possibility. This is particularly true in light of his extreme self-doubt as to whether these experiences were anything other than self-induced.[3] It should also be pointed out that aside from this passage, nowhere else do we read R. Hayyim Vital writing "*Yihadti*" or "*Asiti Yihud*" ["I performed a *yihud*"], although he clearly did perform *yihudim*.[4]

1. On the day before Rosh Hodesh Elul in the year 5331, my teacher of blessed memory sent me to the cave of [the grave of] Abayye and Ravva,

and I stretched myself over the grave of Abayye, may his memory be a blessing for eternal life. First I performed the *yihud* of the mouth and nose of the Ancient Holy One[5] and sleep fell upon me. Then I awakened and saw nothing. Afterward I once again stretched myself over the grave of Abayye and performed the *yihud* [for uniting with the souls of departed saints at their graves] written by my teacher himself.[6] While combining and interlacing the letters YHVH and ADNI as is known, my concentration became confused and I was unable to combine them, and I refrained from thinking out this combination.

2. Then within my consciousness there came a likeness as if a voice was telling me "Retract, retract!" ["Return in yourself, return in yourself!"][7] And then I thought, these are the very words used by Akavyah ben Mehallel to tell his son [on Akavyah's deathbed, to retract his opinions that were contrary to those of the majority].[8] So then I returned to concentrate on this combination and completed it successfully.[9]

3. Then it was as if in my mind they[10] are saying to me, "God will provide Himself the lamb for a burnt offering, my son" [Gen. 22:8],[11] as if they were suggesting to me its explanation: that my concern about not having accomplished the first *yihud* [the cosmic *yihud* of the Ear and Nose of the Ancient One, on account of having fallen asleep] was wrongly placed. For it indeed did succeed before the blessed Name—"God will provide Himself the lamb." And the concept was imprinted in my thought that they are hinting to me that the first *yihud* I performed is implicit in this verse. For the first letters of the first four words equal forty-six numerically, which equals [with the "*Kolel*"] AHYHYHVH, and the first letters of the final three words yield the word "*hevel*" [breath], referring to the breath of the Supernal Mouth [a cosmic pneumatic image], which I intended [to manifest] in this *yihud*. And it seemed to me as if they are telling me that [the first letters of words 3–5] form the name Hillel the Elder but I don't understand its significance.[12] All this occurred to me in my thought.

4. Afterwards, a great and exceeding fright and trembling seized me in all my limbs,[13] and my hands were trembling, knocking against one another, and also my lips were trembling in an exaggerated way and were moving rapidly with forcefulness exceedingly fast.[14] It was as if a voice was sitting on my tongue which was saying exceedingly swiftly, "*mah omar mah omar*" ["What shall I say, what shall I say?"] more than one hundred times![15] And I was trying to take hold of myself and my tongue so that [I] not move them, but I was not able to quiet them at all.

5. Afterward I thought to ask for wisdom. And the sound exploded in my mouth and tongue and said more than twenty times, "*ha-Hokhmah,*

ha-Hokhmah" ["the Wisdom, the Wisdom"]. Then it went on to say "*ha-Hokhmah ve-ha-Madda*" ["the Wisdom and the Knowledge"] many, many times. Then it went on to say "Wisdom and knowledge is given to you like the knowledge of Rabbi Akiva"; then it said, "And more than R. Akiva." Then it said, "And like R. Yeiva Sabba," and then, "And more than R. Yeiva Sabba."[16] And then it said, "Peace be unto you," and then, "From heaven they send you the greeting of peace." All this was with great wondrous speed, many times in the waking state. And I was fallen on my face, spread out on the grave of Abayye.

6. Then I went to my teacher of blessed memory, and he told me that my having performed these two *yihudim* was quite propitious, and that such was the proper order [cosmic and then individual in which to do them]; and that the reason I wasn't answered [with an experience] with the first *yihud* was because they were waiting for me to unify the two *yihudim*. And my teacher of blessed remembrance told me that when I returned from there [the grave of Abayye] and entered his house, he saw the *nefesh* of Benayahu ben Yehoyada walking with me. And he told me that [Benayahu] is not of the same [soul] root as I, but that the reason [he is with me] is because he reveals himself [perhaps "appears"] with each and every person who performs a cosmic *yihud*, because this was his custom during his life [to perform cosmic *yihudim*].[17]

7. And my teacher of blessed memory told me at the time of the afternoon prayer, that if I merit during the coming Sabbath to [cleave to] R. Yeiva Sabba, he will stay with me always and will never depart from me like my other *gilgulim* [he seems here to use *gilgul* and *ibbur* interchangeably], and through him I will merit great illuminations, especially [if I can connect with him] during the Silent Prayer, in the benedictions for the blessing of the year and for the righteous,[18] because R. Yeiva Sabba reveals himself to the *tzaddikim* [such as the AR"I] as is the case with Benayahu ben Yehoyada. In addition, he is of the same soul root as I. Thus, if I merit that he will reveal himself to me, he will reveal great wonders to me, with God's help.[19]

8. On the evening of the close of that Sabbath, I unified a *yihud* after midnight, after rising from bed, and was successful as before.[20] And R. Yeiva Sabba roused me to vigilance, saying that through the manuscript *yihud* of my teacher of blessed memory [to unite with the souls of *tzaddikim*], I will attain by means of wisdom all that I would desire; and that I ought to practice it three times a day as follows: during the *Nefilat Apayim* prayer of the morning and afternoon prayers and during the recitation of the *Shema* of the evening prayer. And by this means I will attain all that I wish.

9. And on the eve of the second day [Sunday night], I again unified a *yihud* after midnight; and R. Yeiva Sabba said to me: "Why did you not practice the *yihud* as I commanded you to do, three times a day? For I told you that by its means you will attain a whole and unlimited state of spiritual consciousness! Go to your teacher R. Yitzhak Ashkenazi and tell him to teach you how to perform it during these three times. And tell him to speak to me, and I will teach him, and he will teach you afterward.[21]

And you don't know how great you are in the eyes of the blessed Name, for you are great as R. Akiva and his colleagues, and you will attain what no one else in your generation has attained, including R. Yitzhak Ashkenazi, your teacher. And in the future you will be spoken to by the angel Elijah of goodly remembrance, face-to-face while awake. Therefore, when you perform this *yihud* [of the Luria manuscript], raise it up in the secret nature of Elijah who is the arcanum of the Name of 52.[22] This is the secret of the Feminine Waters; and raise it up in the secret of Nadav and Avihu, who constitute the secret of the *nefesh* [of Adam].[23] And raise me [R. Yeiva] together with them, and through this you will merit that Elijah and other angels will talk to you. And you have no idea how great your level is—greater than all the other people of this generation.[24] And God will grant you children and wealth, so that you will not need to rely on anyone." So in the morning I went to my teacher of blessed memory and told him all of the above. Afterward he taught me how to perform the aforementioned *yihud* during the three prayers: at *Nefilat Apayim* of the morning and afternoon, and during *Keri'at Shema* of the evening prayers.[25] And I have already explained this *yihud* in its place.[26]

> Thus, at that time, the imaginative psychical ability of R. Hayyim Vital was not yet capable of creative generation, as was clearly the case with his teacher, the AR"I. See, however, *Sefer ha-Hezyonot*, p. 57, where he writes in the year 1610, approximately thirty-eight years after his teacher's demise, that his teacher

... revealed himself to me in dreams on most nights in order to console me so that I not despair. And this occurred until twenty years after he passed away. And since then, for the next ten years, he would come to me only about once a month, and since then he would come only once every three months. And in all the dreams in which he participates he always appears in the same way: to teach me Torah and to console me so that I not despair. ...

> It is thus interesting to consider, in this connection, two instances where R. Hayyim Vital, apparently writing after his teacher's demise, mentions

a doubt that he had with reference to a *Kavvanah* practice by saying: "and I have not yet merited that my teacher explain this to me."[27] In one of these passages, it is implied that R. Hayyim Vital's psychical abilities had improved, and more importantly, that at least some ideas of the Lurianic Kabbalah may have developed by means of what R. Hayyim Vital had perceived as postmortem revelations to him by his teacher. And see *Sefer ha-Hezyonot*,[28] where in a dream approximately fourteen months after his demise, the AR"I reveals to R. Hayyim Vital the phenomenon of a Feminine Divine *Partzuf* that corresponds to the higher aspect of *Ze'ir Anpin*. This, however, is not an innovation; for we come across this idea elsewhere in various forms.[29] Unfortunately, aside from the above, as far as I am aware, we have no further specific information regarding revelation of teachings after the AR"I's demise.

And I already explained this [the various applications of the *yihud*] at the end of the manuscript *yihud* of my teacher of blessed memory; see there.[30] And regarding the matter of the *yihud* of Nadav and Avihu and Elijah of blessed memory, I wrote it after the first *yihud* of the Mouth and Nose of *Atika Kadisha*.[31]

Notes

This appendix is related to the section entitled "A Case Study: The Soul of R. Hayyim Vital" in M. Kallus's essay in this volume, "Pneumatic Mystical Possession and the Eschatology of the Soul in Lurianic Kabbalah."

1. See *Sha'ar Ru'ah ha-Kodesh*, 50a–53a; and for the dating, see *Sha'ar ha-Yihudim* (1855; reprint, Jerusalem: Mekkor Hayyim, [1970]), 5d.
2. See *Sha'ar Ru'ah ha-Kodesh*, 48a–50a.
3. On this see *Sefer ha-Hezyonot*, 162, sec. 25, 193.
4. See *Sha'ar ha-Gilgulim*, 329, and also 339, where he is told by the AR"I on several occasions (prior to his "conscious" attempt to connect with *tzaddikim*) that particular *tzaddikim* are currently temporarily impregnated in him. But see my long comment toward the end of section 9, where it may be implied that his psychical ability did indeed improve. The following translation is from the *Sefer ha-Hezyonot*, pp. 170–73; compare in *Sha'ar ha-Gilgulim*, pp. 341–43.
5. See *Sha'ar Ru'ah ha-Kodesh*, 44a–45a.
6. See ibid. fol. 43a–b.
7. The confusion in translation comes from the phrase *hazor bekha*, which has both connotations, and which was perhaps the first self-induced free association; but considering the free association he was about to have, I placed the other, perhaps more primary meaning in this context, in brackets.
8. See Mishnah *Eduyot* 5:7.

9. This refers to the "lower combination" YHVH and ADNI, corresponding to the *nefesh* and *ru'ah*, as opposed to the "higher combination" of AHYH YHVH that corresponds to the Wisdom and Understanding of the upper worlds and the higher levels of the *neshamah* [i.e. the Hayah] and the *neshamah* of the *neshamah*. These, according to protocol, were to be performed before the "lower combination," and he performed the second part of the *yihud* with confidence.

10. The word *they* keeps appearing, as if referring to the anonymous denizens of heaven.

11. אלהים יראה לו השה לעולה בני; another communication to "the son." See also R. Moses Cordovero, *Sefer ha-Gerushin* (Jerusalem: Ahuzat Yisrael, 1962), for the spontaneous pronouncement of a verse as a form of (self-induced?) speaking in tongues.

12. He is free-associating the name of a great sage who lived about three hundred years before Abayye.

13. See material in my essay above following note 83.

14. See R. Joseph Gikatilla, *Sod ha-Hashmal*, published in R. Sasson ben Moses, *Shemen Sasson*, vol. 2 (Jerusalem: [Mekor Hayyim], 1966), 4a. This is the classic commentary on the *Etz Hayim* from the early-twentieth-century head of the Jerusalem school of R. Shalom Shar'abi (late eighteenth century). Perhaps R. Hayyim Vital is approximating the "cacophony of sounds" described there.

15. See the *yihudim* in *Sha'ar Ru'ah ha-Kodesh*, 45b–46b, nos. 7 and 9 for those who have "the voice" but "no words." This indicates that the AR"I tried various stratagems to free R. Hayyim Vital, so that he could attain to automatic speech.

16. This vouchsafing did not suffice to convince him to abandon doubts in self-confidence.

17. See *Sha'ar Ru'ah ha-Kodesh*, 28a, where it is said that those sages who in the course of their lives were always performing cosmic *yihudim* were uniting "all of the Divine Roots together" so that upon demise, whenever a cosmic *yihud* is practiced, they are present. They are thus connected even with those souls that aren't of their "root." The Divine Throne is never without these souls. See also *Sha'ar Ma'amare RaShB"I*, 12a–d.

18. See material in my essay above around note 29.

19. Apparently, R. Hayyim Vital did not establish contact with R. Yeiva Sabba during his Sabbath afternoon nap and made another attempt after the close of the Sabbath.

20. It is likely that this was the cosmic *yihud* of the "Thirteen Reparations of the Beard," which is designated (50a) as a practice done after midnight.

21. This is highly significant; for here we see how although R. Hayyim Vital was able to convince himself that he had achieved contact with this mythical sage of the Zohar, he did not have the self-confident creativity at that point to directly receive a teaching from him, whereas the AR"I was capable of both.

22. The Tetragrammaton written out in this spelling: Yud=20 + Hh=10 + Vv=12 + Hh=10 =52, denoting the rising of the "Feminine Waters" from the lower levels. See my doctoral dissertation.

23. See *Sha'ar ha-Kavvanot*, drush 1 of *Keri'at Shema*; and see *Sha'ar ha-Gilgulim*, sec. 38, p. 367.

24. Soothing words to a troubled ego!

25. In other words, the AR"I had no trouble "contacting R. Yeiva" and creatively applying his *yihud* to these prayers. And see drush 5 of *Nefilat Apayim* written by the AR"I, 48a–c, where the basic conceptual infrastructure of this is laid out by the AR"I, but without the actual *yihud*.

26. See *Sha'ar Ru'ah ha-Kodesh*, 43b, *yihud* 2.

27. See *Sha'ar ha-Kavvanot, Inyan Kavvanot Keri'at Shema*, 23a, drush 6; and drush 1 of *Tefillat Arvit*, 52c.

28. P. 58, no. 18.

29. I discuss this in my doctoral dissertation. See *Sefer ha-Hezyonot*, 211–12 (and the parallel in *Sha'ar ha-Gilgulim*, sec. 39 p. 375f.); *Sha'ar ha-Kavvanot, Inyan Kavvanot ha-Amidah*, drush 2 on *"be-Ahavah,"* 32d; ibid., *Inyan va-Ya'avor*, 43c–d, drush 2; *Etz Hayim*, gate 29, chap. 1, final version; and elsewhere for parallels and applications.

30. See *Sha'ar Ru'ah ha-Kodesh*, 43b.

31. See ibid., 45a-b, no. 4. For another treatment of this section, stressing Vital's creativity, see Ronit Meroz, "Faithful Transmission versus Innovation: Luria and His Disciples," in *Gershom Scholem's Major Trends; 50 Years After* (Tubingen: Mohr, 1995), 263–66. Clearly, our analyses differ in detail, and the reasons for my opinions are given here in my interpolations and notes.

Appendix E

On the Possession of Rabbi Hayyim Vital from His *Book of Visions*, book 5, chapter 12

Translations and commentary by MORRIS M. FAIERSTEIN

In the year 5332 [1572], we went out in the fields and we passed the grave of a gentile that was more than a thousand years old. His Animus was seen on his tombstone and he tried to harm me and kill me. There were many angels and innumerable souls of *tzaddikim* to my right and left and he was powerless to harm me. My teacher commanded me that when I returned, I should not do so on that road. Afterward, the soul of that gentile followed me at a distance. There in the field I became angry at Rabbi I"M,[1] and the Animus of the gentile began to attach itself to me and cause me to sin even more and I did not want to listen to my teacher z"l's teachings. He began to cry and said: All the souls and angels have left him because of the anger and as a result that Animus rules over him. What shall I do? I wish that he would harm him and let him remain living; then I will be able to heal him. However, I fear that he will kill him and everything that I think will repair the world will be not accomplished by him, as is known to me. I could not tell, since I had not been given permission, whether I have struggled for nothing and the world would be destroyed. He did not eat the whole night out of anguish and worry. I returned on that road alone. When I reached his grave, a wind lifted me and I saw myself in the air, running twenty stories above the ground until I reached a land at nightfall and was left there. I slept soundly until morning. I wanted to get up, but all of my limbs were very weak and painful, but I slowly reached the door of my teacher, z''l. When I arrived, I was barely alive, like Jonah, and my teacher laid me on his bed, closed the door, and prayed. Afterward, he entered the house alone, walked around the house, returned to the bed, and stretched himself over me.[2] He did this until noon, when I was almost dead, and at noon I saw myself that my soul was slowly returning to me until I opened my eyes, got up, and recited the blessing, "He who resurrects the dead." All this is absolutely and undoubtedly true.[3]

Notes

This appendix is related to M. Faierstein's essay in this volume, "*Maggidim, Spirits, and Women in Rabbi Hayyim Vital's Book of Visions*."

1. It is not clear to whom this refers.
2. An allusion to Elisha and the son of the Shunnamite woman in 2 Kings 4:33–35.
3. See also *Book of Visions*, 1.24, quoted in the body of my essay.

Appendix F

Texts from Vital's Autobiography concerning the Vision of Pillars

Translations and commentary by HARRIS LENOWITZ; sources as noted

Here are some pillars that appear in the autobiography of Hayyim Vital (1:12, 19, 26, 27). I am limiting the field, with one exception, by attending only to part 1 of the *Book of Visions*. The work contains four parts: the first, what happened to him; the second, his own dreams; the third, the dreams of others concerning him; the fourth, what his master had to say about him, particularly in the matter of the history of his soul. There is also an appendix of additions and corrections in the original manuscript.

12. 5338. I was preaching before a congregation in Jerusalem one Sabbath morning and Rachel, the sister of R. Yehuda Mish'an, was there and told me that the whole time I was preaching she saw a pillar of fire upon my head, and Elijah of blessed memory was standing to my right and helping me, and that when I finished preaching both of them departed.

In Damascus, too, in 5362 she saw a pillar of fire upon my head while I was acting as the cantor on Yom Hakippurim, praying the *musaf* [additional service] in the Sicilian congregation. And the woman mentioned was accustomed to see visions and demons and spirits and angels and was correct in most of what she said from the time of her childhood through her adulthood.

19. 5364. I became very sick, immeasurably. I remained twenty-one days with no feelings and no sensations. The night of the twenty-second day was the end of the Sabbath and many people came and stayed around me to see the departure of my soul. And at the beginning of the night I opened my mouth four times as at the departure of the soul. And then I

opened my eyes and looked at the eastern wall across from me. I saw two pillars of fire there, one of red fire and the other of green fire, the color of grass. I prostrated myself toward them and looked at them until midnight. Then they moved from where they were to the north wall until morning, and I never took my eyes off them the whole night. I was like a stricken man lacking any sense of this world.

And when the people who were sitting around me saw how I prostrated myself toward the wall and stared there, they said, "This is what our rabbis of blessed memory have said, 'In their life they do not see and at their death they see.'" They said to me, "What do you see?" I said to them that they were telling me that the time of my passing had not yet come, for my house and place in the Garden of Eden had not yet been finished, for it was a great building. I was silent as a stone.

In the morning I forgot everything I had said to the people, but I remembered everything that had happened to me in connection with the two pillars.

The fever left me entirely and all my senses returned except for my vision, for my eyes remained entirely dim for seven days. Then I began to see a little, until forty days had passed. From then on my eyes were dim as if clouds of the color of the flames of those pillars ascended and descended before my eyes, back and forth. . . .

> Vital goes on to say in this passage that he later consulted a (Moslem) sheikh about the dimness of his eyes. He says that the sheikh treated him with extraordinary honor, sending his own disciples away, saying that this man was so powerful a personage in the other world that he had no choice but to attend to him and his wishes.

26. When Hayyim the son of R. Yedidyah Penzieri was born, I was his *sandak* (godfather). At the time of the circumcision Sa'dat, the wife of Yakov Natser, saw a pillar of fire from the sky upon my head. And as best as I recall it was the year 5328 since the creation.

27. 5370. The seventh day of Pesah I went out of the synagogue after prayers and a group of women was walking in front of me. And one woman looked behind her to see my face and saw a pillar of white light on my right side, twice as bright as the light of the sun and filling the whole of that street, and its height was twice the measure of my height and it was altogether a glare and flashed like lightning that blinds the eyes. And she was not able to see my face at all, and because of her great pain she went in at the entrance of a certain courtyard to hide there. And the name of that woman is Simhah, the sister of Zibdah the wife of Cuencas.

Notes

This appendix is related to the section entitled "Heaven Comes Calling" in H. Lenowitz's essay in this volume, "A Spirit Possession Tale as an Account of the Equivocal Insertion of R. Hayyim Vital into the Role of Messiah."

For a different translation of the whole work, see M. M. Faierstein, *Jewish Mystical Autobiographies* (New York: Paulist Press, 1999).

Appendix G

Selections from *Sefer ha-Hezyonot,* by Rabbi Hayyim Vital

Translations and commentary by HARRIS LENOWITZ

Book 1.22–5369 [1609].

1. A great thing happened in Damascus and I will write here only that part that concerns me.

2. It was the eve of the Sabbath of the 29th of Tammuz when pains and fainting overcame the daughter of Rafael Anav and he brought her to magicians, but they could do nothing.

3. It was nighttime, the night of the Sabbath and the New Moon of Av after the Sabbath lamp had been lit, and she was laid out like a dead body, with no feeling at all.

4. Rafael heard a voice come from her mouth, which said, "Rafael, come here." And he asked, "Who are you?"

5. It said, "I am the sage Piso, and why did you only light two lamps according to the custom—when you ought to have lit many lamps in honor of the angels and the souls of the righteous that have come to accompany me and to watch over me? And so arrange chairs for them, for they are six souls." And they arranged them for them.

6. And he said, "I am not like the other spirits, for I am a sage and a righteous man and I have only come on account of a minor sin that remains to me to repair and to be an emissary to you, to bring you to repentance for the multitude of sins that are in you. And it is twenty-one days since I left the Garden of Eden by way of the rivers of the Garden of Eden and came under the ground as far as the rivers of Damascus, and there I entered into the body of a fish, and a fisherman caught me and brought me to be sold in the street of the Jews on the eve of the Sabbath after *minhah*, and a very

evil man came along, al-Tawil, the son-in-law of the Sheikh al-Yahud,[1] and tried to buy me, but the Name be He blessed sent Rafael Anav there and he bought me and divided me into several pieces and gave one piece to R. Ya'akov Ashkenazi. And on the Sabbath night they ate me; and I was in the fish's head and his daughter ate me and I entered her, but I did her no harm at all for I am not like the other spirits. And they have not given me permission to reveal myself and speak until now, for it is the Sabbath and the New Moon; and I am very unhappy that I have not merited ascending on this holy day to my place in the Garden of Eden. And may Yehoshua Al-Boom be excommunicated for not coming to my aid to bring me forth on the Sabbath eve with the operations of the book he possesses, for perhaps I would have merited ascending, as I mentioned. And I am not going to tarry here longer than this day, for I have been given permission to speak only during it, and immediately upon the morning of the first day of the week I will return to my place in the Garden of Eden. Now, all the angels and souls I mentioned are waiting for R. Hayyim the kabbalist to carry out his mission, so call him to come."

7. But Rafael didn't want to come [to me] then, because it was nighttime, and he [Piso] said to him, "Don't worry about what has happened to your daughter, for I am a holy spirit; eat and make *kiddush*."

8. He made *kiddush*, and he [Piso] said to him, "Why aren't you careful to put water in the *kiddush* cup [in preparing to make the blessing]?"[2]

9. R. Ya'akov went home, and he said to him, "Be careful of the ban; say nothing."

10. And when he returned after eating, he [Piso] said, "Let the banned one not enter here for he has transgressed upon my ban."

11. And Rafael too said to him, "Don't come in, perhaps you have eaten saffron, which is bad for things like this."

12. And he said, "I haven't eaten any saffron."

13. And the spirit said to him, "And you're a liar as well, for you have eaten fish.[3] And your wife is more proper than you, for when she asked you why you were late you said, 'On account of an evil spirit that has entered into a certain woman.' And your wife was more proper than you and said to you, 'But if you say that he is a sage, how can you call him an evil spirit?'" Then he said to him, "I know you're a simple man and a fool, so come in." And he came in. And [the spirit] began speaking to all the people of the household, to each a little about his sins, and told the sins of those that had died in that plague as well. And that whole mid-night it seemed to them as if there were flames in the house. And R. Ya'akov dozed and felt as if they were choking him, and awoke. And at midnight [the spirit] said, "I have already suffered for three days on account of the distress I have undergone

in this *gilgul*, and it is improper to suffer on the Sabbath, too. Give me some water to drink and an apple to eat."

14. And they gave it to him. And he said to them, "Now sleep a bit." And they slept until the dawn, and he awoke them and said, "It's dawn; call R. Hayyim." But they didn't want to, until [at last] he decreed a ban of excommunication upon them and said to them, "If he doesn't believe you, give him this sign, that on this night in the morning watch, he dreamed a great dream and doesn't know its meaning and is saddened. Now, you will find him dressed, with his head on the ground, thinking about this dream. And if he will come to me, I will tell him."

15. Now what I had dreamed was that I saw six righteous men coming to my house from the world to come, and they were bringing me a Torah scholar to cure, and I forgot who they were. Then Rafael and R. Ya'akov came and told me all that has been mentioned and I went there. When I came in, [the spirit] said to me three times, "Blessed is he who comes!" And I came near the girl, and there was a veil on her face, and she was like a dead body, and I said to him [Piso], "Where do you know me from?" And he said, "And aren't you R. Hayyim the kabbalist?" And I said to him, "And who are you?" And he said, "I am Piso the sage." And I begged him to tell me his name until [at last] he said to me in a whisper, "I am Ya'akov Piso. In Jerusalem I was married to the daughter of the sage R. Yitzhak Ashkenazi and my wife's sister is named Esther, and I died thirty-five years ago and ascended to my place in the Garden of Eden and dwelled there until now. I have yet to repair a certain small matter and I have now come to repair it, and therefore, woe to him who is not careful in this world not to sin even a minor sin, so that he might not suffer what I do now."

16. And it seemed to me, Hayyim, that his sin was to have caused many others to sin by causing the study of the ways of repentance to be halted, and now he had come to make repair in the matter of repentance.

17. "And here is the dream that you dreamed: I am the Torah scholar they sent you from Heaven to cure and to pray over. [They sent me] in the company of six souls, which are sitting here with you: Elijah of blessed memory, and the master R. Yoseph Karo, and the master Shmuel Amron, and the master Aharon ibn Tifa, and the sage Atiya, and the sage Arha. And even though I studied with our teacher, the master, R. Yitzhak Luria—your master, of blessed memory—he has not come with the souls mentioned, but he too is there above praying for me. Now, you know that the upper beings have no power to make things better without the prayers of the righteous of this world, and so all of them are waiting on you and need you, so pray for me and cure me. Do you not, master of the Torah, see the great fire that burns the world?"

18. I said to him, "Do you want me to gather all those who dwell in the city into your presence?" He said, "If only that they would come and fast the three fasts, of the second, the fifth, and the second day in the same manner as the fast of Yom Hakippurim, men and women, then perhaps the Lord would repent of His wrath upon them for the many transgressions among them."

19. I, Hayyim, who write this, say that this proves what I wrote above, that his sin was the neglect of repentance and that he had come to repair that, but that it had to be done through my agency so that it might be done in this world. And this will suffice those who understand.[4]

20. I said to him, "But see, the people of Damascus do not want my preaching." He said to me, "All this is already known to the Blessed One." I said, "If so, I will gather together the Torah scholars alone." He said to me, "It is good." I said, "I don't know whom I will gather." He said to me, "Do not bring before me any of the Arab Jews, only Sephardic Torah scholars. Except for Yisrael Najjara—let him not look upon my face." I said, "I must go and pray." He said, "This matter is greater than prayer." I said, "I will not cancel my prayer in any circumstance, and the Lord will be merciful thereafter." He said to me, "Do you, master of the Torah, not wish to take pity on my sufferings and repair what I have said? What am I to do?"

21. I went off to pray and [then] I went and ate the morning meal and I thought that Rafael would come back to get me, but he didn't come. I was unable to decide whether to go or not, and I sent for R. Ya'akov. He came back to me and said, "I haven't been there." So we stayed until *minhah*. Then the spirit said to Rafael, "Look, the sage considers whether to come here," and he sent someone. And after *minhah* R. Ya'akov went there and the spirit said to them, "The sage has not wished to come and disdains to come to me and look, pride is fit only for the Blessed One alone, and a man ought not say, 'I don't want to drink from that water,' for perhaps he will need to drink it; and see, the whole matter of my mission is only on his behalf, for they have sent me from Heaven to reveal to him the uppermost secrets of Heaven, which he has not learned from his master of blessed memory, and also so that he may bring the world to repentance, for everything depends upon him to repair the whole world. And I have come to reveal to him matters concerning the messiah, for the matter hangs by a hair. Now, he always preaches that they should repent so that the messiah may come, and R. Y[a'akov] Abulafia, because of his jealousy, says to the people, 'He speaks lies, for the messiah will not come to this generation,' and he ridicules him. And woe to him, for his punishment is great, for due to his words and on account of the great transgressions that are in

this city, they have weighted down the messiah in thick iron ropes and he is delayed another twelve years. And during this time, many sufferings will befall Damascus and it will be overturned like Sodom, and Jerusalem will burn as well; only Safed will be saved. And then Gog and Magog will come, and then the messiah will come with the eight princes of men.[5] And the sage preached three sermons last year before the plague and some few repented; and, because he restrained himself from preaching more, his dear daughter died in the plague, and she was a great soul. And surely his little son will be a great master in Israel. And now he has lost the chance to hear the highest mysteries, for they have sent me from Heaven for that purpose, and when he seeks me, he will not find me, for permission has only been given me to speak on this day, and tomorrow I will return to my place."

22. And at the end of the Sabbath he spoke no more. And in the morning they came and told me everything he said, and I went there. And he did not want to speak any more. And he said to me, "I am going back to my place." And he gave me some indications, like those of spirits that are coming out, and he came out and did not return. And, to be sure, when he said on his own initiative that he was about to come out, Yehoshua Boom was standing there and made his adjurations. And then he did come out. And when he was coming out, I said to him [Yehoshua], "Write such-and-such an amulet that is found in such-and-such of your books and hang it on the girl so that harmful ones might not harm her after his departure." And he did so.

23. Now I will write what I did through the agency of R. Yehoshua Boom, and then I will write some other matters associated with the matter of the girl. This is what pertains to him:

Book 1.23

24. On the 6th of that Av, R. Yehoshua Boom brought down an angel, one of the servants of Tzidkiel, the prince of that day, and he appeared in a glass mirror, as is the custom. I asked him if the art of my teacher, the Ashkenazi, of blessed memory, as well as what he had said to me in the matters of my soul and my attainment, was true. He said, "All his words are true." I said, "Is what the soul of the righteous one that speaks with me by way of the *yihudim* true or a seeming?" He said that the speech was true but that sometimes the soul of the righteous one enters into my heart and raises his speech into my mouth and I hear it, and sometimes he stays outside and draws near me and speaks with me. I said, "Why has he

stayed away from me for such a long time?" He said to me, "You are the cause, for at first you put away all matters of this world from your heart and cleaved entirely to your Maker and would make *yihudim* and engage all day long in Torah and preach reproof to the whole people, and now you have abandoned everything, and he too has abandoned you, for you know what your master, as well as others, told you, that the whole world depends on you, and that you have only come into the world to call them to repent, and the redemption depends on you; and you have already attempted to do this for ten years now, preaching to the people and reproving them. How many people have repented and been attentive to your words? And when you abandoned them, they turned away from the path, and many of them have died in their sin, and the transgression hangs about your own neck; and now you have gone away completely and stay alone and apart in a corner; and *how many people dream marvelous dreams and tell them to you; and all this is from the Name be He blessed, in order to strengthen your heart,* and still your heart hesitates and you cannot make up your mind, and you do not believe strongly in those dreams. And know that your place in the Garden of Eden is with your master the Ashkenazi and two other righteous ones of the first and greatest *tanna'im*. And you are completely righteous before the Blessed One, except for that which I have said, and it [Vital's abandonment of his preaching] is the cause of that righteous one ceasing to speak with you through the *yihudim*. And your master, too, is angered with you somewhat on this account, and therefore you do not dream with him as at first. And, if you return to your labor, you will surely attain all your desire. But there is yet one small transgression in you, and we do not have permission to reveal it in the presence of those who stand here even if you permit it. And see, your daughter who was dear to you, who was a great soul, died in the plague on account of that transgression. Nor do we have permission to reveal to you in the presence of these here the name of the righteous one who speaks with you, because of his honor. But surely there are four letters in his name. And the *yihud* that is most proper for you now is the seventh *yihud* of Metatron, which is written in your book as well as the *yihud* of your master of blessed memory. And thus the righteous one who is most proper for you now is Samuel the prophet, even though he is very great in your eyes. And know that if you do not heed our words to call the people to repent and fast, a fast like that of Yom Hakippurim on the second, fifth, and second days of the week, fasting and weeping and so forth, a great trouble will come upon you. And upon the people of Damascus there will come mighty troubles. And now, the Blessed One has only sent the deed of the spirit in the daughter of Rafael Anav to bring back the people of Damascus to repent, for it was the spirit of a pious man, of great merit in his place, in the Garden of Eden, and due to a minor sin he had yet to repair, they sent him to receive his punishment in a certain river and there he was embodied in a fish, and Rafael bought him, and when his daughter ate its head he came into her and dwelled in her for twelve days. And on the first day of the week, on the New Moon of Av, the time of his ascent arrived and he arose on his own and not through the agency of any human; and on the Sabbath before he sent for you in the morning and you went there. And then you did not return until the first day of the week, when the time of his ascent had already arrived. And he wanted to reveal to you the upper mysteries. And his whole intention was that you call the world back to repent. And how many souls and angels descended together with him that Sabbath night? And all of them were waiting on you, to speak about this to you, and you would not believe their words, and you lost all those mysteries. Now, the Blessed One only sent them to have the people hear how awesome is the doing of the Lord and thereby to repent, so that the Lord might repent of His wrath upon them, for a great evil will come upon them because of the many sins that are theirs. And too, because the Blessed One knows that the people of Damascus would not heed you [alone], for great transgressions are among them that restrain their repentance. Do that which is your duty and gather ten men who are the most fit you can find, even if they are not entirely fit, and bring them back, and do too whatever is in your power to bring the people back, to repent. And he who hears will hear, and he who fails to will fail and you will have saved your own soul."

Book 1.24

25. Now, in section 22 I wrote what happened in the matter of the spirit itself, which was in the daughter of Rafael Anav, what I saw with my own eyes and what Rafael and R. Ya'akov Ashkenazi told me, and this all took place on the Sabbath of the New Moon of Av and on the morning of the first day of the week [the spirit] came out, without doubt, and ascended to its place. Thereafter other things happened that were not through the agency of the spirit mentioned while it was yet clothed in her, for it had already left and the girl was left completely healthy, but occasionally saying that she saw visions awake and in dreams by the agency of angels and,

infrequently, by the agency of the spirit mentioned as well. And therefore I had doubts about her words, whether they were true or mixed of good and evil, for the reason mentioned and for another reason as well: *because I did not see this with my eyes as I saw in the first case.* But what I marveled at was that her words were nothing but [concerning] repentance and the fear of the Lord and words of reproof. So I won't refrain from writing them, as they have been reported by trustworthy people who were present.

26. These are they: She said that after the spirit had left her, she was always seeing a certain angel in her dream who led her to the Garden of Eden and to Gehenna and showed her the places of the righteous. And in most of these visions they would say to her that she should warn me to call the people of Damascus to repentance—that perhaps the Lord would repent His wrath upon them.

27. On the Sabbath of the 28th of Av the spirit said that it really had been true that he had not been able to ascend to his place in the Garden of Eden until the morning of the first day of the week. But surely if R. Y. Boom had helped him to go out with adjurations from the [time of the] eve of the Sabbath, he would then have entered into a glass flask and stayed there all the day of the Sabbath and that thereafter they should have washed it out before using it, so that they might not be hurt through his having been in it.

28. The night of the 7th of Av: they said to her that she should say to me that at first the soul of a particular *tanna* was always appearing to me by means of the *yihud* in which I joined myself to him and that it had been a long time, to be precise two and a half years, since he had been revealed to me. For two reasons: one, that I had abandoned the *yihudim* mentioned; and two, that I had abandoned my preaching and reproving the people to call them to repent as I had at first. And on account of these same two reasons, my daughter had died in that plague. The night of the 8th of Av, Elijah of blessed memory said to her while she was awake,[6] at the time of the Sabbath *kiddush*, "Say to R. Hayyim and the other sages of the city that they are failing to carry out everything that they have heard and a great evil will fall upon the dwellers of Damascus therefore, and in particular to R. Hayyim. Say to him also, 'Why did you sin on the 6th of Av and bring down that angel in a cup to make inquiry of him? Does he [Vital] not believe all that we said to him through the agency of the spirit mentioned?' And see his master of blessed memory in his life also said to him that he had only come to the world to call the people to repentance and that angel he brought down also said all this to him, and he still hesitates and is indecisive and does not altogether believe! I fear for him that there might come upon him, may it not happen, many troubles on account of his urging."

29. The 10th of Av I asked her through her father, "Why has the righteous one known to me ceased speaking with me and what is his name and is there any hope to bring him back?" And she answered me that on the night of the 11th of Av she had seen my teacher of blessed memory and he had said to her, "Say to him on my behalf that he should stop asking these questions so many times. And I am not able to give him an answer except for this, these three words: *'Happy are those who die in your house,'*[7] and he will understand the meaning of the words on his own."

30. The night of the 12th of Av she saw my teacher of blessed memory in a dream, in a cave, and he said to her, "What answer has R. Hayyim given you?" She said to him, "He said to me that he didn't understand those three words." He said to her, "Such a simple thing? Has his mind stopped working so that he doesn't understand? Where is the art that I taught him? Let him recall that evil spirit that I brought forth from him. Now it is four years that he has not seen me in a dream, and now I thought I would return to him, but since he hasn't understood the words of my response, I don't want to return to him."

31. And here in my humble opinion is the meaning of the evil spirit mentioned, a matter of the resurrection of the dead. For he revived me on our walk to the village of Akhbara, because the spirit that was in the grave of the goy had caused me harm, or perhaps it was how my mouth had become twisted in the first *yihud* that I had taught myself.

32. The 24th of Av, Rafael went to Sinim,[8] and Rachel Aberlin went to visit them. And his daughter said to her that on the Sabbath of the New Moon of Av that the entire intention of the spirit's seeking was concerning me and it had been sent to me, and thereafter when I didn't wish to do its will, as mentioned above, and didn't come back there, that he complained against me on account of three things: the first, that when I had gone there I thought that he was an evil spirit like the spirits of other evildoers and so I didn't treat him honorably and spoke disparagingly with him; and the second, because I didn't believe his words when he said to me that there were angels and souls there and all of them waiting upon my prayer and yet I did not linger there and I left; and the third, because I had not come back there afterward to speak with him. And he had come on a mission from the Blessed One to tell me awesome things and supernal mysteries and thus I had lost them and in the end I would regret it and that when I sought him I would not find him.

33. The New Moon of Kislev, 5370, Rafael came from Sinim and said to me that my teacher of blessed memory had appeared to his daughter while she was awake and said to her, "Say to R. Hayyim that he is saddened because he has had no success with his preaching to the people of Damascus in the month of Elul and, at first, I was angered with him because

he would not listen to the words of that spirit and waited until R. Ya'akov Abulafia came from Safed, and thereby the matter became confused, for when the spirit spoke to him, then was the proper time, and thereafter, the moment had passed and thereby his preaching was not successful. Surely, in spite of all this, his sermons are pleasing before the Blessed One, even though they have not been successful."

34. And now I will write what happened to R. Ya'akov Abulafia with that spirit after it had already left her body as mentioned. Now, I held back from calling the people to repentance because he was not in the city then and I thought that the matter would be repaired by both of us, but on the contrary, when he came, he ruined everything. He came there on the Sabbath eve of the 15th of Av and, so that there might not be any special honor paid me on account of the spirit mentioned, he made the whole matter seem nothing in the eyes of the people. Then, on the second day of the week, the 17th of Av, the spirit was revealed to the daughter of Rafael and said to her that she should decree a ban on her father in his name, that he should not eat on the morning of the third day until he brought Abulafia there after prayers to reprove him for what had happened. And on the morning of the third day after prayers, he summoned him and he sat there until midday during the reproof. Rafael and his daughter and all the household and other women and R. Y. Boom and Betzalel and Frajallah his brother were there, and some other people were on the roof to hear. Then the girl said to R. Y. Boom, "Bring the glass mirror before me and summon down the angel Tzidkiel who governs this day." And the angel appeared and four souls of sages to be witnesses to the matter, and they were: R. Yosef Tziag and R. Yitzhak Karo and R. Shmuel Amron and R. Aharon ibn Tifa. And the girl was looking at the mirror and seeing them and was speaking with them.

35. And the angel said to her, "I do not want to reprove him, for R. Y. Abulafia will not believe the matters that appear as [mere] hints in the mirror, but only clear words from the mouth of the spirit himself to him, after he embodies himself in the mouth of the girl; and since he himself came at the first on this mission from above so, therefore, I will ascend and summon him." Then he went away and he stayed there awhile, and returned and descended into the mirror with the four witnesses. He said to her, "Say to R. Ya'akov Abulafia and to Betzalel and to Frajallah that they should go out into the courtyard until the spirit enters the girl." And the three of them went out to the courtyard, and the spirit clothed himself in the girl, and she fainted away as do epileptics. After the spirit had clothed himself, he began to speak and said, "Say to R. Y. Abulafia that he should draw near this window from the outside." He drew near, and

he said to him, "Why did you not clothe yourself [in the girl] until you made me go out?" He said to him, "Because you are not fit to see me as I clothe myself, for you are a sinner. And behold, the messiah is angered with you because you are always ridiculing the matter of the coming of the messiah and saying, 'The messiah will not come in this generation.' And when R. Hayyim the kabbalist preaches repentance to the people concerning matters touching on the messiah, you ridicule him and twist his words because you are jealous of him. And if you think yourself a sage, explain to me the meaning of the commandments of Pesah and Shavu'ot and Rosh Hashanah and Sukkot and so forth."

36. And he told him the simple, well-known meanings. And he said to him, "These things are revealed to the simple people, and if you had wanted to know the truth you ought to have heard the mysteries of the Torah from R. Hayyim. And he wanted to preach on the Sabbath and reprove the people, and you held him back and prevented Israel from repenting. Woe to you, sages of this time, that you do not recall the people to repentance! And behold, I saw disgrace and scandal among the sages of Egypt, too, for there is no wisdom in them at all, and they are destroying the city by the perversion of justice. And the people of Egypt have slaves who serve them, and, when the men leave their homes, the slaves lie down with their wives. They also bury their stews on the Sabbath day[9] and many other things like that. And behold, any who go now to Egypt, even to carry on trade, are excommunicated above, and in the end, all their wealth will be lost on account of the evil deeds that are there. Also in Venice there will come a drawn sword for seven days together, and great sages and righteous men whose like is not to be found in this city will be slain by it. The end of the matter is, woe to you sages of the generation, for you are proud and cast shame and do not attend to the honor of the Blessed One and call the people back to repent, and you cause the world great evil." Then R. Ya'akov Abulafia was somewhat humbled and tears came from his eyes.

37. And he [the spirit] said to him, "Since you have been humbled and shamed because I sent you out, it is enough." And he gave him permission to enter. After he came in, he said to him, "Now you and the inhabitants of Damascus have no portion in the world to come, Heaven forbid, for several reasons. You cause the people to sin by having them take oaths concerning taxes and evaluations, how much wealth each possesses, and they swear falsely[10]—and you already know that they are making false oaths. Moreover, your wives are brazen in their dress and their disgraceful adornments, like the *finjans* [cups] that are upon their heads and their breasts are revealed and they stuff their bosoms with clothes to show off their large breasts and go about in flimsy *lizaris* [shawls] and scarves to

show off their bodies; and put on *khaskhasis* [poppy] and other sorts of balms and fragrances, to stir up the evil impulse among men. And they drag all this through the markets and the streets in order to show all the people their beauty. You must also reprove your children and restrain them from sin. And behold there are forty-eight men who transgress with gentile women and with other men's wives and lying with other men, in addition to other transgressions." And he listed them all. But he only told me about these: Eliyahu Hefetz and the sons of Gandour and the son of Koreidi and Avraham Mosieri—they lie down with gentile women; and the daughter of Komieri, who has converted, whores with Yehoshua Koresh and many other men; and R. Ya'akov Monedas has intercourse with Natan Kholef, and now has given him his daughter and still whores with him—and woe to Ya'akov! for his face is black as pitch in the world to come on account of the multitude of his sins, and he has no portion in the world to come; and Ya'akov Uceda, your brother-in-law, has transgressed with a certain woman; and Nissim Menashe has no portion in the world to come and has no one in Heaven to say a good word about him, and if anyone does him a favor, even to cure him from the illness with which he has been struck by Heaven through an evil spirit, it is proper to cut him apart with a saw; and Rafael Kholeif and Mikhael his son transgress with Jewish and gentile women. And, last Sabbath night, a Torah scholar who is called *hakham* in the congregation of the Sefardim lay with a gentile woman in Jubar. And thereafter we investigated who, at that time, was there on the stove that was there, and it was found that it was R. Avraham, son of R. Moshe Galanté, for he slept there with his wife and also a gentile woman who owned the house. And the wife of Meir Peretz, she and her daughter: complete whores, causing many to sin. And R. David Gavison sinned much, for he left his chaste wife here and married a whore in Egypt, and for his sins, his wife died and his daughter-in-law, both of them chaste. And also one man said to me that they said of him that in Egypt he was transgressing with whores and had lost everything. And perhaps it was the matter of the woman he took in Egypt.

38. "And see R. Y[israel] Najjara. It is true that the poems he has written are themselves good, but it is forbidden to speak with him and to make him sing what he has composed, for his mouth is always filled with filth and he is a lifelong drunk. And behold, on one certain day during the Three Weeks of Mourning for the Temple, he dined at a certain hour in the home of Ya'akov Monedas and put his hat on the ground and played songs loudly and ate meat and drank wine and got drunk too—*and how can he announce the watches in Jubar and preach repentance to them?*" And I, Hayyim, told him of this matter and he confessed that it was so. Even now, while

fleeing from the plague, he has lain with a man on account of his great drunkenness. And on the Sabbath he transgressed twice: once, when he quarreled with his wife and threw her out of the house; and the second time when, after that, a gentile woman came into his house, and she set incense to smolder on the fire, and then he lay with her. And, therefore, it is forbidden to employ him and it is forbidden to give him a *ketubah* or a *get* to write, and it is almost proper to decree them void. And his younger son as well had intercourse with the gentile woman, and he is a complete evildoer, may his bones be ground up fine. But his older son does not sin.

39. "And there is much homosexuality in this city and twistings and perversions of justice, too, in this city."

40. R. Y. Abulafia responded to him, "How do I know all this is true?" And he said to him, "Your son Moshe, he and Menahem Romano brought a gentile woman into a certain house during the past holiday of Shavu'ot, before he went to Aleppo, and lay with her." He said, "How is it possible that my son has sinned in such a manner?" He said, "What the fathers do, the sons inherit. And did you not also do things that were not proper in your youth?" He said, "If it is so, then I shall go to Safed." He said, "You have destroyed Damascus and now you will go to Safed and destroy it as well? First repair the destruction of Damascus and then go where you like." He said, "I will wait until the month of Elul, which is the time of repentance." He said, "You have spoken well, but what you say and what you intend are not the same, for you do not believe these things. Now, when I spoke with the kabbalist R. Hayyim he hesitated at first, until he brought the angel down, and then he believed and was pleased to call the people back to repentance—but you do not believe at all. Therefore, in any case, let all the sages of the city gather together and call the people back in repentance—and leave R. Hayyim the kabbalist out of it and do not call upon him, because he did not believe at first—and fast for seven days." He said, "But is the seventh day not a Sabbath?" He said, "And do you fulfill all the commandments? For the need of the moment—for the wrath of the Lord is upon you—it is necessary for you to fast on the Sabbath, too. But do not preach sermons. But spend the whole day in prayers for forgiveness and pleading and weeping. And if you do not do so, know that hard decrees will befall the people of Damascus, particularly a mass famine, during which a man will eat the flesh of his own arm. And be cautious not to let R. Y. Najjara enter among you in any of these fasts. And this thing I command you with oaths of excommunication and bans. Now, if there were among you a completely righteous and holy man, a holy angel would reveal himself to him to speak with him face-to-face all these things."

41. He also mentioned that Yehoshua Boom was one who knows and is expert in the matter of adjuring the spirits and demons on the basis of that which he had received from R. David of Morocco, his master, who was a God-fearing man and an expert. And, as his student, he was able, if he wished, to cure Shimon the epileptic, the brother of Betzalel.

42. And after the spirit departed, R. Ya'akov Abulafia decreed an order of excommunication [according to the formula of the] *Kol Bo* upon all those who were present there, that they not reveal a word, on account of his own honor and the honor of others whom the spirit had mentioned. But they did not fear a powerless oath, and the matters became known, and then he, too, had to confess. Surely it [the spirit] had cast aspersions on that which was holy, for it had touched upon his honor and had spoken libel against him when he had but said, "that all the Torah is true." And on this account he erected fortresses and excommunications, and excommunicated the spirit before the congregation because it had spoken libel against righteous men. Thereafter, the daughter of Rafael sent to him from Sinim the following, in the name of the spirit: that the spirit stood every day in the Heavenly Academy, excommunicating him and all those who agree with him in what he did.

Notes

This appendix is related to H. Lenowitz's essay in this volume, "A Spirit Possession Tale as an Account of the Equivocal Insertion of R. Hayyim Vital into the Role of Messiah."

1. "The head of the Jewish community" in Arabic.

2. The practice of mixing water and wine for the *kiddush* is a symbolic act, sweetening the red/harsh qualities of the wine with the white/merciful qualities of the water.

3. M. Faierstein suggests that the fish was cooked with saffron.

4. The expression, *dai la-mevin*, serves to conceal Vital's consideration of his role as messiah. The use of such a phrase, as well as other considerations, brings up the question of the audience for which Vital is writing this journal. M. Faierstein is of the opinion that Vital had no intention of the journal's being read by others. If so, here he is concealing his opinion—that he is the messiah (or something else)—from himself, as it were. The fact that the *Book of Visions* is broken down into books and numbered within them likewise provokes inquiry. In considering this matter the incident of the contract (*shtar ha-hitkashrut*) Vital drew up to prevent other disciples from writing or talking about the teachings of Luria and the tale of the copying out of Vital's own notes while he was sick would have to be taken into account. Vital's conduct in these matters leads to a conclusion that in this as well

as in his understanding of his role as messiah, opposing forces were at play in his self-identity.

5. Micah 5.4; see the discussion in Louis Ginzberg, *Legends of the Jews* 7 (Philadelphia: Jewish Publication Society, 1937–1966), 130.

6. The *gilui eliyahu*—the appearance of the prophet Elijah, the harbinger of the messiah—is ordinarily restricted to men who are themselves candidates for the messiahship.

7. *Ashre mete betekha* here is probably a reference to Luria's restoring Vital to life in the incident mentioned below and described in the *Book of Visions*, addenda and corrigenda, sec. 12; M. Faierstein suggests that the source for the phrase is a rewriting of Ps. 84:5, *ashre yoshve betekha*, used as a proof text for the doctrine of the resurrection of the dead in BT Sanhedrin 91b.

8. Tripoli in Lebanon.

9. The objection involves a dispute over avoiding sabbatarian restrictions on cooking.

10. Whether, for the purpose of equalized distribution of the tax burden imposed on the Jewish community by governmental authorities, one could be forced to take an oath that one's wealth and earnings were what one stated was a well-known topos of contemporary rabbinic disputation.

Appendix H

From *Sha'ar Ru'ah ha-Kodesh* (The Gate of Holy Spirit), by Rabbi Hayyim Vital

Translation by MATT GOLDISH

Homily 1: In which the matter of prophecy and holy spirit and their function will be explained, as well as their various levels.

Be aware that inasmuch as a person is righteous and holy, studies Torah, and prays with directed intensity, it is certain that nothing [he does] will lack a tangible outcome. Even the sound emitted during carnal relations is not meaningless, as the Zohar in the portion of *Shlah lekha* mentions. It is, rather, certain that that thing [a person does] does not go to waste, God forbid; it is certain that from it are produced angels and holy spirits that have a permanent existence, as is mentioned in the [Zohar] portion of *Beshalah*, 59. Similarly, the rabbis say, "One who performs one commandment acquires himself one defender [in heaven], etc." The reason is that from a person's speech one creates good or bad angels, depending on what he said.

And thus it is written further: When a person occupies himself with Torah, those sounds and breaths that come from his mouth create a chariot for the souls of righteous men, on which they come down below to teach Torah to that person. So it is written in *Sabba de-Mishpatim*, 100r, concerning breath, speech, and sound. All three will be explained below, God willing.

In any case, it all depends on the actions of the person. For if the Torah he studies is read for its own sake, the angel created thereby is very holy, highly exalted, and trustworthy in all it says to be completely true. Similarly, if he reads it with no errors or mistakes, the angel created will be without mistakes and totally trustworthy in all it says. So, too, if the commandment he performs is done as decreed [by the rabbis], a very holy angel will be created from it. This accords with what is written: "Every person who performs one commandment merits one defender." On the other hand, whatever is lacking in his performance of that commandment will similarly be lacking in the light of that angel. But it is a certainty that the angel created from Torah study is stronger than that of an angel created by [performance of] a commandment. But there is no call to expand on these details.

This is the concept of angels that reveal themselves to people and inform them about future events and secret matters, to which the literature refers as *magidim*. These, then, are created by a person's involvement in Torah and performance of the commandments. There are persons to whom these *magidim* are not revealed at all, and there are those to whom they are revealed—all is a function of the nature of their souls or of their actions, about which there is no call to expand.

There are some completely truthful *magidim*—those created from Torah [study] or commandments perfectly performed. There are some *magidim* that are only partially truthful in their words, with an admixture of lying and deceit. The reason for this is that if a person contaminated his Torah [learning] or commandment performance with an evil aspect or falsehood, the angel created therefrom too will contain both good and evil—its good aspect says true things and its evil aspect says falsehoods.

There are also *magidim* created from the World of Activity [*olam ha-asi'ah*] alone through the unwitting performance of active commandments. Other *magidim* come from the World of Creation [*olam ha-yetzirah*], deriving from Torah study alone. Yet other *magidim* derive from the World of Formation [*olam ha-bri'ah*], deriving from the intentions and thoughts of a person as he studies Torah and performs commandments. In each of these Worlds are many divisions and details, each different from the other, and there is no call to expand.

The sign given me by my teacher [the AR"I; for telling true *magidim* from false ones] is this: we see if the person is truthful in all his words, or if he performs all his deeds for the Name of Heaven, wastes not one word in his speech, and knows how to interpret the hidden matters and secrets of the Torah. We can definitely believe him if so, and as he told me, we are thereby in a position to know and recognize his greatness and qualities according his [level of] knowledge.

Now, the secret of prophecy and holy spirit is certainly that a voice is sent from above to speak with that prophet or possessor of the holy spirit. However, that spiritual voice from above cannot become physically manifest by itself, and thus enter the ears of that prophet, unless it is first "dressed" in that physical voice emitting from that person while he learned Torah or prayer or other such things. It will then be dressed in [his voice], join itself to it, and thus arrive at the ear of that prophet so that he will hear it. But without that person's own physical voice it can't exist.

The explanation of this matter is as follows. The first voice has already been turned into angels and holy spirits, as was already explained. These are themselves the voice of prophecy. Now, when that voice comes to a person to tell him that prophecy, it dresses itself in the physical voice that this man is *now* emitting, when this prophecy descends on him. This is the secret meaning of the passage "The spirit of God speaks in me and His word is on my tongue"—the *spirit* and the *word* refer to the speech that he previously emitted in his Torah learning and commandment observance, as mentioned above....

Notes

This appendix is related to M. Goldish's essay in this volume, "Vision and Possession: Nathan of Gaza's Earliest Prophecies in Historical Context."

Appendix I

On How the Spirits of the Dead Enter the Bodies of the Living, from *Sefer Nishmat Hayyim*, by Rabbi Manasseh ben Israel, book 3, chapter 10

Translation by MATT GOLDISH

In which it will be shown how the spirits of the dead enter the bodies of the living, which is a positive, indubitable proof of the soul's eternity.

The matter of spirits that possess the bodies of the living is a further excellent support for our position on the eternity of the soul. This matter is well accepted and needs no further proof. Indeed, all the books of spells found in the Christians' language, called exorcisms, bear witness and support this, as you will see in Martin del Rio, Bodin, Vieira, and numerous others, both newer and older.

So too was there the Jewish woman in the city of Ferrara quite recently, of whom the whole world heard. People would come to see her from the four corners of the earth because the spirit of a certain Christian, whose name is well known, possessed her for an extended period. R. Eliezer Ashkenazi wrote in his great and most praiseworthy book [*Ma'ase ha-Shem*], in the section "Works of Creation," chapter 2, as follows:

> So also in the year [5]337 [1577] of the minor count came the well-known tale from the mouths of men and women, the elderly and the young, all reporting in an identical manner, which is a proof for the truth of the matter. They stated that in the city of Ferrara a certain Jewish woman swooned and a voice issued from her throat, while her lips did not move. The voice spoke, and when asked who it was, it responded: "I am the Christian so-and-so; I lived in such-and-such a city," giving full, convincing details, such that all those listening identified that Christian, who

had died recently. They asked it how it had entered that woman's body, and it answered "thus-and-thus was the way I entered, and through this [aperture].

Thus far his statement. Rabbi Gedalia ibn Yahia testified about this [case], and in his book entitled *Shalshelet ha-Kabbalah*, 86, he writes as follows.

Behold, now that God has informed you about all this by means of my exertions, I having both gathered them and retold them, He will give my hand strength to write to you and present you with a response to your inquiry concerning strange spirits that enter the bodies of people. By the power of spells they reveal their names and say that they are people who suffered unusual deaths. It is difficult for our power of reason to comprehend how the spirit of another person, who is dead, can act within a different body of someone who is alive—how it can control all his limbs and senses. But in truth, briefly, it appears one of the wonders of our time, and quite strange. The following quite clearly occurred: In the month of Tevet [5]335 [winter 1575] when I was in Ferrara, I went in the company of many upstanding people to visit a certain girl. She was twenty-five years old and married. I found her laid out on her back in bed like a body without a soul. Her eyes were closed, her mouth was open, and her tongue was exceedingly thick from the lip inward. The men and women who were caring for her informed me that the spirit was then lodged in her tongue. I said to myself, "This is the day for which I have hoped—to discover new knowledge about the soul's abandonment of the body." After I argued with the spirit and begged it to answer my queries, it answered in clearly spoken, well-modulated Italian that his name was Battista da Modena, and that he was condemned to be punished for thievery that he had committed. He then began to wail and groan. I comforted him with kind words and he calmed down. I began to ask him questions concerning the soul, to know its nature and the manner of its exit from the body at the moment of death, as well as its subsequent movements and what hell is like. (I didn't ask him about the Garden of Eden, knowing that had been withheld from him.) I asked him many other questions along these lines, and he answered at length, but the conclusion of his reply was, "I don't know." When he reported "I was a farmer and a cowherd," the manner of his words caused me to see him like a cow. I asked about the substance of his body. He replied, "I don't know." I asked if he was more like a goose egg, a chicken egg, or a dove egg. He replied, "Like a chicken's." I asked where he was situated in the woman's body. He answered, "Between the ribs and waist on the right side." I asked who put him there. He answered,

"I don't know." I asked him to come out. He answered, "I am unable." I asked why he entered the Jewish woman's body. He answered because he was suffering, and that he did not know her when he entered there. I asked through what place he entered. He answered, through her vagina. He also informed us how it occurred, which was similar to the way the girl later told of it.

I begged him with great supplication to let the girl remain quietly until I could speak with her, and he agreed. When he left to his place we observed the woman's throat swell enormously. She suffered great pain in all her limbs, jerked and palpitated in astoundingly difficult and bizarre ways, and caused great pity among all those who saw her. Now when the spirit entered its place, the woman's entire body, particularly that side, shook and shuddered continually as occurs in the seizures preceding the onset of malaria. She immediately opened her eyes and looked at us. I asked her how all this had come about. She answered that when she had come out from immersing herself in the ritual bath outside her house, she descended into the courtyard (it was then the second hour of the night) with a lit candle in her hand, intending to draw water from the well so she could prepare food for her husband. She placed the lit candle in a hole near the well, at which point her husband, who had been with her, departed. She had picked up the bucket to draw water when the candle was suddenly extinguished. She [it?] was taken up by the wind and cast halfway down the well, then lifted from there into the air. She knew not what it was nor what was happening and how. She screamed and fainted. The members of her household lifted her onto her bed.

Now she asked us for a cure to her injury. With this the spirit surged back upward before our eyes, causing much pain and anguish to the girl, and it would let her speak no more. Thus far that incident.

Other events of this type occurred, and ones even more marvelous have been recounted to me. I have even seen them signed—one from the sages of Safed (may it be speedily rebuilt!), about which I report elsewhere, and one from the rabbis of Italy, which happened in Ancona. [This concerned] the souls of persons who had been put to death and hanged; [the souls] entered bodies of people, but through spells, sulphur, and similar methods applied to the orifices of the body, these spirits informed [those present], revealing their names, a number of matters concerning them, all their deeds, the places they dwell, and the transgressions for which they [found the need to] enter bodies and wander about. Others have testified that all the [spirits'] words are true. They exorcised them from the bodies with spells, and the spot where the spirit left swelled.

Thus far the aforementioned sage. Now, in order that you be convinced and believe the truth of this matter, I now present you with the letter sent from Safed (may it be speedily rebuilt!) about a similar case. Note who the sage is who testifies for it: Rabbi Solomon Levi ibn Alkabetz, author of *Manot ha-Levi* and *Shoresh Yishai*, and teacher of Rabbi Moses Cordovero (of blessed memory). This is the account as it has long appeared in print:

Notes

The continuation of this chapter can be found in appendix A, above.

BIBLIOGRAPHICAL ESSAY

General Possession Literature

A good place to start reading about spirit possession in the world context is with the work of Erika Bourguignon, the illustrious anthropologist who has contributed a foreword to this volume. In her slim book *Possession* (San Francisco: Chandler & Sharp, 1976), Bourguignon presents a carefully worked out definition of possession in which she differentiates between possession beliefs, possession trances, and other phenomena, categories that she and others had described in *Religion, Altered States of Consciousness, and Social Change*, ed. E. Bourguignon (Columbus: Ohio State University Press, 1973). In *Possession*, Bourguignon also offers an exemplary case of possession beliefs from Haiti and provides a highly illuminating look at continuing possession beliefs in the West, particularly among Christian denominations. Bourguignon's universal anthropological and functionalist approach follows the style of classic possession studies by T. K. Oesterreich, *Possession, Demoniacal and Other—Among Primitive Races in Antiquity, the Middle Ages, and Modern Times* (Secaucus, N.J.: University Books, 1966; originally published in German, 1921); and I. M. Lewis, *Ecstatic Religion: An Anthropological Study of Spirit Possession and Shamanism* (Baltimore: Penguin, 1971). All these works present a much more reasoned and less tendentious picture than that of A. D. White, *History of the Warfare of Science with Theology* (New York: D. Appleton & Co., 1896), chaps. 15–16, which has nevertheless not lost all its value.

While it is impossible to even begin dealing with the vast quantity of work done on possession in varius world contexts here, I will mention two very well-known books of essays that have blazed a path in the field: *Case Studies in Spirit Possession*, ed. V. Crapanzano and V. Garrison (New York: John Wiley & Sons, 1977), with an outstanding introduction by Crapanzano; and *Trance and Possession States*, ed. R. Prince (Montreal: R. M. Bucke Memorial Society, 1968), which includes the important (if rather problematic) paper, "Altered States of Consciousness," by A. M. Ludwig.

There are several important studies concerning possession beliefs in the early modern Christian West that deserve attention here. D. P. Walker, *Unclean Spirits* (Philadelphia: University of Pennsylvania Press, 1981), deals with cases in sixteenth- and seventeenth-century France and England, focusing especially on why Christian possession accounts always concern malevolent spirits in a highly religious context. On the other hand, Clarke Garrett has written an outstanding monograph, *Origins of the Shakers* (Baltimore: Johns Hopkins University Press, 1998; originally published as *Spirit Possession and Popular Religion* [1987]), in which he traces a tradition of prophetic, benevolent possessions from western Europe to New England in the seventeenth and early eighteenth centuries. This tradition bears much resemblance to "positive" Jewish possessions in the same period. Stuart Clark, in his learned book on early modern witchcraft, *Thinking with Demons: The Idea of Witchcraft in Early Modern Europe* (Oxford: Clarendon Press, 1997), includes a sizeable section on spirit possession that places these beliefs in a much broader context of European ideas and popular culture.

Much attention has been focused specifically on the case of the possessed nuns of Loudun, concerning which the popular work by Aldous Huxley, *The Devils of Loudun* (London: Chatto & Windus, 1952 and numerous subsequent printings), still gives an interesting picture. A far more sophisticated study of that event is available in Michel de Certeau, *The Possession at Loudun* (Chicago: University of Chicago Press, 2000).

This is only a sampling of some better-known works. Other studies in all fields concerning possession can be found in the notes to essays in this volume.

Jewish Possession Literature

Without any doubt, the most essential work for understanding the history and phenomenology of Jewish possessions is G. Nigal, *Dybbuk Tales in Jewish Literature* (in Hebrew), 2nd ed. (Jerusalem: Rubin Mass, 1994). Nigal brings together almost all the known texts about malevolent Jewish possession cases. While his analysis has been criticized in a review by J. H. Chajes (*Kabbalah* 1 [1996]: 288–93), everyone interested in the field is beholden to Nigal for his collection of these widely scattered accounts.

References to some of the scattered discussions about ancient and medieval Jewish possessions and exorcisms can be found in the notes to Jonathan Seidel's essay in this volume, but since the phenomenon becomes much better known in the sixteenth century and later, I will mention some of the major scholarship in this period. The definitive work on early modern possession and its meaning is currently J. H. Chajes, "Spirit Possession and the Construction of Early Modern Jewish Religiosity" (Ph.D. diss., Yale University, 1999), a revised version of which is *Histories of the Spirits: Dybbuk Possession, Magical Exorcism and Early Modern Judaism* (Philadelphia: University of Pennsylvania Press, forthcoming). Chajes addresses all the older scholarship and constructs a thorough and broad new perspective. His analyses of documents are particularly useful. Some of these can be found in the present volume and in Chajes, "Judgments Sweetened: Possession and Exorcism in Early Modern Jewish Culture," *Journal of Early Modern History* 1.2 (1997): 124–69.

The most important discussion of "positive" possessions and the Safed context is R. J. Z. Werblowsky, *Joseph Karo: Lawyer and Mystic*, 2nd ed. (Philadelphia: Jewish Publication Society, 1977). Werblowsky lays the groundwork not only for an understanding of Karo but for the whole mystical background of maggidic possession. More specialized studies in this field can be found, for example, in R. Patai, "Exorcism and Xenoglossia among the Safed Kabbalists," *Journal of American Folklore* 91 (1978): 823–35; and L. Fine, "Maggidic Revelation in the Teachings of Isaac Luria," in *Mystics, Philosophers, and Politicians: Essays in Jewish Intellectual History in Honor of Alexander Altmann*, ed. J. Reinharz, D. Swetschinski, and K. Bland (Durham, N.C.: Duke University Press, 1982), 141–57. Among the important primary sources for benevolent possessions in Safed are those found in the appendixes to the present volume and in general in the *Toledoth ha-AR"I*, ed. M. Benayahu (Jerusalem: Ben-Zvi Institute, 1967); R. Hayyim Vital's *Sefer ha-Hezyonot*, ed. A. Z. Aescoly (Jerusalem: Mosad ha-Rav Kook, 1954), now available in English in Morris J. Faierstein, *Jewish Mystical Autobiographies: "Book of Visions" and "Book of Secrets"* (New York: Paulist Press, 2000); and Vital's *Sha'ar ha-Gilgulim* and *Sha'ar Ru'ah ha-Kodesh*, which have gone through various printings.

A sophisticated folkloristic approach to some Ashkenazi possession cases of the seventeenth century can be found in Sara Zfatman-Biller, " 'Tale of an Exorcism in Koretz'—A New Stage in the Development of a Folk-Literary Genre" (in Hebrew), *Jerusalem Studies in Jewish Folklore* 2 (1982): 17–65. ; idem, "Exorcisms in Prague in the Seventeenth Century: The Question of the Historical Authenticity of a Folk Genre"(in Hebrew), *Jerusalem Studies in Jewish Folklore* 3 (1982): 7–33.

The best-known scholarship on Jewish spirit possessions is the anthropological and psychological analysis presented by Yoram Bilu, particularly in his "The Taming of the Deviants and Beyond," which is reprinted at the beginning of this volume. With Benjamin Beit-Hallahmi, Bilu has written about the specific "hysterical" psychological interpretation of *dybbuk* possession in "*Dybbuk* Possession as a Hysterical Symptom: Psychodynamic and Socio-Cultural Factors," *Israel Journal of Psychiatry and Related Sciences* 26.3 (1989): 138–49. In one of Bilu's most important articles, he attempts to place the various forms of Jewish possession into the categories described by Erika Bourguignon in her wide anthropological theories about possession: Bilu, "*Dybbuk* and *Maggid*: Two Cultural Patterns of Altered Consciousness in Judaism," *Association for Jewish Studies Review* 21.2 (1996): 341–66. In another noteworthy paper, Bilu examines the ways in which a specifically Moroccan-Jewish form of possession manifested itself when Moroccan immigrants came to Israel: Bilu, "The Moroccan Demon in Israel: The Case of 'Evil Spirit Disease,'" *Ethos* 8 (1980): 24–39.

The studies in this volume constitute a continuation and expansion of the work done by Bilu, Chajes, and Fine as well as containing new work by many other scholars. The appendixes to the text are an invaluable resource for future work.

GLOSSARY

For terms describing possession, see the preface; for further information on all subjects, see the *Encyclopedia Judaica* [Jerusalem: Keter, 1971].

Adam Kadmon—"Primordial Adam"; a spiritual formation through which the sephirot and partzufim manifested themselves, according to the Lurianic Kabbalah.

Adam ha-Rishon—"The First Adam"; Adam from the book of Genesis, who takes on additional meanings in mystical works.

agunah—A woman whose husband has left her or disappeared and is not known to be dead. She is unable to obtain a divorce and thus cannot remarry.

AR"I *see* Luria, Rabbi Isaac.

Ba'al Shem—"Master of the Name"; a wonder worker, especially in the seventeenth through nineteenth centuries, who was believed to have magical powers through his knowledge of secret divine names.

Ba'al Shem Tov—Rabbi Israel ben Eliezer ((d. 1760), founder of the Hasidic movement. Considered an ignorant dreamer as a young man, he later revealed great spiritual qualities.

Bahir—"Clarity"; the first book of Kabbalah proper.

Babylonian Talmud (BT)—Voluminous, authoritative compendium of Jewish oral law compiled in late antiquity.

Cairo Genizah—A storehouse of discarded papers and books in the Cairo synagogue which contained a wealth of information on Jewish life over at least a millennium.

devekut—"Clinging"; the desirable trait of clinging or cleaving to God, especially in Hasidic thought.

Gehennom *or* **Gehinnom**—Hell; the netherworld. Named for the Valley of the Son of Hinnom in Jerusalem.

Gemarah—Interpretations and discussions of the Mishnah which, together with the Mishnah, comprise the Talmud.

gerush (*pl.* **gerushin**)—"Separation"; in exoteric usage the term refers to divorce, but in cases of possession it means an exorcism.

gilgul—"Rollover"; a reincarnation of a soul.

Great Adam *see* Adam Kadmon.

halakah—A decision on a matter of Jewish law; the legal discussions that appear in the Talmud; the legal side of Judaism.

Hasidim, Hasidism—an eighteenth-century spiritualist movement founded by the Ba'al Shem Tov focusing on the mystical power of prayer and happiness to bring one close to God.

Haskalah—"Enlightenment"; a Jewish rationalist and literary movement which took place in Europe during the eighteenth and nineteenth centuries.

Hekhalot—"Chambers"; a literature of early medieval Jewish mysticism concerning the chambers of God's palace or chariot and the methods through which the mystic can ascend through these to reach the throne of God. Also called *Merkabah mysticism*.

herem—Excommunication; a particularly vehement version of an excommunication appears in the volume *Kol Bo*.

historiolae—Mythological narratives that concern acts of power performed by a victorious deity and are themselves empowering spells or incantations.

Kabbalah—the central Jewish mystical tradition of the medieval and modern periods.

karet—"Cutting off"; removal from one's people or from one's proper life. Karet is the punishment for many sexual sins and other transgressions.

Karo, Rabbi Joseph (*First name also spelled* Yosef; *d*. 1575)—A legal scholar and mystic who lived much of his life in Safed and was involved in the earliest known exorcism there. Karo is also famous for his maggid.

kavvanah (*pl.* kavvanot)—Intense mystical intention or concentration in prayer or performance of the Commandments.

kelippah (*pl.* kelippot)—"husks"; a mystical term from Lurianic Kabbalah denoting shards of the primordial vessels destroyed in the cataclysmic cosmogony. These shards hold back the holy sparks in the world and are therefore evil.

kohen—"Priest"; a descendant of the family of Aaron the High Priest who is commanded to observe an extra level of holiness.

kosher—"Prepared"; made ready for use in accordance with Jewish law.

Luria, R. Isaac (*Also known as* ha-AR"I, "The Lion"; *d*. 1572)—the most famous kabbalist of late-sixteenth-century Safed; created a novel system of Kabbalah focused on a complex cosmogony and theory of souls.

Lurianic—Pertaining to the person or the mystical teachings of Rabbi Isaac Luria.

maggid—A mentor-angel most often granted to great kabbalists.

malbush—"Clothing," especially the garment composed of one's good deeds worn in the next world.

maskil—"Enlightened one"; a practitioner of Haskalah.

Merkabah *see* Hekhalot.

Metatron—An extremely exalted angel mentioned in the Talmud and mystical texts.

Metatron is also identified with Enoch in some traditions.

mezuzah—A small parchment scroll containing certain biblical passages which is attached to the doorpost of Jewish homes in accordance with a biblical commandment.

mhr"r—Acronym for *morenu ha-rav rav*, "our teacher, rabbi [so-and-so]," which is used as a mark of respect in front of the name of a great sage.

Midrash—Homiletic biblical interpretations and legends from the Talmudic period and early Middle Ages.

Minhah—Afternoon prayers.

Mishnah (*pl.* mishnayot)—"Teachings"; the central text of the Jewish oral law, redacted ca. 200 C.E., which, together with the Gemarah, comprises the Talmud.

mitnagged (*pl.* mitnaggedim)—"Opponents"; the Lithuanian-led party of anti-Hasidic talmudists.

mitzvah (*pl.* mitzvot)—A commandment of Jewish law; a good deed.

nabi *or* navi—Prophet.

Nefesh—A soul.

Neshamah—Another term for a soul.

niddui—A level of excommunication somewhat less serious than a herem.

nitzotz (*pl.* nitzotzot)—Sparks of divine light, some of which, according to the Lurianic Kabbalah, were caught in the kelippot during the cataclysm of creation and must be returned to God by human action.

ob"m—Acronym meaning "of blessed memory" which is used before the names of pious people or teachers as a mark of respect.

partzuf (*pl.* partzufim)—"Countenances"; constellations of sephirot with internal hierarchies.

Palestinian Talmud (PT)—Compendium of the Jewish oral law, less authoritative than the version edited in Babylonia but dating from roughly the same period.

R.—Abbreviation for "rabbi."

Raya Mehemna—"Faithful shepherd"; a work in the Zoharic corpus.

reshimu—According to the Lurianic Kabbalah, a trace impression left in the unformed divine matter.

ru'ah tum'ah—An impure spirit.

ru'ah ra'ah—"Evil spirit."

ru'ah ha-kodesh—"Holy spirit"; often identified with a certain level of prophecy.

ru'ah—A spirit of any type.

Sabbatean—Pertaining to the messianic movement of Shabbatai Zvi (1626–1676), a mystic from Smyrna who is considered to be one of the most important messianic pretenders of Judaism.

Safed—A city in Galilee that became a center for Jewish mystics in the sixteenth century.

Samael—Satan; associated with the left side and with God's attribute of strict justice.

Sar ha-Torah—"Prince of the Torah"; an angel or spirit mentioned in early Jewish magical texts, whose realm is the study of the Torah.

sephirah (*pl.* sephirot)—The ten emanated divine powers or potentialities of divine efflux, central to most kabbalistic cosmogonies: Keter (crown), Hokhmah (wisdom), Binah (insight), Gedulah (greatness), Gevurah (might), Tifereth (beauty), Netzah (eternity), Hod (splendor), Yesod (foundation), and Malkhut (kingship).

She'ol—Hell; the netherworld.

Shekhinah—The female presence of God, associated with the Sefirah Malkhut.

Shem ha-Meforash—"The explicit name"; the secret name of God, which holds great magical powers.

sitra ahra—"The other side"; the evil side.

ta'amei ha-mitzvot—"The flavor of the Commandments"; writings discussing the reasons for the Commandments. Practitioners of the genre include Maimonides and Nahmanides.

Talmud—"Teaching"; the central text of the Jewish oral law. *See* Babylonian Talmud *and* Palestinian Talmud.

tanna (*pl.* tannaim)—Rabbis who composed the Mishnah and are considered very holy sages.

Tikkune Zohar—A relatively late layer of the Zoharic corpus.

tvb"b—Acronym for the phrase *tibaneh ve-tikonen bimherah be-yamenu*, "may it be rebuilt and established speedily in our days," a phrase often said by Jews about Jerusalem, Hebron, and other holy cities destroyed by the Romans.

Tzaddik—A righteous man, especially in later times a leader (Rebbe) of a Hasidic sect.

tzimtzum—"Contraction"; the first movement of God's presence in the process of creation, according to the Lurianic cosmogeny: God begins creation by withdrawing into himself.

Vital, R. Hayyim (*d.* 1620)—Main student of the AR"I; author of works on Lurianic Kabbalah and an autobiographical book of visions.

xenoglossia—The production of a voice that is not his or her own from the throat of a possessed person.

Yetzirah—One of the four worlds of existence described by the kabbalists; also, the name of a very early book of Jewish mysticism.

yihud (*pl.* yihudim)—A statement or ritual made before performing a commandment that declares the unity of God but is also designed to conduct mystical power and knowledge to the performer.

z"l—Acronym for the phrase *zikhrono/ah le-vrakhah*, "may his/her memory be a blessing," which is appended to the name of a deceased person.

zivvug—"Match"; a corresponding soul in the Luranic system.

zlh"h—Acronym for the phrase *zikhro lehaye ha-olam ha-ba*, "may his memory live in the World to Come."

Zohar—a mystical commentary on the first five books of the Bible; the central text of Kabbalah, the Jewish mystical tradition, which appeared in Spain in the late thirteenth century.

zt"l—Acronym for the phrase *zekher tzaddik le-vrakhah*, "may the memory of [this] righteous person be a blessing," which is used like z"l, but for a person who had been especially pious.

CONTRIBUTORS

TAMAR ALEXANDER (Ph.D., University of California-Los Angeles) is a professor of Hebrew literature at Ben-Gurion University of the Negev. She has published numerous books and articles on Jewish folklore and gender issues, including *The Beloved Friend-and-a-Half: Studies in Sephardic Folk Literature* (Jerusalem: Magnes Press, 1999).

YORAM BILU is a professor of psychology and anthropology at the Hebrew University of Jerusalem. He has written extensively about spirit possessions in the Jewish context as well as other cultural and psychological aspects of Jewish spiritual beliefs.

J. H. CHAJES (Ph.D., Yale University) is a lecturer in Jewish history at the University of Haifa. His forthcoming book and several articles deal with Jewish spirit possession and Jewish identity in the early modern world.

JOSEPH DAN (Ph.D., Hebrew University of Jerusalem) is Gershom Scholem Professor of Kabbalah at the Hebrew University of Jerusalem, winner of the Israel Prize, and author of numerous books and essays on Jewish mysticism, thought, and literature.

MORRIS M. FAIERSTEIN (Ph.D., Temple University) is an independent scholar in Rockville, Maryland. He has written numerous books and articles dealing with Jewish thought and spirituality and edited *Jewish Mystical Autobiographies* (Mahwah, N.J.: Paulist Press, 1999).

LAWRENCE FINE (Ph.D., Brandeis University) is Irene Kaplan Leiwant Professor of Jewish Studies at Mount Holyoke College. He edited *Safed Spirituality* (Mahwah, N.J.: Paulist Press, 1984) and has written extensively on the Safed kabbalists and other topics.

MATT GOLDISH (Ph.D., Hebrew University) is Samuel M. and Esther Melton Associate Professor of Jewish History at Ohio State University. He has written and edited studies on Christian Hebraism, *conversos*, and Jewish messianism.

MENACHEM KALLUS (Ph.D., Hebrew University) recently finished a dissertation concerning the conception of the soul in Lurianic Kabbalah.

HARRIS LENOWITZ (Ph.D., University of Texas, Austin) is a professor of Hebrew at the University of Utah. In addition to numerous studies in linguistics and poetry, he is the author of *The Jewish Messiahs: From the Galilee to Crown Heights* (New York: Oxford University Press, 1998).

ZVI MARK (Ph.D., Hebrew University) recently finished a dissertation on madness and mystical experience in the thought of Rabbi Nahman of Bratzlav and has published articles on this topic.

JONATHAN SEIDEL (Ph.D., University of California, Berkeley), formerly an adjunct professor of Jewish studies at the University of Arizona, now practices as a spiritual leader in Oregon.

RONI WEINSTEIN (Ph. D., Hebrew University) is a postdoctoral fellow at Harvard University. His dissertation and several articles deal with Jewish customs and family life in early modern Italy.

INDEX

Abba title, 76, 88n. 12
Abel (biblical personage), 160, 168–69, 171, 176n. 13, 322
Aberlin, Rachel, 429
ablutions, 169
Abraham bar Hiyya, R., 38
Abraham ben Amram, R., 275
Abraham ben David of Posquieres, R., 117
Abraham ben Isaac, R., 117
Abraham ibn Ezra, R., 31, 38n. 5
"Absolute Divinity," 172
Abu-'Isa (Persian messiah), 200
Abulafia, R. Abraham, 267–68
Abulafia, R. Jacob (Yakov), 424, 430, 431; humbling of, 211n. 19; as R. Hayyim Vital's nemesis, 189, 204, 205, 207; on sexual misconduct, 433
Abulafia, R. Shlomo, 318
Abulafian mysticism, 110, 114, 116, 219, 220
Adam (biblical personage), 109, 110, 385; *Adam ha-Rishon*, 172; *Adam Kadmon* (Primordial), 171, 172–73, 379; sin of, 390; souls of, 159, 160, 170, 403
Adrianople, rabbis of, 275
adultery, 50, 133, 136, 152n. 60
Africa, 346, 353, 357
Afro-American religions, 47, 232
"Age of the Demoniac," 25, 99, 354
agunah status, of widows, 135, 153n. 72, 373
Aharon ibn Tifa, R., 423, 430
ahorayim ("rear-beings"), 380
Aisha Qandisha, 356
Akavya ben Mehallel, 408

Akiba (Akiva), R., 164, 165, 166, 326, 409, 410; messianism and, 203; on return of souls, 29; on *Ru'ah Tum'ah* (impure spirits), 76
Akkadian language, 80
alchemy, 207, 208
Alexander, Tamar, 10, 14, 16, 17; on exorcism in modern Israel, 305–6; interviews conducted by, 18
Alexis, Léon D', 140
aliyah (ascent), 325–26, 327, 328, 330, 331, 332
Alkabetz, R. Solomon (Shlomo), 108, 130, 187, 199; on R. Karo's maggidic possession, 223; in *Divre Yosef* text, 369, 373; journey to Palestine, 224; letter of, 231; "soul family" and, 175n. 8; speech automatism and, 102, 107; as teacher of R. Cordovero, 444
Alsheikh, R. Moshe, 125
altered consciousness, 77, 78, 101, 228, 251; culture-specific syndromes and, 68; differing views of, 239; positive spirit possessions and, 287
Amidah prayer, 392
amnesia, 228, 232, 287, 351
Amron, R. Shmuel, 430
Amsterdam, 215
Amulets and Magical Bowls (Shaked and Naveh), 93n. 46
Anav, Raphael, daughter of, 203–7, 421, 422, 426, 434; benevolent possession of, 188; as clairvoyant, 189; Messiah events and, 197–98; in R. Vital's account, 421, 427–30; as symbol of marginality, 208
Ancona, Italy, 443

467

angels/angelic beings, 43, 78, 112, 351, 415; adjuration of, 169; communicating, 80; demons and, 309; of destruction, 56, 61, 312, 375–76; as healers, 90n. 26; positive possession and, 188–89; Torah study and, 437–38. *See also specific angels*
animal forms, 350
An-ski, S., 11, 193, 305, 309, 318, 358; *dybbuk* cases influenced by, 305; hagiographic context and, 30; kabbalism and, 34; literary work's influence on reality, 336, 337; performances of play, 41; as Yiddish author, 28
anthropology, 11, 14–15, 16, 68, 77; altered states of consciousness and, 239; critique of cross-cultural universalism, 346; culture-sensitive, 348; views of possession, 149n. 42, 152n. 62
anus, penetration of, 47
Aqiba, R. *See* Akiba (Akiva), R.
Arabic language, 78, 126, 132, 370
Aramaic language, 81, 95n. 60
AR"I. *See* Luria, R. Isaac
Arikh Anpin, 171, 172, 173
Aristotelian philosophy, 33
Aruety, R. Abraham, 130
asceticism, 143
Ashkenazi, R. Eliezer, 128, 129, 441
Ashkenazi, R. Elisha, 224
Ashkenazi, R. Isaac. *See* Luria, R. Isaac
Ashkenazi, R. Joseph Shalom, 272–73, 375
Ashkenazi, R. Ya'akov, 203, 422
Ashkenazi, R. Yizhak. *See* Luria, R. Isaac
Ashkenazic Jews, 126, 315, 350; *dybbuk* possession unique to, 43; *gilgul* doctrine and, 42; hagiographic tales of, 31, 32
Ashkenazy, R. Isaac Luria. *See* Luria, R. Isaac
Ashmedai, 356
Asia, 346
aslai (possession illness), 349, 352–53, 357, 359

Assi'ah (World of Action), 162, 164, 167, 170
assimilation, 361
astrology, 272
Atika Kadisha, 411
Atzilut (Divine Emanation), 162, 171, 172, 386; "new soul" and, 164; parsimony and, 394
autistic children, as mediums, 362
autogenesis (Self-Created God), 172, 178n. 38
autosuggestion, 167
Averroism, 35
Avtalyon, 112, 121n. 31
Azikri, R. Eliezer, 226
Azulai, R. Abraham, 125, 126

Ba'al Shem Tov, 216, 258, 261–62; charisma of, 297n. 75; *devekut* and, 277; as madman, 266–69, 293n. 34; madwoman and, 262–65; as magician, 280, 284; mysticism of, 289; Shabbatai Zvi and, 281, 287–88, 301n. 108; stories about, 287; as wonder-worker, 282, 283, 284, 285
ba'ale shem (wonder-workers), 257, 258, 264, 277, 312
Babylonian Talmud (BT), 111, 385; *golem* narratives and, 40n. 21; on healing, 75; verses from, 389, 391; on volitional possession, 76; on World to Come, 393. *See also* Talmud
Bacchi, R. Samson, 251
Bacharach, R. Naftali, 128, 136, 168, 169, 226
Baghdad, 43, 47, 307, 350, 360; angels of destruction in, 61; cosmological issues in, 62; last historical *dybbuk* cases in, 44; Sabbatean possession case in, 50
Bakhtin, M. M., 309
Balaban, M., 274–75
Bar Kokhba, Simeon, 203, 210n. 11, 301n. 108
Baraqiel (angel), 82
Baruch of Arezzo, R., 221
Basri, R. David, 27, 315, 319, 320, 341
Basri, Judah, 319

Battista da Modena, 442
Bauman, Richard, 308
Being John Malkovich (film), 11
Beirut, 43
Belzer Rebbe, 64
Benayahu, Meir, 201
Benayahu ben Yehoyada, 166, 409
Benjamin ha-Cohen, R., 244, 247
Berab, R. Ya'akov, 212n. 21, 224
Berakiah of Modena, R. Aaron, 218
Bereshit Rabbah, 322
Beri'ah (Creation), 162, 170
Bérulle, Pierre de, 140
Besht, the. *See* Ba'al Shem Tov
Bet Din (Supreme Rabbinical Court), 376
Bet Yosef (R. Joseph Karo), 218, 222
Bialik, H. N., 309
Bible, Hebrew, 13, 322, 326; Ecclesiastes, 29, 311, 385, 388, 393; Exodus, 390; Genesis, 221; Job, 403; Tobit, 81–82, 92n. 43
Bilu, Yoram, 9, 16, 17, 18, 26, 73; on categorization of spirit possession, 78; on *dybbuk* as culturally dependent syndrome, 307; on modern possession cases, 306; on positive possession in Judaism, 286, 287; on possession as sexual urge, 313; on trance possession, 236n. 35; on women as primary "victims," 186
Binah (Understanding), 171, 172, 174n. 5, 388, 395
blasphemy, 141
blood, 322, 333
body/bodies, 33, 155n. 95, 248–49
Bonfil, Robert, 249
Book of Genealogy (A. Zacut), 237
Bourguignon, Erika, 68, 73, 78, 347, 349
Brazil, 15
Brown, Peter, 115
Buddhas/Buddhism, 179n. 55
Byzantine areas, 118

Cain (biblical personage), 160, 168–69, 379; root pathway and, 176n. 13, 387, 388, 396; status in Lurianic Kabbalah, 176n. 17

Cairo, Egypt, 43, 49
Cairo Genizah, 17, 25, 73, 75; on conquest of demons, 79–81; language/rhetoric of exorcism in, 81–84; magical texts in, 78–79
Calabrese, R. Hayyim. *See* Vital, R. Hayyim
Camisard movement, 239
Cardoso, R. Abraham Miguel, 215, 227, 230
Catharism, 29
Catherine (Christian saint), 249
Chajes, J. H., 99–100, 169, 186, 232, 308
Charcot, Jean-Martin, 50
charisma, 77, 117, 205, 277, 297n. 75
charity, 311, 321
children, as trance mediums, 9, 362
Christianity, 12, 13, 14, 85, 308; "Age of the Demoniac," 25, 99, 354; attitude toward death, 115; Catharist heresy, 29; Counter-Reformation, 248; demonic possession in, 354; demonology/witch-hunts and, 35–36; *dybbuk* possession and, 55; European Age of Exploration and, 231; exorcism in, 30, 34, 83, 134, 441; gender issues in possession cases, 249; hagiography in, 39n. 12; influence on Jewish culture, 18–19; Jews converted to, 35, 54, 150n. 51 (*See also conversos*); mourning patterns in, 238; mystical visions in, 219; myth of Revelation, 388; negative possessions and, 305; "superstition" and, 239, 252; Third Order (Tertiaries), 243; urban society and, 250; view of cursing, 141; view of spirit possession, 127; women as possession subjects, 16; *zar* possession among Christians, 357. *See also* New Testament; Roman Catholic Church
Chrysostom, John (Christian saint), 85
circumcision, 190
civility, 249
clairvoyance, 138, 142
cloud, pillar of, 200, 201–2, 207
Cohen, Shaye, 85, 94n. 56

commandments, religious, 241, 244, 323, 439; flouting of, 54–55; interpretation of, 249; *Karet* punishment and, 160; social control and, 62; in Torah, 397; women and, 247
Commentary on the Idra Zutta, 165
community, exorcism and, 316
confession, 250
conformity, 44, 59–64, 65, 67, 307
Conforté, David, 201
consciousness, 10
Constantinople, 58, 60, 135, 217, 374
control, social, 44–64
conversos, 126, 131, 133, 151n. 56, 226
Cordoverian Kabbalah, 245
Cordovero, R. Moses, 102, 107, 118, 140, 444; circle of, 223, 224–25, 231; death of, 200, 201; maggidic possession and, 218; prophecy of, 208
cosmological issues, 62, 67–68
Counter-Reformation, 248
Crapanzano, V., 44, 45, 73
Cuencas, 190
cultural distinctiveness, 349–50, 354, 357
culture-specific syndromes, 64, 67, 68
cursing, 141, 323

Da'at, 388
Damascus, Syria, 17, 43, 307, 433; benevolent possessions in, 19; possession case in (1609), 127; R. Hayyim Vital in, 63, 199, 421, 424, 426;
Dan, Joseph, 16, 17, 26, 143–44, 308
Daniel Ben-Lulu, R., 324–25, 332, 333, 336, 344n. 33
Darkhe No'am [Ways of Pleasantness] (R. Garmison), 128
David, King (biblical personage), 13, 77, 166, 202, 222
David ben Samuel ha-Levi, R., 282
David ben Zimra, R., 178n. 31
David de la Reina, R., 318
David of Morocco, R., 434
Dead Sea Scrolls, 80
death, 242, 316, 323–24; conquest of, 198; *hevrah kadishah* (holy society)

and, 321; longing for, 146n. 13; mourning rituals and, 237, 238; of possession victims, 313, 318; quality of, 60, 125; relation of dead to living, 115; spirits of the dead, 42, 76, 110; wandering souls and, 322. *See also* necromancy
de Certeau, Michel, 130, 131, 183n. 108
Dedieu, J.-P., 141
Deleira, Tuvia, 131, 368
Delmedigo, R. Joseph, 128, 226
del Rio, Martin, 441
demonology, 35–36, 80
demons, 31, 61, 377; adjuration of, 169; in *aslai* (possession illness), 352; gender of, 83; in Greco-Roman accounts, 75, 238–39; madness and, 257; male sexuality and, 46; of Muslim origin, 356; rebuking and threatening of, 79–81; as sources of information, 78; used for divination, 80
devekut ("clinging" to God), 216, 258, 277, 282, 286; implications of, 283–85; madness and, 266–70; in *Me'oreot Zvi*, 278–80
deviance, rectification of, 55–59, 65, 69, 313
deVidas, R. Elijah, 226
devil, the. *See* Satan (the devil)
"devils," 13
diachronic cosmology, 355
Diaspora, Jewish, 129, 307
Dimona (Israel), exorcist in, 315; history of Dimona, 38n. 1; influence of language on events, 37; possession case in, 10, 11, 16, 27, 128
Dina (wife of R. Daniel), 330–32, 335–36
disease, 15, 42, 66, 83, 84
dissociation, 68, 347
divination, 74, 77, 351; in Greco-Roman tradition, 78; by means of angels, 78; by means of demons, 80
Divine Feminine and Masculine levels, 171
divine names, 81, 163, 258, 399n. 11; angelic revelations and, 118; *partzufim* ("countenances") and, 110

divine tree, 29
divorce, exorcism as, 81
Divre Yosef [Words of Joseph] (R. Sambari), 128, 190, 367–79
Dodds, E. R., 238
Dolby-Stahl, Sandra, 339
Dönmeh sect, 274–75
Doresh el ha-Metim, 76, 88n. 14
Dov Baer of Linits, R., 261, 264, 278, 280; book's purpose explained, 259–60; manuscript modified by R. Israel Jaffe, 288; on Sabbateanism, 276–77
Draa Valley (Morocco), 118, 119
dreams, visionary, 118, 190, 206, 230; earlier incarnations and, 169; gender and, 191; from Satan, 267; soul roots and, 159
Dreznitz, R. Shlomiel, 226, 235n. 28
Drishot be-Inyane ha-Malakhim [Inquiries Concerning Angels] (R. Cordovero), 140
dualism, 35, 36, 172, 284, 398
Duran, R. Benjamin, 275
Dybbuk, The: Between Two Worlds (play), 11, 41, 318; in Hebrew translation, 309; influence on reality, 305, 336; performances of, 336, 343n. 9; success of, 193, 358
dybbuk/dybbukkim (malevolent spirits), 13, 198, 240, 350–52; age of victims, 47–48; as articulation of sexual urges, 45–54; cases of possession, 41, 43–44; communal conformity and, 59–64; cultural distinctiveness and, 349; as culture-specific syndrome, 64–69; derided by secular modernists, 358; *devekut* ("clinging" to God) and, 269, 271, 274, 278–80, 286; as disease, 42, 66; exorcism of, 55–59; hagiography and, 30–32, 36; *ibbur* (impregnation) and, 310–12; Jewish cultural idiom and, 354–55; Jews in Islamic countries and, 35; as linguistic phenomenon, 34–35; madness as effect of, 258; modern return of, 319–42, 361–62; narrative function of, 317–19; nonsexual aberrant impulses and, 54–55; reincarnation and, 28–29, 30; research approaches to, 307–8; social control and, 44–45; soul sparks and, 161; as term in general use, 193n. 1; as tradition in Jewish culture, 27–28; transformation of *dybbuk* narrative, 308–10

Eco, Umberto, 11
ecstasies, 251, 280
ego-alien agents, 45, 55
Egypt, 119, 307, 353, 376, 431; R. Isaac Luria in, 167; Exodus of Jews from, 378; Souls of the Seventy in, 170
Ein Dor, female ritual specialist at, 76
Elazar ben Durdaya, R., 391
Elazar ben Shamu'a, R., 165
Eleazar of Worms, R., 32
Elijah (biblical prophet), 117, 118, 326; appearance in dream vision, 428; messiahship candidacy and, 435n. 6; numerical arcanum and, 410; women and, 188, 189, 205
Elisha (biblical prophet), 121n. 21, 222
Emden, R. Jacob, 274, 296n. 69
Emek ha-Melekh [Valley of the King] (R. Naphtali Bacharach), 128, 168, 169, 226, 333; on Eve's primordial sin, 46; widow of Safed case in, 136
emotions, divine inspiration and, 104
En-Sof, 173
epileptic seizures, 50, 257, 275, 434; prophecy and, 276, 277, 279; Saint Teresa of Avila and, 152n. 64
Esau (biblical personage), 221
eschatology, 14, 80, 119, 159, 394; messianic, 396; undecided issues in, 170
Esther (biblical queen), 131, 133
Ethiopia, 15, 353, 354, 355, 360
Ethiopian Jews, 349, 359
ethnography, 10
Etz Hayyim, 168, 172, 391, 400n. 22
Europe, 35–36, 43, 186, 346; cultural distance between Jews and non-Jews, 357; Lurianism in, 225
Eve (biblical personage), 46
Evgeni (father of Menuhah), 328–30, 331

evil, 284, 387; evil eye, 77, 353; evil spirits, 12, 76; overcoming of, 36
excommunication, 312, 316, 370, 434
Exemplary Literature, 250
exorcism, 9, 12, 240, 258, 443; anthropological view of, 15; in *aslai* (possession illness) cases, 352–53; in Christianity, 13, 30, 34, 82, 134, 239–40, 246, 441; in *Divre Yosef* text, 367–75; in early Judaism, 75–77; in Falcon case (1571), 132–33; in Islam, 144; Jewish paraphernalia used in, 354, 357; language and rhetoric of, 81–84; male authority and, 250; in modern Israel, 27, 309–10, 319; normative communal values and, 317–19; performed by Jesus, 42; performed by women, 330–32; in private setting, 320, 353; psychosis and, 65; as public ritual, 351; rabbi as physician, 84–85; as rectification of deviance, 55–59; as sacred theater, 312–17; setting for, in late antiquity, 73–75; speech and, 130; taming of deviance and, 45; as theatrical dialogue, 248–49; as widespread practice, 25; with *yihudim*, 191; *zar* possession and, 355
Exorcist, The (film), 11
Ezekiel (biblical prophet), 78, 79

fabulate (folk literature genre), 316
Faierstein, Morris, 16, 17, 100
fainting, 241, 279
Falcon, R. Elijah, 128, 134, 187, 199, 369, 373
Falcon possession case (1571), 128–35, 140, 187, 240–41, 367–73
fall, the, 170
false Messiah, 50, 314, 355
fasting, 76, 104, 118, 169, 275
fate, 335
father image, 52–53, 334
female-in-female possession, 47, 52, 319, 320–27, 342
female-in-male possession, 47, 309–10, 351
female victims, 46, 48, 52, 83, 313;
culturally specific possession and, 349; exorcism and, 59; Menuhah (1994), 319, 320–27. *See also* Falcon possession case (1571)
feminine divine power, 29, 30
Feminine Waters, raising of, 171, 172
Ferrara, Italy, 248, 307, 441
Fine, Lawrence, 99, 218
fire, pillar of, 190, 201, 202, 211n. 15, 219, 417–18
First Temple, 60, 355
Flynn, M., 141
folklore, 11, 15–16, 33, 257, 307; beliefs about blood, 322; *dybbuk* narrative in, 308, 309; genres of, 337–38; magic and, 75; non-Jewish, 31–32
foreign languages, sudden ability to speak in, 312. *See also* xenoglossia
Foucault's Pendulum (Eco), 11
France, 29, 117, 239
Francisa Sarah, 189–90
Frank, Ewa, 200
Frank, Ya'akov, 200, 275
Frankists, 274
Freud, Sigmund, 52
Freudianism, 65

Gabbai, R. Shlomo, 136
Gabriel (angel), 81, 82, 84
Galanté, R. Jedidiah, 226
Galanté, R. Moses, 212n. 21, 432
Galya Raza, 29, 118
Gano, Judah, 191
Garden of Eden, 125, 146n. 9, 173, 201, 376; fragrance of, 221–22; merit of place in, 422, 427; "neighbor's portion" moral problem and, 385, 386, 389, 395, 397, 404, 405; possessing spirit barred from, 442; as station of reward, 406n. 4
Garmison, R. Samuel, 128
Gaster collection, 80
Gavison, R. David, 432
Geary, Patrick, 115
Gedalia ibn Yahia, R., 30, 129, 148n. 30, 187, 243, 442
Gehinnom/Gehenna (netherworld), 376, 377, 385, 386, 389; spirits' inability to

enter, 134, 139; transgressions and, 396. *See also* Hell
gematriot (numerological interpretations), 274
gender, 228, 249–50, 310, 336–37, 353. *See also* men; sexuality; women
Gentiles, 50, 51, 54; Animus of, 415; killing of Jews by, 60; as possessing spirits, 314, 354; rabbinical exorcisms and, 57, 63; women, fornicating with, 139, 377, 432
Geonic period, 84
German Pietists, 31, 36
Germany, 43, 54, 143
Gershon of Kuty, R., 262, 263, 266–67, 269, 284
gerushin ("peregrinations"), 102, 106, 108
ghosts, 75, 94n. 53, 126, 132
gilgul (reincarnated soul), 12, 34, 168, 186, 350; *golem* narratives and, 36; *ibbur* (impregnation) and, 351; *tzaddikkim* and, 404. *See also* transmigration of souls
Girard, René, 230
gnosis, revelatory, 117–19
Gnosticism, 92n. 38
God, names of, 110
Goldish, Matt, 216
golem narratives, 36–37
graves, 124–25, 144; "beating of," 369; veneration of, 115–16, 159
Great Event in Safed, The (R. Falcon), 129
Greco-Roman antiquity, 9, 52, 73, 74, 79, 85
Greece (Ottoman period), 118, 227
Greek language, ancient, 81

ha-Ramaz. *See* Zacuto, R. Moses
ha-Ramhal (R. Moses Hayyim Luzzatto), 215–16, 251
Habillio, R. David, 218
hagiographic literature, 28, 36, 127, 135; R. Isaac Luria and his circle, 112–13, 186, 200, 207; *dybbuk* narratives in, 30–32; efflorescence of (mid-seventeenth cent.), 128–29;

messianism in, 225; in modern Israel, 333; of successful exorcists, 315
Hagiz, R. Jacob, 279
Haiti, 15
Hakham Zvi, 274
hakhamim, 199
halakhah (Jewish law), 241
Hallewa, R. Judah, 127, 128, 187
Hamadsha, 357
Hamograbi, David, 204
Hamon, R. Ovadiah, 118
Harshish, R., 341
Haside Ashkenaz (German Pietists), 31, 36
Hasidism, 28, 210n. 11, 350; battle with secular modernism, 358; Besh"tian, 395; *devekut* concept in, 216, 283–85; *dybbuk* possession and, 43, 53–54, 284–85; exorcism and, 63–64; founder of, 216, 258, 270, 288; madness and, 258, 259, 262, 263; magic and mysticism in, 69n. 11, 288–89; prophecy and, 287; rabbinical authority in, 390; *tzaddik* concept in, 37. *See also* Judaism
Hayah, 162, 164
Hayyim ha-Kohen, R., 202
Hazut Kashah [Terrible Vision] (R. Alsheikh), 125
healing practices, 73, 75, 81, 240; holy names, 247–48; popular culture and, 25
Heaven, visions of, 190
Heavenly Court, 62
Hebrew Bible. *See* Bible, Hebrew
Hebrew language, 31, 81, 247; *dybbuk* possession and, 309; *golem* narratives in, 36; hagiographic tales in, 32; magical books in, 95n. 60; spoken by spirits, 132
hedonism, 129
Hefetz, Eliyahu, 432
Hekhalot genre, 78, 79, 87n. 9, 286
Hell, 43, 62, 351. *See also* Gehinnom/Gehenna
herem (excommunication), 370
heresy, 134, 141, 239, 275, 368
heroes, 30–31, 32, 36, 164

Hesed (Grace), 171
heterosexuality, 46, 51
Hezekiah, King, 164, 180n. 71
hiner bet (coma), 259, 260, 261, 277, 300n. 92
Hirsch of Zidechov, R. Zvi, 282–83
historical situatedness, 350, 358
history, 11, 15, 16
History of the ARI, Book of the, 201
Hokhmah (Wisdom), 171, 172, 174n. 5, 388, 395
Holocaust, 44, 60
holy names, 241, 247–48, 357
Holy Spirit *(ru'ah ha-kodesh)*, 106, 111, 117, 118, 167; melancholia and, 104; past lives and, 168
homosexuality, 46–47, 50, 51, 52, 433
Horowitz, R. Isaiah, 226
hozeret be-teshuvah (newly observant Jew), 332
humanism, 25
Humiliana dei Cerchi, 249–50
Hungary, 43
hypnosis, 230
hysteria, 15, 50, 52, 65, 230, 257

ibbur (impregnation), 10, 17, 34, 198, 308, 350; R. Cordovero on, 140; by *dybbuk* (malevolent spirit), 310–12; as expansion of *gilgul* concept, 351; *golem* narratives and, 36; good and bad, 309, 317–18; in literary expression, 78; in Lurianic Kabbalah, 160–62; Luria's failed exorcism and, 199; metempsychosis and, 225; as positive form of possession, 186; reincarnation and, 159; as sexual transgression, 46; *tzaddikkim* and, 404; as undetected righteous soul, 12
Iberian Jews. *See* Sephardic (Iberian) Jews
Ibn Musa, 370
Ibn Susan, Avraham, 308, 318
Idel, Moshe, 117–18, 188, 245, 272, 283
idolatry, 60
Iggulim (Circle of Light), 172
Ignatius of Loyola, 248
"ill-fated righteous" problem, 60
illumination *(hasagah)*, 111

Illuminism, 141
incest, 50, 53
individuals, social conformity and, 65
Inquisition, 141, 240
Iraq, 85
Isaac (biblical personage), 221
Isaac the Blind, R., 117, 175n. 9
Islam, 12, 13, 14, 35, 85; Berbers (Marabouts) of Morocco, 118–19; emigration of Jews from Muslim countries, 44; gender of demonic possession in, 47; Jews converted to, 215, 227; *jinn (jnun)* possession in, 144, 352, 353, 356, 357; magic in, 157n. 122; Muslim exorcists, 139–40, 144; origins of *maggidim* and, 127, 231; Ottomans, 25; wonder-workers of, 155n. 100. *See also* Sufism
Israel, premodern, 35, 219, 225, 241; in ancient times, 13; nineteenth-century, 308, 318. *See also* Palestine
Israel, State of, 10, 11, 305; *aslai* (possession illness) in, 359, 361; emigration of Jews from Muslim countries to, 44; exorcists in, 86n. 5; Menuhah's *dybbuk* possession in, 319–42; Moroccan Jews in, 352; spiritual revival in, 362; *zar* possession in, 359, 361. *See also* Dimona (Israel), possession case in
Israel ben Eliezer, R. *See* Ba'al Shem Tov
Israelites, 60
Italy, 25, 35, 216; Christian urban society in, 238; Jewish ghetto in, 248; Jewish tradition of possession in, 242–51; kabbalists in, 99, 215; possession cases in, 127, 238–42, 250; Sabbateans in, 227; significance of Jewish community in, 253–54n. 18

Jacob (biblical personage), 221
Jacob ha-Nazir, R., 117
Jaffa, 44, 350
Jaffe, R. Israel, 278, 280, 282, 283; method as editor of *Shivhe ha-Besht*, 264–65; on Shabbatai Zvi as "holy spark," 287–88
Jerusalem, 43, 44, 48, 220, 307, 360;

captured by Romans (70 C.E.), 25; last *dybbuk* cases reported in, 350; modern possession case in, 319, 320; Sephardic women of, 338
Jesus, 42, 80, 82, 212n. 21; incarnated in men, 140; as messiah, 200, 203, 210n. 11; rebuking of demons, 81
Jewish Enlightenment (secular modernism), 260, 278, 358
jinn (jnun) possession, 144, 352, 353, 356, 357
Joel Ba'al Shem of Zamosc, R., 169
Johnston, Sarah, 9
Jonah, R. Moses, 181n. 85
Jordan, Rosan, 338
Jose of Zaitor, Abba, 87n. 11
Joseph (biblical personage), 202
Joseph, R. Jacob, 266
Joseph ben Tzur, 275
Joseph della Reina, R., 187, 199, 224, 279
Joseph ibn Tabul, R., 119
Josephus Flavius, 9, 200
Joseph of Yokrat, R., 107
Joshua al-Boom, R., 188, 195n. 24, 204
Joshua ben Nun, R., 187, 199
Judah Hasid, R., 36
Judah ibn Tibbon, 38n. 5
Judah the Pious, R., 31
Judaism, 12, 13, 14, 19, 61, 134; commandments regulating Jewish life, 54–55; contrast with Christianity, 39n. 12, 140; East-West contrast in, 44; exorcism in, 75–79, 240, 308; messiah accounts in, 202; positive possession trances in, 286, 287; reform of, 256n. 38; reincarnation and, 28, 29, 30; transformations of, 32, 37; women and possession in, 16, 193; women's legal standing in, 207. *See also* Hasidism
Judeo-Arabic language, 78, 95n. 60
Judgment, Day of, 388
Julius III, Pope, 150n. 51

Kabbalah, 34, 118, 251, 286; apocalyptic, 225; Ba'al Shem Tov and, 264; books of, 29; exorcism and, 354; popularization of, 35, 37; ritualistic patterns and, 238; social/historical change and, 242, 245, 249, 256n. 38; spread of magical practices and, 252; theosophical, 110; transmigration of souls in, 42; view of women in, 208. *See also* Lurianic Kabbalah; Zohar
kabbalism/kabbalists, 9–10, 134, 186; exegesis of commandments, 244; exorcism and, 245, 315; fusion of traditions, 235n. 28; *golem* narratives and, 36–37; on good and evil, 279; hagiographic biographies and, 31; legitimization of possession and, 251; maggidic possession among, 231; as magicians, 188; metempsychosis doctrines, 311; in modern Israel, 324; ontology of, 25; possessions among, 218; reincarnation and, 29; revelatory gnosis and, 117–19; in Safed, 30, 33–34; Saturn (planet) and, 272; view of sexual transgressions, 46
Kalcik, Susan, 338
Kallus, Menachem, 16, 17, 100
Kalonymids, 31
Kapferer, Bruce, 73, 86n. 1
Karaites, 78, 84
Karet (punishment), 160, 177n. 24, 182n. 92, 404
Karo, R. Joseph, 99, 199, 423; as exorcist, 187, 315; longing for martyrdom, 146n. 13; maggidic revelation of, 102, 103, 116, 195n. 22, 222–25, 226, 232, 286; *mishnayot* recitations and, 108, 116; Shekhinah and, 108; Taitatzak circle and, 217–18; transition rites and, 105
Karo, R. Yitzhak, 430
kavvanah/kavvanot (mystical intentions), 163, 165, 375, 379–81, 395; *Reshimu* and, 162, 178n. 38; Sabbateans and, 169; of Silent Prayer, 161
kelippah/kelippot (evil husks), 170, 171, 172, 278, 386; R. Isaac Luria on, 380; prophecy through, 265–66; as serpent, 385; soul sparks and, 164
Ker'iat Shema, 410
Keter (Crown), 162, 173
Kholef, Natan, 432

Kholeif, Rafael and Mikhael, 432
Kirkisani (Karaite), 78
Kiyum Mitzvot (religious commandments), 241
Kohenim (priestly caste), 139, 140, 377–78
Kol Bo, 370, 434
Kook, R. Abraham Isaac, 315
Korets (Koretz-Ostrog), shtetl of, 61, 266, 267, 307
kosher, 369–70, 379, 381
Kotansky, Roy, 81, 85
Kotses, R. Ze'ev, 281
Koznitz shtetl, 54, 60
Krohn, A., 65–66

Ladino language, 95n. 60
Lahmi, R. Avraham, 369
Lambek, Michael, 348
Langness, L. L., 66
language, 37, 117
Lebanon, 205
Leib, R. Judah ("the Rebuker"), 268–69
Leib ben Oyzer, R., 276
Lenowitz, Harris, 16, 17, 100, 215
Lewis, I. M., 73, 77, 347, 355, 357
Liebes, Y., 287
Likkute ha-Shas, 391, 397
Likkute Torah, 172
limbo (transition), 43, 106, 351
limbs (limb-roots), 171, 172
literacy, 232
literature, possession in, 15–16
Lithuania, 43, 44, 54, 350
Loudun, nuns at, 15
love stories, 318
Lover of Lies (Lucian), 74
Lucian, 74
Luria, R. Isaac, 30, 63, 165, 166–68, 170, 220, 307, 410, 423; accounts of practice of, 112–13; on Adam Kadmon, 172–73; alleged to be messiah, 315; Anav's daughter possession case and, 206–7; beholding the dead, 124, 126; circle of, 159; death of, 386, 387, 388, 398; exorcism and, 191, 199; fragrance of Garden of Eden and, 222; hagiographic literature about, 186, 200, 226; influence of, 99; legend of, 19, 188; *maggid* of, 218; messianic soul of, 225; past lives of, 168; possession cases of, 136–44; qualifying rites and, 103–4; relationship to R. Hayyim Vital, 200, 201; revelations about past lives, 168; *Sefer ha-Meshiv* and, 118; self-confidence of, 167; soul root of, 165; widow of Safed and, 375–79; *yihudim* and, 106, 108–9, 111, 116
Lurianic Kabbalah, 29, 43, 160, 169, 215; dualism of, 284; possession and soul impregnation in, 160–62; R. Hayyim Vital's psychical experience, 407–13; on self-rectification of incomplete *tzaddik*, 403–6; soul levels in, 162–63; text concerning moral problem, 385–401; undecided issues in, 169–73; *yihudim* practice and, 167. *See also* Kabbalah; kabbalism/kabbalists
Lurianic school, 17, 34
Lutheranism, 141, 143, 239
Luzzatto, R. Moses Hayyim (ha-Ramhal), 215–16, 251

Ma'ase ha-Shem [Acts of the Lord] (R. Eliezer Ashkenazi), 128, 441
Ma'ase Tzaddikim (Avraham ibn Susan), 308
Ma'aseh Buch (Story Book), 31, 36, 51, 128
Ma'aseh ha-Ru'ah, 38n. 4
ma'asim ("makings"), 395
madness, 246, 257–59, 285–87, 309, 335; sainthood and, 266–70; of Shabbatai Zvi and his prophets, 270–76; in *Shivhe ha-Besht*, 259–62; tales of revelation, 262–66
maggid/maggidim (mentor-angels), 81, 99, 102, 105, 215; decline in accounts of, 305; as divine messengers, 195n. 22; erotic metaphor of penetration and, 251; historical prevalence of, 217–19; instructions of, 103; Torah study and, 438; women possessed by, 188, 190

Maggid Mesharim, 224
magic, 36, 74, 78, 118, 188; antagonism toward, 257; contrasted with Kabbalah, 207, 208; executed persons and, 243, 443; exorcism and, 309–10; growth of, 251–52; Hasidic mysticism and, 283, 285; Hellenistic tradition of, 79; mirror-magic, 204; Nathan of Gaza's spirit possession and, 221; Sabbateans as magicians, 281; synthesis with mysticism, 298n. 76; women and, 333
mahalat ru'ah ra'ah (evil spirit illness), 356
Maharal of Prague, 37
Ma'hlat Bat Agrat, 356
Maimonides, R., 35, 153n. 72, 165, 180n. 63
Makhpelah, Cave of, 125, 146nn. 8–9
Malakh, Hayyim, 200
male-in-female possession, 367–73, 375–79
male-in-male possession, 351, 373–75
male victims, 46, 48, 51–52; exorcism and, 59; she-demons, 309–10; Young Man in Safed, 135–36, 373–75
Malkhut (feminine aspect of divinity), 107, 111, 121n. 17, 395
Manot ha-Levi (R. Solomon Alkabetz), 444
Ma'or va-Shemesh, 287
Mark, Zvi, 16, 216
masculine gaze, 243
Mashan, R. Judah, 190, 417
maskilim (adherents of Jewish Enlightenment), 260, 278, 358
masturbation, 249
materialism, 129
medicine, 15, 80, 82
mediumship, 16, 74, 101, 331; of autistic children, 362; in early Judaism, 77–79; of madpeople, 262, 285; of women, 189, 209n. 1
Me'ir ha-Rofe, R., 221
Me'ir ibn Gabbai, R., 385, 395
melancholy, 238
memorate (folk literature genre), 316, 339
men, 15, 46, 64
Menahem Azariah of Fano, R., 176n. 16, 218, 226
Menashe, Nissim, 432
Menasseh ben Israel, R., 128, 131
Menghi, Gerolamo, 240
menstruation, 50, 61, 139, 333, 334
Menuhah's *dybbuk* (modern Israeli case), 319–20; exorcist's story, 330–32; as narrated event, 332–42; victim's story, 320–27; witness's story, 328–30
Me'oreot Zvi [A Story of Dreams and End of Wonders], 278–83, 288
Me'orot Natan, 168
Merkabah genre, 79
Meroz, R., 170
Meshivat Nefesh [Restoration of the Soul] (R. Zemah), 127–28
Mesopotamia, 80, 81
messianism/messiahs, 17, 100, 164; exiled secrets of the Torah and, 119; exorcism and, 80; false Messiah (Shabbatai Zvi), 50, 219; Kabbalah and, 245; "last generation" and, 396; lineage of messiah, 227; madness and, 271; maggidic possession and, 224; magical attempt to bring messiah, 187; in R. Vital's *Book of Visions*, 197–212; R. Vital as equivocal messiah, 201–3; recognition accounts of messiahs, 200; Safed kabbalists and, 226–27; Sanhedrin and, 224; Saturn (planet) and, 272–74
Metatron (angel), 78–79, 386, 395, 426
metempsychosis, 12, 18, 38n. 7, 225, 311
mezuzah, 142, 157n. 116, 255n. 30, 370; absence of, 379; kosher, 379, 381
Michael (angel), 82, 84
Middle Ages, 9, 13, 14, 16, 32
Midelfort, H.C.E., 130–31, 134, 143
Midrash, 85
midrashim, 28, 75, 76
"migrant illnesses," 361
mimesis, 230–32
Minhat Eliahu (The Gift of Elijah), 46
Minhat Ya'akov Solet, 169
Minhat Yehudah: Ha-Ru'hot Mesaprot, 177n. 25

minyan (quorum), 56, 62
Mish'an, R. Yehuda (R. Judah Mashan), 190, 417
Mishnah, 102, 108, 116, 223, 403
Mishneh Torah (R. Maimonides), 180n. 63
Mitnagedim (anti-Hasidic talmudists), 64, 260
mitzvah/mitzvot (good deeds), 311, 390, 393, 396
"Mixed Multitude," 387, 398, 399n. 5
modernization, 249
Molkho, R. Solomon, 118, 146n. 13, 200, 224
Mondshine, Y., 288
Monedas, Yakov, 432
Montaigne, Michel de, 150n. 51, 151n. 56
Montalto, Elijah, 226
Morocco, 15, 150n. 51, 359; *aslai* illness among Moroccan Jews, 349, 352–53, 356–57; kabbalistic tradition of, 9, 118–19, 318
Moses (biblical personage), 111, 165, 393
Moses of Kuty, R., 263, 264, 265, 266
Moses Saravel, R. (Sabbatean prophet), 276
mourning, 237–38
Mufassal Defterler, 126
murder, 54
Mushka (Persian messiah), 200
music, 77, 89n. 17, 223, 256n. 38
Mustarib (Arabic-speaking) Jews, 126
mysticism, 11, 14, 15

Nablus, city of, 139–40
Nahman of Kosov, R., 265–66
Nahmanides, 30
Najjara, Israel, 205, 206
"Names of Power," 85
narrators, 316–17, 339–40
Nasar, Jacob, 418
Nathan of Gaza, 18, 215, 216, 232, 279; impact of possession of, 225–27; prophetic vision of (1665), 219–20; R. Joseph Karo's *maggid* and, 222–25;

Shabbatai Zvi and, 271–72, 280, 288, 301n. 108; spirit possession of, 217, 220–22
Navarro, R. Solomon, 224
Naveh, Joseph, 79, 82
necromancy, 75, 76, 85, 110. *See also* death
nefesh (soul), 162, 164, 165, 167, 172; attributes of, 385; sparks and, 38
Nefilat Apayim prayer, 409, 410
negative (malevolent) possession, 12, 19, 99, 186–87; cultural interpretation of, 228; in Islam, 14; madness and, 263; in modern Israel, 309–10; narrative function of, 317–18; speech automatism and, 107; xenoglossia during, 130–32. *See also* spirit possession
neshamah (soul), 162, 164, 172, 395
Netivot, 307
Netzah-Hod-Yesod, 392
neutral possession, 12, 14
"New Age," 11
New Souls, 159, 164, 183n. 102
New Testament, 9, 12, 25, 55; exorcism in, 30; Gospels, 13; Jesus rebuking demons in, 81; possession in, 231. *See also* Bible, Hebrew; Christianity
niddui (lesser excommunication), 380
Nigal, Gedaliah, 89n. 19, 240, 307, 350
Nikolsburg, Moravia, 51, 59, 63, 307
Nishmat Hayyim [Soul of Life] (R. Menasseh ben Israel), 128, 149n. 46
nitzotz/nitzotzot (sparks of divine light), 34
nominalism, 170, 172
Nukba de-Ze'ir (feminine gradation), 110
Nuriel (angel), 82

Obeyesekere, G., 44
Oceania, 346
Oedipus myth, 53
Olam ha-Ba (World to Come), 80, 171–72
Old Testament. *See* Bible, Hebrew
ontology, 170
oral tales, 308, 318, 337–38, 342

Ormuz, city of, 139, 140, 155n. 94, 377
Orpheus (mythological character), 77
Ottoman Empire, 25, 126, 200, 216, 254n. 18; Byzantine areas of, 118; contact with European Christians, 231; Lurianism in, 225
Otzar Eden Ganuz (R. Jacob Abulafia), 114
Oughourlian, Jean-Michel, 230, 232

palabra offenses, 141
Palestine, 25, 42, 44, 216, 350; kabbalists in, 99; under Ottoman rule, 126, 200. *See also* Israel
Palestinian Talmud (PT), 87n. 10
Paradise, 43
Parah Adumah (Red Heifer), 85
partzufim ("countenances"), 110, 111, 172, 173, 386; commandments and, 397; as Divine Faces, 181n. 85; higher and lower, 394; of souls of Adam, 403
passivity, myth of, 66
past lives, 168–69
Patai, R., 199
Patriarchs, souls of, 170
pederasty, 51–52, 53
penetration, 45–47, 251, 313, 314
penitential acts, 104
Penzieri, R. Yedidyah, 418
Pereda, R., 393, 394, 396
Peretz, Meir, 432
Persian messiahs, 200
Perush ha-Mitzvot, 244
Petaiah, R. Judah, 177
phenomenology, 44, 285, 289
Philo Judeus, 9
physicians, exorcists as, 15, 246
pietism, 143, 158n. 123
Pines, S., 217, 231
Pinhas ben Ya'ir, R., 311
Pinheiro, R. Moses, 219, 220
Pirke de-Rabbi Eliezer, 76
Piso, R. Jacob, soul of, 189, 204, 208, 421, 422; as heavenly messenger, 188; R. Hayyim Vital's self-doubt and, 207; speech automatism and, 203

Platonic philosophy, 29
pneumatic images, 118, 162, 165, 167
poetry, 78
Poland, 42, 43, 129; Peelts, 63; Stolovitsch possession case, 48, 49, 60
popular culture, 11, 15
Portugal/Portuguese Jews, 60, 126, 215
positive (benign) possession, 12, 48, 101–2, 215, 305; convulsions in, 300n. 101; cultural interpretation of, 230; madness and, 263; Nathan of Gaza and, 219; practice of, 106–17; prophecy and, 222; qualifying rites, 103–4; in R. Vital's *Book of Visions*, 188–90; revelatory gnosis, 117–19; rites of preparation and transition, 105–6; Sabbateanism and, 19; willfully sought after, 78. *See also* spirit possession
prayer, 132, 163, 218, 241, 321, 410; *Amidah* prayer, 392; civilizing process and, 249; falling on the face during, 15n. 7; penitential, 249; Silent prayer, 409
pregnancy, mystical, 330–31, 337
projection, psychological, 45
prophecy, 74, 78, 165; deliberately induced, 219; holy and impure, 279–80; madness and, 258, 261–66, 272–74; maggidic possession and, 222; of Moses, 111; R. Hayyim Vital on, 437–39; through power of *kelippot*, 265–66
prostitutes, 49–50
Protestantism, 239, 246
Provence, kabbalists in, 117
psak din (legal ruling), 76
Psi Factor (television program), 11
psychiatry, folk, 346, 356
psychiatry, western, 361
psychology, 11, 15, 16, 19, 26, 284
psychosis, 65, 68
psychotherapy, 56, 58–59, 60
punishment, 60, 63, 129, 134, 143; *Karet*, 160; of possessing spirit, 312, 314; of sexual transgression, 136;

punishment (*cont.*)
    transmigration into body of animal, 329, 350

Querido, Ya'akov, 200
quietism, 288–89
Qumran, psalms at, 79

rabbis, 53–54, 55, 144; cosmological issues and, 62; as exorcists, 55–59, 133, 244, 312, 315–16, 317, 351; interrogation of possessing spirits, 62, 442–43; moral authority of, 63; mystically oriented, 56; necromancy and, 75–76; opponents of Sabbateanism, 274–76; as physicians, 84–85; public image of, 319. *See also* sages; *specific individuals*
Rachel (sister of R. Judah Mashan), 190, 417
Ranu le-Ya'akov [Joy for Jacob] (R. Zemah), 127
rape, 47, 50, 53, 313, 336
Raphael (angel), 82, 84, 92n. 43
rasha (wicked person), 388, 390
Rashi, 30
rationalists, 34, 35, 346, 348, 358
Rav, the. *See* Luria, R. Isaac
Raya Mehmna, 39n. 8
realism, 170
reincarnation, 28–29, 159, 238, 245, 362
reshimu (trace impression), 162, 165, 178n. 38
Reshit Hokhmah (R. Elijah de Vidas), 226
Reubeni, David, 200
reward and punishment, 60, 63, 129, 285, 318
rgd (scaring away), 80
Ritualum Romanum, 240
role behaviors, 67
Roman Catholic Church, 13, 140; exorcism and, 134, 239–40; feminine religious needs and, 249–50; propaganda use of possession, 239, 246. *See also* Christianity
Romano, Daniel, 187, 191
Romano, Menahem, 433

Rome, ancient, 74
Romeo, Giovanni, 250
Roper, Linda, 239
Rosenberg, Yehuda Yudl, 37
Rozin rabbi, 64
ru'ah (spirits), 12, 13, 27, 164, 198, 395; of *Adam Kadmon*, 172; soul impregnation and, 165; soul levels and, 162, 182n. 102
Ru'ah Tum'ah (impure spirit), 76, 79, 88n. 14
Rubenstein, A., 265, 287
Russia, 43, 53, 60, 320, 336
Russo, Barukhia, 200

Sa'adat (wife of Jacob Nasar), 190, 418
Sabba, R. Hamnuna, 165
Sabba, R. Yeiva, 166
Sabbateanism, 18, 19, 169, 215; amnesia and, 287; believers in, 274–78; cultural interpretation of possessions, 227–30; holy names and, 296n. 69; *maggid* possession and, 216; magic and, 281; mimetic model and, 230, 232; opponents of, 270, 274–78; rise of, 218; trance possession in, 236n. 35. *See also* Shabbatai Zvi
Sabbath duties, 54
Safed, city of, 15, 307, 360; as city of the dead, 124–36; *Divre Yosef* texts, 267–79; *maggidim* in, 217; negative possessions in, 186–87; nephew of R. Yehoshua bin Nun in, 382–83; origin of *dybbuk* tales in, 341; positive possessions in, 17, 101–2, 186; possession cases in, 50–51, 62, 63, 375–79; *Shivhe ha-Ari* text, 379, 381; spread of possession from, 242
Safed, mystics of, 9, 12, 16, 33–34, 226; arrival of, 99; "conventional wisdom" concerning, 192; exorcism and, 240; first reports of *dybbuk* possession and, 43; gender and possession, 192–93; hagiography of, 30; historical background to, 73; induced possession among, 220; *maggidim* and, 218; prophecy and,

225; revelatory gnosis and, 118–19; understanding of the soul, 100
sages, 36, 41, 165, 373, 397. *See also* rabbis; *tanna/tannaim* (Mishnaic sages)
saints, Christian, 242, 243
saints, Muslim, 357
Salem witch accusations, 15, 228
Salonika (Saloniki), 131, 217
Sambari, R. Joseph, 128, 135, 190
Sammael, 76
Samson of Ostropol, R., 218
Samuel the Pious, R., 31, 36
Sar ha-Torah (Prince of the Torah), 78–79, 90n. 27
Sarah (biblical personage), 160
Sarug, R. Israel, 170, 176n. 16
Satan (the devil), 29, 35, 36, 130–31, 229; angels of destruction and, 376; Christian conception of, 140, 308; New England "witches" ascribed to, 228; prophetic incapacitation of, 224; visions and dreams from, 267
Saturn (planet), madness and, 272–74
Saul, King, 13, 77, 93n. 51, 222
Schäfer, Peter, 79, 91n. 32
schizophrenia, 257
scholasticism, 75
Scholem, Gershom, 33, 38n. 8, 225, 245; on ascetic piety of Safed, 143; on Ba'al Shem Tov, 297n. 75; *golem* narratives and, 40n. 21; on maggidic possessions, 223; on *Me'oreot Zvi*, 295n. 62; on origins of *dybbuk* concept, 89n. 19; on past lives, 168, 169; on R. Hayyim Vital, 293–94n. 44; on Shabbatai Zvi, 271–72
science, 36, 208, 341
Second Jewish Commonwealth, 309
Second Temple, 60, 257–58, 272–73
Seegautekar, Judith, 314, 319, 320, 341
Sefer Avodat ha-Kodesh (R. Me'ir ibn Gabbai), 385
Sefer Gilgule Neshamot [Im Perush Me'ir Ayin], 176n. 16
Sefer ha-Bahir, 29, 30, 38n. 5
Sefer ha-Gilgulim, 396
Sefer ha-Goralot, 169
Sefer ha-Haredim, 168
Sefer ha-Hezyonot [Book of Visions] (R. Hayyim Vital), 17, 127, 136, 138, 163; accounts of women possessed, 188–90; dreams recorded in, 191; R. Hayyim Vital's psychical experience and, 410, 411; inconsistencies of, 180n. 57; negative possession in, 191; R. Hayyim Vital's possession in, 192, 415–16; selections from, 421–35; two genres in, 197–200; women as visionaries in, 207
Sefer ha-Meshiv, 118, 217, 224
Sefer ha-Razim, 80
Sefer Haredim (R. Eliezer Azikri), 226
Sefer Hasidim, 31
Sefer ha-Tamar, 217, 231
Sefer Ke vitzat ha-Ruhot [Book of the Gathering of Spirits], 80
Sefer Mif'alot Elohim, 169
Sefer Tzafnat Pane'ah (R. Judah Hallewa), 187
Sefer Yetzirah, 36, 40n. 21
sefira/sefirot (emanated divine powers), 29, 37, 107, 392; commandments and, 397; in realm of Emanation, 165
Seidel, Jonathan, 17, 26
Seiler, Tobias, 130–31
semikhah controversy, 224, 225
Sephardic (Iberian) Jews, 38n. 2, 42, 126, 315, 338, 356; first documented possession cases and, 350; kabbalism and, 43; Torah scholars, 424
Seth, 170
Seven Kings, 173
Seville, Spain, 307
sex-role conflict, 53–54
sexuality, 45–54, 62; adolescent, 334; *dybbuk* and women's sexual urges, 313; in Falcon case (1571), 132–33; sexual transgression, 139, 205–6, 432; as threat to communal leadership, 143
Sha'ar ha-Gilgulim [Gate of Transmigrations] (R. Hayyim Vital), 124, 163, 182n. 102, 231, 388
Sha'ar ha-Kavvanot, 391

Sha'ar ha-Kelalim, 181n. 85
Sha'ar ha-Pesukim, 398
Sha'ar Ru'ah ha-Kodesh (R. Hayyim Vital), 179n. 48, 218, 231, 394–95, 437–39
Sha'are Kedushah (R. Hayyim Vital), 122n. 43
Sha'are Tzedek (R. Jacob Abulafia), 114, 294n. 55
Shabbatai Zvi, 18, 50, 51, 61, 177n. 25, 245; apostasy of (conversion to Islam), 215, 227; as false messiah, 314, 355; historical romance about, 278–80; inheritors of, 200; madness of, 270–74; *maggidim* and, 217; messiahship of, 272; messianism before, 226; Nathan of Gaza's prophetic visions and, 219, 220, 221, 222, 227; opponents of, 275–76; prophecy of messiahship of, 230; as spark of Messiah, 287–88. *See also* Sabbateanism
Shaked, Saul, 79, 91n. 32
Shalshelet ha-Kabbalah [Chain of Tradition] (R. Gedaliah ibn Yahia), 128, 148n. 30, 187–88, 246, 442–43; Falcon possession case in, 129; hagiographic stories in, 30; spirit of executed criminal in, 242–43
shamanism, 66, 84, 221, 239; dissociation of, 347; as inspiration/healing, 251
Shamharush (demon-king), 356
Shapira, R. Nathan, 168
Shas (Israeli political party), 27, 38n. 2–3
shedim, 356
Sheikh al-Yahud, 422
Shekhinah (female aspect of divinity), 30, 117, 208, 224, 285; *gerushin* ("peregrinations") and, 106; impure spirits and, 77, 88n. 14; speech automatism and, 107–8
Shemayah, 112, 121n. 31
Shene Luhot ha-Brit, 226
Sheol (the underworld), 62
Shimon bar Yohai, R., 113, 117, 125, 165

Shivhe ha-Ari, [In Praise of R. Isaac Luria] 112–13, 225, 311, 379–81
Shivhe ha-Besht [In Praise of the Ba'al Shem Tov], 18, 258, 263, 269, 270, 287; influence of *Me'oreot Zvi* on, 280–83; madness in, 259–62; mystical experiences in, 289; on Sabbateans, 276–78
Shivhe R. Hayyim Vital (Praises of R. Hayyim Vital), 127
shofar, blowing of, 241, 312, 316, 354
Shomer Emunim, 60
Shoresh Yishai (R. Solomon Alkabetz), 444
Shukr Kuhayl (I and II), 200
Shulhan Arukh (R. Joseph Karo), 218, 222
Shvili, Yefet, 309
Sifra de-Tzene'uta, 395
Simhah (wife of Cuencas), 190
sin/sinners, 31, 33, 43; commandments and, 392; confessed by possessing spirit, 314; consequences of, 137; exile of the *Shekhinah* and, 107; exposed by *dybbukim*, 63; *ibbur* (impregnation) and, 140; *maggid*'s instructions and, 103; masturbation, 249; penitential acts, 104; primordial sin of Eve, 46; punishment of, 61; repentance and, 160, 161, 265, 319; sexual taboos, 311; strengthening of faith and, 260, 261; *tikkune avonot* (amends of sins), 104
Singer, Isaac Bashevis, 41, 54
Sitre Torah (R. Jacob Abulafia), 114
skepticism, 141, 143, 151n. 56
sleep deprivation, 105
Smyrna, 215
sociology, 11
Solomon, King, 335
"Solomonic" exorcism, 85
somnambulism, 101
soteriology, 174n. 2
soul roots, 17, 159, 165, 396, 409; Lurianic Kabbalah and, 160; past lives and, 168; Sabbatean interest in, 169

souls: conceptions about, 32–34; fate of, 32; in shamanic trance, 347; soul levels, 162–63; soul trees, 164, 167; sparks of, 9–10; transmutation of, 28–29. *See also* transmigration of souls
Souls of the Seventy, 170
Spain, 117, 118; expulsion of Jews from, 25, 37, 43, 174n. 2, 217; Inquisition in, 60, 141
Spanish Kabbalah, 34
sparks of a soul, 9–10
speech automatism, 107, 114, 294n. 55, 351; male-in-female possession, 421; in negative possession, 311. *See also* xenoglossia
spirit possession, 9, 11, 66; agency and, 131, 150n. 49; central and peripheral cults, 347; in Christianity, 239–40; as cross-cultural phenomenon, 346; cultural intrepretation of, 227–30; "diagnosis" of, 238, 240; disciplinary approach to study of, 14–16; gender and, 188, 249–50; historical trajectories of, 358–59; history of possession ideas, 13–14; idiom of, 44, 45, 49, 65; as index of cultural distance, 354–58; manifestations among Jewish communities, 350–54; messiah accounts and, 197–200; mimetic model of, 230–32; propaganda use of, 239, 246; setting for, in late antiquity, 73–75; terms and types, 11–13; as theatrical performance, 359, 361; volitional, 74, 76. *See also* negative (malevolent) possession; positive (benign) possession
Spiro, Melford, 45
spontaneity, possession and, 219, 228, 229
Sudan, 353
Sufism, 219, 220, 225, 357; positive (benevolent) possession and, 14; similarity to maggidic revelation, 231. *See also* Islam
suicide, 54

sulphur smoke, used in exorcisms, 241, 313, 443; described in *Divre Yosef* text, 371; R. Zacuto's description of, 244, 245, 247
supernatural powers, 277, 280, 282, 352
supernatural world, 14
superstition, 358
Suriel (angel), 82
susto (illness role), 67
swollen body parts, 241, 248
Sword of Moses treatise, 82
symbolization, 44
synagogues, 124, 132, 157n. 121; *dybbuk* possession in, 55; exorcisms performed in, 56–57, 249, 316, 354, 357; necromancy in, 85
synchronic cosmology, 358
Syria, 85

Ta'alumot Hokhmah [Mysteries of Wisdom] (R. Solomon Delmedigo), 128, 226
Ta'ame ha-Mitzvot, 33
Taitatzak, R. Joseph, 118, 217, 224, 231
Talmide Hakhamim (scholarly sages), 204, 397
Talmud, 28, 150n. 51, 258, 309, 404. *See also* Babylonian Talmud (BT)
tanna/tannaim (Mishnaic sages), 31, 112, 113, 116, 159
television, 11
Ten Commandments, 370
Teresa of Avila (Christian saint), 152n. 64
"Terrible Happening, A" *(Maaseh Noraah)*, 48
Testament of Solomon, 79
Tetragrammaton, 392, 412n. 22
theodicy, 314
theology, 19
theosophy, 45
theurgic practices, 159, 175n. 7, 183n. 108
Third Order (Tertiaries), 243
Tiberias, 43, 382
Tiferet (male aspect of divinity), 107, 170

tikkun (repair of the world), 160, 163, 166; exorcism and, 315; messianism and, 201, 272, 301n. 108, 396; undecided issues in Lurianic Kabbalah and, 171
tikkune avonot (amends of sins), 104
Tikkune Zohar, 33, 39n. 8
Tikla ("scales of deceit"), 394, 396
Tishby, Isaiah, 117
Tobias the physician, 273
Toledot ha-Ari, 226
Torah, 56, 112, 165, 221; abandonment of, 129; angels and, 437–38; commandments of, 160, 397; exiled secrets of, 119; exorcism and, 354; kabbalistic interpretations of, 102; madness and, 259–60, 277; Oral Torah, 108; sexual transgression and, 134, 135–36; studied in Safed, 125; volitional possession and, 78–79; water as metaphor for, 333; women and, 206, 208, 247
Traicté des Energumènes (Bérulle), 140
trance, 101, 230, 251, 347; as basic component of religious experience, 239; mediums, 9, 79; Sabbateans and, 236n. 35; in *zar* possession, 353
Trani, R. Moses, 151n. 55
transmigration of souls, 33, 34, 42, 140–41, 329; "ill-fated righteous" question and, 60; as punishment, 350; sexual transgressions and, 46. *See also gilgul* (reincarnated soul); soul roots; souls
Tree of Knowledge, 176n. 17, 386, 395
Turkey, 18, 118, 227
Turkish language, 132
Turner, Victor, 106
tzaddik (righteous man), 37, 56; *devekut* and, 287; as exorcist, 310; good/evil sparks and, 389; *ibbur* (impregnation) and, 160–62, 179n. 53, 311, 318; madness and, 260; merits/demerits and, 391–93; "neighbor's portion" moral problem and, 385–86; self-rectification of, 403–6; soul levels and, 163; transgressions of, 388, 390, 391; World to Come and, 171–72; *yihudim* practice and, 109–10, 400n. 26
tzaddikah (righteous woman), 336
Tzadkiel (angel), 188
Tzadok, R., 274
Tzafnat Pa'aneah (Decipherer of Mysteries), 127
Tzelemim (forms), 164
tzeruf (added soul), 198
Tziag, R. Yosef, 430
Tzimtzum, 172–73
Tzoref, Heshel, 200

Uceda, R. Shmu'el, 311
Uceda, Yakov, 432
ultra-orthodox Jews, 27, 38n. 2, 69, 362
Underhill, Evelyn, 228
United States, 11, 336
urban popular culture, 244, 250
Uzzell, D., 67

vagina, penetration of, 47, 48, 51, 133
Van Gennep, Arnold, 106
VaYikra Rabbah, 76
Venice, rabbis of, 276
virginity, 47, 48
visionary experiences, 117, 138–39, 154n. 88
Vital, Hannah, 190
Vital, R. Hayyim, 17, 30, 63, 113, 388; alleged to be messiah, 315; Anav's daughter possession case and, 203–7; archenemy of, 189, 204, 207, 211n. 19; AR"I (R. Isaac Luria) and, 170, 181n. 85; construction of gender, 154n. 90; death of (1620), 218; diary of, 136, 138, 159, 166, 206; as exorcist, 142, 177n. 25, 187, 191; on *gilgul* and *ibbur*, 311; homily from *Sha'ar Ru'ah ha-Kodesh*, 437–39; on R. Isaac Luria, 124, 126; on merit and demerit, 391–93; *mishnayot* recitations and, 102; possessed by evil spirit, 187, 415–16; preparatory rites and, 106; psychical experience

of, 407–13; relationship to R. Isaac Luria, 200, 398; reworking of Lurianic teaching, 390; on self-rectification of *tzaddikkim*, 403–5; in *Shivhe ha-Ari* text, 379; soul of (case study), 163–67; soul pattern of, 160; spiritual diary of, 100; on transmigration of souls, 140–41; vision of pillars, 417–18; *yihudim* practice and, 109, 110, 112, 113–14, 116, 165
Vital, R. Samuel, 215, 399n. 14

Wallace, A., 66
Weinstein, Roni, 16, 18
Weiss, J., 295n. 61
whipping, in exorcism, 312, 313
Wisdom of the Soul, The (Eleazar of Worms), 32
witchcraft, 82, 141, 231–32, 239
witch hunts, Christian, 35–36, 43, 228
women, 15, 16, 46; *agunah* status, of widows, 135, 153n. 72, 373; *aslai* (possession illness) and, 359; dreams of, 191; exemption from studying Torah, 176n. 20; as exorcists, 319; feminine passivity, 243; Gentile, 50, 139, 377, 432; as healers, 246; healing methods practiced upon, 247–48; impurity and, 333; inner-oriented sexuality of, 46; intercourse with spirits, 133; in Jewish society, 249–50; mourning in Christian society, 238; positive (benign) possession of, 188–90, 192–93; as possessed, 64, 83, 245; as primary "victims," 186, 188–89; prophecy of madwoman, 262–66; sexual symbolism of possession and, 348; sexual transgression and, 139; she-demons, 309–10, 318, 377; social identity of, 250–51; spiritual power of, 207–8
Women's Folklore, Women's Culture (Jordan, Kalcik), 338
wonder-workers. *See ba'ale shem* (wonder-workers)
World of Activity *(olam ha-asi'ah)*, 438

World of Creation *(olam ha-yetzirah)*, 438
World to Come, 393, 396, 397, 401n. 37

X-Files (television program), 11
xenoglossia, 228, 245, 248, 313, 351; in Anav's daughter possession case, 203, 206; in *aslai* (possession illness), 352; in Falcon possession case (1571), 130, 132, 151n. 58, 241; maggidic possession and, 224; mimetic model and, 232. *See also* speech automatism

Yannai, R., 112
Yehidah, 162, 171
Yehoshua Al-Boom, R., 422, 425, 430
Yehoshua Bin Nun, R., nephew of, 136, 382–83
Yeiva Sabba, R., 407, 409
Yemenite messiahs, 200
Yetzirah (Energy Formation), 162
Yiddish language, 31, 36, 95n. 60, 132, 266
yihudim (Unifications), 103–4, 108–11, 112, 165, 167; exorcism with aid of, 191; raising of sparks and, 388; ritually enacted death, 115; soul roots and, 163, 409
Yisrael Najjara, R., 432, 433
Yocom, Margaret, 338
Yohanan ben Zakkai, R., 85, 165
Yosher (Straight Light), 172
Young, Allan, 355
Yudeghan (Persian messiah), 200

Zacut, Abraham, 237
Zacuto, R. Moses, 18, 168, 169, 216, 218; interest in magic, 252; letters of, 244–45, 246, 247, 248, 251; as Lurianic propagandist, 215; poem dedicated to, 237
zar possession, 350, 353–54, 360; "assimilation" and, 361; Ethiopian *kessoch* and, 359; gender and, 349
Zarfati, Joseph, 131, 132, 150n. 51, 367
Zarfati, Samuel, 131, 132, 134, 140, 368

Zarri, Gabriella, 243
Zechariah (biblical prophet), 54, 355
Ze'ir Anpin (masculine gradation), 110, 111, 171, 311, 395
Zemah, R. Jacob, 127
Zfatman-Biller, Sarah, 307
Zikkaron Li-vne Yisra'el (R. Baruch of Arezzo), 221
Zionism, 361
Zivvug (cosmic Union), 172, 176n. 9
Zohar, 29, 38n. 8, 117, 389, 395; Age of the Zohar, 33; author of, 125, 165; authorities/commentators on, 200; commentary of AR"I (R. Isaac Luria), 173; on *devekut*, 298–99n. 82; on fragrance of Garden of Eden, 221–22; pillar of cloud symbol in, 211n. 15; *Shlah lekha* portion, 437; view of women, 208; on *yihudim* performance, 163. *See also* Kabbalah
Zohar ha-Raki'a, 394

Books in the Raphael Patai Series in Jewish Folklore and Anthropology

The Myth of the Jewish Race, revised edition, by Raphael Patai and Jennifer Patai, 1989

The Hebrew Goddess, third enlarged edition, by Raphael Patai, 1990

Robert Graves and the Hebrew Myths: A Collaboration, by Raphael Patai, 1991

Jewish Musical Traditions, by Amnon Shiloah, 1992

The Jews of Kurdistan, by Erich Brauer, completed and edited by Raphael Patai, 1993

Jewish Moroccan Folk Narratives from Israel, by Haya Bar-Itzhak and Aliza Shenhar, 1993

For Our Soul: The Ethiopian Jews in Israel, by Teshome G. Wagaw, 1993

Book of Fables: The Yiddish Fable Collection of Reb Moshe Wallich, Frankfurt am Main, 1697, translated and edited by Eli Katz, 1994

From Sofia to Jaffa: The Jews of Bulgaria and Israel, by Guy H. Haskell, 1994

Jadid al-Islam: The Jewish "New Muslims" of Meshhed, by Raphael Patai, 1998

Saint Veneration among the Jews in Morocco, by Issachar Ben-Ami, 1998

Arab Folktales from Palestine and Israel, introduction, translation, and annotation by Raphael Patai, 1998

Profiles of a Lost World: Memoirs of East European Jewish Life before World War II, by Hirsz Abramowicz, translated by Eva Zeitlin Dobkin, edited by Dina Abramowicz and Jeffrey Shandler, 1999

A Global Community: The Jews from Aleppo, Syria, by Walter Zenner, 2000

Without Bounds: The Life and Death of Rabbi Ya'akov Wazana, by Yoram Bilu, 2000

Jewish Poland—Legends of Origin: Ethnopoetics and Legendary Chronicles, by Haya Bar-Itzhak, 2001

Defining the Yiddish Nation: The Jewish Folklorists of Poland, by Itzik Nakhmen Gottesman, 2001

Spirit Possession in Judaism: Cases and Contexts from the Middle Ages to the Present, edited by Matt Goldish, 2002